In the last century, a new way of looking at the Bible developed. Research into the ancient Near East and its texts recreated for us the civilizations out of which the Bible emerged. In this century, there has been a revival of Jewish biblical scholarship; Israeli and American scholars, in particular, concentrating in the fields of archaeology, biblical history, Semitic languages, and the religion of Israel, have opened exciting new vistas into the world of the Scriptures. For the first time in history, we have at our disposal information and methodological tools that enable us to explore the biblical text in a way that could never have been done before. This new world of knowledge, as seen through the eyes of contemporary Jewish scholars and utilizing at the same time the insights of over twenty centuries of traditional Jewish exegesis, is now available for the first time to a general audience in *The JPS Torah Commentary.*

The *Commentary* is published in five volumes, each by a single author who has devoted himself to the study of the text. Given the wide range of perspectives that now exist in biblical scholarship, the JPS has recognized the individual expertise of these authors and made no attempt to impose uniformity on the methodology or content of their work.

The Hebrew text is that of the Leningrad Codex B 19A, the oldest dated manuscript of the complete Hebrew Bible. Copied from a text written by the distinguished Masoretic scholar Aaron ben Moses ben Asher, who lived in the first half of the 10th century C.E., the manuscript was completed in 1009 C.E. In this edition it has been arranged according to the weekly synagogue Torah readings. The format has been adjusted to correspond to that adopted by the TANAKH, the new translation of the Hebrew Bible, published by the Jewish Publication Society and utilized in the present Commentary.

The Jewish Publication Society has completed this project with a full awareness of the great tradition of Jewish Bible commentary, with a profound sense of the sanctity of the biblical text and an understanding of the awe and love that our people has accorded its Bible. The voice of our new *Commentary* resounds with the spirit and concerns of our times—just as the Jewish spirit has always found its most sincere and heartfelt expression in its appreciation of the Bible; yet it acknowledges the intrinsic value of the tools of modern scholarship in helping to establish the original sense and setting of Scripture.

With all this fixed firmly in mind, the Jewish Publication Society commits its good name and its decades of pioneering in the world of English-language Jewish publishing to this *Torah Commentary* with the hope that it will serve as the contemporary addition to the classic commentaries created by Jews during past epochs in Jewish history.

Nahum M. Sarna, GENERAL EDITOR
Chaim Potok, LITERARY EDITOR

וְהַמַּשְׂכִּלִים יַזְהִרוּ כְּזֹהַר הָרָקִיעַ
וּמַצְדִּיקֵי הָרַבִּים כַּכּוֹכָבִים לְעוֹלָם וָעֶד

Sander H., Alan, and David C. Mendelson

Joseph and Rebecca Meyerhoff

Warren G. and Gay H. Miller

Mr. and Mrs. Hershel Muchnick
In memory of Max and Annie Sherman
and Lt. Louis O. Sherman

Joseph Muchnick
In memory of his wife, Mollie

Nancy and Morris W. Offit

Mr. and Mrs. Mitchell E. Panzer
In memory of their parents

Edith and Charles Pascal
In memory of their parents,
Harry and Lena Chidakel
Harry and Marion Pascal

Mr. and Mrs. Frank J. Pasquerilla

Leon J. Perelman

Mr. and Mrs. Ronald O. Perelman

Harry M. and Esther L. Plotkin

Anne and Henry S. Reich

Arleen and Robert S. Rifkind

Judy and Arthur Robbins
In honor of Sheila F. Segal

Mr. and Mrs. Daniel Rose

Sam Rothberg

Rabbi Stephen A. and Nina Berman Schafer
In memory of Joel Michael Schafer

Drs. Amiel and Chariklia-Tziraki Segal

Bernard G. Segal

Norma L. Shapiro
In memory of her parents,
Jane K. and Bert Levy

Lola and Gerald Sherman
In memory of Jean and Al Sherman
and Ada and Jack Kay

Jerome J. and Marciarose Shestack
In memory of Olga and Isadore Shestack
and Clara Ruth Schleifer

Jonathan and Jennifer Shestack
In memory of their great-grandfathers,
Rabbi Israel Shankman and
Rabbi Judah Shestack

Dr. and Mrs. Edward B. Shils

Charles E. Smith
In honor of Mr. and Mrs. Robert P. Kogod
and Mr. and Mrs. Robert H. Smith

Marian Scheuer Sofaer

William and Radine Spier

The Oscar and Lillian Stempler Foundation
In memory of Rose and Isadore Engel
and Lillian Stempler
In honor of Oscar Stempler

David B Sykes
In memory of his wife, Shirley

Mr. and Mrs. Sylvan M. Tobin

Sami and Annie Totah
In honor of their parents

Adele and Bert M. Tracy
In memory of their parents

Elizabeth R. and Michael A. Varet

Edna and Charles Weiner

Simon and Trudy Weker
In honor of their children,
Laurie, Jonathan, and Robert

Morton H. Wilner

Mr. and Mrs. Seymour D. Wolf
In memory of their parents,
Abraham and Dora Wolf
Abraham and Sarah Krupsaw

Dr. Allen M. and Eleanor B. Wolpe

Ben Zevin

Benjamin Bernard Zucker
In honor of Lotty Gutwirth Zucker

PATRONS

And the knowledgeable will be radiant like the bright expanse of sky,
And those who lead the many to righteousness will be like the stars forever and ever.

DANIEL 12:3

Mr. and Mrs. Robert P. Abrams
In memory of Peter Abrams

D.F. Antonelli, Jr.

Mr. and Mrs. Marvin Anzel and Sons
In memory of Rose and Samuel Anzel

Stephen and Stephanie Axinn

Mr. and Mrs. Ronald S. Baron

Dr. Muriel M. Berman

Nancy Berman and Alan Bloch

Philip I. Berman

Steven M. Berman

Herbert and Nancy Bernhard

Mr. and Mrs. Arthur H. Bienenstock

Goldene and Herschel Blumberg
In memory and in honor of their parents

Irvin J. Borowsky and Laurie Wagman

Elmer Cerin
In memory of Sylvia S. Cerin

Dr. and Mrs. D. Walter Cohen
In honor of their parents,
Abram and Goldie Cohen
Joseph and Bessie Axelrod

Melvin and Ryna Cohen

Rosalie and Joseph Cohen

Elsie B. and Martin D. Cohn
In honor of their children and grandchildren

Mr. and Mrs. Charles M. Diker

Carole and Richard Eisner

Edward E. Elson

The Endowment Fund of the
Greater Hartford Jewish Federation

Edith Brenner Everett and Henry Everett
In memory of their father, Eli Brenner,
and brother, Fred Brenner

Federation of Jewish Agencies
of Greater Philadelphia

Peter I. Feinberg

Myer and Adrienne Arsht Feldman
In honor of Bella Feldman

Mr. Joseph M. and Dr. Helen G. First

Libby and Alan Fishman

Selma and William Fishman

The Foundation for Conservative Judaism
of Greater Philadelphia

Bernard and Muriel Frank

Aaron and Cecile Goldman

Evelyn and Seymour C. Graham

Dorothy Gitter Harman
In memory of her parents,
Morris and Maria Gitter

Irving B. Harris

Shirley and Stanley Hayman
In memory of their parents

Evelyn and Sol Henkind

Erica and Ludwig Jesselson

Leonard Kapiloff

Sol and Rita Kimerling

Lillian and Sid Klemow

Mr. and Mrs. Ronald A. Krancer

William B. and Elaine Kremens

Mr. and Mrs. Harvey M. Krueger

Simon and Rosa Laupheimer

Fanney N. Litvin
In memory of her husband, Philip Litvin

Ruth Meltzer
In memory of her husband, Leon

Martha H. and Joseph L. Mendelson

Martha H. and Joseph L. Mendelson
In memory of their parents,
Alexander and Celia Holstein
Abraham and Dora Mendelson

THE JPS TORAH COMMENTARY

LEVITICUS ויקרא

GENERAL EDITOR *Nahum M. Sarna*
LITERARY EDITOR *Chaim Potok*

GENESIS *Nahum M. Sarna*
EXODUS *Nahum M. Sarna*
LEVITICUS *Baruch A. Levine*
NUMBERS *Jacob Milgrom*
DEUTERONOMY *Jeffrey H. Tigay*

THE JPS TORAH COMMENTARY

LEVITICUS ויקרא

The Traditional Hebrew Text with the New JPS Translation

Commentary by BARUCH A. LEVINE

THE JEWISH PUBLICATION SOCIETY
PHILADELPHIA · NEW YORK · JERUSALEM 5749 / 1989

First edition
Manufactured in the United States of America
Composed by Polebridge Press in Galliard (English text) and Keter (Hebrew text).
Printed and bound by Arcata Graphics.

Library of Congress Cataloging-in-Publication Data

Levine, Baruch A.
Leviticus : the traditional Hebrew text with the new JPS translation / commentary by Baruch A. Levine. — 1st ed.
p. cm. — (The JPS Torah commentary)
English and Hebrew; commentary in English
Title on half t.p.: Leviticus = Va-yikra
Includes bibliographical references.
ISBN 0-8276-0328-2
1. Bible. O.T. Leviticus—Commentaries. I. Bible. O.T. Leviticus. Hebrew. 1989. II. Title. III. Title: Va-yikra. IV. Series: Bible. O. T. Pentateuch. Hebrew. 1989.
BS1255.3.L48 1989 89-1841
222'.13077—dc19 CIP

GENESIS *ISBN 0-8276-0326-6*
EXODUS *ISBN 0-8276-0327-4*
NUMBERS *ISBN 0-8276-0329-0*
DEUTERONOMY *ISBN 0-8276-0330-4*
Five-volume set ISBN 0-8276-0331-2

Designed by ADRIANNE ONDERDONK DUDDEN

To my parents-in-law,
Ruth and Bert Godfrey,
in appreciation.

ACKNOWLEDGMENTS

In retrospect, I identify two kinds of support that have enabled me to accomplish the present Commentary to Leviticus: I am grateful to my gifted student, Anne Robertson, for her assistance in preparing this manuscript. I am grateful to certain enabling agencies whose assistance afforded me the time and means to pursue work on the Commentary over an extended period of years. I began work on the Commentary in 1975, during my tenure as a fellow of the John Simon Guggenheim Foundation for the academic year 1975–76. Several years later, in 1979–80, I was a fellow of the Institute of Advanced Studies at the Hebrew University, Jerusalem. Without these two singular opportunities, I would not have been able to immerse myself in the research required by the task. New York University's flexible leave policy also abetted my progress, and I am grateful to my colleagues in the Department of Near East Languages and Literature for their understanding and their willingness to allow me repeated absences for purposes of research.

Intellectual stimulation came from my teachers, colleagues, and students. H. L. Ginsberg influenced me greatly in philology and exegesis during our continuous discussions over the years. Thorkild Jacobsen imparted to me an insightful approach to religious phenomenology. C. H .Gordon introduced me to the languages and cultures of the ancient Near East. The incisive commentary of David Zvi Hoffmann made of that great scholar a teacher of a different sort; his work never left my side! Many questions relevant to the interpretation of Leviticus were addressed in lectures and papers presented before learned societies in North America, as well as in Europe and Israel. My students at New York University and at other institutions of higher learning where I have taught, did me the great service of listening and questioning. The staff of the Library of the Ecole Biblique in Jerusalem were most helpful. My colleague, Nahum Sarna, deserves praise and gratitude for his prudence as general editor of the Commentary, as does Chaim Potok for his guidance as literary editor.

The Jewish Publication Society has once again demonstrated its commitment to Jewish learning. Sheila F. Segal, editor-in-chief, and the editorial staff, Amy M. Gewirtzman, Linda R. Turner, and Ilene Cohen, contributed their invaluable services in the publication of this book. Adrianne Onderdonk Dudden deserves note for her masterful design. My appreciation also goes to Bernard I. Levinson and Nathan Barnett, former executive vice presidents, Jerome J. Shestack, past president and chairman of the Commentary Committee, and Richard Malina, now executive director, for their kind assistance.

My dedicated wife, Corinne, has consistently encouraged me in the preparation of this Commentary and my special thanks go to her. In dedicating the Leviticus Commentary

to my parents-in-law, Ruth and Bert Godfrey, I wish to acknowledge their appreciation of the role of the scholar in the preservation of Judaism.

All who attempt to interpret the words of the Torah must pronounce the blessing of the Amidah, addressed to the Divine Pedagogue:

אַתָּה חוֹנֵן לְאָדָם דַּעַת וּמְלַמֵּד לֶאֱנוֹשׁ בִּינָה

"It is You who graciously imparts knowledge to human beings, and teaches discernment to mortals."

Baruch A. Levine

CONTENTS

THE EXCURSUSES

INTRODUCTION

The Hebrew Bible expresses the central concerns of the minds and hearts of an ancient people. One such concern underlies the question posed by the prophet Micah (6:6–8):

> With what shall I approach the LORD,
> Do homage to God on high?
> Shall I approach Him with burnt offerings,
> With calves a year old? . . .
>
> He has told you, O man, what is good,
> And what the LORD requires of you:
> Only to do justice
> And to love goodness,
> And to walk modestly with your God.

Like other Israelite prophets, Micah questioned the accepted norms of religious behavior, which required that God be worshiped through sacrifice. How shall the human being honor his Creator? What does God require of His creatures? The prophet's response regards burnt offerings as a poor substitute for justice and goodness.

We should regard Leviticus 19:2 as a priestly response to the same question posed by Micah: What does the Lord require of Israel?

> You shall be holy, for I, the LORD your God, am holy!

The priestly traditions emphasized the proper worship of God, undertaken in the pursuit of holiness, which, in turn, could only be realized in the context of an Israelite society governed by religious law. Justice and compassion, too, were a dimension of holiness, and at points, the priestly and the prophetic responses converged. But the priests were concerned with the celebration of holiness, the preservation of purity, and the formation of a religious community that acknowledged the true God.

Leviticus takes its cue from the covenantal charge delivered in Exodus 19:5–6: "Indeed, all the earth is Mine, but you shall be My kingdom of priests and holy nation."[1] How Israel was to realize the divine program is the burden of the Book of Leviticus.

This program is clearly alluded to by the rabbinic name for this book, *torat kohanim*, "instructions *for* the priests," that is, the rules and procedures by which the priests themselves were to perform their tasks.[2] Certain sections of Leviticus are entitled *torah*—chapters 6–7, for instance. These texts are in essence manuals of practice that were used in the training of priests. The same function is evident elsewhere, even where the term *torah* does not appear.

But *torat kohanim* can also be translated as "instructions *of* (or *by*) the priests," that is, the rulings and teachings of the priests that are addressed to the Israelite people. As Jeremiah put it (18:18): "For instruction (*torah*) shall not fail from the priests, nor counsel from the wise, nor oracle from the prophet." In Haggai 2:10–13, we find an actual inquiry on a question of ritual addressed to the priests of Jerusalem during the late sixth century B.C.E., after the Babylonian exile had ended. The ruling the priests issued in that instance was their *torah*, their instructions to the people. The same meaning is present in Malachi 2:6–7. There, Levi, the forefather of the priests, is praised:

> Proper rulings (*torat 'emet*) were in his mouth,
> And nothing perverse was on his lips;
> He served Me with complete loyalty
> And held the many back from iniquity.
> For the lips of a priest guard knowledge,
> And men seek rulings (*torah*) from his mouth;
> For he is a messenger of the LORD of Hosts.

Leviticus addresses the multiple functions of the priesthood: officiation in the sacrificial cult, purification, and administration of sanctuary and consecrated personnel. But its educational role pervades the book: The biblical priests taught the people what God required of them. The two dimensions of the rabbinic name *torat kohanim* not only account for the varied subject matter contained in Leviticus, but they also hold the key to the book's organization and structure.

The more commonly known name, *Va-yikra'*, was intended merely as an aid to memory; it classified the book by referring to the first significant word in its opening verse. (Compare *Shemot* for Exodus, *Devarim* for Deuteronomy, and so on.) On the other hand, the Latin name Leviticus, which goes back to the Greek word *Levitikon*—which, in turn, reflects Hebrew *levi*, "a Levite"—was, indeed, intended to characterize the contents of the book.

To Greek-speaking Jews of antiquity, such as those in Alexandria who produced the ancient Greek translation of the Bible known as the Septuagint, the name *Levitikon* probably meant "priestly" in a general sense and did not refer specifically to the Levites as a group. Leviticus assigns no particular role to the Levites, in contrast to the Book of Numbers, where their role is paramount.

In some way, the name Leviticus was probably conditioned by the terminology in Deuteronomy, which classifies all priests as Levites, using such designations as *ha-kohanim ha-leviyim*, "the Levitical priests" (Deut. 17:9,18; 18:1). It is significant that the prophet Malachi referred to the priests of Jerusalem as "Levi." He speaks of "the covenant of Levi," upheld by the priests in earlier times but abrogated in the prophet's own day. The equation "Levi" = "the priesthood" suggests the very identification expressed by the Greek name, *Levitikon*. Most likely, Greek *Levitikon* expresses the same concept as Hebrew *torat kohanim*.

The Leviticus Text

Content Leviticus begins (chaps. 1–3) with regulations governing the preparation and presentation of the three principal types of sacrifices used in the cult of biblical times:

the burnt offering, the grain offering, and the sacred gift of greeting. These "modes" of sacrificing were utilized separately and in combination in a wide variety of celebrations and occasions for worship, both public and private.

The burnt offering (*ʿolah*) was prepared as a holocaust and, except for the hide, was entirely destroyed on the altar fire. The *ʿolah* consisted of animals and fowl that were slaughtered and sectioned and then placed on the altar of burnt offerings. Blood drawn from the *ʿolah* was dashed and sprinkled on the altar. The object of this sacrifice, as detailed in chapter 1, and of other offerings burnt on the altar, was to send the aromatic smoke of the offering heavenward, where God would, it was popularly believed, breathe in the pleasing aroma of His people's gift.

The grain offering (*minḥah*), discussed in chapter 2, was usually made of semolina flour, olive oil, and aromatic spices, such as frankincense. Originally this type of offering was not meant to be burnt on the altar but was meant to be presented, or shown, to God. In time, however, its mode was adapted to conform to the growing emphasis on burnt altar sacrifices, a trend clearly observable in biblical worship. The priest placed a fistful of dough on the altar as a token, while the rest was baked or fried. Most *minḥah* offerings were made of unleavened dough.

These two types of sacrifices are classified as "most sacred," meaning, in practical terms, that only priests could partake of them—and then only in sacred areas of the Sanctuary. The third type, the sacred gift of greeting (*shelamim*), was a *zevaḥ*, a sacred meal. Certain parts of the sacrifice were burnt on the altar, but most of it was boiled in pots and then apportioned among priests and donors, as detailed in chapter 3. Sacrifices of the *zevaḥ* type were classified as "less sacred," and parts of them could be eaten outside the Sanctuary.

Leviticus then proceeds in chapters 4–5 to address the need for expiation: the need for God's forgiveness. Two principal sacrifices served this need, the sin offering (*ḥattaʾt*) and the guilt offering (*ʾasham*). Both were necessitated by unintentional offenses against God committed by individuals and their families and by the Israelite community and its leadership. Each had its specific varieties, which were classified as "most sacred." Usually, parts of these sacrifices were allocated to the priests.

Chapters 6–7 contain regulations for the distribution of the various sacrifices to priests and to donors, where applicable. A good part of the revenue needed to support the priesthood accrued in the form of sacrifices.

A legitimate priesthood, well trained and properly consecrated, was essential to the conduct of worship. Chapters 8–10 of Leviticus record a series of events in the time of Moses, through which the formal sacrificial worship of the God of Israel on the part of His people, Israel, was initiated. In chapter 8, the priesthood of Aaron and of his sons was officially installed with rites of consecration at the same time that Moses sanctified the Tabernacle and its altar. Thereupon, in chapter 9, the newly invested priests officiated for the first time.

The priestly tradition rarely allowed for celebration without voicing strong admonitions on the conduct of religious worship. Chapter 10, for example, reports on the tragic death of the two of Aaron's sons who officiated improperly; it is followed by a series of instructions to the priests on their functions.

Taken as a whole, chapters 1–10 focus on officiation as a basic function of the priesthood. Chapters 11–16, on the other hand, address the matter of purity, which is a prerequisite of the pursuit of holiness. This section of Leviticus begins, therefore, with the

regimen required for a pure diet; it outlines those sources of food, derived from living creatures, that are forbidden and those that are allowed. (That which grows out of the land is permitted.)

In addition to enumerating the relevant species of living creatures, chapter 11 deals with the contamination of foodstuffs caused by contact with impure vessels, and with impure persons.

Chapters 12–15 delineate the tasks of the priests in purifying persons whose physical conditions were considered impure. Left unattended, such conditions were dangerous: They threatened the purity of the Sanctuary because it was located within the Israelite settlement. The category of *tum'ah*, "impurity," included actual diseases and infections, on the one hand, and the less perceptible phenomenon of impurity, on the other. By subsuming both under the common category of *tum'ah*, it was possible to draw attention to problems of public health, as well as to promote the religious devotion of the community. These priestly concerns were prevalent in many ancient Near Eastern societies.

Chapter 12 deals with the mother and her newborn child and prescribes quarantine, purifications, and sacrifices for the period following childbirth. Chapters 13–14 deal with the treatment and purification of persons suffering from certain skin ailments that were, undoubtedly, regarded as contagious. Similar symptoms occurring in leather, cloth, and plastered building stones also required purification. Finally, the Israelite priesthood was expected to concern itself with persons who suffered from infectious discharges associated with the genital organs. For males, the regulations involved both normal seminal emissions and abnormal discharges from the penis. For females, they involved normal menstruation and abnormal vaginal discharges. It was thought that phenomena associated with the organs of procreation were potentially dangerous if not cared for and purified according to the procedures of chapter 15.

Chapter 16 is perhaps the best-known of all the sections of Leviticus, because it is traditionally read in the synagogue on Yom Kippur. It includes the well-known account of the dispatch of the scapegoat, a practice of great interest to students of religious phenomenology, with analogues in other ancient and recent cultures. The chapter also addresses the need to maintain the purity of the Sanctuary on a regular basis. The sacred space of the Sanctuary and its various artifacts and vessels were indispensable for proper purification, just as were the priests themselves. The High Priest and his family were first purified of guilt for any infractions of religious law on their own part that may have led to the defilement of the Sanctuary. In turn, the priesthood sought expiation for the entire House of Israel, thereby redressing any offenses by the people that may have led to the defilement of the Sanctuary.

Together with the scapegoat, which carried away the sins of the people to a land of no return, blood rites and expiatory sacrifices effectuated the purification of the Sanctuary. This elaborate complex of religious rites was scheduled as an annual event, on Yom Kippur, the tenth day of the seventh month, just prior to the most widely celebrated pilgrimage of the year on the Sukkot festival.

This concludes the first division of Leviticus. Chapters 17–26 consist largely of the Holiness Code, to which chapter 27 was subsequently appended. The Holiness Code constitutes a major statement of law: It is, in effect, a priestly pronouncement of God's will, defining what the God of Israel requires of His people.

As is true of the other principal collections of laws in the Torah, the Holiness Code opens with a Prologue (chap. 17) and ends with an Epilogue (26:3–46). The Prologue

ordains proper worship. All sacrifices are to be presented at the entrance of the Tent of Meeting and are to be offered on the one legitimate altar by a properly consecrated priest. The erstwhile custom of offering sacrifices at multiple shrines and altars is outlawed. No blood is to be consumed. Blood drawn from sacrificial animals and fowl is reserved for ritual utilization on the altar.

In fairly traditional fashion, the Epilogue admonishes the Israelite people to obey God's laws and commandments by predicting the consequences of disobedience. Israel will be exiled from its land and will endure horrible suffering. In a more original vein, the Epilogue goes beyond destruction and exile to hold forth the hope of restoration and national survival if only Israel repents of its disobedience, confesses its sins, and applies the lessons of its tragic experience.

Between Prologue and Epilogue, the Holiness Code preserves important legal texts. Chapters 18 and 20, in their different formulations, define the immediate Israelite family by setting the limits of incest and by forbidding certain sexual unions. In an endogamous society, one in which marriage within the group as defined is normal, if not at all times mandatory, it becomes necessary to regulate the degree of closeness in order to avoid incest and excessive inbreeding. As the family is the foundation of society, all systems of law show concern for its definition.

Chapter 19 is a collection of laws modeled after the Decalogue (the Ten Commandments). It demonstrates the interrelatedness of proper social behavior and a meaningful religious life, two dimensions of life that were never meant to be regarded as separate. Thus, chapter 19 commands the observance of the Sabbath and also respect for parents. It prohibits certain pagan funerary practices involving necromancy and also commands respect for elders. It requires the disposition of sacrificial flesh within a prescribed time, while prohibiting fraudulent economic practices. We are instructed to avoid grafting and blending species that are separate in nature, such as flax and wool and plants and vines, as well as to leave gleanings and corner sections of fields for the needy. Idolatry is condemned, yet Israelites are commanded to show kindness to aliens residing in the Land of Israel, who are idolators by origin. All the above, and more, are identified as milestones on the road to holiness.

The sanctity of the priesthood itself was indispensable to the fulfillment of Israel's mandate to become a holy nation. What was sacrificed to God also had to be suitable. In both instances, physical soundness—that is, the absence of blemishes and disfiguration—served as the normal criterion of suitability (chaps. 21–22).

The "sancta" are basic to the religious character of any society. Chapter 23 presents a calendar of set times, or sacred celebrations, that are marked during the year. This calendar includes the weekly Sabbath, an uninterrupted day of rest from normal tasks. Chapter 23 outlines the annual festivals beginning with the spring of the year. First comes Passover, a seven-day festival during which unleavened bread is eaten and on which a pilgrimage is undertaken. Then we read of the seven-week interval of counting, leading up to the Festival of First Fruits (also known as Shavuot). In the autumn of the year, Israelites celebrated the first day of the seventh month, which later became Rosh Hashanah. And the tenth day of the seventh month is Yom Kippur. The seven-day Sukkot festival and its concluding observance of the eighth day begin on the fifteenth day of the seventh month and were the occasion for pilgrimage. This completed the annual calendar.

Chapter 24 then details two practices associated with the Sanctuary, the eternal light and the bread of display, and it relates an incident of blasphemy and its prompt punish-

ment. Chapter 25 presents a major statement on economic policy: A holy nation treats its members justly and humanely and does not tolerate widespread poverty or disenfranchisement. The chapter declares that sales of land in Israel were to be of limited duration, like long-term leases; all sales would terminate in the year of the Jubilee, which came in the fiftieth year, at the conclusion of a series of seven sabbatical cycles. At that time, all land was to revert to its original owners and all indentures would cease. Indebtedness, too, was regulated, and the imposition of interest prohibited.

Chapter 25 conveys a concept of land ownership according to which all land is theoretically owned by the God of Israel, for it is He who granted the Land of Israel to His people. The Israelites, then, are His stewards and tenants. Moreover, God has first claim on all that the land produces. This theory of ownership sought to promote a sense of collective responsibility for the land by regulating the way of life pursued by its inhabitants, the people of Israel.

The inclusion of chapter 27 in the context of the Holiness Code, where it logically belongs, enables us to observe just how the priesthood was expected to administer the affairs of the Sanctuary. The priests were to establish the valuations of commodities devoted to the Sanctuary that were collected as dues, tithes, and the like.

Structure The outline just presented indicates clearly that the Book of Leviticus was compiled according to a plan, or concept, that reflects both dimensions of the name *torat kohanim* discussed at the outset. Allowing for some anomalies, we can divide Leviticus into two principal parts: Chapters 1–16 consist of manuals of practice addressed to the priesthood, and chapters 17–27 consist of priestly teachings addressed to the Israelite people. The former division represents *torat kohanim* in the sense of instructions *for* the priests, whereas the latter division expresses the notion of instructions *by* the priests. The former division focuses on officiation and purification as particular concerns of the priesthood, whereas the latter section emphasizes holiness as the common concern of all Israelites.

Further patterns of organization are discernible in the former division: Chapters 1–10 deal with officiation, and chapters 11–16, with purification. Furthermore, there is a symmetry in the organization of each of the two subdivisions. We are first told in chapters 1–7 how the principal sacrifices are to be prepared and offered by the priests. Thereupon chapters 8–10 establish the exclusive legitimacy of the Aaronide priesthood as officiants in the sacrificial cult. They record the consecration of the priesthood and the initiation of the Tabernacle cult in the time of Moses.

The same internal pattern is evident in chapters 11–16, as regards purity. First, the duties of the priesthood in effecting required purifications are detailed in chapters 11–15. Then chapter 16 describes how the Sanctuary, whose altar and appurtenances were necessary for most purification rites, was to be kept in a pure state.

Within the former division, chapters 1–16, there is an apparent anomaly. We might have expected to find chapter 11 in the Holiness Code, since it ordains a regimen of dietary prohibitions and regulates the purity of vessels and their contents. These regulations apply to all Israelites, not only to priests. What is more, chapter 11 prescribes no explicit purification rites to be performed by the priests, as is the case of chapters 12–15. On what basis, then, can chapter 11 qualify as a *torah*, or manual, *for* the priesthood?

Actually, it may have originated in the Holiness Code, only to be shifted later on to the former division of Leviticus. This chapter is, after all, the only section of Leviticus outside the Holiness Code that emphasizes the theme of Israel's holiness (vv. 44–45). It employs

the same holiness terminology encountered in the Holiness Code itself, in such verses as 19: 1–2,36, 20:26, and 22:32–33. Perhaps the provisions of chapter 11 were redefined as a *torah* of purity, a manual of procedures for the priests. The postscript of chapter 11, in verses 46–47, implies as much: "These are the instructions (*ha-torah*) concerning animals, birds, all living creatures . . . for distinguishing between the unclean and the clean." Making such distinctions was one of the basic duties of priests, as we read in 10:10: "For you [= the priests] must distinguish between the sacred and the profane, and between the unclean and the clean."

At some point, chapter 11 was perceived to be germane to the training of priests, and its content was redefined in terms of purity, rather than holiness. In substance, the dietary code applied to all Israelites and was requisite to the attainment of holiness on the part of the people as a whole. This much is clear from the similar code of dietary laws preserved in Deuteronomy 14, where the theme of a holy nation predominates. In Leviticus, however, the dietary laws, extended to include the purity of vessels and of persons, came to be perceived as a matter of special concern to the priesthood and were positioned among the *torot* of purity. This is epitomized in the opening verses of chapter 11. In verse 1, God addresses Moses and Aaron, and in verse 2, He commands them to speak in turn to the Israelite people.

The second division of Leviticus consists of chapters 17–27. As regards chapter 27, one assumes that it was appended to Leviticus only after the Holiness Code was compiled, with the Epilogue (26:3–46) already in place. In content, the chapter belongs with the Holiness Code, as it deals with votives, consecrations, and other forms of popular support for the Sanctuary, all administered by the priests.

By and large, the contents of chapters 17–27 are addressed to the Israelite people and relate to the life of the entire community. And yet, we encounter apparent anomalies. Chapters 21–22 are addressed to the priesthood and deal with the physical requirements of priests and sacrificial materials. Also included are marriage restrictions applicable to priests and laws relieving priests of funerary duties: One might have expected to find these chapters in the former division of Leviticus.

Yet the theme of holiness predominates in chapters 21–22 and is reiterated in 21:15,24 and 22:16,32–33. These chapters stand in the same relation to the priesthood as does the rest of the Holiness Code in relation to the Israelite people. There is a symmetry. As an example, Israelites must follow certain marriage practices; the same is true of priests. One may also presume that the sanctity of the priesthood and its governance of its own membership were matters of concern to the entire community.

We are unable to account for the two overlapping versions of the marriage code in chapters 18 and 20. Although each is formulated differently, the presence of both is inevitably repetitious. In chapter 24, we find material arranged rather loosely. But for the most part, chapters 17–27 conform to the notion of *torat kohanim* as teachings *by* the priests that were addressed to the Israelite people.

Formulation Leviticus preserves only one prose composition, the Epilogue to the Holiness Code (26:3–46), and only a few brief reports. Aside from commonplace introductions and postscripts, Leviticus is otherwise devoted entirely to ritual and law. The nature of the content has dictated a particular style of writing that may be called "formulaic," the writing usually encountered in legal documents, in leases and deeds, and in purchase agreements.

Formulaic statements do not read smoothly; rather, they tend to be abrupt and laconic in style. Most important is the fact that the technical vocabulary of such documents is specialized, so that terms and verbal forms do not have their usual meanings. They must be interpreted in context. As an example, the common Hebrew verb *ʿasah*, "to do, make," may mean, in a priestly text, "to perform a ritual"; but, in another specific statement, it can also mean "to assign a sacrifice." It becomes necessary, therefore, to exercise care in reading formulaic texts so as not to overlook such specializations of meaning.

Several examples may serve to illustrate the complexity of language characteristic of Leviticus and of priestly writing in general.

1. In 1:4, we read of a procedure involved in presenting a sacrifice: *ve-samakh yado ʿal roʾsh ha-ʿolah ve-nirtsah lo le-khapper ʿalav*, "He [= the donor] shall lay his hand upon the head of the burnt offering, that it may be acceptable in his behalf, in expiation for him." Analyzing this verse as a formulaic statement must take into account the following factors:

a. The term *ʿolah*, as the name of a particular type of sacrificial offering, must be defined precisely.

b. The verb *samakh*, "to lay upon, lean upon," has a technical meaning in the context of ritual and law. It must be explained how the laying on of the hand functioned as part of the act of sacrifice and why it was necessary. This was a widespread practice both in biblical Israel and in the ancient Near East generally. Extensive Hittite evidence is available on this practice.

c. The Nifal form, *nirtsah*, "to be acceptable, to be regarded favorably," and other forms of the verb *ratsah* characterize both the favorable disposition of God and the suitability of the offering itself. The verb relates to one of the primary concerns of religious experience—the efficacy of ritual.

d. The verb *kipper*, "to expiate," is central to ancient Israelite worship because it relates to divine forgiveness. Its basic sense is that of cleansing, of washing away impurity and sinfulness. In this instance, we must also explain what need there was for expiation when an Israelite donated a burnt offering without any offense against God involved.

e. Finally, we must be precise in understanding the syntax of the verb *kipper* when it is followed by the preposition *ʿal*. In our case, it means to expiate "on behalf of, in relation to," whereas elsewhere it may imply physical contact: "to expiate over, upon."

2. In 25:47, we read of an Israelite indentured to a non-Israelite resident of the land:
ve-khi tassig yad ger ve-toshav ʿimmakh, umakh ʾaḥikha ʿimmo, ve-nimkar le-ger toshav . . . / "If a resident alien among you has prospered, and your kinsman being in straits, comes under his authority and gives himself over to the resident alien . . . ."

Formulaic analysis of this statement leads to the following observations:

a. Hebrew *ger ve-toshav* represents an example of hendiadys, two words that have the force of one, as though written *ger toshav*, a combination we actually find elsewhere; hence the translation "resident (*toshav*) alien (*ger*)." This composite term must be explained in various contexts. Here it refers to a non-Israelite living in the Land of Israel, whereas elsewhere in the same chapter (v. 23) it refers to the Israelites themselves as "residents" in God's land.

b. Hebrew *ʾaḥ*, literally "brother," is a term for a fellow Israelite; hence the translation "kinsman." It expresses the notion that all Israelites are related, as if in one large family. This connotation and its implications must be explored.

c. The verb *makhar*, "to sell," is here used to characterize indenture, a form of bondage

in which the debtor works for the creditor, usually on the creditor's premises, to pay off his debt. So, *nimkar*, the Nifal form, means to put oneself under the authority of another. This specialized meaning is also applicable in other Torah laws.

d. Finally, two other verbs used in this verse have specialized connotations that are particularly relevant to priestly law. The verb *mukh* seems to mean "to become weak." Here, and in similar statements in chapter 25, it connotes financial instability; hence the translation "being in straits." Similarly, the idiom *tassig yad*, literally, "the hand reaches," conveys the notion of acquisition or material gain.

3. In 8:10, we read about how Moses consecrated the Tabernacle: *va-yikkaḥ mosheh 'et shemen ha-mishah va-yimshaḥ 'et ha-mishkan ve-'et kol 'asher bo*/ "Moses took the anointing oil and anointed the Tabernacle and all that was in it, thus consecrating them." Here, again, careful analysis demands attention to technical usage:

a. The specific composition of the oil called *shemen ha-misḥah* must be described; furthermore, the rite of unction must be discussed in terms of its efficacy and function as part of the process of consecration.

b. The term that designates the Sanctuary in this verse is *mishkan*. Elsewhere in Leviticus we also find two other terms for the same structure: *'ohel mo'ed*, "the Tent of Meeting," and *mikdash*, "sanctuary, temple." The character of the projected Sanctuary must be described and the origins of the relevant terms traced.

c. Finally, the verb *kiddesh*, "to consecrate," proves to be of central importance in biblical literature. It expresses a whole complex of concepts and is linked to other forms of the verb *kadash*, "to be holy." The Piel form that we have here is often used to convey the attribution of holiness to persons, spaces, structures, and even special times, such as the Sabbath and festivals, that were "sanctified" in various ways.

The three examples just cited not only illustrate the "deep structure" of formulaic writing but also are informative in other ways. The first example comes from a *prescriptive* ritual, chapter 1. Most of the ritual texts of Leviticus are prescriptive in that they ordain, or command, certain procedures rather than merely describing them. Thus, the verb *vesamakh* conveys an order: "He *shall* lay upon." The second example, 25:47, actually comes from a legal passage. The *casuistic* formulation, which uses "If" or "When," is typical of legal statements. Often the actual requirements of law are expressed as conditions or circumstances: If certain conditions obtain, the law becomes operative.

In a real sense, ritual and law are interrelated because both are expressed in terms of duty and both require compliance with precise procedures.

The third example, 8:10, is taken from a descriptive ritual. The verbs occurring in descriptive rituals are in narrative forms, like *va-yikkaḥ*, "he took," in our verse. Descriptive rituals are formulated as reports, as though written by one who actually observed the performance of a particular celebration.

To summarize: Leviticus is almost entirely composed of prescriptive rituals pertaining to officiation and purification, of laws and commandments, and of descriptive rituals recording important celebrations.

Versions Both the translation and Commentary presented here are based on the Masoretic text of the Hebrew Bible. The term "Masoretic" designates a group of authorized texts of the Hebrew Bible that have been accepted by most Jewish communities since talmudic times, a period roughly corresponding to the early centuries of the Christian Era.

Exactly when and how the received Masoretic text became official is a difficult matter to ascertain. As more evidence emerges, it becomes clear that we are dealing with a complex and protracted process of collating manuscripts and of determining precise readings.[3]

Study of the actual Hebrew text of a given biblical book— its precise wording, spelling (orthography), and vocalization (a factor that directly affects meaning in Semitic languages)—is known as *text criticism*. The text critic attempts to determine what was the original ancient text. An effort is made to identify possible errors that may have crept into the text through miscopying. Ancient copies and early manuscripts are examined for this purpose.

We now know that differing versions of the text of the Torah, and of biblical books generally, circulated within Jewish communities during the Greco-Roman period. This is confirmed by recent discoveries of ancient copies, such as those found at Qumran, that preserve readings that differ from those appearing in our Masoretic text. At that site atop the cliff overlooking the Dead Sea, there lived a sect (or sects) of Jews from about 135 B.C.E. to about 70 C.E., when the Second Temple of Jerusalem was destroyed by the Romans. Those Jews retained copies of biblical texts alongside their contemporary, sectarian compositions. This archive, and similar writings discovered in nearby sites, have come to be known as the Dead Sea Scrolls. They include many texts, such as fragments of Exodus, as well as segments of Samuel, Jeremiah, and Psalms. The most impressive find is the extensive Isaiah scroll.[4] Some of the material has been published—including parts of one or more scrolls of Leviticus, written in a script imitative of earlier centuries—by D. N. Freedman and K. A. Mathews.[5] R. H. Harrison dates the script on paleographic grounds to around 100 B.C.E.

Scholars working with the Leviticus scroll, which preserves legible verses from chapters 4, 10, 11, and 13–27, have carefully tabulated all instances where these ancient fragments differ from our Masoretic text. They have also correlated these variations with the text of the Samaritans, which is an ancient version that differs appreciably from the Masoretic text at many points. The evidence of the Septuagint was also figured into the comparisons. The ancient Jewish translators of the Torah into Greek must have had before them a Hebrew text that differed from the Masoretic text at some points; otherwise their translations would make no sense.[6] The results of these rather complex comparisons indicate that the text of the Torah had not yet been standardized during the last pre-Christian centuries. At that time, its precise wording had not been uniformly accepted by all Jewish communities.

Just how significant this situation is for our understanding of the content of Leviticus is a matter of judgment. The variations between the Qumranic and the Masoretic versions do not reflect a different meaning or intent. Many are simply alternative ways of stating the same laws and rituals and involve little more than different tenses of the same verbs, juxtapositions of syntax, alterations of sequences, and stylistic variations. This is not so with respect to the Samaritan text, where we find substantive variations. (The Septuagint translation also reveals attempts by the translators to interpret the Hebrew text in specific ways.)

Nevertheless, quite early on, it seems, efforts were under way to standardize the text of the Torah, which was read in its entirety in the synagogue. Furthermore, exceptional care was exercised in copying Torah books: Since the laws and rituals of the Torah were basic to the fulfillment of Judaism, their status encouraged great textual precision.

In summary, the copies of Leviticus discovered at Qumran testify to a degree of textual variety around 100 B.C.E. regarding the third book of the Torah. These ancient copies

reinforce our sense that the Masoretic text of the Torah accurately preserves ancient writings. But the Masoretic versions also indicate that important decisions were eventually made in order to fix the wording of passages where variation had previously existed. The Greek Septuagint of Leviticus indicates only a few cases of textual divergence, where the text used by the translators was different from the Masoretic version.[7] These instances are hardly of great significance. When we contrast the situation of Leviticus to that of other biblical books such as Samuel, where whole passages differ, we appreciate how stable the text of the Torah was in late antiquity relative to other sections of the biblical canon.

The Context

Beyond the general guidelines established for the Commentary series as a whole, the present Commentary on Leviticus pursues a particular method. In part, this method was dictated by the distinctive character of the book itself, but it also reflects the approach adopted by the commentator.

In Search of Context: Realistic Interpretation The first matter to be discussed is the new translation, which appears alongside the Masoretic Hebrew text. It was produced under the auspices of the Jewish Publication Society and represents a major advance in our comprehension of the biblical text. In fact, it helped to guide the commentator to a more accurate understanding of the text than might otherwise have been possible in numerous instances. There were, however, cases where the commentator disagreed with the translators, and alternative renderings were proposed. Usually, such disagreements pertained to the syntax and style of the English translation. It was felt that the full import of the formulaic style of Leviticus was occasionally obscured in the translation, and an effort was made to convey with greater precision the meaning of the Hebrew technical terms and formulas. This approach to the process of translation merely underscores the importance of decoding formulaic writing in the effort to reconstruct the rituals and laws of Leviticus.

REALISM AND THE COMPARATIVE METHOD The technical terms and formulas of Leviticus are the very features that lend an air of realism to the written word. Just as in the analysis of legal texts one seeks to define the terms of reference used for crimes and violations or conditions and obligations, so too in studying ritual texts it is imperative to discern what the names of various sacrifices and rites meant to the ancient Israelites. In a significant way, most ritual texts are legal in character because they set down specific procedures and impose exact penalties.

A realistic approach to Leviticus posits that at certain periods of Israelite history, priests offered sacrifices just as they were instructed to do in the opening chapters of the book. On the same basis, it is assumed that priests presided over purifications like those prescribed in chapters 12–16. In other words, we consider the text of Leviticus to be a source of evidence of the actual practice of religion: to be sure, not the practice followed at all periods of biblical history but, rather, what was followed at *certain* periods. It is curious that the realistic approach is, in its way, traditional because the tradition invariably regards all that is written in the Torah as having actually occurred.

Though the traditionalist commentator tends to adopt a view that allows for relatively little development or change in practice, the very belief in the authenticity of Mosaic law

reveals a realistic perspective. In its commitment to realism, this Commentary follows the method of the Mishnah and of rabbinic legal interpretation in the effort to preserve and reconstruct the realia of the biblical cult.

Modern critical scholars have for the most part tended to doubt the realism of the priestly texts of the Torah. Some regard the rituals and laws of Leviticus as artificial or programmatic, as canonical statements of what was thought to be proper rather than as evidence of actual practice. According to this view, the repetitious detail of ritual formulation does not reveal the true nature of religion but merely represents ossified crystallizations of established practices whose inner logic had been largely forgotten and whose forms had lost much of their meaning. The tendency toward homiletical and allegorical interpretation of ritual has also served to distance the study of Leviticus from realistic insights. Without discounting the independent value of such methods of interpretation and the edifying messages they afford, it is more important to retrieve, as best we can, the reality of ancient biblical religion. After all, it is this reality, this actual stage of religious development, that is the basis of all subsequent phases of Jewish religion.

Perhaps the strongest endorsement of realistic interpretation is offered by comparative evidence from other ancient Near Eastern cultures. One who is conversant with the documentary evidence of ancient Egypt, Mesopotamia, and Syria would hardly doubt that the priestly texts of the Torah have a foundation in reality. One would hardly regard as unrealistic an elaborate account of numerous sacrifices listed in repetitious sequence if the tablet on which that account was written had been unearthed in the ruins of a Mesopotamian temple. We now possess thousands of such ancient records.[8]

Nor would one doubt the realism of a Ugaritic temple ritual of the late second millennium B.C.E. that prescribes various sacrifices and recitations for specific days of a given month, listing these in repetition.[9] The same realism is assumed for Hittite festival texts and purifications and for Egyptian wall inscriptions, which often appear alongside pictorial depictions of the very ceremonial scenes referred to in the inscriptions themselves.[10] From a later period, we have the tariffs from Carthage, which inform all who wished to offer sacrifices in the temple of that important city as to what items and amounts had to be remitted to the temple administration. This information pertains, most probably, to the fourth and third centuries B.C.E.[11]

Admittedly, we lack the kind of historical information for Leviticus that we possess for the extrabiblical documents, and this lack seems to diminish our sense of realism. Thus, although the extensive archaeological activity carried out on biblical soil has yielded artifacts and structures in great quantity, relatively little of it is written material. We also lack the graphic depictions of ritual like those that have been found in Egypt, Mesopotamia, and Syria. And there is a tendency to regard canonical texts as being at least once removed from reality since they have undergone some editing and reformulation. Nevertheless, careful utilization of all that we actually possess from biblical Israel combined with examination of comparative sources can at least partially compensate for the scarcity of Hebraic evidence. Though we may never overcome our disadvantages, we ought not to diminish our efforts in search of ancient reality.

In addition to contemporary evidence, we possess later Jewish sources of considerable value for reconstructing biblical rituals. The Mishnah and other rabbinic texts preserve extensive descriptions of ritual celebrations as they were conducted in late Second Temple times. As an example, tractate Yoma of the Mishnah is devoted entirely to the rites of Yom

Kippur. In formulation and arrangement, these rabbinic texts often read like ancient Near Eastern documents. In some respects they resemble the temple records and ritual tablets of the ancient Near East, even more closely than do the priestly texts of the Torah.

The validity of utilizing the Mishnah as evidence of earlier Israelite practice can be argued on the basis of an analogy from elsewhere in the ancient Near East. Thus, it is generally considered valid for students of Mesopotamian religion to utilize as source material the Uruk rituals, much later texts that date from the Seleucid period.[12] We find that, even allowing for changes in religious practice, later material coming from identical locales and pertaining to the same people or society can be highly instructive. It has been found to be so in interpreting Leviticus.

Also suggestive of the realism of Leviticus are the specific terms for the sacrifices that were offered in biblical times, many of which originated in other, nonritual or nonpriestly contexts. They can be studied more precisely in those contexts where their root meanings and basic functions are clearly evident.

Several examples can serve to illustrate the method employed in this Commentary. The term *minḥah* designates grain offerings in the priestly texts. In the Commentary, its various meanings are explored. Ultimately, Hebrew *minḥah* derives from the political and administrative vocabulary, where it has the meaning of "tribute, gift." The *minḥah* was paid to kings of Judah and Israel by tributary peoples and, under less favorable circumstances, by Israelites to foreign, imperial kings (cf. 2 Sam. 8:2–6; 1 Kings 5:1; 2 Kings 8:8–9, 17:3–4). There can be little doubt that the administrative meanings of *minḥah* are primary; priestly and other writers appropriated the term to designate certain types of offerings that were presented in the manner of gifts. A term meaning "tribute, gift" is, after all, highly appropriate for expressing the relationship between the individual worshiper and God and between the Israelite community and the God of Israel. It highlights the themes of sovereignty and subservience, of covenant and mutual obligations, and of loyalty and devotion.

In a similar way, Hebrew *tamid*, "regular, daily sacrifice; daily rite," was appropriated by priestly writers from the administrative vocabulary. In nonritual contexts, *tamid* designates *regular* rations or allocations granted by kings to their retainers (2 Sam. 9:7,10; 2 Kings 25:29–30; Jer. 52:33). What better term for the daily sacrifice in Exodus 29 or in Numbers 28!

A third example may further clarify this process of appropriation. The Hebrew verb *ḥata'*, "to offend, sin," and the nouns derived from it, such as *ḥatta't*, "sin offering," are basic to the vocabulary of cult and ritual. They pertain to one of the principal objectives of ritual, the expiation of religious offenses. In other biblical contexts, the verb *ḥata'* clearly signifies violations of treaties and alliances: the betrayal of trust between nations and between officials and their overlords. In this instance, we are fortunate in having the Akkadian cognate *ḥaṭû* and its derivatives so that we can document their semantic range, extending from the political and administrative to ritual and purificatory contexts.

These examples suggest that the priestly writers and others writing about the practice of religion operated within a larger institutional framework. Like royal scribes (which many were), they used a vocabulary and formulary common to that larger context. The cult, in other words, did not function as something apart or "unreal." Rather, the observable interaction of religion, government, and society that is indicated by the terms and formulas of the priestly texts further enhances our sense of realism.

THE PHENOMENOLOGY OF RELIGION Phenomenology is the study of essence and manifestation. We often observe a manifest act and ask what it "means" in the hope of learning why such an act was performed in specific ways. What did it "mean," for example, to offer a burnt sacrifice on the altar in celebration of a particular occasion? To answer questions of this sort, we attempt to penetrate the inner mentality of the ancient Israelites.

It is extremely difficult in general to attribute meaning to formal acts, especially so regarding those we can no longer observe in practice. Such acts possess inner systemic meaning; that is, they may be seen as "meaningful" only within discrete contexts. Once certain facts are known, the overt behavior makes sense, just as details of law make sense only if we see them as part of an overall legal system based on known principles.

One example will suffice. In this Commentary it is proposed that, by declaring the corpse of an Israelite impure in the extreme, the Torah effectively eliminated any funerary role for the priesthood. No funerary cult was admitted into the Sanctuary, and attending to the burial of the dead was declared a family matter.[13]

On the face of it, one would have expected the Israelite priesthood to be involved in funerary rites, since death has surely been a matter of religious concern in virtually every known human society. But a religious system opposed to pagan cults of the dead, one which regarded worship of dead ancestors as incompatible with worship of the God of Israel, would indeed have sought to distance funerary activity from the Sanctuary and to eliminate any priestly role in such rites.

Perhaps the most valuable insight we might obtain about the phenomenology of biblical religion would be an explanation of the meaning of the act of sacrifice itself. What were the *concerns* that made sacrificial worship so important? Of all the theories that have been advanced to explain the phenomenon of sacrifice, the notion of the sacrifice as a *gift* offered to the Deity tells us most about the purposes of such worship. Again the key is provided by terminology.

When we analyze the names of specific sacrifices, we observe that many of them connote a gift of some sort. We have already seen that *minḥah* basically means "gift, tribute." The term *berakhah*, usually rendered "blessing," means "grant, gift" in contexts relevant to gifts of land and other forms of material wealth.[14] In this Commentary it is proposed that Hebrew *shelamim*, the name given to a popular sacrifice, actually means "sacred gift of greeting," based on comparative evidence from other ancient Semitic languages.[15] These and other examples endorse the notion that a sacrifice is first and foremost a gift. This is so even when a sacrifice is obligatory or when it is prompted by some offense committed against God.[16]

The purpose of sacrifice was to formalize or reaffirm and, at times, to repair the relationship between the worshiper and God and between the community of worshipers and God. It is this relationship and the problems emerging from it that require explanation.

Human beings have always sought the nearness and presence of God (or of the gods, in polytheistic environments). We are filled with anxiety at the prospect of God's withdrawal, or absence, or distance from the human scene. In truth, God is omnipresent: He hears our prayers even from the distant heavens. We are told that He "is near . . . to all who call Him with sincerity" (Ps. 145:18).

Despite the avowed belief in God's omnipresence, it was seldom satisfying or reassuring to the human psyche. Emotionally, we expect that God, as the power who sustains the universe and grants the petitions of His worshipers, responds to our needs more readily if He is near and present and that He is less likely to do so from heaven. This feeling is a

projection of human dependence on God. But to retain the nearness of God it was necessary to provide a sacred environment acceptable to Him. It was feared that if the purity of the earthly environment were compromised, God would become enraged and withdraw His presence from His people, often punishing them as well.

Thus, in Leviticus and in priestly literature generally, we find statements as to what was required to retain God's continuing presence in the midst of His people. If Israel becomes a kingdom of priests and a holy nation, with all that this entails, the God of Israel will abide amidst the people and grant them the blessings of life. This is the inner reality of the rituals and laws of Leviticus, and these are the central concerns that generated all that Leviticus ordains.[17]

Literary History: When Leviticus Was Written Positioned between Exodus and Numbers, the Book of Leviticus is an integral part of the written history that flows through the five books of the Torah. After leaving Egypt, the Israelites experienced the revelation of God at Sinai, where they entered into a covenant with God and received laws and commandments by which to live as a people. One aspect of the covenant was the commandment to initiate the proper worship of the God of Israel. Exodus concludes by recording the construction of the desert Tabernacle and, in anticipation of Leviticus, refers to the investiture of the Aaronide priesthood.

Although Leviticus records some events, it is essentially not a recounting of historical developments and changes. Hence, there is no historiography per se. The book begins with God's call to Moses from the Tent of Meeting (another name for the Tabernacle), and, in its entirety, it pertains to the institution of religious life within the Israelite community before the settlement of Canaan, the promised land. It appears that the sequence of events in Leviticus occurs during a very brief period of time at the beginning of the forty years of wandering. The institution of worship and the ordering of religious life set forth in the book were undertaken before the wanderings began—more precisely, before the decree that the people would have to wander so many years before entering Canaan. The Book of Numbers, by contrast, begins with reference to a specific date, the first day of the second month of the second year after the Exodus from Egypt. Numbers covers a period of some thirty-eight years, and it contains the historiographic climax of the Torah, which occurs in the steppes of Moab, before the crossing of the Jordan (an event recounted as well at the end of Deuteronomy).

The tradition has consistently accepted this literary framework as historical and has considered the many statements in Leviticus—and in the Torah generally, wherein God speaks to Moses, and Aaron, and the Israelites—as historically accurate. According to this view, the entire Torah was revealed, or communicated, through Moses, precisely as stated. Since talmudic antiquity, sages and commentators have been aware of chronological discrepancies and have been willing to concede that the events recorded in the Torah do not always appear in actual sequence. Thus the talmudic dictum: "There is no early or late in the Torah." They also agree that certain laws belonged, more logically, in other contexts. But never is the possibility accepted that the Torah, as we have it, was compiled from separate, sometimes divergent, sources or components, attributable to different authors and historical periods.

Traditional interpreters found it necessary to deal with apparent contradictions in the text itself, a situation that threatened the concept of the unity of transmission in which they believed. Leviticus 1:1 records God's call to Moses from the Tent of Meeting after the

Sinaitic revelation, whereas other statements in Leviticus indicate that certain instructions were communicated at Sinai (7:37–38; 25:1; 26:46; 27:34). In Numbers we find statements of Sinaitic revelation in 36:13, but Numbers 1:1 indicates a communication at the Tent of Meeting, and 26:3, in the steppes of Moab, some thirty-eight years later. D. Z. Hoffmann, a traditionalist scholar writing around the turn of the twentieth century, devotes considerable attention to the problem of transmission.[18] He cites a dispute between sages of the second century C.E., recorded in Zevaḥim 115b: "R. Ishmael says: The generalities were spoken at Sinai, and the specifics at the Tent of Meeting. R. Akiba says: Both the generalities and the specifics were [first] spoken at Sinai. They were reiterated at the Tent of Meeting and stated a third time in the steppes of Moab."

Rabbi Akiba's view has predominated in the Jewish tradition. But the real significance of this ancient debate lies in its presuppositions, not in its proposed resolution. The Torah was revealed by the one divine shepherd to one prophet, Moses, and nothing stated in it should be construed as contradicting this doctrine. There can be no real differences among Exodus, Leviticus, Numbers, and Deuteronomy as to what each records or prescribes as law and commandment. Surely God would not contradict Himself. More consequentially—Moses' transmission of God's words was considered faithful and accurate. The historical implication of this view is that the laws and rites set forth in Leviticus either went into effect in the Israelite society of Moses' day or were intended to take effect once the people entered Canaan and settled there.

For the past several centuries, ever since the Renaissance and the Age of Humanism during the early sixteenth century, a modern method of studying the Hebrew Bible, including the Torah, has been pursued: the critical method.[19] Critical scholarship regards the Bible as ancient literature and understands statements attributing time and place to events and institutions as *traditional*, as conveying what ancient authors and editors would have the reader accept as historical. Whether or not such statements are historically accurate is a determination to be made on the basis of critical investigation and may not be accepted as accurate solely on the evidence of the biblical text.

If there is any degree of consensus among modern critical scholars, who predictably disagree on many questions, it is in the judgment that the institutions legislated in the Torah and the concepts expressed in its historical narratives were promulgated centuries later than the age of Moses and, then, not all at the same time. In substance, certain Torah institutions are very ancient, even antedating the lifetime of Moses, which history would assign to the late thirteenth or early twelfth century B.C.E. Other institutions appear to be relatively late. The critical consensus is that the Torah as we have it is comprised of components, or "sources," and not merely of books. These sources use different language, reflect different historical periods, and express divergent points of view regarding early Israelite history and the biblical message as well. The key factor in the critical approach is development; and its most basic insight is the awareness of difference. Instead of attempting to harmonize divergences, the critical scholar is particularly sensitive to the factor of change.

Generally speaking, critical inquiry is historically oriented in its search for ancient reality. It accepts the validity of comparative evidence derived from other, related societies and cultures. The traditionalist, on the other hand, is more interested in the message of Torah literature. Therefore, whereas the critical scholar seeks to reconstruct the literary processes involved in the composition of the Torah, to trace the actual historical development of Israelite religion and society, the traditionalist is more concerned with Torah

literature as the central document of Judaism, the ultimate foundation upon which later Judaism rests.

The two approaches are not totally irreconcilable. Although traditionalists cannot accept much of what the critical scholar discovers because it may conflict with doctrine, they appreciate the critical scholar's cultural insights on the meaning of the text. And the critical scholar can, indeed, learn much from traditional interpretations and insights, even if he does not share the overall presuppositions underlying traditional interpretations.

As regards Leviticus, the prime representative of priestly literature in the Torah, critical inquiry has added considerably to our understanding of the text, as well as to our historical knowledge about the development of biblical religion.

Critical scholars refer to the priestly component of Torah literature as *Priesterschrift* (commonly called P). The contents of Leviticus emerged from centers of priestly administration in biblical Israel such as Jerusalem, and Leviticus is linked by language and subject matter to other priestly materials preserved in the books of the Torah generally.

Priestly writing in the Torah is of two main types: historiography on the one hand, and law and ritual on the other. In Genesis, Exodus, and Numbers, and even occasionally in Deuteronomy, we find priestly historiography, which, in effect, recasts the early history of Israel in a way that assigns great historic importance to covenants between God and Israel and between God and the patriarchs. Priestly writers were particularly interested in genealogies—in establishing the connection of the generations and in emphasizing the bonds uniting all Israelites. They recorded an unbroken tradition of sacrifice and of the worship of God: from the sacrifices offered by Adam and the patriarchs to the Passover of Egypt and, in the Book of Numbers, to the end of the period of wanderings. Priestly writers were absorbed by ritual detail; they sought to root the proper worship of God and the institutional network required to conduct such worship in the earliest periods of Israelite history.

By studying Leviticus as *priestly* literature, we are also able to assess its relationship to those statements on matters of worship and religious life that are preserved in the historical and prophetic books. Once we accept the possibility that certain of the laws and institutions, as set forth in Leviticus, derive from later periods of biblical history, we may explore, by comparison and contrast, the relationship of Leviticus to Ezekiel, especially the concluding chapters of the latter book. We are also attracted to the dicta of Jeremiah and Deutero-Isaiah and of the postexilic prophets Haggai, Zechariah, and Malachi, all of whom addressed questions of ritual and worship quite extensively. The emphasis on cult and worship and on the Temple as a central institution in Ezra, Nehemiah, and Chronicles is similarly directly relevant.

In summary, the critical analysis of Torah literature has led to the identification of several documentary sources, or textual archives, emanating from different schools of writers in biblical times. Each contributed its content to the Torah and to biblical literature as a whole.

In addition to priestly literature, modern scholarship has identified a source known as E (Elohist), in which the God of Israel is designated by the generic term *'elohim*, "Divinity, God." This collection is presumed to have emerged from the northern Israelite kingdom. More recently, it has been suggested that there is a distinctive Transjordanian component in biblical literature, composed of writings from that area, especially from Gilead. In successive periods of biblical history, large areas of Transjordan were under Israelite domination, and Israelites were settled there.[20]

Another source is known as J, based on "Jehovah," a mistaken reading of the con-

sonants YHVH, the tetragrammaton. This source emerged from Judah and its capital, Jerusalem. At some time in preexilic history, the two sources J and E were combined by Judean editors. Finally, we have what scholars refer to as the Deuteronomic school, which, known as D, continued to function in ancient Israel long after J and E were compiled.

At the present time, there is considerable disagreement among critical scholars as to the history and development of the source known as P. The textual content of P is fairly well defined because priestly language is distinctive and specialized. It is much more difficult to trace the *historic* development of priestly literature—in this instance, of Leviticus, which consists entirely of priestly writings. Several general observations will serve to identify the problems encountered by critical scholars.

1. The canonical order of the books of the Torah (Genesis, Exodus, Leviticus, Numbers, Deuteronomy) may or may not be historically accurate. (Moreover, each of the five books is in itself a composite, preserving materials of differing origins.) For the purposes of this Commentary it is of critical importance to ascertain whether Leviticus antedates Deuteronomy, as the canonical order indicates, or whether the reverse is the case. This determination is important because Deuteronomy 12 and 14–17 expound a new doctrine of religious worship; and worship is of course the principal concern of Leviticus. Thus, the sequence necessarily influences our understanding of Leviticus.

Deuteronomy ordains that all sacrificial worship and cultic activity be conducted at the one central Temple. Such activities would be illegitimate if carried out at any other cult site. No other Torah book states this restriction explicitly, though there may be an allusion to it in Leviticus. Indeed, Exodus 20:22–23 states that sacrifices to the God of Israel may be offered at any proper site.

Deuteronomy, therefore, announces a new pattern of worship, a change in customary practice. In some way, this Deuteronomic doctrine is historically related to the edict of Josiah, king of Judah, issued in 622 B.C.E. and reported in 2 Kings 22–23. Josiah most probably reaffirmed a doctrine known earlier, whose implementation had been neglected or opposed for generations. The Deuteronomic doctrine eventually produced far-reaching changes in religious life.

To return to our question: Is the cultic legislation of Leviticus based on this Deuteronomic doctrine of centralized worship? Some great scholars, including Julius Wellhausen in the nineteenth century, interpreted the provisions of Leviticus 17 as indirectly endorsing the doctrine of cult centralization.[21] We read there that Israelites were forbidden, once in their own land, to continue offering sacrifices wherever they wished, as they had done previously. They were required to bring all sacrifices to the Tent of Meeting, to be offered on the sanctuary altar by a legitimate priest. According to Wellhausen, this regulation, cast in a wilderness setting and with a portable Tent-shrine, reflects the distinctive doctrine of Deuteronomy; that is, its statement in Leviticus would have been inconceivable without the prior promulgation of Deuteronomic law.

More recently, H. L. Ginsberg has argued that the festival legislation of Leviticus 23 represents a response to the same Deuteronomic doctrine of centralized worship.[22] An Israelite intending to celebrate one of the pilgrimage festivals fully would be required to undertake a lengthy trip to a central sanctuary and could no longer celebrate at a local shrine or high place (*bamah*). This logistical problem lies behind the festival legislation of chapter 23, which altered the duration and scheduling of festivals, as well as their cultic character. Most of these changes were instituted against the background of the prior Deuteronomic reforms of worship.

Ginsberg, noting similarities of diction and doctrine between Hosea and Deuteronomy, traces the origin of the law of cult centralization to the northern kingdom of Israel, in the period before the fall of that kingdom to the Assyrians in 722–721 B.C.E. He proposes that Deuteronomic writings (though not the entire Book of Deuteronomy) were transmitted to Judah and Jerusalem and that these ideas influenced King Hezekiah of Judah, who had endeavored to do away with the high places (2 Kings 18:4). This effort apparently failed. Hezekiah was followed by Manasseh, who enjoyed a long reign and was known for his heterodoxy. In the late seventh century, Josiah, who had "returned" to the Lord sincerely (2 Kings 23:25), destroyed the major cult sites in use at the time and altered the role of the priesthood.

Now, if Leviticus mirrors the doctrine of Deuteronomy, then it is most likely a product of the age of Josiah at the earliest, at least in its laws governing proper worship and celebrations. There are scholars who dispute this historical reconstruction and, instead, regard the legislation of Leviticus as being earlier than the time of Josiah and the promulgation of the Deuteronomic doctrine of cult centralization. Foremost among these was Yehezkel Kaufmann.[23] In his monumental work, he argued that the priestly literature of the Torah emerged at an earlier period than the Deuteronomic writings. More recent scholars, who follow this chronology, date P to the early seventh century B.C.E.

2. The relative chronology of the Torah books and of the sources that comprise Torah literature also has a bearing on the significance of the similarities, in language and content, between the writings of Ezekiel and P. Ezekiel, the priest-prophet, was a major spokesman of the priestly school of Jerusalem. He lived at the time of the destruction of the First Temple and went into exile to Babylonia. Some scholars, following Kaufmann and others of his persuasion, maintain that P served as a source for Ezekiel. Others conclude that, for the most part, the relationship was the reverse: It was Ezekiel who introduced some of the themes that found their way into the priestly source of the Torah.

Ginsberg, for example, proposes that themes prominent in the Epilogue to the Holiness Code of Leviticus (26:3–46) were drawn from Ezekiel. Historically, this would mean that, at the very least, parts of the Epilogue were written well into the Babylonian exile, during the sixth century B.C.E.

The most prudent view on the history of Leviticus would approximate that of the late E. A. Speiser: that priestly law and literature took form over a protracted period of time and that it would be inaccurate to assign all of their contents to a single period of ancient history.[24] This approach helps to explain the presence of some relatively early material in Leviticus, while at the same time allowing for the inclusion of exilic and postexilic creativity. It also correlates well with the observable strata within Leviticus and within P as a whole, a subject to be explained in due course.

There are indications that Leviticus may include postexilic material. Certain of its terms of reference are known from extrabiblical documents of the late sixth and fifth centuries B.C.E., after the end of the Babylonian exile. Some of the legislation of Leviticus regarding the jurisdiction of the priesthood fits in well with the preexilic situation—for example, chapter 27, which speaks of priestly accountability for Temple administration, a set of functions compatible with the Judean monarchy. Chapter 25, however, speaks of indebtedness, indenture, and land transactions; it is unrealistic to suppose that under the Judean kings the priesthood would have had jurisdiction over such matters. From the books of Samuel and Kings, it would appear that royal officials and local elders dealt with such transactions. In the postexilic period, however, Jerusalem and Judea were governed by

a priesthood, a "hierocracy," centered in the Temple of Jerusalem, whose heads represented the Jewish community to the Persian authorities. The theory of land tenure set forth in chapter 25 also differs appreciably from that typical of the preexilic period.

There is a certain logic in supposing that, at a time when the Second Temple was being rebuilt, priestly writers would be engaged in recording their interpretation of the historic events that had contributed to the Judean restoration. One hears echoes of exilic prophecy in Leviticus, in such themes as redemption (*ge'ullah*), a major emphasis in the writings of the exilic author, or authors, of Isaiah 40–66.

In summary, Leviticus is part of the priestly component in Torah literature, in keeping with its traditional classification as *torat kohanim*. It is linked to priestly historiography preserved in Genesis, Exodus, and Numbers and even occasionally in Deuteronomy. In their interpretations of early Israelite history, priestly writers placed great emphasis on religious concerns: the covenant between God and Israel, sacrifice and celebration, purification and the quest for holiness. Some of the forms of sacrifice prescribed in Leviticus were quite ancient. This is true of the Sabbath and annual festivals as well—though it is likely that, in Leviticus, they also incorporate later phases of development.

In this regard, Leviticus is like other biblical books. Each has a prehistory as well as a literary history, having undergone various stages of redaction. Ancient Israelite religion incorporated institutions and laws that antedated their committal to writing. A close study of Leviticus shows that although the book is unified by its common priestly derivation, many of its sections and chapters exhibit distinctive features, suggesting that it includes materials written by different authors at different times—a probability strengthened by a careful look at its terminology. The book contains terms for designating the collectivity of Israelites, ranging from the common term *benei yisra'el*, "the Israelites," to the more limited one, *beit yisra'el*, "the household of Israel," a term largely concentrated in chapters 17 and 22 (and once in 10:6). Chapters 17 and 22, both of which are in the Holiness Code, have other elements in common, further indicating that they derive from the same archive or have been written by the same author.

When we examine terms referring to fellow Israelites, we also encounter concentrations of usage in the Holiness Code. The term *re'a*, "companion," is found only in Leviticus 19 and 20, both in the Holiness Code; *'amit*, "kinsman," is restricted to chapter 5 and the Holiness Code. These facts of usage correlate with the overall definition of the Holiness Code as a distinctive collection. Even the frequent biblical term *'aḥ*, "brother, kinsman," as a way of referring to a fellow Israelite, is restricted in Leviticus to the Holiness Code. These patterns suggest the conclusion that Leviticus, in its received form, was compiled from existing documents or archives and that little attempt was made to standardize usage with respect to its basic terminology.

It is also true that in any given chapter or other textual unit one may find passages that were added to a prior version of the text. Taking Leviticus 23 as an example, we note that verse 4 repeats verse 2 in introducing the set times (*mo'adim*) of the liturgical year. We also find two consecutive statements on the Sukkot festival, one in verses 33–38, the other in verses 39–43. The former statement ends with a summary in verses 37–38, and it is quite abrupt to have a second statement appearing after a summary.

Like the other books of the Torah, Leviticus documents significant developments in the celebration of the festivals and other important observances. To identify such developments requires the subtle analysis of the text, its terminology and composition, and its relation to other sources dealing with similar subjects.

Institutional History: Realistic Functions in Leviticus Perhaps the closest we can come to a sense of historical reality regarding the laws and rituals of Leviticus is through an analysis of the institutions to which the book refers. As has been explained, Leviticus lacks the usual information on which critical scholars rely in their effort to date an ancient text. However, we may instead utilize religious institutions as historical indicators. If we can establish when certain practices or procedures went into effect, when certain laws were enacted, or when the Israelites began to order their collective existence as Leviticus requires, we may be able to identify specific periods of biblical history.

Four principal factors are reflected in Leviticus and are presupposed by its laws and rituals: (1) the community, within which the program ordained by Leviticus was to be realized; (2) the priesthood or consecrated fraternity in charge of the religious life of the community and its individual members; (3) the Sanctuary, a structural complex where sacrificial worship, purification rites, and public celebration took place; and (4) the cult, a regimen of worship, purification, and celebration centered in the Sanctuary and conducted by the priesthood.

THE COMMUNITY Leviticus ordains a religious way of life for a community or for a network of communities. As projected in Leviticus, this community was comprised of the Israelites living during the period of the Sinai migrations, prior to the settlement of Canaan. Moses was the leader of the people, with Aaron, the High Priest, at his side. God communicated to Moses, and sometimes to Aaron as well, the regulations by which the Israelites were to live; this is how the community was governed. Also communicated were laws that would take effect once the people settled in the land of Canaan. There is no reference to a king, for the obvious reason that Leviticus is set in a period that antedates the advent of the monarchy.

A traditionalist commentator would tend to interpret the diverse names by which the community is designated in Leviticus as synonymous with each other. By contrast, the critical interpreter would seek to learn what each of these names contributes to our historic knowledge of the ancient Israelites. It would be best to divide these various names into two categories: (1) functional terms that inform us realistically about the nature of the community as conceived in Leviticus, and (2) traditional terms that are common to many biblical traditions and tell us little of specific significance as regards Leviticus.

In the latter group of traditional, or representative, terms we find ***benei yisra'el***, "the Israelite people," and ***beit yisra'el***, "the household of Israel." These names are hardly distinctive; nor is the frequent designation ***ha'am***, "the people." The truly functional terms seem to be ***ha-'edah***, "the community," a specifically priestly term of reference, and ***ha-kahal***, "the congregation," a term of generally wider usage that seems to have a specific function in Leviticus.

A cognate of the term ***'edah*** is known outside the Hebrew Bible. It occurs in Aramaic documents of the fifth century B.C.E. unearthed in Egypt, at the site of the Jewish colony at Elephantine. In those documents, Aramaic ***'edah*** is one way of referring to the socio-religious unit; we read of one who would rise up in the ***'edah*** to press his suit or to take other legal action.[25] The derivation of the word ***'edah*** is not entirely certain, but quite clearly it is a term having no genealogical, familial, or tribal connection. The same is true of ***kahal***, which is also known from extrabiblical sources. Whereas the terms ***benei yisra'el, beit yisra'el***, and ***'am*** express kinship, at least in their original orientation, the terms ***'edah*** and ***kahal*** do not. It is of interest to note that the usual terms for "tribe," ***shevet*** and ***matteh***,

never appear in Leviticus as designations for the internal units that comprised the collectivity, as they frequently do in the Book of Numbers, for example.

Hebrew *mishpaḥah*, "clan," is a functional term in Leviticus. It appears in contexts that speak of the economic ties that bind families together and of land ownership. In significant respects, the functional context of the Israelite clan had broken down, but, as in all communities, clans continued to exist. We also find in Leviticus that the laws governing marriage serve to define the immediate family in terms of both consanguineal (blood) and affinal (marriage) relations. And yet, when it comes to ways of referring to fellow Israelites, we again encounter differing functional and traditional terms and sometimes the same term used in various ways. Leviticus employs the kinship term *'aḥ*, "brother, kinsman," to refer to a member of the same clan, in which cases its use is functional; but it also uses *'aḥ* more loosely to refer to any member of a society. There is also reference to *benei ʿamkha*, "fellow members of your people."

The most definitively functional terms in Leviticus are social in orientation and have no basis in kinship. Thus, a fellow Israelite may be a *reʿa*, "fellow, associate," or an *ʿamit*, "neighbor," a term occurring in Leviticus and only once elsewhere, in Zechariah 13:7, in parallelism with *reʿa*. A community whose members refer to each other as *reʿa* or *ʿamit* is one in which clans and families function in the usual ways but where common ancestry and kinship play much less of a role than do social communality and religious identity. This conclusion is somewhat surprising because we customarily think of the priestly tradition as emphasizing genealogy, whereas what we see in Leviticus is evidence of covenantal community.

Settlement patterns may also point either to traditional conceptions, on the one hand, or to aspects of historical reality, on the other. In the context of the migration through Sinai en route to the promised land, Leviticus often refers to *ha-maḥaneh*, "the encampment," which we may regard as a traditional term in that setting. We also find a rather imprecise term, *moshavot*, "settlements," literally "territories of habitation." In contrast to these, Leviticus also speaks of towns (*ʿir, ʿarim*), referring to urban dwellings and to the Levitical towns. It deals with the legalities of the sale of both urban property and arable land. More curious, perhaps, and possibly more revealing, is the reference to towns in the laws of Leviticus 14:40ff. that require quarantine of diseased persons.[26]

Beneath the surface of traditional terminology in Leviticus we find terms characteristic of an agrarian society that also engaged in pastoral pursuits. An example is *migrash*, "lot," a way of designating both corrals and gardens adjacent to towns. We also encounter the term *ḥatserim*, "open settlements," which designates agricultural and/or pastoral villages. Outside the towns is the *sadeh*, "open country."

Terms for leadership likewise contribute to the picture of the Israelite community projected in Leviticus. There is only one occurrence of the tribal term *nasi'*, "chieftain," and in that instance we are told that the *nasi'* who is guilty of a religious offense must expiate it in the same manner as any other Israelite. In contrast, an offense by the High Priest, called "the anointed priest," is of the same consequence as one committed by the entire community; it therefore requires more elaborate expiation rites. This suggests that the High Priest was the functional head of the community. We occasionally read of the *zekenim*, "elders," but only in ceremonial roles.

In summary, a functional analysis of what Leviticus has to say about the nature of the Israelite community leads to the following conclusions: We have reflected in Leviticus a community functioning as a socioreligious organism, whose members are similar to what

we today would call citizens. This agricultural/pastoral community is governed by the High Priest, and its affairs are administered by the priesthood. In the Commentary, as well as in this Introduction, it is suggested that the community depicted in Leviticus would seem to reflect the life situation of the Judean populace in the early postexilic period. At that time, a hierocracy, or a government by priests, administered Jerusalem and Judea under Persian imperial domination. An alternative model could be the premonarchic pattern of settlement, but there are many reasons to consider such an early provenance unlikely.

Regarding the social character of the projected community, we can say, furthermore, that it was intended to be sacred. Non-Israelite residents were to be treated humanely, but they were prohibited from overt acts that clashed with the strictly monotheistic commitments of Israelite religion. For example, they were required to respect the festivals, which, including the Sabbaths, were to be observed in all the Israelite habitations and celebrated in the public cult.

Great care was to be exercised in diet and in the storage and preparation of food. There was a heightened concern with purity; certain unusual diseases and infections, as well as normal physiological phenomena, were classified as impure and regulated accordingly. The objective of this community was to become a holy nation in every respect, a people unified by a common religion and, in the words of the Epilogue to the Holiness Code, bound by a common destiny. Communal and interpersonal relations were to be conducted on the highest ethical level. Elders and parents were to be shown respect. Dealings were to be honest. The unfortunate had to be cared for. Israelites were expected to be devout in their support for the priesthood and Sanctuary, pious in worship, and God-fearing. All inadvertent offenses against God were to be expiated in the cult, so as to avert God's wrath.

Is it realistic to conclude that *all* the laws and rituals of Leviticus were observed within the community? Of course not! From prophetic denunciations and critiques of religious experience, we gather that there was often cause for complaint. The admonitions against idolatry and its concomitants—sorcery, necromancy, and divination—and the great emphasis on preserving the distinctiveness of Israelite identity indicate that there were ongoing problems. Biblical outcries against social injustice likewise warn the reader against idealizing the ancient Israelite community. Such horrendous stories as the sudden death of two of Aaron's sons at God's hand for a ritual offense suggest the need to admonish the community and the priesthood against improper forms of worship.[27]

The provisions of Leviticus 25 seem to reflect an economically strained, somewhat stratified society, in which the risk of forfeiture of land was ever present and in which indenture was common. The law aimed to protect the rights of landowners, and the ancient duty to preserve land within the clan, so basic to earlier legislation, had given way to an emphasis on private ownership. Charging interest was forbidden, and the right to redeem seized land and indentured persons was guaranteed. There is reference to the special problems involved in doing business with non-Israelites, which suggests a mixed population.

THE PRIESTHOOD The functions of the priesthood have already been discussed in various connections and will be further clarified in the discussion of the Sanctuary and cult, as these are reflected in Leviticus. It has been suggested that in the real—namely, the historic—community of Leviticus, the priesthood occupied a position of leadership. The "anointed priest," or High Priest, was the effective head of the community.

The priesthood filled several primary functions: (1) officiation in the sacrificial cult; (2) purification and related activities, which included attending to the ill and impure; (3) administration of the transactions of the Sanctuary and probably of other transactions involving sales of land, indebtedness, and indenture; and, finally, (4) implicit in all that Leviticus prescribes were the judicial and educational roles of the priesthood.[28] According to Leviticus, officiation in the sacrificial cult was the exclusive prerogative of the priesthood, though donors and communal leaders participated in officiation by the placing of hands on the offering. Certain cultic functions were reserved for the High Priest.

To be fit for cultic officiation in the sacred precincts of the Sanctuary, a priest, once consecrated, was required to remain in a state of ritual purity. Purity also affected the right of the priest to partake of consecrated foodstuffs derived from the offerings of the sanctuary. Priests were subject to certain marital restrictions: They were banned from marrying divorced women, harlots, and women who were degraded as a result of prohibited marriages or from families that were declassed. The High Priest was even further restricted and could marry only a virgin of his own kin. The violation of these restrictions would defile a priest and affect his children's status.

In addition, the notion that blemishes or other physical deformities render a sacrifice unfit to be offered to God also applied to the physical condition of priests. Physical soundness was required of officiating priests, though priests born with deformities, or who had been injured, were not deprived of their support.

Historically, there is every reason to regard such requirements as having been realistic in their time. In fact, they continued to be operative in postbiblical times, and the marital restrictions remain in effect to this day among traditional Jews.

One type of impurity was particularly consequential for priests, although its effects were remediable: the severe impurity resulting from contact with the dead. Priests were effectively eliminated from any funerary role and could attend only to the burial of close, consanguineal relatives and, by implication, to the burial of their wives. The High Priest could never be involved in burial. The dead body of an Israelite was regarded as the most severe generator of impurity. These regulations are known to have been realistic and have persisted throughout the centuries since biblical times.

Also realistic were the therapeutic functions of the priesthood in treating diseases that were regarded as life-threatening as well as impure. In part, we observe in Leviticus the transferral to the official priesthood of certain roles elsewhere associated with prophets and "men of God." In the rituals and laws of Leviticus there is little mention of the customary oracular functions of priests. Whereas Aaron donned the ephod and Urim and Thummim at his investiture—and there is also reference to the casting of lots on Yom Kippur—Leviticus fails to prescribe an oracular role to the priesthood as a whole.

The priesthood was charged with maintaining the purity of the Sanctuary. This involved procedures for restoring its purity once defiled and for replacement of vessels that could not be purified. In reality, maintenance, as it is usually understood, consisted in large part of maintaining purity. Once a year, prior to the Sukkot festival, on the day that came to be known as Yom Kippur, there was an elaborate general purification of the Sanctuary in which the High Priest had a unique role.

Priests issued rulings on the fitness of sacrificial animals and other consecrated materials, so as to prevent the defiling of the Sanctuary through impure offerings. Consecrated substances had to be stored in special ways and removed at specific times. Priests also instructed the people in proper food sources and on the purity of vessels.

On certain levels, purification involved administration, and chapter 27 shows how the priests were to conduct the business of the Sanctuary. Specific market values were placed on many commodities for the purpose of determining the cost of redeeming donations of various sorts to the Sanctuary. Priests registered all that was brought into and dispensed from the Sanctuary. Sanctuary weight was the standard.

Chapter 25 is a code of law that has already been discussed for the information it provides on the Israelite community. Its provisions pertain to sales of land, indebtedness, and indenture. It does not explicitly mention the priesthood. All transactions are expressed as occurring between individual Israelites, occasionally among members of the same clan, and also with non-Israelite residents of the land. There is no direct reference to any legal or administrative authority or agency that might have been in charge of such transactions. Nevertheless, the very inclusion of chapter 25 in Leviticus suggests that the priesthood was undoubtedly expected to administer such transactions. The chapter is introduced by statements on the importance of observing the Sabbatical year; and it is here that the Jubilee year is initiated as an institution in Torah literature. All of this suggests that the laws of chapter 25, though mundane in nature, were of religious concern.

Leviticus tells us little in an explicit way about the training and education of priests, though the *torot* and similar texts undoubtedly served as manuals of procedure to be followed by the priests in the performance of their tasks. A bit more is said about the support of the clergy and their families. The people were, in effect, taxed for that purpose in several ways. Sections from most sacrifices were withheld on behalf of the clergy. We are compelled to rely on sources other than Leviticus for a full outline of this support system, and at times it is not clear whether certain payments went to support the clergy in particular or to the Sanctuary as an institution.

In summary, Leviticus is an important source of information on the realistic functions of the priesthood. In the community projected in Leviticus, the priesthood held most of the leadership roles, administered the Sanctuary, and probably also handled legal transactions of all sorts.

Where realism ends, tradition begins: Leviticus presupposes the exclusive legitimacy of the Aaronide priesthood, a basic tenet of the priestly source of the Torah. But the tradition of the Aaronide priesthood—a family-based fraternity founded by Aaron, Moses' brother, and his sons—does not accord with the overall thrust of biblical evidence. Although consistently associated with the priestly component of Torah literature, this tradition is almost entirely absent from the historical books, Judges through Kings. It reemerges only in the postexilic writings of Ezra, Nehemiah, and Chronicles. Even in Ezekiel we read of the Zadokite priesthood, not of the Aaronide priesthood.

In fact, general references in Leviticus to "the priest" (*ha-kohen*) can be interpreted as referring originally not to Aaron or his sons at all but merely to any legitimate priest, or to the priest in charge. But the priestly writers, wishing to feature the Aaronide priesthood, may have incorporated that material into Leviticus. In chapters 8–10, we find a description, or record, of the original consecration of the Aaronide priesthood and the initial assumption of their duties in the Tabernacle. Elsewhere, as well, priests are often identified as Aaronide priests. Thus, this tradition on the origins of the priesthood begins in Exodus, continues through Leviticus, and finds its most elaborate expression in Numbers. Priestly historiography weaves in the antecedent family background via the early career of Moses and the Egyptian experience. In Numbers, the first succession after Aaron's death is also recounted, thereby establishing the hereditary character of the priesthood.

It is not certain when and how this tradition of an Aaronide priesthood, with its tribal and familial underpinnings, arose. Its historicity in the preexilic period is doubtful, both on literary-historical grounds and in institutional terms. It is not unrealistic, however, to have priestly families or to find priests clustered in their own communities. Even the hereditary principle is realistic, if we allow for the occasional recruitment or adoption of outsiders. Actually, three factors interacted to give structure to ancient priesthoods: place of residence, family origin, and training in the priestly arts. Families tended to reside together and to transmit crafts and professions from generation to generation with some degree of secrecy. Perhaps the least realistic feature of Leviticus is the Aaronide tradition.

In sum, Leviticus is extremely informative about the operation of the priesthood and its involvement not only in the cult but also in communal administration—although we must conclude that the account of the Aaronide tradition is itself historically questionable.

THE SANCTUARY Leviticus presents us with a traditional view, according to which formal worship of the God of Israel was initiated during the days of Moses in a portable tentlike sanctuary. This structural complex, described in the Commentary, is variously named *'ohel mo'ed*, "the Tent of Meeting," and *ha-mishkan*, "the Tabernacle." Leviticus also employs the term *mikdash*, "sanctuary," which, strictly speaking, refers to a stationary building, roofed and enclosed. Because priestly writers also use this term more loosely to designate the Tent of Meeting/Tabernacle, as in Exodus 25:8 and Numbers 1–9 and following, it is not certain how it should be understood in Leviticus.

Priestly literature records that this tentlike structure and its accompanying altars served as the sole legitimate Israelite Sanctuary. It was the repository of the Ark and its contents during the period of the Sinai migrations, and it continued in this function at Shiloh, the first major cult site established by the settling Israelites (Josh. 18:1). The same portable Tabernacle served as the repository of the Ark until it was replaced by the Solomonic Temple and its Shrine in Jerusalem, after a period in which the Ark was moved through several sites (see 2 Sam. 7:4–6; 1 Kings 8:3–6).

This is the tradition as stated and as reflected in Leviticus. The Torah itself is not consistent in its depiction of this tentlike structure. The evident discrepancies have been debated since late antiquity, both by traditionalist and more recently by critical scholars. In fact, critical scholarship has generated the same kinds of questions about the Tabernacle tradition as about the historicity of Leviticus as a whole. It has been proposed that the Tabernacle tradition is merely a feature of the larger recasting of early Israelite history that we encounter in priestly literature. A migratory people, forbidden to follow the customary pattern of offering sacrifices at existing altars and cult sites and barred from erecting new ones, according to the official law of the priests (Lev. 17), would have been well served by a portable sanctuary. This structure, erected within the "encampment" (*maḥaneh*), would have served as the locus of cultic and other communal activity. The oracular function associated with "the Tent" to which Moses repaired in order to communicate with God (Exod. 33) was integrated into the priestly conception of the Sanctuary.

In critical terms, a distinction must be made between the Ark as a cult object and the tradition of a wilderness Tabernacle.

The reality of an Ark containing sacred tablets may be accepted, but the tradition of the Tabernacle, with all its corollary features, is hardly realistic. The effort to find analogues to the priestly Tabernacle has led scholars to structures in use by Bedouins and to Egyptian reliefs that portray a shrine or altar of sorts positioned at the center of the Egyptian military camp.[29] Leviticus probably does not provide us with realistic information about the phys-

ical features of early Israelite cult sites or altars. Archaeological excavations have yielded examples of fairly early Israelite cult sites at Shiloh, Arad, Beer-Sheba, and elsewhere. The pattern seems clearly to have been one of stationary altars and *bamot* (a term designating a larger installation) and of regional temples. The evidence of other biblical books also points in this direction; there are abundant narratives about events occurring at any number of stationary cult sites.

Traditionalist interpretation, undoubtedly beginning in the Bible itself, has always sought to preserve a unified record and to harmonize very different portrayals of early Israelite worship. The critical scholar is willing to admit the existence of differing histories of early Israel. Leviticus belongs to the priestly tradition, which in this respect is less realistic than other biblical records.

Nevertheless, the spatial organization reflected in the design of the priestly Tabernacle has a direct bearing on the realities of worship in biblical times. We observe a progression of graduated zones of sanctity (or taboo) as we proceed closer to the Holy of Holies. Each zone imposes increasingly restricted access and stricter purity requirements.[30]

This principle of incremental spatial sanctity determined, to a considerable extent, the actual design of ancient temples in the Near East and elsewhere. It is clearly noticeable at Iron Age Arad, where the more holy area is demarcated from the rest of the courtyard by a step or ledge. Some scholars have suggested a correlation between the measurements of the main altar at Arad and the dimensions of the priestly altar. The orientation of the priestly altar of burnt offerings toward the entrance to the Shrine clearly reflects actual ancient design.[31]

The desert Tabernacle described in the priestly tradition is modeled after actual temples. It is only from the priestly tradition, however, that we learn so much about the meaning that underlies the design. There is, therefore, a certain irony in our quest for ancient realism: The physical character of the priestly Tabernacle is probably unrealistic, but the apportionment of space in its projected design reveals the concepts underlying the designs of real temples in biblical Israel.

THE CULT There is every reason to accept the cultic practice presented in Leviticus as essentially realistic. The phenomenology of sacrifice has also been described in considerable detail. What is now required is an overview of the nature of Israelite worship, as we learn about it from Leviticus.

In biblical times, until after the destruction of the Second Temple of Jerusalem, public or private prayer was not regarded as a sufficient mode of worship. The requirements of worship included some sacrificial offering. This was true even after the Babylonian exile. In fact, traditional Judaism has never abandoned hope for a restoration of the sacrificial cult. More will be said on this subject later in this introduction.

The regimen of sacrifice shows us how the various available materials utilized as sacrifices were related to food sources and to the formalities of dining and hospitality. After all, sacrifices were provided, so to speak, to the visiting, or resident, divine guest. They were sacred meals of sorts. So we find large and small cattle, fowl, grains, wine and oil, and incense. We also find spices, mostly aromatic, and salt, basically used to remove vestigial blood from meat but prescribed even for grain offerings. Male animals were used predominantly, probably out of economic concerns; females were needed to reproduce the herds and flocks. It remains uncertain as to why females are specifically ordered for a certain relatively few sacrificial rites.

There was definitely a quantitative factor at work in the sacrificial regimen—as if to say,

the more important the rite or the more grievous the offense, the more costly the sacrifice. Allowances were made for those unable to afford the full measure: In cases where individuals could not afford the required item and might be deprived of purification or expiation, they were allowed to substitute less costly sacrifices.

The individual Israelite and his family enjoyed several avenues of access to worship in the Sanctuary. Vowing a sacrifice to God was a common practice, and this may have been the most frequent route to the Sanctuary. Most kinds of sacrifices were available to the individual, including sin offerings of various sorts, which one would be obligated to donate in the event an offense had been committed. One might also devote objects of value, including land, to the Sanctuary; or symbolically the individual could devote himself or herself. A system of commutations is set forth in chapter 27, whereby one would overpay 20 percent for the privilege of repurchasing a donation. We read of offerings of first fruits on an individual basis.

There is every reason to accept as realistic the participation of individuals and their families in the sacrificial and votive cult. There were occasions when such participation was obligatory, and one assumes that a new mother would make every effort to secure the sacrifice she required after her period of quarantine. If anything, the expiatory function may have been overused at times. Individual participation in the cult was determined by the life cycle, by the seasons, and by one's own life experience.

Public worship, as we observe it in Leviticus, centered around the Sabbaths and the festivals celebrated in the Sanctuary. The book does not provide a full picture of such worship. Interestingly, it does not focus on the daily public cult, but refers only to a public daily grain offering by the High Priest and to the lamp kindled by him (6:12–16, 24:2–4). On festivals, the duty of pilgrimage brought large numbers of Israelites to the Sanctuary, where they attended the public celebration. Though the rites were performed by priests, and though the text tells us little of the social dynamics of cultic celebration, the cultic experience was certainly meaningful for all who were present. Since Leviticus is pointedly oriented to the functions of the priesthood, it is to be expected that its rituals and laws emphasize those elements.

Viewing the cult from the perspective of the God of Israel, the divine recipient of sacrificial offerings, might help us arrive at an imaginative method of deepening our understanding of religious phenomenology. The various modes of sacrifice testify to differing perceptions as to how gifts were to be offered to God. The burnt offering expresses, so to speak, the perception that God breathes in the aromatic smoke, which ascends heavenward. An offering presented on a table in the Shrine reflects a different phenomenology, one in which God views the sacrifice with pleasure and thereby accepts it: The gift, in such cases, is shown to Him and is then allocated to the priests, who actually consume it. Offerings of wine and the use of aromatic oil have their obvious meanings.

Most sacrifices combine more than one mode, and we observe significant evidence of development in the manner of worship as prescribed in the rituals of Leviticus. Thus, a small scoop of dough from most grain offerings was burned on the altar, while the rest of the substance of the offering was prepared as human food through baking or frying. Similarly, most burnt offerings were only partially burned on the altar, with the rest prepared as food for priests and, in some cases, for the donors of sacrifices. The object was to celebrate a sacred meal in the presence of God, to share a meal with the Deity. In fact, the sacrifice was generally not efficacious unless the priests and, where applicable, the donors actually partook of their respective shares.

The blood rites prescribed in Leviticus represent a different set of meanings, and,

though part of the same sacrificial cult, they functioned in other ways. Blood was taboo and forbidden for human consumption because it was regarded as *the* vital juice, that part of the physical being of the sacrificial animal that gave it life. Reserved for God, the blood was offered to Him on the altar. Vestigial blood was removed by salting the offerings. Blood substituted for the life of the worshiper and served to avert divine wrath. In the Commentary, the phenomenology of blood rites is explained in considerable detail.

Similar to the role of blood is the role of those parts of sacrificial animals that were consumed on the altar, particularly the fat covering the internal organs. Fat was thought to be desired by the Deity because it was perceived as giving energy. Reference to the fat of an animal or to the "fat" of wheat was a way of referring to their choice parts. In a related matter, all materials used as offerings had to be the choicest, without blemish or physical deformity. One used the best semolina and the best olive oil and spices.

The absence of any recitational texts is conspicuous in Leviticus. And yet, we should not assume that all was done in silence. We find reference to a verbal confession of sins, and we are warranted in assuming that priests recited fixed liturgical formulas at various points in the process of offering sacrifices while performing rites of purification. Although the priestly texts simply do not reproduce these liturgies, it is hard to conceive of a sacrificial cult without instruction and formal statements. In Numbers, we have the Priestly Benediction; and the Mishnah preserves some such recitations, all of a later origin.

Absolutely nothing is recorded in Leviticus about how animals were slaughtered or about the tools used in this process. All sorts of vessels are mentioned, such as bowls and tools for cleaning and scraping. All of these are realistic and may, in some cases, be identified with artifacts unearthed in archaeological excavations.

To conclude: Leviticus affords us only a partial view of the official biblical cult, but its functional evidence is undoubtedly realistic, as far as it goes. It is difficult to pinpoint precisely when the procedures of the cult, as preserved in Leviticus, went into operation. It can be said, however, that the older mode of presentation offerings was clearly accommodated, in Leviticus, to the rising importance of the burnt altar offering in Israelite religion. When compared with the table of sacrifices prescribed for the public cult in Numbers 28–30, Leviticus 23 seems to represent an earlier stage. On the other hand, the emphasis on rites of purification in Leviticus appears to reflect the growing interest in purity evident in exilic and postexilic literature.

Conclusions

Leviticus remains a major source of knowledge about the religion of biblical Israel. By virtue of its abundant detail, it provides information of a kind rarely encountered elsewhere in the Hebrew Bible, except in other priestly texts, such as one finds in Exodus and Numbers.

Studying Leviticus enhances our awareness that, in practice, Israelite religion not only embodied concepts and beliefs that were held by the members of the religious community of Israel but also represented a specific system with prescribed ways of expressing these beliefs and concepts. This awareness should encourage students of biblical religion and society to devote more attention to ritual and symbolism, worship, celebration, and purification as set forth in Leviticus. It is from these aspects of religious experience that we learn what it meant to be an Israelite who believed in and worshiped the God of Israel.

Historically, the laws, celebrations, and purifications of Leviticus served as part of the

structure of later Judaism. Although the modes of Jewish religion underwent significant change over the course of time in response to new historical circumstances and differing perceptions of the meaning of religion, much of the biblical system of religious living has survived. A proper understanding of historical Judaism becomes possible, then, only by way of an understanding of its earliest phases.

For all students of biblical religion and history, Leviticus poses a genuine challenge: Are we able to penetrate forms and actions to arrive at the dimension of their underlying meanings? Are we limited to statements about how religious devotion was expressed, or can we say something as well about why it was expressed in prescribed ways? One of the major purposes of the present Commentary will be the attempt to fathom the significance of biblical religion, in essence and manifestation.

Leviticus speaks to us of purity and holiness and, in effect, commands us to worship God fervently:

O house of Israel, bless the LORD;
  O house of Aaron, bless the LORD;
  O house of Levi, bless the LORD;
  you who fear the LORD, bless the LORD.
Blessed is the LORD from Zion,
  He who dwells in Jerusalem.
  Hallelujah. (Ps. 135:19–21)

Notes to the Introduction

1. See B. A. Levine, "The Language of Holiness: Perceptions of the Sacred in the Hebrew Bible," in *Backgrounds for the Bible,* ed. N. P. O'Connor (Winona Lake, Ind.: Eisenbrauns, 1987), 241–256. The translation given here conveys the sense of the statement more clearly, perhaps, than: "You shall be to Me a kingdom of Priests." The Hebrew idiom *hayah le* means "to belong to" and conveys possession.

2. For the term *torat kohanim* as a way of referring to the Book of Leviticus, see Mish. Meg. 3:5 and Mish. Men. 4:3. The halakhic midrash on Leviticus, the Sifra, often cited in the Commentary, also bears the title "Torat Kohanim."

3. On the term "Masoretic," see the introduction to the NJPS; and EncJud, s.v. "Masorah."

4. See E. Y. Kutscher, *The Language and Linguistic Background of the Isaiah Scroll* (1 Q Isa) (Leiden: E. J. Brill, 1974). See also Joseph A. Fitzmyer, *The Dead Sea Scrolls: Major Publications and Tools for Study* (Missoula, Mont.: Scholars Press, 1975).

5. D. N. Freedman, K. A. Mathews et. al., *The Paleo-Hebrew Leviticus Scroll* (11 QpaleoLev) (Winona Lake, Ind.: American Schools of Oriental Research, 1985).

6. On the Samaritan version see EncJud, s.v. "Samaritans, Literature" and bibliography there. On the Septuagint, see E. Tov, *The Text-Critical Use of the Septuagint in Biblical Research* (Jerusalem: Simor, 1981).

7. For an example of this, see the Commentary to 26:1–2.

8. An example of a temple record from Mesopotamia is analyzed in B. A. Levine and W. W. Hallo, "Offerings to the Temple Gates at Ur," HUCA 38 (1967): 17–58.

9. For examples of Ugaritic temple rituals, see B. A. Levine, "Ugaritic Descriptive Rituals," JCS 17 (1963): 105–111; and idem, "The Descriptive Ritual Texts from Ugarit: Some Formal and Functional Features of the Genre," in *The Word of the Lord Shall Go Forth: Essays in Honor of David Noel Freedman,* ed. C. L. Meyers and M. O'Connor (Winona Lake, Ind.: Eisenbrauns, 1983), 311–326, and literature cited.

10. Examples of Egyptian, Akkadian, and Hittite ritual texts may be found in ANET, 325–361.

11. See the Comments to chap. 1 for information on the Punic tariffs and their similarity to the ritual laws of Leviticus.

12. A collection of temple rituals from the ancient city of Uruk in Mesopotamia was published by F. Thureau-Dangin under the title *Rituels accadiens* (Paris: Editions Ernest Leroux, 1921). For a discussion of the Uruk archives of the Seleucid period, see Lawrence Timothy Doty, *Cuneiform Archives from Hellenistic Uruk* (Ann Arbor, Mich.: University Microfilms, 1980).

13. See the introductory Comments to chaps. 21–22 for a discussion of the laws governing the priesthood.

14. For the sense of *berakhah* as "grant, gift," see Gen. 27:36; Josh. 15:19; Judg. 1:15; 1 Sam. 30:26.

15. See the introductory Comments to chap. 3 for an explanation of the term *shelamim.*

16. This view was advanced by G. B. Gray, *Sacrifice in the Old Testament* (1925; repr., with a prolegomenon by B. A. Levine, Ktav: New York, 1971).

17. For a discussion of this theme, see B. A. Levine, "On the Presence of God in Biblical Religion," in *Religions in Antiquity*, ed. J. Neusner (Leiden: E. J. Brill, 1968), 71–87.

18. Hoffmann's commentary was of great value in the preparation of the present Commentary.

19. Summaries of the methods used in modern Bible criticism may be found in H. Cazelles, IDBSup, s.v. "Bible Criticism, OT"; and in J. A. Whartman, IDBSup, s.v. "Redaction Criticism, OT."

20. See B. A. Levine, "The Balaam Text from Deir ʿAllā: Historical Aspects," in *Biblical Archaeology Today* (Jerusalem: Israel Exploration Society, 1985), 326–339.

21. See J. Wellhausen, *Prolegomena to the History of Ancient Israel* (1878; repr., New York: Meridian Books, 1957), 376–385.

22. H. L. Ginsberg, *The Israelian Heritage of Judaism* (New York: The Theological Seminary of America, 1982).

23. Yehezkel Kaufmann, *Toledot ha-ʾemunnah ha-yisraʾelit,* 8 vols (Jerusalem–Tel Aviv: Mosad Bialik, 1946–1947). Also see the translation and abridgment by Moshe Greenberg, *The Religion of Israel* (Chicago: University of Chicago Press, 1960).

24. E. A. Speiser, "Leviticus and the Critics," in *Yehezkel Kaufmann Jubilee Volume,* ed. M. Haran (Jerusalem: Magnes Press, 1960), 29–45.

25. See Comment to 4:15, where the term *ʿedah* is explained.

26. For other references to towns, see chap. 25.

27. See the introductory Comments to chap. 10 for a discussion of this incident.

28. See B. A. Levine, *Encyclopedia of Religion* (1987), s.v. "Levites."

29. For a recent discussion, see F. M. Cross, Jr., "The Priestly Tabernacle in the Light of Recent Research," *Temples and High Places in Biblical Times* (Jerusalem: Nelson Glueck School of Biblical Archaeology of HUC-JIR, 1981), 169–180.

30. See M. Haran, *Temples and Temple Service in Ancient Israel* (Oxford: Clarendon Press, 1978), 149–259.

31. See the introductory Comments to chap. 1 for a discussion of the design of the Tabernacle.

GLOSSARY

Aggadah The nonhalakhic (nonlegal) homiletic side of rabbinic teaching, mostly anchored to the biblical text.

Akkadian A group of ancient Semitic languages of Syro-Mesopotamian origin related to biblical Hebrew, widely diffused in the ancient Near East from before 3,000 B.C.E. through the biblical period. Most prominent are Assyrian and Babylonian. "Akkadian" derives from the ancient city-state of Aggade (=Akkad) in northern Mesopotamia. Tens of thousands of texts are available to modern scholars, written on clay tablets and on stone in cuneiform.

Aramaic A Semitic language closely related to biblical Hebrew and known in many dialects and phases, including Syriac. Aramaic flourished throughout the biblical period and thereafter and is the language of the Targums, the Gemaras, and large sections of Midrash.

Gemara A commentary on the Mishnah in Aramaic and Hebrew.

Halakhah The individual and collective rabbinic legal rulings that regulate all aspects of Jewish life, both individual and corporate.

Ibn Ezra, Abraham (1089–1164) Poet, grammarian, biblical commentator. Spain and Italy.

Maimonides, Moses ben Maimon, known as Rambam (1135–1204) Halakhic codifier (*Yad Hazakah = Mishneh Torah*), philosopher (*Moreh Nevukhim, Guide of the Perplexed*), and commentator on the Mishnah. Spain and Egypt.

Mekhilta Halakhic midrash on the Book of Exodus in two forms, the Mekhilta de-R. Ishmael and the Mekhilta de-R. Simeon ben Yoḥai, 1st and 2nd centuries C.E.

Midrash Legal and homiletical expositions of the biblical text, and anthologies and compilations of such. Examples are Leviticus Rabba and Midrash Ha-Gadol on Leviticus.

Mishnah The written compilation of orally transmitted legal teachings covering all aspects of Jewish law, arranged in six orders that, in turn, are divided into tractates; executed by Judah ha-Nasi, ca. 200 C.E. Palestine.

Naḥmanides See Ramban.

Punic The phase of the Phoenician language used primarily in the western Phoenician colonies, such as Carthage, in North Africa, from around the beginning of the 5th century B.C.E.

Qumran A site overlooking the Dead Sea where Jewish sects lived in religious communities from ca. 135 B.C.E. to 70 C.E. and from which we have numerous documents.

Rabad Acronym for Rabbi Abraham ben David of Posquières, in Provence (ca. 1125–1198). Commentator of rabbinic texts and noted codifier of rabbinic law. He wrote a commentary on the Sifra.

Rambam See Maimonides.

Ramban Acronym for Rabbi Moses ben Naḥman, known as Naḥmanides (1194–1270) Philosopher, halakhist, biblical commentator. Spain.

Rashbam Acronym for Rabbi Samuel ben Meir (ca. 1080–1174) Grandson of Rashi. Commentator on Bible and Talmud. Northern France.

Rashi Acronym for Rabbi Solomon ben Isaac (1040–1105) Commentator on Bible and Talmud. Troyes, France.

Septuagint The Greek translation of the Torah made for the Jewish community of Alexandria, Egypt, 3rd century B.C.E.

Sifra = Torat Kohanim Tannaitic midrashic commentary to the Book of Leviticus, probably compiled about the end of the 4th century C.E. Palestine.

Sifrei Tannaitic halakhic midrash to the Books of Numbers and Deuteronomy, probably compiled at the end of the 4th century C.E.

Talmud The body of rabbinic law, dialectic, and lore comprising the Mishnah and Gemara, the latter being an exposition and elaboration of the former in Hebrew and Aramaic. Two separate talmudic compilations exist: the Babylonian Talmud and the Palestinian Talmud (also known as Jerusalem Talmud).

Tanna(im) The Palestinian sages of the 1st and 2nd centuries C.E. whose rulings are cited in the Mishnah.

Targum Jonathan An unofficial Aramaic free translation of the Torah, erroneously ascribed to Jonathan ben Uzziel through misinterpretation of the initials "T.Y." (= Targum Yerushalmi). That scholar is the reputed author of the Targum to the Prophets.

Targum Onkelos The standard, official Aramaic translation of the Torah. Attributed to Onkelos, reputed nephew of the Roman emperor Hadrian and convert to Judaism; 2nd century C.E. The name is probably a corruption of Aquila.

Tosefta A compilation of tannaitic rulings either omitted from the Mishnah or containing material parallel or supplementary to it. It is arranged according to the six orders of the Mishnah.

Ugaritic The Semitic language closely related to Hebrew used in the ancient city-state of Ugarit and nearby areas in the period preceding the 12th century B.C.E. Ugarit (Ras Shamra) was located on the Syrian seacoast. Much of the content of the Ugaritic texts, written in alphabetic cuneiform, is topically relevant to biblical studies.

ABBREVIATIONS

AB	Anchor Bible
AHW	W. von Soden, *Akkadisches Handwörterbuch*
Akk.	Akkadian
ANET	J. B. Pritchard, ed., *Ancient Near Eastern Texts*
AP	A. E. Cowley, *Aramaic Papyri of the Fifth Century* B.C.
Ar.	Arakhin
Arab.	Arabic
Aram.	Aramaic
Av. Zar.	Avodah Zarah
BA	*Biblical Archaeologist*
BAP	E. C. Kraeling, ed., *The Brooklyn Museum Aramaic Papyri*
BASOR	*Bulletin of the American Schools of Oriental Research*
Ber.	Berakhot
Bib	*Biblica*
CBQ	*Catholic Biblical Quarterly*
CRAIBL	*Comptes rendus de l'Académie des inscriptions et belles-lettres*
EB	*Encyclopaedia Biblica*
EncJud	*Encyclopaedia Judaica* (1971)
Git.	Gittin
Gk.	Greek
HALAT	W. Baumgartner et al., *Hebräisches und aramäisches Lexicon zum Alten Testament*
Heb.	Hebrew
Hor.	Horayot
Hoffmann	David Zevi Hoffmann, *Sefer Va-Yiqra'*, translated by Aharon Lieberman, (Jerusalem: Mosad Ha-Rav Kook, 1954 [5714]). Originally *Das Buch Leviticus,* Berlin, 1904.
HUCA	*Hebrew Union College Annual*
Ḥul.	Ḥullin
IDB	*Interpreters Dictionary of the Bible*
IDBSup	*Interpreters Dictionary of the Bible,* Supplementary Volume (1976)
JANES	*Journal of the Ancient Near Eastern Society of Columbia University*
JAOS	*Journal of the American Oriental Society*
JBL	*Journal of Biblical Literature*
JCS	*Journal of Cuneiform Studies*
JJS	*Journal of Jewish Studies*
JSS	*Journal of Semitic Studies*
JTS	*Journal of Theological Studies*
KEL	Kelim

Ker.	Keritot
Lev. R.	Leviticus Rabba
LXX	Septuagint
Maʿas. Sh.	Maʿaser Sheni
Meʿil.	Meʿilah
Mekh.	Mekhilta
Men.	Menaḥot
Mid.	Midrash
Mik.	Mikva'ot
Mish.	Mishnah
MK	Moʿed Katan
NJPS	New Jewish Publication Society translation
Or.	Orlah
PAAJR	Proceedings, American Academy of Jewish Research
Phoen.	Phoenician
Q	Qumran
RB	*Revue biblique*
Shab.	Shabbat
Shevu.	Shevuʿot
Sif.	Sifrei
Sifra	Sifra
Syr.	Syriac
Targ.	Onkelos
Targ. Jon.	Targum Jonathan
Tem.	Temurah
Tosef.	Tosefta
TWAT	*Theologisches Wörterbuch zum alten Testament,* G. J. Botterweck and H. Ringgren, eds.
UF	*Ugarit-Forschungen*
Ugar.	Ugaritic
UT	C. H. Gordon, *Ugaritic Textbook* (1965)
VT	*Vetus Testamentum*
VTSup	*Vetus Testamentum: Supplements*
Vulg.	Vulgate
Yad	Yad Ha-Ḥazakah (= Mishnah Torah)
Yev.	Yevamot
Zev.	Zevaḥim

The editors have adopted a popular system for transliteration of Hebrew, except for the following letters, which have no English equivalent:

' = alef
ʿ = ayin
ḥ = ḥet (pronounced as the guttural "ch" in German)
kh = khaf (pronounced as the guttural "ch" in German)

THE COMMENTARY TO LEVITICUS

The Principal Types of Sacrifice (1:1–7:38)

Va-yikra'

Chapters 1–7 constitute the first section of the Book of Leviticus. They outline the basic modes of sacrifice, listing and describing the several classes of offerings to be presented to God in the sanctuary. Chapters 1–5 are addressed to the general populace—to individual Israelites and to their leaders, to all who wished to worship God or who were required by circumstances to offer a particular sacrifice. They tell what may be offered—animals, birds, grain, and so forth—and they lay down the proper procedures for presenting the different sacrifices, a function that was performed primarily by priests but could occasionally require some sort of participation on the part of the donors of the sacrifices. Chapters 6–7, on the other hand, constitute a professional manual for the priesthood; they provide a *torah,* literally "an instruction," for each of the major classes of sacrifices. Although there is some overlapping of specific content between chapters 1–5 and chapters 6–7, the style and the form of each division is distinct.

Chapters 1–5 should be subdivided further. Chapters 1–3 outline the three principal types of sacrifices that were offered regularly by individual Israelites and their families, by kings and other leaders, and often by the entire community. A chapter is devoted to each of them: the burnt offering (*'olah*), the grain offering (*minḥah*), and the sacred gifts of greeting (*zevaḥ ha-shelamim*). These offerings could be included in a variety of celebrations—public and private, voluntary and obligatory. They served a multiplicity of functions since they could be offered singly or as part of more elaborate rites. The sacrifices treated in chapters 4–5, sacrifices of expiation, were of more limited application. Offered for the purpose of securing God's forgiveness, their presentation was obligatory, pursuant to transgressions of religious law, committed either by omission or through inadvertent violations. In most cases, the sacrifice served to remove the charge against the offenders and to restore them to a proper relationship with God and to fit membership in the religious community.

It should be emphasized here, as the workings of the sacrificial system are introduced to the reader, that the laws of the Torah did not permit Israelites to expiate intentional or premeditated offenses by means of sacrifice. There was no vicarious, ritual remedy—substitution of one's property or wealth—for such violations, whether they were perpetrated against other individuals or against God Himself.[1] In those cases, the law dealt directly with the offender, imposing real punishments and acting to prevent recurrences. The entire expiatory system ordained in the Torah must be understood in this light. Ritual expiation was restricted to situations where a reasonable doubt existed as to the willfulness of the offense. Even then, restitution was always required where loss or injury to another person had occurred.[2] The mistaken notion that ritual worship could atone for criminality or intentional religious desecration was persistently attacked by the prophets of Israel, who considered it a major threat to the entire covenantal relationship between Israel and God.[3]

In summary, the prescriptions of chapters 1–7 outline the main components of the biblical sacrificial system, as it was administered by the Israelite priesthood.

CHAPTER 1 THE BURNT OFFERING (*'OLAH*) (vv. 1–17)

Chapter 1 deals with the sacrifice called *'olah,* which was burned to ashes on the altar of burnt offerings. No part of it was eaten, either by priests or donors. The *'olah* could consist of male herd cattle (vv. 3–9), of male flock animals (vv. 10–13), or of certain birds (vv. 14–17). Despite some differences in detail, the procedures for all burnt offerings, or holocausts, were quite similar: The sacrifice was presented at the entrance to the Tent of Meeting; the donor laid his hand on the victim,

1 The Lord called to Moses and spoke to him from the Tent of Meeting, saying: ²Speak to the Israelite people, and say to them:

When any of you presents an offering of cattle to the Lord, he shall choose his offering from the herd or from the flock.

וַיִּקְרָא֙ אֶל־מֹשֶׁ֔ה וַיְדַבֵּ֣ר יְהוָ֔ה אֵלָ֖יו מֵאֹ֣הֶל מוֹעֵ֖ד לֵאמֹֽר: ² דַּבֵּ֞ר אֶל־בְּנֵ֤י יִשְׂרָאֵל֙ וְאָמַרְתָּ֣ אֲלֵהֶ֔ם אָדָ֗ם כִּֽי־יַקְרִ֥יב מִכֶּ֛ם קָרְבָּ֖ן לַֽיהוָ֑ה מִן־הַבְּהֵמָ֗ה מִן־הַבָּקָר֙ וּמִן־הַצֹּ֔אן תַּקְרִ֖יבוּ אֶת־

א' א' זעירא   v. 1.

thereby designating it for a particular rite; and blood from the sacrificial victim was dashed on the altar in appropriate ways.

1. The Lord called to Moses . . . from the Tent of Meeting Although the sense is clear enough, this unusual syntax did not escape the attention of commentators. Rashbam suggested that this opening verse takes up where Exodus 40:34–35 leaves off. There we read that Moses had been unable to enter the Tent because it was filled with God's presence. Here we read that the Lord "called" Moses, that He summoned him from the Tent nonetheless! In this way Leviticus is linked sequentially to Exodus.

Hebrew 'ohel mo'ed is the name given to the portable tent structure that housed the Ark and other cult objects. In other priestly texts this structural complex is called *mishkan,* a term that also means "tent."⁴ Conceived as God's earthly residence, this sanctuary served two principal functions: It was an *oraculum,* where God communicated His word, and it was a cult site, where God was worshiped through sacrifices. The derivation of the word *mo'ed* from the root *y-'-d,* "to meet, come together" at an appointed time or place, expresses the functions of the structure called *'ohel mo'ed.*

This Tent of Meeting was surrounded by an enclosed courtyard, within which stood the altar of burnt offerings. In turn, the altar faced the entrance of the Tent, so that sacrifices were directed toward God's residence. Within, the Tent itself was divided into two sections, separated by a screen (*parokhet*) that was embroidered with cherubs. Behind the screen, in the innermost area, was the Holy of Holies, which housed the Ark covered by its sculptured lid, the *kapporet.* Before the screen, in the front part of the Tent, stood the menorah, the altar of incense, and a table for presentations. The outer entrance of the Tent was also protected by a curtain. All of this information is set forth in Exodus 25:1–27:21 and repeated, with additional detail, in Exodus 35–40.

There is, however, another tradition about *'ohel mo'ed* that differs from what has been reconstructed here from the priestly texts. In Exodus 33:6–11, *'ohel mo'ed* is portrayed as a Tent—pitched far outside the Israelite encampment—that served exclusively as an *oraculum.* Whenever Moses entered the Tent to "meet" with God, a pillar of cloud appeared at its entrance as though to separate the Tent from the people gathered around. What is striking about these verses is the absence of any reference to the sacrificial cult, the Ark, or any other sacred objects. Evidently, the priestly tradition fused several of the known sacred functions of ancient Israel (including the cloud traditions) in their retelling of the history of the *'ohel mo'ed* during the wilderness period. How these traditions are brought together has been widely discussed in recent scholarly literature; nevertheless, we still do not know the whole story.⁵

2. the Israelite people Hebrew *benei yisra'el,* a very common way of referring to the Israelite people, is usually rendered "the children of Israel." But that rendering is unsatisfactory, for it fails to express the concept of peoplehood basic to biblical notions of group organization. The term is constructed in the same way as are several other ethnographic names, such as *benei 'ammon,* "the Ammonite people," and the names of families or clans. Such nomenclature expresses kinship and reflects the notion that nations, like families, are descendants of common ancestors and share a common genealogy. The Israelite people was thought to have descended from the patriarch Israel and his twelve sons.

When any of you presents The syntax of the Hebrew is unusual: "When a person presents, from among you." Here the term for person is *'adam,* whereas elsewhere it may be *'ish* or *nefesh.* All three terms share the same functional connotation, although each preserves individual nuances.⁶ The conditional particle *ki,* "if, when," is the sign of the casuistic formulation so characteristic of biblical

3If his offering is a burnt offering from the herd, he shall make his offering a male without blemish. He shall bring it to the entrance of the Tent of Meeting, for acceptance in his behalf before the LORD. 4He shall lay his hand upon the

קָרְבַּנְכֶם׃ 3 אִם־עֹלָה קָרְבָּנוֹ מִן־הַבָּקָר זָכָר תָּמִים
יַקְרִיבֶנּוּ אֶל־פֶּתַח אֹהֶל מוֹעֵד יַקְרִיב אֹתוֹ לִרְצֹנוֹ
לִפְנֵי יְהוָה׃ 4 וְסָמַךְ יָדוֹ עַל רֹאשׁ הָעֹלָה וְנִרְצָה

and ancient Near Eastern law codes. This syntax projects a hypothetical situation; a particular law applies only "if" or "when" a certain situation arises.[7]

an offering Hebrew *korban,* "offering," is a generic term for anything presented to God when one approaches (*karav*) His sanctuary. A *korban* could consist of artifacts and vessels, votive objects, or sacrificial victims, as is the case here. Archaeological excavations at various sites, including Jerusalem and its environs, have turned up objects inscribed with the word *korban,* indicating that they were used to prepare or present offerings.[8]

cattle . . . herd . . . flock As in many legal formulas, the general category, here represented by *behemah,* "cattle," is stated first. It is further specified by the two usual classes of cattle: *bakar,* "large cattle," and *tso'n,* "flock." In rabbinic interpretation, this rhetorical pattern is known as *kelal u-frat,* "the general followed by the specific." The general category is defined by its specifications. Wild animals (*ḥayyah,* "beast") are unsuitable for sacrifice, as they are not of the category *behemah.*[9]

3. If his offering is a burnt offering The conditional particle *'im,* "if," frequently introduces cultic laws in the Book of Leviticus and is encountered repeatedly in the first three chapters as well as elsewhere in the book. It expresses the options available to those who offer sacrifices—the choice of which type of sacrifice to bring as well as the choice of animal, fowl, or various grain offerings, where applicable.

While the casuistic formulation with "if" is generally characteristic of ancient Near Eastern law codes, its appearance in the Punic "tariffs," so-called, is immediately relevant to our understanding of Leviticus. These statutes, displayed on stone monuments, were discovered in Marseilles but come from Carthage. They are rather imprecisely dated in the fourth or third century B.C.E. and are written in Punic, a dialect of the Phoenician language used in the western Mediterranean colonies that is very similar to biblical Hebrew. These tariffs set down the taxes, or "dues," to be paid by those who offered sacrifice in the temple of Carthage (outside of modern Tunis). Throughout the Leviticus commentary there will be occasion to point out substantive parallels between the laws of Leviticus and the Marseilles tariffs and to illustrate the similarities in composition and formulation between the two sources.

The tariffs repeatedly delineate the various kinds of offerings in the following manner: *b'lp—kll, 'm ṣw't, 'm šlm kll.* This means: "In the case of a head of large cattle—[whether] holocaust, *or* expiatory offering (?), *or* sacred gift of greeting [accompanying] the holocaust. . . ."[10] There is a close resemblance here to the casuistic, or conditional, formulation of our chapter: (1) the options—large or small cattle (v. 2); (2) *'im 'olah korbano*—"If his offering is a burnt offering" (v. 3); (3) *ve-'im min ha-tso'n korbano*—"If his offering for a burnt offering is from the flock" (v. 10); and (4) *ve-'im min ha-'of 'olah korbano*—"If his offering is a burnt offering of birds" (v. 14).

"Burnt offering" is a functional translation of Hebrew *'olah,* which actually derives from the verb *'-l-h,* "to ascend." This type of sacrifice was to be consumed in its entirety (exclusive of the hide) by the altar fire. This could account for its name: The offering may have been called *'olah* because its flames and smoke "ascended" to heaven. Other actions involved in presenting the *'olah* may also help to explain its name. There was the "ascent" of the sacrifice itself onto the altar, and one speaks of "raising up" the *'olah,* conveyed by the Hifil form *he'elah.* There is also the "ascent" of the priest or of the officiant or the donor onto a raised platform where the offering was to be made. This interpretation seems to be corroborated by an ancient Ugaritic epic that tells of a king named Keret who mounted the turret of his city wall to offer a sacrifice; his act is conveyed by a form of the verb *'ly,* "ascend."[11]

The *'olah* was a signal to God that His worshipers desired to bring their needs to His attention; its purpose was to secure an initial response from Him. (God is perceived as breathing the aromatic smoke of the *'olah* and responding favorably to the overtures of His devotees.) Frequently, the *'olah* was the first sacrifice in rites that included other offerings as well, which supports this suggestion

head of the burnt offering, that it may be acceptable in his behalf, in expiation for him. 5The bull shall be slaughtered

לוֹ לְכַפֵּר עָלָיו׃ 5 וְשָׁחַט אֶת־בֶּן הַבָּקָר לִפְנֵי יְהוָה
וְהִקְרִיבוּ בְּנֵי אַהֲרֹן הַכֹּהֲנִים אֶת־הַדָּם וְזָרְקוּ אֶת־

about its purpose. This sacrificial method is known as "attraction," the offering of an inviting gift to God. In those biblical narratives where the *ʿolah* is prominent, or where it is the only sacrifice employed, attraction emerges as its specific purpose, as is clearly illustrated in the Elijah narrative of 1 Kings 18. Elijah prepares the *ʿolah* and the Baal priests prepare their offerings in the same manner, their common objective being to secure a response from the deity they respectively worship. As 1 Kings 18:24 puts it, "The god who *responds* with fire, that one is God." Balaam uses the method of attraction at various sites to induce an encounter with the God of Israel, as we read in Numbers 23:3–6, for example. The priestly texts also understand the function of the *ʿolah* in this way. Leviticus 9:24 relates that after the installation of Aaron and his sons as priests a fire issued forth from the sanctuary and consumed the *ʿolah* and other offerings on the altar, thereby confirming God's acceptance of the rites of installation.

This, then, was the reason for beginning with the *ʿolah,* which was followed in so many instances by the *zevaḥ,* the shared sacred meal. Before God could be expected to accept the invitation of His worshipers, it was necessary to have an indication of His readiness to be present.[12] This phenomenology suggests that the term *ʿolah* refers to the "ascent" of the smoke and flames of the sacrifice itself. The sacrifice, in its transmuted form, reaches God.

for acceptance in his behalf The antecedent of Hebrew *li-rtsono* is the donor of the sacrifice. The sacrifice counts in his favor; it is accredited to him. When a sacrifice is not considered proper the opposite is said of it: *loʾ le-ratson,* "not acceptable, discredited."[13]

before the Lord Hebrew *lifnei YHVH* seems to delineate a defined sacred area, at times the zone beginning at the rear of the altar of burnt offerings in the sanctuary courtyard and continuing to the interior of the Tent. In other passages the zone is less specific, referring to a large space near the entrance of the courtyard. The point is that priestly law strictly limits sacrifice to a particular area and to the legitimate altar.[14]

4. He shall lay his hand This symbolic act, known in later Hebrew as *semikhah,* "the laying on" of hands, served to assign a sacrificial victim for use in a particular rite, in this case an *ʿolah.* This act had other uses as well, and these help to clarify its meaning. By the laying on of hands, those in authority could invest other persons with offices of authority. Moses laid his hands on Joshua when appointing him leader of the Israelite people, as we read in Numbers 27:18–23 and Deuteronomy 34:9. In the same way, in Numbers 8:10 the Israelites are instructed to lay their hands on the Levites. In Leviticus 24:10–16 we read that the members of the community are to lay their hands on a person convicted of blasphemy, thereby identifying him as the guilty party. Thus, the laying on of hands may not have been a cultic rite originally but, rather, a juridic or legal procedure.

The Hittites had a similar procedure. In their *Ritual of Tunnawi* we read that a female worshiper touches the horn of a fertile cow, hoping to transfer the animal's fertility to herself. This is the same process, working in a different direction; other Hittite rituals describe similar acts.[15]

It is important to emphasize that the requirement of *semikhah* for some expiatory sacrificial victims should *not* be interpreted as indicating that the essential function of laying on the hands was necessarily the transferal of impurity or guilt to the victim. In the cult, *semikhah* assured that sacrifices intended for specific rites would be used solely for that purpose. Once assigned in this way, the offering was sacred and belonged to God. The act of *semikhah* was probably accompanied by a recitation that has been lost to us. The Mishnah preserves formulas of assignment from a later period.[16]

that it may be acceptable in his behalf, in expiation for him Rather, "By its acceptance on his behalf it serves as redemption for him." Usually, the formula *le-khapper ʿal* means "to perform rites of expiation *over,* near, or with respect to" a person or group of people or an object, such as the altar. This sense is not suitable here because as a type of sacrifice the *ʿolah* was not occasioned by any offense that would have placed the offender in need of expiation!

In his comments on this verse, Ibn Ezra calls attention to Exodus 30:12, where we read that each Israelite was required to contribute a half-shekel as a head-tax to the sanctuary: "Each shall pay the

before the LORD; and Aaron's sons, the priests, shall offer
the blood, dashing the blood against all sides of the altar
which is at the entrance of the Tent of Meeting. 6The burnt
offering shall be flayed and cut up into sections. 7The sons
of Aaron the priest shall put fire on the altar and lay out
wood upon the fire; 8and Aaron's sons, the priests, shall lay
out the sections, with the head and the suet, on the wood
that is on the fire upon the altar. 9Its entrails and legs shall
be washed with water, and the priest shall turn the whole
into smoke on the altar as a burnt offering, an offering by
fire of pleasing odor to the LORD.

הַדָּם עַל־הַמִּזְבֵּחַ סָבִיב אֲשֶׁר־פֶּתַח אֹהֶל מוֹעֵד׃
6 וְהִפְשִׁיט אֶת־הָעֹלָה וְנִתַּח אֹתָהּ לִנְתָחֶיהָ׃
7 וְנָתְנוּ בְּנֵי אַהֲרֹן הַכֹּהֵן אֵשׁ עַל־הַמִּזְבֵּחַ וְעָרְכוּ
עֵצִים עַל־הָאֵשׁ׃ 8 וְעָרְכוּ בְּנֵי אַהֲרֹן הַכֹּהֲנִים אֵת
הַנְּתָחִים אֶת־הָרֹאשׁ וְאֶת־הַפָּדֶר עַל־הָעֵצִים אֲשֶׁר
עַל־הָאֵשׁ אֲשֶׁר עַל־הַמִּזְבֵּחַ׃ 9 וְקִרְבּוֹ וּכְרָעָיו
יִרְחַץ בַּמָּיִם וְהִקְטִיר הַכֹּהֵן אֶת־הַכֹּל הַמִּזְבֵּחָה
עֹלָה אִשֵּׁה רֵיחַ־נִיחוֹחַ לַיהוָה׃ ס 10 וְאִם־

LORD a *ransom* for *himself* on being enrolled, that no plague may come upon them through their being enrolled." Ibn Ezra is suggesting that here we have an abbreviation of the formula *le-khapper ʿal nefesh,* "to serve as ransom for a life," which occurs in Exodus 30:15 as part of the same instruction. It is not a rite of expiation that figures in our verse but, rather, protection from God's wrath. Proximity to God was inherently dangerous for both the worshiper and the priests, even if there had been no particular offense to anger Him. The favorable acceptance of the *ʿolah* signaled God's willingness to be approached and served as a kind of ransom, or redemption, from divine wrath.[17]

5. The bull shall be slaughtered The Hebrew verb *sh-ḥ-t,* "to slaughter," may connote ritual slaughter, as it does here, or it may simply mean slaughtering in general. The Bible never informs us of which instrument was to be used to slaughter sacrifices. The only possible clue is the type of knife, never actually described, that Abraham was preparing to use on Isaac. It is called *maʾakhelet* in Genesis 22:10.

against all sides of the altar The reference is to the altar of burnt offerings, *mizbaḥ ha-ʿolah,* mentioned by name in Leviticus 4:7. According to Exodus 27:1–8, it was made of acacia wood overlaid with copper. It was hollow and partly filled with earth. At the half point of its interior, there was a copper net, or grate, that served as a grill on which the offerings were placed. The altar had four "horns" at its four corners, and it could be carried with two poles inserted in rings. Horned altars of stone have been discovered in archaeological excavations in Israel.[18]

6. shall be flayed and cut up into sections The hide was not burned. Usually, sacrificial animals were sectioned before being placed on the altar. The verb *nataḥ,* "to section," has a specialized meaning in biblical Hebrew, always referring to the sectioning of living bodies, animal or even human.[19] The salient exception to the sectioning of sacrificial animals was the paschal lamb, which, according to the law of Exodus 12:9, was roasted whole.

7. and lay out wood upon the fire The Hebrew verb *ʿ-r-kh,* "to set up, arrange, lay out" and the nominal form *maʿarakhah,* "layout, array," are part of the technical vocabulary of the cult. In Exodus 29:37 the same verb is used to signify placing offerings on the altar.[20]

8. with the head and the suet The head of the animal had been severed. Hebrew *peder,* "suet," is cognate with Akkadian *pitru,* a term used in cuneiform texts, where it refers to the loose covering of fat over the liver. *Peder* occurs only here, in verse 12, and in 8:20.[21]

9. entrails Hebrew *kerev* is synonymous with *meʿa,* "intestines," in Isaiah 16:11, which helps to define it as an anatomical term.[22]

turn the whole into smoke This is the precise sense of Hebrew *hiktir,* a verb derived from the noun *kiter* or *kitor,* "smoke." In Hebrew and in other Semitic languages, the word for incense (*ketoret*) derives, in turn, from the word for smoke because it appears in the form of smoke. The burned parts of the victim rise as smoke when they are consumed by the altar fire.[23]

an offering by fire of pleasing odor to the LORD The etymology of the term *ʾisheh* is disputed, but it probably derives from *ʾesh,* "fire." It follows the form of certain adjectives and

10If his offering for a burnt offering is from the flock, of
sheep or of goats, he shall make his offering a male without
blemish. 11It shall be slaughtered before the LORD on the
north side of the altar, and Aaron's sons, the priests, shall
dash its blood against all sides of the altar. 12When it has
been cut up into sections, the priest shall lay them out, with
the head and the suet, on the wood that is on the fire upon
the altar. 13The entrails and the legs shall be washed with
water; the priest shall offer up and turn the whole into
smoke on the altar. It is a burnt offering, an offering by fire,
of pleasing odor to the LORD.

14If his offering to the LORD is a burnt offering of birds, he
shall choose his offering from turtledoves or pigeons. 15The
priest shall bring it to the altar, pinch off its head, and turn
it into smoke on the altar; and its blood shall be drained out
against the side of the altar. 16He shall remove its crop with
its contents, and cast it into the place of the ashes, at the
east side of the altar. 17The priest shall tear it open by its

מִן־הַצֹּאן קָרְבָּנוֹ מִן־הַכְּשָׂבִים אוֹ מִן־הָעִזִּים לְעֹלָה
זָכָר תָּמִים יַקְרִיבֶנּוּ׃ 11 וְשָׁחַט אֹתוֹ עַל יֶרֶךְ
הַמִּזְבֵּחַ צָפֹנָה לִפְנֵי יְהוָה וְזָרְקוּ בְּנֵי אַהֲרֹן
הַכֹּהֲנִים אֶת־דָּמוֹ עַל־הַמִּזְבֵּחַ סָבִיב׃ 12 וְנִתַּח
אֹתוֹ לִנְתָחָיו וְאֶת־רֹאשׁוֹ וְאֶת־פִּדְרוֹ וְעָרַךְ הַכֹּהֵן
אֹתָם עַל־הָעֵצִים אֲשֶׁר עַל־הָאֵשׁ אֲשֶׁר עַל־
הַמִּזְבֵּחַ׃ 13 וְהַקֶּרֶב וְהַכְּרָעַיִם יִרְחַץ בַּמָּיִם וְהִקְרִיב
הַכֹּהֵן אֶת־הַכֹּל וְהִקְטִיר הַמִּזְבֵּחָה עֹלָה הוּא אִשֵּׁה
רֵיחַ נִיחֹחַ לַיהוָה׃ פ שני 14 וְאִם מִן־הָעוֹף
עֹלָה קָרְבָּנוֹ לַיהוָה וְהִקְרִיב מִן־הַתֹּרִים אוֹ מִן־בְּנֵי
הַיּוֹנָה אֶת־קָרְבָּנוֹ׃ 15 וְהִקְרִיבוֹ הַכֹּהֵן אֶל־הַמִּזְבֵּחַ
וּמָלַק אֶת־רֹאשׁוֹ וְהִקְטִיר הַמִּזְבֵּחָה וְנִמְצָה דָמוֹ
עַל קִיר הַמִּזְבֵּחַ׃ 16 וְהֵסִיר אֶת־מֻרְאָתוֹ בְּנֹצָתָהּ
וְהִשְׁלִיךְ אֹתָהּ אֵצֶל הַמִּזְבֵּחַ קֵדְמָה אֶל־מְקוֹם
הַדָּשֶׁן׃ 17 וְשִׁסַּע אֹתוֹ בִכְנָפָיו לֹא יַבְדִּיל

literally means "something fiery."[24] The idiom *reaḥ niḥoaḥ* means "a pleasant aroma." The unusual form *niḥoaḥ* probably derives from the verb *nuaḥ,* "to rest, be at ease"—hence "experience pleasure, comfort." In the rabbinic tradition the linguistic connection with *naḥat,* "comfort, ease," is emphasized, expressing the thought that sacrifices offered in accordance with God's instructions bring Him pleasure, *naḥat ruaḥ.*[25]

Aromatic substances were utilized in the biblical cult. There was the daily incense offering prescribed in Exodus 30:7–10, 34–35. Exodus 30:24–28 ordains that the Tent of Meeting be censed with aromatic substances. Numbers 19:6 speaks of casting cedar wood and hyssop, both aromatic, into the fire that burned the red heifer to ashes.

Fumigation was widely employed in the ancient Near East. Maimonides explained the use of incense as a means of removing the stench of the burning sacrifices.[26] Although the priestly texts do not contain the explicit requirement of using aromatics in all sacrifices, the fact that so many offerings are characterized by *reaḥ niḥoaḥ,* "a pleasing odor," certainly gives us reason to suppose that such was intended.[27]

14. turtledoves or pigeons In Genesis 15:9 the turtledove (*tor*) is paired with a young bird (*gozal*). Hebrew *benei yonah* is better translated "young pigeons."

15. pinch off its head The Hebrew verb *m-l-k* means "to break the nape of the neck," usually of a bird. In later periods this was done by the priest with his fingernail.[28] In this case the head of the bird was to be severed after its neck was broken. But in other instances this was not done. When birds were used as sin offerings the heads were not severed; so we are told in 5:8–9. The reason for severing the head of a bird offered as an *ʿolah* may be that this parallels the procedure for executing other animals, as we read in verses 6 and 8.

and its blood shall be drained out The Hebrew verb *matsah* is rare in biblical usage, although it becomes frequent in later phases of the language. It means "to squeeze" or "drain out" a liquid. The same verb is used in 5:9 to describe the draining of blood from sin offerings.[29]

16. He shall remove its crop with its contents Hebrew *mur'ah,* "crop," occurs only here. Its approximate meaning may be learned from Targum Onkelos: the rendering of *zefek,* a form of Greek *oisophagos,* "esophagus." It designates a pocket in the bird's throat where food was retained during digestion.

Hebrew *notsah* usually means "feather," but that connotation is inappropriate here. Targum Onkelos takes it to mean "food," and the Sifra explains it as "gizzard." The crop was too dirty to be

wings, without severing it, and turn it into smoke on the altar, upon the wood that is on the fire. It is a burnt offering, an offering by fire, of pleasing odor to the LORD.

וְהִקְטִיר אֹתוֹ הַכֹּהֵן הַמִּזְבֵּחָה עַל־הָעֵצִים אֲשֶׁר
עַל־הָאֵשׁ עֹלָה הוּא אִשֵּׁה רֵיחַ נִיחֹחַ לַיהוָה׃
ס

2 When a person presents an offering of meal to the LORD, his offering shall be of choice flour; he shall pour oil upon it, lay frankincense on it, [2]and present it to Aaron's sons,

ב וְנֶפֶשׁ כִּי־תַקְרִיב קָרְבַּן מִנְחָה לַיהוָה סֹלֶת
יִהְיֶה קָרְבָּנוֹ וְיָצַק עָלֶיהָ שֶׁמֶן וְנָתַן עָלֶיהָ לְבֹנָה׃

placed on the altar, so it was consigned to the ash heap, near the altar. In the case of animals sacrificed as burnt offerings, the entrails had to be washed before being placed on the altar, as we read in verse 9, to assure that nothing offensive was offered to God.

Like certain other priestly laws, chapter 1 presented the ancient worshiper with several options ranging from expensive large cattle to relatively inexpensive birds. Undoubtedly, this graduated system was intended to enable Israelites of modest means to participate in religious life by presenting offerings at the sanctuary.[30]

CHAPTER 2 THE GRAIN OFFERING (*MINḤAH*) (vv. 1–16)

The subject of chapter 2 is the ***minḥah,*** "grain offering." Like the burnt offering of chapter 1, it was appropriate for a variety of occasions and often served as a less costly alternative to animal sacrifices. Like the burnt offering, the ***minḥah*** was also considered a "most sacred offering," and this status imposed special restrictions.

Chapter 2 outlines the different types of ***minḥah,*** listing them according to their different methods of preparation. The ingredients were usually the same for the various offerings: The ***minḥah*** was made of semolina, the choice part of wheat that was taken from the inner kernels; olive oil was mixed into the dough or smeared on it; and frankincense was applied to it, enhancing the taste. The ***minḥah*** could be prepared on a griddle, in a pan, or in an oven. A fistful of the dough, with the oil and frankincense added, was burned on the altar. The rest was prepared in one of the accepted ways, to be eaten by the priests in the sacred precincts of the sanctuary. Since the fistful of dough was burned on the altar, grain offerings could *not* be made with leavened dough, as is discussed further on, and they had to be salted.

Verses 14–16 digress somewhat from the pattern of the chapter as a whole. They ordain a special ***minḥah*** of first fruits (***bikkurim***), which consisted of nearly ripe grain from the new crop. This grain was roasted and then made into grits.

1. When a person presents The word for "person" is ***nefesh,*** which has often been rendered "soul." We know, however, that the term enjoys a wide range of connotations and should be translated in accordance with its context. Here ***nefesh*** refers to an individual as part of a group.[1]

an offering of meal Rather, "an offering of grain." In modern English usage "meal" hardly ever refers to wheat, and it would be inaccurate to call an offering made of wheat by a name that refers primarily to other grains.[2]

Actually, the term ***minḥah*** has an interesting history. It does not relate to the substances used in preparing the sacrifice. Its basic sense is that of "tribute, gift."[3] Like many names given to sacrifices, the term ***minḥah*** was appropriated by priestly writers from the administrative vocabulary because it effectively expressed the subservient relationship of the worshiper toward God. At the same time, it conveyed the duty of the worshiper to present gifts to God, often in the form of sacrifices.

In the first stage, ***minḥah*** served as a generic term for any type of sacrifice. In Genesis 4:3–5 the different sacrifices of Cain and Abel, one consisting of grain and the other of animals, are both called ***minḥah.***[4] Just how the term came to signify grain offerings, in particular, is not entirely clear. Perhaps the answer lies in the manner of presenting some grain offerings and in the derivation of the term

2 וְהֱבִיאָ֗הּ אֶל־בְּנֵי֮ אַהֲרֹן֒ הַכֹּהֲנִים֒ וְקָמַ֨ץ מִשָּׁ֜ם
מְלֹ֣א קֻמְצ֗וֹ מִסָּלְתָּהּ֙ וּמִשַּׁמְנָ֔הּ עַ֖ל כָּל־לְבֹנָתָ֑הּ
וְהִקְטִ֨יר הַכֹּהֵ֜ן אֶת־אַזְכָּרָתָהּ֙ הַמִּזְבֵּ֔חָה אִשֵּׁ֛ה רֵ֥יחַ
נִיחֹ֖חַ לַיהוָֽה׃ 3 וְהַנּוֹתֶ֙רֶת֙ מִן־הַמִּנְחָ֔ה לְאַהֲרֹ֖ן
וּלְבָנָ֑יו קֹ֥דֶשׁ קָֽדָשִׁ֖ים מֵאִשֵּׁ֥י יְהוָֽה׃ ס 4 וְכִ֧י

the priests. The priest shall scoop out of it a handful of its
choice flour and oil, as well as all of its frankincense; and
this token portion he shall turn into smoke on the altar, as
an offering by fire, of pleasing odor to the LORD. 3And the
remainder of the meal offering shall be for Aaron and his
sons, a most holy portion from the LORD's offerings by fire.

minḥah. It probably derives from the root *n-ḥ-h,* "to lead, conduct," and so the term *minḥah* would signify "what was set before, brought to" a deity or ruler. Biblical evidence indicates that from early times offerings of grain and fruit were not burned on the altar but, rather, placed or set before God. Leviticus 24:5–6 ordain that the "bread of display" was to be presented in this way. According to Leviticus 7:12–13, the thanksgiving offering (*todah*) included two loaves of bread, no part of which was burned on the altar. Deuteronomy 26:1–4 describes how the "first fruits" were placed before God.

What we perceive in chapter 2 is the gradual adaptation of presentation offerings to the prevailing mode of the burnt offerings; that is, a small portion of the dough from the *minḥah* was burned on the altar. Even the bread of display was not unaffected by such developments. Pure frankincense was burned near the loaves of the bread of display when they were placed on the tables in the sanctuary, as we read in 24:7. It is the older, unadapted method of presentation, however, that accounts for the name *minḥah* in the first place. Once applied to grain offerings, it is understandable that the term *minḥah* should refer to sacrifices of the evening or late afternoon, since grain offerings were customary in evening rituals. Indeed, evening became known as the time of the *minḥah.*[5]

choice flour Hebrew *solet* is better translated "semolina flour"; Ibn Ezra translates "flour of clear wheat." Rabbinic law stipulates that wherever the Torah mandates *solet,* wheat must be used (Sifra). The usual translation "fine flour" is, therefore, incorrect. This is not to say that flour for the *minḥah* was not finely ground or pounded in a mortar—it undoubtedly was. However, the point of this verse is to prescribe the *substance* of the offering and not how that substance was to be prepared. Almost all grain offerings had olive oil mixed into the flour; at a later stage, into the dough. The verb describing this procedure is *b-l-l,* "to mix," which appears below, in v. 4, and frequently thereafter. Hebrew *b-l-l* attests to cognates in other Semitic languages, most notably in Akkadian as *balālu,* in similar contexts to ours.

What v. 1 informs us is that oil was initially poured over the semolina flour (the verb *y-ts-q,* "to pour") along with frankincense (Heb. *levonah*). Depending on how the grain offering was to be prepared—by baking, frying, etc.—oil might also be applied in any of several ways to the dough at later stages, as will become evident in the verses to follow.

2. shall scoop out of it a handful Hebrew *komets* is a way of indicating a minute quantity.

as well as all of its frankincense The Hebrew preposition *ʿal* often means "together with, in addition to," not necessarily "on" or "over." The sense here is that the frankincense was used along with other ingredients. Cognates of Hebrew *levonah,* "frankincense," are known in the other Semitic languages.[6]

and this token portion The precise meaning of Hebrew *ʾazkarah,* "token portion," is difficult to ascertain. Some have explained it as "reminder," analyzing this unusual word as an Afel form. On this basis, *ʾazkarah* would mean "that which calls to mind." The fistful of dough is *reminiscent* of the complete offering from which it was taken. The translation "token portion" relates the word *ʾazkarah* to the same verbal root, *z-kh-r,* and to the noun *zekher,* which can mean "a commemorative object." The Akkadian cognate *zikru* has the specialized connotation of "effigy, double," that is, an object that resembles the original. It is this analysis that produced the translation "token portion."[7]

3. a most holy portion Hebrew *kodesh kodashim* is a superlative combination, literally "most holy of the holy offerings." In Mishnah Zevaḥim 5 this category is expressed by the plural: *Kodshei kodashim* is contrasted with *kodashim kallim,* "offerings of lesser sanctity." This latter category includes the offerings prescribed in chapter 3.

4 When you present an offering of meal baked in the oven,
[it shall be of] choice flour: unleavened cakes with oil mixed
in, or unleavened wafers spread with oil.
5 If your offering is a meal offering on a griddle, it shall be
of choice flour with oil mixed in, unleavened. 6 Break it into
bits and pour oil on it; it is a meal offering.
7 If your offering is a meal offering in a pan, it shall be
made of choice flour in oil.
8 When you present to the LORD a meal offering that is
made in any of these ways, it shall be brought to the priest
who shall take it up to the altar. 9 The priest shall remove the
token portion from the meal offering and turn it into
smoke on the altar as an offering by fire, of pleasing odor to
the LORD. 10 And the remainder of the meal offering shall be
for Aaron and his sons, a most holy portion from the
LORD's offerings by fire.

תַקְרִב קָרְבַּן מִנְחָה מַאֲפֵה תַנּוּר סֹלֶת חַלּוֹת
מַצֹּת בְּלוּלֹת בַּשֶּׁמֶן וּרְקִיקֵי מַצּוֹת מְשֻׁחִים
בַּשָּׁמֶן׃ ס 5 וְאִם־מִנְחָה עַל־הַמַּחֲבַת קָרְבָּנֶךָ
סֹלֶת בְּלוּלָה בַשֶּׁמֶן מַצָּה תִהְיֶה׃ 6 פָּתוֹת אֹתָהּ
פִּתִּים וְיָצַקְתָּ עָלֶיהָ שָׁמֶן מִנְחָה הִוא׃ ס
שלישי 7 וְאִם־מִנְחַת מַרְחֶשֶׁת קָרְבָּנֶךָ סֹלֶת
בַּשֶּׁמֶן תֵּעָשֶׂה׃ 8 וְהֵבֵאתָ אֶת־הַמִּנְחָה אֲשֶׁר יֵעָשֶׂה
מֵאֵלֶּה לַיהוָה וְהִקְרִיבָהּ אֶל־הַכֹּהֵן וְהִגִּישָׁהּ אֶל־
הַמִּזְבֵּחַ׃ 9 וְהֵרִים הַכֹּהֵן מִן־הַמִּנְחָה אֶת־אַזְכָּרָתָהּ
וְהִקְטִיר הַמִּזְבֵּחָה אִשֵּׁה רֵיחַ נִיחֹחַ לַיהוָה׃
10 וְהַנּוֹתֶרֶת מִן־הַמִּנְחָה לְאַהֲרֹן וּלְבָנָיו קֹדֶשׁ

4. ***baked in the oven . . . unleavened cakes . . . unleavened wafers*** The law here distinguishes between the two customary varieties of baked goods: *ḥallah,* "a thick, round cake," according to Ibn Ezra's translation; and *rakik,* "a thin cake, cookie, or wafer."[8] The basic meaning of *matsah* remains uncertain. Its functional sense, however, is quite specific. It means "unleavened dough"—the opposite of *ḥamets,* "leavening, leavened dough."[9]

5. ***on a griddle*** Mishnah Menaḥot distinguishes between cakes prepared on a griddle (*maḥavat*) and those prepared in a pan, the subject of verse 7. Cakes prepared on a griddle become crisp and can be broken into *pittim,* "bits," the plural of the better-known word for a slice of dry bread, *pat (leḥem).* In Leviticus 6:14 we find the term *minḥat pittim,* "a grain offering of crisp slices."

7. ***in a pan*** Hebrew *marḥeshet* derives from the verb *r-ḥ-sh,* "to move, agitate," referring in this case to the motion of the dough as it is deep fried in a covered pan. Cakes prepared in this way become soft, as we read in Mishnah Menaḥot 5:8 and as is explained by Ibn Ezra.

8. ***When you present . . . it shall be brought . . . who shall take it up*** Rather, "You shall *bring* any grain offering prepared in any of these ways to the LORD; one shall *present* it to the priest, who shall *deliver* it to the altar." This verse employs three verbs to convey the sequence of actions involved in the process of presenting a grain offering: *hevi',* "to bring"; *hikriv,* "to present"; *higgish,* "to deliver." All three verbs are used elsewhere to describe the presentations of sacrifices. Once the dough is prepared, the offering must be carried through to its completion.

Hebrew *me-'eleh* cannot mean "from any of these," since that would imply that several different substances were used, which was not the case. The translation "in any of these ways" follows Rashi and Malbim, both of whom noted the problem in this phrase.

9. ***The priest shall remove*** This parallels the statement of verse 2: "The priest shall scoop out of it. . . ." Verses 8–10 generally recapitulate the provisions stipulated earlier in verses 2–3. It is not uncommon in codes of law, as well as in narratives, to find some repetition for clarity and emphasis.

10. ***And the remainder of the meal offering shall be for Aaron and his sons*** This rule refers to a basic feature of the Israelite sacrificial system and of most ancient Near Eastern cults. In a few cases, the complete sacrifice was consumed by the altar fire; but, more often than not, large portions of the offerings were to be eaten by the priests and, in some cases, by the donors of the offerings as well. This was considered indispensable to the ritual process because it was important to celebrate a sacred meal in the presence of God. Failure to eat the appropriate portion of the sacrifices in the proper place and within the proper span of time would render the sacrifices themselves ineffectual. There were, therefore, two dimensions to a sacrifice: On the altar (or, in some cases, on a table), the deity received portions of the sacrifice, whereas the officiants (and sometimes donors) partook of their portions soon after. Together, these parallel acts made the celebration complete.

11No meal offering that you offer to the LORD shall be
made with leaven, for no leaven or honey may be turned
into smoke as an offering by fire to the LORD. 12You may
bring them to the LORD as an offering of choice products;
but they shall not be offered up on the altar for a pleasing

קָֽדָשִׁ֖ים מֵאִשֵּׁ֥י יְהוָֽה׃ 11 כָּל־הַמִּנְחָ֗ה אֲשֶׁ֤ר
תַּקְרִ֙יבוּ֙ לַֽיהוָ֔ה לֹ֥א תֵעָשֶׂ֖ה חָמֵ֑ץ כִּ֤י כָל־שְׂאֹר֙
וְכָל־דְּבַ֔שׁ לֹא־תַקְטִ֥ירוּ מִמֶּ֛נּוּ אִשֶּׁ֖ה לַֽיהוָֽה׃
12 קָרְבַּ֥ן רֵאשִׁ֛ית תַּקְרִ֥יבוּ אֹתָ֖ם לַֽיהוָ֑ה וְאֶל־

11. for no leaven or honey may be turned into smoke In other words, no leaven or honey may be burned on the altar.

Hebrew *ḥamets*, "leaven," is cognate with Akkadian *emṣu,* "sour, fermented." In Akkadian, this adjective often describes beer, dough, and vinegar.[10]

Since antiquity, there has been discussion as to the meaning of Hebrew *devash.* From what is known, production of honey in beehives was not much in evidence in biblical Israel. Bees gathered to produce honey in the crevices of rocks, in split tree trunks, and in carcasses of animals.[11] Accordingly, *devash* occasionally refers to the honey of bees. Most authorities—including Rashi, Ibn Ezra, and Maimonides—insist that *devash* in the Bible refers primarily to the nectar of dates and possibly of other fruits. It is, after all, a general term for "sweetness." The Akkadian cognate *dishpu* also had that more general usage.[12] Furthermore, verse 12 must have intended the nectar of fruits because honey processed by bees would hardly have been called "first fruits" (*re'shit*). It is reasonable to conclude that the prohibition set forth in our chapter was inclusive of both bee honey and nectars.

When we attempt to explain the prohibitions against leaven and honey, we confront ancient attitudes that are far from clearly understood. It is not typical of either the Levitical laws or the law codes of the Torah generally to explain the basis for their requirements or prohibitions. Nevertheless, it is clear that leaven and honey were not unsuitable for all offerings, only for those burned on the altar. Only what God was intended to inhale could not contain these substances. It is logical, therefore, to seek an explanation that is tied in specifically with burnt offerings. The explanation that "leavening," or "souring," spoiled foodstuffs is hardly convincing because the best foods were often subjected to leavening. Conversely, *matsah* was poor man's bread. Wine was fermented, and yet it was proper for libations poured onto the altar. As regards leaven, a connection between the prohibition stated here and the Passover laws is certainly to be assumed. And yet nowhere is the *matsah* of Passover explicitly associated with the requirements of grain offerings. The requirement to eat *matsah* and to avoid *ḥamets* on Passover is given an historical or commemorative explanation. It is obvious, in any event, that there was a general aversion to leaven in altar offerings, although, as has been noted, this attitude did not affect offerings presented in *other* ways.

The prohibition against honey may represent a reaction against the widespread use of honey in pagan cults, an explanation actually ventured by Maimonides.[13] Indeed, we possess extensive comparative evidence that honey was frequently offered to pagan gods in the ancient Near East. In the Ugaritic epic of Keret, we read that *nbt* (cognate of Heb. *nofet,* "honey from a honeycomb") was offered to the Syro-Canaanite god El.[14] Cuneiform records from Mesopotamia and ancient Syria often list *dishpu,* "honey-nectar," as an offering.[15] By prohibiting the use of honey on the altar, the priestly laws may have been directed at eliminating pagan practices.

There is a subtle suggestion that the aversion to nectar as a sacrificial substance may have been very ancient in biblical Israel. Whereas wine and olive oil were prized as ingredients for sacrifices, nectar was not. The parable of Jotham in Judges 9:8–13 speaks of the virtues of various trees and vines. The olive tree boasts that its rich oil "honors God and men," and the grapevine says that its wine "gladdens God and men." But it is significant that the fig tree, in speaking of "my sweetness, my delicious fruit," fails to allude to their utilization as offerings to deities!

Until further evidence becomes available, it must be assumed that we do not clearly understand the attitudes reflected in these prohibitions.

12. as an offering of choice products Rather, "as an offering of first fruits." The point is that honey and leaven are unsuitable as altar offerings but are suitable as offerings set before God.

Hebrew *re'shit* is ambiguous. It can mean "first," in order or sequence, or "foremost," in terms of quality. These two meanings are not mutually exclusive, but they differ nonetheless. As in Deuteronomy 26:2,10, *re'shit* is here to be understood as positional: "first fruits," referring to offerings of the

odor. 13You shall season your every offering of meal with salt; you shall not omit from your meal offering the salt of your covenant with God; with all your offerings you must offer salt.

14If you bring a meal offering of first fruits to the LORD, you shall bring new ears parched with fire, grits of the fresh grain, as your meal offering of first fruits. 15You shall add

הַמִּזְבֵּחַ לֹא־יַעֲלוּ לְרֵיחַ נִיחֹחַ׃ 13 וְכָל־קָרְבַּן
מִנְחָתְךָ בַּמֶּלַח תִּמְלָח וְלֹא תַשְׁבִּית מֶלַח בְּרִית
אֱלֹהֶיךָ מֵעַל מִנְחָתֶךָ עַל כָּל־קָרְבָּנְךָ תַּקְרִיב
מֶלַח׃ ס 14 וְאִם־תַּקְרִיב מִנְחַת בִּכּוּרִים
לַיהוָה אָבִיב קָלוּי בָּאֵשׁ גֶּרֶשׂ כַּרְמֶל תַּקְרִיב אֵת
מִנְחַת בִּכּוּרֶיךָ׃ 15 וְנָתַתָּ עָלֶיהָ שֶׁמֶן וְשַׂמְתָּ עָלֶיהָ

first fruits, or produce, of the land. Thus, before the Israelites were permitted to enjoy the bounty of the land, they were required to offer God some of what was His. This process is known as desacralization.[16] Such offerings were, in fact, among those usually placed before God rather than burned on the altar.

13. the salt of your covenant with God According to priestly law, all sacrifices were to be salted. In the case of meat, salt functioned to remove whatever blood remained after slaughter. The unexpected use of salt in grain offerings is likely a reflection of the overall tendency toward uniformity in ritual. The same general requirement is referred to in Numbers 18:19. In Ezra 6:9 and 7:22 we read that large quantities of salt were delivered to the postexilic Temple of Jerusalem for use in the sacrificial cult.[17]

In effect, the phrase *melaḥ berit ʾeloheikha* refers to the binding, God-ordained obligation, or commitment, to use salt. In Leviticus 24:8–9, *berit ʿolam* similarly means "a commitment for all time." There *berit ʿolam* interacts with *ḥok ʿolam,* "due for all time." In the law of Exodus 31:16, the Sabbath is also characterized as *berit ʿolam,* an observance binding forever.

In Numbers 18:19, the requirement of salting sacrifices is repeated, although in somewhat altered form, as *berit melaḥ ʿolam;* but the sense is the same: "an everlasting covenant of salt." Nevertheless, an extensive literature has arisen on the subject of the presumed role of salt in the enactment of treaties and covenants on the assumption that *berit melaḥ* means "a covenant made binding by salt." Scholars have noted references to salt in ancient Near Eastern treaty curses: according to these, if a treaty were violated one's land would be sowed or plowed with salt so as to impair its productivity. Similarly, the symbolic role of salt in rituals of hospitality has been mentioned in support of the notion that the use of salt in the sacrificial cult may have had a covenantal function.[18] It is doubtful, however, whether any of this explicitly concerns the Levitical law requiring the salting of sacrifices.

In any event, *berit* in our text and in Numbers 18:19 should be understood to mean "binding obligation, commitment," making the *use* of salt a duty, rather than attributing any covenantal function to salt per se.

14. first fruits Hebrew *bikkurim* derives from the same verbal root as *bekhor,* "first-born," which refers to both animals and humans. Growth and birth were perceived as dimensions of the same process in all of nature.[19]

new ears . . . grits of the fresh grain The same items are mentioned in Leviticus 23:14–17, where an offering of first fruits is likewise prescribed. Hebrew *ʾaviv,* here translated "grain in season," designates grain just prior to ripening, when the kernels, not yet darkened, still have a greenish color. This is the understanding of Exodus 9:31–32 in a description of the effects of the hailstorm on crops growing in Egypt. There *ʾaviv* is contrasted to *ʾafilot,* literally "grain that darkens late." (Heb. *ʾafelah* means darkness.) Hence, *ʾaviv* refers to grain that was already ripe when the hail struck and was consequently damaged by it. The same word designates the month in the spring when grains ripen and derives from the root *ʾanav,* "to bud." In mishnaic Hebrew, the biblical collective noun *geres,* "grits," is spelled with a *samekh* in the plural form *gerisin.*[20] This helps to define it more precisely. Targum Onkelos translates *geres* by Aramaic *perokhan,* "hulled kernels of grain." Both verbs, *g-r-s* and *p-r-kh,* mean "to crush." Hebrew *kalui,* written *kali* in Leviticus 23:14, derives from a rare Hebrew verb meaning "to burn, parch."[21] The derivation of Hebrew *karmel,* here translated "fresh ear" from context, is uncertain.[22]

The similarity of our text to 23:14–17 has raised the question as to whether both texts are speaking of the same offerings. Both are called *bikkurim,* "first fruits," and most traditional commentators,

oil to it and lay frankincense on it; it is a meal offering. [16]And the priest shall turn a token portion of it into smoke: some of the grits and oil, with all of the frankincense, as an offering by fire to the LORD.

לְבֹנָ֑ה מִנְחָ֖ה הִֽוא׃ 16 וְהִקְטִ֨יר הַכֹּהֵ֜ן אֶת־אַזְכָּרָתָ֗הּ
מִגִּרְשָׂהּ֙ וּמִשַּׁמְנָ֔הּ עַ֖ל כָּל־לְבֹנָתָ֑הּ אִשֶּׁ֖ה לַיהוָֽה׃
פ רביעי

including Rashi and Ramban, have argued for the identity of the two laws, with Ibn Ezra and Luzzatto dissenting. It is probable that the difference lies in the timing and the disposition of the two offerings, not in their essential character. Our text indicates a voluntary, unscheduled sacrifice to be burned on the altar and hence to be prepared with unleavened dough. The offering ordained in 23:14–17 is an obligatory offering, to be baked on Shavuot from the new grain crop, of leavened dough. It is to be placed before the Lord rather than burned on the altar. This prescription more closely resembles the offerings of first fruits ordained in Deuteronomy 26.

CHAPTER 3 THE SACRED GIFT OF GREETING (*ZEVAḤ SHELAMIM*) (vv. 1–17)

Chapter 3 is a code of sacrifice governing the third essential type of offering in Israelite worship, the type called *zevaḥ*. The most frequent *zevaḥ* was known as *zevaḥ shelamim*, "sacred gift of greeting." In order to understand chapter 3 against the background of the first two codes—the law of the burnt offering in chapter 1 and the law of the grain offering in chapter 2—it is necessary to explain each component of the composite term *zevaḥ shelamim* independently.

The *zevaḥ* was presented differently from the burnt offering or grain offering, although there were overlapping features. Some of the same animals used for burnt offerings could be used for the *zevaḥ* as well, and the same altar was used for all three types of offerings. Also, blood from the sacrificial animal offered as a *zevaḥ* was applied to the altar of burnt offerings, in different ways but in the same spirit.

There were, however, significant differences that inform us of the special character of the *zevaḥ*. Whereas the *ʿolah* of chapter 1 was completely consumed by the altar fire, and in this way given over to God entirely, the *zevaḥ* was a sacred meal in which sections of the sacrifice were shared by the priests and donors of the offering. Only certain fatty portions of the animal were burned on the altar as God's share. There is also some evidence that at an early stage in the development of Israelite worship, the *zevaḥ* may have been prepared in a manner that did not require the use of an altar. According to Exodus 12–13, the paschal *zevaḥ* was to be roasted whole over an open fire, in proximity to one's home, a procedure that was probably very ancient.

Whereas the *minḥah* could be eaten only by priests, the eating of the *zevaḥ* was not so restricted. Thus it clearly represents a distinctive mode of sacrifice whose presentation expressed its purpose: to afford the worshipers the experience of joining together with the priests in a sacred meal at which God Himself was perceived to be the honored guest. Viewed as a class of sacrificial offerings, the *zevaḥ* was, however, "an offering of lesser sanctity" because even nonpriests could partake of it, even outside the sanctuary.[1]

The word *shelamim* is difficult to define precisely because the Hebrew verb *sh-l-m,* from which it derives, has many related yet different connotations. The translation "sacrifice of well-being" reflects one of these meanings, based on the rendering of *shalom* as "well-being, wholeness." The preferred rendering "sacred offering of greeting" reflects, on the other hand, the particular role of this sacrifice in the Israelite cult.[2]

In time, *shelamim* became the term for a general category of sacrifices and was virtually interchangeable with *zevaḥ* itself. It had several uses, including the thanksgiving offering (*todah*), the voluntary offering (*nedavah*), and the payment of vows (*neder*). Often the *shelamim* sacrifice was combined with other sacrifices, especially with *ʿolah,* in celebrating important events in the history of the Israelite people. It also served as part of the public celebration of the Shavuot festival (23:19). It was offered most frequently, however, as a personal sacrifice.[3]

3 If his offering is a sacrifice of well-being—
If he offers of the herd, whether a male or a female, he
shall bring before the LORD one without blemish. 2 He shall
lay his hand upon the head of his offering and slaughter it at
the entrance of the Tent of Meeting; and Aaron's sons, the
priests, shall dash the blood against all sides of the altar.
3 He shall then present from the sacrifice of well-being, as an

ג וְאִם־זֶבַח שְׁלָמִים קׇרְבָּנוֹ אִם מִן־הַבָּקָר הוּא
מַקְרִיב אִם־זָכָר אִם־נְקֵבָה תָּמִים יַקְרִיבֶנּוּ לִפְנֵי
יְהֹוָה׃ 2 וְסָמַךְ יָדוֹ עַל־רֹאשׁ קׇרְבָּנוֹ וּשְׁחָטוֹ פֶּתַח
אֹהֶל מוֹעֵד וְזָרְקוּ בְּנֵי אַהֲרֹן הַכֹּהֲנִים אֶת־הַדָּם
עַל־הַמִּזְבֵּחַ סָבִיב׃ 3 וְהִקְרִיב מִזֶּבַח הַשְּׁלָמִים
אִשֶּׁה לַיהֹוָה אֶת־הַחֵלֶב הַמְכַסֶּה אֶת־הַקֶּרֶב וְאֵת

1. ***a sacrifice of well-being*** The Hebrew term *shelamim* is better rendered "a sacred gift of greeting" as will be explained in due course. The noun *zevaḥ* produced the verb *zavaḥ,* which is usually translated "to slaughter." Although in practice a biblical *zevaḥ* consisted of slaughtered animals, it is more accurate to explain this term as "food offering" and to understand the verb *z-v-ḥ* as "to celebrate a sacred meal." The Akkadian cognate is *zību,* which may designate any offering of food. Both Ugaritic and Phoenician texts indicate that other foodstuffs, aside from meat, could be termed *z-b-ḥ/d-b-ḥ*.[4] The widespread circulation of these Semitic terms testifies to the importance of this type of sacrifice, from earliest times, in any number of religious cults.

The most detailed description of the *zevaḥ* sacrifice, apart from the priestly legislation in the Book of Leviticus, is found in 1 Samuel 9:12,14,19,22–25. There participants are referred to as *keru'im,* "invited guests."[5] A priest presided over the celebration—in that instance the prophet Samuel himself, who functioned as a priest on many occasions. Samuel blessed the sacrifice, offered it up, and then distributed portions of it to the invited participants, who partook of it in special rooms. What was eaten by the priests and the invited guests was boiled in pots, whereas the portions offered to God were burned on the altar. Some further details may be deduced from the story concerning the sinful sons of Eli, the priest of Shiloh, as related in 1 Samuel 2:12–16. It was forbidden for the priests or the participants to eat the meat of the *zevaḥ* before God's share had been offered to Him on the altar. That account also makes reference to the kinds of pots and forks that were used.[6]

The term *shelamim* has puzzled commentators since antiquity. The Septuagint gives it no fewer than three different Greek renderings, and midrashic interpretations likewise vary greatly. The usual translation, "peace offering," merely echoes the Latin of the Vulgate, *pacificus,* and the Greek *eirēnikos,* one of the Septuagint's renderings. Both mean "that which relates to peace." Presumably, this translation expresses the peaceful, or harmonious, relationship between the worshiper and God, brought about and reaffirmed by the sacrifice itself. In a similar vein, some scholars have taken their cue from a statement in Solomon's prayer at the dedication of the Temple in Jerusalem included in 1 Kings 8. On that occasion, *shelamim* offerings were sacrificed, and verse 61 states: "And may you be wholehearted with [*shalem 'im*] the LORD our God." In the view of these scholars, this statement, in the context of the dedication ceremony, establishes the meaning of the word *shelamim* as a sacrifice intended to reaffirm the covenant between God and the Israelite people. Still another interpretation, also based on one of the connotations of the verb *sh-l-m,* is preserved in *Midrash ha-Gadol.* There *shelamim* is explained in quantitative terms: *she-ha-kol shelamim bo,* "for all are 'complete' in it," that is, all receive a portion of the sacrifices—priests, participants (or donors), and God. The *New English Bible* seems to have adopted this view, because it translates *shelamim* as "shared offering."

All of the aforementioned interpretations are possible, of course, but there is now comparative evidence to suggest that the term *shelamim* originally meant "tribute, gift of greeting." In a Ugaritic epic, Keret, the king of a besieged city, offered *shalamūma* to the commander of the attacking forces in an effort to induce him to withdraw the siege.[7] In Akkadian texts we find a cognate term, *shulmānu*, that literally means "a gift of greeting," such as was presented by vassals to their suzerains when they visited them or by emissaries on a mission to their allies. This meaning reflects the word of greeting, which is *shalom* in Hebrew and is expressed by similar words in Ugaritic and Akkadian. The *shelamim* is offered when one greets another by saying *"shalom!"* In the cult, the *shelamim* assumed the form of an animal sacrifice offered to God when one came before Him to greet Him at a sacred meal. It was adopted as the name of a particular sacrifice because it expressed the fellowship experienced by the worshipers and priests in God's presence, as they greeted their divine guest.

offering by fire to the LORD, the fat that covers the entrails and all the fat that is about the entrails; [4]the two kidneys and the fat that is on them, that is at the loins; and the protuberance on the liver, which he shall remove with the kidneys. [5]Aaron's sons shall turn these into smoke on the altar, with the burnt offering which is upon the wood that is on the fire, as an offering by fire, of pleasing odor to the LORD.

[6]And if his offering for a sacrifice of well-being to the LORD is from the flock, whether a male or a female, he shall offer one without blemish. [7]If he presents a sheep as his offering, he shall bring it before the LORD [8]and lay his hand upon the head of his offering. It shall be slaughtered before the Tent of Meeting, and Aaron's sons shall dash its blood against all sides of the altar. [9]He shall then present, as an offering by fire to the LORD, the fat from the sacrifice of well-being: the whole broad tail, which shall be removed close to the backbone; the fat that covers the entrails and all the fat

כָּל־הַחֵלֶב אֲשֶׁר עַל־הַקֶּרֶב׃ 4 וְאֵת שְׁתֵּי הַכְּלָיֹת
וְאֶת־הַחֵלֶב אֲשֶׁר עֲלֵהֶן אֲשֶׁר עַל־הַכְּסָלִים וְאֶת־
הַיֹּתֶרֶת עַל־הַכָּבֵד עַל־הַכְּלָיוֹת יְסִירֶנָּה׃
5 וְהִקְטִירוּ אֹתוֹ בְנֵי־אַהֲרֹן הַמִּזְבֵּחָה עַל־הָעֹלָה
אֲשֶׁר עַל־הָעֵצִים אֲשֶׁר עַל־הָאֵשׁ אִשֵּׁה רֵיחַ נִיחֹחַ
לַיהוָה׃ פ 6 וְאִם־מִן־הַצֹּאן קָרְבָּנוֹ לְזֶבַח
שְׁלָמִים לַיהוָה זָכָר אוֹ נְקֵבָה תָּמִים יַקְרִיבֶנּוּ׃
7 אִם־כֶּשֶׂב הוּא־מַקְרִיב אֶת־קָרְבָּנוֹ וְהִקְרִיב אֹתוֹ
לִפְנֵי יְהוָה׃ 8 וְסָמַךְ אֶת־יָדוֹ עַל־רֹאשׁ קָרְבָּנוֹ
וְשָׁחַט אֹתוֹ לִפְנֵי אֹהֶל מוֹעֵד וְזָרְקוּ בְּנֵי אַהֲרֹן
אֶת־דָּמוֹ עַל־הַמִּזְבֵּחַ סָבִיב׃ 9 וְהִקְרִיב מִזֶּבַח
הַשְּׁלָמִים אִשֶּׁה לַיהוָה חֶלְבּוֹ הָאַלְיָה תְמִימָה
לְעֻמַּת הֶעָצֶה יְסִירֶנָּה וְאֶת־הַחֵלֶב הַמְכַסֶּה אֶת־
הַקֶּרֶב וְאֵת כָּל־הַחֵלֶב אֲשֶׁר עַל־הַקֶּרֶב׃ 10 וְאֵת

3. ***the fat that covers the entrails*** Hebrew *ḥelev* has the general sense of "fat," but here it refers specifically to the fat that covers or surrounds the kidneys, the liver, and the entrails. It does not refer, in its legal usage, to ordinary fat that adheres to the flesh of an animal, which is called *shuman* in rabbinic Hebrew.[8] *Ḥelev,* like sacrificial blood, is forbidden for human consumption. Although not regarded as choice food for humans, under normal circumstances, *ḥelev* was desired by God. From the cultic perspective, a food's desirability was not a function of the usual dietary considerations but of its symbolic value. Deuteronomy 32:14, for example, refers to the finest quality of wheat as the "fat" of the wheat, where fatness is a symbol of energy and blessing.[9]

Hebrew *kesalim,* translated loins, is better rendered "sinews, tendons." It has cognates in several other Semitic languages, where it occurs in detailed religious and medical texts. This has helped to establish the precise meaning of an otherwise rare term in Hebrew.[10]

4. ***the protuberance on the liver*** The sense is more precisely conveyed by variations of this term such as, "the protuberance of the liver" (8:16; 9:10). The "protuberance" (*yoteret*) was not at the top of the liver. According to Maimonides, the reference is to "the lower end of the liver, which protrudes from it, like the thumb from the hand." In Latin nomenclature, this appendage is known as *lobus caudatus;* in Hebrew, *'etsba' ha-kaved,* "the 'finger' of the liver," as it is called in Mishnah Tamid 4:3. In Leviticus 1:8 this protuberance is called *peder.*[11]

5. ***with the burnt offering*** Not "on top, over the burnt offering." According to Rashi, the point is, rather, that the same altar of burnt offerings was used for the *'olah* and the *zevaḥ shelamim.* The Hebrew preposition *'al* does not necessarily mean "on, upon," so that here *'al ha-'olah* may be rendered "with the *'olah.*"

6–8. The terms and procedures prescribed here have been explained in the Comments to chapter 1.

9. ***the fat from the sacrifice . . . the whole broad tail*** Literally, "its fat." Hebrew *'alyah* has cognates in Aramaic and Arabic that clarify its precise meaning. It is the large, broad tail of certain species of sheep that are still raised in Israel and in neighboring countries.

In 8:25 we have "the fat and the broad tail," which indicates that *ḥelev* and *'alyah* are two separate parts of the sheep. Here it would appear that *ḥelbo,* "its fat," is the general category, then specified by two of its components: (1) the broad tail, and (2) other fat that covers the internal organs. It is likely, therefore, that here the word *ḥelev* is used in a more general sense first, whereas further on in the verse it is used technically to signify the fat covering the internal organs.[12]

that is about the entrails; [10]the two kidneys and the fat that
is on them, that is at the loins; and the protuberance on the
liver, which he shall remove with the kidneys. [11]The priest
shall turn these into smoke on the altar as food, an offering
by fire to the LORD.

[12]And if his offering is a goat, he shall bring it before the
LORD [13]and lay his hand upon its head. It shall be slaughtered before the Tent of Meeting, and Aaron's sons shall
dash its blood against all sides of the altar. [14]He shall then
present as his offering from it, as an offering by fire to the
LORD, the fat that covers the entrails and all the fat that is
about the entrails; [15]the two kidneys and the fat that is on
them, that is at the loins; and the protuberance on the liver,
which he shall remove with the kidneys. [16]The priest shall
turn these into smoke on the altar as food, an offering by
fire, of pleasing odor.

All fat is the LORD's. [17]It is a law for all time throughout
the ages, in all your settlements: you must not eat any fat or
any blood.

שְׁתֵּי הַכְּלָיֹת וְאֶת־הַחֵלֶב אֲשֶׁר עֲלֵהֶן אֲשֶׁר עַל־
הַכְּסָלִים וְאֶת־הַיֹּתֶרֶת עַל־הַכָּבֵד עַל־הַכְּלָיֹת
יְסִירֶנָּה׃ 11 וְהִקְטִירוֹ הַכֹּהֵן הַמִּזְבֵּחָה לֶחֶם אִשֶּׁה
לַיהוָה׃ פ 12 וְאִם עֵז קָרְבָּנוֹ וְהִקְרִיבוֹ לִפְנֵי
יְהוָה׃ 13 וְסָמַךְ אֶת־יָדוֹ עַל־רֹאשׁוֹ וְשָׁחַט אֹתוֹ
לִפְנֵי אֹהֶל מוֹעֵד וְזָרְקוּ בְּנֵי אַהֲרֹן אֶת־דָּמוֹ עַל־
הַמִּזְבֵּחַ סָבִיב׃ 14 וְהִקְרִיב מִמֶּנּוּ קָרְבָּנוֹ אִשֶּׁה
לַיהוָה אֶת־הַחֵלֶב הַמְכַסֶּה אֶת־הַקֶּרֶב וְאֵת כָּל־
הַחֵלֶב אֲשֶׁר עַל־הַקֶּרֶב׃ 15 וְאֵת שְׁתֵּי הַכְּלָיֹת
וְאֶת־הַחֵלֶב אֲשֶׁר עֲלֵהֶן אֲשֶׁר עַל־הַכְּסָלִים וְאֶת־
הַיֹּתֶרֶת עַל־הַכָּבֵד עַל־הַכְּלָיֹת יְסִירֶנָּה׃
16 וְהִקְטִירָם הַכֹּהֵן הַמִּזְבֵּחָה לֶחֶם אִשֶּׁה לְרֵיחַ
נִיחֹחַ כָּל־חֵלֶב לַיהוָה׃ 17 חֻקַּת עוֹלָם לְדֹרֹתֵיכֶם
בְּכֹל מוֹשְׁבֹתֵיכֶם כָּל־חֵלֶב וְכָל־דָּם לֹא תֹאכֵלוּ׃
פ חמישי

Hebrew *temimah* may mean "complete" in contrast to "partial." This is its meaning, for instance, in 23:15: "seven complete Sabbaths (*shabbatot temimot*)." Usually this adjective means "faultless, without blemish," but that meaning is unsuitable here.

the backbone Hebrew *ʿatseh,* which occurs only here in all of the Hebrew Bible, is rendered by Targum Onkelos as *shidretaʾ,* "spine."

11. on the altar as food Hebrew *leḥem* not only means "bread" but is a more general word for food.[13] In Leviticus 21:6 and Numbers 28:2, the sacrifices are referred to as *leḥem,* because they are offered to God in the same way as food is served to humans. In most ancient societies it was believed that gods required food for their sustenance and relied on sacrifices for energy and strength. Rituals for feeding the statues of gods are known from Egypt and Mesopotamia.[14]

The Torah codes, while preserving the idiom common to ancient religions, understand the process somewhat differently. God desires the sacrifices of His worshipers not because He requires sustenance but because He desires their devotion and their fellowship.

16. All fat is the LORD's This verse states the general rule, applicable to all animal sacrifices of which sections were burnt on the altar. *Ḥelev,* "fat," is prohibited for human consumption because it belongs to God as His share.

17. a law for all time Hebrew *ḥukkah,* "law," like the masculine form *ḥok,* derives from the verbal root *ḥ-k-k,* "to inscribe, incise," and reflects the practice of inscribing statutes on stone.[15] The priestly codes often stipulate that what is ordained in a specific instance is meant as a permanent statute. This formula not only adds emphasis but meets a basic requirement in codified laws, namely, a statement as to time limits, if applicable.[16]

in all your settlements The regulations prescribed here regarding fat and blood are not restricted to the cult of the sanctuary but are obligatory, as well, in the homes of the Israelites, in the conduct of their private lives. In this respect, the prohibition against eating fat and blood differs from the other laws governing sacrificial rites, which are only applicable to the cult proper.

you must not eat any fat or any blood The principal statement on the prohibition against eating blood occurs in 17:10–12, where its rationale is given and where its larger implications will be explained. The fact that the two prohibitions are listed together here has led some to seek a common basis for prohibiting both. They both belong to God as sacrificial offerings. There is, however, much that is distinctive to the blood prohibition over and above the utilization of blood in sacrificial rites.

The Expiatory Sacrifices (4:1–5:26)

Chapters 4 and 5 contain the laws governing expiatory sacrifices, the purpose of which is to secure atonement and forgiveness from God. These offerings are efficacious only when offenses are inadvertent or unwitting. They do not apply to defiant acts or premeditated crimes.[1] Whenever an individual Israelite, a tribal leader, a priest, or even the chief priest, or the Israelite community at large is guilty of an inadvertent offense or of failing to do what the law requires, expiation through sacrifice is required.

The laws of chapters 4–5 do not specify all the offenses for which such sacrifices are mandated. We may assume, as did the rabbinic sages, that there is a correspondence between those offenses requiring the expiatory offerings and those punishable by the penalty known as ***karet,*** the "cutting off" of the offender from the community: The expiatory sacrifices are required for inadvertent transgressions that, if committed defiantly, would bring upon the offender the penalty of ***karet.***

At some early stage ***karet*** probably involved actual banishment. *Karet* was often combined with more stringent punishments, even death. It is sometimes perceived as punishment meted out directly by God, in contrast to that imposed by the community and its leaders for offenses committed against God. *Karet* was inflicted for a variety of religious sins, such as desecration of the Sabbath, eating leaven on Passover, or committing adultery. Although this group excluded most crimes against persons, it included certain crimes "between man and man" when these involved oaths taken in God's name or the misappropriation of sanctuary property. Even the withholding of testimony had a sacred aspect to it.[2]

In substance, chapters 4–5 prescribe two principal sacrifices: the ***ḥatta't*** and ***'asham.*** The object of the ***ḥatta't,*** usually translated "sin offering," was to remove the culpability borne by the offender, that is, to purify the offender of his guilt (4:1–5:13). The ***'asham,*** usually translated "guilt offering," was actually a penalty paid in the form of a sacrificial offering to God. It applied when one had unintentionally misappropriated property that belonged to the sanctuary or had been contributed to it; or, in certain cases, when one had sworn falsely concerning his responsibility toward the property of others. A false oath brings God into the picture directly. The sacrifice did not relieve the offender of his duty to make full restitution for the loss he had caused another. In fact, the offender was fined 20 percent of the lost value. The ***'asham*** merely squared the offender with his God, whose name he had taken in vain (5:14–26).

A further distinction must be drawn with respect to the term ***ḥatta't*** itself. Two different sacrificial rites are actually subsumed under the name ***ḥatta't.*** Although both share the common objective of expiating religious offenses, each accomplishes this end through its own particular ritual means. The first ***ḥatta't,*** prescribed in 4:3–21, consisted of a young bull, offered in the case when the chief priest or the collective community of Israelites was guilty. It was accompanied by unusual rites in which blood taken from the sacrificial victim was brought inside the Shrine, reflecting the severity of the offense committed against God and His sanctuary. Furthermore, no part of the sacrifice was consumed by the priests; instead, whatever was not placed on the altar was removed from the camp and burned, a procedure that anthropologists call "riddance."

The second type of ***ḥatta't,*** prescribed in 4:22–5:13, consisted of a goat or sheep, but in certain instances offerings of birds or grain could be substituted for an animal. Such an offering was mandated in the event an individual Israelite or a tribal chief inadvertently committed a forbidden act (4:22–35) or failed to perform a required duty (5:1–13). This type of ***ḥatta't,*** of which there were several varieties, had the twofold effect of propitiating God through an altar sacrifice and of com-

4 The LORD spoke to Moses, saying: ²Speak to the Israelite people thus:

When a person unwittingly incurs guilt in regard to any of the LORD's commandments about things not to be done, and does one of them—

ד וַיְדַבֵּ֥ר יְהוָ֖ה אֶל־מֹשֶׁ֥ה לֵּאמֹֽר׃ 2 דַּבֵּ֞ר אֶל־בְּנֵ֣י
יִשְׂרָאֵ֘ל לֵאמֹר֒ נֶ֗פֶשׁ כִּֽי־תֶחֱטָ֤א בִשְׁגָגָה֙ מִכֹּל֙
מִצְוֹ֣ת יְהוָ֔ה אֲשֶׁ֖ר לֹ֣א תֵעָשֶׂ֑ינָה וְעָשָׂ֕ה מֵאַחַ֖ת
מֵהֵֽנָּה׃ 3 אִ֣ם הַכֹּהֵ֧ן הַמָּשִׁ֛יחַ יֶחֱטָ֖א לְאַשְׁמַ֣ת הָעָ֑ם

pensating the priesthood for its services on behalf of the people. Portions of the offering were consumed by the priests in sacred precincts.

All told, chapters 4–5 reflect a deep concern for sanctity—for maintaining the purity of the sanctuary against all forms of defilement caused by the priesthood and the people and for assuring the acceptability of all Israelites in God's sight. Further information on the expiatory sacrifices is presented in 6:17–7:10. The laws of chapters 4–5 see an inherent connection between sinfulness and impurity, a connection that is apparent in a variety of situations. Many technical terms can mean both "sin" and "impurity." Since antiquity there has been a tendency in many languages to juxtapose ritual and legal concepts. Even today, we use the word "fault" to connote both a physical or structural imperfection as well as a misdeed. In the context of ritual, one is perceived as either pure or impure, which implies a physical, or nearly physical, state. In the context of law, one is innocent or guilty, which relates primarily to behavior. In the Levitical codes of the Torah, as in many other ancient traditions, these two contexts have been blended, so that what is sinful is at the same time impure; conversely, the forgiven person is at the same time purified. Consequently, the *ḥatta't* sacrifice can be viewed both as a form of purification and as the removal of one's guilt. There is also a cause-and-effect relationship to be considered: Sinful acts are often, though not always, the very ones that cause impurity.

CHAPTER 4   FORMS OF THE *ḤATTA'T* SACRIFICE
_____

FOR SINS COMMITTED (vv. 1–35)

*2. **When a person unwittingly incurs guilt*** Literally, "When a person unwittingly commits an offense." The translation "incurs guilt" more properly expresses the consequences of the act, not the act itself. The Hebrew verb *shagag*, "to err," and its adverbial derivative *bishgagah*, "unwittingly," were understood by the rabbis to have two related aspects: (1) inadvertence with respect to the facts of law; and (2) inadvertence with respect to the nature of the act. In the first situation, the offender might be unaware that the act was in violation of the law, or, at the very least, might not know the specific penalties for such actions. In both the biblical and rabbinic traditions, it was conceded that ignorance of the law was a mitigating circumstance, and this was especially true in ritual or religious matters. Inadvertence with respect to the nature of the act itself would occur if, for example, a person ate forbidden fat, *ḥelev*, thinking it was merely ordinary fat, *shuman*, which is permitted.[3] In both cases, the presumption is that an Israelite possessed of full awareness and knowledge would seek to obey God's laws, not violate them. Such unwitting offenses could therefore be expiated by ritual means.

The verb *ḥ-t-'* has a wide range of meanings in biblical Hebrew and in cognate languages, especially Akkadian. Comparative evidence in this case enables us to trace the various usages of this verb in Hebrew. Akkadian *ḥaṭû* means "to err, be at fault, betray." It is used in treaties and legal documents to refer to violations of trust or breaches of treaty. When the concepts expressed by the verb *ḥ-t-'* are applied to religious offenses, they refer to violations of the covenant between God and Israel and to those who fail to fulfill their religious duties.[4]

in regard to . . . things not to be done, and does one of them In rabbinic terminology this circumstance is referred to as *shiggat ha-ma'aseh*, "an inadvertent violation that involves committing an act."[5] Note the repeated use of the verb *'asah*, "to do, commit," in verses 13, 22, and 29. Such

[3]If it is the anointed priest who has incurred guilt, so that
blame falls upon the people, he shall offer for the sin of
which he is guilty a bull of the herd without blemish as a sin
offering to the LORD. [4]He shall bring the bull to the
entrance of the Tent of Meeting, before the Lord, and lay
his hand upon the head of the bull. The bull shall be
slaughtered before the LORD, [5]and the anointed priest shall
take some of the bull's blood and bring it into the Tent of
Meeting. [6]The priest shall dip his finger in the blood, and

וְהִקְרִ֗יב עַ֣ל חַטָּאתוֹ֩ אֲשֶׁ֨ר חָטָ֜א פַּ֣ר בֶּן־בָּקָ֥ר
תָּמִ֛ים לַיהוָ֖ה לְחַטָּֽאת׃ 4 וְהֵבִ֣יא אֶת־הַפָּ֗ר אֶל־
פֶּ֛תַח אֹ֥הֶל מוֹעֵ֖ד לִפְנֵ֣י יְהוָ֑ה וְסָמַ֤ךְ אֶת־יָדוֹ֙ עַל־
רֹ֣אשׁ הַפָּ֔ר וְשָׁחַ֥ט אֶת־הַפָּ֖ר לִפְנֵ֥י יְהוָֽה׃ 5 וְלָקַ֛ח
הַכֹּהֵ֥ן הַמָּשִׁ֖יחַ מִדַּ֣ם הַפָּ֑ר וְהֵבִ֥יא אֹת֖וֹ אֶל־אֹ֥הֶל
מוֹעֵֽד׃ 6 וְטָבַ֧ל הַכֹּהֵ֛ן אֶת־אֶצְבָּע֖וֹ בַּדָּ֑ם וְהִזָּ֨ה מִן־
הַדָּ֜ם שֶׁ֣בַע פְּעָמִ֗ים לִפְנֵ֣י יְהוָ֔ה אֶת־פְּנֵ֖י פָּרֹ֥כֶת

transgressions stand in contrast to "sins of omission," where the fault lies in the failure to act or to do what is required by law.

3. *If it is the anointed priest* The title *ha-kohen ha-mashiaḥ* is synonymous with *ha-kohen ha-gadol,* "the High Priest," which occurs in 21:10. According to the primary laws of Leviticus, he is the only priest anointed with the oil of unction, and this accounts for his title here and in 6:15.[6]

so that blame falls upon the people The errors and possible offenses of the chief cultic official, the individual in charge of the sanctuary and the priesthood, had an effect on the entire community. Here the law refers to offenses occurring in the performance of the priestly office, not to the personal sins of the chief priest (which he had to expiate independently). And yet later commentators, such as Rashi and Rashbam, were not far from the mark in stressing that the chief priest's personal behavior was relevant to his sacerdotal office. In the Yom Kippur ritual, set forth in chapter 16, we read that he had first to atone for his own sins and those of his family before he could secure atonement for the entire Israelite community.

The noun *'ashmah,* "blame," derives from the same root as the sacrifice known as *'asham.*[7] In the Levitical codes, cultic notions of guilt do not correspond exactly to legal norms of innocence and guilt. Human judges, who must proceed on the basis of evidence, dare not prejudge a person's guilt. But the divine Judge, who knows our deepest thoughts, is not so limited. In religious terms, even inadvertent offenses where there is not any intent to violate the commandments might immediately arouse God's wrath and result in divine punishment.

Thus, priestly texts hold that God's wrath is easily kindled by carelessness in maintaining the purity of His earthly sanctuary and by the improper execution of religious duties, even if unintentional. Although this is, of course, only one of the viewpoints encountered in biblical literature (elsewhere, we are assured that God is slow to anger),[8] in Leviticus the sense of the reality of divine wrath should not be underestimated. Mitigating and preventing that wrath is a major objective of the religious life.

for the sin of which he is guilty Rather, "for the sin that he has committed." As in verse 3 it is preferable to convey in the translation the sense of the act itself rather than the consequent guilt that results from the act. It is important to explain that the Hebrew consonantal root *ḥ-t-'-t* is ambiguous. The Masoretes consistently pointed the second root consonant, *tet,* with a *dagesh,* but in fact the Hebrew consonants allow for two distinct nouns: (1) *ḥata't,* a noun based on the Kal stem and a variant of *ḥata'ah,* "sin, fault, offense";[9] (2) *ḥatta't,* a noun based on the Piel stem, literally "an offering to remove an offense, to purify."[10] In biblical Hebrew, the Piel stem may signify the undoing, or elimination, of the very act, or state, conveyed by the Kal stem of the same verb. Thus, Hebrew *ḥitte'* means "to remove impurity," as in 6:19 and 8:15. Here the phrase *ha-ḥatta't 'asher ḥat'u 'aleiha* means "the offense which they committed," not, of course, "the sin offering."

a bull of the herd The Sifra defines *ben bakar* as a three-year-old bull. As in the case of *benei yonah,* "young pigeons," in 1:14, the designation *ben,* "son, offspring," indicates the relative age of the sacrificial victim.

4. *and lay his hand upon the head of the bull* The rite of laying on the hand is explained in the Comment to 1:4.

sprinkle of the blood seven times before the LORD, in front
of the curtain of the Shrine. [7]The priest shall put some of
the blood on the horns of the altar of aromatic incense,
which is in the Tent of Meeting, before the LORD; and all the
rest of the bull's blood he shall pour out at the base of the
altar of burnt offering, which is at the entrance of the Tent
of Meeting. [8]He shall remove all the fat from the bull of sin
offering: the fat that covers the entrails and all the fat that is
about the entrails; [9]the two kidneys and the fat that is on
them, that is at the loins; and the protuberance on the liver,
which he shall remove with the kidneys—[10]just as it is
removed from the ox of the sacrifice of well-being. The
priest shall turn them into smoke on the altar of burnt
offering. [11]But the hide of the bull, and all its flesh, as well
as its head and legs, its entrails and its dung—[12]all the rest

הַקֹּדֶשׁ׃ 7 וְנָתַן הַכֹּהֵן מִן־הַדָּם עַל־קַרְנוֹת מִזְבַּח
קְטֹרֶת הַסַּמִּים לִפְנֵי יְהוָה אֲשֶׁר בְּאֹהֶל מוֹעֵד
וְאֵת ׀ כָּל־דַּם הַפָּר יִשְׁפֹּךְ אֶל־יְסוֹד מִזְבַּח הָעֹלָה
אֲשֶׁר־פֶּתַח אֹהֶל מוֹעֵד׃ 8 וְאֶת־כָּל־חֵלֶב פַּר
הַחַטָּאת יָרִים מִמֶּנּוּ אֶת־הַחֵלֶב הַמְכַסֶּה עַל־
הַקֶּרֶב וְאֵת כָּל־הַחֵלֶב אֲשֶׁר עַל־הַקֶּרֶב׃ 9 וְאֵת
שְׁתֵּי הַכְּלָיֹת וְאֶת־הַחֵלֶב אֲשֶׁר עֲלֵיהֶן אֲשֶׁר עַל־
הַכְּסָלִים וְאֶת־הַיֹּתֶרֶת עַל־הַכָּבֵד עַל־הַכְּלָיוֹת
יְסִירֶנָּה׃ 10 כַּאֲשֶׁר יוּרַם מִשּׁוֹר זֶבַח הַשְּׁלָמִים
וְהִקְטִירָם הַכֹּהֵן עַל מִזְבַּח הָעֹלָה׃ 11 וְאֶת־עוֹר
הַפָּר וְאֶת־כָּל־בְּשָׂרוֹ עַל־רֹאשׁוֹ וְעַל־כְּרָעָיו וְקִרְבּוֹ
וּפִרְשׁוֹ׃ 12 וְהוֹצִיא אֶת־כָּל־הַפָּר אֶל־מִחוּץ

6. *in front of the curtain of the Shrine* The Comment to 1:3 explains that the Tent of Meeting was of two parts, separated from each other by a curtain called *parokhet.* The *parokhet* was held up by four poles, inserted into sockets in the ground; it reached from one side of the Tent to the other and all the way to its top. It concealed from view the innermost section of the Tent, which was called *kodesh ha-kodashim,* "the Holy of Holies." The *parokhet* also marked off the first section, encountered upon entering the Tent, which was called simply *kodesh,* "sanctuary." According to Exodus 26:31–35, the *parokhet* was made of embroidered fabric, with representations of cherubs woven into it.[11]

The blood rites prescribed here and in verses 16–21 are highly unusual and are reserved elsewhere for the Yom Kippur ritual, as set forth in chapter 16. Only here, and in the law of 16:18, was sacrificial blood to be dabbed on the horns of the incense altar, which stood inside "the Shrine," not outside in the courtyard.

7. *on the horns of the altar of aromatic incense* For the design of the altar, see Exodus 30:1–10, and for the recipe for the incense to be used on it, see Exodus 30:34–38. Only incense was to be offered on this altar, which stood inside the Tent proper, whereas all other sacrifices were to be burned on the altar that stood in the courtyard, facing the entrance to the Tent. Examples of ancient incense altars and of horned altars as well have been unearthed in archaeological excavations.[12]

10. *just as it is removed from the ox of the sacrifice of well-being* The relevant procedures are discussed in the Comments to 3:3–4. The point is that in this case the same parts of the animal are placed on the altar as in the case of the *shelamim* sacrifice. The difference here is that the rest of the animal is not eaten but destroyed.

11. *But the hide of the bull* In this rite, as in the Yom Kippur ritual, we find the combination of two methods of expiation, or purification: an offering by fire on the altar for the purpose of propitiating God; and a riddance ritual by which impurity is eliminated from the Israelite camp and physically destroyed. The best example of a complete riddance ritual is the procedure for purification after contamination by a corpse, as set forth in Numbers 19. The entire red heifer, selected for this purpose, was burned outside the camp, and no part of it was offered to God. By comparing that rite with the *ḥatta't* sacrifice prescribed in 4:3–21 and with the Yom Kippur sacrifice, we can appreciate how two modes of purification were combined. Here impurity is destroyed by the destruction of the entire victim, even its hide—a very extreme procedure, for the hides were not burned even in the execution of the *'olah,* prescribed in chapter 1.[13]

Underlying rituals such as this one is a concept known in the phenomenology of religion as "substitution": The sacrificial victim substitutes for the person, or persons, who offended God or who are impure. Impurity is transferred from them to the sacrificial victim, thus freeing the offenders from

of the bull—he shall carry to a clean place outside the camp, to the ash heap, and burn it up in a wood fire; it shall be burned on the ash heap.

¹³If it is the whole community of Israel that has erred and the matter escapes the notice of the congregation, so that they do any of the things which by the LORD's commandments ought not to be done, and they realize their guilt—

לַֽמַּחֲנֶ֜ה אֶל־מָק֤וֹם טָהוֹר֙ אֶל־שֶׁ֣פֶךְ הַדֶּ֔שֶׁן וְשָׂרַ֥ף אֹת֛וֹ עַל־עֵצִ֖ים בָּאֵ֑שׁ עַל־שֶׁ֥פֶךְ הַדֶּ֖שֶׁן יִשָּׂרֵֽף׃ פ ¹³ וְאִ֞ם כָּל־עֲדַ֤ת יִשְׂרָאֵל֙ יִשְׁגּ֔וּ וְנֶעְלַ֣ם דָּבָ֔ר מֵעֵינֵ֖י הַקָּהָ֑ל וְ֠עָשׂוּ אַחַ֨ת מִכָּל־מִצְוֺ֧ת יְהֹוָ֛ה אֲשֶׁ֥ר לֹא־תֵעָשֶׂ֖ינָה וְאָשֵֽׁמוּ׃ ¹⁴ וְנֽוֹדְעָה֙ הַֽחַטָּ֔את

God's punishment. God accepts the sacrifice in lieu of the life of the offenders, whom He then pardons.¹⁴

and its dung As in 8:17, Hebrew *peresh* designates the undigested contents of the stomach.¹⁵

12. ***to a clean place outside the camp*** Literally, "to a pure place." In the Levitical texts of the Bible, Hebrew *tahor* is better understood in the cultic sense of "pure," rather than in the hygienic sense of cleanliness, although it was certainly important to maintain cleanliness in performing all cultic rites, and in the sanctuary generally. But "cleanliness," as it is usually understood, is an inadequate term here, since one could be "clean" but still "impure," and the same was true of objects and sacred areas if certain rites had not been performed properly. Although the primary sense of *tahor* pertains to the "purity" of physical properties or physical effects (such as "pure" light or "pure" color), its cultic connotation has more to do with a state of ritual purity.

to the ash heap There was an ash heap outside the camp, just as in 1:16 we read that there was one located near the altar of burnt offerings.

13. ***the whole community of Israel*** Hebrew *'edah,* "community," one of the terms for the Israelites as a whole, is regularly used in this sense in the priestly codes of the Torah. It probably derives from the verb *y-'-d* "to meet"—at an appointed time, or place. (The same verbal root underlies the term *'ohel mo'ed,* "the Tent of Meeting," and Hebrew *mo'ed,* "annual festival, appointed time.") The term *'edah* conveys the sense that the group was unified as a community on the basis of set principles. The Hebrew verb *y-'-d* never connotes a random phenomenon. The character of the Israelite community was determined by a shared history and a common religion. Hebrew *'edah* is known outside the Bible, primarily in the Aramaic papyri from Elephantine, in Upper Egypt (present-day Aswan). There, a Jewish mercenary community lived through most of the fifth century B.C.E., and this community is referred to as *'edah.*¹⁶

and they realize their guilt Rather, "and thereby incur guilt." The precise sense of *ve-'ashemu* here and of the singular form *ve-'ashem* in verses 22, 27 and in 5:2, 4, 17, and 23, has been the subject of extensive scholarly argument. These forms all occur in the transitional verses of chapter 4, following descriptions of various hypothetical offenses. When certain transgressions occur—*ve-'ashemu.* If subsequently the offenses become known, special rites are to be performed. And so the entire process of ritual expiation hinges on this pivotal verb.

There are several conclusions that can be stated at the outset, so as to eliminate unlikely interpretations. The verb *'asham,* as it is used in this law, does not imply any spiritual or psychological change in the offender, which might induce him to admit to an offense he had previously concealed or denied. It is simply that facts have become known that were unknown before. Furthermore, the conjunctive *vav* in the transition from verse 13 to verse 14 with the Hebrew verb *ve-nod'ah* does not mean "or it became known" but, rather, "when it became known" (or possibly "if it became known"). There is no contrast implied, as between one's own recollection versus being informed by others.¹⁷ A state of guilt exists because of the fact of the misdeed. If and when the offense becomes known, expiation must be undertaken.

The main problem concerns the concept of culpability, or guilt, itself. In the cultic conception, guilt exists whether or not the offender is aware of it at the time. God's wrath is aroused by the offense against Him. Guilt may "begin" even before the offender realizes what he has done. Undoubtedly, an offender has to become aware of his sins at some point, if expiation is to be undertaken at all. But, this awareness is not expressed in our text by the verb *'asham,* which refers only to the state of guilt as

[14]when the sin through which they incurred guilt becomes known, the congregation shall offer a bull of the herd as a sin offering, and bring it before the Tent of Meeting. [15]The elders of the community shall lay their hands upon the head of the bull before the LORD, and the bull shall be slaughtered before the LORD. [16]The anointed priest shall bring some of the blood of the bull into the Tent of Meeting, [17]and the priest shall dip his finger in the blood and sprinkle of it seven times before the LORD, in front of the curtain. [18]Some of the blood he shall put on the horns of the altar which is before the LORD in the Tent of Meeting, and all the rest of the blood he shall pour out at the base of the altar of burnt offering, which is at the entrance of the Tent of Meeting. [19]He shall remove all its fat from it and turn it into smoke on the altar. [20]He shall do with this bull just as is done with the [priest's] bull of sin offering; he shall do the same with it. Thus the priest shall make expiation for them, and they shall be forgiven. [21]He shall carry the bull outside

אֲשֶׁר חָטְאוּ עָלֶיהָ וְהִקְרִיבוּ הַקָּהָל פַּר בֶּן־בָּקָר
לְחַטָּאת וְהֵבִיאוּ אֹתוֹ לִפְנֵי אֹהֶל מוֹעֵד׃
15 וְסָמְכוּ זִקְנֵי הָעֵדָה אֶת־יְדֵיהֶם עַל־רֹאשׁ הַפָּר
לִפְנֵי יְהוָה וְשָׁחַט אֶת־הַפָּר לִפְנֵי יְהוָה׃ 16 וְהֵבִיא
הַכֹּהֵן הַמָּשִׁיחַ מִדַּם הַפָּר אֶל־אֹהֶל מוֹעֵד׃
17 וְטָבַל הַכֹּהֵן אֶצְבָּעוֹ מִן־הַדָּם וְהִזָּה שֶׁבַע
פְּעָמִים לִפְנֵי יְהוָה אֵת פְּנֵי הַפָּרֹכֶת׃ 18 וּמִן־הַדָּם
יִתֵּן עַל־קַרְנֹת הַמִּזְבֵּחַ אֲשֶׁר לִפְנֵי יְהוָה אֲשֶׁר
בְּאֹהֶל מוֹעֵד וְאֵת כָּל־הַדָּם יִשְׁפֹּךְ אֶל־יְסוֹד מִזְבַּח
הָעֹלָה אֲשֶׁר־פֶּתַח אֹהֶל מוֹעֵד׃ 19 וְאֵת כָּל־חֶלְבּוֹ
יָרִים מִמֶּנּוּ וְהִקְטִיר הַמִּזְבֵּחָה׃ 20 וְעָשָׂה לַפָּר
כַּאֲשֶׁר עָשָׂה לְפַר הַחַטָּאת כֵּן יַעֲשֶׂה־לּוֹ וְכִפֶּר
עֲלֵהֶם הַכֹּהֵן וְנִסְלַח לָהֶם׃ 21 וְהוֹצִיא אֶת־הַפָּר

determined by God, the supreme judge. Awareness is expressed by the verb *yada'*, "to know." Therefore, in all the transitional verses the verb *'asham* means "to be in a state of guilt," whereas the verb *yada'* connotes awareness of guilt.

*15. **The elders of the community shall lay their hands . . .*** The "elders" (*zekenim*) represent a very ancient institution in biblical Israel, comparable to councils of elders known from other ancient Near Eastern societies. Several early biblical sources represent the *zekenim* as part of the tribal system, in a role similar to the Bedouin or Arab sheikhs.[18] The "elders" hark back to preurban and premonarchic periods of Israelite settlement in Canaan, but this institution continued to function during later periods as well and never fully lost its authority.[19] Here the elders act on behalf of the Israelite community in expiating collective offenses against God, as is often their responsibility.

16–19. The rites required in the event the whole community sins are identical to those prescribed for the expiation of the anointed priest, as set forth in verses 3–12.

*20. **the priest shall make expiation for them*** Expiation by means of sacrificial blood-rites is a prerequisite for securing God's forgiveness. As the rabbis expressed it, *'ein kapparah 'ella' be-dam,* "There is no ritual expiation except by means of blood."[20]

The Hebrew verb *k-p-r* expressed in the Piel stem as *kipper,* "to expiate," has cognates in several other Semitic languages, most notably in Akkadian. It expresses a central theme in the Levitical texts, and a correct understanding of the process of expiation, in all its aspects, hinges upon its proper interpretation. The Akkadian verb *kuppuru,* which corresponds to Hebrew *kipper,* means "to wipe off, burnish, cleanse." In cultic terms this means that expiation is conceived of as cleansing, as wiping away impurity, contamination, and, by extension, sinfulness itself. This interpretation differs from the concept endorsed by many scholars that the verb *kipper* means "to cover, conceal" the sin or impurity from God's view. Such an idea is of course well known in biblical literature, as it is in most other religious traditions, but it is not the idea conveyed by the verb *kipper.* Not all biblical concepts of atonement and forgiveness reflect the same perception. The Levitical texts use the verb *kipper* to express the concept that through expiation one is "wiped clean" of impurities that adhere or cling to a person—infect him, we might say.

If this is the underlying sense of the verb *kipper,* how are we to understand the indirect object formulation *ve-khipper 'aleihem* used in this verse? The direct object formulation *kipper 'et* clearly means "to wipe clean," but a less graphic meaning would be required for indirect-object formulations. The sense here is functional: "to perform rites of expiation over, with respect to. . . ." Sinfulness, or impurity, is removed from the offender by means of specific rites. In this case they do not in-

the camp and burn it as he burned the first bull; it is the sin offering of the congregation.

²²In case it is a chieftain who incurs guilt by doing unwittingly any of the things which by the commandment of the LORD his God ought not to be done, and he realizes his guilt—²³or the sin of which he is guilty is brought to his knowledge—he shall bring as his offering a male goat without blemish. ²⁴He shall lay his hand upon the goat's head, and it shall be slaughtered at the spot where the burnt offering is slaughtered before the LORD; it is a sin offering. ²⁵The priest shall take with his finger some of the blood of the sin offering and put it on the horns of the altar of burnt offering; and the rest of its blood he shall pour out at the base of the altar of burnt offering. ²⁶All its fat he shall turn into smoke on the altar, like the fat of the sacrifice of well-being. Thus the priest shall make expiation on his behalf for his sin, and he shall be forgiven.

אֶל־מִחוּץ֙ לַֽמַּחֲנֶ֔ה וְשָׂרַ֣ף אֹת֔וֹ כַּאֲשֶׁ֣ר שָׂרַ֔ף אֵ֖ת הַפָּ֣ר הָרִאשׁ֑וֹן חַטַּ֥את הַקָּהָ֖ל הֽוּא: פ

²² אֲשֶׁ֥ר נָשִׂ֖יא יֶֽחֱטָ֑א וְעָשָׂ֡ה אַחַ֣ת מִכָּל־מִצְוֺת֩ יְהֹוָ֨ה אֱלֹהָ֜יו אֲשֶׁ֧ר לֹא־תֵעָשֶׂ֛ינָה בִּשְׁגָגָ֖ה וְאָשֵֽׁם: ²³ אֽוֹ־הוֹדַ֤ע אֵלָיו֙ חַטָּאת֔וֹ אֲשֶׁ֥ר חָטָ֖א בָּ֑הּ וְהֵבִ֧יא אֶת־קָרְבָּנ֛וֹ שְׂעִ֥יר עִזִּ֖ים זָכָ֥ר תָּמִֽים: ²⁴ וְסָמַ֤ךְ יָדוֹ֙ עַל־רֹ֣אשׁ הַשָּׂעִ֔יר וְשָׁחַ֣ט אֹת֔וֹ בִּמְק֛וֹם אֲשֶׁר־ יִשְׁחַ֥ט אֶת־הָעֹלָ֖ה לִפְנֵ֣י יְהֹוָ֑ה חַטָּ֖את הֽוּא: ²⁵ וְלָקַ֨ח הַכֹּהֵ֜ן מִדַּ֤ם הַֽחַטָּאת֙ בְּאֶצְבָּע֔וֹ וְנָתַ֕ן עַל־ קַרְנֹ֖ת מִזְבַּ֣ח הָעֹלָ֑ה וְאֶת־דָּמ֣וֹ יִשְׁפֹּ֔ךְ אֶל־יְס֖וֹד מִזְבַּ֥ח הָעֹלָֽה: ²⁶ וְאֶת־כָּל־חֶלְבּוֹ֙ יַקְטִ֣יר הַמִּזְבֵּ֔חָה כְּחֵ֖לֶב זֶ֣בַח הַשְּׁלָמִ֑ים וְכִפֶּ֨ר עָלָ֧יו הַכֹּהֵ֛ן מֵֽחַטָּאתֽוֹ

volve physical purification, such as bathing or changing garments; nor do they require the application of blood or other substances to a person, garments, or immediate environment. The purification comes from God in response to the proper performance of required rituals undertaken in good faith.[21]

and they shall be forgiven   The verb *salaḥ* has been variously explained. Most likely, the proposed derivation from a verb meaning "to wash, sprinkle with water" (with attested cognates in Ugaritic and Akkadian) is correct. The basic concept would be that of cleansing with water, a concept then extended, of course, to connote God's forgiveness and acceptance of expiation.[22]

21. of the congregation   Hebrew *kahal*, like *'edah,* encountered in verse 13, is a term for the Israelites as a whole. It derives from the verb *kahal,* "to assemble," and characterizes a group living together.[23]

22. a chieftain who incurs guilt   Literally, "who commits an offense." Hebrew *nasi',* "chieftain," is a passive form of the verb *nasa',* "to elevate, raise up." The *nasi'* is one who has been "elevated" above others. This originally reflected the practice of electing tribal leaders.[24] Unlike the priest, the *nasi'* was a secular leader, not one who held a sacred office, although at times he might bear special sacral responsibilities. He was not, therefore, directly responsible for the religious offenses of the whole community, as was the chief priest. Consequently, his sacrifice of expiation was basically the same as that of any other Israelite. On the other hand, he was not free of punishment by virtue of his eminent position and was, in every respect, subject to religious law.

23. a male goat   Hebrew *sa'ir,* literally "a hairy goat." The rabbis defined the law as requiring a yearling goat, just as in other cases a yearling sheep was required. The utilization of goats for sin offerings, which was relatively frequent in biblical worship, is a development from the premonotheistic worship of the wilderness goat as a demonic being. This is implied in the law of 17:7, which warns Israelites not to worship "goat demons" (*se'irim*) as they had once done. In the Yom Kippur ritual of chapter 16, this practice has been transposed into a component of a monotheistic rite consisting of the dispatch of the scapegoat.

25-26.   The same portions of the sacrificial animal are placed on the altar as for the *shelamim,* prescribed in 3:3-4. The difference is that here some of the sacrificial blood is dabbed on the horns of the altar of burnt offerings, and the rest is poured out at the base of the altar. In the case of the *'olah* and the *shelamim,* all sacrificial blood is dashed against the sides of the altar. It seems that here the horns of the outside altar receive blood to parallel the horns of the incense altar inside the Shrine, which receive blood from the more severe *hatta't* prescribed in verses 3-21. The priests received portions of this type of *hatta't,* as outlined in the legislation of 6:17-7:10.

27 If any person from among the populace unwittingly
incurs guilt by doing any of the things which by the LORD's
commandments ought not to be done, and he realizes his
guilt— 28 or the sin of which he is guilty is brought to his
knowledge—he shall bring a female goat without blemish
as his offering for the sin of which he is guilty. 29 He shall lay
his hand upon the head of the sin offering, and the sin
offering shall be slaughtered at the place of the burnt
offering. 30 The priest shall take with his finger some of its
blood and put it on the horns of the altar of burnt offering;
and all the rest of its blood he shall pour out at the base of
the altar. 31 He shall remove all its fat, just as the fat is
removed from the sacrifice of well-being; and the priest
shall turn it into smoke on the altar, for a pleasing odor to
the LORD. Thus the priest shall make expiation for him, and
he shall be forgiven.

32 If the offering he brings as a sin offering is a sheep, he
shall bring a female without blemish. 33 He shall lay his
hand upon the head of the sin offering, and it shall be
slaughtered as a sin offering at the spot where the burnt
offering is slaughtered. 34 The priest shall take with his
finger some of the blood of the sin offering and put it on
the horns of the altar of burnt offering, and all the rest of its
blood he shall pour out at the base of the altar. 35 And all its

וְנִסְלַח לוֹ׃ פ ששי 27 וְאִם־נֶפֶשׁ אַחַת
תֶּחֱטָא בִשְׁגָגָה מֵעַם הָאָרֶץ בַּעֲשֹׂתָהּ אַחַת
מִמִּצְוֺת יְהוָה אֲשֶׁר לֹא־תֵעָשֶׂינָה וְאָשֵׁם׃ 28 אוֹ
הוֹדַע אֵלָיו חַטָּאתוֹ אֲשֶׁר חָטָא וְהֵבִיא קָרְבָּנוֹ
שְׂעִירַת עִזִּים תְּמִימָה נְקֵבָה עַל־חַטָּאתוֹ אֲשֶׁר
חָטָא׃ 29 וְסָמַךְ אֶת־יָדוֹ עַל רֹאשׁ הַחַטָּאת וְשָׁחַט
אֶת־הַחַטָּאת בִּמְקוֹם הָעֹלָה׃ 30 וְלָקַח הַכֹּהֵן
מִדָּמָהּ בְּאֶצְבָּעוֹ וְנָתַן עַל־קַרְנֹת מִזְבַּח הָעֹלָה
וְאֶת־כָּל־דָּמָהּ יִשְׁפֹּךְ אֶל־יְסוֹד הַמִּזְבֵּחַ׃ 31 וְאֶת־
כָּל־חֶלְבָּהּ יָסִיר כַּאֲשֶׁר הוּסַר חֵלֶב מֵעַל זֶבַח
הַשְּׁלָמִים וְהִקְטִיר הַכֹּהֵן הַמִּזְבֵּחָה לְרֵיחַ נִיחֹחַ
לַיהוָה וְכִפֶּר עָלָיו הַכֹּהֵן וְנִסְלַח לוֹ׃ פ
32 וְאִם־כֶּבֶשׂ יָבִיא קָרְבָּנוֹ לְחַטָּאת נְקֵבָה תְמִימָה
יְבִיאֶנָּה׃ 33 וְסָמַךְ אֶת־יָדוֹ עַל רֹאשׁ הַחַטָּאת
וְשָׁחַט אֹתָהּ לְחַטָּאת בִּמְקוֹם אֲשֶׁר יִשְׁחַט אֶת־
הָעֹלָה׃ 34 וְלָקַח הַכֹּהֵן מִדַּם הַחַטָּאת בְּאֶצְבָּעוֹ
וְנָתַן עַל־קַרְנֹת מִזְבַּח הָעֹלָה וְאֶת־כָּל־דָּמָהּ יִשְׁפֹּךְ
אֶל־יְסוֹד הַמִּזְבֵּחַ׃ 35 וְאֶת־כָּל־חֶלְבָּהּ יָסִיר כַּאֲשֶׁר

27. any person from among the populace From here to the end of chapter 4, the form of the *ḥatta't* sacrifice is essentially the same as the one prescribed for the *nasi'*, with the difference that an individual Israelite could choose to offer a female goat or a female sheep instead of a male animal. The term *'am ha-'arets* literally means "the people of the land," but it had diverse social and political applications in biblical society, where it served to distinguish the populace at large from such individuals as officials and priests. It did not, however, convey a lowly status by any means. In fact, *'am ha-'arets* often refers to the landed gentry of ancient Israel, those who elected kings. This gentry continued to govern as a council in Jerusalem until the destruction of the First Temple.[25]

28. a female goat It is not certain why female animals were required for certain offerings and not for others. Most animal sacrifices consisted of males for the probable reason that fewer males than females were necessary to reproduce the herds and flocks. This pattern is common to most ancient Near Eastern religions.

32–35. The procedures prescribed for a female sheep offered as a *ḥatta't* sacrifice are identical to those pertaining to a female goat.

CHAPTER 5 ADDITIONAL MEANS OF EXPIATION (vv. 1–13)

The theme of expiation, introduced in chapter 4, continues through chapter 5, which may be divided topically into four sections. (1) Verses 1–13, an adaptation of the *ḥatta't,* "sin offering," first prescribed in 4:27–35. Here a similar sacrifice is ordained for "sins of omission" rather than for active violations of the law, as in chapter 4. (2) Verses 14–16, the *'asham,* "guilt offering," imposed on those who inadvertently misappropriate sanctuary property. (3) Verses 17–19, an adaptation of the *'asham* for situations where a possible violation has occurred, but not a certain one. (4) Verses 20–26, an

fat he shall remove just as the fat of the sheep of the sacrifice of well-being is removed; and this the priest shall turn into smoke on the altar, over the LORD's offering by fire. Thus the priest shall make expiation on his behalf for the sin of which he is guilty, and he shall be forgiven.

יוּסַ֣ר חֵ֣לֶב־הַכֶּ֗שֶׂב מִזֶּ֤בַח הַשְּׁלָמִים֙ וְהִקְטִ֨יר הַכֹּהֵ֤ן אֹתָם֙ הַמִּזְבֵּ֔חָה עַ֖ל אִשֵּׁ֣י יְהוָ֑ה וְכִפֶּ֨ר עָלָ֤יו הַכֹּהֵ֛ן עַל־חַטָּאת֥וֹ אֲשֶׁר־חָטָ֖א וְנִסְלַ֥ח לֽוֹ׃ פ

5 If a person incurs guilt—

When he has heard a public imprecation and—although able to testify as one who has either seen or learned of the matter—he does not give information, so that he is subject to punishment;

ה וְנֶ֣פֶשׁ כִּֽי־תֶחֱטָ֗א וְשָֽׁמְעָה֙ ק֣וֹל אָלָ֔ה וְה֣וּא עֵ֔ד א֥וֹ רָאָ֖ה א֣וֹ יָדָ֑ע אִם־ל֥וֹא יַגִּ֖יד וְנָשָׂ֥א עֲוֺנֽוֹ׃ 2 א֣וֹ

'asham offered in expiation of any of a series of deceitful acts involving an oath and the loss of property to others.

These varied laws make of chapter 5 a legal mosaic that has interested commentators since antiquity. There is, first of all, the problem regarding the laws of verses 1, 4, and 20–26. On the face of it, these are not cultic laws but, rather, laws of testimony. More significant is the fact that in the laws of verses 1 and 20–26 there is no reference to inadvertence, which is a basic precondition for ritual atonement.[1] Everywhere else in chapters 4–5 there is some reference to the fact that the offense involved was unintentional or had escaped notice. Finally, verses 17–19 seem to be repetitive, rephrasing the essential provisions of 4:27–35, and one is hard put to explain the necessity for such a restatement unless a new legal principle is being introduced.

Once these difficulties are acknowledged, an attempt can be made to relate the entire content of chapter 5 to the central theme of expiation.

FOR SINS OF OMISSION (vv. 1–13)

1. ***When he has heard a public imprecation*** One who heard a proclamation adjuring all who possessed information in a certain case to come forward and testify, but who failed to assist the judicial process and withheld evidence, was liable to a penalty. Hebrew *kol,* which simply means "voice, sound," here has the technical sense of "oral proclamation." Thus we read in Ezra 1:1: "He [Cyrus] issued a proclamation [*va-ya'aver kol*] throughout his realm."[2] In later Hebrew usage the idiom *yatsa' kol,* literally "the voice went forth," means "a *proclamation* was issued." According to talmudic law, one could be held legally responsible once the facts of a certain case or situation had been publicly proclaimed.[3]

An "adjuration" (*'alah*) consisted of a statement pronouncing a curse over anyone who failed to uphold the law. In this respect an *'alah* had the same force as an oath that a person might take to clear himself of a charge, swearing that he had indeed fulfilled his obligation.[4] In Genesis 24:41 we read that Abraham charged his steward Eliezer, under terms of an *'alah,* not to agree to any marriage arrangement that would require Isaac to leave Canaan and return to Aram-naharaim. In Deuteronomy 7 we read that the people of Israel were adjured not to worship other gods, under threat of the devastation of their land. In both cases, those bound by an *'alah* could free themselves of the threatened penalties by fulfilling the terms of the adjuration.[5] In our case, a person would be clear of the penalties stipulated in the *'alah* by coming forth to testify. But if he failed to do so, he would bear the punishment of the adjuration.

so that he is subject to punishment Rather, "He shall bear the punishment for his sin." The Hebrew formula *nasa' 'avon* reflects a semantic process by which the same word can designate both the act and its effect, the crime and its punishment. In this way *'avon* can be translated "sin" and also "the wages of sin," meaning punishment. Compare the equivalent formula *nasa' het',* "to bear the punishment of an offense," in 22:9.[6] There is a symmetry to the legal formulation. Verse 1 concludes with *ve-nasa' 'avono,* "He shall bear the punishment for his sin," and verse 2 with *ve-'ashem,* "He shall be *held guilty.*"

[2]Or when a person touches any unclean thing—be it the carcass of an unclean beast or the carcass of unclean cattle or the carcass of an unclean creeping thing—and the fact has escaped him, and then, being unclean, he realizes his guilt;

[3]Or when he touches human uncleanness—any such uncleanness whereby one becomes unclean—and, though he has known it, the fact has escaped him, but later he realizes his guilt;

נֶפֶשׁ אֲשֶׁר תִּגַּע בְּכָל־דָּבָר טָמֵא אוֹ בְנִבְלַת חַיָּה
טְמֵאָה אוֹ בְּנִבְלַת בְּהֵמָה טְמֵאָה אוֹ בְּנִבְלַת
שֶׁרֶץ טָמֵא וְנֶעְלַם מִמֶּנּוּ וְהוּא טָמֵא וְאָשֵׁם׃ 3 אוֹ
כִּי יִגַּע בְּטֻמְאַת אָדָם לְכֹל טֻמְאָתוֹ אֲשֶׁר יִטְמָא
בָּהּ וְנֶעְלַם מִמֶּנּוּ וְהוּא יָדַע וְאָשֵׁם׃ 4 אוֹ נֶפֶשׁ כִּי

The presence of a law on testimony in a cultic code requires explanation. The same problem concerns verse 4 and verses 20–26. In fact, chapter 5 demonstrates the interaction between two themes in biblical law: (1) purity and respect for what is sacred, which are essential if there is to be reverence for God, and (2) trust, as expressed in oaths taken in God's name. In the ancient Near East courts and archives generally were located in temple complexes, and this was true of ancient Israel as well. Deuteronomy 1:16–17 states that judgment is God's prerogative, and Deuteronomy 16:8–12 ordains that the central court be located in the Temple. In Deuteronomy 33:8–10 we read that the Levitical priests were assigned the task of instructing the people in the laws of God; they also served oracular functions that involved determinations of innocence and guilt. Thus there is an institutional connection between testimony and related juridical procedures, on the one hand, and expiation for what we usually refer to as religious sins, on the other. Whenever God's name was involved, religion was involved. This is true even today, notwithstanding the constitutional separation of church and state operative in modern democracies.[7]

Verse 1 poses still another problem, which it shares with verses 20–26: the absence of any reference to inadvertence. Ancient commentators were aware of this; the Sifra, for instance, responded by extending the provisions of verse 1 to include unintentional sins as well.[8]

If properly understood, verse 1 may resolve its own problem. We should understand the failure to come forth as a form of inadvertence, namely, *negligence.* In this case, the omission was, moreover, one that involved speech, not deed, a distinction also noted by traditional commentators[9] and one that would not apply to the laws in verses 20–26, although it seems likely in verse 1.

2. *when a person touches any unclean thing* The general category *kol davar tame'*, "every impure thing," is followed by three specific types of impure carcasses: impure animals, beasts, and swarming creatures (*sherets*).[10] The main source for these prohibitions of contact is chapter 11, especially verses 24–31, where their significance is discussed. In rabbinic law such objects are known as *'avot ha-tum'ah,* "primary sources of impurity," which have the effect of defiling whatever touches them.[11]

and the fact has escaped him, and then, being unclean, he realizes his guilt Rather, "and insofar as he was impure, he had incurred guilt." The point is that impurity is the basis of the offender's guilt. For a time one had been impure without realizing it and therefore had also been culpable without knowing it.

3. *Or when he touches human uncleanness* Hebrew *tum'at 'adam,* "human impurity," refers to such forms of impurity as affect a woman after childbirth (12:2), a person who experiences a bodily discharge (15:2, 19), or a man who has sexual intercourse with a menstruating woman (18:19). It also applies to a person who has eaten the meat of a dead animal or an animal torn by beasts (17:15–16). This category must be distinguished from the more severe impurity caused by contact with a corpse (Num. 19:13), which caused a person to be "defiled by a corpse" (Heb. *tame' la-nefesh*), the term used in Numbers 9:10.[12]

and, though he has known it, the fact has escaped him, but later he realizes his guilt Rather, "and though the fact escaped him, he ultimately knew of his *having been guilty.*" As has been emphasized repeatedly, according to cultic law guilt is not a function of awareness; it is a function of committing an act or failing to commit one (see Comments to 4:13–14). Therefore, the *vav* in *ve-'ashem* does *not* create a sequence of knowledge followed by guilt. That *vav* is not conjunctive but,

4Or when a person utters an oath to bad or good purpose —whatever a man may utter in an oath—and, though he has known it, the fact has escaped him, but later he realizes his guilt in any of these matters— 5when he realizes his guilt in any of these matters, he shall confess that wherein he has sinned. 6And he shall bring as his penalty to the Lord, for the sin of which he is guilty, a female from the flock, sheep or goat, as a sin offering; and the priest shall make expiation on his behalf for his sin.

תִשָּׁבַע֩ לְבַטֵּ֨א בִשְׂפָתַ֜יִם לְהָרַ֣ע׀ א֣וֹ לְהֵיטִ֗יב
לְכֹל֩ אֲשֶׁ֨ר יְבַטֵּ֧א הָאָדָ֛ם בִּשְׁבֻעָ֖ה וְנֶעְלַ֣ם מִמֶּ֑נּוּ
וְהוּא־יָדַ֥ע וְאָשֵׁ֖ם לְאַחַ֥ת מֵאֵֽלֶּה׃ 5 וְהָיָ֥ה כִֽי־יֶאְשַׁ֖ם
לְאַחַ֣ת מֵאֵ֑לֶּה וְהִתְוַדָּ֕ה אֲשֶׁ֖ר חָטָ֥א עָלֶֽיהָ׃
6 וְהֵבִ֣יא אֶת־אֲשָׁמ֣וֹ לַיהוָ֡ה עַ֣ל חַטָּאתוֹ֩ אֲשֶׁ֨ר
חָטָ֜א נְקֵבָ֨ה מִן־הַצֹּ֥אן כִּשְׂבָּ֛ה אֽוֹ־שְׂעִירַ֥ת עִזִּ֖ים
לְחַטָּ֑את וְכִפֶּ֥ר עָלָ֛יו הַכֹּהֵ֖ן מֵחַטָּאתֽוֹ׃ 7 וְאִם־לֹ֨א

rather, circumstantial; literally, "He, being guilty, knew." According to Mishnah Shevuʿot 1:2 and 2:1f., the sacrifices referred to in 5:1–13 apply only when there exists "initial knowledge," "ultimate knowledge," and "lack of notice in the interim." In other words, something originally known was ignored or forgotten and then later recalled. It was at that point that the offender undertook to expiate for his offense.[13]

The concern in verses 2–3 is the protection of the sanctuary and all within it from any sort of impurity "carried" by an impure person. If the offense had been intentional, the contamination of the sanctuary would subject the offender to the more severe penalty of being "cut off" from the community, as stated in 7:19–21.

4. ***an oath to bad or good purpose*** The Hebrew idiom *le-haraʿ oʾ le-hetiv* means "to any purpose at all." It is a merism, which is a way of expressing generalities by stating them as polarities.[14] The oath referred to here bound the person to do or not to do something and was similar to "the oath of self-denial" stipulated in Numbers 30. One must fulfill an oath, and if one neglects to do so or allows the matter to escape his notice, he offends God, in whose name the oath was taken, as well as those affected by it. As Deuteronomy 23:24 states, ". . . you must fulfill what has crossed your lips," a thought echoed in Ecclesiastes 5:3–5.[15]

5. ***when he realizes his guilt . . . he shall confess that wherein he has sinned*** Alternatively, "when he incurs guilt, and has confessed how he has sinned, he shall bring. . . ." The requirement of making confession is not the main thrust of this statement. The verb *hitvaddah,* "to confess," is more likely indicative than subjunctive; it is conveying a fact rather than expressing a requirement.

All those who wished to expiate offenses against God admitted their guilt at some point, and yet this is the only explicit reference to confession in all of chapters 4–5, and for a good reason. In this case the confession was material to the judicial process. In other cases, projected in chapters 4–5, there are indications as to what prompted the offender to undertake expiation. In 4:2–23, and again in 27–28, we are told that the matter was brought to the attention of the offender, and this may also be true of the situation reflected in 4:13. Similarly, in 5:14–16 it had probably been discovered that property was missing. In 5:20–26 the deceit involved other persons, and the suspect had been accused. Here we are dealing with private acts and the failure to act, which might never have come to light had the offender himself not come forth to confess. The motivation for doing so was religious and moral —the desire to be purified and to avert God's wrath for having failed to fulfill one's commitments.

The essence of the confessional is the exposure, or revelation, of one's sins. The confessional is basic to the Yom Kippur ritual, and its phenomenological character is explained in the Comment to 16:21. A confession is also required in the summary laws of Numbers 5:5–7, as regards the *ʾasham* penalty.

6. ***And he shall bring as his penalty . . . a sin offering*** The word *ʾasham* has two connotations: "penalty" and "guilt offering" (see Comment to v. 15). The term *ʾasham* in the sense of "penalty" thus can designate a sin offering, as is the case here. The sacrifice prescribed in this instance consisted of a female from the flock. It was to "sins of omission" what the sacrifice prescribed in 4:27–35 was to "sins of commission." Here the offender had the option of offering either a sheep or a goat. One who could afford the full *ḥattaʾt* sacrifice was to offer it even for sins of omission, which were deemed less severe.

7. ***But if his means do not suffice*** This is the functional sense of the Hebrew idiom *ʾim ʾein yado masseget,* literally "if his 'hand' cannot reach." In rabbinic parlance, this type of sacrifice was

7But if his means do not suffice for a sheep, he shall bring to the LORD, as his penalty for that of which he is guilty, two turtledoves or two pigeons, one for a sin offering and the other for a burnt offering. 8He shall bring them to the priest, who shall offer first the one for the sin offering, pinching its head at the nape without severing it. 9He shall sprinkle some of the blood of the sin offering on the side of the altar, and what remains of the blood shall be drained out at the base of the altar; it is a sin offering. 10And the second he shall prepare as a burnt offering, according to regulation. Thus the priest shall make expiation on his behalf for the sin of which he is guilty, and he shall be forgiven.

11And if his means do not suffice for two turtledoves or two pigeons, he shall bring as his offering for that of which he is guilty a tenth of an *ephah* of choice flour for a sin offering; he shall not add oil to it or lay frankincense on it, for it is a sin offering. 12He shall bring it to the priest, and

תַגִּיעַ יָדוֹ דֵּי שֶׂה וְהֵבִיא אֶת־אֲשָׁמוֹ אֲשֶׁר חָטָא
שְׁתֵּי תֹרִים אוֹ־שְׁנֵי בְנֵי־יוֹנָה לַיהוָה אֶחָד
לְחַטָּאת וְאֶחָד לְעֹלָה׃ 8 וְהֵבִיא אֹתָם אֶל־הַכֹּהֵן
וְהִקְרִיב אֶת־אֲשֶׁר לַחַטָּאת רִאשׁוֹנָה וּמָלַק אֶת־
רֹאשׁוֹ מִמּוּל עָרְפּוֹ וְלֹא יַבְדִּיל׃ 9 וְהִזָּה מִדַּם
הַחַטָּאת עַל־קִיר הַמִּזְבֵּחַ וְהַנִּשְׁאָר בַּדָּם יִמָּצֵה
אֶל־יְסוֹד הַמִּזְבֵּחַ חַטָּאת הוּא׃ 10 וְאֶת־הַשֵּׁנִי
יַעֲשֶׂה עֹלָה כַּמִּשְׁפָּט וְכִפֶּר עָלָיו הַכֹּהֵן מֵחַטָּאתוֹ
אֲשֶׁר־חָטָא וְנִסְלַח לוֹ׃ ס שביעי 11 וְאִם־
לֹא תַשִּׂיג יָדוֹ לִשְׁתֵּי תֹרִים אוֹ לִשְׁנֵי בְנֵי־יוֹנָה
וְהֵבִיא אֶת־קָרְבָּנוֹ אֲשֶׁר חָטָא עֲשִׂירִת הָאֵפָה
סֹלֶת לְחַטָּאת לֹא־יָשִׂים עָלֶיהָ שֶׁמֶן וְלֹא־יִתֵּן
עָלֶיהָ לְבֹנָה כִּי חַטָּאת הִיא׃ 12 וֶהֱבִיאָהּ אֶל־

called *korban ʿoleh ve-yored,* "the ascending and descending offering," that is, one whose cost was determined on a sliding scale,[16] a concept that was basic to the system of vows in ancient Israel. If one donated to the sanctuary a fixed amount of silver as his "valuation," symbolically making himself God's servant, he could have that amount reduced if the attending priest assessed his means as inadequate (27:1–8). The same sliding scale also applied to certain obligatory sacrifices unconnected with any offense at all; otherwise inability to meet the full cost might deny purification to one who was diseased (14:21) or to a woman impure after childbirth (12:6–8). We know, from comparative evidence, that the sliding scale was also employed in the Punic temple at Carthage during the fourth and third centuries B.C.E.[17]

The distribution of the two birds of the reduced *ḥattaʾt* is significant: One was to be offered as a *ḥattaʾt* and the other as an *ʿolah.* The same distribution is prescribed in 15:15,30 for instances of impurity. Ibn Ezra, later cited by Maimonides, explains this distribution as a way of compensating for the fatty portions of the sacrificial animals, which would have been burned on the altar as God's share had the full *ḥattaʾt* been offered. By burning one of the birds to ashes, the share offered to God was at least increased.

8–9. pinching its head at the nape without severing For the specialized sense of the Hebrew verb *m-l-k,* see Comment to 1:15. The utilization of sacrificial blood prescribed here is similar to the procedure used for the *ḥattaʾt* generally, as prescribed in 4:25,30, except that in this instance the blood was not sprinkled on the horns of the altar of burnt offerings but on its side (*kir*).

There is logic to the order of the two sacrifices: The *ḥattaʾt* preceded the *ʿolah* because one was obliged to be in good standing before he could properly worship God. Coming immediately after the *ḥattaʾt,* which was expiatory in character, the *ʿolah* symbolized the restoration of the offender and constituted his first act of worship after forgiveness.[18]

10. according to regulation Hebrew *ka-mishpat,* used quite frequently in the priestly legislation of the Torah, obviates the need for restating the complete ritual. It is a form of cross-reference that assumes the reader will know where the complete regulation is stated.[19]

the priest shall make expiation on his behalf See Comment to 4:20 on the sense of the verb *kipper,* "to expiate."

11. a tenth of an ephah of choice flour for a sin offering The quantity of flour used in this offering is equivalent to what is prescribed for the grain offering in 6:12 and Numbers 28:5. Hebrew *solet* more accurately means "semolina flour."[20] The usual embellishments of oil and frankincense,

the priest shall scoop out of it a handful as a token portion
of it and turn it into smoke on the altar, with the LORD's
offerings by fire; it is a sin offering. 13 Thus the priest shall
make expiation on his behalf for whichever of these sins he
is guilty, and he shall be forgiven. It shall belong to the
priest, like the meal offering.
14 And the LORD spoke to Moses, saying:
15 When a person commits a trespass, being unwittingly
remiss about any of the LORD's sacred things, he shall bring
as his penalty to the LORD a ram without blemish from the
flock, convertible into payment in silver by the sanctuary

הַכֹּהֵן וְקָמַץ הַכֹּהֵן מִמֶּנָּה מְלוֹא קֻמְצוֹ אֶת־
אַזְכָּרָתָהּ וְהִקְטִיר הַמִּזְבֵּחָה עַל אִשֵּׁי יְהוָה חַטָּאת
הִוא׃ 13 וְכִפֶּר עָלָיו הַכֹּהֵן עַל־חַטָּאתוֹ אֲשֶׁר־חָטָא
מֵאַחַת מֵאֵלֶּה וְנִסְלַח לוֹ וְהָיְתָה לַכֹּהֵן כַּמִּנְחָה׃
ס 14 וַיְדַבֵּר יְהוָה אֶל־מֹשֶׁה לֵּאמֹר׃
15 נֶפֶשׁ כִּי־תִמְעֹל מַעַל וְחָטְאָה בִּשְׁגָגָה מִקָּדְשֵׁי
יְהוָה וְהֵבִיא אֶת־אֲשָׁמוֹ לַיהוָה אַיִל תָּמִים מִן־
הַצֹּאן בְּעֶרְכְּךָ כֶּסֶף־שְׁקָלִים בְּשֶׁקֶל־הַקֹּדֶשׁ

prescribed for the grain offering in 2:1 and elsewhere, are not included here. The same austerity is noticeable in the grain offering required of the wife suspected of infidelity in the code of Numbers 5:15. Although this omission may be explained in part as a reduction in the cost of the offering, there is probably another factor involved: It was thought that God took no delight in receiving such offerings and would have preferred, so to speak, that they had not been necessary in the first place!

USES OF THE *'ASHAM* SACRIFICE (vv. 14–26)

FOR SINS AGAINST THE SANCTUARY (vv. 14–16)

15. When a person commits a trespass The etymology of Hebrew *ma'al* is uncertain. All biblical occurrences of this term relate directly or indirectly to ancient notions of sacrilege and impurity; as such, it is an appropriate term for misappropriation of sanctuary property. It may also refer to betrayal of trust, involving marital infidelity; to acts of deceit; and to violation of the covenant between God and Israel by the worship of foreign gods.[21] In legal texts, the crime of *ma'al* involves actual loss of property to other persons or agencies. This is the view of the Mishnah Me'ilah, and it is borne out by an analysis of other cases where the *'asham* is required in expiation of *ma'al.*

The law of verses 14–16 applies only to unintentional misuse or destruction of sanctuary property. That is the force of *bishgagah,* "inadvertently," in this verse. Intentional theft of sacred property or damage to it was a heinous crime. The story about Achan, preserved in Joshua 7, epitomizes the severity of intentional *ma'al.* Achan was caught looting the spoils of Jericho, which had been devoted to God, and he was put to death in punishment for his crime.[22]

remiss about any of the LORD's sacred things The term *kodshei YHVH*, "the LORD's sacred things," has general as well as specific connotations. In this context it refers to sanctuary property, not to priestly allocations or tithes, which belonged to the priests and Levites, and not to the sanctuary proper. According to 22:14, misappropriation of what belonged to the priests required the offender to make restitution and to pay a penalty, but there is no mention of an *'asham* sacrifice. The precise sense of the idiom *ḥata' min,* "to be remiss about," receives some clarification through comparison with verse 16, where we read *'et 'asher ḥata' min ha-kodesh,* literally "that which he sinfully detracted from sanctuary property." In this context *ḥata'* conveys the notion of causing a loss. Similarly, the Piel stem of the same verb *ḥitte'* may mean "to make up a loss."[23]

he shall bring as his penalty As in verse 6, the term *'asham* is used here in the sense of "penalty." Actually, in this one verse we have both meanings of the term *'asham*: as fulfillment of the duty to offer an *'asham* sacrifice and as fulfillment of the duty of a *ḥatta't* sacrifice.

convertible into payment in silver Rather, "according to the equivalent in silver." The term *'erekh* means "assessed value, equivalent." The second person masculine form *'erkekha,* "your equivalent," became a fixed term, what linguists call a "bound form." As a result, we can refer to *ha-'erkekha* literally as "the 'your equivalent.'" A feminine plural *'rkt,* "equivalents," is attested in a Punic votive inscription, where the verb *n-d-r,* "to pledge, vow," also occurs. In still another Punic text, a tax official bears the title *r [b] 'rkt,* "supervisor of taxes." These are rare, extrabiblical attesta-

weight, as a guilt offering. ¹⁶He shall make restitution for that wherein he was remiss about the sacred things, and he shall add a fifth part to it and give it to the priest. The priest shall make expiation on his behalf with the ram of the guilt offering, and he shall be forgiven.

¹⁷And when a person, without knowing it, sins in regard to any of the LORD's commandments about things not to be done, and then realizes his guilt, he shall be subject to punishment. ¹⁸He shall bring to the priest a ram without

לָאָשָׁם: 16 וְאֵ֣ת אֲשֶׁר֩ חָטָ֨א מִן־הַקֹּ֜דֶשׁ יְשַׁלֵּ֗ם וְאֶת־חֲמִֽישִׁתוֹ֙ יוֹסֵ֣ף עָלָ֔יו וְנָתַ֥ן אֹת֖וֹ לַכֹּהֵ֑ן וְהַכֹּהֵ֗ן יְכַפֵּ֥ר עָלָ֛יו בְּאֵ֥יל הָאָשָׁ֖ם וְנִסְלַ֥ח לֽוֹ: פ 17 וְאִם־נֶ֙פֶשׁ֙ כִּ֣י תֶֽחֱטָ֔א וְעָֽשְׂתָ֗ה אַחַת֙ מִכָּל־מִצְוֺ֣ת יְהֹוָ֔ה אֲשֶׁ֖ר לֹ֣א תֵעָשֶׂ֑ינָה וְלֹֽא־יָדַ֥ע וְאָשֵׁ֖ם וְנָשָׂ֥א עֲוֺנֽוֹ: 18 וְ֠הֵבִ֠יא אַ֣יִל תָּמִ֧ים מִן־הַצֹּ֛אן

tions of terms similar to biblical ʿerekh.²⁴ In 27:1 we therefore find the formulation be-ʿerkekha nefashot, "in the 'your equivalent' of lives." Compare 2 Kings 12:5: ʾish kesef nafshot ʿerko, "the silver of each person's life equivalent."²⁵ The offender had the option of either providing a ram of his own or remitting the cost of one so that a proper sacrificial ram could be secured on his behalf. The form of the sacrifice was not optional, however, and is set forth in 7:1–10.

The term ʿerekh (or ʿerekha) is central to the system of cultic administration in ancient Israel. It occurs in two contexts: the votive system, set forth primarily in chapter 27, and the ʾasham sacrifice, as prescribed here. The problem is to explain the puzzling formulation of the law. Why is it stressed that the ram offered as an ʾasham sacrifice corresponded to a value in silver shekels, especially when the actual amount of the valuation is not stated?

Biblical literature provides evidence for the development of the ʾasham from a votive offering of expiation, which could take any number of forms, to an altar sacrifice of fixed form. In 1 Samuel 6:3–5, we are told that the Philistines, suspecting that they were being punished by the God of Israel for failing to return the Ark they had captured in battle, sent it back to the Israelite camp as an act of restitution. In addition, they sent objects of value as an ʾasham to appease God's wrath.

This background helps to explain how terminology originating in the votive system came to be applied to the ʾasham as an altar sacrifice: Expiation is common to both systems. The ʾasham began as a votive offering, as we gather from the Philistine episode, but it subsequently developed into an altar offering as well. Perhaps for this reason, it is stated that the ʾasham sacrifice, consisting of one ram, represented an assessment in silver shekels. Reference to silver is more traditional than realistic. So it is that a votive offering, figured in silver shekels, became an altar offering, specified in terms of animals, as one would expect.²⁶

Hebrew shekel ha-kodesh, "sanctuary weight," was the prevalent standard in ancient Israel at certain periods. In fact, Ezekiel 45:12, in listing official weights and measures, gives the silver content of the shekel as 20 gerahs, "grains," which is identical to the sanctuary weight of a shekel according to 27:25 and as stated in Exodus 31:13.²⁷

16. He shall make restitution . . . and he shall add a fifth part to it The penalty of one-fifth was a common feature of Temple administration.²⁸ The provisions of this law are reformulated in verse 24 where the specific terminology is explained.

The priest shall make expiation on his behalf On the sense of the verb kipper, see Comment to 4:20. It is to be assumed that the blood from the ʾasham sacrifice was disposed of in the same way as that of the ḥattaʾt of the people in 4:25,30.

One is prompted to ask how instances of maʿal came to light in the first place. To establish the intentional theft of sanctuary property, the testimony of witnesses was necessary. In Joshua 7:14–15, the person guilty of maʿal was "trapped" by the casting of lots and compelled to confess his crime. Here, in the case of unintentional maʿal, it is possible that the missing property was discovered during an inventory; and although there was no evidence, suspects were questioned. This may be a situation in which a person used foodstuffs or other materials of value for his private purposes, presuming they were not "sacred things." Examples are provided in Mishnah Meʿilah.²⁹

THE ʾASHAM OF CONTINGENCY (vv. 17–19)

17. And when a person, without knowing it, sins . . . and then realizes his guilt Alternatively, "And when a person sins, but did not subsequently realize that he had incurred guilt." The

blemish from the flock, or the equivalent, as a guilt offering. The priest shall make expiation on his behalf for the error that he committed unwittingly, and he shall be for-

בְּעֶרְכְּךָ לְאָשָׁם אֶל־הַכֹּהֵן וְכִפֶּר עָלָיו הַכֹּהֵן עַל
שִׁגְגָתוֹ אֲשֶׁר־שָׁגָג וְהוּא לֹא־יָדַע וְנִסְלַח לוֹ׃

ambiguity in this verse derives from its negative formulation. In verses 3–4 the formulation is positive, "and he knew," whereas here we have *ve-lo' yada'*, "he did not know." The new JPS translation understands this negative formulation to refer to lack of initial knowledge and the following verb, *ve-'ashem,* to refer to the subsequent realization or awareness of guilt—in this way resolving the problem of explaining how one was obliged to expiate a sin of which he never became aware.

There remain, however, several problems in this translation. As explained in the Comment to 5:3 *yada'*, "he knew," refers to ***ultimate*** knowledge, not ***initial*** knowledge, and the verb *ve-'ashem* refers to the *fact* of guilt, not the ***awareness*** of it. Furthermore, the translation above would make of this verse a repetition of 4:27–35. In both cases a person inadvertently violated a law, a violation of which he later became aware. But since the language of legislative formulation is exceedingly precise, one would expect there to be a significant difference between the positive formulation of 4:27f. and the negative formulation of our verse. Wherein does that difference lie?

The rabbinic tradition understands the laws of 5:17–19 to mean that the offender did not know *for certain,* but only suspected, that he may have committed an offense. In effect, he had no positive, ultimate knowledge of the offense, and this is the sense of the clause *ve-hu' lo' yada'*, "he did not know"—for certain. Most of Mishnah Keritot is devoted to a discussion of cases where the *'asham* of 5:17–19 would apply. There it is called *'asham talui,* "the contingent *'asham.*" Certain knowledge of an offense committed would invoke the law of 4:27–35, but where there was uncertainty about past trespasses, an *'asham* consisting of a ram was prescribed in order to avert God's wrath in a preventive way.

There is some biblical evidence that sacrifices were offered on this basis. The Mishnah speaks of *'asham ḥasidim,* "the guilt offering of the devout";[30] and Job 1:5 recounts how one devout person, who was tested by God, brought daily burnt offerings on behalf of his children because of the likelihood that in the midst of their feasting and revelry they would unwittingly commit blasphemy.

18. for the error that he committed unwittingly Rather, "for the inadvertent sin he committed, but did not subsequently realize."

THE *'ASHAM* FOR ROBBERIES (vv. 20–26)

Verses 20–26 comprise laws about the expiation of false oaths involving deceitful acts of theft, robbery, fraud, and so on, which cause actual loss of property to another. These parallel, with respect to crimes "between man and man," the provisions of 5:14–16 regarding the inadvertent misappropriation of sanctuary property, but with an important difference: The offenses outlined here were quite definitely intentional! A person misappropriated property or funds entrusted to his safekeeping, or defrauded another, or failed to restore lost property he had located. As there were no witnesses to the crime, the usual laws of testimony were not applicable. When sued, the defendant lied under oath and claimed no responsibility. Without witnesses, the aggrieved party had no further recourse and sustained an irretrievable loss.

But if, subsequently, the accused came forth on his own and admitted to having lied under oath—thus assuming liability for the unrecovered property—he was given the opportunity to clear himself by making restitution and by paying a fine of 20 percent to the aggrieved party. Having lied under oath, he had also offended God and was obliged to offer an *'asham* sacrifice in expiation.[31]

The practice of allowing pleas of guilty "after the fact," or of allowing one to offer to make restitution, is accepted in many legal systems. According to Mishnah Bava Metsia 3:1, a person who failed to produce what had been entrusted to him had to swear that he had not abused his trust. If he wished to avoid the prescribed oath, imposed in Exodus 22:6–13, he could offer to make restitution, and that satisfied the law. Here the more serious case of admission after a false oath accounts for the penalty of 20 percent and the requirement of an *'asham* sacrifice.

But how are we to explain the opportunity for the ritual expiation of an intentional false oath,

given. 19 It is a guilt offering; he has incurred guilt before the Lord.

20 The LORD spoke to Moses, saying: 21 When a person sins and commits a trespass against the LORD by dealing deceitfully with his fellow in the matter of a deposit or a pledge, or through robbery, or by defrauding his fellow, 22 or by finding something lost and lying about it; if he swears falsely regarding any one of the various things that one may do and sin thereby— 23 when one has thus sinned and, realizing his guilt, would restore that which he got through robbery or fraud, or the deposit that was entrusted to him, or the lost thing that he found, 24 or anything else about which he swore falsely, he shall repay the principal amount and add a fifth part to it. He shall pay it to its owner when he realizes his guilt. 25 Then he shall bring to the priest, as his penalty to the LORD, a ram without blemish from the flock, or the equivalent, as a guilt offering. 26 The priest shall

19 אָשָׁם הוּא אָשֹׁם אָשַׁם לַיהוָה׃ פ
20 וַיְדַבֵּר יְהוָה אֶל־מֹשֶׁה לֵּאמֹר׃ 21 נֶפֶשׁ כִּי
תֶחֱטָא וּמָעֲלָה מַעַל בַּיהוָה וְכִחֵשׁ בַּעֲמִיתוֹ
בְּפִקָּדוֹן אוֹ־בִתְשׂוּמֶת יָד אוֹ בְגָזֵל אוֹ עָשַׁק אֶת־
עֲמִיתוֹ׃ 22 אוֹ־מָצָא אֲבֵדָה וְכִחֶשׁ בָּהּ וְנִשְׁבַּע עַל־
שָׁקֶר עַל־אַחַת מִכֹּל אֲשֶׁר־יַעֲשֶׂה הָאָדָם לַחֲטֹא
בָהֵנָּה׃ 23 וְהָיָה כִּי־יֶחֱטָא וְאָשֵׁם וְהֵשִׁיב אֶת־
הַגְּזֵלָה אֲשֶׁר גָּזָל אוֹ אֶת־הָעֹשֶׁק אֲשֶׁר עָשָׁק אוֹ
אֶת־הַפִּקָּדוֹן אֲשֶׁר הָפְקַד אִתּוֹ אוֹ אֶת־הָאֲבֵדָה
אֲשֶׁר מָצָא׃ מפטיר 24 אוֹ מִכֹּל אֲשֶׁר־יִשָּׁבַע
עָלָיו לַשֶּׁקֶר וְשִׁלַּם אֹתוֹ בְּרֹאשׁוֹ וַחֲמִשִׁתָיו יֹסֵף
עָלָיו לַאֲשֶׁר הוּא לוֹ יִתְּנֶנּוּ בְּיוֹם אַשְׁמָתוֹ׃
25 וְאֶת־אֲשָׁמוֹ יָבִיא לַיהוָה אַיִל תָּמִים מִן־הַצֹּאן
בְּעֶרְכְּךָ לְאָשָׁם אֶל־הַכֹּהֵן׃ 26 וְכִפֶּר עָלָיו הַכֹּהֵן

given that both versions of the Decalogue, in Exodus 20:7 and Deuteronomy 5:11, state that God will not exonerate one who swears falsely in His name but will surely punish him?[32] Mishnah Bava Metsia 6 explains that the expiation allowable under this law applied only when the offender came forth on his own and confessed his crime. This is made explicit in Numbers 5:5–7, another version of the same law, where there is reference to the confessional of the guilty party. If instead, however, witnesses appear and testify to the guilt of the offender, expiation is not possible. The guilty party would then face God's punishment as well as the imposition of multiple penalties.[33]

The admission by the guilty party enables the victim of a crime to recover his lost property in a case where there is no other legal recourse; that is, although the criminal is under suspicion, there is no proof of his guilt. Whereas, in the first place, the overriding objective in biblical law is to prevent theft, fraud, robbery, and other crimes, in the event they occur, it becomes of prime importance to recover what was lost or damaged on behalf of the victim. God accepts the expiation even of one who swears falsely in His name because the guilty person is willing to make restitution to the victim of his crime, for God is offended less by the desecration of His name than by disobedience of His law, which produces violence among men.

The terminology of verses 22–23 is of particular interest: Hebrew *kiḥḥesh,* "to act with deceit," is a synonym for *shikker,* "to lie," in 13:11. It may variously connote denial of the truth, as in Genesis 18:15, or the fabrication of an untruth, as in 1 Kings 13:18, as well as faithlessness in general. Hebrew *ʿamit,* "fellow," suggests, by its context, a social relationship.[34]

Verses 21–23 project three kinds of deceit: (1) Misappropriation of what was entrusted to one's safekeeping (*pikkadon*) or of a pledge (*tesumet yad*). The latter term literally refers to what is "placed" in one's "hand," and it is difficult to define specifically. Rashi interprets it as a loan or business investment, and Ibn Ezra, as a partnership arrangement. (2) Robbery (*gezelah*), which gave its name to the *ʾasham* in rabbinic law, *ʾasham gezelot,* "the *ʾasham* of robberies."[35] (3) Fraud (*ʿoshek*), which does not refer to taking from another what is already his, which is theft or robbery, but, as Erhlich and Hoffmann state, to withholding what he is entitled to receive. Rashi interprets *ʿoshek* as illegally withholding the wages of a laborer, forbidden in the law of 19:13; this is called "restraint."

23. when one has thus sinned and, realizing his guilt, would restore that which he got Rather, "When one has thus sinned, thereby incurring guilt, he *must* restore that which he got.' This corresponds to the formulation in Numbers 5:7, where the verb *ve-heshiv,* "he must remit," expresses what the criminal is *required* to do, not what he may prefer to do.

24. he shall repay the principal amount. . . . He shall pay it to its owner when he realizes his guilt Alternatively, "when his guilt is established." Hebrew *be-yom ʾashmato,* literally "on the day of

make expiation on his behalf before the LORD, and he shall be forgiven for whatever he may have done to draw blame thereby.

לִפְנֵ֥י יְהוָ֖ה וְנִסְלַ֣ח ל֑וֹ עַל־אַחַ֛ת מִכֹּ֥ל אֲשֶׁר־יַעֲשֶׂ֖ה לְאַשְׁמָ֥ה בָֽהּ׃ פ

his guilt," refers to the time when the guilt is proved, not when one realizes it. Only after acting to make good on his obligation and by paying a fine may the offender undertake ritual expiation. The provisions of verses 25–26 are identical to those of the *'asham* as prescribed in verse 16 but one formulated differently. Here, Hebrew *ro'sh,* "head," like English "capital," refers to principal, in contrast to interest or other additional payments and revenues. Cf. usage in Numb. 5:7. In Aramaic legal documents, *re'sha',* literally "the head," has the same financial connotation.[36]

The Disposition of Sacrifices (6:1–7:38)

Tsav

As noted in the introductory Comment to chapters 1–7, the last two chapters of this section present the *torah,* the "ritual," for each one of the several types of sacrifices already outlined in chapters 1–5. The earlier chapters emphasize the mechanics—the preparation of sacrifices and their ingredients—as well as the special conditions that made certain sacrifices necessary.

Chapters 6–7, on the other hand, focus on the role of the priesthood as officiants in the sanctuary and detail the special care that must attend the sacrificial offerings in order to prevent impurity. Most of all, these chapters specify that certain portions of the sacrifices (with the exception of the burnt offerings, or holocausts) were to be allocated to the priests as their share.

Some repetition of content is noticeable when we compare chapters 6–7 with chapters 1–5. Unique to chapters 6–7, however, is the glimpse they offer of the system whereby priests partook of sacred meals within the precincts of the sanctuary, meals that were at least in part supported or sustained by sacrificial offerings. In this connection it should be remembered that—except for the burnt offering of chapter 1, the priestly *minḥah* of 6:12–16, and the priestly *ḥatta't* of 4:1–21—most sacrifices were meant to be eaten, usually by priests and on occasion even by the donors.

Most sections of the sacrificial animals (except for the holocausts) were prepared as food, and only relatively small parts of the victims were burned on the altar as "God's share." Relevant procedures such as the boiling of sacrificial flesh and the baking or frying of grain offerings have already been set forth and explained in chapters 2–3 and 4:22f.

The priests received their emoluments in several forms, all in return for their services on behalf of the Israelite people. This principle is reflected in the provisions of 6:12–16, namely, the law governing the High Priest's grain offering, which was completely burned on the altar. That passage illustrates the rule that priests may not be compensated for sacrifices performed on their own behalf but only for services rendered to others.

The occurrence of this law in chapter 6 has been viewed as a problem because it seems to interrupt the continuity of the rest of the chapter. It was most likely inserted here because of its general topical relationship to grain offerings, the subject of verses 7–11, which immediately precede it.

The key term in chapters 6–7 is *torah,* which requires clarification precisely because the more general term Torah is so familiar.[1] Hebrew *torah* derives from the verb *y-r-h,* "to cast, shoot"—an arrow, for instance.[2] The verb in the Hifil form, *horah,* means "to aim, direct toward"—hence "to show the way, instruct."[3] As used here, *torah* signifies the content of the instruction. Frequently reference is to priestly instruction, including what the priests have been taught as well as what they, in turn, teach the Israelite people regarding the performance of religious rituals. It is a term that appears throughout the priestly writings of the Bible.[4] A classic example pertains to the foreigners who had been settled in Samaria by the Assyrian conquerors after the fall of the northern kingdom of Israel in 721 B.C.E. These new arrivals sought instruction in the proper worship of the God of Israel, and in 2 Kings 17:28 we read that an Israelite priest, who had been exiled from Samaria, was sent back there and engaged in "instructing" (*va-yehi moreh*) the newcomers.

Chapters 6–7 consist of a series of discernible units of the *torot,* "ritual instructions," which are ordered differently from those of chapters 1–5. The *'olah* and *minḥah* are discussed first in 6:1–16, since

TSAV

6 The LORD spoke to Moses, saying: ²Command Aaron and his sons thus:

This is the ritual of the burnt offering: The burnt offering itself shall remain where it is burned upon the altar all night until morning, while the fire on the altar is kept going on it. ³The priest shall dress in linen raiment, with linen breeches

ו וַיְדַבֵּ֥ר יְהֹוָ֖ה אֶל־מֹשֶׁ֥ה לֵּאמֹֽר: 2 צַ֤ו אֶת־אַהֲרֹן֙
וְאֶת־בָּנָ֣יו לֵאמֹ֔ר זֹ֥את תּוֹרַ֖ת הָעֹלָ֑ה הִ֣וא הָעֹלָ֡ה
עַל֩ מוֹקְדָ֨ה* עַל־הַמִּזְבֵּ֤חַ כָּל־הַלַּ֙יְלָה֙ עַד־הַבֹּ֔קֶר
וְאֵ֥שׁ הַמִּזְבֵּ֖חַ תּ֥וּקַד בּֽוֹ: 3 וְלָבַ֨שׁ הַכֹּהֵ֜ן מִדּ֣וֹ בַ֗ד
וּמִֽכְנְסֵי־בַד֮ יִלְבַּ֣שׁ עַל־בְּשָׂרוֹ֒ וְהֵרִ֣ים אֶת־הַדֶּ֗שֶׁן

מ' זעירא   v. 2.

they were part of the public cult.[5] Chapters 6:17–7:10 treat the sin offering and the guilt offering, which were not a regular feature of the public cult but, rather, expiatory rituals usually performed by individual Israelites. (The guilt offering ['asham] had no role at all in the public cult.)[6] The first unit extends, therefore, from 6:1–7:10 and concludes with the allocations of sacrificial foods to the priests. This completes the category of *kodesh kodashim,* "most sacred offerings."

It is followed by the category of *kodashim kallim,* "offerings of lesser sanctity," as it is known in the Mishnah, and is represented by *zevah ha-shelamim,* "the sacred gift of greeting," treated in 7:11–34.[7] Except for the unique *shelamim* offered on Shavuot and ordained in Leviticus 23:19, this type of sacrifice was utilized primarily in private worship (its public use was reserved for commemorating special occasions).[8]

We observe in chapters 6–7 an administrative order that begins with the most sacred public offerings and continues with other most sacred offerings that are usually relegated to private worship. The law then proceeds to outline offerings of lesser sanctity that also fall within the category of private worship. Finally, 7:35–38 summarizes the allocations of parts of the sacrificial offerings as the "share" (*mishhah*) of the priests, their portions of the Lord's offerings by fire.

CHAPTER 6   THE BURNT OFFERING (*'OLAH*)   (vv. 1–6)

2.   Command Aaron and his sons   According to the Sifra, the imperative form of the verb *tsav,* "command," emphasizes the duty to provide for the needs of sanctuary worship, the administration of which was the responsibility of the priests. Similar emphatic formulations occur in Leviticus 24:2 and in Numbers 28:2, both statements that introduce new sections of the law.

This is the ritual of the burnt offering   The preparation and presentation of the *'olah* have been explained in chapter 1.

The burnt offering itself shall remain   The Hebrew syntax is unusual. The construction *hi' ha-'olah* is usually rendered "it is the burnt offering," but this sense would not be suitable here. The translation reflects the fact that in certain contexts the pronouns "he" and "she" are used for emphasis, in the sense of "himself" and "herself." Compare Jeremiah 6:6 *hi' ha-'ir,* "the city itself."[9]

where it is burned   Rather, "on its fireplace." Hebrew *moked,* from the verb *yakad,* "to burn, blaze," designates the spot on top of the altar grill where the firewood was placed. The same verb accounts for the Hofal form *tukad,* "is kept burning," at the end of the verse and in verses 5–6 below.[10]

all night until morning, while the fire on the altar is kept going on it   The daily holocaust (burnt offering) consisted of two yearling lambs, one offered in the morning and the other in the evening, as ordained in Exodus 29:38f. and Numbers 28:3–4. The morning holocaust, with its accompanying grain offering and libation, were the first offerings placed on the altar of burnt offerings each day, and the evening holocaust and its accompaniments were the final ones (Sifra). The latter offering was left burning on the altar during the night; first thing in the morning the ashes of the previous day's sacrifices were removed and new firewood was added, as we are told in verse 3.

All of this occurred before the fresh holocaust was placed on the altar. Although the same altar was used for other sacrifices during the day, it was logical to provide instructions for tending the altar at this point since each day the public cult began and concluded with the holocaust.

אֲשֶׁר תֹּאכַל הָאֵשׁ אֶת־הָעֹלָה עַל־הַמִּזְבֵּחַ וְשָׂמוֹ
אֵצֶל הַמִּזְבֵּחַ׃ 4 וּפָשַׁט אֶת־בְּגָדָיו וְלָבַשׁ בְּגָדִים
אֲחֵרִים וְהוֹצִיא אֶת־הַדֶּשֶׁן אֶל־מִחוּץ לַמַּחֲנֶה אֶל־
מָקוֹם טָהוֹר׃ 5 וְהָאֵשׁ עַל־הַמִּזְבֵּחַ תּוּקַד־בּוֹ לֹא
תִכְבֶּה וּבִעֵר עָלֶיהָ הַכֹּהֵן עֵצִים בַּבֹּקֶר בַּבֹּקֶר
וְעָרַךְ עָלֶיהָ הָעֹלָה וְהִקְטִיר עָלֶיהָ חֶלְבֵי הַשְּׁלָמִים׃
6 אֵשׁ תָּמִיד תּוּקַד עַל־הַמִּזְבֵּחַ לֹא תִכְבֶּה׃ ס
7 וְזֹאת תּוֹרַת הַמִּנְחָה הַקְרֵב אֹתָהּ בְּנֵי־

next to his body; and he shall take up the ashes to which the fire has reduced the burnt offering on the altar and place them beside the altar.
4 He shall then take off his vestments and put on other vestments, and carry the ashes outside the camp to a clean place.
5 The fire on the altar shall be kept burning, not to go out: every morning the priest shall feed wood to it, lay out the burnt offering on it, and turn into smoke the fat parts of the offerings of well-being.
6 A perpetual fire shall be kept burning on the altar, not to go out.

7 And this is the ritual of the meal offering: Aaron's sons

3. linen raiment, with linen breeches Israelite priests customarily wore linen garments, as is prescribed specifically for the Yom Kippur ritual in 16:4.[11] Linen was first imported into ancient Israel from Egypt, where it was also worn by priests.[12]

The Hebrew construction *middo bad,* literally "his raiment of linen," is unusual because in Hebrew the pronominal suffix is expressed in the object, but the sense is clear nonetheless.[13]

and he shall take up the ashes The Hebrew verb *herim* often means "to take away, remove," as is true in 2:9, where the text speaks of removing a portion of the grain offering so that it may be burned on the altar. This meaning of the verb is reflected in the postbiblical term *terumat ha-deshen,* "the removal of the ashes," a ritual described in Mishnah Tamid 1:2–2:2, as it was practiced in Second Temple times.

to which the fire has reduced the burnt offering The common verb *'akhal,* "to eat," when referring to the action of fire, means "to consume, destroy."[14]

4. take off his vestments As we are told in Exodus 28:43, the priestly vestments were to be worn only in the precincts of the sanctuary.

and carry the ashes outside the camp to a clean place The pure place outside the camp is called *shefekh ha-deshen,* "the ash heap" in 4:12.

In 1:16 the spot near the eastern side of the altar where the ashes were dumped is called *mekom ha-deshen,* "the place for the ashes."

5. every morning In the Hebrew idiom *ba-boker ba-boker,* which also occurs in Exodus 30:7, repetition conveys continuity. Compare the idiom *yom yom,* "every day," in Psalms 68:20.

the priest shall feed wood to it In late biblical times wood for the altar fire was secured through a special collection called *kurban ha-etsim,* "the donation of wood," in Nehemiah 10:35 and 13:31. This procedure is also mentioned in Mishnah Tamid 2:3–5.

lay out the burnt offering on it The Hebrew verb *'arakh,* "to set up, arrange," has already been explained in the Comments to 1:7–8.

6. A perpetual fire shall be kept burning on the altar, not to go out The requirement of keeping the fire burning at all times is also implied in verse 2 above. Here the rendering "perpetual" is appropriate because our verse states explicitly that the fire is not to go out but must burn incessantly. The term *tamid* does not always have this specific meaning, as is explained in the Comment to verse 12 below. Its usual sense is regularity.[15] The perpetual fire on the altar expressed the devotion of the Israelite people to God by indicating that they were attendant upon God at all times in the sanctuary.

THE GRAIN OFFERING (*MINḤAH*) (vv. 7–11)

7. And this is the ritual of the meal offering The preparation of the *minḥah* is set forth in chapter 2.

shall present it before the Lord, in front of the altar. ⁸A handful of the choice flour and oil of the meal offering shall be taken from it, with all the frankincense that is on the meal offering, and this token portion shall be turned into smoke on the altar as a pleasing odor to the Lord. ⁹What is left of it shall be eaten by Aaron and his sons; it shall be eaten as unleavened cakes, in the sacred precinct; they shall eat it in the enclosure of the Tent of Meeting. ¹⁰It shall not be baked with leaven; I have given it as their portion from My offerings by fire; it is most holy, like the sin offering and the guilt offering. ¹¹Only the males among Aaron's descendants may eat of it, as their due for all time throughout the ages from the Lord's offerings by fire. Anything that touches these shall become holy.

אַהֲרֹן֙ לִפְנֵ֣י יְהֹוָ֔ה אֶל־פְּנֵ֖י הַמִּזְבֵּֽחַ׃ 8 וְהֵרִ֨ים מִמֶּ֜נּוּ בְּקֻמְצ֗וֹ מִסֹּ֤לֶת הַמִּנְחָה֙ וּמִשַּׁמְנָ֔הּ וְאֵת֙ כׇּל־הַלְּבֹנָ֔ה אֲשֶׁ֖ר עַל־הַמִּנְחָ֑ה וְהִקְטִ֣יר הַמִּזְבֵּ֗חַ רֵ֧יחַ נִיחֹ֛חַ אַזְכָּרָתָ֖הּ לַיהֹוָֽה׃ 9 וְהַנּוֹתֶ֣רֶת מִמֶּ֔נָּה יֹאכְל֖וּ אַהֲרֹ֣ן וּבָנָ֑יו מַצּ֤וֹת תֵּֽאָכֵל֙ בְּמָק֣וֹם קָדֹ֔שׁ בַּחֲצַ֥ר אֹֽהֶל־מוֹעֵ֖ד יֹאכְלֽוּהָ׃ 10 לֹ֤א תֵֽאָפֶה֙ חָמֵ֔ץ חֶלְקָ֛ם נָתַ֥תִּי אֹתָ֖הּ מֵֽאִשָּׁ֑י קֹ֤דֶשׁ קׇֽדָשִׁים֙ הִ֔וא כַּחַטָּ֖את וְכָֽאָשָֽׁם׃ 11 כׇּל־זָכָ֞ר בִּבְנֵ֤י אַהֲרֹן֙ יֹֽאכְלֶ֔נָּה חׇק־עוֹלָם֙ לְדֹרֹ֣תֵיכֶ֔ם מֵֽאִשֵּׁ֖י יְהֹוָ֑ה כֹּ֛ל אֲשֶׁר־יִגַּ֥ע בָּהֶ֖ם יִקְדָּֽשׁ׃ פ 12 וַיְדַבֵּ֥ר יְהֹוָ֖ה אֶל־מֹשֶׁ֥ה לֵּאמֹֽר׃ שני

The syntax of the Hebrew in this verse is somewhat unusual: *hakrev 'otah benei 'aharon*, "to offer it, the sons of Aaron." In biblical Hebrew, the infinitive absolute, here represented by the form *hakrev*, can stand for other forms of the verb and may be translated accordingly.

8. *A handful of the choice flour* The procedure for presenting the grain offering is set forth in chapter 2.

9. *What is left of it shall be eaten by Aaron and his sons* The *torah* of the grain offering here adds an important requirement, not stressed in chapter 2, that the priests must partake of the grain offering. This was considered indispensable to the efficacy of the ritual, and this requirement is repeated in verses 11 and 19 below, with reference to the sin offering. The same duty is dramatized in Moses' criticism of the priests recorded in 10:17f. The priests had not partaken of the sin offering as they should have on the occasion of their investiture. Portions of the sacrifices that remained uneaten after a specified period of time were to be destroyed.[16]

in the enclosure of the Tent of Meeting As described in Exodus 27:9–19 and 35:17 and in other priestly texts, the Tabernacle had an enclosed courtyard, just as did the Temple of Jerusalem. And yet, in all of Leviticus, it is only here and in verse 19 below that this sacred area is called *ḥatser*, "courtyard." Usually this area is referred to as *petaḥ 'ohel mo'ed*, "the entrance of the Tent of Meeting," which included a large part of the courtyard.

10. *I have given it as their portion from My offerings by fire* The notion that God granted parts of the sacrifices to the priests is explained in the Comment to 2:3.

11. *Only the males among Aaron's descendants* Sacrificial foods could be eaten only by the priests themselves, although other foodstuffs collected for their support and other forms of priestly revenue could be used to feed their families. These are summarized in Numbers 18:8–20.[17]

as their due for all time Hebrew *ḥok* (fem. *ḥukkah*), "due," derives from the verb *ḥ-k-k*, "to inscribe, engrave," and signifies that which is ordained by written statute. By extension, it connotes one's lawful share or amount, a rightful due, which is the meaning of *ḥok* here.

Anything that touches these shall become holy Rather, "Anyone who is to touch these must be in a holy state."

Similar statements pertaining to the sanctity of the altar occur in Exodus 29:37 and 30:39 and in verse 20 below. The problem of interpretation concerns the verb *yikdash*. Does it mean "will become holy—as a result of contact with sanctified substances and objects—or "must be in a holy state"—before being allowed to come into contact with sacred substances and objects? Several scholars, most notably M. Haran, have argued for the former interpretation. Haran has formulated a theory of "contagious" holiness, according to which the sanctity of holy objects and substances is communicated, or conducted, to all that comes into contact with them.[18]

Although the verb *k-d-sh* itself often connotes resultant holiness, it is more likely that here it

12The LORD spoke to Moses, saying: 13This is the offering that Aaron and his sons shall offer to the LORD on the occasion of his anointment: a tenth of an *ephah* of choice flour as a regular meal offering, half of it in the morning and half of it in the evening, 14shall be prepared with oil on

13 זֶה קָרְבַּן אַהֲרֹן וּבָנָיו אֲשֶׁר־יַקְרִיבוּ לַיהוָה בְּיוֹם
הִמָּשַׁח אֹתוֹ עֲשִׂירִת הָאֵפָה סֹלֶת מִנְחָה תָּמִיד
מַחֲצִיתָהּ בַּבֹּקֶר וּמַחֲצִיתָהּ בָּעָרֶב׃ 14 עַל־מַחֲבַת

refers to what must occur prior to contact with the sacred. Our verse simply means that only consecrated persons may have contact with sacrificial materials, a notion that reinforces the opening of the verse: Only Aaronide priests may partake of the sacrifices. Similarly, in Exodus 29:37 and 30:29 the sense is that only consecrated persons may have contact with the altar. In fact, there are indications that holiness was *not* regarded as "contagious" at all, unlike impurity, which was thought to be highly communicable. This contrast is brought out clearly in Malachi 2:11–13, where we read the actual text of an inquiry on questions of purity, addressed to the priesthood of Jerusalem in the early postexilic period.

The priests were asked, hypothetically, whether foodstuffs carried by a man would be rendered holy through physical contact with sacrificial flesh borne by the same man in the folds of his garment. They answered in the negative. But, when the priests were asked whether the same foodstuffs would be defiled if touched by a man impure through contact with a corpse, they replied in the affirmative. The point is that whereas impurity is transferred through physical contact alone, substances do not become holy merely through contact with sacred materials. An act of consecration is required.

THE GRAIN OFFERING OF THE HIGH PRIEST (vv. 12–16)

13. This is the offering that Aaron and his sons shall offer The term *korban* is explained in the Comment to 1:2.

on the occasion of his anointment Hebrew *be-yom,* literally "on the day of," simply means "when," as is typical of many units of time.

The rite of unction was essential to the status of the High Priest and is described in 8:10ff. Not only he but the altar as well was anointed. According to chapters 8–9, where the investiture of the priesthood is described in detail, only the High Priest was anointed with the special oil prepared for this purpose. This is also the intent of Exodus 29:17, a similar investiture text, and of the Holiness Code, according to 21:10f. But another tradition, reflected in Exodus 34:30; 40:14–19; and Leviticus 7:36, indicates that Aaron's sons were also to receive the rite of unction. Our verse agrees with the tradition that only Aaron was to be anointed because it refers to "his anointment" (*himmashaḥ 'oto*); Aaron's sons joined in the offering, but only he was anointed.[19]

tenth of an ephah of choice flour For this standard content of the grain offering, see Numbers 28:5 and Comments to Leviticus 5:11 and 6:8.

as a regular meal offering The term *tamid* connotes regularity and for the most part is used to characterize daily offerings. There was an entire regimen of daily rites called *tamid:* (1) the daily holocausts accompanied by grain offerings and libations, as prescribed in Exodus 29:38ff. and Numbers 28:3f.; and (2) the kindling of the "regular light" (*ner tamid*) every morning, as is ordained in Exodus 27:20–21; 30:7–8; and 40:25; Leviticus 24:1–4; and Numbers 8:2;[20] (3) the regular incense offering, ordained in Exodus 30:7–10 and 40:27, to be presented each morning when the High Priest tended the menorah.

The problem in verse 13 is glaring: A grain offering to be presented on the day of Aaron's anointment, as part of his initiation, is called *tamid!* There is evidence from Second Temple times of a daily grain offering presented by the High Priest as a holocaust, just as this passage ordains. In Ben Sira 45:14 we read: ". . . his [the High Priest's] grain offering shall be burned to smoke in its entirety, twice every day." In Mishnah Menaḥot 4:5 and 6:2, this daily grain offering is called *ḥavitei kohen gadol,* "the griddle cakes of the High Priest." Josephus, in his Antiquities of the Jews (4.10.7) also refers to this rite.

The problem is further complicated by the fact that a grain offering, presented as a holocaust, is indeed ordained as part of the initiation of the priesthood in 8:26–28, but its ingredients are different

a griddle. You shall bring it well soaked, and offer it as a
meal offering of baked slices, of pleasing odor to the LORD.
15And so shall the priest, anointed from among his sons to
succeed him, prepare it; it is the LORD's—a law for all
time—to be turned entirely into smoke. 16So, too, every
meal offering of a priest shall be a whole offering: it shall
not be eaten.

17The LORD spoke to Moses, saying: 18Speak to Aaron and
his sons thus: This is the ritual of the sin offering: the sin
offering shall be slaughtered before the LORD, at the spot
where the burnt offering is slaughtered: it is most holy.

בַּשֶּׁמֶן תֵּעָשֶׂה מֻרְבֶּכֶת תְּבִיאֶנָּה תֻּפִינֵי מִנְחַת
פִּתִּים תַּקְרִיב רֵיחַ־נִיחֹחַ לַיהוָה׃ 15 וְהַכֹּהֵן
הַמָּשִׁיחַ תַּחְתָּיו מִבָּנָיו יַעֲשֶׂה אֹתָהּ חָק־עוֹלָם
לַיהוָה כָּלִיל תָּקְטָר׃ 16 וְכָל־מִנְחַת כֹּהֵן כָּלִיל
תִּהְיֶה לֹא תֵאָכֵל׃ פ 17 וַיְדַבֵּר יְהוָה אֶל־
מֹשֶׁה לֵּאמֹר׃ 18 דַּבֵּר אֶל־אַהֲרֹן וְאֶל־בָּנָיו לֵאמֹר
זֹאת תּוֹרַת הַחַטָּאת בִּמְקוֹם אֲשֶׁר תִּשָּׁחֵט הָעֹלָה
תִּשָּׁחֵט הַחַטָּאת לִפְנֵי יְהוָה קֹדֶשׁ קָדָשִׁים הִוא׃

from what is specified here. So there is evidence both for an offering of initiation and for a regular offering, and yet the specifications are problematic in both cases.

Ibn Ezra, attempting to solve the problem by interpreting the prepositional *bet* in the formula *be-yom himmashaḥ 'oto* as "direction from," so rendered this formula: "*from* the day of his anointment." This corresponds to some extent with the view of Maimonides in his Mishneh Torah (Hilkhot Kelei Ha-mikdash 5:16) that Leviticus 8:26–28 concerns the singular offering of the High Priest upon his initiation, whereas our passage speaks of the regular incense offering presented by the High Priest.

These attempted resolutions fall short, however, because verse 15 of our chapter states that each successive High Priest was to make the same grain offering, which seems to mean that the initiation rite was permanent, not that the grain offering was to be a regular feature of the public cult. Furthermore, we are still left with the difference in content between this grain offering and what is ordained in 8:26–28. It is likely that these are parallel traditions on the investiture of the High Priest. Our rite became the pattern for the daily grain offering of the High Priest, whereas that of chapter 8 remained associated specifically with his investiture.

14. ***You shall bring it well soaked, and offer it as a meal offering of baked slices*** Hebrew *murbekhet,* "well soaked," occurs only here, in Leviticus 7:12, and in 1 Chronicles 23:23, all with reference to the treatment of flour. The Sifra explains *murbekhet* as "fully prepared in boiling water." The Akkadian cognate, the verb *rabāku,* means "to mix, extract," and it is used with reference to the preparation of herbs and drugs. This is also the sense of Arabic *rabaka.*[21]

Hebrew *tufinim,* here rendered "baked (slices)," is as yet unexplained. Commentators have assumed that it derives from the root *'-f-h,* "to bake," but that the *alef* of that root was elided. The term *pittim,* "slices," is explained in the Comment to 2:6.

15. ***to be burned entirely into smoke*** Hebrew *kalil* conveys the notion of being entirely consumed by fire. It is an early term for a holocaust offering, as in Deuteronomy 33:10: "They [the Levites] shall offer You incense to savor and whole-offerings [*kalil*] on Your altar." In the cult of Carthage, as we know it from inscriptions dating to the fourth or third century B.C.E., there is also mention of an offering called *kll.*[22]

16. ***So, too, every meal offering of a priest*** Every grain offering brought by a priest on his own behalf, or on behalf of the priesthood, in expiation or as a voluntary offering, was to be burned entirely on the altar. This affirms the rule that priests could benefit only for services undertaken on behalf of other Israelites, not on their own behalf. When the offering served only the priests themselves, the usual share of the priests had to be surrendered to God.[23]

THE SIN OFFERING (*ḤATTA'T*) (6:17–23)

18. ***the sin offering shall be slaughtered*** In 1:11 it is ordained that the *'olah* is to be slaughtered at the northern side of the altar, and this practice is recorded for the Second Temple in Mishnah Zevaḥim 5:1f. We are informed here that this rule also applies to the sin offering.

19The priest who offers it as a sin offering shall eat of it; it shall be eaten in the sacred precinct, in the enclosure of the Tent of Meeting. 20Anything that touches its flesh shall become holy; and if any of its blood is spattered upon a garment, you shall wash the bespattered part in the sacred precinct. 21An earthen vessel in which it was boiled shall be broken; if it was boiled in a copper vessel, [the vessel] shall be scoured and rinsed with water. 22Only the males in the priestly line may eat of it: it is most holy. 23But no sin offering may be eaten from which any blood is brought into the Tent of Meeting for expiation in the sanctuary; any such shall be consumed in fire.

19 הַכֹּהֵן הַמְחַטֵּא אֹתָהּ יֹאכְלֶנָּה בְּמָקוֹם קָדֹשׁ
תֵּאָכֵל בַּחֲצַר אֹהֶל מוֹעֵד׃ 20 כֹּל אֲשֶׁר־יִגַּע
בִּבְשָׂרָהּ יִקְדָּשׁ וַאֲשֶׁר יִזֶּה מִדָּמָהּ עַל־הַבֶּגֶד אֲשֶׁר
יִזֶּה עָלֶיהָ תְּכַבֵּס בְּמָקוֹם קָדֹשׁ׃ 21 וּכְלִי־חֶרֶשׂ
אֲשֶׁר תְּבֻשַּׁל־בּוֹ יִשָּׁבֵר וְאִם־בִּכְלִי נְחֹשֶׁת בֻּשָּׁלָה
וּמֹרַק וְשֻׁטַּף בַּמָּיִם׃ 22 כָּל־זָכָר בַּכֹּהֲנִים יֹאכַל
אֹתָהּ קֹדֶשׁ קָדָשִׁים הִוא׃ 23 וְכָל־חַטָּאת אֲשֶׁר
יוּבָא מִדָּמָהּ אֶל־אֹהֶל מוֹעֵד לְכַפֵּר בַּקֹּדֶשׁ לֹא
תֵאָכֵל בָּאֵשׁ תִּשָּׂרֵף׃ פ

it is most holy The sin offering is of the class of ***kodesh kodashim,*** "most sacred offerings." This class was first encountered in 2:3 and was mentioned in this chapter in verse 10. It recurs in verse 22 and in 7:6.

19. The priest who offers it as a sin offering Hebrew *meḥatte',* a denominative form deriving from the noun *ḥatta't* itself, means "to perform a sin offering."

In the enclosure of the Tent of Meeting The entire courtyard is sacred. See Comment to verse 9.

20. Anything that touches its flesh shall become holy Rather, "Anyone who is to touch its flesh must be in a holy state." This preferred translation is explained in the Comment to verse 11.

and if any of its blood is spattered upon a garment The form *yizzeh* represents the Kal stem and means "to spatter," as in 2 Kings 9:33 and Isaiah 63:3. Usually, we find the Hifil form, ***hizzah,*** "to sprinkle, cast," as is explained in the Comment to 15:19. Should any sacrificial blood stain a garment, that garment must be laundered because it would be improper if any blood of the sacrifice was not used for its only legitimate purpose. The blood of the sin offering was to be placed on the horns of the altar and the rest poured down its side, as is ordained in 4:25. It was sufficient to launder garments to rid them of the blood. This is also the later law of Mishnah Zevaḥim 11:1–5.

21. An earthen vessel in which it was boiled shall be broken Earthenware, being more porous than metal, absorbs particles of the flesh boiled in it. Technically speaking, some of the sacrificial flesh would remain in the vessel. Such flesh would constitute *notar,* "leftovers of the sacrifice," forbidden for consumption according to 7:15–17. Now, according to Hoffmann, if other foodstuffs were subsequently boiled in the same ceramic vessel, the forbidden sacrificial particles would contaminate the rest. To prevent this, the earthenware vessel had to be broken, because there was no possible way to purify it. This accords with the later legislation of Mishnah Kelim 2:1.

if it was boiled in a copper vessel, [the vessel] shall be scoured and rinsed with water Hebrew *marak,* which is cognate with Akkadian *marāqu* and Aramaic *meraq,* means "to cleanse" by rubbing or abrasive action, at times using boiling water. This is how the procedure is described in Mishnah Zevaḥim 5:7. Rabbinic law, in Mishnah Zevaḥim 11:7–8, actually extended these procedures to include all prepared sacrificial offerings.

Similar procedures continue to be used to this day. In fact, they are required, according to traditional Jewish practice, for rendering some types of cooking vessels and eating utensils fit (*kasher*) for use.[24]

23. from which any blood is brought into the Tent of Meeting This rule refers to the priestly *ḥatta't* as set forth in 4:1–21, to the rites prescribed in 8:17 for the investiture of the priests, and in chapter 16 for the Yom Kippur ritual. Similar rites are involved in purification from the contamination communicated by a corpse in Numbers 19.

This rule is the issue addressed in Moses' criticism of Aaron and his sons in 10:17–18. In that

7 This is the ritual of the guilt offering: it is most holy.
2 The guilt offering shall be slaughtered at the spot where
the burnt offering is slaughtered, and the blood shall be
dashed on all sides of the altar. 3 All its fat shall be offered:
the broad tail; the fat that covers the entrails; 4 the two
kidneys and the fat that is on them at the loins; and the
protuberance on the liver, which shall be removed with the
kidneys. 5 The priest shall turn them into smoke on the altar
as an offering by fire to the LORD; it is a guilt offering. 6 Only
the males in the priestly line may eat of it; it shall be eaten in
the sacred precinct: it is most holy.

7 The guilt offering is like the sin offering. The same rule
applies to both: it shall belong to the priest who makes
expiation thereby. 8 So, too, the priest who offers a man's
burnt offering shall keep the skin of the burnt offering that
he offered. 9 Further, any meal offering that is baked in an
oven, and any that is prepared in a pan or on a griddle, shall
belong to the priest who offers it. 10 But every other meal

ז וְזֹאת תּוֹרַת הָאָשָׁם קֹדֶשׁ קָדָשִׁים הוּא׃
2 בִּמְקוֹם אֲשֶׁר יִשְׁחֲטוּ אֶת־הָעֹלָה יִשְׁחֲטוּ אֶת־
הָאָשָׁם וְאֶת־דָּמוֹ יִזְרֹק עַל־הַמִּזְבֵּחַ סָבִיב׃ 3 וְאֵת
כָּל־חֶלְבּוֹ יַקְרִיב מִמֶּנּוּ אֵת הָאַלְיָה וְאֶת־הַחֵלֶב
הַמְכַסֶּה אֶת־הַקֶּרֶב׃ 4 וְאֵת שְׁתֵּי הַכְּלָיֹת וְאֶת־
הַחֵלֶב אֲשֶׁר עֲלֵיהֶן אֲשֶׁר עַל־הַכְּסָלִים וְאֶת־
הַיֹּתֶרֶת עַל־הַכָּבֵד עַל־הַכְּלָיֹת יְסִירֶנָּה׃ 5 וְהִקְטִיר
אֹתָם הַכֹּהֵן הַמִּזְבֵּחָה אִשֶּׁה לַיהוָה אָשָׁם הוּא׃
6 כָּל־זָכָר בַּכֹּהֲנִים יֹאכְלֶנּוּ בְּמָקוֹם קָדוֹשׁ יֵאָכֵל
קֹדֶשׁ קָדָשִׁים הוּא׃ 7 כַּחַטָּאת כָּאָשָׁם תּוֹרָה
אַחַת לָהֶם הַכֹּהֵן אֲשֶׁר יְכַפֶּר־בּוֹ לוֹ יִהְיֶה׃
8 וְהַכֹּהֵן הַמַּקְרִיב אֶת־עֹלַת אִישׁ עוֹר הָעֹלָה
אֲשֶׁר הִקְרִיב לַכֹּהֵן לוֹ יִהְיֶה׃ 9 וְכָל־מִנְחָה אֲשֶׁר
תֵּאָפֶה בַּתַּנּוּר וְכָל־נַעֲשָׂה בַמַּרְחֶשֶׁת וְעַל־מַחֲבַת
לַכֹּהֵן הַמַּקְרִיב אֹתָהּ לוֹ תִהְיֶה׃ 10 וְכָל־מִנְחָה

episode the priests should have partaken of the sin offering presented at the initiation of the Tabernacle cult, none of which had been brought inside the Tent. Their failure to partake of it might have affected the efficacy of the offering.[25]

CHAPTER 7 THE GUILT OFFERING (*'ASHAM*) (vv. 1–10)

1. *This is the ritual of the guilt offering* The procedures specified in verses 1–6 for the *'asham*, "guilt offering," complement those already stipulated for the sin offering in 6:17. The provisions are identical for both offerings, a fact made explicit in verse 7, and it is therefore unnecessary to comment on them in detail. Verses 1–6 provide particulars absent from chapter 6; they are, however, anticipated in 4:28f. and in chapter 5. The anatomical terms that occur in verses 3–4 are explained in the Comments to 3:3–4.

7. *it shall belong to the priest who makes expiation thereby* This statement is significant because it indicates that the expiatory sacrifices eaten by the priests are actually their property. This principle is further expounded in verses 8–10.[1]

8. *So, too, the priest . . . shall keep the skin of the burnt offering that he offered* Chapter 1, which sets forth the procedures relevant to the burnt offering, meticulously avoids mentioning that the hide of the sacrificial animal should be burned because, in fact, it was not to be destroyed. Only in the case of the priestly *ḥatta't*, ordained in 4:1–21 and in similar riddance rituals, was the hide to be destroyed—and that was done outside the camp, not on the altar.[2] In most cases, the officiating priest could keep the hide as his own and profit from its value.

9. *Further, any meal offering* The text seems to prescribe various grain offerings. Verse 9 speaks of those prepared in an oven, in a pan, or on a griddle, all of which belong to the officiating priest; verse 10 speaks of other grain offerings that belong to *all* priests. Although traditional commentaries are hard pressed to reconcile verses 9 and 10, Mishnah Menaḥot 6:1 does not record any difference in the allocation of the various grain offerings. This suggests that we simply have two merisms, that is, two different ways of saying, in effect, that *all* types of grain offerings, parts of which went to the priests, belonged to the various groups of officiants at these rites; this according to Hoffmann.

offering, with oil mixed in or dry, shall go to the sons of
Aaron all alike.
11This is the ritual of the sacrifice of well-being that one
may offer to the LORD:
12If he offers it for thanksgiving, he shall offer together
with the sacrifice of thanksgiving unleavened cakes with oil
mixed in, unleavened wafers spread with oil, and cakes of
choice flour with oil mixed in, well soaked. 13This offering,
with cakes of leavened bread added, he shall offer along
with his thanksgiving sacrifice of well-being. 14Out of this

בְלוּלָה־בַשֶּׁמֶן וַחֲרֵבָה לְכָל־בְּנֵי אַהֲרֹן תִּהְיֶה אִישׁ
כְּאָחִיו׃ פ שלישי 11 וְזֹאת תּוֹרַת זֶבַח
הַשְּׁלָמִים אֲשֶׁר יַקְרִיב לַיהוָה׃ 12 אִם עַל־תּוֹדָה
יַקְרִיבֶנּוּ וְהִקְרִיב ׀ עַל־זֶבַח הַתּוֹדָה חַלּוֹת מַצּוֹת
בְּלוּלֹת בַּשֶּׁמֶן וּרְקִיקֵי מַצּוֹת מְשֻׁחִים בַּשָּׁמֶן
וְסֹלֶת מֻרְבֶּכֶת חַלֹּת בְּלוּלֹת בַּשָּׁמֶן׃ 13 עַל־חַלֹּת
לֶחֶם חָמֵץ יַקְרִיב קָרְבָּנוֹ עַל־זֶבַח תּוֹדַת שְׁלָמָיו׃

THE SACRED GIFT OF GREETING (*ZEVAḤ HA-SHELAMIM*) (7:11–34)

11. ***This is the ritual of the sacrifice of well-being*** Rather, "of the sacred gift of greeting." The preferred translation of *zevaḥ ha-shelamim* is explained in the Comment to 3:1.

Beginning in this verse attention shifts to the sacrifices of lesser sanctity. Donors could eat parts of these sacrifices outside the sacred precincts of the sanctuary; the priests could eat them inside the sanctuary precincts.[3] As in chapter 3, our section employs the term *shelamim* in a general sense, referring to all sacrifices of the *zevaḥ* type.

12. ***If he offers it for thanksgiving*** The sacrifice is offered as an expression of gratitude. In this single verse, the term *todah* has two meanings. Here we have the more general sense of "thanksgiving" as a religious attitude. Further on in the verse, *zevaḥ todah* is a technical term that designates the thanksgiving offering, as in verses 13–15 below.

the sacrifice of thanksgiving This use of *zevaḥ todah,* "the thanksgiving sacrifice," technically refers to the animal sacrifice that was ordained in chapter 3, namely, a sheep or goat of either sex. Nevertheless, the ritual first considers the preparation and disposition of the grain offerings of both unleavened and leavened cakes that accompanied the animal sacrifice, a matter not dealt with elsewhere in Leviticus. The ritual then proceeds to deal with the animal sacrifice itself, for which basic information is available in chapter 3.

Thanksgiving offerings were appropriate for expressing one's gratitude to God for deliverance from danger or misfortune.[4] Amos (4:5) mentioned them as frequent offerings in his day. The prophet Jeremiah (17:29; 33:11) envisioned a faithful people streaming into Jerusalem from all over the land to offer sacrifices of thanksgiving.

The prescriptions of our chapter subsume the *todah* under the general category of *shelamim* and yet indicate that it was originally distinct from the other kinds of *shelamim,* such as votaries and freewill offerings, discussed in verses 16–18. Not only did the *todah* itself undergo development, as we shall presently see, but its classification undoubtedly changed as well. Whereas here the *todah* is considered a kind of *shelamim* offering, in the Holiness Code, as represented by 22:21f., it is even listed separately from the *shelamim.*

According to our verse the *todah* must be accompanied by a grain offering of unleavened cakes. Combining grain offerings with animal sacrifices is a well-known pattern, not only in the regular public cult as it developed in ancient Israel but in specific celebrations as well. According to 8:26, a grain offering accompanied the *zevaḥ* in the ordination rites of the Aaronide priesthood. The requirement of eating unleavened cakes (*matsah*) together with the paschal *zevaḥ* may also represent the same combination.[5] The grain offering ordained here is patterned after the one presented in 2:4f., except that it was to be prepared with "soaked" flour, like the priestly *minḥah*—the holocaust of 6:14.

13. ***This offering, with cakes of leavened bread added*** The preposition *ʿal* occurs twice in this verse, and in both instances it means "in addition to."[6]

The *minḥah* of leavened cakes (*ḥamets*) is actually what the prophet Amos (4:5) referred to as the thanksgiving offering, which indicates that it was, at certain periods, a self-sufficient rite, independent of animal sacrifice. The different disposition of the grain offering prescribed here follows the rule of

he shall offer one of each kind as a gift to the LORD; it shall go to the priest who dashes the blood of the offering of well-being. 15And the flesh of his thanksgiving sacrifice of well-being shall be eaten on the day that it is offered; none of it shall be set aside until morning.

16If, however, the sacrifice he offers is a votive or a freewill offering, it shall be eaten on the day that he offers his sacrifice, and what is left of it shall be eaten on the morrow.

14 וְהִקְרִיב מִמֶּנּוּ אֶחָד מִכָּל־קָרְבָּן תְּרוּמָה לַיהוָה
לַכֹּהֵן הַזֹּרֵק אֶת־דַּם הַשְּׁלָמִים לוֹ יִהְיֶה׃ 15 וּבְשַׂר
זֶבַח תּוֹדַת שְׁלָמָיו בְּיוֹם קָרְבָּנוֹ יֵאָכֵל לֹא־יַנִּיחַ
מִמֶּנּוּ עַד־בֹּקֶר׃ 16 וְאִם־נֶדֶר ׀ אוֹ נְדָבָה זֶבַח
קָרְבָּנוֹ בְּיוֹם הַקְרִיבוֹ אֶת־זִבְחוֹ יֵאָכֵל וּמִמָּחֳרָת
וְהַנּוֹתָר מִמֶּנּוּ יֵאָכֵל׃ 17 וְהַנּוֹתָר מִבְּשַׂר הַזָּבַח

2:11 that no leaven may ascend the altar of burnt offerings. Thus, the leavened cakes are not offered on the altar, only the unleavened ones. This ***minḥah*** of leavened cakes is one of two such offerings recorded in the Torah, the other being the ***minḥah*** of new grain, prescribed in 23:17, to be presented on Pentecost.[7] In a sense, the bread of display (*leḥem ha-panim*), made of leavened dough, is yet another example, although strictly speaking it is not called a ***minḥah*** in 24:8.

Our verse employs the unusual composite term *zevaḥ todat shelamav,* "his sacred thanksgiving gifts of greeting." It epitomizes the incorporation of the ***todah*** within the general category of *shelamim* sacrifices.

We are not told precisely how many cakes of the several varieties were to be offered during the entire rite. Mishnah Menaḥot 7:1 mentions ten of each variety. This totals forty cakes and wafers, thirty unleavened and ten leavened. All were made from the same dough, according to Mishnah Menaḥot 5:1; the dough for the leavened cakes differed only in its being allowed to rise.

14. one of each kind as a gift to the LORD Literally, "one of each offering," that is, four pieces in all were allotted to the officiating priest. Hebrew *terumah,* translated here and in verse 32 as "gift," more precisely means "levy, what is raised." The verb ***herim*** sometimes connotes "raising" funds.[8]

It may not appear logical to designate the priests' allocation as an offering to the Lord. Nevertheless, sacrificial procedures in biblical Israel, and in the Near East generally, often dictated that the offering was first presented to the deity for acceptance, at which time, having been devoted to him, it belonged to him in its entirety. Only then did the deity grant portions of the same offerings to the priests and, occasionally, to the donors as well. Consequently, even in cases such as ours, where no part of the leavened grain offering was placed on the altar, it could be considered, nonetheless, as an offering to the Lord. This theory of the transfer of gifts initially offered to the Lord underlies the grants to the priesthood outlined in Numbers 18:8ff. and is also reflected in verses 34 and 35 below. These passages state explicitly that the Lord granted to the Aaronide priesthood portions of the sacrifices as their measure, or share, from what had been offered to Him in the first instance.[9]

15. And the flesh of his thanksgiving sacrifice This indicates yet another difference between the *todah* and other *shelamim* sacrifices. In the case of the *todah,* the flesh must be eaten on the day the altar sacrifice is made; if not consumed then, it must be burned. This rule is also stated in 22:29–30, and is reminiscent of the paschal sacrifice. Exodus 12:5–10 tells us that no part of it could be left over until the following morning. And in disposing of the ram of investiture, a rite included in the ordination of the Aaronide priesthood in Leviticus 8:31–32, the sacrificial flesh also had to be eaten with dispatch.

The *todah* occupied a special position in the rabbinic tradition because it symbolized the pure expression of gratitude to God. It was not obligatory; nor was it occasioned by sinfulness or guilt, nor even by the motives that induced Israelites to pledge votive sacrifices when confronted by danger. According to rabbinic teaching, it would continue to be offered in the messianic era, when the rest of the sacrificial system was no longer operative.[10]

16. If, however, the sacrifice he offers is a votive Except in the case of the *todah,* the flesh of *shelamim* sacrifices may be eaten until the third day, a rule also stated in 19:5–8.

Hebrew *neder,* "votive," can be used both for the original pronouncement of the vow and for the act of fulfillment. Here *neder* has the latter meaning, referring to the payment of the vow in the form of sacrifice.[11]

[17]What is then left of the flesh of the sacrifice shall be
consumed in fire on the third day. [18]If any of the flesh of his
sacrifice of well-being is eaten on the third day, it shall not
be acceptable; it shall not count for him who offered it. It is
an offensive thing, and the person who eats of it shall bear
his guilt.

[19]Flesh that touches anything unclean shall not be eaten;
it shall be consumed in fire. As for other flesh, only he who
is clean may eat such flesh. [20]But the person who, in a state
of uncleanness, eats flesh from the LORD's sacrifices of well-
being, that person shall be cut off from his kin. [21]When a

בַּיּוֹם הַשְּׁלִישִׁי בָּאֵשׁ יִשָּׂרֵף׃ 18 וְאִם הֵאָכֹל יֵאָכֵל
מִבְּשַׂר־זֶבַח שְׁלָמָיו בַּיּוֹם הַשְּׁלִישִׁי לֹא יֵרָצֶה
הַמַּקְרִיב אֹתוֹ לֹא יֵחָשֵׁב לוֹ פִּגּוּל יִהְיֶה וְהַנֶּפֶשׁ
הָאֹכֶלֶת מִמֶּנּוּ עֲוֺנָהּ תִּשָּׂא׃ 19 וְהַבָּשָׂר אֲשֶׁר־יִגַּע
בְּכָל־טָמֵא לֹא יֵאָכֵל בָּאֵשׁ יִשָּׂרֵף וְהַבָּשָׂר כָּל־
טָהוֹר יֹאכַל בָּשָׂר׃ 20 וְהַנֶּפֶשׁ אֲשֶׁר־תֹּאכַל בָּשָׂר
מִזֶּבַח הַשְּׁלָמִים אֲשֶׁר לַיהוָה וְטֻמְאָתוֹ עָלָיו
וְנִכְרְתָה הַנֶּפֶשׁ הַהִוא מֵעַמֶּיהָ׃ 21 וְנֶפֶשׁ כִּי־תִגַּע

Vows were an important element in Israelite religion, and making a vow, in itself a private act, was often interrelated with public worship. In 1 Samuel 1 it is recounted that Elkanah and his family, on a pilgrimage to Shiloh to offer the annual sacrifices, attended to their private vows on the same occasion. The payment of a vow could take the form of sacrifice. The appropriateness of the *shelamim* for such payment is suggested by Proverbs 7:14. There we read that a harlot might lure an unsuspecting young man to her house by offering him a portion of her *shelamim* sacrifice: "I owe *shelamim* offerings; for today I have paid my vows" (literally). This was admittedly a pretext, but a credible one in terms of accepted practice.

There were no restrictions regarding where the donor of a *shelamim* sacrifice could eat his portion of the offering, so long as this was done promptly and no impure person partook of the flesh, a rule stated in verse 19 below.

or a freewill offering Hebrew *nedavah,* "freewill offering," also serves as a generic term for many types of voluntary contributions to the sanctuary.[12] Like the *todah,* it expresses gratitude to God and is often mentioned together with the *neder.*[13] Amos 4:5 mentions the *todah* and the *nedavah* together.

18. If any of the flesh . . . is eaten on the third day, it shall not be acceptable The formula *lo' yeratseh,* "it shall not be acceptable," is explained in the Comment to 1:3. Because the sacrificial flesh was left uneaten for an improper period of time, the sacrifice itself was not efficacious: "It shall not be counted for him who offered it." This rule is also stated in 19:5 and in 22:10.

The precise meaning of Hebrew *piggul,* here translated "an offensive thing," remains uncertain.[14] In Ezekiel 4:14, it is used, together with references to carcasses and torn flesh, in a more general sense as something forbidden.[15] In Isaiah 55:4 the plural form *piggulim* seems to designate flesh offered in idolatrous worship, regarded as abominable, like the flesh of swine.

In this verse the penalty for eating flesh remaining from the *shelamim* sacrifice after the third day is stated merely as "bearing one's guilt," whereas in 19:5–8 the penalty of being "cut off" from the religious community is imposed for the same offense.[16]

19. Flesh that touches anything unclean shall not be eaten Beginning in verse 19, the text proceeds to deal more fully with the subject of impurity, a concern that was particularly relevant to the *shelamim* because parts of it were handled by ordinary Israelites outside the sanctuary. This warranted an explicit admonition. In chapter 22, the law addressed to the priests includes all sacrifices in the admonition.

At the end of this verse, the Hebrew syntax is unusual. The text reads *ve-ha-basar kol tahor yo'khal basar,* literally "and the flesh—any pure person may eat flesh." This rhetorical device is known as anacoluthon, wherein the sentence starts out to say one thing and then abruptly switches to another.

20. But the person who, in a state of uncleanness, eats flesh "Flesh" (*basar*) means *sacrificial* flesh, of course.

21. When a person touches anything unclean, be it human uncleanness The term *tum'at 'adam,* "human uncleanness," is explained in the Comment to 5:2–3.[17]

person touches anything unclean, be it human uncleanness or an unclean animal or any unclean creature, and eats flesh from the LORD's sacrifices of well-being, that person shall be cut off from his kin.

22And the LORD spoke to Moses, saying: 23Speak to the Israelite people thus: You shall eat no fat of ox or sheep or goat. 24Fat from animals that died or were torn by beasts may be put to any use, but you must not eat it. 25If anyone eats the fat of animals from which offerings by fire may be made to the LORD, the person who eats it shall be cut off from his kin. 26And you must not consume any blood, either of bird or of animal, in any of your settlements. 27Anyone who eats blood shall be cut off from his kin.

28And the LORD spoke to Moses, saying: 29Speak to the

בְּכָל־טָמֵא בְּטֻמְאַת אָדָם אוֹ בִּבְהֵמָה טְמֵאָה אוֹ
בְּכָל־שֶׁקֶץ טָמֵא וְאָכַל מִבְּשַׂר־זֶבַח הַשְּׁלָמִים
אֲשֶׁר לַיהוָה וְנִכְרְתָה הַנֶּפֶשׁ הַהִוא מֵעַמֶּיהָ׃
פ 22 וַיְדַבֵּר יְהוָה אֶל־מֹשֶׁה לֵּאמֹר׃ 23 דַּבֵּר
אֶל־בְּנֵי יִשְׂרָאֵל לֵאמֹר כָּל־חֵלֶב שׁוֹר וְכֶשֶׂב וָעֵז
לֹא תֹאכֵלוּ׃ 24 וְחֵלֶב נְבֵלָה וְחֵלֶב טְרֵפָה יֵעָשֶׂה
לְכָל־מְלָאכָה וְאָכֹל לֹא תֹאכְלֻהוּ׃ 25 כִּי כָּל־
אֹכֵל חֵלֶב מִן־הַבְּהֵמָה אֲשֶׁר יַקְרִיב מִמֶּנָּה אִשֶּׁה
לַיהוָה וְנִכְרְתָה הַנֶּפֶשׁ הָאֹכֶלֶת מֵעַמֶּיהָ׃ 26 וְכָל־
דָּם לֹא תֹאכְלוּ בְּכֹל מוֹשְׁבֹתֵיכֶם לָעוֹף וְלַבְּהֵמָה׃
27 כָּל־נֶפֶשׁ אֲשֶׁר־תֹּאכַל כָּל־דָּם וְנִכְרְתָה הַנֶּפֶשׁ
הַהִוא מֵעַמֶּיהָ׃ פ 28 וַיְדַבֵּר יְהוָה אֶל־מֹשֶׁה

any unclean creature Hebrew *shekets,* literally "abomination," is translated "unclean creature" in accordance with ancient versions of the Torah. Several Hebrew manuscripts read *sherets,* "swarming creature," instead. This is understandable, even apart from the similarity in spelling and sound, because swarming creatures are often referred to as abominable.[18]

23. You shall eat no fat of ox or sheep or goat Verses 22–27 contain prohibitions against eating blood (vv. 26–27) and against eating *ḥelev,* the animal fat that is offered on the altar. As was noted in the Comment to 3:3–4, *ḥelev* does not refer to ordinary fat that adheres to meat but to fat that covers the internal organs and entrails. It was also explained that the prohibition of *ḥelev* derived from the assignment of the fatty portions of the victim to God as His share of the offering. This made *ḥelev* forbidden for any other use. Like 3:17, this legislation extends the prohibition of *ḥelev* so as to "build a fence" around the law. Once the *ḥelev* of sacrificial animals was forbidden, the *ḥelev* of all pure animals was forbidden as well, whether or not the animals in question were actually sacrificed. Regarding the penalty of *karet* for violating these as well as other prohibitions, see Excursus 1.

The blood prohibition is more comprehensive and applies to all but the blood of fish and certain permitted insects, according to the Sifra. More about the basis for the prohibition is explained in the Comments to 3:17 and 17:11.

24. Fat from animals that died This would seem to be an unnecessary statement, since an animal torn by beasts (*terefah*) and the carcass of a dead animal (*nevelah*) were forbidden in their entirety, according to the laws of Exodus 22:30 and Leviticus 17:15; 22:18. In turn, therefore, any part of them would also be forbidden. It is likely that this rule was included for emphasis, to reinforce the ban on eating *ḥelev*. According to rabbinic interpretation the verse served to limit the prohibition to the consumption of *ḥelev;* its use for other purposes was permitted.[19]

25. from which offerings by fire may be made This clarifies the provisions of verse 22. The *ḥelev* of large and small cattle is forbidden because such animals are of the kind offered as sacrifices.

26. And you must not consume any blood . . . in any of your settlements The formula *bekhol moshvoteikhem,* "in any of your settlements," often appears in the instructions regarding activities that are not limited to the sanctuary and priesthood but that nevertheless involve violations of religious law. Examples are the Passover law, requiring Israelites to eat *matsah* during the festival, and laws governing the observance of the Sabbath and other holy days.[20] These duties were not limited to the sacred cult of the sanctuary and applied as well to Israelites, wherever they lived.

29. The offering to the LORD . . . sacrifice of well-being to the LORD Verses 29–30 ordain that the donor of the *shelamim* sacrifice must actually participate in the presentation of the offering.

לֵאמֹר׃ 29 דַּבֵּר אֶל־בְּנֵי יִשְׂרָאֵל לֵאמֹר הַמַּקְרִיב
אֶת־זֶבַח שְׁלָמָיו לַיהוָה יָבִיא אֶת־קָרְבָּנוֹ לַיהוָה
מִזֶּבַח שְׁלָמָיו׃ 30 יָדָיו תְּבִיאֶינָה אֵת אִשֵּׁי יְהוָה
אֶת־הַחֵלֶב עַל־הֶחָזֶה יְבִיאֶנּוּ אֵת הֶחָזֶה לְהָנִיף
אֹתוֹ תְּנוּפָה לִפְנֵי יְהוָה׃ 31 וְהִקְטִיר הַכֹּהֵן אֶת־
הַחֵלֶב הַמִּזְבֵּחָה וְהָיָה הֶחָזֶה לְאַהֲרֹן וּלְבָנָיו׃
32 וְאֵת שׁוֹק הַיָּמִין תִּתְּנוּ תְרוּמָה לַכֹּהֵן מִזִּבְחֵי
שַׁלְמֵיכֶם׃ 33 הַמַּקְרִיב אֶת־דַּם הַשְּׁלָמִים וְאֶת־
הַחֵלֶב מִבְּנֵי אַהֲרֹן לוֹ תִהְיֶה שׁוֹק הַיָּמִין לְמָנָה׃
34 כִּי אֶת־חֲזֵה הַתְּנוּפָה וְאֵת ׀ שׁוֹק הַתְּרוּמָה
לָקַחְתִּי מֵאֵת בְּנֵי־יִשְׂרָאֵל מִזִּבְחֵי שַׁלְמֵיהֶם וָאֶתֵּן
אֹתָם לְאַהֲרֹן הַכֹּהֵן וּלְבָנָיו לְחָק־עוֹלָם מֵאֵת בְּנֵי

Israelite people thus: The offering to the LORD from a sacrifice of well-being must be presented by him who offers his sacrifice of well-being to the LORD:
30his own hands shall present the LORD's offerings by fire. He shall present the fat with the breast, the breast to be elevated as an elevation offering before the LORD;
31the priest shall turn the fat into smoke on the altar, and the breast shall go to Aaron and his sons.
32And the right thigh from your sacrifices of well-being you shall present to the priest as a gift;
33he from among Aaron's sons who offers the blood and the fat of the offering of well-being shall get the right thigh as his portion.
34For I have taken the breast of elevation offering and the thigh of gift offering from the Israelites, from their sacrifices of well-being, and given them to Aaron the priest and to his sons as their due from the Israelites for all time.

In contrast to the "most sacred offerings" discussed in 6:1–7:10, at which only priests officiated, the presentation of the *shelamim* sacrifices was to involve ordinary Israelites as well. Since nonpriests could not actually place sacrifices on the altar—access to the adjacent area was banned to them—the rite of *tenufah,* "presentation," was employed to afford them some measure of participation in sacrifices of lesser sanctity. (Although Israelites normally laid their hand on sacrifices that they offered, as is stipulated in 1:4, this was merely a preliminary assignment of the victim, not part of the sacrificial presentation itself.)

30. the breast to be elevated as an elevation offering before the LORD A sacrifice designated *tenufah,* derived from the verb *henif,* "to lift, raise." As Mishnah Menaḥot 5:6 describes it, the offering was carried to and fro in a raised position, the intent being to show the offering to God for His acceptance.[21] The rite of *tenufah* was a sufficient mode of sacrifice, although in our case it merely precedes the burning of certain parts of the offering on the altar and the burning of other parts in pots. These two modes, presentation and burning (here *'isheh,* "offering by fire") are discussed in the Comment to 2:1. *Tenufah* was a method of presentation suitable for the dedication of the Levites as servants in the sanctuary, according to Numbers 8:11, and for the consecration of precious metals contributed to the sanctuary, as recorded in Exodus 35:22 and 38:24,29. It was likewise prescribed for certain grain offerings, no part of which was placed on the altar, such as the offering from the new crop ordained in Leviticus 23:11,17.

What we observe in our legislation is the sequential combining of modes of sacrifice that were originally independent. Even here, however, the parts of the sacrifice that were "presented" were not burned on the altar, as we read in verse 34 below. They were assigned to the priests and the donors and were boiled in pots.[22]

31. the priest shall turn the fat into smoke The order of the procedure is significant here: The priest was entitled to take the breast and the right thigh of the sacrificial animal only after God's share of the offering, that is, the fatty portions, had been burned on the altar. As related in 1 Samuel 2:15–17, the sons of Eli, the priest of Shiloh, failed to observe this law. They seized their portions of the sacrifices from the cooking pots, even before the altar sacrifice had been performed, thereby provoking God's wrath.

33. shall get the right thigh as his portion Hebrew *manah,* "portion," is a synonym for *ḥok,* "due," the term used in verse 34 and, previously, in 6:11. In verse 35 below, a third term, *mishḥah,* "measure," is used.[23]

34. and the thigh of gift offering Hebrew *terumah* is explained in the Comment to verse 14.

35Those shall be the perquisites of Aaron and the perquisites of his sons from the LORD's offerings by fire, once they have been inducted to serve the LORD as priests; 36these the LORD commanded to be given them, once they had been anointed, as a due from the Israelites for all time throughout the ages.

37Such are the rituals of the burnt offering, the meal offering, the sin offering, the guilt offering, the offering of ordination, and the sacrifice of well-being, 38with which the LORD charged Moses on Mount Sinai, when He commanded that the Israelites present their offerings to the LORD, in the wilderness of Sinai.

יִשְׂרָאֵֽל׃ 35 זֹ֣את מִשְׁחַ֤ת אַהֲרֹן֙ וּמִשְׁחַ֣ת בָּנָ֔יו
מֵאִשֵּׁ֖י יְהוָ֑ה בְּיוֹם֙ הִקְרִ֣יב אֹתָ֔ם לְכַהֵ֖ן לַיהוָֽה׃
36 אֲשֶׁר֩ צִוָּ֨ה יְהוָ֜ה לָתֵ֣ת לָהֶ֗ם בְּיוֹם֙ מָשְׁח֣וֹ אֹתָ֔ם
מֵאֵ֖ת בְּנֵ֣י יִשְׂרָאֵ֑ל חֻקַּ֥ת עוֹלָ֖ם לְדֹרֹתָֽם׃ 37 זֹ֣את
הַתּוֹרָ֗ה לָֽעֹלָה֙ לַמִּנְחָ֔ה וְלַֽחַטָּ֖את וְלָאָשָׁ֑ם
וְלַ֨מִּלּוּאִ֔ים וּלְזֶ֖בַח הַשְּׁלָמִֽים׃ 38 אֲשֶׁ֨ר צִוָּ֧ה יְהוָ֛ה
אֶת־מֹשֶׁ֖ה בְּהַ֣ר סִינָ֑י בְּי֨וֹם צַוֺּת֜וֹ אֶת־בְּנֵ֣י יִשְׂרָאֵ֗ל
לְהַקְרִ֧יב אֶת־קָרְבְּנֵיהֶ֛ם לַיהוָ֖ה בְּמִדְבַּ֥ר סִינָֽי׃

פ רביעי

SUMMARY (7:35–38)

35. *Those shall be the perquisites of Aaron* Rather, "they shall constitute the share of Aaron." The translation derives Hebrew *mishḥah* from the verb *mashaḥ,* "to anoint," and explains it as referring to the gifts and honors received by the priests as a consequence of their anointment. This interpretation seems to be supported by the following verse, which states that God commanded that such emoluments be given the priests once they had been anointed.

What we have, however, is a case of homonyms, two roots that appear alike but that have separate derivations: (1) *mashaḥ,* "to anoint," and (2) *mashaḥ,* "to measure," a verb more common in Aramaic and Akkadian than in Hebrew. The noun *mishḥah* simply means "measure," hence "share," and is a synonym for *manah* and *ḥok,* terms used earlier. Numbers 18:8 has *le-moshḥah,* "as a share," where this meaning is clear. In that passage there is nothing to suggest a connection with anointing. The Aramaic noun *misheta',* "measure," occurs in Egyptian documents dating from the fifth century B.C.E. In Late Babylonian documents we find the Akkadian forms *mišiḫtu* or *mešḫātu.* This is the very Semitic root expressed here.[24]

37. *Such are the rituals* Hebrew *zo't ha-torah* has collective force, although in form it is singular. It refers to all of the rituals set forth in chapters 6–7.

the offering of ordination Whereas there is a *torah* in chapters 6–7 for the other items summarized in this verse, there is none for the ordination of the priests. The only possible point of reference in chapters 6–7 would be the *minḥah* holocaust offered by the High Priest and prescribed in 6:12–16. The ordination rites themselves are described in chapters 8–9. Hebrew *millu'im,* "ordination," is explained in the Comment to 8:22.

38. *with which the LORD charged Moses on Mount Sinai* The main thrust of this verse is the assertion that, already in the wilderness of Sinai, the Israelites worshiped God with sacrifices.[25]

The Initiation of Formal Worship (chaps. 8–9)

Chapters 8 and 9 of Leviticus present a detailed description of the religious celebrations marking the initiation of formal worship in ancient Israel. This description is part of a larger historiography: an interpretation of the history of Israel from the perspective of its priesthood. The priesthood had a particular interest in the origin of worship because of its own central role in this area of Israelite life.

Subsequent to the Exodus from Egypt and the revelation of laws and commandments at Mount Sinai, the Tabernacle was erected, and Moses was instructed by God on the proper modes of worship. A priesthood had to be ordained and the altar and Tabernacle consecrated to God's service.

In their detailing of these issues, therefore, chapters 8 and 9 differ from the preceding chapters of Leviticus and from most of what follows. Unlike the other sections, they are not legal in formulation but, rather, descriptive of special ritual events; they serve to describe the fulfillment of what was ordained in Exodus 29:1–37 and also overlap in content with the final chapters of Exodus.[1]

Chapter 8, in verses 1–3, briefly outlines what is to follow. This introduction (and also the introduction that opens chapter 9) functions to reinforce the principle that all the specific rituals were commanded by God. Indeed, we encounter the recurrent formula: "As the LORD had commanded Moses" at various points in these chapters (8:9,13,17,21,29; 9:10). The effect is to portray Moses, Aaron and his sons, and the Israelites as obedient to God's command and to attribute Israelite modes of worship to divine command, not to custom and convention.

Most of chapter 8 (vv. 6–36) is devoted to a description of two distinct yet related ceremonies: the consecration of the altar and Tabernacle and of Aaron, the High Priest (vv. 6–12); and the ordination of Aaron and his sons as priests, which was accomplished by a series of sacrificial and purificatory rites, performed over a period of seven days (vv. 13–36).

The High Priest is represented as the bearer of a distinct office. He wore special vestments not worn by ordinary priests, and he alone was anointed with the "oil of anointing," the same oil used to consecrate the altar and Tabernacle and its sacred vessels. In effect, he was the human counterpart of the altar. Following the consecration of the altar and the High Priest, the altar was purified preparatory to its utilization, just as the priests themselves would soon be purified. The altar was then used for the first time in a kind of trial run: an *ʿolah,* "burnt offering," was sacrificed on it (vv. 18–21), and when a favorable response was received from God, the actual ordination ceremonies, which were to last seven days, could proceed (vv. 22–36). As the main event, the "ram of ordination," whose blood was used to initiate the priests, was offered on the altar.

Chapter 9, after an introduction (vv. 1–7), describes the ritual for the eighth day. Moses plays a key role, for it is he who issues the detailed instructions for the performance of various rites, just as he had issued orders to Aaron and his sons regarding the celebration of the first seven days. The rites described in this chapter are dedicatory in character, performed on behalf of the entire people. They celebrate the entry of God's "presence" (*kavod*) into the newly consecrated Tabernacle, an earthly residence for the God of Israel. Hebrew *mishkan,* translated "Tabernacle," means "tent"; but it derives from the verb *shakhan,* "to dwell, reside." The dedication of the Tabernacle was not complete, therefore, until God's presence rested upon it, as is stated in Exodus 29:43: "It [the Tabernacle] shall be sanctified by My presence." In the same way, the Temple of Jerusalem is called *bayit,* "house," and was declared to be sacred only after God's presence entered it.[2]

There are diverse traditions regarding the precise form assumed by God's presence when it became visible or manifest. It is described variously as a blazing fire,[3] and as a thick cloud that took on a fiery glow at night.[4] In the traditions concerning the wilderness Tabernacle, the cloud of God's presence hovered over the structure when it was stationary and filled it. (In the biblical conception of God, His presence filled the entire universe and could not be contained in any earthly temple. Yet God's presence in the Tabernacle and, later, in the Temple of Jerusalem was not thought to contradict the fact of His omnipresence. Rather, His nearness to the human community was regarded as evidence of His concern for those who called upon Him.)

As the presence of God was welcomed at the Tabernacle, extreme care had to be exercised to protect it from impurity. Both the priests and the people, represented on this occasion by the elders (*zekenim*), offered their respective sin offerings, an indication that the Tabernacle existed for the benefit of all, not solely for the priesthood.[5]

Once the purificatory sacrifices were completed and the first *ʿolah* offered, the sacred gifts of greeting (*shelamim*) were placed on the altar in celebration of the dedication of the altar and

8 The LORD spoke to Moses, saying: [2]Take Aaron along with his sons, and the vestments, the anointing oil, the bull of sin offering, the two rams, and the basket of unleavened bread; [3]and assemble the whole community at the entrance of the Tent of Meeting. [4]Moses did as the LORD commanded him. And when the community was assembled at the entrance of the Tent of Meeting, [5]Moses said to the community, "This is what the LORD has commanded to be done."

[6]Then Moses brought Aaron and his sons forward and

ח וַיְדַבֵּר יְהוָה אֶל־מֹשֶׁה לֵּאמֹר: 2 קַח אֶת־
אַהֲרֹן וְאֶת־בָּנָיו אִתּוֹ וְאֵת הַבְּגָדִים וְאֵת שֶׁמֶן
הַמִּשְׁחָה וְאֵת׀ פַּר הַחַטָּאת וְאֵת שְׁנֵי הָאֵילִים
וְאֵת סַל הַמַּצּוֹת: 3 וְאֵת כָּל־הָעֵדָה הַקְהֵל אֶל־
פֶּתַח אֹהֶל מוֹעֵד: 4 וַיַּעַשׂ מֹשֶׁה כַּאֲשֶׁר צִוָּה יְהוָה
אֹתוֹ וַתִּקָּהֵל הָעֵדָה אֶל־פֶּתַח אֹהֶל מוֹעֵד:
5 וַיֹּאמֶר מֹשֶׁה אֶל־הָעֵדָה זֶה הַדָּבָר אֲשֶׁר־צִוָּה
יְהוָה לַעֲשׂוֹת: 6 וַיַּקְרֵב מֹשֶׁה אֶת־אַהֲרֹן וְאֶת־בָּנָיו

Tabernacle. The people received a blessing, and God's presence appeared before them. Miraculously, the altar fire was ignited to consume the sacred gifts of greeting, and the people prostrated themselves before God and rejoiced greatly (vv. 22–24).

Chapters 8 and 9 present Moses as the "priest-maker." As the first of the prophets, he ordains the first priests. In the priestly historiography, he also instructs them in their duties and later, when Aaron dies, transfers the office of High Priest from Aaron to his son Eleazar (Num. 20:22–29). Only once in biblical literature, in Psalms 99:6, is Moses himself called *kohen,* "priest": "Moses and Aaron among His priests, Samuel, among those who call on His name." It would be incorrect, however, to regard Moses as a priest, and the passage undoubtedly does not use the term ***kohen*** in its technical sense.[6]

CHAPTER 8 THE CONSECRATION OF PRIESTS AND TABERNACLE (vv. 1–36)

Moses is instructed to assemble Aaron and his sons and all the materials to be used in the celebrations to follow: the vestments, the anointing oil, the sacrificial animals, and the unleavened bread. Then the congregation assembles.

2. ***the vestments, the anointing oil*** The vestments and the robing of the priests are described in verses 7–9. The "anointing oil" (*shemen ha-mishḥah*) was blended according to a special recipe (prescribed in Exod. 30:22–25) that could not be imitated for any other purpose. Verses 10–12 and 23–24 specify exactly how this oil was utilized in the celebrations.

3. ***and assemble the whole community*** On the term *ʿedah,* see Comment to 4:13. The verb ***hakhel,*** "to assemble," is a form of the root from which ***kahal,*** "congregation," derives.

at the entrance of the Tent of Meeting The designation ***petaḥ ʾohel moʿed,*** "at the entrance of the Tent of Meeting," should not be taken literally. The actual place of assembly of the people was in the outer section of the courtyard, not directly in front of the Tent. According to accepted procedures, it was forbidden for any except priests to advance beyond the altar of burnt offerings, which stood in the courtyard about halfway between the outer gate and the entrance to the Tent proper. There were gradations of sanctity, as one moved from the interior of the Tent toward the outer gate of the Tabernacle complex. The outer section of the courtyard was reserved for activities preparatory to sacrifice and for the assembly of the people, which undoubtedly overflowed beyond the outer gate.

At the site of Arad in the Negeb, archaeologists have unearthed an Israelite sanctuary dating from the period of the First Temple of Jerusalem. In its courtyard stood an altar, and aligned with the front of the altar there was a row of stones indicating a step onto a higher surface. Most likely, this step marked the division between the two sections of the courtyard.[7] The Temple of Jerusalem likewise had both an inner and an outer courtyard at certain periods of its history.[8]

5. ***This is what the LORD has commanded*** The description that follows is what the Lord has commanded, according to Hoffmann.

6. ***Then Moses brought Aaron and his sons*** The verb *va-yakrev,* here translated "he brought," has the general sense of presentation and does not necessarily imply a sacrificial offering. In

washed them with water. 7He put the tunic on him, girded
him with the sash, clothed him with the robe, and put the
ephod on him, girding him with the decorated band with
which he tied it to him. 8He put the breastpiece on him, and
put into the breastpiece the Urim and Thummim. 9And he

וַיִּרְחַץ אֹתָם בַּמָּיִם׃ 7 וַיִּתֵּן עָלָיו אֶת־הַכֻּתֹּנֶת
וַיַּחְגֹּר אֹתוֹ בָּאַבְנֵט וַיַּלְבֵּשׁ אֹתוֹ אֶת־הַמְּעִיל וַיִּתֵּן
עָלָיו אֶת־הָאֵפֹד וַיַּחְגֹּר אֹתוֹ בְּחֵשֶׁב הָאֵפֹד וַיֶּאְפֹּד
לוֹ בּוֹ׃ *8 וַיָּשֶׂם עָלָיו אֶת־הַחֹשֶׁן וַיִּתֵּן אֶל־הַחֹשֶׁן
אֶת־הָאוּרִים וְאֶת־הַתֻּמִּים׃ 9 וַיָּשֶׂם אֶת־הַמִּצְנֶפֶת

v. 8. חצי התורה בפסוקים

Numbers 8:9 we read that the Levites, like the priests, were brought into God's presence when they were to be consecrated.

and washed them with water Ablutions are a universal feature of religious ritual. Beyond the obvious hygienic advantages of water, its utilization in ritual also serves to purify symbolically. Ibn Ezra indicates that the formula "to wash the body" refers to bathing, but the verb *r-ḥ-ts,* "to wash," used alone, refers to only the hands and feet. In rabbinic idiom this rite is called ***kiddush yadayim ve-raglayim,*** "the sanctification of hands and feet."[9] Water for ablutions was provided in a basin (*kiyyor*) that was located in the inner section of the Tabernacle courtyard.[10] In the Temple of Jerusalem there was a large basin called *yam,* "sea," as well as ten mobile basins.[11] Purification by water continued to have great significance in postbiblical Judaism, as it did in Christianity and Islam.

7. ***He put the tunic on him*** There were, in all, eight vestments worn by the High Priest, of which four were unique to him. They are described in Exodus 28 and again in Exodus 39; here they are merely mentioned by name.

It is to be assumed that at the beginning of the robing the priests were wearing their linen breeches (*mikhnasayim*).[12] There is no mention of sandals, for they undoubtedly officiated barefoot, which would conform to ancient Israelite notions of proper dress in sacred places. According to Exodus 3:5 and Joshua 5:15, Moses and Joshua, respectively, were instructed to remove their sandals when standing on sacred ground.[13]

The High Priest donned a fringed linen tunic (*kuttonet*)[14] that was tied with a sash (*'avnet*). This was followed by the robe (*me'il*), also known as *me'il ha-'efod,* "the *'efod* robe," because the *'efod* was worn over it. This robe was made of purple wool and had golden bells attached to it. Between each bell was a cloth pomegranate. The *'efod* was attached to the robe by a decorated band called *ḥeshev.* The *'efod* itself was made of wool and linen with gold threads woven into the fabric, giving it a golden appearance. Two lapis lazuli stones (*shoham*), each engraved with the names of six of the twelve tribes of Israel, were attached to the shoulder pads, called *kitfot ha-'efod.*

The word *'efod* is cognate with Akkadian *epattu,* "a costly garment." Not all biblical descriptions of it are consistent. At times it appears that the Bible is speaking of something other than a garment, perhaps a statue or an upright object. In Judges 8:7, Gideon "sets up" an *'efod* in his hometown, and in Judges 18:18, the term *pesel ha-'efod,* "the *'efod* statue," is used in reference to the idol of Micah. Actually, all biblical references to the *'efod* probably indicate the same phenomenon, but represent its changing manifestation at different stages of Israelite history. The term itself is pre-Israelite and was originally used in the context of robing statues of gods in richly ornamented, golden garments. This explains the usage in Judges, where Micah's *'efod* meets with disapproval. It was a vestige of pre-monotheistic practice, like the idol of Micah itself. Because priests, and occasionally kings, were deemed sacred persons, it was customary to utilize garments of the types that had been common to both priests and statues of gods, even though there was no longer any place for the statues themselves in the legitimate Israelite cult.[15]

8. ***He put the breastpiece on him*** The breastpiece (*ḥoshen*) was made of wool and linen. Gold threads were woven into the fabric, and twelve gem stones were set into the almost metallic cloth. The name of one tribe of Israel was engraved on each stone. The *ḥoshen* was fashioned in the form of a square pouch, which served as a container for the Urim and Thummim.

and put into the breastpiece the Urim and Thummim The meanings of these terms, as well as the objects they designate, remain elusive. In form, the Urim and Thummim may have been fairly flat stones, similar to the *pūrū* used in Mesopotamia, and known in Hebrew as *purim* in the Megillah of Esther. Examples of such objects, which worked in the manner of dice or lots, have been

set the headdress on his head; and on the headdress, in front, he put the gold frontlet, the holy diadem—as the LORD had commanded Moses.

10Moses took the anointing oil and anointed the Tabernacle and all that was in it, thus consecrating them. 11He

עַל־רֹאשׁוֹ וַיָּשֶׂם עַל־הַמִּצְנֶפֶת אֶל־מוּל פָּנָיו אֵת
צִיץ הַזָּהָב נֵזֶר הַקֹּדֶשׁ כַּאֲשֶׁר צִוָּה יְהוָה אֶת־
מֹשֶׁה׃ 10 וַיִּקַּח מֹשֶׁה אֶת־שֶׁמֶן הַמִּשְׁחָה וַיִּמְשַׁח
אֶת־הַמִּשְׁכָּן וְאֶת־כָּל־אֲשֶׁר־בּוֹ וַיְקַדֵּשׁ אֹתָם׃

recovered in archaeological excavations.[16] In 1 Samuel 14:43 the verb used to describe their operation is *happilu,* "throw down!" Casting lots was the only form of divining the word of God sanctioned in the official monotheistic cult, which normally objected to the use of omens for predicting the future.[17]

Whereas the meaning of the word Thummim (*tummim*) is clear, deriving from a root meaning "to be complete, innocent," the etymology of Urim (*'urim*) has been disputed. Logically, it should mean the opposite of *tummim,* and on this basis it has been suggested that it derives from the root *'arar,* "to curse." If the face of the stones called *'urim* comes up in both of the lots, the verdict is unfavorable. A classic instance of the use of the Urim and Thummim is preserved in 1 Samuel 14: King Saul's orders have been disobeyed, and in order to discover the guilty parties, he has recourse to oracular inquiry of God. Hoping that his son, Jonathan, will not be identified by lot, he says to the Lord: "Show the Thummim," a verdict that would have cleared his son.[18]

The High Priest wore the Urim and Thummim when he entered the Tent, thereby calling attention to his oracular function in guiding the destiny of the Israelite people. Numbers 27:21 relates that when Joshua was appointed as Moses' successor, he was instructed to inquire of Eleazar, son of Aaron, the new High Priest, as to the verdict of the Urim.

9. And he set the headdress on his head Ordinary priests wore turbans (*migba'ot*), as we are told in verse 13, and only the High Priest wore the royal headdress (*mitsnefet*).[19] The diadem (*tsits*) was a crown of gold reserved for the High Priest and worn when he officiated inside the Tent of the Tabernacle complex.[20] On it were engraved the words *kodesh le-YHVH*, "Sacred to the LORD," indicating that the High Priest himself was a sanctified person, entirely devoted to his sacred functions.

Archaeologists have found artifacts and storage jars containing materials used in Temple ritual and bearing the word *kodesh* marked on them.[21] This practice is reflected in the prophecy of Zechariah 14:20–21. When the nations come to Jerusalem to celebrate the Sukkot festival, the bells of the horses will have the words *kodesh le-YHVH* inscribed on them, and every pot in Jerusalem will be *kodesh* so that offerings can be cooked in them. In Jeremiah 2:3 the entire people of Israel is symbolically referred to as *kodesh le-YHVH,* God's own people.

In verses 10–12 we read of two parallel acts: the consecration of Aaron, the High Priest, and the consecration of the altar and the Tabernacle with its vessels. Both were accomplished by the same means—anointing with (the same) oil. In this way Aaron, too, became a sacred vessel.

Oil, universally used as an unguent and cleanser, has, like water, also assumed a religious, and even legal, significance. Pouring oil over cultic objects, as over persons—kings and priests—confers a special status. In biblical Israel kings were anointed by prophets, and Elisha was anointed by his master, Elijah. The oil was usually poured from a bowl or a horn. The consecration of Aaron, the High Priest, by the prophet Moses parallels the anointing of kings by prophets.[22]

After the sons of Aaron were robed, the sacrifices of ordination commenced. A sin offering, along the lines of what is prescribed in 4:3–12, was brought. It was of the type required when the High Priest inadvertently committed an offense and was thus suitable for his initial purification (vv. 13–17). Then the ordination rites commenced. Two rams were used, one as an *'olah,* "burnt offering," and the other as the actual sacrifice of investiture. The sacrifice of investiture was offered in a manner similar to the *shelamim,* "sacred gifts of greeting," as prescribed in chapter 3 and in 7:11f. Unleavened cakes and wafers were employed as an additional sacrificial ingredient.

Blood from the sacrifice of investiture was applied to the extremities of the priests, a rite of purification elsewhere prescribed for those suffering from certain dangerous ailments (vv. 18–29). Finally, a mixture of oil and water was dabbed on the persons of Aaron and his sons, after they had donned their respective vestments. The priests then partook of portions of the sacrifice of investiture; they were to remain inside the Tabernacle for seven days (vv. 30–36).

sprinkled some of it on the altar seven times, anointing the altar, all its utensils, and the laver with its stand, to consecrate them. 12He poured some of the anointing oil upon Aaron's head and anointed him, to consecrate him. 13Moses then brought Aaron's sons forward, clothed them in tunics, girded them with sashes, and wound turbans upon them, as the LORD had commanded Moses.

14He led forward the bull of sin offering. Aaron and his sons laid their hands upon the head of the bull of sin offering, 15and it was slaughtered. Moses took the blood and with his finger put some on each of the horns of the altar, cleansing the altar; then he poured out the blood at the base of the altar. Thus he consecrated it in order to make expiation upon it.

16Moses then took all the fat that was about the entrails, and the protuberance of the liver, and the two kidneys and their fat, and turned them into smoke on the altar. 17The rest of the bull, its hide, its flesh, and its dung, he put to the fire outside the camp—as the LORD had commanded Moses.

18Then he brought forward the ram of burnt offering. Aaron and his sons laid their hands upon the ram's head, 19and it was slaughtered. Moses dashed the blood against all sides of the altar. 20The ram was cut up into sections and Moses turned the head, the sections, and the suet into smoke on the altar; 21Moses washed the entrails and the

11 וַיַּז מִמֶּנּוּ עַל־הַמִּזְבֵּחַ שֶׁבַע פְּעָמִים וַיִּמְשַׁח
אֶת־הַמִּזְבֵּחַ וְאֶת־כָּל־כֵּלָיו וְאֶת־הַכִּיֹּר וְאֶת־כַּנּוֹ
לְקַדְּשָׁם׃ 12 וַיִּצֹק מִשֶּׁמֶן הַמִּשְׁחָה עַל רֹאשׁ אַהֲרֹן
וַיִּמְשַׁח אֹתוֹ לְקַדְּשׁוֹ׃ 13 וַיַּקְרֵב מֹשֶׁה אֶת־בְּנֵי
אַהֲרֹן וַיַּלְבִּשֵׁם כֻּתֳּנֹת וַיַּחְגֹּר אֹתָם אַבְנֵט וַיַּחֲבֹשׁ
לָהֶם מִגְבָּעוֹת כַּאֲשֶׁר צִוָּה יְהוָה אֶת־מֹשֶׁה׃
חמישי 14 וַיַּגֵּשׁ אֵת פַּר הַחַטָּאת וַיִּסְמֹךְ אַהֲרֹן
וּבָנָיו אֶת־יְדֵיהֶם עַל־רֹאשׁ פַּר הַחַטָּאת׃
15 וַיִּשְׁחָט וַיִּקַּח מֹשֶׁה אֶת־הַדָּם וַיִּתֵּן עַל־קַרְנוֹת
הַמִּזְבֵּחַ סָבִיב בְּאֶצְבָּעוֹ וַיְחַטֵּא אֶת־הַמִּזְבֵּחַ
וְאֶת־הַדָּם יָצַק אֶל־יְסוֹד הַמִּזְבֵּחַ וַיְקַדְּשֵׁהוּ לְכַפֵּר
עָלָיו׃ 16 וַיִּקַּח אֶת־כָּל־הַחֵלֶב אֲשֶׁר עַל־הַקֶּרֶב
וְאֵת יֹתֶרֶת הַכָּבֵד וְאֶת־שְׁתֵּי הַכְּלָיֹת וְאֶת־חֶלְבְּהֶן
וַיַּקְטֵר מֹשֶׁה הַמִּזְבֵּחָה׃ 17 וְאֶת־הַפָּר וְאֶת־עֹרוֹ
וְאֶת־בְּשָׂרוֹ וְאֶת־פִּרְשׁוֹ שָׂרַף בָּאֵשׁ מִחוּץ לַמַּחֲנֶה
כַּאֲשֶׁר צִוָּה יְהוָה אֶת־מֹשֶׁה׃ 18 וַיַּקְרֵב אֵת אֵיל
הָעֹלָה וַיִּסְמְכוּ אַהֲרֹן וּבָנָיו אֶת־יְדֵיהֶם עַל־רֹאשׁ
הָאָיִל׃ 19 וַיִּשְׁחָט וַיִּזְרֹק מֹשֶׁה אֶת־הַדָּם עַל־
הַמִּזְבֵּחַ סָבִיב׃ 20 וְאֶת־הָאַיִל נִתַּח לִנְתָחָיו וַיַּקְטֵר
מֹשֶׁה אֶת־הָרֹאשׁ וְאֶת־הַנְּתָחִים וְאֶת־הַפָּדֶר׃

14. He led forward the bull of sin offering Large cattle were used in sin offerings associated with purification when the entire community and the High Priest, in particular, were affected. We observe this in 4:3–12 and in chapter 16.

15. and it was slaughtered Literally, *va-yishḥat,* meaning "he slaughtered"; but third person verbs can be translated as passives when no subject is specified. The verb *y-ts-k,* "to pour," usually refers to water, and only here and in 9:9 is it used with respect to pouring sacrificial blood. The usual verb is *sh-f-kh,* "to pour."[23]

cleansing the altar Rather, "removing the altar's impurities." Hebrew *ḥitte',* a verb in the Piel stem, has the force of undoing or removing the effects of the action conveyed by the Kal stem. Thus, *ḥata'* means "to commit an offense," and *ḥitte'* means "to remove an offense."[24]

Thus he consecrated it in order to make expiation upon it Rather, "Thus he consecrated it for making expiation upon it." Hebrew *le-khapper* always means "to expiate, to perform rites of expiation." The sense here is that the altar was consecrated for the purpose of making expiation, since expiatory sacrifices required an altar.

16. Moses then took all the fat For the procedures involved in the laws of verses 16–20, see Comments to 4:8–12, 19–20, and 16:6.

17. he put the fire outside the camp This requirement is rephrased in Ezekiel 43:21.

18. Then he brought forth the ram of burnt offering The procedures for the *'olah* correspond to what is prescribed in chapter 1. The function of the *'olah* was to evoke a favorable response from the Deity prior to approaching Him with other sacrifices.[25]

legs with water and turned all of the ram into smoke. That
was a burnt offering for a pleasing odor, an offering by fire
to the LORD—as the LORD had commanded Moses.
22He brought forward the second ram, the ram of ordination. Aaron and his sons laid their hands upon the ram's
head, 23and it was slaughtered. Moses took some of its
blood and put it on the ridge of Aaron's right ear, and on
the thumb of his right hand, and on the big toe of his right
foot. 24Moses then brought forward the sons of Aaron, and
put some of the blood on the ridges of their right ears, and
on the thumbs of their right hands, and on the big toes of
their right feet; and the rest of the blood Moses dashed
against every side of the altar. 25He took the fat—the broad
tail, all the fat about the entrails, the protuberance of the
liver, and the two kidneys and their fat—and the right
thigh. 26From the basket of unleavened bread that was
before the LORD, he took one cake of unleavened bread, one
cake of oil bread, and one wafer, and placed them on the fat
parts and on the right thigh. 27He placed all these on the
palms of Aaron and on the palms of his sons, and elevated
them as an elevation offering before the LORD. 28Then

21 וְאֶת־הַקֶּרֶב וְאֶת־הַכְּרָעַיִם רָחַץ בַּמָּיִם וַיַּקְטֵר
מֹשֶׁה אֶת־כָּל־הָאַיִל הַמִּזְבֵּחָה עֹלָה הוּא לְרֵיחַ־
נִיחֹחַ אִשֶּׁה הוּא לַיהוָה כַּאֲשֶׁר צִוָּה יְהוָה אֶת־
מֹשֶׁה׃ ששי 22 וַיַּקְרֵב אֶת־הָאַיִל הַשֵּׁנִי אֵיל
הַמִּלֻּאִים וַיִּסְמְכוּ אַהֲרֹן וּבָנָיו אֶת־יְדֵיהֶם עַל־
רֹאשׁ הָאָיִל׃ 23 וַיִּשְׁחָט ׀ וַיִּקַּח מֹשֶׁה מִדָּמוֹ וַיִּתֵּן
עַל־תְּנוּךְ אֹזֶן־אַהֲרֹן הַיְמָנִית וְעַל־בֹּהֶן יָדוֹ הַיְמָנִית
וְעַל־בֹּהֶן רַגְלוֹ הַיְמָנִית׃ 24 וַיַּקְרֵב אֶת־בְּנֵי אַהֲרֹן
וַיִּתֵּן מֹשֶׁה מִן־הַדָּם עַל־תְּנוּךְ אָזְנָם הַיְמָנִית וְעַל־
בֹּהֶן יָדָם הַיְמָנִית וְעַל־בֹּהֶן רַגְלָם הַיְמָנִית וַיִּזְרֹק
מֹשֶׁה אֶת־הַדָּם עַל־הַמִּזְבֵּחַ סָבִיב׃ 25 וַיִּקַּח אֶת־
הַחֵלֶב וְאֶת־הָאַלְיָה וְאֶת־כָּל־הַחֵלֶב אֲשֶׁר עַל־
הַקֶּרֶב וְאֵת יֹתֶרֶת הַכָּבֵד וְאֶת־שְׁתֵּי הַכְּלָיֹת
וְאֶת־חֶלְבְּהֶן וְאֵת שׁוֹק הַיָּמִין׃ 26 וּמִסַּל הַמַּצּוֹת
אֲשֶׁר ׀ לִפְנֵי יְהוָה לָקַח חַלַּת מַצָּה אַחַת וְחַלַּת
לֶחֶם שֶׁמֶן אַחַת וְרָקִיק אֶחָד וַיָּשֶׂם עַל־הַחֲלָבִים
וְעַל שׁוֹק הַיָּמִין׃ 27 וַיִּתֵּן אֶת־הַכֹּל עַל כַּפֵּי אַהֲרֹן
וְעַל כַּפֵּי בָנָיו וַיָּנֶף אֹתָם תְּנוּפָה לִפְנֵי יְהוָה׃

22. He brought forward the second ram, the ram of ordination The Hebrew term *millu'im,* "ordination," literally means "filling" the hands, a symbolic act that transfers or confers status or office.[26] Further on, in verses 27–29, we read that parts of the offerings were actually placed on the palms of Aaron and his sons, who raised them in a presentation to God. The biblical formula *mille' yad,* "to fill the hand," is limited to the appointment of priests and cultic officials.[27]

The ram of ordination was offered in the manner of the *shelamim,* "sacred gifts of greeting," with certain differences arising from the particular character of this occasion.

23. Moses took some of its blood . . . Aaron's right ear Dabbing sacrificial blood on certain extremities of the body is essentially a rite of purification, a procedure that was followed in the case of one who suffered from an acute skin disease, according to the legislation of 14:14f., where this rite is explained in greater detail. In this manner Aaron and his sons were purified as they entered into their new status.

24. and the rest of the blood Moses dashed against every side of the altar It is significant that the remainder of the blood taken from the ram of ordination is cast upon the altar. This is analogous to what occurred at the enactment of the Sinaitic covenant, as recounted in Exodus 24:6–8. On that occasion part of the blood was cast upon the altar, which represented God as one of the "parties" to the covenant, and the rest of the blood was cast over the people, the other party. In the ordination of the priests, the sacrificial blood served a dual function: It purified the priests and also bound them in a covenant of service to God in His Tabernacle.[28]

Perhaps the grain offerings of unleavened dough, of cakes and wafers, were included here so that a representation of all the major classes of sacrifices would be offered by the newly ordained priests. The names of the specific ingredients are explained in the Comment to 2:4.

27. He placed all these on the palms of Aaron . . . and elevated them Rather, the Hebrew term *tenufah* is explained in the Comment to 7:30.

Included here among the parts of the ordination sacrifice burned on the altar was the thigh (*shok*), which, according to the provisions of 7:32f., belonged to the priests. In the rites of ordination, the priests surrendered their own portion to God, since it had been offered on their behalf, and it would have been improper for the priests to benefit from what was offered on their own behalf. Only

Moses took them from their hands and turned them into smoke on the altar with the burnt offering. This was an ordination offering for a pleasing odor; it was an offering by fire to the LORD. 29Moses took the breast and elevated it as an elevation offering before the LORD; it was Moses' portion of the ram of ordination—as the LORD had commanded Moses.

30And Moses took some of the anointing oil and some of the blood that was on the altar and sprinkled it upon Aaron and upon his vestments, and also upon his sons and upon their vestments. Thus he consecrated Aaron and his vestments, and also his sons and their vestments.

31Moses said to Aaron and his sons: Boil the flesh at the entrance of the Tent of Meeting and eat it there with the bread that is in the basket of ordination—as I commanded: Aaron and his sons shall eat it; 32and what is left over of the flesh and the bread you shall consume in fire. 33You shall not go outside the entrance of the Tent of Meeting for seven days, until the day that your period of ordination is completed. For your ordination will require seven days. 34Everything done today, the LORD has commanded to be done [seven days], to make expiation for you. 35You shall

28 וַיִּקַּח מֹשֶׁה אֹתָם מֵעַל כַּפֵּיהֶם וַיַּקְטֵר הַמִּזְבֵּחָה
עַל־הָעֹלָה מִלֻּאִים הֵם לְרֵיחַ נִיחֹחַ אִשֶּׁה הוּא
לַיהוָה׃ 29 וַיִּקַּח מֹשֶׁה אֶת־הֶחָזֶה וַיְנִיפֵהוּ תְנוּפָה
לִפְנֵי יְהוָה מֵאֵיל הַמִּלֻּאִים לְמֹשֶׁה הָיָה לְמָנָה
כַּאֲשֶׁר צִוָּה יְהוָה אֶת־מֹשֶׁה׃ שביעי 30 וַיִּקַּח
מֹשֶׁה מִשֶּׁמֶן הַמִּשְׁחָה וּמִן־הַדָּם אֲשֶׁר עַל־הַמִּזְבֵּחַ
וַיַּז עַל־אַהֲרֹן עַל־בְּגָדָיו וְעַל־בָּנָיו וְעַל־בִּגְדֵי בָנָיו
אִתּוֹ וַיְקַדֵּשׁ אֶת־אַהֲרֹן אֶת־בְּגָדָיו וְאֶת־בָּנָיו וְאֶת־
בִּגְדֵי בָנָיו אִתּוֹ׃ 31 וַיֹּאמֶר מֹשֶׁה אֶל־אַהֲרֹן וְאֶל־
בָּנָיו בַּשְּׁלוּ אֶת־הַבָּשָׂר פֶּתַח אֹהֶל מוֹעֵד וְשָׁם
תֹּאכְלוּ אֹתוֹ וְאֶת־הַלֶּחֶם אֲשֶׁר בְּסַל הַמִּלֻּאִים
כַּאֲשֶׁר צִוֵּיתִי לֵאמֹר אַהֲרֹן וּבָנָיו יֹאכְלֻהוּ׃
32 וְהַנּוֹתָר בַּבָּשָׂר וּבַלָּחֶם בָּאֵשׁ תִּשְׂרֹפוּ׃ מפטיר
33 וּמִפֶּתַח אֹהֶל מוֹעֵד לֹא תֵצְאוּ שִׁבְעַת יָמִים
עַד יוֹם מְלֹאת יְמֵי מִלֻּאֵיכֶם כִּי שִׁבְעַת יָמִים
יְמַלֵּא אֶת־יֶדְכֶם׃ 34 כַּאֲשֶׁר עָשָׂה בַּיּוֹם הַזֶּה צִוָּה
יְהוָה לַעֲשֹׂת לְכַפֵּר עֲלֵיכֶם׃ 35 וּפֶתַח אֹהֶל מוֹעֵד

when they were of service to others could they benefit in this way.[29] Therefore, the procedure was altered, and Moses, as the officiant, received his portion (*manah*), consisting of the breast (*ḥazeh*), which he, in turn, contributed to the priests as a gift.

30. *And Moses took some of the anointing oil* A mixture of anointing oil and sacrificial blood was sprinkled on Aaron and his sons and upon their vestments, and this completed their ordination.[30]

31. *Moses said to Aaron* Moses instructed Aaron and his sons on how to dispose of the meat of the ordination sacrifice, that is, the breast, Moses' own portion of the sacrifice. We are probably to read the passive form, *tsuvveiti,* "I was commanded," instead of *tsivveiti,* "I have commanded." This passive form occurs in verse 35 in a similar context. It was vital to the efficacy of the ordination sacrifice that the priests actually partake of it. Only in this way would they join in the sacred meal in the presence of the Lord.[31]

32. *and what is left over* What was not eaten had to be destroyed. See Comment to 7:17.

33. *You shall not go outside the entrance of the Tent of Meeting for seven days* Here again, the designation "entrance of the Tent" has to be understood in context. The priests were not inside the Tent but, rather, near its entrance, in the inner section of the Tabernacle courtyard. They were not to leave this sanctified area for seven days in order to avoid contact with anything or anyone impure.[32]

for seven days, until the day that your period of ordination is completed The practical impact of this statement is difficult to ascertain. In the parallel passages of Exodus 29:35–37 it is explicitly ordained that a sin offering was to be offered each day for seven days and that the altar was to be repeatedly anointed for seven days. Here it merely states that the "filling of the hands" was to last for seven days. Does this mean that the ordination sacrifice was to be repeated each day, for seven days, and does the beginning of verse 34 indicate that what was done on the first day was to be repeated seven times? Most traditional commentaries are of this opinion.[33]

remain at the entrance of the Tent of Meeting day and
night for seven days, keeping the LORD's charge—that you
may not die—for so I have been commanded.
36And Aaron and his sons did all the things that the LORD
had commanded through Moses.

תֵּשְׁבוּ יוֹמָם וָלַיְלָה שִׁבְעַת יָמִים וּשְׁמַרְתֶּם אֶת־
מִשְׁמֶרֶת יְהוָה וְלֹא תָמוּתוּ כִּי־כֵן צֻוֵּיתִי׃ 36 וַיַּעַשׂ
אַהֲרֹן וּבָנָיו אֵת כָּל־הַדְּבָרִים אֲשֶׁר־צִוָּה יְהוָה
בְּיַד־מֹשֶׁה׃ ס

SHEMINI

9 On the eighth day Moses called Aaron and his sons, and
the elders of Israel. 2He said to Aaron: "Take a calf of the
herd for a sin offering and a ram for a burnt offering,
without blemish, and bring them before the LORD. 3And
speak to the Israelites, saying: Take a he-goat for a sin
offering; a calf and a lamb, yearlings without blemish, for a
burnt offering; 4and an ox and a ram for an offering of well-
being to sacrifice before the LORD; and a meal offering with
oil mixed in. For today the LORD will appear to you."
5They brought to the front of the Tent of Meeting the
things that Moses had commanded, and the whole community came forward and stood before the LORD. 6Moses said:
"This is what the LORD has commanded that you do, that
the Presence of the LORD may appear to you." 7Then Moses

שמיני

ט וַיְהִי בַּיּוֹם הַשְּׁמִינִי קָרָא מֹשֶׁה לְאַהֲרֹן וּלְבָנָיו
וּלְזִקְנֵי יִשְׂרָאֵל׃ 2 וַיֹּאמֶר אֶל־אַהֲרֹן קַח־לְךָ עֵגֶל
בֶּן־בָּקָר לְחַטָּאת וְאַיִל לְעֹלָה תְּמִימִם וְהַקְרֵב
לִפְנֵי יְהוָה׃ 3 וְאֶל־בְּנֵי יִשְׂרָאֵל תְּדַבֵּר לֵאמֹר קְחוּ
שְׂעִיר־עִזִּים לְחַטָּאת וְעֵגֶל וָכֶבֶשׂ בְּנֵי־שָׁנָה
תְּמִימִם לְעֹלָה׃ 4 וְשׁוֹר וָאַיִל לִשְׁלָמִים לִזְבֹּחַ
לִפְנֵי יְהוָה וּמִנְחָה בְּלוּלָה בַשָּׁמֶן כִּי הַיּוֹם יְהוָה
נִרְאָה אֲלֵיכֶם׃ 5 וַיִּקְחוּ אֵת אֲשֶׁר צִוָּה מֹשֶׁה אֶל־
פְּנֵי אֹהֶל מוֹעֵד וַיִּקְרְבוּ כָּל־הָעֵדָה וַיַּעַמְדוּ לִפְנֵי
יְהוָה׃ 6 וַיֹּאמֶר מֹשֶׁה זֶה הַדָּבָר אֲשֶׁר־צִוָּה יְהוָה
תַּעֲשׂוּ וְיֵרָא אֲלֵיכֶם כְּבוֹד יְהוָה׃ 7 וַיֹּאמֶר מֹשֶׁה

35. keeping the LORD's charge The "charge" consisted of following the instructions given on this occasion. Hebrew *mishmeret* may connote "guarding" against violations.[34]

CHAPTER 9 THE FIRST CELEBRATION OF SACRIFICE (vv. 1–24)

Shemini

Chapter 9 describes what occurred after the seven days of ordination. At that time, on the eighth day, the Tabernacle altar was used for the first time in the performance of sacrificial worship on behalf of the people of Israel. As in chapter 8, this chapter too is introduced (vv. 1–7) by instructions regarding the rites to be described subsequently. All the necessary materials are assembled and the congregation gathers in the outer section of the Tabernacle courtyard.

1. On the eighth day Moses called Aaron . . . and the elders of Israel The "elders" (*zekenim*) represented the people. Their functions and status are discussed in the Comment to 4:15.

2. He said to Aaron: "Take a calf of the herd" In the Comment to 8:18 the combination of sin offering and burnt offering is explained. The difference is that here the entire people is involved, not only the priesthood, as in chapter 8. A sequence of sin offering and burnt offering was ordained both for the priesthood and for the people.

4. For today the LORD will appear to you This is the main purpose of the celebrations, as we read explicitly in verse 6.

5. that Moses had commanded Moses had an enhanced role in this celebration as the transmitter of God's commands. In Leviticus, it is usually God who commands, not Moses.

said to Aaron: "Come forward to the altar and sacrifice
your sin offering and your burnt offering, making expiation
for yourself and for the people; and sacrifice the people's
offering and make expiation for them, as the LORD has
commanded."
8 Aaron came forward to the altar and slaughtered his calf
of sin offering. 9 Aaron's sons brought the blood to him; he
dipped his finger in the blood and put it on the horns of the
altar; and he poured out the rest of the blood at the base of
the altar. 10 The fat, the kidneys, and the protuberance of
the liver from the sin offering he turned into smoke on the
altar—as the LORD had commanded Moses; 11 and the flesh
and the skin were consumed in fire outside the camp.
12 Then he slaughtered the burnt offering. Aaron's sons
passed the blood to him, and he dashed it against all sides
of the altar. 13 They passed the burnt offering to him in
sections, as well as the head, and he turned it into smoke on
the altar. 14 He washed the entrails and the legs, and turned
them into smoke on the altar with the burnt offering.
15 Next he brought forward the people's offering. He took
the goat for the people's sin offering, and slaughtered it,
and presented it as a sin offering like the previous one. 16 He
brought forward the burnt offering and sacrificed it according to regulation. 17 He then brought forward the meal
offering and, taking a handful of it, he turned it into smoke
on the altar—in addition to the burnt offering of the morning. 18 He slaughtered the ox and the ram, the people's

אֶל־אַהֲרֹן קְרַב אֶל־הַמִּזְבֵּחַ וַעֲשֵׂה אֶת־חַטָּאתְךָ
וְאֶת־עֹלָתֶךָ וְכַפֵּר בַּעַדְךָ וּבְעַד הָעָם וַעֲשֵׂה אֶת־
קָרְבַּן הָעָם וְכַפֵּר בַּעֲדָם כַּאֲשֶׁר צִוָּה יְהוָה׃
8 וַיִּקְרַב אַהֲרֹן אֶל־הַמִּזְבֵּחַ וַיִּשְׁחַט אֶת־עֵגֶל
הַחַטָּאת אֲשֶׁר־לוֹ׃ 9 וַיַּקְרִבוּ בְּנֵי אַהֲרֹן אֶת־הַדָּם
אֵלָיו וַיִּטְבֹּל אֶצְבָּעוֹ בַּדָּם וַיִּתֵּן עַל־קַרְנוֹת
הַמִּזְבֵּחַ וְאֶת־הַדָּם יָצַק אֶל־יְסוֹד הַמִּזְבֵּחַ׃ 10 וְאֶת־
הַחֵלֶב וְאֶת־הַכְּלָיֹת וְאֶת־הַיֹּתֶרֶת מִן־הַכָּבֵד מִן־
הַחַטָּאת הִקְטִיר הַמִּזְבֵּחָה כַּאֲשֶׁר צִוָּה יְהוָה אֶת־
מֹשֶׁה׃ 11 וְאֶת־הַבָּשָׂר וְאֶת־הָעוֹר שָׂרַף בָּאֵשׁ
מִחוּץ לַמַּחֲנֶה׃ 12 וַיִּשְׁחַט אֶת־הָעֹלָה וַיַּמְצִאוּ בְּנֵי
אַהֲרֹן אֵלָיו אֶת־הַדָּם וַיִּזְרְקֵהוּ עַל־הַמִּזְבֵּחַ סָבִיב׃
13 וְאֶת־הָעֹלָה הִמְצִיאוּ אֵלָיו לִנְתָחֶיהָ וְאֶת־
הָרֹאשׁ וַיַּקְטֵר עַל־הַמִּזְבֵּחַ׃ 14 וַיִּרְחַץ אֶת־הַקֶּרֶב
וְאֶת־הַכְּרָעָיִם וַיַּקְטֵר עַל־הָעֹלָה הַמִּזְבֵּחָה׃
15 וַיַּקְרֵב אֵת קָרְבַּן הָעָם וַיִּקַּח אֶת־שְׂעִיר
הַחַטָּאת אֲשֶׁר לָעָם וַיִּשְׁחָטֵהוּ וַיְחַטְּאֵהוּ כָּרִאשׁוֹן׃
16 וַיַּקְרֵב אֶת־הָעֹלָה וַיַּעֲשֶׂהָ כַּמִּשְׁפָּט׃ שני
17 וַיַּקְרֵב אֶת־הַמִּנְחָה וַיְמַלֵּא כַפּוֹ מִמֶּנָּה וַיַּקְטֵר
עַל־הַמִּזְבֵּחַ מִלְּבַד עֹלַת הַבֹּקֶר׃ 18 וַיִּשְׁחַט אֶת־

7. ***Then Moses said to Aaron: "Come forward to the altar"*** At this point, Moses turned over the conduct of the ritual to Aaron by inviting him to officiate at the altar for the first time.

making expiation for yourself and for the people This formulation is suggestive of what we find in 16:15–17 regarding the role of the High Priest on Yom Kippur. The sin offering of the priesthood indirectly served the people as well, but an additional sin offering on their behalf was required nevertheless.

9. ***Aaron's sons brought the blood to him*** This is a detail of procedure missing elsewhere. In 8:14,22 it is merely stated that the officiating priests "took" the blood. Practically speaking, it was necessary for another priest to assist the officiant; in Mishnah Yoma 4:3, 5:3, it is explained that a second priest held the sacrificial blood in a bowl and, later on in the ritual, handed it back to the officiant.

12. ***Aaron's sons passed the blood to him*** The rare form *va-yamtsi'u,* "they handed over, passed on," is unique to this chapter in all of Leviticus. In verse 9 the verb used is *va-yakrivu,* "they brought."

16. ***according to regulation*** On the meaning of Hebrew *ka-mishpat,* "according to regulation," see Comment to 5:10.

17. ***He then brought forward the meal offering and, taking a handful of it*** The Comment to 2:1 explains that Hebrew *minḥah* is better rendered "grain offering." A literal rendering of *va-yemalle' kappo mi-mennah* would read "He filled his palm with it," namely, with a fistful of the dough. Usually this act is described as "scooping a fistful," as in 2:2 and in 6:8, but the procedure is the same.

sacrifice of well-being. Aaron's sons passed the blood to him—which he dashed against every side of the altar—[19]and the fat parts of the ox and the ram: the broad tail, the covering [fat], the kidneys, and the protuberances of the livers. [20]They laid these fat parts over the breasts; and Aaron turned the fat parts into smoke on the altar, [21]and elevated the breasts and the right thighs as an elevation offering before the LORD—as Moses had commanded.

[22]Aaron lifted his hands toward the people and blessed them; and he stepped down after offering the sin offering, the burnt offering, and the offering of well-being. [23]Moses and Aaron then went inside the Tent of Meeting. When they came out, they blessed the people; and the Presence of the Lord appeared to all the people. [24]Fire came forth from

הַשּׁוֹר וְאֶת־הָאַ֫יִל זֶ֫בַח הַשְּׁלָמִ֫ים אֲשֶׁר לָעָ֑ם
וַיַּמְצִ֫אוּ בְּנֵ֣י אַהֲרֹן֙ אֶת־הַדָּם֙ אֵלָ֔יו וַיִּזְרְקֵ֖הוּ עַל־
הַמִּזְבֵּ֖חַ סָבִֽיב: 19 וְאֶת־הַחֲלָבִ֖ים מִן־הַשּׁ֔וֹר וּמִן־
הָאַ֔יִל הָֽאַלְיָ֤ה וְהַֽמְכַסֶּה֙ וְהַכְּלָיֹ֔ת וְיֹתֶ֖רֶת הַכָּבֵֽד:
20 וַיָּשִׂ֥ימוּ אֶת־הַחֲלָבִ֖ים עַל־הֶחָז֑וֹת וַיַּקְטֵ֥ר
הַחֲלָבִ֖ים הַמִּזְבֵּֽחָה: 21 וְאֵ֣ת הֶחָזוֹת֮ וְאֵת֮ שׁ֣וֹק
הַיָּמִין֒ הֵנִ֧יף אַהֲרֹ֛ן תְּנוּפָ֖ה לִפְנֵ֣י יְהוָ֑ה כַּאֲשֶׁ֖ר צִוָּ֥ה
מֹשֶֽׁה: 22 וַיִּשָּׂ֨א אַהֲרֹ֧ן אֶת־יָדָ֛ו אֶל־הָעָ֖ם וַֽיְבָרֲכֵ֑ם
וַיֵּ֗רֶד מֵעֲשֹׂ֧ת הַֽחַטָּ֛את וְהָעֹלָ֖ה וְהַשְּׁלָמִֽים: 23 וַיָּבֹ֨א
מֹשֶׁ֤ה וְאַֽהֲרֹן֙ אֶל־אֹ֣הֶל מוֹעֵ֔ד וַיֵּ֣צְא֔וּ וַיְבָרֲכ֖וּ אֶת־
הָעָ֑ם וַיֵּרָ֥א כְבוֹד־יְהוָ֖ה אֶל־כָּל־הָעָֽם: שלישי

v. 22. יָדָיו ק'

he turned it into smoke on the altar—in addition to the burnt offering of the morning   The formula ʿolat ha-boker, "the burnt offering of the morning," occurs several times in the Bible. It occurs in 2 Kings 16:15 as well as in Numbers 28:23 and Ezekiel 46:15. In all instances, ʿolat ha-boker refers to the daily burnt offering of the morning. Here such a sense would be problematic because the daily cult was not in force before the rites of investiture and dedication had been performed. Reference to "the burnt offering of the morning" would be anticipatory.

This difficulty is addressed in the Sifra, which identifies "the burnt offering of the morning" with the sacrifice just offered by the people on this very occasion, as described in verses 12–16. The grain offering specified here would have been made in addition to the special burnt offering, conforming to the common pattern whereby grain offerings accompany burnt offerings. The regimen here would then resemble the rites described in Exodus 40:29f., where both a burnt offering and a grain offering were performed at the dedication of the Tabernacle altar.

Nevertheless, it would be questionable to adopt a meaning for ʿolat ha-boker in this instance that differs from its meaning everywhere else. Critical scholarship raises the possibility that a later editor added this wording on the suggestion of Numbers 28–29, or perhaps of Exodus 29:38–46, where the daily burnt offerings are specifically ordained. Certainly, the wording here is strange, and traditional attempts to explain its occurrence are less than satisfactory.

18.   *He slaughtered the ox and the ram, the people's sacrifice of well-being*   Rather, "the people's sacred gifts of greeting." The extent of the sacrifice was greater than usual on this occasion, including both an ox and a ram. The procedures correspond to the provisions of chapter 3 and of 7:11f.

22.   *Aaron lifted his hands toward the people and blessed them*   According to the Sifra, followed by Rashi and some other commentators, the priestly blessing preserved in Numbers 6:22–27 was pronounced on this occasion: "The LORD bless you and keep you. . . ." Raising the hands was a characteristic gesture of prayer, directed toward God,[1] whereas here Aaron faced the people and raised his hands over them as he blessed them. This represents a variation on the usual significance of the act. In rabbinic Hebrew, this act is called nesiʾat kappayim, "the raising of the palms."[2]

and he stepped down   The sequence here is unclear. Aaron should first have stepped down and then blessed the people. Sensing this problem, Ibn Ezra took the verb va-yered as a pluperfect: "having stepped down," he blessed the people.

23.   *Moses and Aaron then went inside the Tent of Meeting*   It is unclear why Moses and Aaron entered the Tent at this time. The Sifra assumes that it was in order to pray for the anticipated appearance of God's presence (kavod). Ibn Ezra states that it was in order to pray for the miraculous ignition of the altar fire. The two views are not inconsistent. When God's presence appeared, a flame came forth from inside the Tent and ignited the altar fire, as we read in the following verse.

before the LORD and consumed the burnt offering and the fat parts on the altar. And all the people saw, and shouted, and fell on their faces.

24 וַתֵּצֵא אֵשׁ מִלִּפְנֵי יְהוָה וַתֹּאכַל עַל־הַמִּזְבֵּחַ
אֶת־הָעֹלָה וְאֶת־הַחֲלָבִים וַיַּרְא כָּל־הָעָם וַיָּרֹנּוּ
וַיִּפְּלוּ עַל־פְּנֵיהֶם׃

10 Now Aaron's sons Nadab and Abihu each took his fire
pan, put fire in it, and laid incense on it; and they offered
before the LORD alien fire, which He had not enjoined upon
them. 2And fire came forth from the LORD and consumed

י וַיִּקְחוּ בְנֵי־אַהֲרֹן נָדָב וַאֲבִיהוּא אִישׁ מַחְתָּתוֹ
וַיִּתְּנוּ בָהֵן אֵשׁ וַיָּשִׂימוּ עָלֶיהָ קְטֹרֶת וַיַּקְרִבוּ לִפְנֵי
יְהוָה אֵשׁ זָרָה אֲשֶׁר לֹא צִוָּה אֹתָם׃ 2 וַתֵּצֵא אֵשׁ

24. Fire came forth from before the LORD The Sifra interprets this as a fire from heaven. Rashbam more accurately identifies it as the fire of God that was inside the Tent, the same fire that would subsequently scald Nadab and Abihu, Aaron's two sons, when they entered the Tent improperly, according to 10:2. In both verses we have the same formulation: *va-tetse' 'esh mi-lifnei YHVH,* "Fire came forth from before the LORD." God's fire issued from the ***kavod,*** which itself was a fire that was enveloped in a thick cloud and pervaded the Tent. It was a blessing to those who pleased God but destructive to those who angered Him. On this occasion the ignition of the altar fire was cause for rejoicing.

CHAPTER 10

Admonitions on Priestly Conduct

Chapter 10, following the ordination of Aaron and his sons and the appearance of God's presence (***kavod***) at the newly consecrated Tabernacle, sets forth various regulations regarding appropriate priestly conduct. To emphasize the necessity of precise compliance with all the ritual laws, this chapter preserves a brief narrative of the untimely death of two of Aaron's sons, Nadab and Abihu; having made an improper incense offering, they were struck down by God's fire.

Like the story of Korah in Numbers 16–17, the story about Nadab and Abihu served as an admonition and as an object lesson. The tragedy of their punishment is echoed in several other Torah passages.[1]

The chapter may be divided into four discernible sections: (1) the death of Nadab and Abihu and its aftermath (vv. 1–7); (2) the regulations prohibiting priests from imbibing intoxicants prior to officiating in the cult (vv. 8–11); (3) a restatement of the requirement that priests eat their allotted portions from the sacrifices within specified areas (vv. 12–15); (4) Moses' instructions to Aaron and his remaining sons regarding the disposition of the sin offering that had been brought by the people as part of the dedication of the Tabernacle (vv. 16–20). Reference is to the sacrifice mentioned in 9:3 and described in 9:15–21.

Chapter 10 seems to bring to a conclusion the account of the traditions regarding the initiation and consecration of the Israelite priesthood that was treated in chapters 8–10.

THE DEATH OF NADAB AND ABIHU: A DRAMATIC PRECEDENT (vv. 1–7)

1. each took his fire pan, put fire in it Rather, "and put coals in it." Hebrew *'esh,* "fire," in fact refers to the embers placed on the fire pans (*maḥtot*). In Numbers 17:2, *'esh* is correctly translated "coals" and should be so rendered here as well.

alien fire, which He had not enjoined upon them Hebrew *'esh zarah,* "alien fire," refers to the incense itself. It could be translated "an alien [incense offering by] fire." The sense of Hebrew *zarah,* "alien," is elusive, and the "strangeness" implied has been variously interpreted. The text does not specify the offense committed by the two young priests; it merely states that they brought an

them; thus they died at the instance of the LORD. [3]Then Moses said to Aaron, "This is what the LORD meant when He said:

Through those near to Me I show Myself holy,
And gain glory before all the people."

מִלִּפְנֵי יְהוָה וַתֹּאכַל אוֹתָם וַיָּמֻתוּ לִפְנֵי יְהוָה׃
3 וַיֹּאמֶר מֹשֶׁה אֶל־אַהֲרֹן הוּא אֲשֶׁר־דִּבֶּר יְהוָה׀
לֵאמֹר בִּקְרֹבַי אֶקָּדֵשׁ וְעַל־פְּנֵי כָל־הָעָם אֶכָּבֵד
וַיִּדֹּם אַהֲרֹן׃ 4 וַיִּקְרָא מֹשֶׁה אֶל־מִישָׁאֵל וְאֶל

offering that had not been specifically ordained. The Sifra speculates that they brought a voluntary offering in celebration of the Tabernacle dedication. Various suggestions in the midrashim produce a composite of several possible offenses. In Leviticus Rabba we read: "Because of nearness (*kirvah*)—for they penetrated into the innermost section [of the sanctuary]. Because of 'sacrificing' (*krivah*)—for they brought an offering they were not enjoined to bring. Because of 'alien fire'—they brought coals inside [the sanctuary] which came from an oven (and not from the sacrificial altar)."[2]

The principle of this last interpretation has been adopted by a modern scholar, M. Haran, who suggests that the offense of the two priests lay in using incense brought from outside the sacred area between the altar and the entrance of the Tent of Meeting. It was therefore impure.[3] For the others, the midrashic interpretations play on the verb *k-r-v,* "to draw near, approach," reflected in *va-yakrivu,* "they brought near, presented," in verse 1. The first of these interpretations, that the offense consisted of penetrating too far into the sanctuary, is supported by the reference to this episode in 16:1–2. There Aaron is warned not to repeat the offense of his two sons by proceeding beyond the curtain (*parokhet*) in the sanctuary on any occasion other than Yom Kippur—"lest he die."

A possible key to the precise nature of the offense lies in the equivalence of two descriptive terms: *'esh zarah* in our text and *ketoret zarah,* "an alien incense offering," in Exodus 30:9. If *'esh zarah* is equivalent to *ketoret zarah* we may learn from Exodus 30:9 that it was forbidden to offer on the golden incense altar anything other than the daily incense offering. Aaron's two sons, then, violated the law of Exodus 30:9: Entering the Tent for an improper purpose, they met with death.

2. ***And fire came forth from the LORD*** This refers to the fire mentioned in 9:24, which came forth from inside the Tent of Meeting and consumed the sacrifices offered at the dedication of the Tabernacle, as explained by Rashbam. The phraseology here is similar to that of Numbers 16:35, where it is said that God's fire consumed Korah and his faction as they stood near the Tent of Meeting to offer incense that had been rejected by God. This suggests a similarity of theme, as well.

at the instance of the LORD Rather, "before the Lord." This formula identifies the place of death. Verses 4–5 state that Aaron's relatives removed the bodies of Nadab and Abihu "away from the front of the sanctuary," namely, from the spot where they died. It is logical, therefore, to conclude that verse 2 is also identifying the place of death, rather than informing us who caused their death.

3. ***Through those near to Me I show Myself holy*** The duly consecrated priests are "near" to God. Thus, we read in Ezekiel 42:13: "The northern chambers and the southern chambers . . . are the consecrated chambers in which the priests who have access to the LORD (*'asher kerovim le-YHVH*) shall eat the most holy offerings." Hebrew *karov* also serves as an official title, designating the courtier who is permitted to approach the king, as in Esther 1:14 or in Ezekiel 23:12, where governors and provincial rulers are called *kerovim,* members of the official inner circle. The priests enjoy a comparable position in the sanctuary.

Priests who adhere to the regulations of their office and protect the purity of the sanctuary sanctify God; and, in turn, the sanctuary is favored by God's presence. When, as happened in this case, they flout God's will, He exercises His punitive power, compelling all to recognize His authority.

The two sides of the coin are expressed quite clearly in other passages of the Torah. In 22:31–32 we read: "You shall faithfully observe My commandments: I am the LORD. You shall not profane My holy name, that I may be sanctified in the midst of the Israelite people. . . ." In contrast, we read in Numbers 20:12–13: "But the LORD said to Moses and Aaron, 'Because you did not trust Me enough to affirm My sanctity in the sight of the Israelite people, therefore you shall not lead this congregation into the land that I have given them.' Those are the Waters of Meribah—meaning that the Israelites quarrelled with the Lord—through which He affirmed His sanctity."

And Aaron was silent.
4Moses called Mishael and Elzaphan, sons of Uzziel the uncle of Aaron, and said to them, "Come forward and carry your kinsmen away from the front of the sanctuary to a place outside the camp."
5They came forward and carried them out of the camp by their tunics, as Moses had ordered.
6And Moses said to Aaron and to his sons Eleazar and Ithamar, "Do not bare your heads and do not rend your clothes, lest you die and anger strike the whole community. But your kinsmen, all the house of Israel, shall bewail the burning that the LORD has wrought.
7And so do not go

אֶלְצָפָן בְּנֵי עֻזִּיאֵל דֹּד אַהֲרֹן וַיֹּאמֶר אֲלֵהֶם קִרְבוּ
שְׂאוּ אֶת־אֲחֵיכֶם מֵאֵת פְּנֵי־הַקֹּדֶשׁ אֶל־מִחוּץ
לַמַּחֲנֶה׃ 5 וַיִּקְרְבוּ וַיִּשָּׂאֻם בְּכֻתֳּנֹתָם אֶל־מִחוּץ
לַמַּחֲנֶה כַּאֲשֶׁר דִּבֶּר מֹשֶׁה׃ 6 וַיֹּאמֶר מֹשֶׁה אֶל־
אַהֲרֹן וּלְאֶלְעָזָר וּלְאִיתָמָר ׀ בָּנָיו רָאשֵׁיכֶם אַל־
תִּפְרָעוּ ׀ וּבִגְדֵיכֶם לֹא־תִפְרֹמוּ וְלֹא תָמֻתוּ וְעַל
כָּל־הָעֵדָה יִקְצֹף וַאֲחֵיכֶם כָּל־בֵּית יִשְׂרָאֵל יִבְכּוּ
אֶת־הַשְּׂרֵפָה אֲשֶׁר שָׂרַף יְהוָה׃ 7 וּמִפֶּתַח אֹהֶל

Either way, God emerges triumphant, for He will not allow His sanctity to be compromised.[4]

And Aaron was silent Aaron accepted God's harsh judgment and did not cry out or complain at his painful loss.

4. ***sons of Uzziel the uncle of Aaron*** Aaron's cousins, who were the uncles of Nadab and Abihu, had the task of attending to the bodies of the two dead priests.

In ancient Israel, certain funerary functions may have been the traditional responsibility of one's close relatives. Amos 6:10 mentions that, in the destruction to come, one's uncle and his "burner" (*mesarefo'*), who may have been one and the same person, would remove from dwellings ravaged by fire the bones of those caught in the devastation. Thus, it may not have been coincidental that the uncles of Nadab and Abihu undertook to remove their bodies.

Ramban explains that it was necessary for Aaron's cousins to remove the bodies of the dead priests in this instance because the two remaining sons of Aaron, Eleazar and Ithamar, had just been consecrated as priests and could not defile themselves by contact with corpses. Normally, ordinary priests were permitted contact with corpses of close relatives, but not in this case.[5]

from the front of the sanctuary The sequence of events is difficult to reconstruct. The two priests had entered the Tent of Meeting. They were probably struck down as they were departing, when they were already in the courtyard outside the Tent.

to a place outside the camp The corpses had to be removed from the camp as was required in the case of any impure object. Relatively little is known of ancient Israelite burial customs, except that impurity resulting from contact with corpses was the most severe kind and a major concern in religious law. The dead were buried away from the settled areas.[6]

5. ***by their tunics*** This significant detail indicates that the bodies of the two priests were not completely consumed by God's fire. The faces of the priests were probably blasted by the flame, which killed them, but their bodies were not burned fully. The Hebrew verb *'akhal* usually means "to consume, destroy."[7] But when it is used to describe the action of fire, it may simply mean "to burn, blaze." The clothing worn by the priests was intact.[8]

6. ***"do not bare your heads and do not rend your clothes"*** The sense of the Hebrew verb *para'* is "to dishevel" the hair.[9] Such an act of mourning obviously involved baring the head. The verb *param,* "to rend," was interpreted in the Talmud as tearing along the seams of one's garment.[10]

lest you die This refers to death at the hand of God, as a punishment.[11]

and anger strike the whole community *Ketsef,* "wrath," and the verb *katsaf* have a particular force in biblical Hebrew, often suggesting a plague sent by God to punish those who have angered Him.[12]

As noted above, the particular circumstances surrounding the death of Nadab and Abihu—occurring at the time of their consecration and purification—prevented, indeed forbade, their father and brothers from mourning for them. Their sanctification took precedence. The rest of the people, however, were to mourn. The Hebrew verb *b-kh-h,* "to weep," means "to mourn" in the context of bereavement.[13] The period of mourning was customarily seven days.[14]

outside the entrance of the Tent of Meeting, lest you die, for the LORD's anointing oil is upon you." And they did as Moses had bidden.

⁸And the LORD spoke to Aaron, saying: ⁹Drink no wine or other intoxicant, you or your sons, when you enter the Tent of Meeting, that you may not die. This is a law for all time throughout the ages, ¹⁰for you must distinguish between the sacred and the profane, and between the unclean and the clean; ¹¹and you must teach the Israelites all the laws which the LORD has imparted to them through Moses.

¹²Moses spoke to Aaron and to his remaining sons, Eleazar and Ithamar: Take the meal offering that is left over from the LORD's offerings by fire and eat it unleavened beside the altar, for it is most holy. ¹³You shall eat it in the sacred precinct, inasmuch as it is your due, and that of your

מוֹעֵד֙ לֹ֣א תֵצֵ֔אוּ פֶּן־תָּמֻ֑תוּ כִּי־שֶׁ֛מֶן מִשְׁחַ֥ת יְהוָ֖ה עֲלֵיכֶ֑ם וַֽיַּעֲשׂ֖וּ כִּדְבַ֥ר מֹשֶֽׁה׃ פ 8 וַיְדַבֵּ֣ר יְהוָ֔ה אֶֽל־אַהֲרֹ֖ן לֵאמֹֽר׃ 9 יַ֣יִן וְשֵׁכָ֞ר אַל־תֵּ֣שְׁתְּ ׀ אַתָּ֣ה ׀ וּבָנֶ֣יךָ אִתָּ֗ךְ בְּבֹאֲכֶ֛ם אֶל־אֹ֥הֶל מוֹעֵ֖ד וְלֹ֣א תָמֻ֑תוּ חֻקַּ֥ת עוֹלָ֖ם לְדֹרֹתֵיכֶֽם׃ 10 וּֽלֲהַבְדִּ֔יל בֵּ֥ין הַקֹּ֖דֶשׁ וּבֵ֣ין הַחֹ֑ל וּבֵ֥ין הַטָּמֵ֖א וּבֵ֥ין הַטָּהֽוֹר׃ 11 וּלְהוֹרֹ֖ת אֶת־בְּנֵ֣י יִשְׂרָאֵ֑ל אֵ֚ת כָּל־הַ֣חֻקִּ֔ים אֲשֶׁ֨ר דִּבֶּ֧ר יְהוָ֛ה אֲלֵיהֶ֖ם בְּיַד־מֹשֶֽׁה׃ פ רביעי 12 וַיְדַבֵּ֨ר מֹשֶׁ֜ה אֶֽל־אַהֲרֹ֗ן וְאֶ֣ל אֶלְעָזָ֣ר וְאֶל־אִֽיתָמָ֣ר ׀ בָּנָיו֮ הַנּֽוֹתָרִים֒ קְח֣וּ אֶת־הַמִּנְחָ֗ה הַנּוֹתֶ֙רֶת֙ מֵאִשֵּׁ֣י יְהוָ֔ה וְאִכְל֥וּהָ מַצּ֖וֹת אֵ֣צֶל הַמִּזְבֵּ֑חַ כִּ֛י קֹ֥דֶשׁ קָֽדָשִׁ֖ים הִֽוא׃ 13 וַאֲכַלְתֶּ֤ם אֹתָהּ֙ בְּמָק֣וֹם

7. *And so do not go outside the entrance of the Tent of Meeting*   Here, as in other references to *petaḥ 'ohel mo'ed,* "the entrance of the Tent of Meeting," the Tent designates a large area, which included the inner section of the courtyard. It is not that the priests were restricted to the inside of the Tent throughout the period of mourning; they were merely forbidden to leave the sacred precinct of the inner court.[15]

for the LORD's anointing oil is upon you   The precise intent of this verse is not clear. According to 8:10–12 only Aaron was anointed with the special oil. Although he along with his sons had a mixture of the oil and sacrificial blood sprinkled on them (8:30) it is questionable whether that procedure would be referred to as anointment.

Actually, there are two distinct traditions concerning the anointing of the priesthood. According to chapter 8 and 21:10, the High Priest was distinguished because only he was anointed. But according to 7:35–36 and certain other traditions (cf. Exod. 40:15), Aaron's sons were also anointed. Our passage may reflect this second tradition.[16]

RULES FOR THE PRIESTHOOD   (vv. 8–15)

9. *Drink no wine or other intoxicant*   In biblical Hebrew *shekhar* does not usually mean "beer," as does Akkadian *shikāru,* for instance. Hebrew *shekhar* always occurs together with *yayin,* "wine," as is the case here.[17] The reference to *shekhar* in connection with the Nazirite in Numbers 6:3 makes it clear that beer is not intended because the Nazirite is prohibited only from drinking any grape product. Targum Onkelos translates *yayin ve-shekhar* as Aramaic *ḥamar u-meravvei,* "wine or intoxicant."

10. *for you must distinguish*   Verses 10 and 11 begin with infinitives, literally "to distinguish" and "to teach," but the force of these infinitives is imperative, as the translation indicates. Intoxicants were forbidden to the priests precisely because imbibing them would impair their faculties and they would not be able to distinguish between the sacred and the profane. This responsibility is emphasized throughout Leviticus and in Ezekiel 44:23 as well. It is likely that, in using this occasion to stress the major roles of the priesthood, the text is linking the restriction on intoxicants to the horrendous deaths of Aaron's two sons.

12. *Take the meal offering*   This refers to the grain offering presented by the people as part of the Tabernacle dedication, as stipulated in 9:4,17.

and eat it unleavened beside the altar   This procedure was ordained in 2:3 and in 6:7–11. That is the sense of "for so I have been commanded" at the end of verse 13 and the formula "as the

children, from the LORD's offerings by fire; for so I have been commanded. [14]But the breast of elevation offering and the thigh of gift offering you, and your sons and daughters with you, may eat in any clean place, for they have been assigned as a due to you and your children from the Israelites' sacrifices of well-being. [15]Together with the fat of fire offering, they must present the thigh of gift offering and the breast of elevation offering, which are to be elevated as an elevation offering before the LORD, and which are to be your due and that of your children with you for all time—as the LORD has commanded.

[16]Then Moses inquired about the goat of sin offering, and it had already been burned! He was angry with Eleazar and Ithamar, Aaron's remaining sons, and said, [17]"Why did you not eat the sin offering in the sacred area? For it is most holy, and He has given it to you to remove the guilt of the community and to make expiation for them before the LORD. [18]Since its blood was not brought inside the sanc-

קֹדֶשׁ כִּי חָקְךָ וְחָק־בָּנֶיךָ הוּא מֵאִשֵּׁי יְהוָה כִּי־כֵן
צֻוֵּיתִי׃ 14 וְאֵת חֲזֵה הַתְּנוּפָה וְאֵת ׀ שׁוֹק הַתְּרוּמָה
תֹּאכְלוּ בְּמָקוֹם טָהוֹר אַתָּה וּבָנֶיךָ וּבְנֹתֶיךָ אִתָּךְ
כִּי־חָקְךָ וְחָק־בָּנֶיךָ נִתְּנוּ מִזִּבְחֵי שַׁלְמֵי בְּנֵי
יִשְׂרָאֵל׃ 15 שׁוֹק הַתְּרוּמָה וַחֲזֵה הַתְּנוּפָה עַל אִשֵּׁי
הַחֲלָבִים יָבִיאוּ לְהָנִיף תְּנוּפָה לִפְנֵי יְהוָה וְהָיָה לְךָ
וּלְבָנֶיךָ אִתְּךָ לְחָק־עוֹלָם כַּאֲשֶׁר צִוָּה יְהוָה׃
חמישי 16 וְאֵת ׀ שְׂעִיר הַחַטָּאת דָּרֹשׁ דָּרַשׁ*
מֹשֶׁה וְהִנֵּה שֹׂרָף וַיִּקְצֹף עַל־אֶלְעָזָר וְעַל־אִיתָמָר
בְּנֵי אַהֲרֹן הַנּוֹתָרִם לֵאמֹר׃ 17 מַדּוּעַ לֹא־אֲכַלְתֶּם
אֶת־הַחַטָּאת בִּמְקוֹם הַקֹּדֶשׁ כִּי קֹדֶשׁ קָדָשִׁים
הִוא וְאֹתָהּ ׀ נָתַן לָכֶם לָשֵׂאת אֶת־עֲוֺן הָעֵדָה
לְכַפֵּר עֲלֵיהֶם לִפְנֵי יְהוָה׃ 18 הֵן לֹא־הוּבָא אֶת־

v. 16. דרש בראש שיטה והיא חצי התורה בתיבות

LORD has commanded" in verse 15. In 6:7 we are told that the priests must eat what is left of the grain offerings brought on behalf of Israelites "in front of the altar" (*'el penei ha-mizbeaḥ*). The difference in wording is probably insignificant.

inasmuch as it is your due On the meaning of the Hebrew term *ḥok,* see Comment to 6:11.

14. ***But the breast of elevation offering*** Rather, "of the presentation offering." The regulations governing the priests' allocation of portions from certain sacrifices are stipulated in 7:11–38, especially in 7:34f. The text of chapter 10 thus acknowledges the earlier ritual legislation in Leviticus as the source for what the Lord commands. It records compliance with what had been ordained.

MOSES MONITORS THE PRIESTS AND THE CULT (vv. 16–20)

16. ***Then Moses inquired about the goat of sin offering*** Reference is to the sin offering provided by the people as part of the dedication rites in 9:3,15. Rabbi Akiba makes this connection in the Sifra: The priests were required to eat certain portions of sin offerings within the sacred precincts, as is stipulated in 6:18,22.

Upon inquiry, Moses learned that on this occasion the priestly portions of the sin offering had been burned on the altar—the priests had not eaten them as they were supposed to. Having disobeyed their instructions, they incurred Moses' anger. He spoke to Aaron's sons in deference to Aaron himself.

17. ***For it is most holy, and He has given it to you to remove the guilt of the community*** On one level, the priestly emoluments represent the compensation due the priests for their services in securing expiation, for officiating in the cult, and so forth. There is, however, another dimension: It was the duty of the priests to eat their assigned portions of the *ḥatta't,* "sin offering," of the people. This *ḥatta't* was an indispensable component of the expiatory process. As the Sifra puts it: "The priests eat (of the *ḥatta't*) and the donors thereby secure expiation." Therefore, although the blood rites incorporated in the offering of the *ḥatta't* constituted the primary means of expiation, the sacred meals of the priests were also essential.

tuary, you should certainly have eaten it in the sanctuary, as
I commanded." 19And Aaron spoke to Moses, "See, this
day they brought their sin offering and their burnt offering
before the LORD, and such things have befallen me! Had I
eaten sin offering today, would the LORD have approved?"
20And when Moses heard this, he approved.

דָּמָהּ אֶל־הַקֹּדֶשׁ פְּנִימָה אָכוֹל תֹּאכְלוּ אֹתָהּ
בַּקֹּדֶשׁ כַּאֲשֶׁר צִוֵּיתִי׃ 19 וַיְדַבֵּר אַהֲרֹן אֶל־מֹשֶׁה
הֵן הַיּוֹם הִקְרִיבוּ אֶת־חַטָּאתָם וְאֶת־עֹלָתָם לִפְנֵי
יְהוָה וַתִּקְרֶאנָה אֹתִי כָּאֵלֶּה וְאָכַלְתִּי חַטָּאת הַיּוֹם
הַיִּיטַב בְּעֵינֵי יְהוָה׃ 20 וַיִּשְׁמַע מֹשֶׁה וַיִּיטַב
בְּעֵינָיו׃ פ ששי

Hebrew *lase't 'avon* is ambiguous because the verb *nasa'* can mean both "to bear, carry" and also "to remove; carry away," which is the sense here. The priests effectively removed the sins of the people by attending to the sacrifices of expiation. But they were not to be punished for the sins of the community.

18. Since its blood was not brought inside the sanctuary Reference is to the rule of 6:23: "But no sin offering may be eaten from which any blood is brought into the Tent of Meeting for expiation in the sanctuary; any such shall be consumed in fire." Since the blood of the dedicatory sin offering had not been brought inside the sanctuary, the proper portions of the sacrifice were to be eaten by the priests. For a discussion of the various types of sin offerings and the disposition of the blood in each case, see introductory Comment to chapters 4–5.

19. they brought their sin offering . . . and such things have befallen me Aaron sought to excuse the failure of the priests to eat their portions of the sacrifice by explaining to Moses that his sons thought they should not eat of the sacrifice because they were in mourning. From Deuteronomy 26:14 we may infer that mourners who had just sustained a loss were not allowed to partake of devoted foods. Hebrew *ve-'akhalti* is to be understood here as a pluperfect, contrary to fact: "Had I eaten."

20. And when Moses heard this, he approved The Hebrew idiom "to find favor in the sight of" conveys approval. Moses reassured Aaron that the priestly duties, requiring the priests to partake of the sacrifice, took precedence over personal bereavement. Consequently, as had been stressed in verse 6, the priests were forbidden to mourn.

CHAPTER 11

The Laws of Kashrut: Proper Foods and Vessels

Chapter 11 of Leviticus ordains a system of dietary laws that specify what an Israelite may and may not eat as food. All that grows in the soil of the earth may be eaten, but a complex regimen of permitted and forbidden types governs the consumption of air, land, and water creatures. Leviticus 11 is one of two major collections of dietary laws in the Torah, the other being Deuteronomy 14. For a discussion of the meaning of the dietary laws, see Excursus 2.

In enumerating the various types of animals, birds, fish, insects, and reptiles, this chapter, like its counterpart in Deuteronomy, follows well-known ancient Near Eastern traditions. The school texts of ancient Syria and Mesopotamia, used for the training of ancient scribes, include columns that list the names of animals, birds, and other living creatures according to class and species. In several respects, Leviticus 11 goes further than the dietary laws of Deuteronomy 14. First of all, it deals with one of the primary concerns of the priesthood, the impurity that results from physical contact with that which is intrinsically impure. Not only would contact with carcasses of prohibited creatures render an Israelite impure, a principle present in Deuteronomy 14, but such impurity would in turn be transmitted to vessels and foodstuffs. Whereas Deuteronomy 14 merely classifies creatures that are considered impure, Leviticus 11, in addition, legislates the status of humans, vessels, and foodstuffs contaminated by contact with impure creatures.

During the early rabbinic period, both of these subjects—the dietary laws and the purity of vessels and foodstuffs—developed into major categories of religious law, and they have remained

important elements of Jewish religious life ever since. These prescribed patterns of behavior, usually referred to as *kashrut,* meaning "fitness" (of foods and vessels), is discussed in "Leviticus in the Ongoing Jewish Tradition." Here emphasis is on the priestly legislation of the biblical period, as seen in its historical context.

The Dietary Laws: Two Collections (vv. 1–23) The dietary restrictions reflect the idea, known the world over, that what one eats is a matter of religious significance. In later Jewish tradition, the impurity resulting from the consumption of forbidden foods became known as *tum'at kodesh*, "impurity pertaining to sanctity."[1] The key word in chapter 11 is *tame',* an adjective meaning "impure"; and the chapter concerns itself with the prevention of impurity and with its elimination, once contracted. No rituals of purification involving water, oil, or blood are prescribed for cleansing a person of impurity that resulted from eating forbidden foods per se. Nevertheless, the physical contact necessarily involved in eating forbidden foods required sacrificing a sin offering, according to the law of 5:2.

A comparison of Leviticus 11 with Deuteronomy 14 reveals that the two sources are closely related in form and content. In Leviticus 11, the dietary laws are viewed as part of a larger purity system that is basic to the priestly tradition. A detailed comparison of the two chapters yields the following information:

THE DIETARY LAWS: TWO COLLECTIONS

Deuteronomy 14	***Leviticus 11***
1 *Permitted land animals* A list of ten animals, domesticated and hunted. CRITERIA: Fully cleft hoofs and chew their cud. *Prohibited land animals* The camel, hare, daman, and swine. (vv. 3–8)	1 The same two criteria, and the same list of prohibited land animals. (vv. 3–8)
2 *Water creatures* CRITERIA: Both fins and scales. (vv. 9–10)	2 The same two criteria, stated both positively and negatively. (vv. 9–12)
3 *Birds* A list of prohibited birds. No general criteria stated. (vv. 11–18)	3 Essentially the same list of prohibited birds. No general criteria stated. (vv. 13–19)
4 *Winged, swarming creatures* A general statement prohibiting all creatures of this type. (vv. 19–20)	4 The same general statement. However, four types of permitted locusts are listed. CRITERION: Jointed legs. (vv. 20–23)
5 *Prohibited* Eating the dead body of any animal. (v. 21)	5 This prohibition is not explicitly stated, but it may be inferred from other provisions of the law.
6 *Prohibited* Seething a kid in its mother's milk. (v. 21)	6 No such prohibition is stated.

Deuteronomy 14	*Leviticus 11*
7 Not specifically stated.	7 *Prohibited* Consumption or tactile contact with the dead bodies of land and amphibious creatures. Eight creatures are listed, including several types of lizards. (vv. 29–31)
8 Not specifically stated.	8 *Prohibited* (a) All creatures that walk on their bellies; (b) all four-legged creatures that walk on paws; (c) all many-legged creatures. (vv. 41–43)

With respect to land animals, birds, and fish, the two sources have essentially the same provisions. Chapter 11 introduces specific provisions in two categories: (1) land and amphibious swarming creatures, known collectively as *sherets,* and (2) reptiles and animals having many legs.

Impurity (vv. 24–40) Leviticus 11 also deals with the subject of the impurities that result from various kinds of contact with the dead bodies of prohibited creatures. This subject first appears in verses 24–28, where such contact renders an Israelite impure until evening. Similarly, carrying any part of such dead creatures renders one impure until evening and requires the laundering of one's clothing. Verses 29–39 deal with the impurity resulting from contact with the dead bodies of eight specified swarming creatures (*sherets*). This impurity is of even greater consequence, as not only are humans rendered impure but also functional vessels and their edible contents. The differing effects of water, as set forth in chapter 11, are particularly important. Water purifies impure persons and vessels, and the water of cisterns and springs is not inherently susceptible to contamination by swarming creatures. At the same time, because water conditions the seeds used for planting, it renders them susceptible to contamination. Therefore, seed that has been dampened with water and that subsequently comes in contact with the dead body of any prohibited swarming creature is then considered impure. If, on the other hand, no water has dampened the seed in the first place, it is not subject to contamination and remains pure in the event of such contact.

Leviticus 11:39–40 prohibits contact with the corpse (*nevelah*) of a pure animal, that is, one permitted as food if properly slaughtered; such contact renders an Israelite impure. One who eats any part of it is impure and must launder his clothing. As in the case of prohibited foodstuffs, the above impurities require the person affected to offer a sacrifice in expiation, according to the laws of 5:2. Verses 41–44 contain general admonitions that reinforce the impurity associated with swarming creatures. The chapter concludes with an exhortation to observe the laws of purity, a prerequisite to becoming a holy people. In practical terms, an Israelite or priest who was in the state of impurity was prevented from entering or approaching the sanctuary—which, in turn, protected the sanctuary. Obviously, priests, who frequented the sanctuary, were more likely to defile it. Nevertheless the laws of chapter 11 are addressed to all Israelites, since impurity anywhere in the settlement had the effect of provoking God's wrath and at least indirectly threatening the purity of the sanctuary.

Both Deuteronomy 14 and Leviticus 11 are concerned with the category of *tame',* "impure." Deuteronomy uses the term *to'evah,* "abomination," in characterizing violations of purity, whereas Leviticus employs the synonymous term *shekets.*

11 The LORD spoke to Moses and Aaron, saying to them:
2Speak to the Israelite people thus:
These are the creatures that you may eat from among all
the land animals: 3any animal that has true hoofs, with
clefts through the hoofs, and that chews the cud—such you
may eat. 4The following, however, of those that either chew
the cud or have true hoofs, you shall not eat: the camel—
although it chews the cud, it has no true hoofs: it is unclean
for you; 5the daman—although it chews the cud, it has no
true hoofs: it is unclean for you; 6the hare—although it
chews the cud, it has no true hoofs: it is unclean for you;
7and the swine—although it has true hoofs, with the hoofs
cleft through, it does not chew the cud: it is unclean for

י״א וַיְדַבֵּר יְהוָה אֶל־מֹשֶׁה וְאֶל־אַהֲרֹן לֵאמֹר
אֲלֵהֶם: 2 דַּבְּרוּ אֶל־בְּנֵי יִשְׂרָאֵל לֵאמֹר זֹאת
הַחַיָּה אֲשֶׁר תֹּאכְלוּ מִכָּל־הַבְּהֵמָה אֲשֶׁר עַל־
הָאָרֶץ: 3 כֹּל ׀ מַפְרֶסֶת פַּרְסָה וְשֹׁסַעַת שֶׁסַע
פְּרָסֹת מַעֲלַת גֵּרָה בַּבְּהֵמָה אֹתָהּ תֹּאכֵלוּ: 4 אַךְ
אֶת־זֶה לֹא תֹאכְלוּ מִמַּעֲלֵי הַגֵּרָה וּמִמַּפְרִיסֵי
הַפַּרְסָה אֶת־הַגָּמָל כִּי־מַעֲלֵה גֵרָה הוּא וּפַרְסָה
אֵינֶנּוּ מַפְרִיס טָמֵא הוּא לָכֶם: 5 וְאֶת־הַשָּׁפָן כִּי־
מַעֲלֵה גֵרָה הוּא וּפַרְסָה לֹא יַפְרִיס טָמֵא הוּא
לָכֶם: 6 וְאֶת־הָאַרְנֶבֶת כִּי־מַעֲלַת גֵּרָה הִוא
וּפַרְסָה לֹא הִפְרִיסָה טְמֵאָה הִוא לָכֶם: 7 וְאֶת־
הַחֲזִיר כִּי־מַפְרִיס פַּרְסָה הוּא וְשֹׁסַע שֶׁסַע פַּרְסָה

PERMITTED AND FORBIDDEN FOOD SOURCES (vv. 1–23)

LAND ANIMALS (vv. 2–8)

2. *These are the creatures that you may eat* The Hebrew terms *ḥayyah,* "creature," and *behemah,* "animal," have varying connotations. Here *ḥayyah* is a generic term meaning "living creature," whereas *behemah* is defined as that "which inhabits the land" (*'asher 'al ha-'arets*). This definition is corroborated by the contrasting category "all that live in the water" in verse 9.

3. *any animal that has true hoofs* Our chapter does not list the ten permitted land animals as does Deuteronomy 14:4. Only the general rule is stated here, as in Deuteronomy 14:6. There is no reason, however, to doubt that both sources permit the same land animals as food.

Hebrew *mafreset parsah* means literally "that grows hoofs," just as in the continuation of the verse *ve-shosa'at shesa'* means literally "that cleaves a cleavage," the verb *shasa'* meaning "to split, cut through."[2] Grammarians refer to this syntax as the cognate accusative since both the verbal form and its object derive from the same root. Deuteronomy 14:6 is more explicit: *ve-shosa'at shesa' shetei perasot,* "and exhibits the cleavage of two hoofs." To qualify as pure, an animal's hoofs must be split all the way through, producing two toes, of a sort, so that the animal in question does not walk on paws, called *kappayim* in verse 27 below.

Hebrew *ma'aleh gerah* means literally "which brings up the cud." Rashi explains this as follows: "The animal brings up and regurgitates its food from its intestines back into its mouth, to fragmentize and grind it." This describes a class of animal known as ruminants, those whose stomach has four compartments. The Hebrew word *gerah,* "cud," derives from the verb *garar,* "to pull, drag along," and it may be related to the word *garon,* "throat."

4. *The following . . . you shall not eat* The list of four unclean land animals consists of what may be called borderline cases, animals that exhibit one but not both of the required physical criteria. The likelihood of mistaking such animals for pure animals was greater.

the camel The camel (an English word that derives from the common Semitic word *gamal*) does not have fully cleft hoofs. Its hoof is split in its upper part, but bound together in its lower part.[3]

it is unclean for you Hebrew *tame'* is better translated "impure" because at issue is not a notion of hygienic cleanliness, as we know it, but of purity as a ritual condition.[4]

5. *the daman* Hebrew *shafan* designates the Syrian hyrax, a small mammal. It does not actually chew its cud, but gives that impression because it has protrusions in its stomach, which suggest that its stomach might have compartments, as is characteristic of the ruminants.[5]

6. *the hare* Hebrew *'arnevet,* "hare," is actually a rodent. It is not a ruminant but gives the impression of being one because it munches its food so noticeably.

you. 8You shall not eat of their flesh or touch their carcasses; they are unclean for you.

9These you may eat of all that live in water: anything in water, whether in the seas or in the streams, that has fins and scales—these you may eat. 10But anything in the seas or in the streams that has no fins and scales, among all the swarming things of the water and among all the other living creatures that are in the water—they are an abomination for you 11and an abomination for you they shall remain: you shall not eat of their flesh and you shall abominate their carcasses. 12Everything in water that has no fins and scales shall be an abomination for you.

13The following you shall abominate among the birds—they shall not be eaten, they are an abomination: the eagle,

וְהוּא גֵּרָה לֹא־יִגָּר טָמֵא הוּא לָכֶם: 8 מִבְּשָׂרָם לֹא
תֹאכֵלוּ וּבְנִבְלָתָם לֹא תִגָּעוּ טְמֵאִים הֵם לָכֶם:
9 אֶת־זֶה תֹּאכְלוּ מִכֹּל אֲשֶׁר בַּמָּיִם כֹּל אֲשֶׁר־לוֹ
סְנַפִּיר וְקַשְׂקֶשֶׂת בַּמַּיִם בַּיַּמִּים וּבַנְּחָלִים אֹתָם
תֹּאכֵלוּ: 10 וְכֹל אֲשֶׁר אֵין־לוֹ סְנַפִּיר וְקַשְׂקֶשֶׂת
בַּיַּמִּים וּבַנְּחָלִים מִכֹּל שֶׁרֶץ הַמַּיִם וּמִכֹּל נֶפֶשׁ
הַחַיָּה אֲשֶׁר בַּמָּיִם שֶׁקֶץ הֵם לָכֶם: 11 וְשֶׁקֶץ יִהְיוּ
לָכֶם מִבְּשָׂרָם לֹא תֹאכֵלוּ וְאֶת־נִבְלָתָם תְּשַׁקֵּצוּ:
12 כֹּל אֲשֶׁר אֵין־לוֹ סְנַפִּיר וְקַשְׂקֶשֶׂת בַּמָּיִם שֶׁקֶץ
הוּא לָכֶם: 13 וְאֶת־אֵלֶּה תְּשַׁקְּצוּ מִן־הָעוֹף לֹא
יֵאָכְלוּ שֶׁקֶץ הֵם אֶת־הַנֶּשֶׁר וְאֶת־הַפֶּרֶס וְאֵת

7. ***the swine*** Hebrew *ḥazzir,* "pig, swine," was widely domesticated in ancient Canaan and even raised for food. No distinction is made here between the wild and the domesticated species of the swine.[6] It is the only domesticated animal used as food in biblical times that has a truly split hoof but does not chew its cud.

The verbal form written *yiggar* is probably to be vocalized *yagor,* "brings up," from the root *garar.* The clause *ve-gerah-yiggar* (that is, *yagor*) is an alternate way of stating *ma'aleh gerah,* "brings up the cud," as in verse 3 above.

8. ***You shall not eat of their flesh or touch their carcasses*** The term *nevelah* is ambiguous because it can designate the carcass of an animal or human being and because it does not indicate the cause of death—whether by natural means or by being killed or slaughtered in some way. However, in some contexts it refers specifically to animals that died a natural death.[7]

Here the sense is general: Not only is one prohibited from *eating* the meat of forbidden animals but also from *touching* or *handling* any part of their bodies, as would normally occur in preparing meat as food. This rule was undoubtedly intended as a safeguard against possible consumption of meat from such prohibited animals. In Leviticus 17:15 and Deuteronomy 14:21 we find the prohibition against eating the flesh of any animal that died or was torn by beasts.

WATER CREATURES (vv. 9–12)

9. ***that has fins and scales*** Hebrew *senappir* is a word of uncertain origin occurring only here and in Deuteronomy 14:9–10. It may be cognate with Akkadian *sappartu,* "a horny protrusion."[8] Hebrew *kaskeset* is translated by Targum Onkelos as *kelifan,* "peels," and probably refers to the soft scales of the fish.[9]

10. ***among all the swarming things of the water*** The Hebrew verb *sharats,* cognate with Akkadian *sharātsu,* means "to come to life, crawl, swarm."[10] All those water creatures that do not swim by the usual means of fins but, instead, crawl are considered impure. In the later tradition it was explained that fish were considered pure if they had fins and scales at any time, even if they shed them at some point in their life cycle, or only developed them in the course of their growth.[11]

they are an abomination for you Hebrew *shekets* is cognate with the Akkadian verb *shaqātsu,* "to be of bad appearance"—hence "detestable."[12] Here again, as in verse 8 above, the prohibition affects both eating and touching.

CREATURES OF THE SKY (vv. 13–17)

13. ***The following you shall abominate among the birds*** There are no overall physical criteria by which to distinguish pure birds from impure birds. Rather, a long list of prohibited birds is

the vulture, and the black vulture; [14]the kite, falcons of every variety; [15]all varieties of raven; [16]the ostrich, the nighthawk, the sea gull; hawks of every variety; [17]the little owl, the cormorant, and the great owl; [18]the white owl, the pelican, and the bustard; [19]the stork; herons of every variety; the hoopoe, and the bat.

[20]All winged swarming things that walk on fours shall be an abomination for you. [21]But these you may eat among all the winged swarming things that walk on fours: all that have, above their feet, jointed legs to leap with on the ground—[22]of these you may eat the following: locusts of every variety; all varieties of bald locust; crickets of every

הָעָזְנִיָּה׃ 14 וְאֶת־הַדָּאָה וְאֶת־הָאַיָּה לְמִינָהּ׃
15 אֵת כָּל־עֹרֵב לְמִינוֹ׃ 16 וְאֵת בַּת הַיַּעֲנָה וְאֶת־
הַתַּחְמָס וְאֶת־הַשָּׁחַף וְאֶת־הַנֵּץ לְמִינֵהוּ׃ 17 וְאֶת־
הַכּוֹס וְאֶת־הַשָּׁלָךְ וְאֶת־הַיַּנְשׁוּף׃ 18 וְאֶת־
הַתִּנְשֶׁמֶת וְאֶת־הַקָּאָת וְאֶת־הָרָחָם׃ 19 וְאֵת
הַחֲסִידָה הָאֲנָפָה לְמִינָהּ וְאֶת־הַדּוּכִיפַת וְאֶת־
הָעֲטַלֵּף׃ 20 כֹּל שֶׁרֶץ הָעוֹף הַהֹלֵךְ עַל־אַרְבַּע
שֶׁקֶץ הוּא לָכֶם׃ ס 21 אַךְ אֶת־זֶה תֹּאכְלוּ
מִכֹּל שֶׁרֶץ הָעוֹף הַהֹלֵךְ עַל־אַרְבַּע אֲשֶׁר־לא
כְרָעַיִם מִמַּעַל לְרַגְלָיו לְנַתֵּר בָּהֵן עַל־הָאָרֶץ׃

v. 21. לוֹ ק׳

provided, the assumption being that all others would be permitted. Determining which birds are permitted has been in some cases a matter of custom and has resulted in persistent discrepancies among various communities in the course of Jewish history. Based on information provided in the Hebrew Bible, especially from religious law, we know that all permitted birds fall into the following classes: (1) *Columbiformes:* various types of doves and pigeons; (2) *Galliformes:* hens and quail (*selav*), gathered as food in the Sinai desert as told in the narratives of Exodus 16:13 and Numbers 11:31–32;[13] (3) *Anseriformes:* domestic geese and ducks; and (4) *Passerines:* specifically the house sparrow (*deror*).[14]

The list of prohibited birds given here is virtually identical with that of Deuteronomy 14. It does not correspond exactly to zoological classifications and even includes the bat (*ʿatallef*), which is technically a winged rodent, not a bird. The impure birds are virtually all birds of prey. They include the following: (1) Four types of falcons: *taḥmas,* "falcon"; *nets,* "sparrow hawk"; *daʾah* (*dayyah* in Deut. 14:13), "kite"; and *ʾayyah,* "buzzard." These eat living flesh and carrion. (2) Four types of vultures or eagles: *nesher,* "eagle, griffin, vulture"; *ʿozniyyah,* "black vulture"; *raḥam,* "Egyptian vulture"; *peres,* "bearded vulture." These eat carrion.[15] (3) Six types of owls: *yanshuf,* "long-eared owl"; *bat yaʿanah,* "dark, desert eagle owl"; *tinshemet,* "barn, screech owl"; *kos,* "little owl"; *kaʾat,* "Saharan owl"; and *shalakh,* "fish owl, ostrich." These are nocturnal birds of prey. (4) The raven, *ʿorev.* Ravens eat living flesh and carrion. Several types of ravens were known in biblical lands. (5) Marsh, or sea birds: *ḥasidah,* "stork"; *ʾanafah,* "heron"; and *shaḥaf,* "sea gull."

There is some uncertainty about nomenclature, which is why the renderings given here differ in some cases from those provided in the translation. The general classifications, however, are fairly clear.

WINGED INSECTS (vv. 20–23)

20. All winged swarming things The section on winged insects (vv. 20–23) provides a classic instance of what students of literature call *inclusio.* The section begins in verse 20 with a general statement, which is repeated with only slight variations in verse 23. Both statements are prohibitive, whereas the intervening two verses (21–22) state exceptions to the overall prohibition. The expression "winged swarming things" (*sherets haʿof*) is a roundabout way of describing insects.

21. But these you may eat . . . all that have, above their feet, jointed legs to leap with on the ground The Hebrew is to be read *ʾasher lo* (אשר לו), "which has," not *ʾasher loʾ* (אשר לא), "which is not," as the Masoretic text is written. There are other similar cases in the Hebrew Bible, some already noted by ancient and medieval scribes, of the confusion of these two short homophones. Hebrew *keraʿayim,* "jointed legs," is a term for the hind legs, or hocks, of animals.[16] Hebrew *nitter,* "to leap," is unique in biblical Hebrew and is translated on the basis of the context.

Four types of locusts, each in turn comprising several varieties, are permitted: (1) *ʾarbeh,* a general term for locust, as in Joel 2:25; (2) *solʿam,* grasshopper; (3) *ḥargol,* cricket, grasshopper; and (4) *ḥagav,* bald locust, grasshopper.

variety; and all varieties of grasshopper. ²³But all other winged swarming things that have four legs shall be an abomination for you.

²⁴And the following shall make you unclean—whoever touches their carcasses shall be unclean until evening, ²⁵and whoever carries the carcasses of any of them shall wash his clothes and be unclean until evening—²⁶every animal that has true hoofs but without clefts through the hoofs, or that does not chew the cud. They are unclean for you; whoever touches them shall be unclean. ²⁷Also all animals that walk on paws, among those that walk on fours, are unclean for you; whoever touches their carcasses shall be unclean until evening. ²⁸And anyone who carries their carcasses shall wash his clothes and remain unclean until evening. They are unclean for you.

²⁹The following shall be unclean for you from among the things that swarm on the earth: the mole, the mouse, and great lizards of every variety; ³⁰the gecko, the land crocodile, the lizard, the sand lizard, and the chameleon. ³¹Those are for you the unclean among all the swarming things; whoever touches them when they are dead shall be unclean

22 אֶת־אֵ֤לֶּה מֵהֶם֙ תֹּאכֵ֔לוּ אֶת־הָֽאַרְבֶּ֖ה לְמִינ֑וֹ
וְאֶת־הַסָּלְעָם֙ לְמִינֵ֔הוּ וְאֶת־הַחַרְגֹּ֖ל לְמִינֵ֑הוּ וְאֶת־
הֶחָגָ֖ב לְמִינֵֽהוּ׃ 23 וְכֹל֙ שֶׁ֣רֶץ הָע֔וֹף אֲשֶׁר־ל֖וֹ
אַרְבַּ֣ע רַגְלָ֑יִם שֶׁ֥קֶץ ה֖וּא לָכֶֽם׃ 24 וּלְאֵ֖לֶּה תִּטַּמָּ֑אוּ
כָּל־הַנֹּגֵ֥עַ בְּנִבְלָתָ֖ם יִטְמָ֥א עַד־הָעָֽרֶב׃ 25 וְכָל־
הַנֹּשֵׂ֖א מִנִּבְלָתָ֑ם יְכַבֵּ֥ס בְּגָדָ֖יו וְטָמֵ֥א עַד־הָעָֽרֶב׃
26 לְכָל־הַבְּהֵמָ֡ה אֲשֶׁר֩ הִ֨וא מַפְרֶ֤סֶת פַּרְסָה֙
וְשֶׁ֣סַע ׀ אֵינֶ֣נָּה שֹׁסַ֗עַת וְגֵרָה֙ אֵינֶ֣נָּה מַעֲלָ֔ה טְמֵאִ֥ים
הֵ֖ם לָכֶ֑ם כָּל־הַנֹּגֵ֥עַ בָּהֶ֖ם יִטְמָֽא׃ 27 וְכֹ֣ל ׀ הוֹלֵ֣ךְ
עַל־כַּפָּ֗יו בְּכָל־הַֽחַיָּה֙ הַהֹלֶ֣כֶת עַל־אַרְבַּ֔ע טְמֵאִ֥ים
הֵ֖ם לָכֶ֑ם כָּל־הַנֹּגֵ֥עַ בְּנִבְלָתָ֖ם יִטְמָ֥א עַד־הָעָֽרֶב׃
28 וְהַנֹּשֵׂ֙א אֶת־נִבְלָתָ֜ם יְכַבֵּ֤ס בְּגָדָיו֙ וְטָמֵ֣א עַד־
הָעָ֑רֶב טְמֵאִ֥ים הֵ֖מָּה לָכֶֽם׃ ס 29 וְזֶ֥ה לָכֶ֙ם
הַטָּמֵ֔א בַּשֶּׁ֖רֶץ הַשֹּׁרֵ֣ץ עַל־הָאָ֑רֶץ הַחֹ֥לֶד וְהָעַכְבָּ֖ר
וְהַצָּ֥ב לְמִינֵֽהוּ׃ 30 וְהָאֲנָקָ֥ה וְהַכֹּ֖חַ וְהַלְּטָאָ֑ה וְהַחֹ֖מֶט
וְהַתִּנְשָֽׁמֶת׃ 31 אֵ֧לֶּה הַטְּמֵאִ֛ים לָכֶ֖ם בְּכָל־הַשָּׁ֑רֶץ
כָּל־הַנֹּגֵ֧עַ בָּהֶ֛ם בְּמֹתָ֖ם יִטְמָ֥א עַד־הָעָֽרֶב׃ 32 וְכֹ֣ל ׀

23.   *But all other winged swarming things*   The types of locusts listed above are permitted but all others (*ve-khol*) are forbidden. Even today, grasshoppers are part of the diet in some countries.

THE CONDUCTIVITY OF IMPURITY   (vv. 24–40)

This part of chapter 11 deals with impurity resulting from several kinds of contact—such as touching, carrying, containing—that render persons, vessels, and foodstuffs impure in varying degrees. Verses 24–28 establish the principle that mere contact with the carcasses of impure creatures causes impurity, even without consumption of them. Verses 29–38 introduce a new category of impure creatures: reptiles, whose impurity is even more consequential than that of land, water, and sky creatures. Verses 39–40 deal with the impurity resulting from contact with the carcasses of pure land animals.

24.   *And the following shall make you unclean*   Hebrew *u-le-'elleh*, "and to these," refers to what follows. Again we have an *inclusio*: Verses 24–25 are virtually repeated in verses 27b–28; what intervenes here in verses 26–27a does not state the exceptions but, rather, details the rule.

27.   *Also all animals that walk on paws . . . whoever touches their carcasses*   Hebrew *kaf* here refers to paws, as distinct from toes or from completely split hoofs. Tactile contact with the carcass of an impure creature serves to render only the person involved impure, whereas carrying something impure results in the contamination of one's clothing as well.

29.   *The following shall be unclean for you*   Eight types of swarming land creatures are listed, including four types of lizards: *holed,* "mole"; *'akhbar,* "mouse"; *tsav,* "great lizard"; *'anakah,* "gecko"; *koah,* "land crocodile, monitor"; *leta'ah,* "lizard"; *homet,* "sand lizard"; and *tinshemet,* "chameleon." The name of this last reptile is identical with that of the barn, screech owl, listed in verse 18. Both are so called for the sounds they make, despite their differing natures.

31.   *whoever touches them when they are dead*   This anticipates the references to *nevelah,* "carcass," as an alternative way of describing a dead creature in verses 35–40.

until evening. 32 And anything on which one of them falls when dead shall be unclean: be it any article of wood, or a cloth, or a skin, or a sack—any such article that can be put to use shall be dipped in water, and it shall remain unclean until evening; then it shall be clean. 33 And if any of those falls into an earthen vessel, everything inside it shall be unclean and [the vessel] itself you shall break. 34 As to any food that may be eaten, it shall become unclean if it came in contact with water; as to any liquid that may be drunk, it shall become unclean if it was inside any vessel. 35 Everything on which the carcass of any of them falls shall be unclean: an oven or stove shall be smashed. They are un-

אֲשֶׁר־יִפֹּל־עָלָיו מֵהֶם׀ בְּמֹתָם יִטְמָא מִכָּל־כְּלִי־עֵץ
אוֹ בֶגֶד אוֹ־עוֹר אוֹ שָׂק כָּל־כְּלִי אֲשֶׁר־יֵעָשֶׂה
מְלָאכָה בָּהֶם בַּמַּיִם יוּבָא וְטָמֵא עַד־הָעֶרֶב וְטָהֵר׃
שביעי 33 וְכָל־כְּלִי־חֶרֶשׂ אֲשֶׁר־יִפֹּל מֵהֶם אֶל־
תּוֹכוֹ כֹּל אֲשֶׁר בְּתוֹכוֹ יִטְמָא וְאֹתוֹ תִשְׁבֹּרוּ׃
34 מִכָּל־הָאֹכֶל אֲשֶׁר יֵאָכֵל אֲשֶׁר יָבוֹא עָלָיו מַיִם
יִטְמָא וְכָל־מַשְׁקֶה אֲשֶׁר יִשָּׁתֶה בְּכָל־כְּלִי יִטְמָא׃
35 וְכֹל אֲשֶׁר־יִפֹּל מִנִּבְלָתָם׀ עָלָיו יִטְמָא תַּנּוּר
וְכִירַיִם יֻתָּץ טְמֵאִים הֵם וּטְמֵאִים יִהְיוּ לָכֶם׃

32. ***And anything on which one of them falls when dead*** Beginning in this verse, and continuing through verse 38, we have the biblical basis of what later was to become an elaborate system of purity in Judaism (affecting vessels and foodstuffs) to which an entire tractate of the Mishnah, Kelim, is devoted.[17]

The clause *'asher yippol 'alav,* "that falls upon it," is to be contrasted with what is stated in verse 33: *'asher yippol mehem 'el tokho,* "into which one of them falls." Under priestly law, vessels made of wood, leather, and certain types of cloth become impure by means of exterior contact alone, whereas ceramic vessels (with the exception of stoves and ovens) become impure only if the contaminating substance enters their interior space. This is explained in Mishnah Kelim 2:1. For this reason, ceramic vessels could be protected from impurity by having a lid fastened on them, according to the law of Numbers 19:15, explained in Mishnah Kelim 10:1.

Be it any article of wood, or a cloth, or a skin, or a sack Rather, "But if any vessel of wood, of cloth, or of skin, or of sackcloth." In a legal text such as this, a technical translation is preferable, and this verse is speaking specifically of a vessel (*keli*). In the later tradition, *keli* is defined as a functional object *'asher ye'aseh mela'khah bahem,* "with which a task can be performed," as our verse explains; and as that which has interior space, a "receptacle," *beit kibbul,* in rabbinic terminology.[18] Verse 32, referring to vessels made of such materials as cloth, wood, or leather, indicates that such vessels may be cleansed in water and that they remain impure only until evening.

Hebrew *beged* is defined as something woven of cloth, and *sak,* as something made of goat's hair or the hair of a similar animal. That such vessels of cloth, leather, and goat's hair can be purified in water may also be learned from Numbers 31:20, which deals with the purification of spoils of war: "You shall also purify everything woven of cloth, every vessel of leather, everything made of goat's hair, and every vessel of wood." It is implicit that food contained in such contaminated vessels is also impure.

33. ***And if any of those falls into an earthen vessel*** A ceramic vessel does not become impure until the dead swarming creatures enter inside it; should this happen, there is no remedy but to smash the vessel.

34. ***As to any food that may be eaten*** Solid food that has been dampened by water and then comes into contact with dead swarming creatures becomes impure because water is a conductor of impurity.[19] Similarly, liquids inside contaminated vessels become impure.

35. ***Everything on which the carcass of any of them falls*** This statement, which refers directly to verse 32 above, in effect restates the general rule governing forbidden swarming creatures and then applies it to stoves and ovens. Like vessels of wood, cloth, leather, and animal hair, and in contradistinction to ceramic vessels generally, ovens and stoves become contaminated as soon as dead swarming creatures fall onto them, a condition for which there is no remedy. Impure stoves and ovens must be smashed.

The word *tanur* is defined as a large, covered ceramic oven, whereas *kirayim* designates a grate or stove top in which fire is kindled and upon which two pots could be placed for cooking.[20] Often such

clean and unclean they shall remain for you. ³⁶However, a spring or cistern in which water is collected shall be clean, but whoever touches such a carcass in it shall be unclean. ³⁷If such a carcass falls upon seed grain that is to be sown, it is clean; ³⁸but if water is put on the seed and any part of a carcass falls upon it, it shall be unclean for you.

³⁹If an animal that you may eat has died, anyone who touches its carcass shall be unclean until evening; ⁴⁰anyone who eats of its carcass shall wash his clothes and remain unclean until evening; and anyone who carries its carcass shall wash his clothes and remain unclean until evening.

⁴¹All the things that swarm upon the earth are an abomination; they shall not be eaten. ⁴²You shall not eat, among all things that swarm upon the earth, anything that crawls on its belly, or anything that walks on fours, or anything that has many legs; for they are an abomination. ⁴³You shall not draw abomination upon yourselves through anything that swarms; you shall not make yourselves unclean there-

36 אַ֣ךְ מַעְיָ֥ן וּב֛וֹר מִקְוֵה־מַ֖יִם יִהְיֶ֣ה טָה֑וֹר וְנֹגֵ֥עַ בְּנִבְלָתָ֖ם יִטְמָֽא׃ 37 וְכִ֤י יִפֹּל֙ מִנִּבְלָתָ֔ם עַל־כָּל־ זֶ֥רַע זֵר֖וּעַ אֲשֶׁ֣ר יִזָּרֵ֑עַ טָה֖וֹר הֽוּא׃ 38 וְכִ֤י יֻתַּן־מַ֙יִם֙ עַל־זֶ֔רַע וְנָפַ֥ל מִנִּבְלָתָ֖ם עָלָ֑יו טָמֵ֥א ה֖וּא לָכֶֽם׃

39 וְכִ֤י יָמוּת֙ מִן־הַבְּהֵמָ֔ה אֲשֶׁר־הִ֥יא לָכֶ֖ם לְאָכְלָ֑ה הַנֹּגֵ֥עַ בְּנִבְלָתָ֖הּ יִטְמָ֥א עַד־הָעָֽרֶב׃ 40 וְהָֽאֹכֵל֙ מִנִּבְלָתָ֔הּ יְכַבֵּ֥ס בְּגָדָ֖יו וְטָמֵ֣א עַד־ הָעָ֑רֶב וְהַנֹּשֵׂא֙ אֶת־נִבְלָתָ֔הּ יְכַבֵּ֥ס בְּגָדָ֖יו וְטָמֵ֥א עַד־הָעָֽרֶב׃ 41 וְכָל־הַשֶּׁ֖רֶץ הַשֹּׁרֵ֣ץ עַל־הָאָ֑רֶץ שֶׁ֥קֶץ ה֖וּא לֹ֥א יֵאָכֵֽל׃ 42 כֹּל֩ הוֹלֵ֨ךְ עַל־גָּח֜וֹן* וְכֹ֣ל ׀ הוֹלֵ֣ךְ עַל־אַרְבַּ֗ע עַ֚ד כָּל־מַרְבֵּ֣ה רַגְלַ֔יִם לְכָל־ הַשֶּׁ֖רֶץ הַשֹּׁרֵ֣ץ עַל־הָאָ֑רֶץ לֹ֥א תֹֽאכְל֖וּם כִּי־שֶׁ֥קֶץ הֵֽם׃ 43 אַל־תְּשַׁקְּצוּ֙ אֶת־נַפְשֹׁ֣תֵיכֶ֔ם בְּכָל־הַשֶּׁ֖רֶץ

v. 42. נ׳ רבתי והיא חצי התורה באותיות

---

appliances were installed in the floor of a room, set in a corner flush with the walls. It was probably thought that the intense heat generated in stoves and ovens made the ceramic material more susceptible to impurity than was the case with ceramic storage vessels.

From Numbers 31:22 we learn that metal vessels may be purified in fire. Stone vessels are not susceptible to impurity in any case.

36. *However, a spring or cistern in which water is collected shall be clean* The Hebrew adverb 'akh, "however," draws a contrast: Whereas water generally renders foodstuffs susceptible to impurity, this is true only of water "placed in them," that is, water emitting from a vessel that is detached from the earth. By contrast, neither rainwater in a cistern nor natural bodies of water transmit impurity. Hebrew *bor* is a technical term for a "cistern" in which rainwater is collected from the surrounding area.²¹ The Hebrew term *mikveh ha-mayim* designates natural bodies of water, as is evident from Genesis 1:10: "And the gathering of waters *(mikveh ha-mayim)* He called seas."

38. *But if water is put on the seed* Water conditions seed, rendering it susceptible to impurity. The verbal form *yuttan* actually represents the fairly rare internal Kal passive, but its true morphology was probably not recognized. More precisely, the form is *yutan*.²² Dampened seed—but not dry seed—becomes impure if the dead body of a forbidden swarming creature falls onto it. It is not entirely clear why the impurity associated with the *sherets*, "swarming creature," discussed in verses 29–37 is more severe in its effects than that associated with the dead bodies of other creatures.

39. *If an animal that you may eat has died* Physical contact with the *nevelah*, "carcass," even of a permitted animal, renders a person impure until evening.

40. *anyone who eats of its carcass ... and anyone who carries its carcass* This statement reiterates the prohibition, encountered earlier in verse 8, against eating meat of any animal, even a permitted one, that has died a natural death.²³ Similarly, carrying the carcass or any part of it produces impurity. In both cases the person involved must launder his clothes.

41. *All things that swarm upon the earth are an abomination* Verses 41–44 express the concept of *shekets*, "abomination." They repeat the definition of forbidden swarming creatures and warn Israelites against becoming contaminated by the impurity of these creatures. The key verb in these verses is *shikkets*, "to make abominable, declare abominable." The Israelites must regard the *sherets* as abominable, lest they themselves become abominable, which is to say, impure.²⁴

with and thus become unclean. 44For I the LORD am your
God: you shall sanctify yourselves and be holy, for I am
holy. You shall not make yourselves unclean through any
swarming thing that moves upon the earth. 45For I the LORD
am He who brought you up from the land of Egypt to be
your God: you shall be holy, for I am holy.

46These are the instructions concerning animals, birds,
all living creatures that move in water, and all creatures that
swarm on earth, 47for distinguishing between the unclean
and the clean, between the living things that may be eaten
and the living things that may not be eaten.

הַשֹּׁרֵץ וְלֹא תִטַּמְּאוּ בָּהֶם וְנִטְמֵתֶם* בָּם׃ 44 כִּי
אֲנִי יְהוָה אֱלֹהֵיכֶם וְהִתְקַדִּשְׁתֶּם וִהְיִיתֶם קְדֹשִׁים
כִּי קָדוֹשׁ אָנִי וְלֹא תְטַמְּאוּ אֶת־נַפְשֹׁתֵיכֶם בְּכָל־
הַשֶּׁרֶץ הָרֹמֵשׂ עַל־הָאָרֶץ׃ מפטיר 45 כִּי׀ אֲנִי
יְהוָה הַמַּעֲלֶה אֶתְכֶם מֵאֶרֶץ מִצְרַיִם לִהְיֹת לָכֶם
לֵאלֹהִים וִהְיִיתֶם קְדֹשִׁים כִּי קָדוֹשׁ אָנִי׃ 46 זֹאת
תּוֹרַת הַבְּהֵמָה וְהָעוֹף וְכֹל נֶפֶשׁ הַחַיָּה הָרֹמֶשֶׂת
בַּמָּיִם וּלְכָל־נֶפֶשׁ הַשֹּׁרֶצֶת עַל־הָאָרֶץ׃
47 לְהַבְדִּיל בֵּין הַטָּמֵא וּבֵין הַטָּהֹר וּבֵין הַחַיָּה
הַנֶּאֱכֶלֶת וּבֵין הַחַיָּה אֲשֶׁר לֹא תֵאָכֵל׃ פ

TAZRIAʿ

12 The LORD spoke to Moses, saying: 2Speak to the
Israelite people thus: When a woman at childbirth bears a

תזריע

י״ב וַיְדַבֵּר יְהוָה אֶל־מֹשֶׁה לֵּאמֹר׃ 2 דַּבֵּר אֶל־
בְּנֵי יִשְׂרָאֵל לֵאמֹר אִשָּׁה כִּי תַזְרִיעַ וְיָלְדָה זָכָר

חסר א׳ v. 43.

44. ***you shall sanctify yourselves and be holy, for I am holy*** This statement is explained in the Comment to 19:2, where it introduces the theme of Israel's imperative to become a holy nation.[25]

POSTSCRIPT (vv. 46–47)

46. ***These are the instructions*** This is a fairly typical postscript, which often appears at the conclusion of a major code of law.

47. ***for distinguishing between . . . the living things that may be eaten*** A similar admonition occurs in 20:25. The purpose of the code of law promulgated in chapter 11 is to enable the Israelites to distinguish (*hivdil*) between the permitted and forbidden foodstuffs under priestly instruction.

CHAPTER 12

Regulations Concerning the New Mother

Tazriaʿ

Chapter 12 defines the ritual status of an Israelite mother after childbirth. Whereas her child is born pure, she is considered to be impure for varying periods of time depending on the sex of the child—seven days for a son, fourteen days for a daughter. The text is not explicit about the precise nature of the impurity sustained by a new mother during this initial period, although her impurity is compared with that of a menstruating woman. It is to be assumed that she was not permitted to have marital relations with her husband and that her impure condition would cause defilement through certain types of contact.

Subsequent to the initial seven days of impurity, there was an additional period of thirty-three days after the birth of a son and sixty-six days after the birth of a daughter during which the new mother awaited her final purification. Although she could engage in marital relations, she was barred from entry into the sanctuary and from contact with "sacred things," pending her final purification by rites of expiation. At the conclusion of this extended time period, the new mother was required to present a sin offering (*ḥatta't*), accompanied by a burnt offering, to signify the elimination of all impurity. The priest performed these rites of expiation on the woman's behalf, and she was declared pure again.

The legislation of chapter 12 is of additional interest because in verse 3 it also includes the requirement that a male child be circumcised on the eighth day after birth.

male, she shall be unclean seven days; she shall be unclean as at the time of her menstrual infirmity.—[3]On the eighth day the flesh of his foreskin shall be circumcised.—[4]She shall remain in a state of blood purification for thirty-three days: she shall not touch any consecrated thing, nor enter the sanctuary until her period of purification is completed.

וְטָֽמְאָה֙ שִׁבְעַ֣ת יָמִ֔ים כִּימֵ֛י נִדַּ֥ת דְּוֺתָ֖הּ תִּטְמָֽא׃
3 וּבַיּ֖וֹם הַשְּׁמִינִ֑י יִמּ֖וֹל בְּשַׂ֥ר עָרְלָתֽוֹ׃ 4 וּשְׁלֹשִׁ֥ים
י֙וֹם֙ וּשְׁלֹ֣שֶׁת יָמִ֔ים תֵּשֵׁ֖ב בִּדְמֵ֣י טָהֳרָ֑ה בְּכָל־קֹ֣דֶשׁ
לֹֽא־תִגָּ֗ע וְאֶל־הַמִּקְדָּשׁ֙ לֹ֣א תָבֹ֔א עַד־מְלֹ֖את יְמֵ֥י

2. *When a woman at childbirth bears a male* Rather, "when a woman is inseminated and bears a male." The formulation *'ishah ki tazria' ve-yaledah* is ambiguous. The translation takes the form of the verb *tazria'* as causative, "to bear seed." This is its sense in Genesis 1:11–12: *'esev mazria' zera'*, literally "plants that bear seed." On this basis, our verse describes a unitary event: childbirth. An alternative would be to understand the verb *tazria'* as describing conception by childbirth, much in the same way as the commonplace idiom "she conceived and bore" conveys the two sequential stages of the process.[1] Since in Numbers 5:28 the passive *ve-nizr'ah zera'* means "she is able to retain seed," the form *tazria'* should also be understood as referring to conception. The Hifil form of the verb often connotes physical conditions and is not consistently causative. It is worth noting that the Samaritan version reads *t-z-r-'* instead of *t-z-r-y-'*, the Masoretic version. This suggests that the Samaritan version understood a Nifal form here: *tizzara'*, literally "She shall be inseminated." In fact, the Torah recitation of the Samaritans, as recorded phonetically by Z. Ben-Hayyim, has *tizzara'*. This information would seem to endorse the interpretation proposed here.[2]

she shall be unclean as at the time of her menstrual infirmity The implication is that not only the duration but the actual nature of the impurity resembles that of a menstruating woman. As Hoffmann notes, it is as though the text read *ke-vi-ymei,* "as in the days of. . . ." This is more clearly expressed in verse 5, literally, "She shall be unclean two weeks in a manner like her menstruation (*ke-niddatah*)."

The impurity of the menstruating woman is defined in 15:19–24, where the term *niddah,* "menstruation," is explained. A menstruating woman was impure primarily with respect to marital relations, though there were certain additional restrictions.

Hebrew *devotah,* "her infirmity," derives from the root *davah,* "to be ill, weak." In 15:33, the menstruating woman is called *davah,* "infirm."[3]

3. *On the eighth day the flesh of his foreskin shall be circumcised* The Hebrew verb *yimmol* is passive (Nifal), from the root *m-w-l,* "to cut off." It is used only with respect to the foreskin (*'orlah*) or its metaphorical expressions.[4] The essential law of circumcision is stated in Genesis 17:10–14, within the context of the covenant between God and Abraham. The practice of circumcision was extant in other ancient cultures, but it assumed a new significance in Israelite religion.[5]

There is undoubtedly a correlation between the eight-day period between birth and circumcision and the duration of the initial period of the mother's impurity after giving birth to a male child, as Hoffmann states.

The verb *yashav,* "to sit, dwell," can also mean "to await, remain inactive," as it does here.[6]

4. *blood purification* The meaning of this translation for Hebrew *demei toharah* is not clear. Perhaps a more literal rendering is preferable: "pure blood." The sense of the statement is that discharges of blood that occur *after* the initial period of impurity are unlike menstrual blood and are not regarded as being impure.

she shall not touch any consecrated thing The rabbinic sages debated the meaning of *kodesh,* "consecrated thing." A broad definition would include within this category such items as *terumah,* the allocations to the priests. According to that definition the wife of a priest who had just given birth would be prohibited from partaking of these foodstuffs.[7]

until her period of purification is completed Rather, "until her period of purity is completed." The noun *tohar,* "purity," is masculine. For this reason the Masoretes inserted a dot (*mappik*) in the final *heh,* producing *tohar-ah,* "her purity." It is not the purification that lasts so long but, more precisely, the time required until the woman is declared pure again.

5 If she bears a female, she shall be unclean two weeks as
during her menstruation, and she shall remain in a state of
blood purification for sixty-six days.
6 On the completion of her period of purification, for
either son or daughter, she shall bring to the priest, at the
entrance of the Tent of Meeting, a lamb in its first year for a
burnt offering, and a pigeon or a turtledove for a sin
offering. 7 He shall offer it before the LORD and make expiation on her behalf; she shall then be clean from her flow of
blood. Such are the rituals concerning her who bears a

טָהֳרָהּ׃ 5 וְאִם־נְקֵבָה תֵלֵד וְטָמְאָה שְׁבֻעַיִם
כְּנִדָּתָהּ וְשִׁשִּׁים יוֹם וְשֵׁשֶׁת יָמִים תֵּשֵׁב עַל־דְּמֵי
טָהֳרָה׃ 6 וּבִמְלֹאת ׀ יְמֵי טָהֳרָהּ לְבֵן אוֹ לְבַת
תָּבִיא כֶּבֶשׂ בֶּן־שְׁנָתוֹ לְעֹלָה וּבֶן־יוֹנָה אוֹ־תֹר
לְחַטָּאת אֶל־פֶּתַח אֹהֶל־מוֹעֵד אֶל־הַכֹּהֵן׃
7 וְהִקְרִיבוֹ לִפְנֵי יְהוָה וְכִפֶּר עָלֶיהָ וְטָהֲרָה מִמְּקֹר
דָּמֶיהָ זֹאת תּוֹרַת הַיֹּלֶדֶת לַזָּכָר אוֹ לַנְּקֵבָה׃

The status of a new mother during this extended period of time was complex. On the one hand, she was no longer impure because of discharges. On the other hand, she was still barred from entry into the sanctuary and from contact with consecrated things. The rabbinic sages compared her status to that of a person impure for a day. Until sunset, rites of purification could not be undertaken; and yet such a person was on his way to final purification, and only time separated him from it. Similarly, the new mother had to wait until a specific period of time had elapsed before she could be declared pure, a period referred to as *yama' 'arikha'*, "an extended day." Rashi comments that her sun would set, so to speak, only after thirty-three or sixty-six days, as the case may be.

5. ***If she bears a female*** The time periods are doubled for a female, but the provisions are the same. See Excursus 3 for more on the sex differentiation and on the impurity of the new mother.

6. ***On the completion of her period of purification*** Rather, "of her period of purity." After the termination of the second period (during which the new mother was essentially pure for private purposes) rites are performed so as to readmit her into the sanctuary and into the religious life of the community.

she shall bring to the priest, at the entrance of the Tent of Meeting As prescribed in 17:3f., all sacrifices are to be offered at one cult site, the Tent of Meeting, on the altar of burnt offerings.

a lamb . . . for a burnt offering On the manner of presenting a burnt offering (*ʿolah*) see chapter 1. The requirement of two offerings, the burnt offering and the sin offering (*ḥatta't*), requires clarification. The type of *ḥatta't* offered by individual Israelites, as in this case, served a dual function. It propitiated God and also compensated the priesthood for its indispensable services in securing expiation. This is why the priests partake of sections of the *ḥatta't* sacrifice.

a pigeon or a turtledove for a sin offering The translation "sin offering" for Hebrew *ḥatta't* is acceptable if understood properly, as it is in our verse. Ancient man seldom distinguished between "sin" and "impurity." In man's relation to God, all sinfulness produced impurity. All impurity, however contracted, could lead to sinfulness if not attended to, and failure to deal properly with impurity aroused God's anger. The point is that the requirement to present a sin offering does not necessarily presume any offense on the part of the person so obligated. This offering was often needed solely to remove impurity. Childbirth, for example, was not sinful—it involved no violation of law—yet a sin offering was required.

The sequence and combination of the two offerings also requires comment. The same rites are required in purification after certain diseases and for the Nazirite.[8] The *ḥatta't,* in removing the impurity, restored to the person the right of access to the sanctuary; and the *ʿolah* that followed immediately upon it symbolized this renewed acceptability. It served as an invocation to God, the first act of worship after being restored to purity. God's acceptance of the *ʿolah* signaled the readmission of the individual into the religious life of the community.

7. ***and make expiation on her behalf*** For the meaning of this formulation, see Comment to 4:20.

from her flow of blood See Comment to 20:18. Hebrew *makor* is a synonym of *maʿayan,*

child, male or female. [8]If, however, her means do not suffice for a sheep, she shall take two turtledoves or two pigeons, one for a burnt offering and the other for a sin offering. The priest shall make expiation on her behalf, and she shall be clean.

8 וְאִם־לֹ֨א תִמְצָ֣א יָדָהּ֮ דֵּ֣י שֶׂה֒ וְלָקְחָ֣ה שְׁתֵּֽי־
תֹרִ֗ים א֤וֹ שְׁנֵי֙ בְּנֵ֣י יוֹנָ֔ה אֶחָ֥ד לְעֹלָ֖ה וְאֶחָ֣ד
לְחַטָּ֑את וְכִפֶּ֥ר עָלֶ֛יהָ הַכֹּהֵ֖ן וְטָהֵֽרָה׃ פ

"spring" (Jer. 2:13; 17:13; Hos. 13:15), and can refer to a source of liquid flowing from the body, for instance, tears, as in Jeremiah 8:23: "Oh, that my head were water, My eyes a fount of tears (*mekor dimʿah*)."[9]

8. ***If, however, her means do not suffice*** The provision for a reduction in the cost of the sacrifice is standard for a number of required purifications and religious obligations. Insistence on the full sacrifice would have deprived poor Israelites of expiation when impurity was incurred through no fault of their own.[10]

The Purification of Skin Diseases (13:1–14:57)

Chapters 13–14 prescribe the role of the Israelite priesthood in diagnosing and purifying persons afflicted with a skin disease known as *tsaraʿat.* This disease also contaminated fabrics and leather as well as plastered or mud-covered building stones. The identification of biblical *tsaraʿat* with "leprosy" is unlikely, if by "leprosy" is meant Hansen's disease;[1] for the symptomatology provided in chapter 13 does not conform to the nature or course of that disease. Undoubtedly, a complex of various ailments was designated by the term *tsaraʿat.*

Chapters 13–14 may be outlined as follows: (1) acute and transient *tsaraʿat* in humans (13:1–46); (2) acute and transient *tsaraʿat* in fabrics and leather (13:47–59); (3) purification rites for a person who has healed after acute *tsaraʿat* (14:1–32); (4) *tsaraʿat* in plastered or mud-covered building stones (14:33–53); and (5) a postscript to chapters 13–14 (14:54–57).

The legislation of chapters 13–14 highlights one of the lesser-understood functions of the Israelite priesthood, whose role went beyond officiating in the cult and attending to the administration of the sanctuary. In 14:11 we read of *ha-kohen ha-metahher,* "the purificatory priest," who regularly dealt with visible, usually contagious illnesses. He combined medical and ritual procedures in safeguarding the purity of the sanctuary and of the Israelite community, which was threatened by the incidence of disease. He instructed the populace and was responsible for enforcing the prescribed procedures.

In the laws of chapters 13–14, acute diseases are subsumed under the category of impurity (*tumʾah*). The afflicted person was treated as an impure substance would be and was quarantined until such time as it could be ascertained, on the basis of observable symptoms, whether the ailment was acute or transient. If it was not acute, the sufferer could be pronounced pure (*ṭahor*) after a given period and be readmitted to the area of settlement. If, however, the symptoms indicated acute *tsaraʿat* (*tsaraʿat mamʾeret*), there was no cure, and the sufferer was banished from the settlement for as long as the disease persisted: in many cases, for life.[2]

Generally speaking, all disease was regarded as a punishment from God for some wrongdoing. In the case of *tsaraʿat* specifically, there was a tradition that it represented a punishment from God for acts of malice such as Miriam's malicious criticism of Moses, reported in Numbers 12:1–3. Precisely why skin diseases were singled out in the priestly codes is not certain. *Tsaraʿat* was undoubtedly quite prevalent in biblical Israel, and there are also the factors of its visibility and its presumed contagion.

13 The LORD spoke to Moses and Aaron, saying:

²When a person has on the skin of his body a swelling, a rash, or a discoloration, and it develops into a scaly affection on the skin of his body, it shall be reported to Aaron the priest or to one of his sons, the priests. ³The priest shall examine the affection on the skin of his body: if hair in the affected patch has turned white and the affection appears to be deeper than the skin of his body, it is a leprous affection; when the priest sees it, he shall pronounce him unclean.

יג א וַיְדַבֵּ֣ר יְהֹוָ֔ה אֶל־מֹשֶׁ֥ה וְאֶֽל־אַהֲרֹ֖ן לֵאמֹֽר׃ 2 אָדָ֗ם כִּֽי־יִהְיֶ֤ה בְעוֹר־בְּשָׂרוֹ֙ שְׂאֵ֤ת אֽוֹ־סַפַּ֙חַת֙ א֣וֹ בַהֶ֔רֶת וְהָיָ֥ה בְעוֹר־בְּשָׂר֖וֹ לְנֶ֣גַע צָרָ֑עַת וְהוּבָא֙ אֶל־אַהֲרֹ֣ן הַכֹּהֵ֔ן א֛וֹ אֶל־אַחַ֥ד מִבָּנָ֖יו הַכֹּהֲנִֽים׃ 3 וְרָאָ֣ה הַכֹּהֵ֣ן אֶת־הַנֶּ֣גַע בְּעֽוֹר־הַ֠בָּשָׂ֠ר וְשֵׂעָ֨ר בַּנֶּ֜גַע הָפַ֣ךְ ׀ לָבָ֗ן וּמַרְאֵ֤ה הַנֶּ֙גַע֙ עָמֹק֙ מֵע֣וֹר בְּשָׂר֔וֹ נֶ֥גַע צָרַ֖עַת ה֑וּא וְרָאָ֥הוּ הַכֹּהֵ֖ן וְטִמֵּ֥א אֹתֽוֹ׃ 4 וְאִם־בַּהֶ֩רֶת֩

CHAPTER 13   THE SYMPTOMATOLOGY (vv. 1–8)

The initial problem faced by the priest was to determine whether the sufferer had acute *tsaraʿat* or some less acute ailment with which it might be confused, but which would heal. If the initial examination did not immediately reveal symptoms of acute *tsaraʿat*, the person was held for further observation for two successive periods of seven days. The text describes the symptoms and prescribes the procedure to be followed. Acute *tsaraʿat* is indicated by a whitish discoloration of the body hair in the infected areas of the skin and by lesions that appear to be recessed or lower than the surrounding skin. If, after seven days, the lesions do not become enlarged, and if, within fourteen days, the hair in the infected areas reverts to a more normal, darker color, a determination may be made that the infection is not acute *tsaraʿat*. Otherwise, further quarantine is imposed; if the rash continues to spread, the person is considered to have acute *tsaraʿat* and is declared impure indefinitely.

2. *When a person has on the skin of his body*   In this verse we find most of the recurring technical terms for the infections referred to in chapters 13–14, and it would be helpful to define these terms here.

(1) *Seʾet,* translated "swelling." A more precise rendering is "local inflammation, boil, mole." This is a generic classification for diverse local inflammations or protrusions, which may assume any one of several forms. In 13:28, Hebrew *seʾet ha-mikhvah,* "the *seʾet* of the burn," is synonymous with *tsarevet ha-mikhvah,* "the scab, scar of the burn." So, *seʾet* and *tsarevet* both designate similar protrusions.

(2) *Sapaḥat* or *mispaḥat,* translated "rash." Literally, *sapaḥat* characterizes the ailment as "growing" out of the skin, that is, "breaking out." This term is not the name of a specific disease of the skin but, rather, identifies a symptomatology in the same way that "rash" does in English.

(3) *Baheret,* translated "discoloration," but more literally "white, shiny spot." It may designate a disease known as *vitiligo,* a whitish ailment of the skin called *bohak* in 13:39. Hebrew *baheret* derives from the adjective *bahir,* "shiny," just as *bohak* derives from a verb meaning "to shine."[3]

(4) *Negaʿ,* translated "affection." This is the generic term for plague and for various sorts of diseases. Literally, it means "touch" and reflects the widespread, ancient belief that gods afflicted persons by their touch. The biblical example closest to expressing this belief occurs in the story of Jacob's contact with the angel of God. The angel "touched" Jacob's hip, which caused Jacob to limp (Gen. 32:26,32f.). The "touch" of divine beings thus became a general term for affliction, and it expressed the belief that one suffered disease as a punishment from God.[4]

(5) *Tsaraʿat,* translated "scaly affection." This rendering of *tsaraʿat* is based on the given symptomatology. The etymology is uncertain.[5]

it shall be reported to Aaron the priest   Alternatively, "He shall be brought to the priest." The point is that the afflicted person must be brought before the priest. The antecedent of the verb *ve-huvaʾ,* "he shall be brought," is *ʾadam,* "a person." This interpretation correlates with verse 6: *ve-nirʾah shenit ʾel ha-kohen,* "he shall appear a second time before the priest."

3. *If hair in the affected patch has turned white*   Hebrew *hafakh lavan,* "has turned white," is the opposite of *kehah,* "has faded," in verse 6. Usually Hebrew *hafakh* means "to cause a

4But if it is a white discoloration on the skin of his body
which does not appear to be deeper than the skin and the
hair in it has not turned white, the priest shall isolate the
affected person for seven days. 5On the seventh day the
priest shall examine him, and if the affection has remained
unchanged in color and the disease has not spread on the
skin, the priest shall isolate him for another seven days. 6On
the seventh day the priest shall examine him again: if the
affection has faded and has not spread on the skin, the
priest shall pronounce him clean. It is a rash; he shall wash
his clothes, and he shall be clean. 7But if the rash should
spread on the skin after he has presented himself to the
priest and been pronounced clean, he shall present himself
again to the priest. 8And if the priest sees that the rash has

לְבָנָה הִוא בְּעוֹר בְּשָׂרוֹ וְעָמֹק אֵין־מַרְאֶהָ מִן־
הָעוֹר וּשְׂעָרָה לֹא־הָפַךְ לָבָן וְהִסְגִּיר הַכֹּהֵן אֶת־
הַנֶּגַע שִׁבְעַת יָמִים׃ 5 וְרָאָהוּ הַכֹּהֵן בַּיּוֹם הַשְּׁבִיעִי
וְהִנֵּה הַנֶּגַע עָמַד בְּעֵינָיו לֹא־פָשָׂה הַנֶּגַע בָּעוֹר
וְהִסְגִּירוֹ הַכֹּהֵן שִׁבְעַת יָמִים שֵׁנִית׃ שני 6 וְרָאָה
הַכֹּהֵן אֹתוֹ בַּיּוֹם הַשְּׁבִיעִי שֵׁנִית וְהִנֵּה כֵּהָה הַנֶּגַע
וְלֹא־פָשָׂה הַנֶּגַע בָּעוֹר וְטִהֲרוֹ הַכֹּהֵן מִסְפַּחַת הִיא
וְכִבֶּס בְּגָדָיו וְטָהֵר׃ 7 וְאִם־פָּשֹׂה תִפְשֶׂה הַמִּסְפַּחַת
בָּעוֹר אַחֲרֵי הֵרָאֹתוֹ אֶל־הַכֹּהֵן לְטָהֳרָתוֹ וְנִרְאָה
שֵׁנִית אֶל־הַכֹּהֵן׃ 8 וְרָאָה הַכֹּהֵן וְהִנֵּה פָּשְׂתָה

change, overturn, reverse," and Ibn Ezra observes that its stative usage here is unusual. In verses 16 and 25 we find the usual passive form of the verb: *ve-nehefkhah le-lavan,* literally "it turned into white."

appears to be deeper than the skin The meaning of Hebrew *ʿamok,* "deep," is explained by verse 20 and by 14:37, where this symptom is characterized as *shafal min ha-ʿor,* "lower than the skin."

When the priest sees it, he shall pronounce him unclean In these codes Hebrew *timme'* means "to declare, pronounce impure," just as, in verses 6, 13, and 17, *tihher* means "to declare pure, purified." Literally, the object of the verb is the disease, not the person, but here and in some following verses we find instances of metonymy, a literary device whereby, in this instance, the disease is interchangeable with its victim. In referring to the disease, the text also refers to the person.

4. ***the priest shall isolate the affected person*** More precisely, Hebrew *ve-hisgir* means "he shall confine, lock up." Rashi notes that a special house was used for this purpose. The incident of Miriam's affliction with *tsaraʿat,* as recounted in Numbers 12:14–15, informs us that the place of quarantine was outside the camp. This is only to be expected, since the afflicted person may have been impure. Here again we have an instance of metonymy. Literally the text states that the disease is quarantined, meaning, actually, the diseased individual.

5. ***and if the affection has remained unchanged in color*** Hebrew *ʿamad be-ʿeinav* literally means "it retained its appearance." The alternative way of stating this condition is *ve-'im taḥteiha taʿamod,* "and if it remains in its place," as in verse 23.

Our verse is somewhat redundant, reading literally ". . . and if the affection remains unchanged in appearance, and has not become enlarged." The statement as a whole pertains to both size and shape.

and the disease has not spread on the skin The Hebrew verb *pasah* more precisely means "to increase"—in size or in number. This symptom describes the enlargement of localized lesions, whereas "spreading" over the body is conveyed by the verb *paraḥ,* "to break out," as in verse 12.

6. ***if the affection has faded*** Hebrew *kehah* is the third person masculine perfect form of the verb "has faded."

he shall wash his clothes Laundering one's garments was a procedure frequently used in purification rites.[6]

7. ***and been pronounced clean*** Literally, Hebrew *le-tohorato* means "for pronouncing him pure."

he shall present himself again to the priest Hebrew *shenit* can mean "again," not only "for a second time."[7]

spread on the skin, the priest shall pronounce him unclean; it is leprosy.

9When a person has a scaly affection, it shall be reported to the priest. 10If the priest finds on the skin a white swelling which has turned some hair white, with a patch of undiscolored flesh in the swelling, 11it is chronic leprosy on the skin of his body, and the priest shall pronounce him unclean; he need not isolate him, for he is unclean. 12If the eruption spreads out over the skin so that it covers all the skin of the affected person from head to foot, wherever the priest can see—13if the priest sees that the eruption has

הַמִּסְפַּחַת בָּעוֹר וְטִמְּאוֹ הַכֹּהֵן צָרַעַת הִוא׃
פ 9 נֶגַע צָרַעַת כִּי תִהְיֶה בְּאָדָם וְהוּבָא
אֶל־הַכֹּהֵן׃ 10 וְרָאָה הַכֹּהֵן וְהִנֵּה שְׂאֵת־לְבָנָה
בָּעוֹר וְהִיא הָפְכָה שֵׂעָר לָבָן וּמִחְיַת בָּשָׂר חַי
בַּשְׂאֵת׃ 11 צָרַעַת נוֹשֶׁנֶת הִוא בְּעוֹר בְּשָׂרוֹ
וְטִמְּאוֹ הַכֹּהֵן לֹא יַסְגִּרֶנּוּ כִּי טָמֵא הוּא׃ 12 וְאִם־
פָּרוֹחַ תִּפְרַח הַצָּרַעַת בָּעוֹר וְכִסְּתָה הַצָּרַעַת אֵת
כָּל־עוֹר הַנֶּגַע מֵרֹאשׁוֹ וְעַד־רַגְלָיו לְכָל־מַרְאֵה
עֵינֵי הַכֹּהֵן׃ 13 וְרָאָה הַכֹּהֵן וְהִנֵּה כִסְּתָה הַצָּרַעַת

8. ***it is leprosy*** That is to say, it is acute *tsaraʿat.*

CHRONIC AILMENTS (vv. 9–17)

If a person with an "old" ailment, or what we would call a *chronic* condition, is brought to the priest, a different set of diagnostic criteria is applied. Exposed ("raw") flesh in an infected area indicates that the old ailment never healed properly. If, however, the exposed flesh is subsequently covered by new skin (referred to by the text as "turning completely white"), this indicates that the chronic *tsaraʿat* has healed.

9. ***When a person has a scaly affection*** That is to say, when a person shows the priest an old ailment of the skin that may represent the recurrence of chronic *tsaraʿat.*

10. ***a white swelling which has turned some hair white*** Rather, "a white inflammation, in which the hair has turned white." The antecedent of *hafekhah lavan,* "has turned white," is *seʾet,* "inflammation." The verb is stative, not transitive, or active, just as in verse 3.

with a patch of undiscolored flesh Rather, "of exposed flesh." This approximates the translation "quick raw flesh," noted previously. The present translation could confuse the symptomatology, both here and in verses 13–16. The point is that when healing occurs, white, normal skin grows over the infected area, as indicated in verse 13. But, as verse 14 promptly informs us, the recurrence of infection is indicated by the reappearance of "raw" flesh. This interpretation is virtually confirmed by verse 24, where *miḥyat ha-mikhvah* clearly means "the *exposed* flesh of the burn," and *miḥyah* derives from the same verbal root as *ḥai* in verse 10.

11. ***it is chronic leprosy*** Hebrew *noshenet* means "old, prior." In this case, there is no need for a period of quarantine because it is determined at the outset that acute *tsaraʿat* has recurred.

12. ***If the eruption spreads out over the skin*** Hebrew *p-r-ḥ* means "to blossom." Compare Exodus 9:9: *sheḥin poreaḥ ʾabaʿbuʿot,* "dermatitis breaking out into boils."

so that it covers all the skin of the affected person Literally, "all the skin of the infection." This is another instance of metonymy.

The idiom "from head to foot," suggested here, is proverbial.[8] In Isaiah 1:6 we read "from head to foot, no spot is sound." An identical expression occurs frequently in Akkadian medical texts: *ištu qaqqādišu adi šēpēšu,* "from his head to his feet."[9]

wherever the priest can see Rather, "after the priest's complete examination." The sense is temporal, not spatial.

13. ***for he has turned all white*** Exposed, or "raw," flesh is a reddish color, not white, like normal skin. This, then, is the criterion: Skin turned white is new skin that has grown over the "raw" area.

covered the whole body—he shall pronounce the affected person clean; he is clean, for he has turned all white. 14 But as soon as undiscolored flesh appears in it, he shall be unclean; 15 when the priest sees the undiscolored flesh, he shall pronounce him unclean. The undiscolored flesh is unclean; it is leprosy. 16 But if the undiscolored flesh again turns white, he shall come to the priest, 17 and the priest shall examine him: if the affection has turned white, the priest shall pronounce the affected person clean; he is clean.

18 When an inflammation appears on the skin of one's body and it heals, 19 and a white swelling or a white discoloration streaked with red develops where the inflammation was, he shall present himself to the priest. 20 If the priest finds that it appears lower than the rest of the skin and that the hair in it has turned white, the priest shall pronounce him unclean; it is a leprous affection that has broken out in the inflammation. 21 But if the priest finds that there is no white hair in it and it is not lower than the rest of the skin, and it is faded, the priest shall isolate him for seven days. 22 If it should spread in the skin, the priest shall pronounce him unclean; it is an affection. 23 But if the

אֶת־כָּל־בְּשָׂרוֹ וְטִהַר אֶת־הַנָּגַע כֻּלּוֹ הָפַךְ לָבָן
טָהוֹר הוּא׃ 14 וּבְיוֹם הֵרָאוֹת בּוֹ בָּשָׂר חַי יִטְמָא׃
15 וְרָאָה הַכֹּהֵן אֶת־הַבָּשָׂר הַחַי וְטִמְּאוֹ הַבָּשָׂר
הַחַי טָמֵא הוּא צָרַעַת הוּא׃ 16 אוֹ כִי יָשׁוּב
הַבָּשָׂר הַחַי וְנֶהְפַּךְ לְלָבָן וּבָא אֶל־הַכֹּהֵן׃
17 וְרָאָהוּ הַכֹּהֵן וְהִנֵּה נֶהְפַּךְ הַנֶּגַע לְלָבָן וְטִהַר
הַכֹּהֵן אֶת־הַנֶּגַע טָהוֹר הוּא׃ פ שלישי
18 וּבָשָׂר כִּי־יִהְיֶה בוֹ־בְעֹרוֹ שְׁחִין וְנִרְפָּא׃ 19 וְהָיָה
בִּמְקוֹם הַשְּׁחִין שְׂאֵת לְבָנָה אוֹ בַהֶרֶת לְבָנָה
אֲדַמְדָּמֶת וְנִרְאָה אֶל־הַכֹּהֵן׃ 20 וְרָאָה הַכֹּהֵן וְהִנֵּה
מַרְאֶהָ שָׁפָל מִן־הָעוֹר וּשְׂעָרָהּ הָפַךְ לָבָן וְטִמְּאוֹ
הַכֹּהֵן נֶגַע־צָרַעַת הִוא בַּשְּׁחִין פָּרָחָה׃ 21 וְאִם ׀
יִרְאֶנָּה הַכֹּהֵן וְהִנֵּה אֵין־בָּהּ שֵׂעָר לָבָן וּשְׁפָלָה
אֵינֶנָּה מִן־הָעוֹר וְהִיא כֵהָה וְהִסְגִּירוֹ הַכֹּהֵן שִׁבְעַת
יָמִים׃ 22 וְאִם־פָּשֹׂה תִפְשֶׂה בָּעוֹר וְטִמֵּא הַכֹּהֵן
אֹתוֹ נֶגַע הִוא׃ 23 וְאִם־תַּחְתֶּיהָ תַּעֲמֹד הַבַּהֶרֶת

14. But as soon as undiscolored flesh appears on it Rather, "as soon as exposed flesh reappears on it." Exposed flesh, if it persists or recurs, is symptomatic of chronic *tsaraʿat.* It means that the old infection has not been covered by new skin and will not heal properly.

16. But if the undiscolored flesh again turns white Rather, "But if the exposed flesh recedes and resumes its whiteness." On the sense of Hebrew *yashuv,* "recedes," see 2 Kings 20:9: "Shall the shadow advance ten steps or recede ten steps?" The meaning here is that new ("white") skin has grown over the infected, exposed flesh.

TSARAʿAT AS A COMPLICATION (vv. 18–46)

This section of the code deals with *tsaraʿat* as a complication arising out of other conditions, that is, as a secondary development. These symptoms are (1) *sheḥin,* a term characterizing a number of conditions similar to dermatitis (vv. 18–23);[10] (2) a burn that became infected (vv. 24–28); (3) diseases of the hair (vv. 29–37); (4) a skin condition identified as vitiligo (vv. 38–39); and (5) ailments of the scalp and forehead (vv. 40–46).

18. When an inflammation appears on the skin of one's body and it heals Rather, "When a dermatitis infection had occurred on one's skin but had healed." The primary condition, dermatitis (*sheḥin*), had healed, but a secondary infection had developed in the same area.

19. streaked with red The reduplicative form *ʾadamdam* is diminutive: hence "reddish, pink," or the like. Similar forms recur in verses 23, 43, 49, and elsewhere.

20. If the priest finds The symptomatology here is essentially the same as that applicable to the diagnosis of an initial condition of *tsaraʿat,* in verses 1–8. This prescription employs the adjective *shafal,* "low, deep," instead of *ʿamok,* "deep," as in verse 3.

22. If it should spread in the skin Rather, "If it should become enlarged on the skin."[11]

discoloration remains stationary, not having spread, it is
the scar of the inflammation; the priest shall pronounce
him clean.

24 When the skin of one's body sustains a burn by fire, and
the patch from the burn is a discoloration, either white
streaked with red, or white, 25 the priest shall examine it. If
some hair has turned white in the discoloration, which
itself appears to go deeper than the skin, it is leprosy that
has broken out in the burn. The priest shall pronounce him
unclean; it is a leprous affection. 26 But if the priest finds
that there is no white hair in the discoloration, and that it is
not lower than the rest of the skin, and it is faded, the priest
shall isolate him for seven days. 27 On the seventh day the
priest shall examine him: if it has spread in the skin, the
priest shall pronounce him unclean; it is a leprous affection. 28 But if the discoloration has remained stationary, not
having spread on the skin, and it is faded, it is the swelling
from the burn. The priest shall pronounce him clean, for it
is the scar of the burn.

29 If a man or a woman has an affection on the head or in
the beard, 30 the priest shall examine the affection. If it
appears to go deeper than the skin and there is thin yellow
hair in it, the priest shall pronounce him unclean; it is a
scall, a scaly eruption in the hair or beard. 31 But if the priest
finds that the scall affection does not appear to go deeper
than the skin, yet there is no black hair in it, the priest shall

לֹא פָשָׂתָה צָרֶבֶת הַשְּׁחִין הִוא וְטִהֲרוֹ הַכֹּהֵן׃
ס רביעי [שני כשהן מחוברות]
24 אוֹ בָשָׂר כִּי־יִהְיֶה בְעֹרוֹ מִכְוַת־אֵשׁ וְהָיְתָה
מִחְיַת הַמִּכְוָה בַּהֶרֶת לְבָנָה אֲדַמְדֶּמֶת אוֹ לְבָנָה׃
25 וְרָאָה אֹתָהּ הַכֹּהֵן וְהִנֵּה נֶהְפַּךְ שֵׂעָר לָבָן
בַּבַּהֶרֶת וּמַרְאֶהָ עָמֹק מִן־הָעוֹר צָרַעַת הִוא
בַּמִּכְוָה פָּרָחָה וְטִמֵּא אֹתוֹ הַכֹּהֵן נֶגַע צָרַעַת הִוא׃
26 וְאִם ׀ יִרְאֶנָּה הַכֹּהֵן וְהִנֵּה אֵין־בַּבַּהֶרֶת שֵׂעָר
לָבָן וּשְׁפָלָה אֵינֶנָּה מִן־הָעוֹר וְהִוא כֵהָה וְהִסְגִּירוֹ
הַכֹּהֵן שִׁבְעַת יָמִים׃ 27 וְרָאָהוּ הַכֹּהֵן בַּיּוֹם
הַשְּׁבִיעִי אִם־פָּשֹׂה תִפְשֶׂה בָּעוֹר וְטִמֵּא הַכֹּהֵן
אֹתוֹ נֶגַע צָרַעַת הִוא׃ 28 וְאִם־תַּחְתֶּיהָ תַעֲמֹד
הַבַּהֶרֶת לֹא־פָשְׂתָה בָעוֹר וְהִוא כֵהָה שְׂאֵת
הַמִּכְוָה הִוא וְטִהֲרוֹ הַכֹּהֵן כִּי־צָרֶבֶת הַמִּכְוָה הִוא׃
פ חמישי 29 וְאִישׁ אוֹ אִשָּׁה כִּי־יִהְיֶה בוֹ
נָגַע בְּרֹאשׁ אוֹ בְזָקָן׃ 30 וְרָאָה הַכֹּהֵן אֶת־הַנֶּגַע
וְהִנֵּה מַרְאֵהוּ עָמֹק מִן־הָעוֹר וּבוֹ שֵׂעָר צָהֹב דָּק
וְטִמֵּא אֹתוֹ הַכֹּהֵן נֶתֶק הוּא צָרַעַת הָרֹאשׁ אוֹ
הַזָּקָן הוּא׃ 31 וְכִי־יִרְאֶה הַכֹּהֵן אֶת־נֶגַע הַנֶּתֶק
וְהִנֵּה אֵין־מַרְאֵהוּ עָמֹק מִן־הָעוֹר וְשֵׂעָר שָׁחֹר אֵין
בּוֹ וְהִסְגִּיר הַכֹּהֵן אֶת־נֶגַע הַנֶּתֶק שִׁבְעַת יָמִים׃

23. *it is the scar of the inflammation* On the meaning of Hebrew *tsarevet,* see Comment to verse 2.

24. *When the skin of one's body sustains a burn by fire* Hebrew *mikhvah,* "burn," is derived from the same root as *keviyah,* "a burn," in Exodus 21:25.

and the patch from the burn is a discoloration Rather, "and the exposed skin of the burn is a pink or white shiny spot." See Comment to verse 2.

29. *If a man or woman has an affection on the head or in the beard* According to dermatologists, the hair, which is rooted in layers of the skin, is directly affected by such conditions as acne, which disturb the hair follicles.[12]

30. *and there is thin yellow hair in it* The symptomatology is generally similar to that of skin ailments, except that yellow, not white hair, is the discoloration to be watched for. Mishnah Nega'im 10:1 explains that the adjective *dak* indicates that the growth of the hair was stunted, that the hair was shorter than usual.

it is a scall As the name of a particular disease, Hebrew *netek,* "scall," occurs only here in the Hebrew Bible. Technically, it refers to the condition of the hair follicles, not of the skin. It describes the follicles of hair as being "torn" from the scalp after "splitting." This occurs in certain skin ailments.

The noun *netek* derives from a verb that means "to tear apart" and is used, curiously enough, with reference to string, or stringy substances, similar to the hair follicles. Thus we read in Judges 16:9: "as a strand of tow comes apart (*yinnatek*)." Also, compare Ecclesiastes 4:12: "a threefold cord is not readily broken (*yinnatek*)." Some have identified the ailment called *netek* as *acne vulgaris.*

isolate the person with the scall affection for seven days. [32]On the seventh day the priest shall examine the affection. If the scall has not spread and no yellow hair has appeared in it, and the scall does not appear to go deeper than the skin, [33]the person with the scall shall shave himself, but without shaving the scall; the priest shall isolate him for another seven days. [34]On the seventh day the priest shall examine the scall. If the scall has not spread on the skin, and does not appear to go deeper than the skin, the priest shall pronounce him clean; he shall wash his clothes, and he shall be clean. [35]If, however, the scall should spread on the skin after he has been pronounced clean, [36]the priest shall examine him. If the scall has spread on the skin, the priest need not look for yellow hair: he is unclean. [37]But if the scall has remained unchanged in color, and black hair has grown in it, the scall is healed; he is clean. The priest shall pronounce him clean.

[38]If a man or a woman has the skin of the body streaked with white discolorations, [39]and the priest sees that the discolorations on the skin of the body are of a dull white, it is a tetter broken out on the skin; he is clean.

32 וְרָאָה הַכֹּהֵן אֶת־הַנֶּגַע בַּיּוֹם הַשְּׁבִיעִי וְהִנֵּה
לֹא־פָשָׂה הַנֶּתֶק וְלֹא־הָיָה בוֹ שֵׂעָר צָהֹב וּמַרְאֵה
הַנֶּתֶק אֵין עָמֹק מִן־הָעוֹר׃ 33 וְהִתְגַּלָּח* וְאֶת־
הַנֶּתֶק לֹא יְגַלֵּחַ וְהִסְגִּיר הַכֹּהֵן אֶת־הַנֶּתֶק שִׁבְעַת
יָמִים שֵׁנִית׃ 34 וְרָאָה הַכֹּהֵן אֶת־הַנֶּתֶק בַּיּוֹם
הַשְּׁבִיעִי וְהִנֵּה לֹא־פָשָׂה הַנֶּתֶק בָּעוֹר וּמַרְאֵהוּ
אֵינֶנּוּ עָמֹק מִן־הָעוֹר וְטִהַר אֹתוֹ הַכֹּהֵן וְכִבֶּס
בְּגָדָיו וְטָהֵר׃ 35 וְאִם־פָּשֹׂה יִפְשֶׂה הַנֶּתֶק בָּעוֹר
אַחֲרֵי טָהֳרָתוֹ׃ 36 וְרָאָהוּ הַכֹּהֵן וְהִנֵּה פָּשָׂה הַנֶּתֶק
בָּעוֹר לֹא־יְבַקֵּר הַכֹּהֵן לַשֵּׂעָר הַצָּהֹב טָמֵא הוּא׃
37 וְאִם־בְּעֵינָיו עָמַד הַנֶּתֶק וְשֵׂעָר שָׁחֹר צָמַח־בּוֹ
נִרְפָּא הַנֶּתֶק טָהוֹר הוּא וְטִהֲרוֹ הַכֹּהֵן׃ ס
38 וְאִישׁ אוֹ־אִשָּׁה כִּי־יִהְיֶה בְעוֹר־בְּשָׂרָם בֶּהָרֹת
בֶּהָרֹת לְבָנֹת׃ 39 וְרָאָה הַכֹּהֵן וְהִנֵּה בְעוֹר־בְּשָׂרָם
בֶּהָרֹת כֵּהוֹת לְבָנֹת בֹּהַק הוּא פָּרַח בָּעוֹר טָהוֹר
הוּא׃ ס ששי [שלישי כשהן מחוברות]

v. 33. ג׳ רבתי

31. yet there is no black hair in it This verse appears to be problematic. As it stands, it does not represent the exact reverse of verse 30, which sets forth two criteria: recessed lesions and yellowish hair in the infected areas. The reverse symptoms would be no recessed lesions and no yellow hair. Verse 31, however, states: no recessed lesions and no black hair. Some modern scholars assume a scribal error and read *tsahov,* "yellow," instead of *shaḥor,* "black, dark," in verse 31. The Septuagint deletes one of the negatives in the verse, leaving only one relevant symptom—the recessed lesions.

These changes do not reflect a correct understanding of the verse. This passage is describing the progressive stages of a complication whose treatment differs somewhat from acute *tsaraʿat* because of the background condition involved. Verse 30 stipulates that if both positive symptoms appear, acute *tsaraʿat* is indicated. Verse 31 states that if only one symptom occurs—the absence of black, normal hair, which is equivalent to the presence of yellow infected hair—quarantine is imposed because a final determination cannot yet be made. (Recessed lesions alone are also not sufficient to indicate acute *tsaraʿat.*) At a later stage, dark hair might still grow back and the lesions remain unenlarged, a situation described in verse 37.

32. On the seventh day the priest shall examine the affection Three conditions must obtain for a declaration of purity at this stage: no yellow hair, no enlargement of the lesions, and no recessed lesions. To allow for clearer observation, the hair is shaved around the infected areas, leaving the infected areas themselves unshaven.

36. If the scall has spread on the skin Any enlargement of the lesions after fourteen days is sufficient to warrant a diagnosis of acute *tsaraʿat.* The priest need look no further for yellow hair. Hebrew *yevakker* means "to attend, examine."[13]

37. But if the scall has remained unchanged If normal-colored hair grows back in the infected area and there has been no subsequent enlargement of the lesions, the *netek* infection has healed.

38. the skin of the body streaked with white discolorations This brief section (vv. 38–39) deals with an ailment known as *bohak,* "brightness," which has been identified by some medical authorities as vitiligo. It is a rash that is not acute.[14]

⁴⁰If a man loses the hair of his head and becomes bald, he is clean. ⁴¹If he loses the hair on the front part of his head and becomes bald at the forehead, he is clean. ⁴²But if a white affection streaked with red appears on the bald part in the front or at the back of the head, it is a scaly eruption that is spreading over the bald part in the front or at the back of the head. ⁴³The priest shall examine him: if the swollen affection on the bald part in the front or at the back of his head is white streaked with red, like the leprosy of body skin in appearance, ⁴⁴the man is leprous; he is unclean. The priest shall pronounce him unclean; he has the affection on his head.

⁴⁵As for the person with a leprous affection, his clothes shall be rent, his head shall be left bare, and he shall cover over his upper lip; and he shall call out, "Unclean! Unclean!" ⁴⁶He shall be unclean as long as the disease is on him. Being unclean, he shall dwell apart; his dwelling shall be outside the camp.

40 וְאִ֕ישׁ כִּ֥י יִמָּרֵ֖ט רֹאשׁ֑וֹ קֵרֵ֥חַ ה֖וּא טָה֥וֹר ה֑וּא: 41 וְאִם֙ מִפְּאַ֣ת פָּנָ֔יו יִמָּרֵ֖ט רֹאשׁ֑וֹ גִּבֵּ֥חַ ה֖וּא טָה֥וֹר ה֑וּא: 42 וְכִֽי־יִהְיֶ֤ה בַקָּרַ֙חַת֙ א֣וֹ בַגַּבַּ֔חַת נֶ֖גַע לָבָ֣ן אֲדַמְדָּ֑ם צָרַ֤עַת פֹּרַ֙חַת֙ הִ֔וא בְּקָרַחְתּ֖וֹ א֥וֹ בְגַבַּחְתּֽוֹ: 43 וְרָאָ֨ה אֹת֜וֹ הַכֹּהֵ֗ן וְהִנֵּ֤ה שְׂאֵת־הַנֶּ֙גַע֙ לְבָנָ֣ה אֲדַמְדֶּ֔מֶת בְּקָרַחְתּ֖וֹ א֣וֹ בְגַבַּחְתּ֑וֹ כְּמַרְאֵ֥ה צָרַ֖עַת ע֥וֹר בָּשָֽׂר: 44 אִישׁ־צָר֥וּעַ ה֖וּא טָמֵ֥א ה֑וּא טַמֵּ֧א יְטַמְּאֶ֛נּוּ הַכֹּהֵ֖ן בְּרֹאשׁ֥וֹ נִגְעֽוֹ: 45 וְהַצָּר֜וּעַ אֲשֶׁר־בּ֣וֹ הַנֶּ֗גַע בְּגָדָ֞יו יִהְי֤וּ פְרֻמִים֙ וְרֹאשׁוֹ֙ יִהְיֶ֣ה פָר֔וּעַ וְעַל־שָׂפָ֖ם יַעְטֶ֑ה וְטָמֵ֥א ׀ טָמֵ֖א יִקְרָֽא: 46 כָּל־יְמֵ֞י אֲשֶׁ֨ר הַנֶּ֥גַע בּ֛וֹ יִטְמָ֖א טָמֵ֣א ה֑וּא בָּדָ֣ד יֵשֵׁ֔ב מִח֥וּץ לַֽמַּחֲנֶ֖ה מֽוֹשָׁבֽוֹ: ס 47 וְהַבֶּ֕גֶד כִּֽי־יִהְיֶ֥ה ב֖וֹ נֶ֣גַע צָרָ֑עַת בְּבֶ֣גֶד צֶ֔מֶר א֖וֹ בְּבֶ֥גֶד פִּשְׁתִּֽים:

40.　*If a man loses the hair of his head and becomes bald* This section (vv. 40–44) deals with cases where a person had already become bald prior to the outbreak of the ailment in question. The terms of reference here are interesting. Hebrew *yimmaret* means "to be rubbed, scratched"—so that the hair is plucked out. The Akkadian cognate *maraṭu* is frequently used with this meaning in medical texts.¹⁵ Whereas Hebrew *karahat* designates the bald area at the top and back part of the head, Hebrew *gabahat* refers to the front part of the head and the forehead. In verse 41, *gabahat* is synonymous with *pe'at panav*, "his temples, forehead." According to 2 Chronicles 26:19, *tsara'at* shone on the forehead of an afflicted king. This is the very condition described in our code.

43.　*The priest shall examine him* If the inflamed infection is whitish on the bald pate or on the forehead, the person is suffering from acute *tsara'at*. Hebrew *tsaru'a* means "one suffering from *tsara'at*." An alternative form is *metsora'*, as in verse 42.

44.　*he has the affection on his head* Hebrew *be-ro'sh nig'o*, literally "at the head of his infection," represents transposition, or reverse order. The correct sense is *be-nega' ro'sho*, "on account of the infection on his head."

45.　*As for the person with a leprous affection* Verses 45–46 prescribe what is to be done with one whose ailments have not healed, namely, one who suffers from the acute condition stipulated in verse 8. Up to this point, the code has set forth procedures prerequisite to a declaration of purity. Here, by contrast, is the treatment for one who is finally declared *tame'*, "impure," due to acute *tsara'at* of any of the varieties discussed in verses 1–44.

his clothes shall be rent Hebrew *parum*, "torn," is explained in the Comment to 10:6.

his head shall be left bare Baring the head so that the hair hung loose was a customary way of shaming a person, as was covering the upper lip. A wife suspected of adultery had her head bared (Num. 5:18), and the prophet Micah (3:7) states: "The seers shall be shamed and the diviners unfounded; They shall cover their upper lips." Here, although no comparable disgrace was involved, these symbols could serve as a means of keeping others distant from the diseased person.

and he shall call out, "Unclean!" The sufferer must warn all who approach that he is impure. Compare Isaiah 52:11: "Turn, turn away, touch naught unclean."

46.　*as long as the disease is on him* The Hebrew reads *kol yemei 'asher*, "all the days while. . . ." The upshot of this provision is that an individual suffering from acute *tsara'at* may be

47When an eruptive affection occurs in a cloth of wool or linen fabric, 48in the warp or in the woof of the linen or the wool, or in a skin or in anything made of skin; 49if the affection in the cloth or the skin, in the warp or the woof, or in any article of skin, is streaky green or red, it is an eruptive affection. It shall be shown to the priest; 50and the priest, after examining the affection, shall isolate the affected article for seven days. 51On the seventh day he shall examine the affection: if the affection has spread in the cloth—whether in the warp or the woof, or in the skin, for whatever purpose the skin may be used—the affection is a malignant eruption; it is unclean. 52The cloth—whether warp or woof in wool or linen, or any article of skin—in which the affection is found, shall be burned, for it is a malignant eruption; it shall be consumed in fire. 53But if

48 אוֹ בִשְׁתִי אוֹ בְעֵרֶב לַפִּשְׁתִּים וְלַצָּמֶר אוֹ
בְעוֹר אוֹ בְּכָל־מְלֶאכֶת עוֹר׃ 49 וְהָיָה הַנֶּגַע
יְרַקְרַק ׀ אוֹ אֲדַמְדָּם בַּבֶּגֶד אוֹ בָעוֹר אוֹ־בַשְּׁתִי
אוֹ־בָעֵרֶב אוֹ בְכָל־כְּלִי־עוֹר נֶגַע צָרַעַת הוּא
וְהָרְאָה אֶת־הַכֹּהֵן׃ 50 וְרָאָה הַכֹּהֵן אֶת־הַנָּגַע
וְהִסְגִּיר אֶת־הַנֶּגַע שִׁבְעַת יָמִים׃ 51 וְרָאָה אֶת־
הַנֶּגַע בַּיּוֹם הַשְּׁבִיעִי כִּי־פָשָׂה הַנֶּגַע בַּבֶּגֶד אוֹ־
בַשְּׁתִי אוֹ־בָעֵרֶב אוֹ בָעוֹר לְכֹל אֲשֶׁר־יֵעָשֶׂה
הָעוֹר לִמְלָאכָה צָרַעַת מַמְאֶרֶת הַנֶּגַע טָמֵא הוּא׃
52 וְשָׂרַף אֶת־הַבֶּגֶד אוֹ אֶת־הַשְּׁתִי ׀ אוֹ אֶת־הָעֵרֶב
בַּצֶּמֶר אוֹ בַפִּשְׁתִּים אוֹ אֶת־כָּל־כְּלִי הָעוֹר אֲשֶׁר־
יִהְיֶה בוֹ הַנָּגַע כִּי־צָרַעַת מַמְאֶרֶת הִוא בָּאֵשׁ
תִּשָּׂרֵף׃ 53 וְאִם יִרְאֶה הַכֹּהֵן וְהִנֵּה לֹא־פָשָׂה הַנֶּגַע

permanently banished; in 2 Kings 15:5 a Judean king afflicted with acute *tsaraʿat* remained all his life in a place called *beit ha-ḥofshit,* "the house of quarantine."[16]

TSARAʿAT IN FABRICS AND LEATHER (vv. 47–59)

This section deals with *tsaraʿat*-type infections that damage fabrics and worked leather. These phenomena had the same appearance as those that attacked humans and it was probably believed that they were dangerous. Some have suggested that they were perhaps fungoid or sporoid infections. The same would be true of the mold that attacked plastered or mud-covered building stones, the subject of 14:33f. The terminology and procedures concerning fabrics and leather were deliberately modeled on the code for human diseases, even to the point of referring to the inner and outer surfaces of fabrics and leather as *karaḥat* and *gabaḥat,* "the back and the front" of the bald head![17]

The procedures themselves are fairly simple. On the basis of a seven-day period of observation, the priest determines whether or not the infection is *tsaraʿat mamʾeret,* "acute, malignant *tsaraʿat*" (vv. 51–52). In such a case, the item must be entirely burned. If it is determined that the infected, discolored areas have not become enlarged, the item is laundered and held for an additional period of observation, after which it is laundered again. If, then, the infected areas still remain, even though not enlarged, the infection is diagnosed as *peḥetet,* a form of acute *tsaraʿat.* In such a case, the fabric or leather must be entirely burned. Throughout the course of this procedure, every effort is made to save as much as possible of the materials by cutting away only the infected areas in the hope of containing the spread of the infection. However, the item as a whole can only be declared pure if the infection finally remits or disappears entirely.

47. in a cloth of wool or linen fabric Wool and linen were the two fibers from which most cloth was woven in biblical times. The two, wool and linen, were not woven into the same fabric.[18]

48. in the warp or in the woof Hebrew *sheti* designates the vertical, drawn threads on the loom, whereas *ʿerev* designates those threads that are woven in by means of the shuttle, the horizontal action.[19]

or in anything made of skin Hebrew *meleʾkhet ʿor* means "worked leather." Compare verse 51: *limlaʾkhah,* "for working."

51. the affection is a malignant eruption Hebrew *mamʾeret* means "destructive, pricking." Compare *sillon mamʾir,* "a prickly brier," in Ezekiel 28:24.

בַּבֶּגֶד אוֹ בַשְּׁתִי אוֹ בָעֵרֶב אוֹ בְּכָל־כְּלִי־עוֹר׃
54 וְצִוָּה הַכֹּהֵן וְכִבְּסוּ אֵת אֲשֶׁר־בּוֹ הַנָּגַע וְהִסְגִּירוֹ
שִׁבְעַת־יָמִים שֵׁנִית׃ שביעי [רביעי כשהן
מחוברות] 55 וְרָאָה הַכֹּהֵן אַחֲרֵי ׀ הֻכַּבֵּס אֶת־
הַנֶּגַע וְהִנֵּה לֹא־הָפַךְ הַנֶּגַע אֶת־עֵינוֹ וְהַנֶּגַע לֹא־
פָשָׂה טָמֵא הוּא בָּאֵשׁ תִּשְׂרְפֶנּוּ פְּחֶתֶת הִוא
בְּקָרַחְתּוֹ אוֹ בְגַבַּחְתּוֹ׃ 56 וְאִם רָאָה הַכֹּהֵן וְהִנֵּה
כֵּהָה הַנֶּגַע אַחֲרֵי הֻכַּבֵּס אֹתוֹ וְקָרַע אֹתוֹ מִן־
הַבֶּגֶד אוֹ מִן־הָעוֹר אוֹ מִן־הַשְּׁתִי אוֹ מִן־הָעֵרֶב׃
מפטיר 57 וְאִם־תֵּרָאֶה עוֹד בַּבֶּגֶד אוֹ־בַשְּׁתִי אוֹ־
בָעֵרֶב אוֹ בְכָל־כְּלִי־עוֹר פֹּרַחַת הִוא בָּאֵשׁ
תִּשְׂרְפֶנּוּ אֵת אֲשֶׁר־בּוֹ הַנָּגַע׃ 58 וְהַבֶּגֶד אוֹ־הַשְּׁתִי
אוֹ־הָעֵרֶב אוֹ־כָל־כְּלִי הָעוֹר אֲשֶׁר תְּכַבֵּס וְסָר
מֵהֶם הַנָּגַע וְכֻבַּס שֵׁנִית וְטָהֵר׃ 59 זֹאת תּוֹרַת
נֶגַע־צָרַעַת בֶּגֶד הַצֶּמֶר ׀ אוֹ הַפִּשְׁתִּים אוֹ הַשְּׁתִי
אוֹ הָעֵרֶב אוֹ כָּל־כְּלִי־עוֹר לְטַהֲרוֹ אוֹ לְטַמְּאוֹ׃
פ

the priest sees that the affection in the cloth—whether in warp or in woof, or in any article of skin—has not spread, 54 the priest shall order the affected article washed, and he shall isolate it for another seven days. 55 And if, after the affected article has been washed, the priest sees that the affection has not changed color and that it has not spread, it is unclean. It shall be consumed in fire; it is a fret, whether on its inner side or on its outer side. 56 But if the priest sees that the affected part, after it has been washed, is faded, he shall tear it out from the cloth or skin, whether in the warp or in the woof; 57 and if it occurs again in the cloth—whether in warp or in woof—or in any article of skin, it is a wild growth; the affected article shall be consumed in fire. 58 If, however, the affection disappears from the cloth—warp or woof—or from any article of skin that has been washed, it shall be washed again, and it shall be clean.

59 Such is the procedure for eruptive affections of cloth, woolen or linen, in warp or in woof, or of any article of skin, for pronouncing it clean or unclean.

55. *it is a fret, whether on its inner side or its outer side* Hebrew *peḥetet,* translated "fret," derives from the verb *paḥat,* "to dig out, furrow." In biblical Hebrew, it occurs only here, but the verb is common in Late Hebrew and in Aramaic.[20] Reference to the bodily areas, *karaḥat* ("bald head") and *gabaḥat* ("bald forehead"), to describe surfaces of fabric and leather shows that the symptomatology is modeled directly on the symptoms of human disease.

56. *after it has been washed* Hebrew *hukkabbes* is a rare form of the verb, although its meaning is clear.[21]

CHAPTER 14

Metsoraʿ

Chapter 14 is a continuation of the laws of chapter 13. Its contents may be divided into two main sections: (1) purification rites for a person declared impure under the provisions of 13:8–46 (vv. 1–32) (a person declared pure after seven, or even fourteen, days required no such elaborate rites and had only to launder his clothing, as prescribed in 13:6); and (2) *tsaraʿat* in plastered or mud-covered building stones (vv. 32–53). Verses 54–57 are a postscript to chapters 13–14.

PURIFICATION RITES FOR INDIVIDUALS (vv. 1–32)

The rites ordained for the purification of a person who had suffered from acute *tsaraʿat* are among the most elaborate in the priestly laws. They demonstrate how seriously the infections referred to as *tsaraʿat* were taken in biblical Israel; and they combine cultic procedures in the sanctuary area with those to be performed outside the camp.

The priest began by visiting the person whose condition had apparently healed in order to ascertain that this had actually occurred. There he prepared two live birds, a cedar stick, a hyssop branch, and a piece of crimson cloth—the same materials that, according to Numbers 19:6f., were employed in the purification of an Israelite who came into contact with a corpse.

One of the birds was to be slaughtered over running spring water, so that whatever blood was not caught up in an earthen vessel employed for this purpose would run down into the earth. The second

METSORAʿ

14 The LORD spoke to Moses, saying: 2This shall be the ritual for a leper at the time that he is to be cleansed.

When it has been reported to the priest, 3the priest shall go outside the camp. If the priest sees that the leper has been healed of his scaly affection, 4the priest shall order two live clean birds, cedar wood, crimson stuff, and hyssop to be brought for him who is to be cleansed. 5The priest shall

מצרע

י״ד וַיְדַבֵּר יְהוָה אֶל־מֹשֶׁה לֵּאמֹר׃ 2 זֹאת תִּהְיֶה
תּוֹרַת הַמְּצֹרָע בְּיוֹם טָהֳרָתוֹ וְהוּבָא אֶל־הַכֹּהֵן׃
3 וְיָצָא הַכֹּהֵן אֶל־מִחוּץ לַמַּחֲנֶה וְרָאָה הַכֹּהֵן וְהִנֵּה
נִרְפָּא נֶגַע־הַצָּרַעַת מִן־הַצָּרוּעַ׃ 4 וְצִוָּה הַכֹּהֵן
וְלָקַח לַמִּטַּהֵר שְׁתֵּי־צִפֳּרִים חַיּוֹת טְהֹרוֹת וְעֵץ
אֶרֶז וּשְׁנִי תוֹלַעַת וְאֵזֹב׃ 5 וְצִוָּה הַכֹּהֵן וְשָׁחַט אֶת־

bird, cedar stick, hyssop branch, and crimson cloth were dipped in the blood that had been collected in the earthen vessel. The live bird was set free to carry away the evil of the disease into the open field. Some of the blood of the slaughtered bird was then sprinkled seven times on the person being purified, who had to launder his clothing, shave off all his hair, and bathe.

The individual was then permitted to reenter the camp, although he had to remain outside his own house for seven more days, after which he would, once again, shave off all his hair, including his beard and eyebrows, launder his clothing, and bathe. He was then purified of the disease and ready to commence the sacrificial rites of the eighth day, to be performed at the entrance of the Tent of Meeting. Those rites closely parallel the purification of the priests at the time of their investiture, as set forth in chapter 8. In both instances the use of blood and oil is specified, and in both some of the extremities of the body are singled out for special purification.

Three animals were utilized in the rites of the eighth day: two male sheep and one ewe. One of the sheep served as a guilt offering (*'asham*), and the other as a burnt offering (*ʿolah*); the ewe served as a sin offering (*ḥatta't*). A *log* of oil and a grain offering were employed as accompaniment to some of the sacrifices. The *'asham* sacrifice and the oil were offered together in the manner of a presentation (*tenufah*).

Some of the blood from the *'asham* sacrifice was applied to the extremities of the person being purified—on the ridge of his right ear, on his right thumb, and on his right metatarsal toe. Then the priest poured oil on his own left palm and, with his right forefinger, sprinkled some of the oil seven times in the direction of the Tent of Meeting. Oil was applied to the extremities of the person being purified, over the blood of the *'asham,* at the same places. The remainder of the oil was poured on the individual's head.

Finally, the sin offering and the burnt offering were performed in the usual manner on behalf of the person being purified, accompanied by the grain offering. Those unable to afford the full regimen of animal sacrifices were allowed to substitute two doves or two young pigeons for the ewe and the male sheep of the sin offering and the burnt offering, respectively. The sheep of the *'asham* could not be substituted, however, for it was essential for purification.

2. ***This shall be the ritual for a leper*** The term *torah,* "ritual," is explained in the Comment to 6:2. In that sense, the *torah* served as a manual of procedure for the priests, who administered the purification rites.

When it had been reported to the priest Rather, "He shall be brought to the priest." As in 13:2, the afflicted person must be examined by the priest. In this case the priest went out of the camp to the afflicted person who, having been declared impure, could not enter the camp. Nevertheless, the formulation of 13:2 is repeated here, although the circumstances are somewhat different.

4. ***the priest shall order two live clean birds*** The birds must be physically sound and of a pure species. The impure species of birds are listed in 11:13–20 and in Deuteronomy 14:11–19. Rabbinic traditions specify certain birds for these rites. The Sifra, in the name of Rabbi Ishmael, identifies the bird as *deror,* "which lives [as freely] in a house as it does in the open field." As its name conveys, it is a bird that, once set free, will not return.

cedar wood, crimson stuff, and hyssop Hyssop (*'ezov*) is associated with purification: "Purge me with hyssop till I am pure," says the psalmist (51:9). Hyssop was also employed in the purification of a person contaminated by contact with a corpse, according to Numbers 19:6.

order one of the birds slaughtered over fresh water in an
earthen vessel; 6and he shall take the live bird, along with
the cedar wood, the crimson stuff, and the hyssop, and dip
them together with the live bird in the blood of the bird
that was slaughtered over the fresh water. 7He shall then
sprinkle it seven times on him who is to be cleansed of the
eruption and cleanse him; and he shall set the live bird free
in the open country. 8The one to be cleansed shall wash his
clothes, shave off all his hair, and bathe in water; then he
shall be clean. After that he may enter the camp, but he
must remain outside his tent seven days. 9On the seventh
day he shall shave off all his hair—of head, beard, and
eyebrows. When he has shaved off all his hair, he shall wash
his clothes and bathe his body in water; then he shall be
clean. 10On the eighth day he shall take two male lambs
without blemish, one ewe lamb in its first year without
blemish, three-tenths of a measure of choice flour with oil
mixed in for a meal offering, and one *log* of oil. 11These
shall be presented before the LORD, with the man to be

הַצִּפּוֹר הָאֶחָת אֶל־כְּלִי־חֶרֶשׂ עַל־מַיִם חַיִּים׃
6 אֶת־הַצִּפֹּר הַחַיָּה יִקַּח אֹתָהּ וְאֶת־עֵץ הָאֶרֶז
וְאֶת־שְׁנִי הַתּוֹלַעַת וְאֶת־הָאֵזֹב וְטָבַל אוֹתָם וְאֵת
הַצִּפֹּר הַחַיָּה בְּדַם הַצִּפֹּר הַשְּׁחֻטָה עַל הַמַּיִם
הַחַיִּים׃ 7 וְהִזָּה עַל הַמִּטַּהֵר מִן־הַצָּרַעַת שֶׁבַע
פְּעָמִים וְטִהֲרוֹ וְשִׁלַּח אֶת־הַצִּפֹּר הַחַיָּה עַל־פְּנֵי
הַשָּׂדֶה׃ 8 וְכִבֶּס הַמִּטַּהֵר אֶת־בְּגָדָיו וְגִלַּח אֶת־
כָּל־שְׂעָרוֹ וְרָחַץ בַּמַּיִם וְטָהֵר וְאַחַר יָבוֹא אֶל־
הַמַּחֲנֶה וְיָשַׁב מִחוּץ לְאָהֳלוֹ שִׁבְעַת יָמִים׃ 9 וְהָיָה
בַיּוֹם הַשְּׁבִיעִי יְגַלַּח אֶת־כָּל־שְׂעָרוֹ אֶת־רֹאשׁוֹ
וְאֶת־זְקָנוֹ וְאֵת גַּבֹּת עֵינָיו וְאֶת־כָּל־שְׂעָרוֹ יְגַלֵּחַ
וְכִבֶּס אֶת־בְּגָדָיו וְרָחַץ אֶת־בְּשָׂרוֹ בַּמַּיִם וְטָהֵר׃
10 וּבַיּוֹם הַשְּׁמִינִי יִקַּח שְׁנֵי־כְבָשִׂים תְּמִימִם
וְכַבְשָׂה אַחַת בַּת־שְׁנָתָהּ תְּמִימָה וּשְׁלֹשָׁה
עֶשְׂרֹנִים סֹלֶת מִנְחָה בְּלוּלָה בַשֶּׁמֶן וְלֹג אֶחָד
שָׁמֶן׃ 11 וְהֶעֱמִיד הַכֹּהֵן הַמְטַהֵר אֵת הָאִישׁ

Hebrew *sheni tolaʿat* literally means "the scarlet of the worm." (The reverse, *tolaʿat shani,* also occurs.) More precisely, reference is to an insect that lives in the leaves of palm trees and from whose eggs the crimson dye is extracted. Hebrew *shani* designates the scarlet color.[1] It does not inform us which kind of cloth is to be used, but the tradition is that it was wool.

5. ***over fresh water in an earthen vessel*** Whatever blood of the slaughtered bird was not collected in the vessel would flow down into the earth. Hebrew *mayim ḥayim* means "living water," namely, water that flows continually, like that of springs, and is not stagnant.[2]

6. ***together with the live bird*** Here the preposition *ʿal* does not mean "on, upon, over" but, rather, "together with, near." This is often its precise meaning in the formulation of the ritual texts.[3]

7. ***on him who is to be cleansed*** The verbal form *mittahher* is reflexive (Hitpael), "one who purifies himself, who undergoes purification."

and he shall set the live bird free The Piel form *ve-shillaḥ* means "to drive off, dispatch," hence "to set free." The Kal stem of the same verb merely means "to send."[4]

in the open country Hebrew *ʿal penei ha-sadeh* contrasts elsewhere with the town or the settled area.[5] In verse 53 below, this is actually stated: ". . . he shall set the live bird free outside the city, in the open country." There reference is to the purification of a stone dwelling, and the setting is necessarily within a town.

9. ***of head, beard, and eyebrows*** It was normally forbidden to shave the beard or the sidelocks of the head, as we read in 19:27. These purification rites are exceptional, however. Hebrew *gabbot,* "[eye] brows," literally means "rims, what is above, over. . . ."

10. ***three-tenths of a measure of choice flour with oil mixed in for a meal offering*** As explained in the Comment to 2:1f., "grain offering" is a more precise translation of Hebrew *minḥah,* and Hebrew *solet* is better rendered "semolina flour." Three-tenths is the total amount required, so that each head of small cattle would be accompanied by one-tenth of an *ʾefah,* the usual amount. Hebrew *log* was a liquid measure of volume that consisted of approximately three-tenths of a liter.

cleansed, at the entrance of the Tent of Meeting, by the priest who performs the cleansing.

12 The priest shall take one of the male lambs and offer it with the *log* of oil as a guilt offering, and he shall elevate them as an elevation offering before the LORD. 13 The lamb shall be slaughtered at the spot in the sacred area where the sin offering and the burnt offering are slaughtered. For the guilt offering, like the sin offering, goes to the priest; it is most holy. 14 The priest shall take some of the blood of the guilt offering, and the priest shall put it on the ridge of the right ear of him who is being cleansed, and on the thumb of his right hand, and on the big toe of his right foot. 15 The priest shall then take some of the *log* of oil and pour it into the palm of his own left hand. 16 And the priest shall dip his right finger in the oil that is in the palm of his left hand and sprinkle some of the oil with his finger seven times before the LORD. 17 Some of the oil left in his palm shall be put by

הַמִּטַּהֵר וְאֹתָם לִפְנֵי יְהוָה פֶּתַח אֹהֶל מוֹעֵד׃
12 וְלָקַח הַכֹּהֵן אֶת־הַכֶּבֶשׂ הָאֶחָד וְהִקְרִיב אֹתוֹ
לְאָשָׁם וְאֶת־לֹג הַשָּׁמֶן וְהֵנִיף אֹתָם תְּנוּפָה לִפְנֵי
יְהוָה׃ שני 13 וְשָׁחַט אֶת־הַכֶּבֶשׂ בִּמְקוֹם אֲשֶׁר
יִשְׁחַט אֶת־הַחַטָּאת וְאֶת־הָעֹלָה בִּמְקוֹם הַקֹּדֶשׁ
כִּי כַּחַטָּאת הָאָשָׁם הוּא לַכֹּהֵן קֹדֶשׁ קָדָשִׁים
הוּא׃ 14 וְלָקַח הַכֹּהֵן מִדַּם הָאָשָׁם וְנָתַן הַכֹּהֵן
עַל־תְּנוּךְ אֹזֶן הַמִּטַּהֵר הַיְמָנִית וְעַל־בֹּהֶן יָדוֹ
הַיְמָנִית וְעַל־בֹּהֶן רַגְלוֹ הַיְמָנִית׃ 15 וְלָקַח הַכֹּהֵן
מִלֹּג הַשָּׁמֶן וְיָצַק עַל־כַּף הַכֹּהֵן הַשְּׂמָאלִית׃
16 וְטָבַל הַכֹּהֵן אֶת־אֶצְבָּעוֹ הַיְמָנִית מִן־הַשֶּׁמֶן
אֲשֶׁר עַל־כַּפּוֹ הַשְּׂמָאלִית וְהִזָּה מִן־הַשֶּׁמֶן
בְּאֶצְבָּעוֹ שֶׁבַע פְּעָמִים לִפְנֵי יְהוָה׃ 17 וּמִיֶּתֶר

11. These shall be presented The person undergoing purification is stationed near the entrance of the Tent of Meeting, together with the material assembled for use in his purification.

by the priest who performs the cleansing Hebrew *ha-kohen ha-metahher* may have a more technical sense: "the purificatory priest." Quite probably, there was specialization of priestly functions, so that certain priests were specifically trained for such purifications and were routinely assigned to administer them. This was so in Egypt and Mesopotamia.

12. as a guilt offering The essential character and function of the guilt offering (*'asham*) are discussed in the introductory Comment to chapters 4–5. It is not clear just why this type of sacrifice was required in the purification of one afflicted with acute *tsara'at,* since the usual purpose of an *'asham* was to expiate an offense that caused a loss to the sanctuary or to another person as a result of a false oath. In the case of one who suffered from acute *tsara'at,* what loss had occurred? The traditional answer is that the sufferer must have committed some offense, such as maligning others, that made an *'asham* appropriate. From the context, however, it is more likely that the *'asham* served as a sacrifice of purification. It provided sacrificial blood for sprinkling on the extremities of the individual being purified; blood from the burnt offering and the sin offering could not be applied to the body of a human being.[6]

and he shall elevate them as an elevation offering This manner of sacrifice, called *tenufah,* is described in the Comment to 7:30.

13. at the spot in the sacred area In 1:11 it is specified that the burnt offering is presented on the north side of the altar; according to 6:18 and 7:2 the same is true of the sin offering and the guilt offering.

For the guilt offering . . . it is most holy This restates the rule of 7:7. Those sacrifices considered "most holy," in contrast to those regarded as "of lesser sanctity," are listed in the Comment to 2:3.

14. on the ridge of the right ear Compare the procedures in 8:23–24 for the purification of Aaron and his sons on the occasion of their investiture as priests. The person being purified was treated literally from head to foot. The term *tenukh,* "ridge" of the ear, and *bohen,* "big toe," are known to us only from priestly texts, such as 8:23–24 and Exodus 29:20, which describe the installation of the Aaronide priesthood. These texts are, thus, very important sources for our knowledge of ancient anatomical terms.

the priest on the ridge of the right ear of the one being cleansed, on the thumb of his right hand, and on the big toe of his right foot—over the blood of the guilt offering. [18]The rest of the oil in his palm the priest shall put on the head of the one being cleansed. Thus the priest shall make expiation for him before the LORD. [19]The priest shall then offer the sin offering and make expiation for the one being cleansed of his uncleanness. Last, the burnt offering shall be slaughtered, [20]and the priest shall offer the burnt offering and the meal offering on the altar, and the priest shall make expiation for him. Then he shall be clean.

[21]If, however, he is poor and his means are insufficient, he shall take one male lamb for a guilt offering, to be elevated in expiation for him, one-tenth of a measure of choice flour with oil mixed in for a meal offering, and a *log* of oil; [22]and two turtledoves or two pigeons, depending on his means, the one to be the sin offering and the other the burnt offering. [23]On the eighth day of his cleansing he shall bring them to the priest at the entrance of the Tent of Meeting, before the LORD. [24]The priest shall take the lamb of guilt offering and the *log* of oil, and elevate them as an elevation offering before the LORD. [25]When the lamb of guilt offering has been slaughtered, the priest shall take some of the blood of the guilt offering and put it on the ridge of the right ear of the one being cleansed, on the thumb of his right hand, and on the big toe of his right foot. [26]The priest shall then pour some of the oil into the palm of his own left hand, [27]and with the finger of his right hand the priest shall sprinkle some of the oil that is in the palm of his left hand seven times before the LORD. [28]Some of the oil in his palm shall be put by the priest on the ridge of the right ear of the one being cleansed, on the thumb of his right hand, and on the big toe of his right foot, over the same places as the blood of the guilt offering; [29]and what is

הַשֶּׁ֜מֶן אֲשֶׁ֣ר עַל־כַּפּ֗וֹ יִתֵּ֤ן הַכֹּהֵן֙ עַל־תְּנ֞וּךְ אֹ֤זֶן
הַמִּטַּהֵר֙ הַיְמָנִ֔ית וְעַל־בֹּ֤הֶן יָדוֹ֙ הַיְמָנִ֔ית וְעַל־בֹּ֖הֶן
רַגְל֣וֹ הַיְמָנִ֑ית עַ֖ל דַּ֥ם הָאָשָֽׁם׃ 18 וְהַנּוֹתָ֗ר בַּשֶּׁ֙מֶן֙
אֲשֶׁר֙ עַל־כַּ֣ף הַכֹּהֵ֔ן יִתֵּ֖ן עַל־רֹ֣אשׁ הַמִּטַּהֵ֑ר וְכִפֶּ֥ר
עָלָ֛יו הַכֹּהֵ֖ן לִפְנֵ֥י יְהוָֽה׃ 19 וְעָשָׂ֤ה הַכֹּהֵן֙ אֶת־
הַֽחַטָּ֔את וְכִפֶּ֕ר עַל־הַמִּטַּהֵ֖ר מִטֻּמְאָת֑וֹ וְאַחַ֖ר
יִשְׁחַ֥ט אֶת־הָעֹלָֽה׃ 20 וְהֶעֱלָ֧ה הַכֹּהֵ֛ן אֶת־הָעֹלָ֥ה
וְאֶת־הַמִּנְחָ֖ה הַמִּזְבֵּ֑חָה וְכִפֶּ֥ר עָלָ֛יו הַכֹּהֵ֖ן וְטָהֵֽר׃
ס שלישי [חמישי כשהן מחוברות]
21 וְאִם־דַּ֣ל ה֗וּא וְאֵ֣ין יָדוֹ֮ מַשֶּׂגֶת֒ וְ֠לָקַח כֶּ֣בֶשׂ
אֶחָ֥ד אָשָׁ֛ם לִתְנוּפָ֖ה לְכַפֵּ֣ר עָלָ֑יו וְעִשָּׂר֨וֹן סֹ֜לֶת
אֶחָ֨ד בָּל֧וּל בַּשֶּׁ֛מֶן לְמִנְחָ֖ה וְלֹ֥ג שָֽׁמֶן׃ 22 וּשְׁתֵּ֣י
תֹרִ֗ים א֤וֹ שְׁנֵי֙ בְּנֵ֣י יוֹנָ֔ה אֲשֶׁ֥ר תַּשִּׂ֖יג יָד֑וֹ וְהָיָ֤ה
אֶחָד֙ חַטָּ֔את וְהָאֶחָ֖ד עֹלָֽה׃ 23 וְהֵבִ֨יא אֹתָ֜ם בַּיּ֧וֹם
הַשְּׁמִינִ֛י לְטָהֳרָת֖וֹ אֶל־הַכֹּהֵ֑ן אֶל־פֶּ֥תַח אֹֽהֶל־מוֹעֵ֖ד
לִפְנֵ֥י יְהוָֽה׃ 24 וְלָקַ֧ח הַכֹּהֵ֛ן אֶת־כֶּ֥בֶשׂ הָאָשָׁ֖ם
וְאֶת־לֹ֣ג הַשָּׁ֑מֶן וְהֵנִ֨יף אֹתָ֥ם הַכֹּהֵ֛ן תְּנוּפָ֖ה לִפְנֵ֥י
יְהוָֽה׃ 25 וְשָׁחַט֮ אֶת־כֶּ֣בֶשׂ הָאָשָׁם֒ וְלָקַ֣ח הַכֹּהֵ֗ן
מִדַּ֣ם הָאָשָׁ֔ם וְנָתַ֥ן עַל־תְּנ֥וּךְ אֹֽזֶן־הַמִּטַּהֵ֖ר הַיְמָנִ֑ית
וְעַל־בֹּ֤הֶן יָדוֹ֙ הַיְמָנִ֔ית וְעַל־בֹּ֖הֶן רַגְל֥וֹ הַיְמָנִֽית׃
26 וּמִן־הַשֶּׁ֖מֶן יִצֹ֣ק הַכֹּהֵ֑ן עַל־כַּ֥ף הַכֹּהֵ֖ן
הַשְּׂמָאלִֽית׃ 27 וְהִזָּ֤ה הַכֹּהֵן֙ בְּאֶצְבָּע֣וֹ הַיְמָנִ֔ית מִן־
הַשֶּׁ֕מֶן אֲשֶׁ֥ר עַל־כַּפּ֖וֹ הַשְּׂמָאלִ֑ית שֶׁ֥בַע פְּעָמִ֖ים
לִפְנֵ֥י יְהוָֽה׃ 28 וְנָתַ֨ן הַכֹּהֵ֜ן מִן־הַשֶּׁ֣מֶן ׀ אֲשֶׁ֣ר עַל־
כַּפּ֗וֹ עַל־תְּנוּךְ֙ אֹ֤זֶן הַמִּטַּהֵר֙ הַיְמָנִ֔ית וְעַל־בֹּ֤הֶן יָדוֹ֙
הַיְמָנִ֔ית וְעַל־בֹּ֖הֶן רַגְל֣וֹ הַיְמָנִ֑ית עַל־מְק֖וֹם דַּ֥ם
הָאָשָֽׁם׃ 29 וְהַנּוֹתָ֗ר מִן־הַשֶּׁ֙מֶן֙ אֲשֶׁר֙ עַל־כַּ֣ף הַכֹּהֵ֔ן

18. Thus the priest shall make expiation The above rites were essential to securing expiation, or purification. On the sense of the verb *kipper,* "to make expiation," see Comment to 4:21. The verb is repeated in verses 19–20 because the sin offering and the burnt offering were also part of the overall purification. The sin offering served to put the individual in good standing with God, and the burnt offering symbolized his renewed acceptability as a worshiper—that is, with God's acceptance of the burnt offering, the individual was fully reinstated.

21. If, however, he is poor Verses 21–32 repeat the rites prescribed in verses 1–20, except that birds are substituted for animals in the burnt offering and the sin offering. This system allowed persons unable to afford several animals at one time to substitute less expensive animals; it enabled those rendered impure through no fault of their own to be reinstated as worshipers in good standing. The formulation of this allowance is explained in the Comments to 5:11–13. Such reductions are provided for the new mother in 12:8 and for expiating sins of omission in 5:11–13. Votive payments may also be reduced in this way, according to the provisions of chapter 27. The *'asham* sacrifice, however, could not be substituted.

left of the oil in his palm the priest shall put on the head of the one being cleansed, to make expiation for him before the LORD. 30He shall then offer one of the turtledoves or pigeons, depending on his means—31whichever he can afford—the one as a sin offering and the other as a burnt offering, together with the meal offering. Thus the priest shall make expiation before the LORD for the one being cleansed. 32Such is the ritual for him who has a scaly affection and whose means for his cleansing are limited.

33The LORD spoke to Moses and Aaron, saying:

34When you enter the land of Canaan that I give you as a possession, and I inflict an eruptive plague upon a house in the land you possess, 35the owner of the house shall come

יִתֵּ֖ן עַל־רֹ֣אשׁ הַמִּטַּהֵ֑ר לְכַפֵּ֥ר עָלָ֖יו לִפְנֵ֥י יְהוָֽה׃
30 וְעָשָׂ֤ה אֶת־הָֽאֶחָד֙ מִן־הַתֹּרִ֔ים א֖וֹ מִן־בְּנֵ֣י הַיּוֹנָ֑ה
מֵאֲשֶׁ֥ר תַּשִּׂ֖יג יָדֽוֹ׃ 31 אֵ֣ת אֲשֶׁר־תַּשִּׂ֞יג יָד֗וֹ אֶת־
הָאֶחָ֥ד חַטָּ֛את וְאֶת־הָאֶחָ֥ד עֹלָ֖ה עַל־הַמִּנְחָ֑ה
וְכִפֶּ֧ר הַכֹּהֵ֛ן עַ֥ל הַמִּטַּהֵ֖ר לִפְנֵ֥י יְהוָֽה׃ 32 זֹ֣את
תּוֹרַ֔ת אֲשֶׁר־בּ֖וֹ נֶ֣גַע צָרָ֑עַת אֲשֶׁ֛ר לֹא־תַשִּׂ֥יג יָד֖וֹ
בְּטָהֳרָתֽוֹ׃ פ רביעי [ששי כשהן
מחוברות] 33 וַיְדַבֵּ֣ר יְהוָ֔ה אֶל־מֹשֶׁ֥ה וְאֶֽל־אַהֲרֹ֖ן
לֵאמֹֽר׃ 34 כִּ֤י תָבֹ֙אוּ֙ אֶל־אֶ֣רֶץ כְּנַ֔עַן אֲשֶׁ֥ר אֲנִ֛י
נֹתֵ֥ן לָכֶ֖ם לַאֲחֻזָּ֑ה וְנָתַתִּי֙ נֶ֣גַע צָרַ֔עַת בְּבֵ֖ית אֶ֥רֶץ
אֲחֻזַּתְכֶֽם׃ 35 וּבָא֙ אֲשֶׁר־ל֣וֹ הַבַּ֔יִת וְהִגִּ֥יד לַכֹּהֵ֖ן

32. Such is the ritual for him who has a scaly affection The syntax of the Hebrew is unusual: *zo'ṭ torat 'asher bo,* literally "This is the ritual for one in whom there is" a scaly affection.

TSARA'AT IN BUILDING STONES (vv. 33–53)

This section deals with some sort of mold, blight, or rot, perhaps of a fungoid character, which produced recessed lesions and discoloration in the plaster or mud used to cover building stones. The symptoms resembled *tsara'at* in humans and were similar to conditions affecting leather and fabric. The condition was considered to be something like a plague and was thought to be contagious and dangerous.

A homeowner had to report the condition to the priest, who immediately ordered the house to be cleaned of its contents. He then inspected the interior of the house: If he detected greenish or reddish lesions on the plastered facing of any of the stones, he imposed a quarantine on the house for seven days. At the end of that period, he returned to inspect the house a second time. If the infected areas had become enlarged, he then ordered the infected stones to be dislodged and taken outside the camp. The rest of the stones of the house were scraped on the interior side, and the mud or plaster was removed from the camp. New stones were installed, and the entire interior of the house plastered anew.

Now if, after all these precautions had been taken, the plague persisted in breaking out, the condition was declared to be acute *tsara'at;* the house had to be leveled, and all its stones, its wood, and its mud, removed outside the city. Retroactively, in such a case, all who had entered the house during its period of quarantine, or who had lain down inside it, or partaken of food inside it were to launder their clothing.

If, on the other hand, the priest observed no enlargement of the infected areas after the proper measures had been taken, he could pronounce the house pure. In that event, rites of purification were necessary. These rites largely conformed to the procedures performed for a person whose acute *tsara'at* had healed, as set forth in 14:1–7. The slaughtering of a bird, the freeing of a bird, and the use of a cedar stick, and hyssop, and crimson cloth paralleled what was done to purify a human being. The shaving of hair in humans is even paralleled by the scraping of the mud from the building stones! The only difference between the rites for a person and those for a house was that, instead of applying blood and oil to the house, blood and "living water" were used in a combined ritual.

34. the land . . . that I give you as a possession The Hebrew term *'aḥuzzah,* "possession, land holding," is central to the theory of land tenure in the Book of Leviticus. Chapter 25 sets forth the rights and duties of the owner of an *'aḥuzzah.*

and I inflict an eruptive plague upon a house It is God who inflicts the plague as a punishment. The term *nega',* "plague," literally "touch," is explained in the Comment to 13:2.

and tell the priest, saying, "Something like a plague has
appeared upon my house." 36The priest shall order the
house cleared before the priest enters to examine the
plague, so that nothing in the house may become unclean;
after that the priest shall enter to examine the house. 37If,
when he examines the plague, the plague in the walls of the
house is found to consist of greenish or reddish streaks that
appear to go deep into the wall, 38the priest shall come out
of the house to the entrance of the house, and close up the
house for seven days. 39On the seventh day the priest shall
return. If he sees that the plague has spread on the walls of
the house, 40the priest shall order the stones with the plague
in them to be pulled out and cast outside the city into an
unclean place. 41The house shall be scraped inside all
around, and the coating that is scraped off shall be dumped
outside the city in an unclean place. 42They shall take other
stones and replace those stones with them, and take other
coating and plaster the house.

לֵאמֹר כְּנֶגַע נִרְאָה לִי בַּבָּיִת׃ 36 וְצִוָּה הַכֹּהֵן וּפִנּוּ
אֶת־הַבַּיִת בְּטֶרֶם יָבֹא הַכֹּהֵן לִרְאוֹת אֶת־הַנֶּגַע
וְלֹא יִטְמָא כָּל־אֲשֶׁר בַּבָּיִת וְאַחַר כֵּן יָבֹא הַכֹּהֵן
לִרְאוֹת אֶת־הַבָּיִת׃ 37 וְרָאָה אֶת־הַנֶּגַע וְהִנֵּה
הַנֶּגַע בְּקִירֹת הַבַּיִת שְׁקַעֲרוּרֹת יְרַקְרַקֹּת אוֹ
אֲדַמְדַּמֹּת וּמַרְאֵיהֶן שָׁפָל מִן־הַקִּיר׃ 38 וְיָצָא
הַכֹּהֵן מִן־הַבַּיִת אֶל־פֶּתַח הַבָּיִת וְהִסְגִּיר אֶת־
הַבַּיִת שִׁבְעַת יָמִים׃ 39 וְשָׁב הַכֹּהֵן בַּיּוֹם הַשְּׁבִיעִי
וְרָאָה וְהִנֵּה פָּשָׂה הַנֶּגַע בְּקִירֹת הַבָּיִת׃ 40 וְצִוָּה
הַכֹּהֵן וְחִלְּצוּ אֶת־הָאֲבָנִים אֲשֶׁר בָּהֵן הַנָּגַע
וְהִשְׁלִיכוּ אֶתְהֶן אֶל־מִחוּץ לָעִיר אֶל־מָקוֹם טָמֵא׃
41 וְאֶת־הַבַּיִת יַקְצִעַ מִבַּיִת סָבִיב וְשָׁפְכוּ אֶת־
הֶעָפָר אֲשֶׁר הִקְצוּ אֶל־מִחוּץ לָעִיר אֶל־מָקוֹם
טָמֵא׃ 42 וְלָקְחוּ אֲבָנִים אֲחֵרוֹת וְהֵבִיאוּ אֶל־תַּחַת
הָאֲבָנִים וְעָפָר אַחֵר יִקַּח וְטָח אֶת־הַבָּיִת׃ 43 וְאִם־

35. "Something like a plague has appeared upon my house." The appearance of what the owner observed reminded him of a disease of the skin.

36. The priest shall order the house cleared Once the priest arrives and quarantines the house, everything inside it becomes impure as well—at the very least, those vessels whose form and function make them susceptible to contamination.

37. to consist of greenish or reddish streaks that appear to go deep into the wall More precisely, ". . . lesions that appear to be recessed within the surface of the wall." Hebrew *sheka'arurot,* "streaks" or "lesions," is most likely derived from the verb *shaka',* "to sink, recede," as Targum Onkelos indicates by his Aramaic rendering *peḥatin,* "furrows." Targum Jonathan translates *meshak'an,* "recessed, sunk," taking the Hebrew word as an adjective derived from *shaka'*. This is also the view of the Sifra: "their appearance is recessed." Others have derived Hebrew *sheka'arurot* from a presumed verb *ka'ar,* "to dig out a bowl" (cf. Heb. *ke'arah,* "bowl"). We have information on the magical treatment of similar fungoid conditions in Mesopotamian texts.[7]

38. close up the house A diseased person is closed up in a house. Here, the house itself is "locked up" in order to keep people out. The use of the Hifil form *hisgir* to connote closure is purposely suggestive of the parallelism of the procedures for both humans and houses.

39. If he sees that the plague has spread As indicated in the Comment to 13:5, the sense of Hebrew *pasah* is "to become enlarged." If the lesions became enlarged, it is likely that the blight, or fungus, had penetrated to the stones themselves.

40. to be pulled out Alternatively, "to be pushed out, dislodged." The Hebrew verb *ḥalats* is cognate with Akkadian *ḫalāṣu,* "to press, squeeze out." As a practical consideration, it is likely that the infected stones were pushed out from the interior of the house.[8]

41. The house shall be scraped . . . the coating . . . shall be dumped The Hebrew verb *katsa',* meaning "to chisel, cut," is cognate with Aramaic *kaṭa'* and is used in connection with the work of a sculptor or craftsman. The second part of the verse uses the verb *ve-hiktsu,* which is of similar meaning.[9] The purpose of scraping the mud coating off of the interior facing of the rest of the stones was to ascertain whether the infection had penetrated beneath the coating into the stones themselves.

42. and replace those stones with them The Hebrew is stated in an unusual manner: "They shall insert in place of those stones."

[43]If the plague again breaks out in the house, after the stones have been pulled out and after the house has been scraped and replastered, [44]the priest shall come to examine: if the plague has spread in the house, it is a malignant eruption in the house; it is unclean. [45]The house shall be torn down—its stones and timber and all the coating on the house—and taken to an unclean place outside the city.

[46]Whoever enters the house while it is closed up shall be unclean until evening. [47]Whoever sleeps in the house must wash his clothes, and whoever eats in the house must wash his clothes.

[48]If, however, the priest comes and sees that the plague has not spread in the house after the house was replastered, the priest shall pronounce the house clean, for the plague has healed. [49]To purge the house, he shall take two birds, cedar wood, crimson stuff, and hyssop. [50]He shall slaughter the one bird over fresh water in an earthen vessel. [51]He shall take the cedar wood, the hyssop, the crimson stuff, and the live bird, and dip them in the blood of the slaughtered bird and the fresh water, and sprinkle on the house seven times. [52]Having purged the house with the blood of the bird, the fresh water, the live bird, the cedar wood, the hyssop, and the crimson stuff, [53]he shall set the live bird free outside the

יָשׁוּב הַנֶּגַע וּפָרַח בַּבַּיִת אַחַר חִלֵּץ אֶת־הָאֲבָנִים
וְאַחֲרֵי הִקְצוֹת אֶת־הַבַּיִת וְאַחֲרֵי הִטּוֹחַ׃ 44 וּבָא
הַכֹּהֵן וְרָאָה וְהִנֵּה פָּשָׂה הַנֶּגַע בַּבָּיִת צָרַעַת
מַמְאֶרֶת הִוא בַּבַּיִת טָמֵא הוּא׃ 45 וְנָתַץ אֶת־
הַבַּיִת אֶת־אֲבָנָיו וְאֶת־עֵצָיו וְאֵת כָּל־עֲפַר הַבָּיִת
וְהוֹצִיא אֶל־מִחוּץ לָעִיר אֶל־מָקוֹם טָמֵא׃ 46 וְהַבָּא
אֶל־הַבַּיִת כָּל־יְמֵי הִסְגִּיר אֹתוֹ יִטְמָא עַד־הָעָרֶב׃
47 וְהַשֹּׁכֵב בַּבַּיִת יְכַבֵּס אֶת־בְּגָדָיו וְהָאֹכֵל בַּבַּיִת
יְכַבֵּס אֶת־בְּגָדָיו׃ 48 וְאִם־בֹּא יָבֹא הַכֹּהֵן וְרָאָה
וְהִנֵּה לֹא־פָשָׂה הַנֶּגַע בַּבַּיִת אַחֲרֵי הִטֹּחַ אֶת־
הַבָּיִת וְטִהַר הַכֹּהֵן אֶת־הַבַּיִת כִּי נִרְפָּא הַנָּגַע׃
49 וְלָקַח לְחַטֵּא אֶת־הַבַּיִת שְׁתֵּי צִפֳּרִים וְעֵץ
אֶרֶז וּשְׁנִי תוֹלַעַת וְאֵזֹב׃ 50 וְשָׁחַט אֶת־הַצִּפֹּר
הָאֶחָת אֶל־כְּלִי־חֶרֶשׂ עַל־מַיִם חַיִּים׃ 51 וְלָקַח
אֶת־עֵץ־הָאֶרֶז וְאֶת־הָאֵזֹב וְאֵת ׀ שְׁנִי הַתּוֹלַעַת
וְאֵת הַצִּפֹּר הַחַיָּה וְטָבַל אֹתָם בְּדַם הַצִּפֹּר
הַשְּׁחוּטָה וּבַמַּיִם הַחַיִּים וְהִזָּה אֶל־הַבַּיִת שֶׁבַע
פְּעָמִים׃ 52 וְחִטֵּא אֶת־הַבַּיִת בְּדַם הַצִּפּוֹר וּבַמַּיִם
הַחַיִּים וּבַצִּפֹּר הַחַיָּה וּבְעֵץ הָאֶרֶז וּבָאֵזֹב וּבִשְׁנִי
הַתּוֹלָעַת׃ 53 וְשִׁלַּח אֶת־הַצִּפֹּר הַחַיָּה אֶל־מִחוּץ

and take other coating and plaster the house As in the previous verses, Hebrew *ʿafar* literally means "dirt, mud." Hebrew *ve-taḥu,* "they shall plaster," indicates that the laws are speaking of streaks or lesions that first appeared on the plaster or mud that covered the stones. These latter could be retained if the blight had not penetrated to them.

43. after the stones have been . . . replastered The verbal form *hittoaḥ* is the infinitive absolute of the Nifal stem "to be plastered."

44. it is a malignant eruption Hebrew *tsaraʿat mamʾeret,* "malignant, acute *tsaraʿat,*" is explained in the Comment to 13:51.

45. The house shall be torn down The Hebrew verb *natats,* "to tear down," has a specialized meaning in the Hebrew Bible, being reserved for the utter destruction, or razing, of buildings and artifacts.[10]

46. Whoever enters the house The provisions of verses 46–47 resemble those of Numbers 19:14f. They pertain to the communication of an impurity present in a closed structure (a "tent") to those who are inside the structure while it is impure. In Numbers the presence of a corpse makes the impurity much more severe than it is in the present case, but the dynamics of communicating impurity are the same in both instances.

49. To purge the house The verb used here is *ḥitteʾ,* "to remove the sin, impurity." The Piel stem may often connote the elimination of what the Kal, or simple stem, connotes in the first place. This verb is almost synonymous with *kipper,* used in verse 53, except that in this sense it always involves actual physical contact with the object to be purified, and it is never used with regard to the purification of a human being.

The procedures for purifying the house that has "healed," so to speak, are almost identical to those prescribed in verses 1–32 for purifying a diseased person. A bird is slaughtered and a live bird is set free; cedar wood, hyssop, and crimson cloth, too, are utilized. The only difference is that instead of oil and blood, water and blood are sprinkled on the house.

city in the open country. Thus he shall make expiation for the house, and it shall be clean.

54Such is the ritual for every eruptive affection—for scalls, 55for an eruption on a cloth or a house, 56for swellings, for rashes, or for discolorations—57to determine when they are unclean and when they are clean.

Such is the ritual concerning eruptions.

לָעִ֔יר אֶל־פְּנֵ֖י הַשָּׂדֶ֑ה וְכִפֶּ֥ר עַל־הַבַּ֖יִת וְטָהֵֽר׃
חמישי 54 זֹ֖את הַתּוֹרָ֑ה לְכָל־נֶ֥גַע הַצָּרַ֖עַת
וְלַנָּֽתֶק׃ 55 וּלְצָרַ֥עַת הַבֶּ֖גֶד וְלַבָּֽיִת׃ 56 וְלַשְׂאֵ֥ת
וְלַסַּפַּ֖חַת וְלַבֶּהָֽרֶת׃ 57 לְהוֹרֹ֕ת בְּי֥וֹם הַטָּמֵ֖א וּבְי֣וֹם
הַטָּהֹ֑ר זֹ֥את תּוֹרַ֖ת הַצָּרָֽעַת׃ ס

53. outside the city in the open country See Comment to verse 6.

Thus he shall make expiation for the house, and it shall be clean See the same formulation in verse 20 in the purification of humans. Also see Comment to verse 18.

54. Such is the ritual Verses 54–57 are a postscript to the entire contents of chapters 13–14. Often the Hebrew formula *zo't ha-torah* serves to introduce a manual of practice, as in verse 2. Here it serves as a concluding statement, summarizing the subject matter of the two chapters in the order of its presentation: humans, leather and fabrics, and stone houses.

57. when they are unclean and when they are clean The Hebrew *be-yom ha-tame' u-ve-yom ha-tahor* is literally "at the time of the impure and at the time of the pure." On the basis of the usual syntax, one could read here, without altering the consonants of the Masoretic text, as follows: *be-yom hittame' u-ve-yom hittahher,* "when they *become* impure, and when they *become* pure." The sense is clear, nonetheless. The principal task of the purificatory priest is to monitor diseases.

CHAPTER 15

Discharges from Sexual Organs

Chapter 15 sets forth the procedures required when an Israelite male or female experiences discharges from the sexual organs. Most of the chapter deals with discharges that are the result of illness or infection, not to be confused with the normal menstruation of the female or the seminal emissions of the male. Evidently, the purpose of chapter 15 is to distinguish among physical phenomena that share some of the same symptoms but that are understood differently in terms of their physical and religious significance.

In chapter 15 we observe, perhaps more clearly than elsewhere in Leviticus, the virtual interchangeability of two conditions: illness and impurity. The laws here may refer to illness simply as impurity and to the termination of illness and the regaining of health as the resumption of purity. By classifying illness and disease as forms of impurity, the Israelite priesthood placed them in the realm of religious concern. It was probably thought that impurity was contagious or, to put it another way, that the effects of abnormal discharges—and, to a lesser degree, of normal emissions and menstruation—were contagious. Impure persons were prohibited from entering the sanctuary. In stark contrast, it must be remembered that in all other ancient Near Eastern religions everything that pertained to sexuality had a role in cult and ritual.[1]

All that was associated with the sexual organs was a matter of religious concern in ancient Israel, but one assumes that little was known about treatment for abnormal bodily discharges apart from bathing, laundering clothing, and careful observation of the course taken by the ailment itself. As described in chapter 15, such discharges of the male consisted of pus, or some similar substance, which appeared as a clear liquid running from the penis or as a dense substance that caused stoppage in the penis. Hebrew *zov,* literally "flowing," is most likely a term for any number of similar infections of the urinary tract or of the internal organs. It is most likely not to be identified with gonorrhea, as some have suggested. The abnormal vaginal discharges of the female, as described here, consisted of blood

15 The LORD spoke to Moses and Aaron, saying: [2]Speak
to the Israelite people and say to them:
When any man has a discharge issuing from his member,
he is unclean. [3]The uncleanness from his discharge shall
mean the following—whether his member runs with the
discharge or is stopped up so that there is no discharge, his
uncleanness means this: [4]Any bedding on which the one

ט״ו וַיְדַבֵּר יְהוָה אֶל־מֹשֶׁה וְאֶל־אַהֲרֹן לֵאמֹר׃
2 דַּבְּרוּ אֶל־בְּנֵי יִשְׂרָאֵל וַאֲמַרְתֶּם אֲלֵהֶם אִישׁ
אִישׁ כִּי יִהְיֶה זָב מִבְּשָׂרוֹ זוֹבוֹ טָמֵא הוּא׃ 3 וְזֹאת
תִּהְיֶה טֻמְאָתוֹ בְּזוֹבוֹ רָר בְּשָׂרוֹ אֶת־זוֹבוֹ אוֹ־
הֶחְתִּים בְּשָׂרוֹ מִזּוֹבוֹ טֻמְאָתוֹ הִוא׃ 4 כָּל־הַמִּשְׁכָּב

and persisted beyond, or outside, the menstrual period "for many days," as the text states. Most likely, these discharges were related to uterine disorders. Like menstruation itself, they are also called *zov.*[2]

Chapter 15 also includes laws governing normal seminal emissions in the male and menstruation in the female. It was characteristic of all who experienced abnormal discharges from the sexual organs, as well as of the menstruating woman, that their impurity extended to persons and objects that came into contact with them. The details of such transmitted impurity will be discussed in the Commentary. The general rule here is that persons experiencing the relevant discharges remain impure for seven days after the disappearance of the observable symptoms—as verse 13 puts it: after the person becomes "pure." At the end of the seventh day, the person must bathe the entire body in "living" water, launder clothing worn during the period of the illness, and on the eighth day undergo ritual purification at the sanctuary.

All the impurities dealt with in this chapter, like any prevailing impurity within the Israelite community, threatened, directly or indirectly, the purity of the sanctuary, which was located within the area of settlement. This is stated explicitly in verse 31: "You shall put the Israelites on guard against their uncleanness, lest they die through their uncleanness by defiling My Tabernacle which is among them."

The specific topics in chapter 15 may be outlined as follows:

1. The Israelite male (vv. 1–18)
   a. Abnormal discharges from the penis (vv. 1–15)
   b. Normal seminal emissions (vv. 16–18)
2. The Israelite female (vv. 19–30)
   a. The menstrual period (vv. 19–24)
   b. Abnormal vaginal discharges of blood (vv. 25–30)
3. Conclusion (vv. 31–33)

THE ISRAELITE MALE (vv. 1–18)

1. When any man has a discharge issuing from his member Literally, "when any man has a discharge, his discharge being from his 'flesh.'" Hebrew *basar,* the usual word for "body, flesh," is here recognized as a euphemism for the penis, an interpretation stated in most of the traditional commentaries.[3] The form *zovo* means "his discharging." Throughout the chapter, the term *zov* is the name given both to ailments and to menstruation itself.

3. The uncleanness from his discharge shall mean the following Rather, "This is his impurity during his discharging." This statement defines the physical symptoms of the ailment. Here "impurity" refers to the ailment itself, not to a separate matter, since "impurity" and "ailment" are synonymous.

whether his member runs with the discharge or is stopped up These are the two forms usually taken by the ailment. The participle *rar,* from the noun *rir,* means "to flow, run," as with a bodily liquid. In 1 Samuel 21:4, this word describes a running mouth.[4] The Hifil form *heḥtim,* meaning "to seal itself up," occurs only here in the Hebrew Bible; it functions uniquely as a medical usage.[5] In other forms, this verb usually refers to the sealing of documents or of spaces and containers.

with the discharge lies shall be unclean, and every object on
which he sits shall be unclean. 5Anyone who touches his
bedding shall wash his clothes, bathe in water, and remain
unclean until evening. 6Whoever sits on an object on which
the one with the discharge has sat shall wash his clothes,
bathe in water, and remain unclean until evening. 7Who-
ever touches the body of the one with the discharge shall
wash his clothes, bathe in water, and remain unclean until
evening. 8If one with a discharge spits on one who is clean,
the latter shall wash his clothes, bathe in water, and remain
unclean until evening. 9Any means for riding that one with
a discharge has mounted shall be unclean; 10whoever
touches anything that was under him shall be unclean until
evening; and whoever carries such things shall wash his
clothes, bathe in water, and remain unclean until evening.

אֲשֶׁר יִשְׁכַּב עָלָיו הַזָּב יִטְמָא וְכָל־הַכְּלִי אֲשֶׁר־
יֵשֵׁב עָלָיו יִטְמָא׃ 5 וְאִישׁ אֲשֶׁר יִגַּע בְּמִשְׁכָּבוֹ
יְכַבֵּס בְּגָדָיו וְרָחַץ בַּמַּיִם וְטָמֵא עַד־הָעָרֶב׃
6 וְהַיֹּשֵׁב עַל־הַכְּלִי אֲשֶׁר־יֵשֵׁב עָלָיו הַזָּב יְכַבֵּס
בְּגָדָיו וְרָחַץ בַּמַּיִם וְטָמֵא עַד־הָעָרֶב׃ *7 וְהַנֹּגֵעַ
בִּבְשַׂר הַזָּב יְכַבֵּס בְּגָדָיו וְרָחַץ בַּמַּיִם וְטָמֵא עַד־
הָעָרֶב׃ 8 וְכִי־יָרֹק הַזָּב בַּטָּהוֹר וְכִבֶּס בְּגָדָיו וְרָחַץ
בַּמַּיִם וְטָמֵא עַד־הָעָרֶב׃ 9 וְכָל־הַמֶּרְכָּב אֲשֶׁר
יִרְכַּב עָלָיו הַזָּב יִטְמָא׃ 10 וְכָל־הַנֹּגֵעַ בְּכֹל אֲשֶׁר
יִהְיֶה תַחְתָּיו יִטְמָא עַד־הָעָרֶב וְהַנּוֹשֵׂא אוֹתָם
יְכַבֵּס בְּגָדָיו וְרָחַץ בַּמַּיִם וְטָמֵא עַד־הָעָרֶב׃

v. 7. חצי הספר בפסוקים

his uncleanness means this Rather, "This is his impurity." Namely, this is the illness. The clause merely recapitulates what has just been described.

4. ***Any bedding on which the one with the discharge lies*** Hebrew *mishkav* means "bed, an object on which one lies." The two sorts of objects rendered impure by contact with the one who has the discharge are those upon which he lies and those on which he sits, called *moshav* in rabbinic Hebrew. These objects must be cleansed.

In this verse the impurity is communicated by the affected person to certain objects, whereas in verses 5–7 we read that contact with such objects, in turn, communicates the impurity to other persons.

5. ***Anyone who touches his bedding*** Verses 5–6 prescribe that a person who comes in contact with impure bedding, chairs, and so forth remains impure until evening and must bathe and launder his or her clothing.

bathe in water Even though the Hebrew verb *raḥats,* "to wash," has no direct object, as it does in verse 13 below, it is clear from the context that here the law requires bathing oneself completely. A good illustration of this usage is provided in 2 Kings 5:14. Naaman, instructed by the prophet Elisha to "wash" (*raḥats*) in the waters of the Jordan, understood this to mean complete immersion, a point noted by Hoffmann.

7. ***Whoever touches the body of the one with the discharge*** Direct contact with the affected person renders one impure.

8. ***If one with a discharge spits on one who is clean*** Verses 8–9 change direction and speak of contact initiated by the affected person. Spittle was considered to carry infection and disease.

9. ***Any means for riding*** Hebrew *merkav* means "an object on which one rides," such as a saddle or other appurtenance located under the rider. If one with a discharge rides on these objects, they become impure.

10. ***whoever touches anything that was under him*** The antecedent of Hebrew *taḥtav,* "under *him,*" is the affected person, not any object. In this case, the impurity does not extend to the clothing of the person who touches such objects, only to his body.

and whoever carries such things Contact by carrying objects requires the usual severity. In rabbinic law, *massa'*, "carrying," is one of the major categories of contact that renders persons and objects impure. The other four are: *magga'*, "touching"; *moshav,* "sitting"; *mishkav,* "lying"; and *merkav,* "riding." Furthermore, rabbinic law carefully distinguishes between different levels of impurity. *'Av ha-tum'ah,* "a primary category of impurity," renders other persons and objects actively impure, which is to say, capable of transmitting impurity on their own. The second category

[11]If one with a discharge, without having rinsed his hands
in water, touches another person, that person shall wash his
clothes, bathe in water, and remain unclean until evening.
[12]An earthen vessel that one with a discharge touches shall
be broken; and any wooden implement shall be rinsed with
water.

[13]When one with a discharge becomes clean of his discharge, he shall count off seven days for his cleansing, wash
his clothes, and bathe his body in fresh water; then he shall
be clean. [14]On the eighth day he shall take two turtledoves
or two pigeons and come before the LORD at the entrance of
the Tent of Meeting and give them to the priest. [15]The

11 וְכֹל אֲשֶׁר יִגַּע־בּוֹ הַזָּב וְיָדָיו לֹא־שָׁטַף בַּמָּיִם
וְכִבֶּס בְּגָדָיו וְרָחַץ בַּמַּיִם וְטָמֵא עַד־הָעָרֶב׃
12 וּכְלִי־חֶרֶשׂ אֲשֶׁר־יִגַּע־בּוֹ הַזָּב יִשָּׁבֵר וְכָל־כְּלִי־
עֵץ יִשָּׁטֵף בַּמָּיִם׃ 13 וְכִי־יִטְהַר הַזָּב מִזּוֹבוֹ וְסָפַר
לוֹ שִׁבְעַת יָמִים לְטָהֳרָתוֹ וְכִבֶּס בְּגָדָיו וְרָחַץ
בְּשָׂרוֹ בְּמַיִם חַיִּים וְטָהֵר׃ 14 וּבַיּוֹם הַשְּׁמִינִי יִקַּח־
לוֹ שְׁתֵּי תֹרִים אוֹ שְׁנֵי בְּנֵי יוֹנָה וּבָא ׀ לִפְנֵי יְהוָה
אֶל־פֶּתַח אֹהֶל מוֹעֵד וּנְתָנָם אֶל־הַכֹּהֵן׃ 15 וְעָשָׂה

concerns those persons and objects that are contaminated through such primary impurity. Called *ri'shon le-tum'ah,* "impurity of the first order," this category does not render other persons or objects sources of impurity.[6]

11. If one with a discharge, without having rinsed his hands Verse 11 concerns contact between a person with a discharge and another person. It projects the reverse direction of the situation specified in verse 7 above, where a pure person initiates contact with one who is impure. The wording of the verse is at first glance puzzling because it implies that the impure person needed only wash his hands, whereas verse 13 explicitly requires that the impure person bathe his entire body in fresh water in order to become pure. Various resolutions to this apparent inconsistency have been proposed since antiquity. It might be preferable, however, to take verse 11 less literally than has usually been done. The sense seems to be that one with a discharge who touches another person with his hands (hence the reference to hands) prior to purification renders that person and his clothing impure. The resultant impurity lasts until evening and is removed by bathing and the laundering of clothing.[7]

12. An earthen vessel Earthen vessels touched by a person who has had a discharge cannot be purified and must be destroyed, whereas wooden vessels may be soaked in water and used again. The same distinction between earthen and wooden vessels is drawn in the law of 11:32f. governing vessels that come into contact with a swarming creature (*sherets*).

In summary, verses 1–12 outline the direct and indirect effects of the impurity attendant upon an Israelite male who has a discharge from his penis. Verses 13–15 prescribe the purification required under such circumstances.

13. When one with a discharge becomes clean of his discharge As Hoffmann notes, becoming clean (or pure) is a way of saying that the affected person is well again.

he shall count off seven days for his cleansing Rather, "He shall count off seven days of being pure." Hebrew *le-tohorato* means "of his being in a state of purity." Seven consecutive days must pass ***after*** the termination of the ailment before ritual purification can be undertaken. At the end of the seven days, the person must bathe his body in living water, namely, naturally flowing water, and launder his clothing. This is an extraordinary requirement because usually immersion is allowed in a "gathering of water" (*mikveh mayim*), in which only a certain quantity of the total amount of water need be "living."[8] After these acts, the *zav* is pure and is ready to undergo the appropriate rituals at the sanctuary.

14. On the eighth day Two birds, turtledoves or young pigeons (see Comment to 1:14), are presented to the priest at the entrance of the Tent of Meeting. Once again, the designation *petaḥ 'ohel mo'ed,* "the entrance of the Tent of Meeting," includes a rather large area that reached all the way to the outer gate of the sanctuary courtyard. The person who had been affected could hardly have approached the inner courtyard prior to purification.

This expiatory offering resembles, in substance, the one required for the purification of a new mother who was unable to afford a more substantial offering, as specified in 12:8.

priest shall offer them, the one as a sin offering and the other as a burnt offering. Thus the priest shall make expiation on his behalf, for his discharge, before the LORD.

¹⁶When a man has an emission of semen, he shall bathe his whole body in water and remain unclean until evening. ¹⁷All cloth or leather on which semen falls shall be washed in water and remain unclean until evening. ¹⁸And if a man has carnal relations with a woman, they shall bathe in water and remain unclean until evening.

¹⁹When a woman has a discharge, her discharge being blood from her body, she shall remain in her impurity seven days; whoever touches her shall be unclean until evening.

אֹתָם֙ הַכֹּהֵ֔ן אֶחָ֣ד חַטָּ֗את וְהָאֶחָ֖ד עֹלָ֑ה וְכִפֶּ֨ר עָלָ֧יו הַכֹּהֵ֛ן לִפְנֵ֥י יְהוָ֖ה מִזּוֹבֽוֹ׃ ס   ששי [שביעי כשהן מחוברות] ¹⁶ וְאִ֕ישׁ כִּֽי־תֵצֵ֥א מִמֶּ֖נּוּ שִׁכְבַת־זָ֑רַע וְרָחַ֥ץ בַּמַּ֛יִם אֶת־כָּל־בְּשָׂר֖וֹ וְטָמֵ֥א עַד־הָעָֽרֶב׃ ¹⁷ וְכָל־בֶּ֣גֶד וְכָל־ע֔וֹר אֲשֶׁר־יִהְיֶ֥ה עָלָ֖יו שִׁכְבַת־זָ֑רַע וְכֻבַּ֥ס בַּמַּ֖יִם וְטָמֵ֥א עַד־הָעָֽרֶב׃ פ ¹⁸ וְאִשָּׁ֕ה אֲשֶׁ֨ר יִשְׁכַּ֥ב אִ֛ישׁ אֹתָ֖הּ שִׁכְבַת־זָ֑רַע וְרָחֲצ֣וּ בַמַּ֔יִם וְטָמְא֖וּ עַד־הָעָֽרֶב׃ ¹⁹ וְאִשָּׁה֙ כִּֽי־תִהְיֶ֣ה זָבָ֔ה דָּ֛ם יִהְיֶ֥ה זֹבָ֖הּ בִּבְשָׂרָ֑הּ שִׁבְעַ֤ת יָמִים֙ תִּהְיֶ֣ה בְנִדָּתָ֔הּ וְכָל־הַנֹּגֵ֥עַ בָּ֖הּ יִטְמָ֥א

15. The priest shall offer them In this case, it is the priest who designates which bird shall be used for each offering. As has been explained in several instances, the sequence "sin offering" followed by "burnt offering" expresses a specific phenomenology. The relationship of the *zav* to God is first rectified by means of the sin offering, which purifies him; only then does he present a sacrifice on his own as a restored member of the religious community. He resumes the role of a proper worshiper through his burnt offering, and its acceptance by God confirms his reinstatement.

A sin offering is required here not because the person in question offended God by any intentional or unintentional act but because the impurity, which is to say the ailment, threatened the purity of the sanctuary.

Thus the priest shall make expiation on his behalf The sense of the formula *ve-khipper ʿalav* is: "He shall perform rites of expiation *over him*," namely, with respect to him or on his behalf.

16. When a man has an emission of semen The sense of Hebrew *shikhvat zeraʿ* is "a flowing of semen." As Ibn Ezra explains, this statement pertains to an involuntary emission of semen. In Deuteronomy 23:11 this is called *mikreh lailah*, "a nocturnal emission." In rabbinic law, a person in this situation is called *tevul yom*, "one who is to immerse himself on the same day."⁹

17. All cloth or leather on which semen falls Clothing and other objects of cloth and leather, susceptible to contamination, must be cleansed. They remain impure until evening, which means that they may not be used until that time.

18. And if a man has carnal relations with a woman Hoffmann explains that the woman in this case does not become impure as a result of semen entering her body. This is important to emphasize, because the sequence of verses 16–18 might suggest just such an interpretation. Verse 16 tells us that a man becomes impure after a seminal emission, and verse 17 states that cloth and leather become impure through contact with semen. The fact is, however, that the true function of semen is realized when a man inseminates his wife in fulfillment of the divine command to be fruitful and multiply, as we read in Genesis 1:28. It is merely that the law declared her, like her male partner, to be impure after intercourse. Both must bathe after the sex act.

As a matter of fact, the impurity of semen made it forbidden ever to have sex within sacred precincts, once again creating a distance between the process of procreation and the cult. In other ancient Near Eastern religions, fertility was celebrated in the cult—on special occasions, sexual intercourse might even be dramatized and myths telling of the mating of the gods were recited. Not so in the cult of Israelite monotheism.¹⁰

THE ISRAELITE FEMALE   (vv. 19–30)

In this section (vv. 19–30), the law begins with the subject of a woman's normal menstruation and then proceeds to deal with abnormal discharges of blood. There is a logic to this order because, with respect to women, the normal and the abnormal are of the same substance, namely, blood, and are

[20]Anything that she lies on during her impurity shall be
unclean; and anything that she sits on shall be unclean.
[21]Anyone who touches her bedding shall wash his clothes,
bathe in water, and remain unclean until evening; [22]and
anyone who touches any object on which she has sat shall
wash his clothes, bathe in water, and remain unclean until
evening. [23]Be it the bedding or be it the object on which she
has sat, on touching it he shall be unclean until evening.
[24]And if a man lies with her, her impurity is communicated
to him; he shall be unclean seven days, and any bedding on
which he lies shall become unclean.

[25]When a woman has had a discharge of blood for many
days, not at the time of her impurity, or when she has a
discharge beyond her period of impurity, she shall be
unclean, as though at the time of her impurity, as long as
her discharge lasts. [26]Any bedding on which she lies while

עַד־הָעָרֶב׃ 20 וְכֹל אֲשֶׁר תִּשְׁכַּב עָלָיו בְּנִדָּתָהּ
יִטְמָא וְכֹל אֲשֶׁר־תֵּשֵׁב עָלָיו יִטְמָא׃ 21 וְכָל־הַנֹּגֵעַ
בְּמִשְׁכָּבָהּ יְכַבֵּס בְּגָדָיו וְרָחַץ בַּמַּיִם וְטָמֵא עַד־
הָעָרֶב׃ 22 וְכָל־הַנֹּגֵעַ בְּכָל־כְּלִי אֲשֶׁר־תֵּשֵׁב עָלָיו
יְכַבֵּס בְּגָדָיו וְרָחַץ בַּמַּיִם וְטָמֵא עַד־הָעָרֶב׃
23 וְאִם עַל־הַמִּשְׁכָּב הוּא אוֹ עַל־הַכְּלִי אֲשֶׁר־הִוא
יֹשֶׁבֶת־עָלָיו בְּנָגְעוֹ־בוֹ יִטְמָא עַד־הָעָרֶב׃ 24 וְאִם
שָׁכֹב יִשְׁכַּב אִישׁ אֹתָהּ וּתְהִי נִדָּתָהּ עָלָיו וְטָמֵא
שִׁבְעַת יָמִים וְכָל־הַמִּשְׁכָּב אֲשֶׁר־יִשְׁכַּב עָלָיו
יִטְמָא׃ פ 25 וְאִשָּׁה כִּי־יָזוּב זוֹב דָּמָהּ יָמִים
רַבִּים בְּלֹא עֶת־נִדָּתָהּ אוֹ כִי־תָזוּב עַל־נִדָּתָהּ כָּל־
יְמֵי זוֹב טֻמְאָתָהּ כִּימֵי נִדָּתָהּ תִּהְיֶה טְמֵאָה הִוא׃

often related to the timing of the menstrual period. In the case of males, there is a perceptible difference between seminal emissions and pus or other substances issuing from the penis as a result of infection. Perhaps it is for this reason that the laws governing males begin with abnormalities and then proceed to deal with normal emissions of semen.

19. When a woman has a discharge, her discharge being blood from her body Menstruation is called *zov,* "discharge," and some of the same terms of reference are used here as in the case of abnormal discharges of the male in verses 1–12. Normal seminal emissions, however, would not be called *zov.*

she shall remain in her impurity seven days Rather, "she shall remain in her menstrual condition seven days." The term *niddah*, which previously appeared in 12:2, derives from the root *n-d-h* (cognate to Akk. *nadû*), "to cast, hurl, throw." It represents a variation of *n-z-h*, "to spatter," discussed in the Comment to 6:20, a connection suggested by Rashi in his comment to Numbers 19:9. It does not connote impurity in and of itself but, rather, describes the physiological process of the flow of blood. The status of the menstruating woman is that she is ritually impure during that period, according to regulation.

Anyone who has contact with a woman during her menstrual period is impure until evening. Verses 20–23 repeat some of the same forms of transmitted impurity as we observed in the case of the male who had a discharge. Whatever the woman sits on or lies on becomes impure, and one who touches such objects becomes impure in turn.

23. Be it the bedding or be it the object on which she has sat This verse has occasioned a good deal of comment because of its unusual syntax. The translation understands the phrase *ve-'im 'al ha-mishkav hu'* to mean "if it is a case of touching her bedding" or a case of touching a vessel, and so forth. The pronoun *hu'* does not refer to a person or object but to a situation. Hoffmann notes that verse 23 contrasts with verse 24: Touching an object on which a menstruating woman has either sat or lain renders one impure only until evening, whereas having sexual intercourse with a menstruating woman renders a man impure for seven days. Although the formulation is not explicit in every case, it is clear from context that when any one of these impurities occurs, the requirement is to bathe and launder one's clothing. This is explicitly stated in verses 21–22 but not in verses 20 and 23.

24. her impurity is communicated to him Rather, "her menstrual impurity is communicated to him."

The essential prohibition against having sexual intercourse with a menstruating woman is stated in 18:19 and again in 20:18. The penalty is being "cut off" from the community of Israel.[11] Here the concern is with impurity. One who has sexual relations with a woman during her menstrual period becomes impure for seven days, and his impurity is severe enough to contaminate his bedding as well. He must, of course, bathe and launder his clothing after seven days.

26 כָּל־הַמִּשְׁכָּב אֲשֶׁר־תִּשְׁכַּב עָלָיו כָּל־יְמֵי זוֹבָהּ
כְּמִשְׁכַּב נִדָּתָהּ יִהְיֶה־לָּהּ וְכָל־הַכְּלִי אֲשֶׁר תֵּשֵׁב
עָלָיו טָמֵא יִהְיֶה כְּטֻמְאַת נִדָּתָהּ׃ 27 וְכָל־הַנּוֹגֵעַ
בָּם יִטְמָא וְכִבֶּס בְּגָדָיו וְרָחַץ בַּמַּיִם וְטָמֵא עַד־
הָעָרֶב׃ 28 וְאִם־טָהֲרָה מִזּוֹבָהּ וְסָפְרָה לָּהּ שִׁבְעַת
יָמִים וְאַחַר תִּטְהָר׃ שביעי 29 וּבַיּוֹם הַשְּׁמִינִי
תִּקַּח־לָהּ שְׁתֵּי תֹרִים אוֹ שְׁנֵי בְּנֵי יוֹנָה וְהֵבִיאָה
אוֹתָם אֶל־הַכֹּהֵן אֶל־פֶּתַח אֹהֶל מוֹעֵד׃ 30 וְעָשָׂה
הַכֹּהֵן אֶת־הָאֶחָד חַטָּאת וְאֶת־הָאֶחָד עֹלָה וְכִפֶּר
עָלֶיהָ הַכֹּהֵן לִפְנֵי יְהוָה מִזּוֹב טֻמְאָתָהּ׃ מפטיר
31 וְהִזַּרְתֶּם אֶת־בְּנֵי־יִשְׂרָאֵל מִטֻּמְאָתָם וְלֹא
יָמֻתוּ בְּטֻמְאָתָם בְּטַמְּאָם אֶת־מִשְׁכָּנִי אֲשֶׁר

her discharge lasts shall be for her like bedding during her impurity; and any object on which she sits shall become unclean, as it does during her impurity:
27 whoever touches them shall be unclean; he shall wash his clothes, bathe in water, and remain unclean until evening.

28 When she becomes clean of her discharge, she shall count off seven days, and after that she shall be clean.
29 On the eighth day she shall take two turtledoves or two pigeons, and bring them to the priest at the entrance of the Tent of Meeting.
30 The priest shall offer the one as a sin offering and the other as a burnt offering; and the priest shall make expiation on her behalf, for her unclean discharge, before the LORD.

31 You shall put the Israelites on guard against their uncleanness, lest they die through their uncleanness by defiling My Tabernacle which is among them.

25. for many days, not at the time of her impurity Rather, "not at the period of her menstruation." This is the primary symptom: irregularity of blood discharges, which either persist beyond the regular menstrual period or are unconnected with it altogether. A woman who has discharges of blood not due to her menstruation bears the same impurity as a menstruating woman for as long as the discharges last.

26–27. These verses repeat the law that whatever the woman with the discharge sits on or lies on becomes impure and that whoever touches these items becomes impure and remains so until evening.

28. When she becomes clean of her discharge Like the male, the female must count off seven days subsequent to the termination of her abnormal discharge of blood.

29–30. These verses repeat the laws applicable to the Israelite male. The categorical difference between abnormal and normal conditions is that abnormalities ultimately require ritual expiation as part of the purification process, whereas normal conditions, though inducing impurity, require only bathing and laundering of clothing and observance of the proper period of waiting. Such normal conditions do not of themselves involve the sanctuary directly, unless a person in such a state actually enters the sacred precincts.

CONCLUSION (vv. 31–33)

31. You shall put the Israelites on guard The verbal form *ve-hizzartem,* which is unique in the Hebrew Bible, means "you shall cause . . . to avoid; to be separate from. . . ." In 22:2 we read that the Israelites are instructed to keep themselves separate (*ve-yinnazru*) from the sacred offerings that are forbidden to them. The root is ***n-z-r,*** from which the term ***nazir,*** "a Nazirite," derives.[12]

lest they die . . . by defiling My Tabernacle As noted in the introductory Comment to the chapter, this is a major statement of policy. Although an impure person may not be guilty of any offense against God, as is true in these laws dealing with illnesses and natural physiological processes, such impurities nevertheless threaten the status of the entire community if left unattended. If the sanctuary were defiled, God's wrath would be aroused against the entire community. This is the sense of the warning "lest they die." It is not the condition of impurity per se that evokes God's punishment, but the failure to rectify that condition so as to restore a state of purity.

32 Such is the ritual concerning him who has a discharge: concerning him who has an emission of semen and becomes unclean thereby, 33 and concerning her who is in menstrual infirmity, and concerning anyone, male or female, who has a discharge, and concerning a man who lies with an unclean woman.

בְּתוֹכָֽם׃ 32 זֹ֥את תּוֹרַ֖ת הַזָּ֑ב וַאֲשֶׁ֨ר תֵּצֵ֥א מִמֶּ֛נּוּ
שִׁכְבַת־זֶ֖רַע לְטָמְאָה־בָֽהּ׃ 33 וְהַדָּוָה֙ בְּנִדָּתָ֔הּ וְהַזָּב֙
אֶת־זוֹב֔וֹ לַזָּכָ֖ר וְלַנְּקֵבָ֑ה וּלְאִ֕ישׁ אֲשֶׁ֥ר יִשְׁכַּ֖ב עִם־
טְמֵאָֽה׃ פ

32. ***Such is the ritual*** Hebrew *torah* means "instruction, prescribed ritual." This term is frequently used to designate a particular rule in which the priests are to be instructed. Verse 32 serves as a concluding statement, as if to say: "The preceding is the prescribed ritual." Similar statements occur elsewhere after specific rituals have been prescribed, for example, in 7:37, following the rites of chapters 6–7, and in 14:54, following the rituals of chapters 13–14.[13]

33. ***and concerning her who is in menstrual infirmity*** The adjective *davah,* meaning "weak," is explained in the Comment to 12:2.

In the subsequent development of Jewish religion, chapter 15 of Leviticus is best remembered for the limitations placed on sexual relations between man and wife during her menstrual period. The requirement that a woman bathe after her period has continued to be upheld by observant Jewish women just prior to marriage, and thereafter.[14]

CHAPTER 16

The Yom Kippur Ritual

Aḥarei Mot

Leviticus 16, which is read in synagogues on Yom Kippur, is well known in the Jewish tradition, and the significance of the ritual of the scapegoat for religious studies in general has drawn widespread attention to this chapter.[1]

The distinctive rites prescribed here involve rare practices called rites of riddance, which effect the removal and destruction of impurity. The transgressions of the Israelites and their priests, which produce impurity, are dramatically transferred to the scapegoat, which is driven into the wilderness, never to return. Certain parts of sin offerings are burned to ashes outside the encampment rather than on the altar. Chapter 16 also ordains the use of sacrificial blood in unusual ways during the purification of the sanctuary. These two processes—purification through sacrificial blood and purification by riddance—are woven into one of the most complex rituals to have reached us from any ancient society.

The primary objective of expiatory rites like the ones set forth in chapter 16 was to maintain a pure sanctuary. An impure, or defiled, sanctuary induced God to withdraw His presence from the Israelite community. Obviously, the greatest threat to the purity of the sanctuary came from the priesthood itself, whose members functioned within its sacred precincts and who bore primary responsibility for its maintenance.[2] The sanctuary was also threatened by major transgressions of the laws of purity involving the entire Israelite community or by the failure of individual Israelites to attend to their own purification—for example, after contamination by a corpse. This occurred because such serious impurities were considered to be contagious and thereby ultimately affected the sanctuary, which was located within the area of settlement. As long as impurity persisted, God remained offended, so to speak, and the danger of His wrath and possible alienation was imminent.[3]

This ancient view of Yom Kippur is somewhat different from that which came to predominate in later Judaism, especially in the centuries following the destruction of the Second Temple of Jerusalem in 70 C.E. Atonement for the sins of the people eventually replaced the purification of the sanctuary per se as the central theme of Yom Kippur.[4] This shift of emphasis is already suggested in verse 30: "For on this day atonement shall be made for *you* to cleanse *you* of all your sins; *you* shall be clean before the LORD." The purification of the sanctuary was understood to extend to the people—to relieve them of their transgressions as well. However, no ritual of purification was actually performed over the people, as was the case on other occasions.[5]

In chapter 16 we observe a dynamic interaction between the priesthood/community, on the one

AHAREI MOT

16 The LORD spoke to Moses after the death of the two sons of Aaron who died when they drew too close to the presence of the LORD. 2The LORD said to Moses:

Tell your brother Aaron that he is not to come at will into the Shrine behind the curtain, in front of the cover that is upon the ark, lest he die; for I appear in the cloud over the cover. 3Thus only shall Aaron enter the Shrine: with a bull

אחרי מות

ט״ז וַיְדַבֵּ֤ר יְהוָה֙ אֶל־מֹשֶׁ֔ה אַחֲרֵ֣י מ֔וֹת שְׁנֵ֖י בְּנֵ֣י
אַהֲרֹ֑ן בְּקָרְבָתָ֥ם לִפְנֵי־יְהוָ֖ה וַיָּמֻֽתוּ׃ 2 וַיֹּ֨אמֶר יְהוָ֜ה
אֶל־מֹשֶׁ֗ה דַּבֵּר֮ אֶל־אַהֲרֹ֣ן אָחִ֒יךָ֒ וְאַל־יָבֹ֤א בְכָל־
עֵת֙ אֶל־הַקֹּ֔דֶשׁ מִבֵּ֖ית לַפָּרֹ֑כֶת אֶל־פְּנֵ֨י הַכַּפֹּ֜רֶת
אֲשֶׁ֤ר עַל־הָאָרֹן֙ וְלֹ֣א יָמ֔וּת כִּ֚י בֶּֽעָנָ֔ן אֵרָאֶ֖ה עַל־

hand, and the omnipresence of God, on the other. Out of love for His people Israel, God manifests His presence among them, but only on condition that the Israelite sanctuary be maintained in a state of purity.[6] God's forgiveness, coming at the end of the expiatory process, can be anticipated only after the purification of the sanctuary is satisfactorily accomplished.

This chapter presents us with difficult problems not only because of the complexity of the rituals themselves but also because certain verses anticipate rites to be performed further on, whereas others merely recapitulate what has already occurred. The chapter may be divided into six sections that present a reconstruction of the complete Yom Kippur ritual. Here the Commentary draws heavily from talmudic literature, which often preserves descriptions of very ancient rites and fills in details absent from the chapter itself.

Verses 1–2 introduce the rites prescribed in chapter 16 by referring to the untimely deaths of Nadab and Abihu, the two sons of Aaron who improperly entered the sanctuary, as recounted in chapter 10. This reference served as an admonition to the priesthood since the purification of the sanctuary required the High Priest to enter its innermost part. If extreme care were not exercised in this endeavor, he risked death.

1. after the death of the two sons of Aaron who died when they drew too close The offense of Aaron's sons is discussed in the Comment to 10:1.

2. Tell your brother Aaron that he is not to come at will into the Shrine Hebrew *be-khol ʿet,* literally "at any time, at all times" is not to be taken to mean that the High Priest was never to enter the Holy of Holies, which would contradict the procedures of this chapter, but, rather, that he was only to enter the Holy of Holies on this unique occasion. In this context, Hebrew *ha-kodesh* refers to the innermost part of the sanctuary, whereas the entire structure is called *ʾohel moʿed,* "the Tent of Meeting." This is evident from verse 16.

into the Shrine behind the curtain That is to say, on the inward side of the *parokhet,* the name given to the curtain that divided the Shrine, or Holy of Holies, from the larger area first encountered upon entering the sanctuary. The layout of the Tent of Meeting, or Tabernacle, is described in the Comment to 1:1.

in front of the cover that is upon the ark The Hebrew term *kapporet,* "cover," has been variously explained. As described in Exodus 25:17–22, it was a sculptured lid for the Ark, fashioned with two cherubs facing each other. It was called *kapporet* because of its function in the expiatory process, not because of its physical function as a covering for the Ark. The Septuagint renders *kapporet* by Greek *hilastērion,* "instrument of propitiation." The lid of the Ark was called *kapporet,* a noun that derives from the verb *k-p-r,* "to wipe clean, purify," hence "to expiate," because it was God's seat of mercy whence atonement was granted.

for I appear in the cloud over the cover Most of the traditional commentaries—including Rashi, Ibn Ezra, and Rashbam—understood the cloud (*ʿanan*) to refer to God's presence (*kavod*). This was also the rendering of Targum Jonathan. As explained in the introductory Comment to chapters 8–9, the *kavod* was depicted as a cloud with fire burning inside it. The cloud pervaded the sanctuary and was visible above it. By contrast, certain talmudic sources identify the cloud of this verse with the "cloud of incense" produced by the High Priest inside the Shrine, as described in verse 13.[7] If that is the case, then verse 2 anticipates what is to follow and is stating that God appeared to the High Priest only when the incense cloud had filled the Shrine.

of the herd for a sin offering and a ram for a burnt offering.—[4]He shall be dressed in a sacral linen tunic, with linen breeches next to his flesh, and be girt with a linen sash, and he shall wear a linen turban. They are sacral vestments; he shall bathe his body in water and then put them on.—[5]And from the Israelite community he shall take two he-goats for a sin offering and a ram for a burnt offering.

[6]Aaron is to offer his own bull of sin offering, to make expiation for himself and for his household. [7]Aaron shall

הַכַּפֹּֽרֶת׃ 3 בְּזֹ֛את יָבֹ֥א אַהֲרֹ֖ן אֶל־הַקֹּ֑דֶשׁ בְּפַ֧ר בֶּן־
בָּקָ֛ר לְחַטָּ֖את וְאַ֥יִל לְעֹלָֽה׃ 4 כְּתֹֽנֶת־בַּ֨ד קֹ֜דֶשׁ
יִלְבָּ֗שׁ וּמִֽכְנְסֵי־בַד֮ יִהְי֣וּ עַל־בְּשָׂרוֹ֒ וּבְאַבְנֵ֥ט בַּד֙
יַחְגֹּ֔ר וּבְמִצְנֶ֥פֶת בַּ֖ד יִצְנֹ֑ף בִּגְדֵי־קֹ֣דֶשׁ הֵ֔ם וְרָחַ֥ץ
בַּמַּ֛יִם אֶת־בְּשָׂר֖וֹ וּלְבֵשָֽׁם׃ 5 וּמֵאֵ֗ת עֲדַת֙ בְּנֵ֣י
יִשְׂרָאֵ֔ל יִקַּ֛ח שְׁנֵֽי־שְׂעִירֵ֥י עִזִּ֖ים לְחַטָּ֑את וְאַ֥יִל
אֶחָ֖ד לְעֹלָֽה׃ 6 וְהִקְרִ֧יב אַהֲרֹ֛ן אֶת־פַּ֥ר הַחַטָּ֖את
אֲשֶׁר־ל֑וֹ וְכִפֶּ֥ר בַּעֲד֖וֹ וּבְעַ֥ד בֵּיתֽוֹ׃ 7 וְלָקַ֥ח אֶת־

The wording of verse 2 argues against the second interpretation, however. The statement "For *I* appear in the cloud" explains the restriction of entry. Aaron is normally prohibited from entering the Holy of Holies precisely because that is where God's *kavod* abides. Furthermore, identifying the cloud as the incense cloud would not accord with the purpose of the incense in this case. The incense cloud in verse 13 protected the High Priest when he came into God's immediate presence, whereas in this verse the cloud envelope, represented by the *kavod* itself, protected God, so to speak.

PREPARATIONS FOR PURIFICATION (vv. 3–10)

The main celebrant in the purification of the sanctuary was the High Priest. Although he was assisted at certain points in the proceedings, the efficacy of the entire ritual depended primarily on him. He prepared himself by bathing his body and donning his special white linen vestments. For the rites of purification, he provided, out of his own resources, a young bull for the sin offering. The Israelite community, for its part, provided two he-goats and one ram for a burnt offering. The bull was to be used in securing expiation for the sins of the priesthood, and one of the he-goats, selected by lot, became the sin offering of the people. The other he-goat was not slaughtered. It became the scapegoat, to be driven into the wilderness.

3. ***Thus only shall Aaron enter the Shrine*** Hebrew *be-zo't yavo'* is emphatic: "only in this way shall he enter . . ."—strict adherence to the prescribed procedures and the use of proper materials are indispensable to the efficacy of the purification rites.

4. ***He shall be dressed in a sacral linen tunic*** The regular vestments of the High Priest, described in 8:7f., were made of gold and rare gems and woven of costly dyed fabrics. For the rites described here, the High Priest donned unadorned white linen vestments that were fashioned especially for the occasion and that, undoubtedly, were of particular significance. They symbolized the abject state of the High Priest, the representative of the Israelite people, in seeking expiation of sins and making confession. Although the text does not say where the High Priest was to don his vestments and perform his ablutions, it is probable that these procedures were performed in a screened area near the Tent of Meeting.[8]

5. ***And from the Israelite community . . . two he-goats*** Sin offerings on behalf of the entire community usually consisted of large cattle, as, for example, in 4:1–21; those offered by individual Israelites were usually from the flocks, as in 4:22f. The Yom Kippur ritual was an exception—he-goats from the flocks served as sin offerings for the entire people.

It is not entirely clear why both of the he-goats, the scapegoat and the one designated "for the LORD," were referred to as sin offerings. Perhaps it is because at this point the lots had not yet been cast to determine which he-goat would be marked "for the LORD" and which "for Azazel." Potentially, then, both were sin offerings. Verses 9–10 explain that only the he-goat marked "for the LORD" served as an actual sin offering.

6. ***Aaron is to offer his own bull*** This statement is anticipatory. This is what Aaron would do at the appropriate time. On the formulation *kipper be'ad,* "to make expiation for, on behalf of," see Comment to 4:20, where several indirect-object constructions with *kipper* are discussed.

take the two he-goats and let them stand before the LORD at the entrance of the Tent of Meeting; 8and he shall place lots upon the two goats, one marked for the LORD and the other marked for Azazel. 9Aaron shall bring forward the goat designated by lot for the LORD, which he is to offer as a sin offering; 10while the goat designated by lot for Azazel shall

שְׁנֵ֣י הַשְּׂעִירִ֑ם וְהֶעֱמִ֤יד אֹתָם֙ לִפְנֵ֣י יְהֹוָ֔ה פֶּ֖תַח
אֹ֥הֶל מוֹעֵֽד׃ 8 וְנָתַ֧ן אַהֲרֹ֛ן עַל־שְׁנֵ֥י הַשְּׂעִירִ֖ם
גֹּרָל֑וֹת גּוֹרָ֤ל אֶחָד֙ לַיהֹוָ֔ה וְגוֹרָ֥ל אֶחָ֖ד לַעֲזָאזֵֽל׃
9 וְהִקְרִ֤יב אַהֲרֹן֙ אֶת־הַשָּׂעִ֔יר אֲשֶׁ֨ר עָלָ֥ה עָלָ֛יו
הַגּוֹרָ֖ל לַיהֹוָ֑ה וְעָשָׂ֖הוּ חַטָּֽאת׃ 10 וְהַשָּׂעִ֗יר אֲשֶׁ֨ר

7. Aaron shall take the two he-goats and let them stand before the LORD A note to the translation explains that the Hebrew text reads *ve-lakaḥ,* "He shall take," but that the sense of the verse is clearer if the antecedent "Aaron" is inserted, based on its occurrence at the beginning of verse 8.

Hebrew *heʿemid,* "to station" (see v. 10), is used with respect to persons who were made to stand in the presence of the Lord, near the altar, when purificatory rites were about to be performed on their behalf. God was to view them and find them deserving of purification.

In this case the two he-goats were stationed near the altar so that one could be chosen by lot as a sacrifice and the other one could be selected as the scapegoat. Further on in the proceedings, in verses 19–20, as the High Priest pronounced the confessional over the designated scapegoat, he also "brought it near" to the altar. The verb *heʿemid* designates preparatory acts, whereas *hikriv,* "to bring near, offer," may signify the act of sacrifice itself or merely moving an object nearer to the altar, as it does in verse 20.

8. and he shall place lots upon the two goats On the utilization of lots in ancient Israel, see Comment to 8:8.

one marked for the LORD and the other marked for Azazel One lot bore the inscription *le-YHVH,* "for the LORD," and the other the inscription *la-ʿazaʾzel,* "for Azazel," that is, *belonging* to the Lord and to Azazel, respectively. Archaeological excavations have unearthed many objects with names inscribed on them, with the prepositional *lamed* indicating the names of their owners.[9]

The precise meaning of Hebrew *ʿazaʾzel,* found nowhere else in the Bible, has been disputed since antiquity and remains uncertain even to the present time. Over the centuries, exegesis of this name has followed three lines of interpretation. According to the first, Azazel is the name of the place in the wilderness to which the scapegoat was dispatched; the term is taken as synonymous with *ʾerets gezerah,* "inaccessible region," in verse 22. Verse 10 may also suggest this interpretation. When translated literally it reads: "and send it [the he-goat] off *to* Azazel, to the wilderness." Yoma 67b understands *ʿazaʾzel* as "a fierce, difficult land," taking the first part of the word to mean *ʿazz,* "strong, fierce." According to the second line of interpretation, Azazel describes the goat. The word *ʿazaʾzel* is a contraction (*notarikon*) comprised of *ʿez,* "goat," and *ʾazal,* "to go away," hence "the goat that goes away." This interpretation occurs in both the Septuagint and the Vulgate and underlies the rabbinic characterization *saʿir ha-mishtalleaḥ,* "the goat that is dispatched," in Mishnah Yoma 6:2. This is, in fact, the interpretation that led to the English rendering "scapegoat" (from *"escape*-goat"), which first appeared in Tyndale's English translation of the Bible in 1530.

Both of the above interpretations are contrived. The third line of interpretation is preferable. Azazel in later myth was the name given to the demonic ruler of the wilderness. The derivation of the word is uncertain, but the thematic relationship of Azazel to the *seʿirim,* "goat-demons," of 17:7 suggests that the word *ʿez,* "goat," is represented in it. The form *ʿazaʾzel* may have developed through reduplication of the letter *zayin: ʿez-ʾel,* "mighty goat," was pronounced *ʿezezʾel* and, finally, *ʿazaʾzel.* The ritual of the scapegoat is discussed in Excursus 4.

9. the goat designated by lot for the LORD The idiom *ʿalah ʿalav ha-goral,* literally "the lot came up for him/it," is an idiom for describing the outcome of casting lots. It probably indicates that the side of the lot bearing the affirmative sign came up on top. The working of lots is explained in the Comment to 8:8.

which he is to offer as a sin offering Rather, "and he shall designate it a sin offering." Assigning an animal as a sacrifice was a formal act accompanied by a declaration. The Sifra, cited by Rashi, explains the procedure as follows: "When he [the High Priest] places the lot upon it [the goat]

be left standing alive before the LORD, to make expiation with it and to send it off to the wilderness for Azazel.

11Aaron shall then offer his bull of sin offering, to make expiation for himself and his household. He shall slaughter his bull of sin offering, 12and he shall take a panful of

עָלָ֨ה עָלָ֤יו הַגּוֹרָל֙ לַעֲזָאזֵ֔ל יָֽעֳמַד־חַ֛י לִפְנֵ֥י יְהוָ֖ה
לְכַפֵּ֣ר עָלָ֑יו לְשַׁלַּ֥ח אֹת֛וֹ לַעֲזָאזֵ֖ל הַמִּדְבָּֽרָה:
יא וְהִקְרִ֧יב אַהֲרֹ֛ן אֶת־פַּ֥ר הַֽחַטָּ֖את אֲשֶׁר־ל֑וֹ וְכִפֶּ֥ר
בַּעֲד֖וֹ וּבְעַ֣ד בֵּית֑וֹ וְשָׁחַ֛ט אֶת־פַּ֥ר הַֽחַטָּ֖את אֲשֶׁר־

he gives it a name and states: To the Lord as a sin offering (*le-YHVH ḥatta't*)." No such formulas have survived from biblical times.

10. shall be left standing alive   The text emphasizes that the he-goat designated for Azazel was not slaughtered in the manner of a sacrifice as was the other goat, which was designated as a sin offering. Its disposition represented a different means of securing expiation, according to Ramban.

to make expiation with it   The idiom *le-khapper 'alav,* translated "to make expiation with it," is actually perplexing, as used in this verse. Almost without exception, *kipper 'al* has to do with the use of sacrificial blood as a means of expiation, which is clearly not the case here.[10] The scapegoat was not part of the expiation rites proper and was not slaughtered. It was merely stationed alongside the other goat and, like it, selected by lot.

Traditional commentaries express diverse views regarding this statement, which they recognize as representing exceptional usage. Targum Jonathan translates: "to atone for the sinfulness of the people, the House of Israel," in which case the preposition *'alav,* "upon it," refers to the people, not the goat. Rashi notes that the verb *kipper* invokes confession, not only atonement, so that this verse could refer to the confession pronounced "over" the scapegoat, as prescribed in verse 21. Ibn Ezra emphasizes function: "That the goat takes on itself the expiation." This is closer to what is being proposed here. The goat was an instrument of expiation—no rite of expiation involving blood was performed near it.[11]

and to send it off to the wilderness for Azazel   The scapegoat was not an offering *to* Azazel; it was being dispatched to his realm, the wilderness.

THE PURIFICATION OF THE SANCTUARY   (vv. 11–19)

In anticipation of the purification of the sanctuary, chapter 16 sets forth the necessary procedures for those rites. The most notable feature was the unique practice of bringing sacrificial blood into the Holy of Holies. It was there that the Ark, with its sculptured lid, the *kapporet,* stood. The *kapporet* was envisioned as God's throne and the Ark as His footstool as He sat astride the cherubs of the *kapporet.*[12]

The High Priest first slaughtered the bull he had provided for the sin offering on behalf of the priesthood. He then drained its blood into a bowl that was held by an assisting priest until it was needed. This detail of the procedure, unmentioned in the Torah text, is supplied by Mishnah Yoma 4:3. Next, the High Priest took a fire pan full of coals from the altar of burnt offerings and two handfuls of a special incense and made his way toward the Holy of Holies. He ignited the incense, which filled the sanctuary with smoke, and left the fire pan just inward of the *parokhet* curtain. He was now ready to bring the blood of the sin offering into the Holy of Holies. He left the Holy of Holies momentarily, took the bowl of bull's blood, and reentered the Holy of Holies, where he sprinkled some of the blood once over the eastern side of the *kapporet.* On his way out, he left the bowl on a stand provided for that purpose. The same procedure was repeated with the blood of the he-goat, provided by the people as their sin offering.

The preceding reconstruction of the purification procedures is based on a fusion of the biblical and mishnaic evidence, as preserved in Mishnah Yoma 5:3.

At this point the text of 16:16 specifies: "And he shall do the same for the Tent of Meeting." This was interpreted by Mishnah Yoma 5:4 to mean that the High Priest sprinkled some of the blood from each of the two sin offerings onto the outer side of the *parokhet* curtain, a practice known from Leviticus 4:16–17. Mixing the blood of the bull and the he-goat into one bowl, he proceeded to purify

glowing coals scooped from the altar before the LORD, and
two handfuls of finely ground aromatic incense, and bring
this behind the curtain. [13]He shall put the incense on the
fire before the LORD, so that the cloud from the incense
screens the cover that is over [the Ark of] the Pact, lest he
die. [14]He shall take some of the blood of the bull and

לוֹ׃ 12 וְלָקַח מְלֹא־הַמַּחְתָּה גַּחֲלֵי־אֵשׁ מֵעַל
הַמִּזְבֵּחַ מִלִּפְנֵי יְהֹוָה וּמְלֹא חׇפְנָיו קְטֹרֶת סַמִּים
דַּקָּה וְהֵבִיא מִבֵּית לַפָּרֹכֶת׃ 13 וְנָתַן אֶת־הַקְּטֹרֶת
עַל־הָאֵשׁ לִפְנֵי יְהֹוָה וְכִסָּה ׀ עֲנַן הַקְּטֹרֶת אֶת־
הַכַּפֹּרֶת אֲשֶׁר עַל־הָעֵדוּת וְלֹא יָמוּת׃ 14 וְלָקַח

the golden incense altar that stood just outside the *parokhet* curtain, as the aforementioned Mishnah Yoma explains. He did this by "applying" blood to each of the four horns of the incense altar and, then, by sprinkling the rest of the blood on the altar seven times.

The purification of the sanctuary was thus completed in two stages, represented first by the bull and then by the he-goat, or to put it in another way, by the sin offering of the priesthood and of the people, respectively. It represents the only instance in the priestly laws of the Torah in which sacrificial blood is brought into the Holy of Holies. What we observe is the purification, or sealing up, of a route of entry leading inward from the incense altar to the *parokhet* curtain to the Ark and *kapporet.* This unique procedure was necessitated by the entry of a mortal being, the High Priest, into the Holy of Holies—an act required for the proper purification of the sanctuary but one that, at the same time, endangered that very condition of purity.[13]

*11. **Aaron shall then offer his bull of sin offering*** Nothing was actually placed on the altar at this point. The verb *hikriv,* "to offer," here indicates that the bull was slaughtered and prepared for sacrifice. The actual sacrifice is described in verse 25. Our verse follows up on the preparations already initiated in verse 6. Once the bull provided by the High Priest was designated a sin offering, it was called *par ha-ḥatta't,* "the bull for the sin offering." A similar formal designation occurs in 8:18: *'el ha-'olah,* "the ram for the burnt offering."

to make expiation for himself and his household The construction *kipper be'ad* previously appeared in verse 6. Here, again, the text anticipates the purpose of the sin offering in advance of its actual performance.

*12. **And he shall take a panful of glowing coals scooped from the altar before the LORD*** Fire pans were used for several purposes, as is explained in the Comment to 10:1. Here, the designation "the altar before the LORD" must refer to the altar of burnt offerings in the sanctuary courtyard, since the High Priest brings the coals from there into the sanctuary. In another context, in verse 18, the golden incense altar is referred to in the same way as "the altar that is before the LORD."

finely ground aromatic incense The prescription for blending this incense is provided in Exodus 30:34–38. The same blend was used for the daily incense offering, ordained in Exodus 30:26. The rabbinic tradition explains that for the rites of purification on Yom Kippur, the incense was ground more finely than usual.

*13. **the cover that is over [the Ark of] the Pact*** The term *kapporet,* "cover," is explained in the Comment to verse 2. Hebrew *ha-'edut,* "the Pact," is an abbreviation of *'aron ha-'edut,* "the Ark of the Pact," a term frequently used in the Tabernacle texts (for example, in Exod. 25:22; 26:33), but also occurring in other passages, such as Leviticus 24:3. The Ark is referred to in this way because "the tablets of the Pact" (*luḥot ha-'edut*) were deposited in it, as is stated in Exodus 31:7.

lest he die The incense cloud served to protect the High Priest while he stood in the immediate area of God's *kavod,* "presence." Incense was widely used as an apotropaic substance, or means of protection. In Numbers 17:11–13, we read that Moses instructed Aaron to burn incense in a fire pan to protect the Israelites from a plague sent against them by God, who had become enraged at the rebellion of Korah and his group. Aaron stood with the incense "between the dead and the living," and the plague subsided.

In the ritual of Yom Kippur, the High Priest drew extremely close to God's throne in the Holy of Holies and was therefore in danger—even though he had committed no wrongdoing and was in the Holy of Holies in accordance with God's instructions. As discussed in the Comment to 1:4, all who stand in God's presence are in need of expiation in order to avert His wrath.[14]

sprinkle it with his finger over the cover on the east side; and in front of the cover he shall sprinkle some of the blood with his finger seven times.
15He shall then slaughter the people's goat of sin offering, bring its blood behind the curtain, and do with its blood as he has done with the blood of the bull: he shall sprinkle it over the cover and in front of the cover.

16Thus he shall purge the Shrine of the uncleanness and transgression of the Israelites, whatever their sins; and he shall do the same for the Tent of Meeting, which abides with them in the midst of their uncleanness.
17When he goes in to make expiation in the Shrine, nobody else shall be in the Tent of Meeting until he comes out.

When he has made expiation for himself and his household, and for the whole congregation of Israel,
18he shall go out to the altar that is before the LORD and purge it: he shall take some of the blood of the bull and of the goat and apply it to each of the horns of the altar;
19and the rest of the blood he shall sprinkle on it with his finger seven times. Thus he shall cleanse it of the uncleanness of the Israelites and consecrate it.

מִדַּם הַפָּר וְהִזָּה בְאֶצְבָּעוֹ עַל־פְּנֵי הַכַּפֹּרֶת קֵדְמָה
וְלִפְנֵי הַכַּפֹּרֶת יַזֶּה שֶׁבַע־פְּעָמִים מִן־הַדָּם
בְּאֶצְבָּעוֹ: 15 וְשָׁחַט אֶת־שְׂעִיר הַחַטָּאת אֲשֶׁר
לָעָם וְהֵבִיא אֶת־דָּמוֹ אֶל־מִבֵּית לַפָּרֹכֶת וְעָשָׂה
אֶת־דָּמוֹ כַּאֲשֶׁר עָשָׂה לְדַם הַפָּר וְהִזָּה אֹתוֹ עַל־
הַכַּפֹּרֶת וְלִפְנֵי הַכַּפֹּרֶת: 16 וְכִפֶּר עַל־הַקֹּדֶשׁ
מִטֻּמְאֹת בְּנֵי יִשְׂרָאֵל וּמִפִּשְׁעֵיהֶם לְכָל־חַטֹּאתָם
וְכֵן יַעֲשֶׂה לְאֹהֶל מוֹעֵד הַשֹּׁכֵן אִתָּם בְּתוֹךְ
טֻמְאֹתָם: 17 וְכָל־אָדָם לֹא־יִהְיֶה ׀ בְּאֹהֶל מוֹעֵד
בְּבֹאוֹ לְכַפֵּר בַּקֹּדֶשׁ עַד־צֵאתוֹ וְכִפֶּר בַּעֲדוֹ וּבְעַד
בֵּיתוֹ וּבְעַד כָּל־קְהַל יִשְׂרָאֵל: שני 18 וְיָצָא אֶל־
הַמִּזְבֵּחַ אֲשֶׁר לִפְנֵי־יְהוָה וְכִפֶּר עָלָיו וְלָקַח מִדַּם
הַפָּר וּמִדַּם הַשָּׂעִיר וְנָתַן עַל־קַרְנוֹת הַמִּזְבֵּחַ
סָבִיב: 19 וְהִזָּה עָלָיו מִן־הַדָּם בְּאֶצְבָּעוֹ שֶׁבַע
פְּעָמִים וְטִהֲרוֹ וְקִדְּשׁוֹ מִטֻּמְאֹת בְּנֵי יִשְׂרָאֵל:

14. and sprinkle it with his finger Sprinkling sacrificial blood was a frequent procedure.[15] Mishnah Yoma 5:3 interprets the verse to mean that the High Priest sprinkled the blood once over the *kapporet* and seven times in front of it. The first sprinkling was done with an upward motion and the other seven sprinklings, with a downward motion. Verse 15 adds that these rites were repeated, using some of the blood from the he-goat provided by the people.

16. of the uncleanness and transgression of the Israelites, whatever their sins Uncleanness is equated with sinfulness; thus, according to the biblical conception, sinfulness was regarded as a form of impurity. The verb *ḥitte'*, literally "to remove the sin," effectively means "to purify," as in 14:52.

which abides with them in the midst of their uncleanness This was the concession made by God out of His love for Israel. He allowed His people to build an earthly residence for Him, on condition that its purity be strictly maintained. In a very real sense, this was the primary purpose of the entire biblical ritual of Yom Kippur.

17. nobody else shall be in the Tent of Meeting On the occasion of this ritual, only the High Priest, who had undergone meticulous purification for his role on Yom Kippur and who held a special status, was permitted inside the Tent. At other times, ordinary priests officiated in the larger section of the Tent, where the menorah, the presentation table, and the altar of incense stood.

18. he shall go out to the altar that is before the LORD In verse 12, "the altar before the LORD" referred to the altar of burnt offerings; here, according to the context, it must refer to the incense altar. The sense of "going out" should, therefore, be understood not as an indication that the High Priest left the Tent itself, but only that he came out of the Holy of Holies to the outer chamber of the Tent.

19. Thus he shall cleanse it . . . and consecrate it The verb *tihher,* "to cleanse, purify," describes a variety of acts. Purification in this instance was accomplished by the use of sacrificial blood from the sin offerings, although blood has no real cleansing properties. (Water, for instance, does, and it was also frequently used in the purification process, along with detergent, in laundering clothing.[16] As a process, fire also purifies.[17] Even oil, used in rites of consecration, possesses cleansing properties, as noted in the Comment to 8:2.) But, all acts of purification went beyond whatever

20 וְכִלָּה מִכַּפֵּר אֶת־הַקֹּדֶשׁ וְאֶת־אֹהֶל מוֹעֵד
וְאֶת־הַמִּזְבֵּחַ וְהִקְרִיב אֶת־הַשָּׂעִיר הֶחָי׃ 21 וְסָמַךְ
אַהֲרֹן אֶת־שְׁתֵּי ידו עַל רֹאשׁ הַשָּׂעִיר הַחַי
וְהִתְוַדָּה עָלָיו אֶת־כָּל־עֲוֺנֹת בְּנֵי יִשְׂרָאֵל וְאֶת־
כָּל־פִּשְׁעֵיהֶם לְכָל־חַטֹּאתָם וְנָתַן אֹתָם עַל־רֹאשׁ
הַשָּׂעִיר וְשִׁלַּח בְּיַד־אִישׁ עִתִּי הַמִּדְבָּרָה׃ 22 וְנָשָׂא

v. 21. יָדָיו ק׳

20 When he has finished purging the Shrine, the Tent of Meeting, and the altar, the live goat shall be brought forward.
21 Aaron shall lay both his hands upon the head of the live goat and confess over it all the iniquities and transgressions of the Israelites, whatever their sins, putting them on the head of the goat; and it shall be sent off to the wilderness through a designated man.
22 Thus the goat shall

physical properties were possessed by the substances employed and expressed notions of a religious character. In the case of blood, the religious factor is more conspicuous than it is with respect to other substances that have actual cleansing power. It is therefore preferable to translate *tihher* as "to purify" rather than as "to cleanse." The root *t-h-r* has, as its primary connotation, a physical purity, like that of the sky or of pure metals, such as gold, which contain little or no alloy. It is also said of the pure water of springs.[18]

The verb ***kiddesh,*** "to consecrate," often figures in the initial dedication of sacred places and persons.[19] Here, the rites performed on Yom Kippur served to reconsecrate the sanctuary, thus restoring it to its pristine state of purification.

THE DISPATCH OF THE SCAPEGOAT (vv. 20–22)

After completing the purification of the sanctuary by means of the blood rites, the High Priest turned his attention to the second mode of purification, that of riddance. Repeatedly, the scapegoat is referred to as "the live goat," emphasizing the difference between its manner of disposition and that of the sin offerings, which were slaughtered.

The High Priest laid his hands on the scapegoat and confessed over it the sins of the people, ***not*** his own transgressions or those of the priesthood. (Those would be adequately expiated by the blood rites associated with the sin offering of the priesthood and by the final destruction of parts of that offering by fire outside the camp, as set forth in verses 23–28.) The scapegoat served only the people, not the priesthood itself. By laying his hands on the scapegoat, the High Priest transferred to it the sins of the people, which were carried with it into the wilderness, to a land of no return.

20. ***shall be brought forward*** The scapegoat was brought near to the altar of burnt offerings. It stood facing the entrance of the courtyard, from which it would depart.

21. ***and confess over it all the iniquities and transgressions of the Israelites*** The verb *hitvaddah,* from the root *y-d-h* (or *v-d-h*), means "to reveal oneself" and connotes the opposite of concealment.[20] Originally, the confessional enumerated the various sins in order to expose them. Once isolated in this way—identified by name—the sins could be exorcised. Ancient peoples believed that sinfulness, like impurity, was an external force that had clung to them; it was necessary, therefore, to "drive out," or detach, sins. This view is expressed in the literal wording of an ancient prayer preserved in Psalms 65:4: "All sorts of sins have overwhelmed me: it is you, O Lord, who will wipe them away!"[21]

There was undoubtedly a formula for the confessional that was used in biblical times, although the priestly laws of the Torah preserve very little recitational material. A later version of the confessional, still recited in the traditional Jewish liturgy, is preserved in Mishnah Yoma 4:2f. An earlier confession is found in Daniel 9:4f.

a designated man The exact meaning of Hebrew *'ish 'itti* is uncertain. The noun *'et* means "time, appointed time." The sense here is "a person available at a specific time." According to Mishnah Yoma 6:3, a priest was assigned this task in order to make certain that the scapegoat did not return to the settled area. The Bible does not provide information on what, if anything, was done with the scapegoat in the wilderness. Mishnah Yoma 6:6,8 also records the later practice of hurling the scapegoat from a cliff.

carry on it all their iniquities to an inaccessible region; and the goat shall be set free in the wilderness.

[23]And Aaron shall go into the Tent of Meeting, take off the linen vestments that he put on when he entered the Shrine, and leave them there. [24]He shall bathe his body in

הַשָּׂעִ֥יר עָלָ֛יו אֶת־כָּל־עֲוֺנֹתָ֖ם אֶל־אֶ֣רֶץ גְּזֵרָ֑ה
וְשִׁלַּ֥ח אֶת־הַשָּׂעִ֖יר בַּמִּדְבָּֽר׃ 23 וּבָ֤א אַהֲרֹן֙ אֶל־
אֹ֣הֶל מוֹעֵ֔ד וּפָשַׁט֙ אֶת־בִּגְדֵ֣י הַבָּ֔ד אֲשֶׁ֥ר לָבַ֖שׁ
בְּבֹא֣וֹ אֶל־הַקֹּ֑דֶשׁ וְהִנִּיחָ֖ם שָֽׁם׃ 24 וְרָחַ֨ץ אֶת־

The verb *shillaḥ* may mean "to set free," but when used with reference to animals it more likely means "to drive."[22] This translation more accurately conveys the role of the person designated to accompany the scapegoat.

RITES SUBSEQUENT TO THE DISPATCH OF THE SCAPEGOAT (vv. 23–28)

After the High Priest had performed all the rites of purification and had dispatched the scapegoat, he removed his white linen vestments, bathed, and donned his golden vestments. He then sacrificed the two burnt offerings (one for himself and one for the people), each consisting of a ram. He placed the fatty portions of the two sin offerings, along with the burnt offerings, on the altar. Those parts of the two sin offerings not burned on the altar were taken outside the camp and burned to ashes.

In addition to the High Priest, two other persons were required to undergo a form of purification: the man designated to accompany the scapegoat and the person who attended to burning the remaining parts of the sin offerings outside the camp. Both were required to bathe before returning to the camp because they had become contaminated in the process of performing a riddance ritual. Similarly, we read in Numbers 19:8 that the person assigned to burn the red heifer outside the encampment was required to bathe; he too had become impure in the process of performing a riddance ritual. Although this may seem paradoxical, it is not. Animals used in riddance rituals had taken on the impurities transferred to them and anyone having contact with such required purification.

Both the High Priest and the people offered a burnt offering, following a pattern characteristic of the Israelite cult. The burnt offering was an invocation; it sought God's favorable attention and confirmed the purification of His people. In the initial purification of the sanctuary, recorded in chapters 8–10, we also observe that once burnt offerings had been accepted, worship of God could legitimately take place.[23]

*23. **And Aaron shall go into the Tent of Meeting*** Since antiquity, commentators have been puzzled by this statement. Taken literally, it means that Aaron was to reenter the Tent, disrobe, and leaving his vestments, proceed in a nude state to the place of bathing, as indicated in verse 24. This procedure is hardly conceivable. The law of Exodus 20:26 expressly forbids exposure of nakedness near the altar. Exodus 28:42–43 indicates that the priestly vestments were fashioned in such a manner as to avoid possible exposure of private parts.

The sages were, of course, fully aware of this problem. Yoma 32a states that the chapter records the proper order up to verse 23. However, the first part of verse 23, in which Aaron is instructed to enter the Tent, is out of order and belongs after verse 25—that is, Aaron was to disrobe after he had already performed the burnt offerings and had placed the fatty portions of the sin offerings on the altar. Rashi also refers to this talmudic interpretation. The purpose of Aaron's reentry later was to retrieve the fire pan that he had left in the Holy of Holies, as is explained in Mishnah Yoma 7:4.

This interpretation leaves certain questions unanswered. If the reentry of the High Priest is deferred to the end of verse 25, how is it that in verse 24 we read that he is to "come out"? Come out of where? To put it simply: The acts prescribed in verses 23–24 would seem to be in their proper sequence, but they are improper in themselves. A change of vestments would be appropriate following purification rites, and so would ablutions. What is improper is the place of the acts, inside the Tent, since disrobing there would constitute a serious breach of propriety. To resolve this problem it is necessary to assume that certain details are left unspecified in our chapter. We have already observed this in other connections. In such instances, we may employ later, rabbinic descriptions and speci-

water in the holy precinct and put on his vestments; then he shall come out and offer his burnt offering and the burnt offering of the people, making expiation for himself and for the people. [25]The fat of the sin offering he shall turn into smoke on the altar.

[26]He who set the Azazel-goat free shall wash his clothes and bathe his body in water; after that he may reenter the camp.

[27]The bull of sin offering and the goat of sin offering whose blood was brought in to purge the Shrine shall be taken outside the camp; and their hides, flesh, and dung shall be consumed in fire. [28]He who burned them shall wash his clothes and bathe his body in water; after that he may reenter the camp.

בְּשָׂרוֹ בַמַּיִם בְּמָקוֹם קָדוֹשׁ וְלָבַשׁ אֶת־בְּגָדָיו וְיָצָא
וְעָשָׂה אֶת־עֹלָתוֹ וְאֶת־עֹלַת הָעָם וְכִפֶּר בַּעֲדוֹ
וּבְעַד הָעָם׃ שלישי [שני כשהן מחוברות]
25 וְאֵת חֵלֶב הַחַטָּאת יַקְטִיר הַמִּזְבֵּחָה׃
26 וְהַמְשַׁלֵּחַ אֶת־הַשָּׂעִיר לַעֲזָאזֵל יְכַבֵּס בְּגָדָיו
וְרָחַץ אֶת־בְּשָׂרוֹ בַּמָּיִם וְאַחֲרֵי־כֵן יָבוֹא אֶל־
הַמַּחֲנֶה׃ 27 וְאֵת פַּר הַחַטָּאת וְאֵת ׀ שְׂעִיר
הַחַטָּאת אֲשֶׁר הוּבָא אֶת־דָּמָם לְכַפֵּר בַּקֹּדֶשׁ
יוֹצִיא אֶל־מִחוּץ לַמַּחֲנֶה וְשָׂרְפוּ בָאֵשׁ אֶת־עֹרֹתָם
וְאֶת־בְּשָׂרָם וְאֶת־פִּרְשָׁם׃ 28 וְהַשֹּׂרֵף אֹתָם יְכַבֵּס
בְּגָדָיו וְרָחַץ אֶת־בְּשָׂרוֹ בַּמָּיִם וְאַחֲרֵי־כֵן יָבוֹא
אֶל־הַמַּחֲנֶה׃ 29 וְהָיְתָה לָכֶם לְחֻקַּת עוֹלָם בַּחֹדֶשׁ

fications, so long as we bear in mind that the Mishnah is describing a temple in Jerusalem, whereas chapter 16 is speaking of a tentlike structure surrounded by a courtyard. With this understanding, the following reconstruction of the acts of the High Priest is proposed.

After dispatching the scapegoat, the High Priest was standing near the altar of burnt offerings, in the courtyard. He proceeded to a screened area, adjacent to the Tent, where he disrobed, bathed, and donned his golden vestments. Mishnah Middot 5:3 and Mishnah Yoma 3:3 refer to a bureau in the temple complex on whose roof was a place for ablutions, called *beit ha-tevilah,* "the place of immersion." One assumes that in the Tabernacle described by the priestly tradition there was also an area for disrobing and bathing, acts quite frequently called for in the performance of the sacrificial cult.

On this basis, we would have to understand the opening words of verse 23, *u-va' 'aharon 'el 'ohel moʿed,* to mean "And Aaron shall *approach* the Tent of Meeting," not that he was actually to enter it at that point. The Hebrew idiom *ba' 'el* usually means "to enter," but the proposed translation is acceptable. Similarly, in verse 24, the words "then he shall come out" would refer to the egress of the High Priest from the screened area, not to his exit from the Tent altogether. To summarize: Verses 23–24 are best understood as recording that the High Priest approached the Tent, entered a screened area, disrobed, bathed, and donned his golden vestments; he then left that area to perform the burnt offering. There was no need for him to enter the Tent itself.

24. *making expiation for himself and for the people* The *ʿolah,* "burnt offering," was not directly involved in the rites of expiation. This is a general statement referring to all that the High Priest had done by way of expiation, rather than to the *ʿolah* specifically.

25. *The fat of the sin offering* The fatty portions of the sin offerings, the bull and the he-goat, were burned on the altar, and the rest was burned outside the camp. This procedure is first prescribed in 4:8–10,19,20.

26. *He who set the Azazel-goat free shall . . . bathe* Rather, "He who drove out the Azazel-goat." The requirement to bathe before reentering the camp applied to various impure persons, including those impure by reason of disease.

27. *whose blood was brought in to purge the Shrine* Rather, "whose blood was introduced to perform rites of expiation within the Shrine." The formula *le-khapper be-* means "to expiate in, within," indicating *where* the rites are to be performed. The sense of "purging the Shrine" is conveyed by the direct object construction, as in verse 20: *le-khapper 'et ha-kodesh.* Reference to bringing blood inside the Shrine emphasizes the distinction between this rite and the sin offerings of lesser gravity. The same distinction between the two types of sin offerings is made in 4:11–12,21; 6:23; and 10:18.

29And this shall be to you a law for all time: In the
seventh month, on the tenth day of the month, you shall
practice self-denial; and you shall do no manner of work,
neither the citizen nor the alien who resides among you.
30For on this day atonement shall be made for you to
cleanse you of all your sins; you shall be clean before the
LORD. 31It shall be a sabbath of complete rest for you, and
you shall practice self-denial; it is a law for all time. 32The

הַשְּׁבִיעִי בֶּעָשׂוֹר לַחֹדֶשׁ תְּעַנּוּ אֶת־נַפְשֹׁתֵיכֶם
וְכָל־מְלָאכָה לֹא תַעֲשׂוּ הָאֶזְרָח וְהַגֵּר הַגָּר
בְּתוֹכְכֶם׃ 30 כִּי־בַיּוֹם הַזֶּה יְכַפֵּר עֲלֵיכֶם לְטַהֵר
אֶתְכֶם מִכֹּל חַטֹּאתֵיכֶם לִפְנֵי יְהוָה תִּטְהָרוּ׃
31 שַׁבַּת שַׁבָּתוֹן הִיא לָכֶם וְעִנִּיתֶם אֶת־
נַפְשֹׁתֵיכֶם חֻקַּת עוֹלָם׃ 32 וְכִפֶּר הַכֹּהֵן אֲשֶׁר־

DESIGNATION OF AN ANNUAL ATONEMENT DAY (vv. 29–34)

Up to this point in chapter 16, nothing has been said about when or how often the sanctuary was to be purified. Nor has there been instruction regarding the conduct required of the Israelite community on such occasions. Common sense would prompt us to assume that periodic purifications were necessary once the sanctuary was in operation. Indeed, verses 29–34 supply this information. Addressed to the entire people, not only to the priesthood, they ordain an annual Day of Atonement for all time and provide regulations to govern the conduct of the people on that day. Verse 30 states that, through the purification of the sanctuary, the entire people was relieved of its iniquities.

29. a law for all time What is ordained here is to be practiced in all future generations. Similar provisions occur throughout Leviticus, as in 3:17, 6:11, and in this chapter in verses 31 and 34.

In the seventh month, on the tenth day of the month Until a relatively late period in biblical history, the months of the year were counted from the spring season, the month of Passover, which was the first month. The seventh month was, therefore, the month of the autumn Sukkot festival and, of course, of Yom Kippur.[24] It is not known with certainty exactly when the counting of the months shifted to the autumn of the year, so that Yom Kippur and Sukkot would, accordingly, occur in the first month of the year, then named Tishrei.[25]

you shall practice self-denial In biblical literature the idiom *ʿinnah nefesh* always connotes fasting, as Ibn Ezra observed and as we may deduce from the contexts of Isaiah 58:3,10 and Psalms 35:13. Mishnah Yoma 8:1 interprets self-denial to involve five abstentions: from food and drink, bathing, use of oil or unguent on the body, wearing leather shoes, and sexual intercourse.

and you shall do no manner of work In verse 31, the Day of Atonement is called a Sabbath, on which work is forbidden. But, even on festival days, labor was forbidden. This is repeated for emphasis in the laws of chapter 23, where Yom Kippur appears in the list of annual festivals.

Including the alien in the prohibition of labor follows a characteristic pattern in the laws of Leviticus, whose purpose was to legislate for a religious community or network of communities. If resident aliens, such as merchants and craftsmen, were to continue their daily pursuits, the Israelite community would be affected as well. Aliens were not, however, expected to practice self-denial, only to honor the day by abstaining from work. Aliens who wished to take part in annual celebrations, such as the Passover, could do so only if their males had been circumcised, and the rites in which they then participated would have to be performed in the manner proper for Israelites.[26] The considerations underlying this law governing non-Israelites undoubtedly guided the founders of the modern state of Israel to declare the Sabbath the weekly day of rest and to proclaim the festivals and holy days of the year national holidays, throughout the land.

30. For on this day atonement shall be made for you The name *yom ha-kippurim* (or *yom kippur*) is suggested by this verse and by 23:27–28. This verse introduces the purification of the people. (Until this time, the purification of the sanctuary had been the object of the various rites.) It is probably for this reason that the verse enjoys such prominence in the liturgy of Yom Kippur until this day.[27]

31. a sabbath of complete rest The construction *shabbat shabbaton* has the force of a superlative. This is explained by Rashi in his comment to Exodus 31:15: "Scripture doubled its

יִמְשַׁח אֹתוֹ וַאֲשֶׁר יְמַלֵּא אֶת־יָדוֹ לְכַהֵן תַּחַת
אָבִיו וְלָבַשׁ אֶת־בִּגְדֵי הַבָּד בִּגְדֵי הַקֹּדֶשׁ׃ 33 וְכִפֶּר
אֶת־מִקְדַּשׁ הַקֹּדֶשׁ וְאֶת־אֹהֶל מוֹעֵד וְאֶת־הַמִּזְבֵּחַ
יְכַפֵּר וְעַל הַכֹּהֲנִים וְעַל־כָּל־עַם הַקָּהָל יְכַפֵּר׃
34 וְהָיְתָה־זֹּאת לָכֶם לְחֻקַּת עוֹלָם לְכַפֵּר עַל־בְּנֵי
יִשְׂרָאֵל מִכָּל־חַטֹּאתָם אַחַת בַּשָּׁנָה וַיַּעַשׂ כַּאֲשֶׁר
צִוָּה יְהוָה אֶת־מֹשֶׁה׃ פ רביעי

priest who has been anointed and ordained to serve as priest in place of his father shall make expiation. He shall put on the linen vestments, the sacral vestments.
33He shall purge the innermost Shrine; he shall purge the Tent of Meeting and the altar; and he shall make expiation for the priests and for all the people of the congregation.

34This shall be to you a law for all time: to make atonement for the Israelites for all their sins once a year.

And Moses did as the LORD had commanded him.

wording to indicate that it [= the Sabbath] carries the prohibition of all manner of labor, even the preparation of food necessary for subsistence. The same is true of the Day of Atonement, of which it is also said: *shabbat shabbaton*—for all forms of labor are prohibited on that occasion, as stated in Leviticus 23:32. But, regarding the festivals, it says only that on the first day and the eighth day a *shabbaton* occurs (not *shabbat shabbaton*), indicating that Israelites are prohibited from any type of laborious toil, but may prepare food to sustain life."

Words ending in *-on* tend to have an abstract sense. Thus, *zikkaron* means "memorial," *herayon,* "pregnancy," and so forth. On this basis, *shabbaton* would mean "restfulness." As Rashi, in his comment to Exodus 31:15 puts it: *menuḥat margoʿa,* "a rest of relaxation."[28]

32. ***The priest who has been anointed and ordained*** On the meaning of *milleʾ yad,* "to fill the hand, appoint," see Comment to 8:22.

He shall purge the innermost Shrine This verse illustrates the rule that in the priestly laws, the verb *kipper,* "to purge," takes the direct object only when said of inanimate objects, such as the altar, the sanctuary, and so forth. When said of persons, or even of sacrificial victims, *kipper* takes an object of preposition in constructions such as *kipper ʿal,* "to make expiation over, for." In this verse it is the Shrine that is being purged, so the construction with the direct object is used: *ve-khipper ʾet ha-kodesh,* "he shall purge the Shrine."

The primary sense of the verb *kipper* is "to wipe off, cleanse," essentially a physical process, like cleansing with detergents or abrasives. In the biblical conception, expiation was not an automatic result of performing certain acts. Purification resulted because God accepted the acts of the priests and of the people and granted expiation. The same is true of forgiveness, as we read in 4:31: "Thus the priest shall make expiation for him, and he shall be forgiven." As a result of God's acceptance of the rites of expiation one is forgiven by God.[29]

34. ***And Moses did as the LORD had commanded him*** The syntax of the Hebrew is unusual. Literally, it reads: "And he did as the LORD commanded Moses." The sense is clear, nonetheless. Formulas of compliance are quite frequent in the priestly laws of the Torah. They epitomize the piety of the early Israelites and of their leaders, who were swift to obey God's commandments. Such formulas also emphasize the doctrine that all of the details of the cult were communicated directly by God to Moses at the very beginning of Israel's history as a people.[30]

The Pursuit of Holiness (17:1–26:46)

Chapters 17–26 of Leviticus constitute a distinct unit whose dominant theme is holiness. For this reason the section has been known by the name "Holiness Code," a term first used by A. Klosterman in 1877.[1] The thematic unity of the Code is further enhanced by the unique style that characterizes these chapters.

The central idea of the Holiness Code is that the people of Israel bears the collective responsibility to seek to achieve holiness, as expressed in 19:2: "You shall be holy, for I, the LORD your God, am holy." This idea, rarely encountered in the rest of Leviticus, is here stated repeatedly and emphatically.[2] Given the prominence of the idea of a holy people, the laws and commandments are usually addressed to all of Israel, not merely to Moses, Aaron, or the priesthood. Virtually all sections of the Holiness Code open with the injunction to speak to the Israelite people; chapters 17, 18, 19, 20, and 22 begin in this way. Elsewhere in Leviticus, by contrast, the people of Israel is addressed collectively on matters of ritual practice, exclusively. This is true in 1:2, 4:1, and 7:28, all of which prescribe the proper modes of sacrifice. And in 11:2 the entire people is instructed on the matter of forbidden foodstuffs.

The Holiness Code, with its emphasis on the interdependence of all Israelites in every aspect of life, including their history and shared destiny, resembles the other two major collections of laws and commandments found in the Torah, the Book of the Covenant (Exod. 20:19–23:33) and the Deuteronomic laws (primarily Deut. 12–28). These similarities may be tabulated graphically as follows:

Theme	*Holiness Code*	*Book of the Covenant*	*Deuteronomy*
Prologue: proper modes of worship	Lev. 17	Exod. 20:19–23	Deut. 12
Epilogue: blessings and execrations	Lev. 26:3–46	Exod. 23:20–33	Deut. 27–30[3]
Duties that pertain to the land	Lev. 19:9f.; 25	Exod. 23:10–11	Deut. 15; 24:19–22; 26
A calendar of sacred occasions	Lev. 23	Exod. 23:12–19	Deut. 16:1–7

Following is a brief outline of the Holiness Code. More detailed information is provided in the introductory Comments to the individual chapters and sections: (1) The Prologue (chap. 17). (2) Commandments governing forbidden sexual unions—incest, adultery, sodomy, homosexuality, etc. All such forbidden acts are designated *to'evah,* "abhorrent things," inconsistent with holiness (chap. 18). (3) A code of religious and secular laws, including matters pertaining to agriculture, testimony, social ethics, and certain rituals associated with sacrifice (chap. 19). (4) A legally formulated restatement of chapter 18, with the addition of some new laws (chap. 20). (5) Ordinances governing the priesthood in matters of ritual purity, marriage, and the physical prerequisites of officiating in a priestly capacity (21:1–22:16). (6) Requirements for sacrificial animals and regulations for the *shelamim* offering that was frequently brought by individual Israelites (22:17–33). (7) A liturgical calendar of the year's festivals and sacred occasions, including the Sabbath (chap. 23). (8) Several laws regarding the eternal light, the bread of display, and the offense of blasphemy. In addition there is a priestly account of an instance of blasphemy during the lifetime of Moses (chap. 24). (9) Laws governing agriculture and the ownership of land, including the law of the Sabbatical year. This section concludes with an admonition against idolatry (25:1–26:2). (10) The Epilogue (26:3–46).

CHAPTER 17 PROLOGUE: PROPER FORMS OF WORSHIP (vv. 1–16)

Chapter 17 introduces the Holiness Code. Verses 1–9 state the requirement that all sacrifices be offered at the one, legitimate altar, located near the entrance of the Tent of Meeting. Verses 10–12 prescribe the proper disposition of sacrificial blood, to which is added the prohibition against consumption of all blood. Verses 13–15 require that the blood of animals and fowl caught in the hunt be drained and covered with earth. Finally, verses 15–16 prohibit the eating of flesh from carcasses of animals that died or were torn by beasts.

17 The LORD spoke to Moses, saying:
2Speak to Aaron and his sons and to all the Israelite people and say to them:
This is what the LORD has commanded: 3if anyone of the house of Israel slaughters an ox or sheep or goat in the camp, or does so outside the camp, 4and does not bring it

י״ז וַיְדַבֵּר יְהוָה אֶל־מֹשֶׁה לֵּאמֹר׃ 2 דַּבֵּר אֶל־
אַהֲרֹן וְאֶל־בָּנָיו וְאֶל כָּל־בְּנֵי יִשְׂרָאֵל וְאָמַרְתָּ
אֲלֵיהֶם זֶה הַדָּבָר אֲשֶׁר־צִוָּה יְהוָה לֵאמֹר׃ 3 אִישׁ
אִישׁ מִבֵּית יִשְׂרָאֵל אֲשֶׁר יִשְׁחַט שׁוֹר אוֹ־כֶשֶׂב
אוֹ־עֵז בַּמַּחֲנֶה אוֹ אֲשֶׁר יִשְׁחַט מִחוּץ לַמַּחֲנֶה׃

2. ***and to all the Israelite people*** These ordinances are addressed not only to the leaders and the priesthood but to the people as a whole.

This is what the LORD has commanded This characteristic formula in the priestly texts expresses the idea that all of the details of worship and ritual were directly commanded by God.[4]

3. ***if anyone of the house of Israel*** The complete formula *'ish 'ish mi-beit yisra'el,* "any man of the house of Israel," occurs only in this chapter (also in vv. 8 and 10) and in Ezekiel 14:4,7. The characterization of the Israelite people as "the house of Israel," occurs very frequently, however, in the prophecies of Jeremiah and Ezekiel, where it expresses the close relationship and common descent of Israelites, even in exile.[5]

slaughters an ox or sheep or goat The precise wording "an ox or sheep or goat" recurs in 22:27, where it also relates to laws of sacrifice.[6]

Because the Hebrew verb *shaḥat,* "to slaughter," has two meanings, its specific usage in this verse is of crucial importance for an understanding of the chapter as a whole. The verb can mean "to slaughter," in the general sense. In that case, the verse would indicate that whenever an Israelite slaughtered an animal for whatever reason—including for food—that act of slaughter had to be carried out at the one, legitimate altar located at the entrance of the Tent of Meeting. The verb can also mean "to slaughter a sacrifice." As such, the sense would be that all sacrifices had to be made at the legitimate altar; but the general slaughter of animals for food, which is nonsacrificial, would be permitted anywhere.

The significance of verses 3–4 has been debated since late antiquity. It was always apparent that verses 3–4 could be taken to contradict the laws of Deuteronomy 12:15f. The latter clearly state that the Israelites were allowed to slaughter animals for food without recourse to the sacrificial altar, so long as they took care to drain the blood from the slaughtered animal and refrained from eating blood. Such nonsacrificial slaughter of animals for food became known in the later Jewish tradition as *ha-shoḥet ḥullin,* "one who slaughters nonsacrally."[7]

Thus, the question of whether Leviticus 17 and Deuteronomy 12 agree or disagree on the permissibility of nonsacral slaughter away from the altar hinges on the meaning of the verb *shaḥat* in this verse. This issue was the subject of a dispute between Rabbi Akiba and Rabbi Ishmael.[8] Ishmael held that Leviticus 17 intended to forbid all forms of slaughter away from the central altar and that subsequently the Torah, in Deuteronomy 12, granted a dispensation permitting what had earlier been forbidden. Clearly, he understood the verb in its general sense. Akiba insisted, on the other hand, that the Torah had never forbidden nonsacral slaughter and that the intent of Leviticus 17 was that only slaughter was permissible, but not the "stabbing" to death of animals, called *neḥirah* in Hebrew. Understanding the verb *shaḥat* in its narrow, technical sense of sacrificial slaughter, Akiba was of the view that chapter 17 did not require all slaughter of animals for food to be sacrificial in character. Only animals intended for sacrifice had to be slaughtered at the entrance of the Tent of Meeting.

The Sifra, commenting on 17:3–4, adopted the main thrust of Akiba's view: "Israelites are liable under the law governing one who slaughters and offers sacrifices in the open field, but the gentiles are not. . . . Furthermore, gentiles are permitted to build a *bamah* (high place) anywhere and ascend to the heavens!" The Sifra thus understood Leviticus 17 to refer specifically to matters of sacrifice, not to ordinary slaughtering for food, in which case Deuteronomy 12 did not permit something that the Torah had earlier forbidden. Both chapters, then, require essentially the same procedure: sacrifice restricted to one, legitimate altar.[9] This interpretation seems to be borne out by the Sifra's exegesis of chapter 17, according to which verses 5–7 provide the rationale for verses 3–4. Thus, in verse 5, the purpose of the law was to prevent sacrifices "in the open field." Similarly, the Sifra understands verses

to the entrance of the Tent of Meeting to present it as an offering to the LORD, before the LORD's Tabernacle, blood-guilt shall be imputed to that man: he has shed blood; that man shall be cut off from among his people. [5]This is in order that the Israelites may bring the sacrifices which they have been making in the open—that they may bring them before the LORD, to the priest, at the entrance of the Tent of Meeting, and offer them as sacrifices of well-being to the LORD; [6]that the priest may dash the blood against the altar

4 וְאֶל־פֶּ֜תַח אֹ֤הֶל מוֹעֵד֙ לֹ֣א הֱבִיא֔וֹ לְהַקְרִ֥יב
קׇרְבָּן֙ לַֽיהֹוָ֔ה לִפְנֵ֖י מִשְׁכַּ֣ן יְהֹוָ֑ה דָּ֣ם יֵחָשֵׁ֞ב לָאִ֤ישׁ
הַהוּא֙ דָּ֣ם שָׁפָ֔ךְ וְנִכְרַ֛ת הָאִ֥ישׁ הַה֖וּא מִקֶּ֥רֶב עַמּֽוֹ׃
5 לְמַ֩עַן֩ אֲשֶׁ֨ר יָבִ֜יאוּ בְּנֵ֣י יִשְׂרָאֵ֗ל אֶת־זִבְחֵיהֶם֮
אֲשֶׁ֣ר הֵ֣ם זֹבְחִים֮ עַל־פְּנֵ֣י הַשָּׂדֶה֒ וֶהֱבִיאֻ֣ם לַֽיהֹוָ֗ה
אֶל־פֶּ֛תַח אֹ֥הֶל מוֹעֵ֖ד אֶל־הַכֹּהֵ֑ן וְזָ֣בְח֗וּ זִבְחֵ֤י
שְׁלָמִים֙ לַֽיהֹוָ֔ה אוֹתָֽם׃ 6 וְזָרַ֨ק הַכֹּהֵ֤ן אֶת־הַדָּם֙

8–10 to represent a restatement of verses 3–7, meaning that one who "slaughters" (in the language of verse 3) is identical to one who "offers" (in the language of verse 8).

In the ritual texts of the Torah the verb *sh-ḥ-t* never has the general sense of "slaughtering" that it has in other, less detailed biblical texts. In 22:26f., for example, in a formulation identical to that found here, we read that the offspring of large and small cattle may not be "slaughtered" until the eighth day after birth, at which time they first become acceptable as sacrifices. In keeping with this understanding, the verb *sh-ḥ-t* may replace *z-v-ḥ,* "to celebrate a sacrifice." Compare, for example, the laws concerning the paschal sacrifice. Exodus 23:18 uses the verb *z-v-ḥ;* the almost verbatim restatement in Exodus 34:35 uses the verb *sh-ḥ-t.*[10]

It is proper, therefore, to view the verb *sh-ḥ-t* in this verse as a term for sacrificing and to conclude that there is basic agreement between Leviticus 17 and Deuteronomy 12. Nonetheless, a large body of scholars, following Rabbi Ishmael, continues to regard Leviticus 17 as representing an earlier stage in the history of Israelite worship, when all slaughter of animals for food had to be of a sacral character.[11]

4. *to present it as an offering to the LORD* The formula *le-hakriv korban,* "to present an offering," is typical of the priestly texts of the Torah.[12] The term *korban* itself is generic, designating various types of offerings that are "brought near."[13]

before the LORD's Tabernacle This verse primarily concerns the place of sacrifice; it is to be restricted to the Tabernacle altar.

bloodguilt shall be imputed to that man: he has shed blood Elsewhere the idiom *shafakh dam,* "to shed blood," refers to homicide, usually intentional murder.[14] Its usage here in the case of an individual who slaughters a sacrifice improperly is exceptional and an example of hyperbole. According to Hoffmann, it serves to dramatize the extreme seriousness of improper sacrifice.

When this verse is compared with Genesis 9:1–6, an interesting difference emerges. Genesis 9:1–4 grants permission to humans to consume the meat of living creatures, so long as no blood is *eaten.* Immediately following this dispensation, in verses 5–6, is the statement that all who *shed* the blood of other humans shall be put to death. The two situations are thus contrasted: It is permitted to slaughter animals for food but prohibited to shed blood. In our verse, slaughter of animals for sacrifice at the wrong site is equated with the shedding of blood. As is often the case, biblical statements draw on other, preceding verses, lending a different nuance to traditional language.

that man shall be cut off from among his people Excursus 1 explains the penalty called *karet,* "cutting off."

5. *in the open* Hebrew *ʿal penei ha-sadeh* does not mean "on the ground," but rather "in the open field." It is the opposite of "in a tent" or "in town."[15] The Israelites had formerly offered sacrifices both inside and outside the camp (*maḥaneh*), the term used in verse 3 for the area of Israelite settlement. In Judges 6:21 and 13:19, we read of sacrifices offered on rocks. Elsewhere, we find local and private altars in use during the early periods of Israelite history. It was difficult for the legitimate priesthood to regulate such cult sites, where idolatry and other improper activities might take place.

that they may bring them before the LORD, to the priest According to Ibn Ezra this is the rationale for prohibiting sacrifice away from the Tabernacle altar, as conveyed in the words of verses 3–4 above. In other words, sacrifices should be offered by a proper priest at the sole, legitimate altar.

עַל־מִזְבַּח יְהוָה פֶּתַח אֹהֶל מוֹעֵד וְהִקְטִיר הַחֵלֶב
לְרֵיחַ נִיחֹחַ לַיהוָה׃ 7 וְלֹא־יִזְבְּחוּ עוֹד אֶת־זִבְחֵיהֶם
לַשְּׂעִירִם אֲשֶׁר הֵם זֹנִים אַחֲרֵיהֶם חֻקַּת עוֹלָם
תִּהְיֶה־זֹּאת לָהֶם לְדֹרֹתָם׃ חמישי [שלישי
כשהן מחוברות] 8 וַאֲלֵהֶם תֹּאמַר אִישׁ אִישׁ
מִבֵּית יִשְׂרָאֵל וּמִן־הַגֵּר אֲשֶׁר־יָגוּר בְּתוֹכָם אֲשֶׁר־
יַעֲלֶה עֹלָה אוֹ־זָבַח׃ 9 וְאֶל־פֶּתַח אֹהֶל מוֹעֵד לֹא

of the Lord at the entrance of the Tent of Meeting, and turn the fat into smoke as a pleasing odor to the Lord;
7 and that they may offer their sacrifices no more to the goat-demons after whom they stray. This shall be to them a law for all time, throughout the ages.

8 Say to them further: If anyone of the house of Israel or of the strangers who reside among them offers a burnt offering or a sacrifice,
9 and does not bring it to the entrance

and offer them as sacrifices of well-being to the Lord Rather, "as sacred gifts of greeting." This rendering is explained in the Comment to 3:1. The *shelamim* offering became the foremost type of *zevaḥ,* especially for individual donations. The intent of this verse is that Israelites must present their offerings as proper *shelamim* at the Tabernacle altar.

6. ***that the priest may dash the blood*** Concern for the proper use of sacrificial blood is basic to the regulations of chapter 17, especially in verses 10f. Except for sacrifices burned to ashes on the altar, most other sacrifices were divided between the altar fire and humans. The altar received the blood and the fatty portions of animal sacrifices, and priests, and sometimes donors, received other portions of the sacrifices. For a detailed outline of these allotments, see introductory Comment to chapters 6–7. The formula *le-reaḥ niḥoaḥ,* "of a pleasing odor," is explained in the Comment to 1:8.

The designation of the Tabernacle altar as *mizbaḥ YHVH,* "the altar of the Lord," is significant. It is based on the view that there is only one, legitimate altar at which the God of Israel may be worshiped. Similarly, Deuteronomy 12:27, 16:21, and so forth designate the one, legitimate altar to be erected in the settled land as *mizbaḥ YHVH 'eloheikha,* "the altar of the Lord your God." In the ritual texts, this unique altar is usually referred to simply as *ha-mizbeaḥ, "the* altar," there being no need to specify that the altar is the Tabernacle altar, that fact being understood.[16]

that they may offer their sacrifices no more to the goat-demons after whom they stray The ancient worship of goat-demons (*se'irim*), thought to be rulers of the wilderness and associated with illness and death, is discussed in the Comment to 16:8 and in Excursus 4.

The regulations of chapter 17 refer to the milieu of the Sinai wilderness during the period that preceded the entry of the Israelites into Canaan. At that time it would have been important to uproot prior religious customs and to enforce strict adherence to the monotheistic religion of Israel. As the rabbis put it: "it was difficult in their perception to withdraw from idolatry."[17]

The verb *z-n-h,* "to go astray," in this verse is appropriate in the context of the early wilderness period. Although the verb literally means "to commit harlotry,"[18] its various connotations and those of its derivatives afford insight into the religious mentality of biblical writers. In most of its occurrences the verb is used metaphorically to express disloyalty and betrayal, conveyed as marital infidelity. The most frequent image is that of the unfaithful wife or the woman of bad character who sells herself to her lovers. Placing unwarranted trust in them, she finds herself abandoned by them in her hour of need. This image is employed to characterize Israel's repeated behavior as a people, although it may be applied to any other people as well. In Isaiah 23:15–18, for example, the city-state of Tyre is called a harlot because of its typically deceitful mercantile dealings. In most cases, however, reference is to Israel, God's chosen people, who is likened to a bride. At certain periods of her history, she showed great fidelity, but at other times she betrayed God by turning to idolatry. She also entered into alliances with other nations who later failed her in a time of need.[19] Against this background, use of the verb *z-n-h* here to characterize the worship of goat-demons reflects a concern for the proper worship of God and urges the avoidance of all practices that may lead to idolatry.[20]

This shall be to them a law for all time On the significance of this formula, see Comment to 3:17.[21]

8. ***If anyone of the house of Israel*** This is a restatement of verses 3–5. Here, however, there is no ambiguity as to the intent of the law. Its purpose is to outlaw sacrifices anywhere except at the Tabernacle altar. The verse also includes the "resident stranger" (*ger*) in this prohibition.[22]

of the Tent of Meeting to offer it to the LORD, that person
shall be cut off from his people.
10 And if anyone of the house of Israel or of the strangers
who reside among them partakes of any blood, I will set My
face against the person who partakes of the blood, and I
will cut him off from among his kin. 11 For the life of the
flesh is in the blood, and I have assigned it to you for
making expiation for your lives upon the altar; it is the
blood, as life, that effects expiation. 12 Therefore I say to the

יְבִיאֶ֔נּוּ לַעֲשׂ֥וֹת אֹת֖וֹ לַיהוָ֑ה וְנִכְרַ֛ת הָאִ֥ישׁ הַה֖וּא
מֵעַמָּֽיו׃ 10 וְאִ֨ישׁ אִ֜ישׁ מִבֵּ֣ית יִשְׂרָאֵ֗ל וּמִן־הַגֵּר֙
הַגָּ֣ר בְּתוֹכָ֔ם אֲשֶׁ֥ר יֹאכַ֖ל כָּל־דָּ֑ם וְנָתַתִּ֣י פָנַ֗י
בַּנֶּ֙פֶשׁ֙ הָאֹכֶ֣לֶת אֶת־הַדָּ֔ם וְהִכְרַתִּ֥י אֹתָ֖הּ מִקֶּ֥רֶב
עַמָּֽהּ׃ 11 כִּ֣י נֶ֣פֶשׁ הַבָּשָׂר֮ בַּדָּ֣ם הִוא֒ וַאֲנִ֞י נְתַתִּ֤יו
לָכֶם֙ עַל־הַמִּזְבֵּ֔חַ לְכַפֵּ֖ר עַל־נַפְשֹׁתֵיכֶ֑ם כִּֽי־הַדָּ֥ם
ה֖וּא בַּנֶּ֥פֶשׁ יְכַפֵּֽר׃ 12 עַל־כֵּ֤ן אָמַ֙רְתִּי֙ לִבְנֵ֣י

10. partakes of any blood There are several statements in the Torah forbidding the consumption of blood.[23] In this chapter, the prohibition is explicitly related to the performance of the cult: Sacrificial blood is to be dashed against the altar as God's share of the sacrifices along with the fatty portions of the sacrificial animals. It serves to secure expiation for the Israelites. But, like Genesis 9, the statement goes beyond the cultic basis for prohibiting the consumption of blood in forbidding *kol dam,* "all blood," a point noted by Rashi. Violation carries the penalty of being "cut off" from the community of Israel. The active verb *ve-hikhratti,* "I shall cut off," is used instead of the usual passive form of the verb, as in verses 4 and 9, making it absolutely clear that the punishment comes directly from God.[24]

11. For the life of the flesh is in the blood This is repeated in verse 14, and similar formulations occur elsewhere in the Torah. Thus, Deuteronomy 12:23 states: "For the blood is the life, and you must not consume the life with the flesh." Genesis 9:4 implies the same rationale for not eating blood: "You must not, however, eat flesh with its life-blood in it."

and I have assigned it to you for making expiation for your lives upon the altar Rashi states: "Blood represents life, and it can therefore expiate for life." Basic to the theory of sacrifice in ancient Israel, as in many other ancient societies, was the notion of substitution. The sacrifice substituted for an individual human life or for the lives of the members of the community in situations where God could have exacted the life of the offender, or of anyone else, for that matter. Indeed, all who stood in God's immediate presence risked becoming the object of divine wrath.[25] But substitution could avert the danger, with sacrificial blood being especially instrumental because it was the symbol of life.

This explains the specific intent of the Hebrew formula *le-khapper ʿal nafshoteikhem,* "for making expiation for your lives." Literally, this formula means "to serve as *kofer* (ransom) for your lives." God accepts the blood of the sacrifices in lieu of human blood.[26] The practice of offering blood on the altar may have been very ancient, harking back to the worship of chthonic deities of the netherworld. In biblical religion, it appears to have been an act of contrition, an acknowledgment of God's power over life and death.

Substitution was allowed only in cases of inadvertence. Where the offense against God had been intentional, ritual expiation did not apply. This distinction corresponds to the norms of biblical criminal law, which allowed no ransom for the life of a murderer.[27] A bridge between the two systems, the criminal and the cultic, can be observed in Deuteronomy 21:1–9. When the corpse of a slain person whose murderer was unknown was discovered outside the territorial jurisdiction of any town, a quasi-sacrificial rite was required. Since no established community could be held accountable for the act of murder, it became necessary to deal with it in a manner that satisfied at least the religious abhorrence of bloodshed. A young heifer was decapitated near a flowing stream, and its blood poured into the water so that it flowed into the earth. Had this not been done, the earth would not have "accepted" the blood of the murdered person, just as in Genesis 4:10–13, the earth "protested" at having the blood of Abel, slain by Cain, poured over it because Cain had gone unpunished.

This legal case clearly illustrates how animal blood can substitute for the life of an offender in situations where criminal penalties cannot be imposed. The use of sacrificial blood on the altar has a similar effect in cases of unintentional religious offenses.

it is the blood, as life, that effects expiation Alternatively, "for it is the blood that effects

Israelite people: No person among you shall partake of blood, nor shall the stranger who resides among you partake of blood.

13 And if any Israelite or any stranger who resides among them hunts down an animal or a bird that may be eaten, he shall pour out its blood and cover it with earth. 14 For the life of all flesh—its blood is its life. Therefore I say to the Israelite people: You shall not partake of the blood of any flesh, for the life of all flesh is its blood. Anyone who partakes of it shall be cut off.

יִשְׂרָאֵל כָּל־נֶפֶשׁ מִכֶּם לֹא־תֹאכַל דָּם וְהַגֵּר הַגָּר
בְּתוֹכְכֶם לֹא־יֹאכַל דָּם׃ ס 13 וְאִישׁ אִישׁ
מִבְּנֵי יִשְׂרָאֵל וּמִן־הַגֵּר הַגָּר בְּתוֹכָם אֲשֶׁר יָצוּד
צֵיד חַיָּה אוֹ־עוֹף אֲשֶׁר יֵאָכֵל וְשָׁפַךְ אֶת־דָּמוֹ
וְכִסָּהוּ בֶּעָפָר׃ 14 כִּי־נֶפֶשׁ כָּל־בָּשָׂר דָּמוֹ בְנַפְשׁוֹ
הוּא וָאֹמַר לִבְנֵי יִשְׂרָאֵל דַּם כָּל־בָּשָׂר לֹא
תֹאכֵלוּ כִּי נֶפֶשׁ כָּל־בָּשָׂר דָּמוֹ הִוא כָּל־אֹכְלָיו

expiation in exchange for life." This clause has been interpreted in various ways and is critical for a proper understanding of the entire Israelite sacrificial system. Ibn Ezra understands it as follows: "By means of the 'life' that is in it, it (meaning 'the blood') effects expiation." This interpretation has been accepted by modern scholars and probably underlies the given translation, which takes the prepositional *bet* in the word *ba-nefesh* to be *bet instrumentii,* "the *bet* of means." Expiation is effected *by means* of blood.

The alternative rendering takes prepositional *bet* as *bet pretii,* "the *bet* of price." There is a subtle but significant difference between the two functions. *Bet pretii* occurs in legal statements, where its meaning is clear. In Exodus 21:23 we read *nefesh taḥat nefesh,* "a life in place of a life." But in Deuteronomy 19:33 the same provision is restated as *nefesh be-nefesh,* "a life in exchange for a life."[28]

In our passage, blood is considered efficacious because it represents life, not because it has special properties. Creatures cannot live without blood, and killing is expressed as shedding blood. On this basis, the blood of the sacrifice offered on the altar is the "life" of the sacrifice and can stand in place of human life. God accepts it in lieu of human life and grants expiation or refrains from wrath.

12. No person among you shall partake of blood This is a restatement of the blood prohibition, for emphasis. These prohibitions of consumption of blood provide the scriptural basis for later regulations in historical Judaism governing the slaughter and preparation of meat. To this day, the purpose of such ritual practice is to remove the blood from meat.[29]

13. And if any Israelite . . . hunts down an animal or bird . . . he shall pour out its blood The Masoretic text has *mi-benei yisra'el,* (literally) "of the Israelites," but the Samaritan version has *mi-beit yisra'el,* "of the House of Israel," as in verses 3, 8, and 13. The Septuagint, however, agrees with the Masoretic reading, which diverges from the pattern of the chapter as a whole. The blood of all animals and fowl caught in the hunt must be drained of blood before the meat may be eaten. This is also implied in the laws of Deuteronomy 12:15–16,22f., where we are told that the meat of slaughtered animals may be eaten in the same way as one may eat the meat of animals caught in the hunt, the deer and the gazelle. The law in both cases forbids eating any of the blood, and it does not require an act of sacrifice for what is caught in the hunt. Despite the fact that Deuteronomy 12 goes further in its provisions than does this code—explicitly stating that animals slaughtered for food need not be sacrificed—it is likely that both codes operated on the same principle.[30]

14. For the life of all flesh—its blood is its life This is yet another restatement of the principle that blood represents life.

Any person . . . who eats what has died or has been torn by beasts Hebrew *nevelah* means "a dead animal." This is precisely established by its Akkadian cognate *napultu,* which in the ancient Mesopotamian dictionaries is translated by *mitti* or *mittitum,* "dead body."[31] Hebrew *terefah,* "torn flesh," is derived from the verb *t-r-f,* which in biblical usage always describes the action of wild beasts or those resembling them in their rapaciousness.[32] The two prohibitions of *nevelah* and *terefah* are frequently listed together because dead flesh would often come from an animal that had been killed by wild beasts.[33]

There are two aspects to these prohibitions: (1) Eating flesh of carcasses or torn animals is forbidden, and (2) tactile contact with carcasses renders one impure and requires purificatory

[15]Any person, whether citizen or stranger, who eats what has died or has been torn by beasts shall wash his clothes, bathe in water, and remain unclean until evening; then he shall be clean. [16]But if he does not wash [his clothes] and bathe his body, he shall bear his guilt.

יִכָּרֵת׃ 15 וְכָל־נֶ֗פֶשׁ אֲשֶׁ֨ר תֹּאכַ֤ל נְבֵלָה֙ וּטְרֵפָ֔ה
בָּאֶזְרָ֖ח וּבַגֵּ֑ר וְכִבֶּ֨ס בְּגָדָ֜יו וְרָחַ֥ץ בַּמַּ֛יִם וְטָמֵ֥א עַד־
הָעֶ֖רֶב וְטָהֵֽר׃ 16 וְאִם֙ לֹ֣א יְכַבֵּ֔ס וּבְשָׂר֖וֹ לֹ֣א יִרְחָ֑ץ
וְנָשָׂ֖א עֲוֺנֽוֹ׃ פ

ablutions. Leviticus 5:25 includes contact with carcasses in a list of inadvertent or neglectful sins that obligate the offender to bring a sin offering and confess his wrongdoing.

Here, we find the duty to bathe and launder one's garments. Laundering was a procedure often included in rites of purification.[34]

16. he shall bear his guilt The legal significance of this formula is explained in the Comment to 5:1.

CHAPTER 18

Definition of the Family

Chapter 18 is the most systematic and complete collection of laws within the Torah dealing with the subject of incest and other forbidden sexual unions. It outlines in detail which unions among relatives within the ancient Israelite clan are forbidden on grounds of incest, adultery, and so on; and in so doing, it indirectly defines the limits of the immediate family. By way of contrast, marriages within the extended clan, called *mishpaḥah* in Hebrew, were actually encouraged.

Chapter 18 seeks to draw that critical line of distinction between the immediate family and the larger clan. The underlying concern of its laws is the continuity of the Israelite family over successive generations. The immediate family was formed by a man who married one or more wives, thereby initiating the process of procreation. This conception of the family explains why the regulations governing sexual behavior were addressed to the male as the head of the family. The biblical family was organized along patrilineal lines; that is, a person was related primarily to his father and to his father's kin. Although primacy was given to relationships on the paternal side, the system nonetheless afforded the mother and her kin a certain status as well, as we observe in the laws of chapter 18. Excursus 5 provides further discussion of the Israelite family.

Two principles govern the definition of incest in the code of chapter 18 and throughout the rest of the Torah: (1) *she'er,* "flesh relations," sometimes known as consanguineal or blood relations and (2) *'ervah,* "nakedness," a euphemism for sexuality. The nuclear family was founded on six *she'er* relatives: mother, father, son, daughter, brother, and sister. We learn this indirectly from the code of purity governing the Israelite priesthood. According to 21:2–3, an ordinary priest, usually forbidden to defile himself through contact with a corpse, was, nevertheless, permitted to attend to the burial of any one of these six relatives. The *she'er* relationship is extended in 18:12–13 to include the sister of one's father or mother.

The *she'er* relatives are in a different category from members of the family related by affinity, those who become a man's relatives by marriage. (A man's wife is his affinal relative par excellence and her sisters and her children from other marriages are also included in this category.) The basic principle regulating sexual union with affinal relatives is conveyed by the term *'ervah.* The only exception is levirate marriage, which, according to Deuteronomy 25:5–10, dispenses with the prohibition of *'ervah* in cases when a brother dies without leaving a male heir. In such an event, it is actually incumbent on a man to marry his brother's widow.

The interaction of these two principles, *she'er* relationship and *'ervah* (exclusive sexual access), account directly and by extension for all of the prohibited sexual unions within the Israelite family. Their scope was, in addition, affected by the polygamous character of the Israelite family. A man who was married to more than one wife would bring into the range of potentially prohibited marriages a large number of women from the clan, or tribe, than would be the case under a monogamous system.

18 The Lord spoke to Moses, saying: ²Speak to the Israelite people and say to them:

I the Lord am your God. ³You shall not copy the practices of the land of Egypt where you dwelt, or of the land of Canaan to which I am taking you; nor shall you follow their

י״ח וַיְדַבֵּ֥ר יְהוָ֖ה אֶל־מֹשֶׁ֥ה לֵּאמֹֽר׃ 2 דַּבֵּר֙ אֶל־
בְּנֵ֣י יִשְׂרָאֵ֔ל וְאָמַרְתָּ֖ אֲלֵהֶ֑ם אֲנִ֖י יְהוָ֥ה אֱלֹהֵיכֶֽם׃
3 כְּמַעֲשֵׂ֧ה אֶֽרֶץ־מִצְרַ֛יִם אֲשֶׁ֥ר יְשַׁבְתֶּם־בָּ֖הּ לֹ֣א
תַעֲשׂ֑וּ וּכְמַעֲשֵׂ֣ה אֶֽרֶץ־כְּנַ֡עַן אֲשֶׁ֣ר אֲנִי֩ מֵבִ֨יא

As an example, a man with several wives could not marry the sister of any one of them while that wife was alive. Further discussion of family structure is found in Excursus 5.

Chapter 18 is one of three legal collections in the Torah that deal in detail with incest and sexuality. Leviticus 20 restates chapter 18 in almost all of its particulars, and Deuteronomy 27:20–23 enumerates prohibitions of the same sort. But each of these texts is formulated in a distinctive way. Deuteronomy 27:20–23 is part of an execration, its dicta expressed as: "Cursed be he . . ." or "Any man who. . . ." As is typical in legal codes, Leviticus 20 specifies penalties for each of the offenses. By contrast, chapter 18 represents a series of commandments formulated in a style similar to the Decalogue: "Do not . . ." or "Thou shalt not. . . ." Although there is comment on the nature of the offenses and their gravity, no specific penalties are stipulated, as they almost always are in legal codes.

A subject not discussed explicitly in any of the codes is the status of children born out of incestuous or adulterous relationships. Deuteronomy 23:3 forbids a bastard (*mamzer*) or his direct descendants to marry within the Israelite community (*kahal*), but the term *mamzer* is never defined legally. In the biblical period Israelite children of uncertain paternity—those born out of incest and adultery or to harlots—were undoubtedly ostracized. In Judges 11:1–12 we read that Jephthah, who was a harlot's son, was driven away from home by the legitimate sons of his father. Mishnah Kiddushin 3:12 defines the status of children in terms of the circumstances surrounding their conception, that is, in terms of which prohibitions had been violated; thus the status of *mamzer* is applied to offspring born out of adultery or incest. But, according to Jewish law, one born out of wedlock (when there is not adultery or incest) is not considered a *mamzer*.

Chapter 18 opens (vv. 1–5) and closes (vv. 24–30) with admonitions that state the consequences of transgressing against God's commandments in the area of forbidden sexual activity. Such offenses would undermine Israel's right to the land of Canaan and would eventually bring about the exile. The main section of the chapter may be divided into three classes of forbidden sexual activity: (1) incest (vv. 6–16); (2) unions with women who are closely related to each other (vv. 17–18); and (3) other forbidden sexual activity, including adultery (vv. 19–20,22–23). Verse 21 stands out as a special prohibition of Molech worship. It may have been included here because the Molech cult involved the sacrifice of children.

2. ***Speak to the Israelite people***   The regulations of chapter 18 were meant to govern the conduct of the entire people.

I the Lord am your God   Chapter 18 begins and ends (v. 30) with this assertion, which, with variations, appears frequently as a recurrent theme in the Holiness Code.[1] It emphasizes that all of the commandments come directly from God and are to be obeyed with utmost strictness.

3. ***You shall not copy the practices of the land of Egypt . . . or of the land of Canaan***   This statement is puzzling in a code dealing primarily with incest, since there is no explicit evidence that incest was widespread in Canaan or Egypt. At certain periods in the history of ancient Egypt, it was the custom among the royal class to encourage brother-sister marriages. This was not likely to be imitated by the common people of another culture. Some of the tangential prohibitions of chapter 18, however, such as homosexuality and bestiality, were apparently quite common in Canaanite culture.

nor shall you follow their laws   Elsewhere, injunctions against following the laws or practices of other nations refer primarily to idolatry. Thus, in 2 Kings 17:7–8, *ḥukkot ha-goyim*, "the laws of the nations," refer specifically to the worship of other deities.[2] It is likely, therefore, that here the injunctions against following the laws of the nations represent generalizations rather than precise, historical references. The references to the sexual misconduct characteristic of the former inhabitants are probably to be attributed to the vehemence of the negative attitude of the priestly literature

laws. ⁴My rules alone shall you observe, and faithfully follow My laws: I the Lord am your God.

⁵You shall keep My laws and My rules, by the pursuit of which man shall live: I am the Lord.

⁶None of you shall come near anyone of his own flesh to uncover nakedness: I am the Lord.

אֶתְכֶ֖ם שָׁ֑מָּה וּבְחֻקֹּתֵיהֶ֖ם לֹ֥א תֵלֵֽכוּ׃
4 אֶת־מִשְׁפָּטַ֧י תַּעֲשׂ֛וּ וְאֶת־חֻקֹּתַ֥י תִּשְׁמְר֖וּ לָלֶ֣כֶת
בָּהֶ֑ם אֲנִ֖י יְהוָ֥ה אֱלֹהֵיכֶֽם׃ 5 וּשְׁמַרְתֶּ֤ם אֶת־חֻקֹּתַי֙
וְאֶת־מִשְׁפָּטַ֔י אֲשֶׁ֨ר יַעֲשֶׂ֥ה אֹתָ֛ם הָאָדָ֖ם וָחַ֣י בָּהֶ֑ם
אֲנִ֖י יְהוָֽה׃ ס   ששי 6 אִ֥ישׁ אִישׁ֙ אֶל־כָּל־
שְׁאֵ֣ר בְּשָׂר֔וֹ לֹ֥א תִקְרְב֖וּ לְגַלּ֣וֹת עֶרְוָ֑ה אֲנִ֖י יְהוָֽה׃

toward pagan ways of life. It would be in character for the priestly codes to enlarge on the sense of revulsion toward idolatrous religions, going beyond mere references to idolatry itself.

The full significance of the association between incest and the sins of the Canaanites is conveyed in the closing admonition of verses 24–28. There, possession of the land is made contingent on the quality of family life; should the land be defiled it would reject the Israelites as it had the former Canaanites.³

4. *My rules alone shall you observe, and faithfully follow My laws*   The terms *ḥok, ḥukkah,* and *mishpat* are often used synonymously in exhortations such as this. And yet, in its original meaning *mishpat* differs considerably from *ḥok* and *ḥukkah*. When these latter are used technically, they express the recording and promulgation of the law, since they derive from the verb *ḥ-k-k*, "to engrave, inscribe." The term *mishpat,* on the other hand, derives from the verb *sh-f-t,* "to judge, pronounce judgment."⁴ It refers primarily to rules, or norms, that govern the judicial process and to laws that are decided as part of that process.

The Hebrew verb *h-l-kh,* "to go, walk," is often used to connote adherence to God's commandments. It expresses a metaphor, common to many literary traditions, of life as a journey on which one embarks or a path on which one walks. God's commandments direct a person in the right path and represent the "way" in which one should "walk." There is nothing particularly theological about this metaphor, which may characterize any course of action, so long as it is considered to be normative, or proper.⁵

5. *by the pursuit of which man shall live*   The simple sense of the clause *va-ḥai ba-hem,* "he shall live by them," is that one should live his life in accordance with God's laws and commandments and that he should obey them all his life or while he is alive. This clause has, however, stimulated other interpretations reflecting its unusual syntax and its semantic nuances. Syntax allows us to understand this clause as one of result: "that man shall perform, so that [as a result] he may acquire life by them." Performance of God's laws and commandments holds forth the reward of life, whereas their violation threatens man with death.⁶ This interpretation is the basis for the traditional understanding of our verse by later commentaries, which state that observance of the commandments is rewarded by life in the world to come.⁷ We also find a nuanced rabbinic interpretation that stresses the sanctity of life itself: *va-ḥai ba-hem ve-lo' she-yamut ba-hem,* "That one may *live* by them, not that one should die because of them."⁸ In situations directly threatening human life, one should set aside the commandments in order to preserve human life. This principle was known as *pikkuaḥ nefesh,* "the sparing or rescue of human life."⁹

6. *None of you shall come near anyone of his own flesh to uncover nakedness*   This verse contains terms of reference that are essential for a proper understanding of the legislation of chapter 18 as a whole. The Hebrew verb *k-r-v,* "to come near, approach," often has the connotation of sexual intercourse.¹⁰ The terms most in need of interpretation are *she'er,* "flesh," and *'ervah,* "nakedness." The simple meaning of *she'er* is "meat, food," as we learn from Exodus 21:10, where this word refers to the food a man must provide for a slave girl in his charge. This is also the meaning of the Akkadian cognate *širu.*¹¹ Much in the way that *basar,* "meat," approximates the sense of blood relative, so *she'er* is used to characterize consanguineal relatives within the family.¹² This meaning is also conveyed by the Ugaritic cognate *tar.* The composite term *she'er besaro,* literally "the flesh of his flesh," is a redundancy, used for emphasis. The noun *'ervah,* "nakedness," is a euphemism for sexuality that is related to the verb *'-r-h,* "to uncover," and is cognate with the Akkadian adjective *eru(m),* "empty, bereft, naked."¹³ To "uncover nakedness" means "to have sexual intercourse."¹⁴

ס 7 עֶרְוַת אָבִיךָ וְעֶרְוַת אִמְּךָ לֹא תְגַלֵּה
אִמְּךָ הִוא לֹא תְגַלֶּה עֶרְוָתָהּ׃ ס 8 עֶרְוַת
אֵשֶׁת־אָבִיךָ לֹא תְגַלֵּה עֶרְוַת אָבִיךָ הִוא׃ ס
9 עֶרְוַת אֲחוֹתְךָ בַת־אָבִיךָ אוֹ בַת־אִמֶּךָ מוֹלֶדֶת
בַּיִת אוֹ מוֹלֶדֶת חוּץ לֹא תְגַלֶּה עֶרְוָתָן׃ ס
10 עֶרְוַת בַּת־בִּנְךָ אוֹ בַת־בִּתְּךָ לֹא תְגַלֶּה עֶרְוָתָן
כִּי עֶרְוָתְךָ הֵנָּה׃ ס 11 עֶרְוַת בַּת־אֵשֶׁת

7Your father's nakedness, that is, the nakedness of your mother, you shall not uncover; she is your mother—you shall not uncover her nakedness.

8Do not uncover the nakedness of your father's wife; it is the nakedness of your father.

9The nakedness of your sister—your father's daughter or your mother's, whether born into the household or outside—do not uncover their nakedness.

10The nakedness of your son's daughter, or of your daughter's daughter—do not uncover their nakedness; for their nakedness is yours.

Verse 6 is an opening statement that establishes a general category to be spelled out in the following verses. A basic rule of rabbinic hermeneutics states: "The general category includes only what is in its specific components." As applied to our case, this means that the circle of forbidden, incestuous relatives could not be extended to include any who are not explicitly mentioned in the laws of chapter 18. The only exception is a man's own daughter, who is, of course, forbidden to him sexually, but who is not listed among the incestuous relations. The law does mention granddaughters, however (v. 10), and it is to be assumed that since a daughter is more closely related than a granddaughter, she would be forbidden, *a fortiori*. The daughter is one of the six *she'er* relations listed in 21:2–3.[15]

7. Your father's nakedness, that is, the nakedness of your mother This verse forbids sexual relations with one's natural mother, according to Ramban. The prefixed *vav* in the word *ve-ʿervat* is to be translated "that being the nakedness of." It does not add another element, but rather defines further what immediately preceded it. This *vav* is, therefore, called "circumstantial." In this case, *ʿervat ʾavikha* means "the nakedness reserved for your father, belonging to your father." Only one's father has access to one's mother's sexuality.[16] This is also the meaning of *ʿervat,* "the nakedness of," in the following verse.

8. the nakedness of your father's wife This refers to one who has sexual relations with a wife of his father who is not his own mother. By so doing, he would also uncover his father's "nakedness," namely, the nakedness of a woman who had been reserved for his father.[17] This regulation most obviously applied in polygamous societies, but it also related to cases of divorce. A man may never marry his father's divorcée, as noted by the translators. The sin of Reuben, as recounted in Genesis 35:22 and referred to in Genesis 49:4, was that he cohabited with one of his father's wives.

9. The nakedness of your sister—your father's daughter or your mother's, whether born into the household or outside Targum Onkelos renders this verse as follows: "who is born from your father by another woman, or by your mother from another man." This rendering takes the definition *moledet bayit ʾo moledet ḥuts,* "whether born into the household or outside," as parenthetical and redundant, not as adding another category. In other words, "your father's daughter" was born into your household, whereas your mother's daughter was born outside of it at a time when your mother was not part of your father's household. On this basis, *moledet bayit* of our verse is equivalent in meaning to *moledet ʾavikha,* "born to your father," in verse 11. Elsewhere, Hebrew *moledet* usually refers to place of birth.[18] The provisions of verse 11 partially duplicate those of this verse.

10. The nakedness of your son's daughter, or of your daughter's daughter It is not entirely clear why the prohibition of union with one's own daughter was not made explicit, but it is obvious that such a union would have been incestuous, as noted in the introductory Comment and in the Comment to verse 6.

11. The nakedness of your father's wife's daughter This is an alternative way of formulating verse 9, namely, "your father's daughter," a half sister with whom one shares a common father

11The nakedness of your father's wife's daughter, who was born into your father's household—she is your sister; do not uncover her nakedness.

12Do not uncover the nakedness of your father's sister; she is your father's flesh.

13Do not uncover the nakedness of your mother's sister; for she is your mother's flesh.

14Do not uncover the nakedness of your father's brother: do not approach his wife; she is your aunt.

15Do not uncover the nakedness of your daughter-in-law: she is your son's wife; you shall not uncover her nakedness.

16Do not uncover the nakedness of your brother's wife; it is the nakedness of your brother.

אָבִ֙יךָ֙ מוֹלֶ֣דֶת אָבִ֔יךָ אֲחוֹתְךָ֖ הִ֑וא לֹ֥א תְגַלֶּ֖ה
עֶרְוָתָֽהּ׃ ס 12 עֶרְוַ֥ת אֲחוֹת־אָבִ֖יךָ לֹ֣א תְגַלֵּ֑ה
שְׁאֵ֥ר אָבִ֖יךָ הִֽוא׃ ס 13 עֶרְוַ֥ת אֲחוֹת־אִמְּךָ֖
לֹ֣א תְגַלֵּ֑ה כִּֽי־שְׁאֵ֥ר אִמְּךָ֖ הִֽוא׃ ס 14 עֶרְוַ֥ת
אֲחִֽי־אָבִ֖יךָ לֹ֣א תְגַלֵּ֑ה אֶל־אִשְׁתּוֹ֙ לֹ֣א תִקְרָ֔ב
דֹּדָתְךָ֖ הִֽוא׃ ס 15 עֶרְוַ֥ת כַּלָּתְךָ֖ לֹ֣א תְגַלֵּ֑ה
אֵ֤שֶׁת בִּנְךָ֙ הִ֔וא לֹ֥א תְגַלֶּ֖ה עֶרְוָתָֽהּ׃ ס
16 עֶרְוַ֥ת אֵֽשֶׁת־אָחִ֖יךָ לֹ֣א תְגַלֵּ֑ה עֶרְוַ֥ת אָחִ֖יךָ
הִֽוא׃ ס 17 עֶרְוַ֥ת אִשָּׁ֛ה וּבִתָּ֖הּ לֹ֣א תְגַלֵּ֑ה

but not the same mother. The overlapping of verses 9 and 11 has attracted critical attention since talmudic times. In Yevamot 22b, Rabbi Yose b. Judah, noting the presence of the word "wife" in verse 11 and its absence in verse 9, concludes that verse 9 is speaking of a daughter born of one's father's mistress, not wife! Verse 11 would refer, then, to a legal half sister. This is unlikely, however, because chapter 18 does not deal with the institution of concubinage. Hoffmann understands verse 11 differently, as adding a prohibition to verse 9. In his view, verse 9 forbids marriage only to a full sister or at least to one with the same mother, whereas verse 11 adds the prohibition of a sister with whom one shared only a common father, and who was less closely related.[19] This, too, is a forced explanation that would require understanding verse 9 as "your father's daughter, or only your mother's daughter," which is not what the verse says.

It is preferable to concede that there was some overlap or repetition in chapter 18 rather than to distort the simple sense of verse 9 in order to preserve a semblance of consistency within the chapter.

12–13. the nakedness of your father's sister . . . the nakedness of your mother's sister The two sides of the family are differentiated, with the two aunts mentioned separately. Their relationship represents an extension of the *she'er* principle. Verse 14 adds an affinal aunt, the wife of one's uncle.

14. the nakedness of your father's brother: do not approach his wife The formation *ʿervat 'aḥi 'avikha,* "the nakedness of your father's brother," means the sexual access to his wife. This is explained in verses 7–8, regarding the meaning of the term *ʿervah.*

15. the nakedness of your daughter-in-law Hebrew ***kallah,*** like its Akkadian cognate ***kallatu,*** basically means "daughter-in-law."[20] Nevertheless, usage was fluid. Viewed from the perspective of the son's generation, the ***kallah*** was the "bride," just as the masculine counterpart ***ḥatan*** means both "son-in-law" and "bridegroom."[21]

16. the nakedness of your brother's wife; it is the nakedness of your brother Here again, as in verses 7–8, *ʿervah* refers to sexual access. The *ʿervah* of one's brother is the nakedness of the brother's wife, who is forbidden in marriage. Deuteronomy 25:5–10 provides a significant exception. In the event a man dies without leaving a male heir, his brother is commanded to take the widow in order to produce an heir and assure the continuity of his brother's "name." This is known as levirate marriage.

Verse 16 completes the primary list of incestuous relatives. Verses 17–18 deal with two cases where marriage into the family engenders additional prohibitions, on the principle that certain of the *she'er* relatives of a man's wife are also forbidden. This combines the affinal and consanguineal principles, so that a man may not marry his wife's daughter nor her granddaughters. In effect, the cumulative provisions of Leviticus 18 and 20 and of Deuteronomy 27 prohibit marriage with three generations of the wife's *she'er* relatives: her mother, her sister (in verse 18, which follows), and her daughter. This is even extended to a fourth generation, with the prohibition of her granddaughters.

¹⁷Do not uncover the nakedness of a woman and her daughter; nor shall you marry her son's daughter or her daughter's daughter and uncover her nakedness: they are kindred; it is depravity. ¹⁸Do not marry a woman as a rival to her sister and uncover her nakedness in the other's lifetime.

¹⁹Do not come near a woman during her period of uncleanness to uncover her nakedness.

²⁰Do not have carnal relations with your neighbor's wife and defile yourself with her.

²¹Do not allow any of your offspring to be offered up to Molech, and do not profane the name of your God: I am the LORD.

אֶת־בַּת־בְּנָ֤הּ וְאֶת־בַּת־בִּתָּהּ֙ לֹ֣א תִקַּ֔ח לְגַלּ֖וֹת עֶרְוָתָ֑הּ שַׁאֲרָ֥ה הֵ֖נָּה זִמָּ֥ה הִֽוא: ¹⁸ וְאִשָּׁ֥ה אֶל־אֲחֹתָ֖הּ לֹ֣א תִקָּ֑ח לִצְרֹ֗ר לְגַלּ֤וֹת עֶרְוָתָהּ֙ עָלֶ֔יהָ בְּחַיֶּֽיהָ: ¹⁹ וְאֶל־אִשָּׁ֖ה בְּנִדַּ֣ת טֻמְאָתָ֑הּ לֹ֣א תִקְרַ֔ב לְגַלּ֖וֹת עֶרְוָתָֽהּ: ²⁰ וְאֶל־אֵ֙שֶׁת֙ עֲמִֽיתְךָ֔ לֹא־תִתֵּ֥ן שְׁכָבְתְּךָ֖ לְזָ֑רַע לְטָמְאָה־בָֽהּ: ²¹ וּמִֽזַּרְעֲךָ֥ לֹא־תִתֵּ֖ן לְהַעֲבִ֣יר לַמֹּ֑לֶךְ וְלֹ֧א תְחַלֵּ֛ל אֶת־שֵׁ֥ם אֱלֹהֶ֖יךָ אֲנִ֥י יְהוָֽה: [רביעי] שביעי כשהן מחוברות

Whereas Leviticus 20:14 and Deuteronomy 27:23 project the prohibition back to the parent generation and forbid marriage with one's mother-in-law, our text looks forward and forbids marriage with the daughter and granddaughter of one's wife.

The new JPS translation understands the form *sha'arah* as an abstract feminine noun meaning "kindred, kinship," the sense being that the wife's daughters and granddaughters are part of her kinship circle. One could, however, vocalize the word *she'erah* with a *mappik* (dot) in the final *heh* of the word,²² and render it "*her* flesh." Actually, such a reading makes sense because the basis of these prohibitions is that a wife's daughter and her granddaughter are *her she'er* relatives.

17. *it is depravity* Hebrew *zimmah,* from the root *z-m-m,* "to plot, conspire," usually refers either to sexual immorality or, as a metaphor, to Israel's infidelity in committing idolatry.²³

18. *Do not marry a woman as a rival to her sister* Hebrew *li-tsror* reflects the noun *tsarah,* "rival wife," which, in turn, derives from the verb *ts-r-r,* "to assail, attack." In polygamous marriages, the interests of the several wives inevitably conflicted.

and uncover her nakedness in the other's lifetime The syntax requires clarification. The literal sense is "to uncover her nakedness (that is, the wife's sister's nakedness) *in addition to her,* during her lifetime (that is, the wife's lifetime)." The preposition *'al* in this statement has the same meaning as *'al nashav,* "in addition to his wives," in Genesis 28:9.²⁴ Marrying two sisters would create an extremely unhealthy rivalry. The prohibition continues so long as the first sister remains alive, even if she had been divorced from the man in question. It is not certain why the text dispenses with the rule of permanent prohibition in this case.²⁵

19. *Do not come near a woman during her period of uncleanness* Rather, "during her period of impurity." As has been noted, the polar terms *tame',* "impure," and *tahor,* "pure," do not describe sanitary conditions, but, rather, ritual conditions. This prohibition, which initiates the section on sexual activity other than incest, is distinctive in that it governs a man's sexual relations with his own wife. On the precise meaning of Hebrew *niddah,* "period of menstruation," see Comments to 12:2 and 15:19.

20. *Do not have carnal relations with your neighbor's wife* The literal Hebrew formula for impregnation is "to place your layer of semen" (*natan shekhovtekha le-zera'*). The offspring of an adulterous union was undoubtedly illegitimate. Apart from the immorality of adultery, children born out of such unions were stigmatized. The prohibition of adultery is basic to biblical law and religion. It is included in the Decalogue, in Exodus 20:14 and Deuteronomy 5:18, where it is associated with the commandment not to covet one's neighbor's wife. The prophets of Israel were likewise very vocal in its condemnation. The act of adultery also became the basis for a widely used prophetic metaphor expressing the poignancy of Israel's faithlessness. According to that metaphor, it is Israel, the bride, who is wayward.

21. *Do not allow any of your offspring to be offered up to Molech* Rather, "Do not dedicate any of your offspring to Molech." The verb *n-t-n* used in this statement may mean "to devote,

[22]Do not lie with a male as one lies with a woman; it is an abhorrence.

[23]Do not have carnal relations with any beast and defile yourself thereby; and let no woman lend herself to a beast to mate with it; it is perversion.

[24]Do not defile yourselves in any of those ways, for it is by such that the nations that I am casting out before you defiled themselves. [25]Thus the land became defiled; and I called it to account for its iniquity, and the land spewed out its inhabitants. [26]But you must keep My laws and My rules,

22 וְאֶת־זָכָר לֹא תִשְׁכַּב מִשְׁכְּבֵי אִשָּׁה תּוֹעֵבָה
הִוא׃ 23 וּבְכָל־בְּהֵמָה לֹא־תִתֵּן שְׁכָבְתְּךָ לְטָמְאָה־
בָהּ וְאִשָּׁה לֹא־תַעֲמֹד לִפְנֵי בְהֵמָה לְרִבְעָהּ תֶּבֶל
הוּא׃ 24 אַל־תִּטַּמְּאוּ בְּכָל־אֵלֶּה כִּי בְכָל־אֵלֶּה
נִטְמְאוּ הַגּוֹיִם אֲשֶׁר־אֲנִי מְשַׁלֵּחַ מִפְּנֵיכֶם׃
25 וַתִּטְמָא הָאָרֶץ וָאֶפְקֹד עֲוֺנָהּ עָלֶיהָ וַתָּקִא
הָאָרֶץ אֶת־יֹשְׁבֶיהָ׃ מפטיר 26 וּשְׁמַרְתֶּם אַתֶּם
אֶת־חֻקֹּתַי וְאֶת־מִשְׁפָּטַי וְלֹא תַעֲשׂוּ מִכֹּל

dedicate" as an offering to a deity.[26] Molech is the name given to a deity worshiped by some of Israel's ancient neighbors. According to 2 Kings 23:10, King Josiah destroyed a cult site in the environs of Jerusalem where children had been sacrificed to Molech during the earlier reign of Manasseh, king of Judah. The biblical evidence on the subject of the Molech cult is difficult to interpret clearly and has occasioned controversy among biblical scholars. These problems are explored in Excursus 7.

*22. **Do not lie with a male as one lies with a woman*** Hebrew *mishkevei 'ishshah* means literally "after the manner of lying with a woman" by the introduction of the male member. Male homosexuality is associated with the ancient Canaanites, if we are to judge from biblical literature. Two biblical narratives highlight this theme, one about the men of Sodom in Genesis 19, and the other concerning the fate of the concubine at Gibeah in Judges 19. Although Gibeah was an Israelite town, the story clearly implies that Gibeah's Israelite residents had descended to the abominable ways of the surrounding Canaanites.

Both of these accounts place the phenomenon of male homosexuality in a particular context: xenophobia. This extreme fear of strangers induces a community to attack visitors. In both of the stories cited here, the form of attack was homosexual assault. It is also thought that the pagan priests, called *kedeshim,* regularly engaged in homosexual acts.[27] The term *meḥir kelev,* "the pay of a dog," mentioned in Deuteronomy 23:18–19, refers to the wages of a male prostitute, who usually serviced men, not women, in ancient societies. Male homosexuality is called *to'evah,* "abhorrence, abomination," a term that occurs frequently in the admonitions of Deuteronomy. It occurs no fewer than four times in this concluding section of our chapter. In Genesis 46:34 and Exodus 8:22, it serves to characterize what Egyptians considered abhorrent, principally pastoral pursuits.[28] There has been considerable speculation as to why lesbianism is not explicitly forbidden in the Torah. In due course, rabbinic interpretation added this prohibition, as well.[29]

*23. **Do not have carnal relations with any beast . . . and let no woman lend herself to a beast*** This is the only instance in chapter 18 where a commandment is addressed to the woman. Elsewhere in the laws the second person masculine singular form of address is consistently employed. Here, the statement speaks, as well, of what a woman may not do. In ancient Israel women would have had little access to men on their own initiative, but would have had the opportunity to engage in bestiality with animals if they chose to. It is understood, of course, that such conduct was forbidden to both men and women, as is explicit in the formulation of 20:15. Hebrew *tevel,* "perversion," derives from the root *b-l-l,* "to mix." The sense is that sexual activity between man and beast is a forbidden "mixture" of the species.

With this the laws of forbidden sexual activity are complete. The closing section (vv. 24–30) is an admonition against violating any of the sexual prohibitions stated in the chapter.

*24. **Do not defile yourselves in any of those ways*** The prohibited sexual acts set forth in chapter 18 fall within the scope of impurity. Although incest and the other sexual offenses involve interpersonal relations, they are also offenses against God.

*25. **Thus the land became defiled*** The interdependence of the people and the land is a prominent theme in prophetic teaching. Those who violate the code of family life commit an outrage that defiles the land—which, in turn, will spew them out. This is, of course, one way of explaining the exile of a people from its land, a threat intrinsic to chapter 18. It is as though the land, personified, is angered by its defilement at man's hand.

and you must not do any of those abhorrent things, neither the citizen nor the stranger who resides among you; [27]for all those abhorrent things were done by the people who were in the land before you, and the land became defiled. [28]So let not the land spew you out for defiling it, as it spewed out the nation that came before you. [29]All who do any of those abhorrent things—such persons shall be cut off from their people. [30]You shall keep My charge not to engage in any of the abhorrent practices that were carried on before you, and you shall not defile yourselves through them: I the LORD am your God.

הַתּוֹעֵבֹת הָאֵלֶּה הָאֶזְרָח וְהַגֵּר הַגָּר בְּתוֹכְכֶם׃
27 כִּי אֶת־כָּל־הַתּוֹעֵבֹת הָאֵל עָשׂוּ אַנְשֵׁי־הָאָרֶץ
אֲשֶׁר לִפְנֵיכֶם וַתִּטְמָא הָאָרֶץ׃ [מפטיר
לספרדים] 28 וְלֹא־תָקִיא הָאָרֶץ אֶתְכֶם
בְּטַמַּאֲכֶם אֹתָהּ כַּאֲשֶׁר קָאָה אֶת־הַגּוֹי אֲשֶׁר
לִפְנֵיכֶם׃ 29 כִּי כָּל־אֲשֶׁר יַעֲשֶׂה מִכֹּל הַתּוֹעֵבוֹת
הָאֵלֶּה וְנִכְרְתוּ הַנְּפָשׁוֹת הָעֹשֹׂת מִקֶּרֶב עַמָּם׃
30 וּשְׁמַרְתֶּם אֶת־מִשְׁמַרְתִּי לְבִלְתִּי עֲשׂוֹת
מֵחֻקּוֹת הַתּוֹעֵבֹת אֲשֶׁר נַעֲשׂוּ לִפְנֵיכֶם וְלֹא
תִטַּמְּאוּ בָּהֶם אֲנִי יְהוָה אֱלֹהֵיכֶם׃ פ

Exile is punishment for an abhorrent way of life, not only as regards Israel, but also for all other nations. So, for example, until the prior inhabitants of Canaan reach the limit of their sinfulness, the Israelites cannot occupy their land, and the fulfillment of God's promise of Genesis 15:16 must be delayed: "And they shall return here in the fourth generation, for the iniquity of the Amorites is not yet complete." In the admonition of chapter 18, this theme is applied to Israel itself.

26. neither the citizen nor the stranger who resides among you The goal of establishing a holy community required that all who lived within it, both Israelites and aliens, uphold a standard of proper sexual behavior. Here, as in other instances, the admonition is worded so as to include non-Israelites.

29. such persons shall be cut off from their people On the penalty known as *karet,* "cutting off," see Excursus 1. Possibly, this statement requires that foreign enclaves in the Land of Israel also banish members of these groups who violated the sexual laws governing Israelites. This is suggested by the third-person formulation: "from their people."

30. You shall keep My charge On the specialized connotations of Hebrew *mishmeret,* "charge," see Comment to 8:35.

CHAPTER 19

The Laws of Holiness

Kedoshim

Chapter 19 may be characterized as a brief *torah* (instruction). It states the duties incumbent on the Israelites as a people and includes a wide range of laws and commandments that are representative of the basic teachings of the Torah. More specifically, it echoes the Ten Commandments. These features were noted by the ancient sages. In Leviticus Rabba 24, we read as follows: "Speak to the entire Israelite people and say to them: 'You shall be holy. . . .' Rabbi Ḥiyya taught: These words inform us that this section is to be read before the people in an assembly. And why is it to be read before the people in an assembly? Because most of the essential laws of the Torah can be derived from it. Rabbi Levi said: Because the Ten Commandments are embodied in it." The midrash then proceeds to list a series of parallels between chapter 19 and the Ten Commandments. Some of the parallels require homiletical license, but even according to the strictest exegesis the following can be established:

Leviticus 19	***The Ten Commandments***
Reverence for parents (v. 3a)	Honoring parents (no. 5)
The Sabbath (v. 3b)	The Sabbath (no. 4)
Idolatry (v. 4)	Idolatry; worship of other Gods (no. 2)

KEDOSHIM
19 The LORD spoke to Moses, saying: 2Speak to the whole
Israelite community and say to them:
You shall be holy, for I, the LORD your God, am holy.
3You shall each revere his mother and his father, and keep
My sabbaths: I the LORD am your God.

קדשים
י״ט וַיְדַבֵּ֥ר יְהוָ֖ה אֶל־מֹשֶׁ֥ה לֵּאמֹֽר׃ 2 דַּבֵּ֞ר אֶל־
כָּל־עֲדַ֧ת בְּנֵֽי־יִשְׂרָאֵ֛ל וְאָמַרְתָּ֥ אֲלֵהֶ֖ם קְדֹשִׁ֣ים
תִּהְי֑וּ כִּ֣י קָד֔וֹשׁ אֲנִ֖י יְהוָ֥ה אֱלֹהֵיכֶֽם׃ 3 אִ֣ישׁ אִמּ֤וֹ
וְאָבִיו֙ תִּירָ֔אוּ וְאֶת־שַׁבְּתֹתַ֖י תִּשְׁמֹ֑רוּ אֲנִ֖י יְהוָ֥ה

Leviticus 19	*The Ten Commandments*
Stealing and deceitful conduct (vv. 11a,13,15,35)	Stealing (no. 8)
False oaths (v. 12)	False oaths (no. 3)
"I am the LORD your God who freed you from the land of Egypt" (v. 36)	"I am the LORD . . ." (no. 1)

There are, in addition, further parallels of a less precise nature to be noted in the Comments.

In Ezekiel 22:6–12 we find a prophetic condemnation of the Israelite people and its "princes" that refers to some of the laws and commandments set forth in this chapter as well as to those characteristic of other parts of the Holiness Code. In most cases, the parallels are so precise that a literary connection between chapter 19 and Ezekiel 22:6–12 is most probable. In the prophecy there is reference to the following six items prominent in chapter 19: (1) humiliation of parents, (2) cheating strangers, (3) despising Sabbaths and sacred offerings, (4) depravity, (5) defrauding one's own kinsfolk, and (6) baseness. Chapter 19 thus emerges as a major biblical statement on the duties of the Israelite people. The entire people is addressed in the plural, and all of what is said relates directly to the opening statement: "You shall be holy. . . ." The emphasis on duties basic to collective existence stands out in bold relief; the concept of "a kingdom of priests and a holy nation," expressed in the words of Exodus 19:6, is the unifying theme of chapter 19.

The composition of the chapter requires some comment. It is organized around a series of primarily apodictic statements: "Do not . . ." or "You shall. . . ." Each is of one to three verses in length and usually concludes with the formula "I the LORD am your God" or simply "I am the LORD." This collection employs both second and third person formulations and both singular and plural forms of address. Taken as a whole, it appears to have been compiled from previously recorded laws and commandments, which have been preserved in their original form. Both the introduction and conclusion are utterly brief when compared with other chapters in the Holiness Code, lending this chapter a dramatic quality.

2. ***The LORD spoke to Moses . . . You shall be holy*** Rather, "You must be holy!" The verse is distinctive in that it provides a rationale for a commandment: Israel must be holy because God is holy. To have a close relationship to God, the people must emulate God. As one of the sages put it: "It is comparable to the court of a king. What is the court's duty? To imitate the king!" In theological terminology this doctrine is known as *imitatio dei,* "the imitation of God."[1] For further discussion, see Excursus 6.

3. ***You shall each revere his mother and his father, and keep My sabbaths*** Literally, "Each one, his mother and his father, you shall revere." In biblical Hebrew, sentences beginning with *'ish,* "a person," may shift to second person address, as is the case here. More significant is the fact that mother precedes father, whereas elsewhere father usually comes first, as one would expect in a patrilineal society. There are a few exceptions to the normal pattern, however, suggesting that in familial contexts, deference is shown to the mother. In 21:2, one's mother comes first in a list of consanguineal relatives. In Genesis 35:18 we observe that the name given a newborn child by its mother is recorded prior to the name given by the father. The traditional resolution of the unusual order evident in our verse is based on a comparison with the Fifth Commandment, where father precedes mother. The two statements, when combined, amount to an equitable estimation of both parents.[2]

4Do not turn to idols or make molten gods for yourselves: I the LORD am your God.

5When you sacrifice an offering of well-being to the LORD, sacrifice it so that it may be accepted on your behalf. 6It shall be eaten on the day you sacrifice it, or on the day following; but what is left by the third day must be consumed in fire. 7If it should be eaten on the third day, it is an offensive thing, it will not be acceptable. 8And he who eats of it shall bear his guilt, for he has profaned what is sacred to the LORD; that person shall be cut off from his kin.

אֱלֹהֵיכֶם׃ 4 אַל־תִּפְנוּ אֶל־הָאֱלִילִים וֵאלֹהֵי
מַסֵּכָה לֹא תַעֲשׂוּ לָכֶם אֲנִי יְהוָה אֱלֹהֵיכֶם׃ 5 וְכִי
תִזְבְּחוּ זֶבַח שְׁלָמִים לַיהוָה לִרְצֹנְכֶם תִּזְבָּחֻהוּ׃
6 בְּיוֹם זִבְחֲכֶם יֵאָכֵל וּמִמָּחֳרָת וְהַנּוֹתָר עַד־יוֹם
הַשְּׁלִישִׁי בָּאֵשׁ יִשָּׂרֵף׃ 7 וְאִם הֵאָכֹל יֵאָכֵל בַּיּוֹם
הַשְּׁלִישִׁי פִּגּוּל הוּא לֹא יֵרָצֶה׃ 8 וְאֹכְלָיו עֲוֺנוֹ
יִשָּׂא כִּי־אֶת־קֹדֶשׁ יְהוָה חִלֵּל וְנִכְרְתָה הַנֶּפֶשׁ

4. Do not turn to idols The Hebrew idiom *'al tifnu 'el,* "Do not turn to," conveys the sense of reliance on a power, human or divine. It is frequently used with reference to idolatrous tendencies.[3] The etymology of Hebrew *'elil,* "idol," is uncertain. Some derive it from *'al*, "nothingness," as in Job 24:25. Others take it as a diminutive form of *'el,* "god, deity," used derogatorily. The form *'elil* also occasionally functions as an adjective rather than as a noun. In Job 13:4 we find *rofe'ei 'elil,* "ineffectual physicians," and in Jeremiah 14:14 *kesem ve-'elil,* "an empty divination." These usages seem to argue for the derivation from *'al,* "nothingness."

molten gods Hebrew *massekhah* derives from the verb *n-s-kh,* "to pour into a mold, cast."

5. When you sacrifice an offering of well-being Rather, "a sacred gift of greeting."[4] Verses 5–8 contain the first of the casuistic statements in chapter 19. They are addressed primarily to the individual Israelites who donated *shelamim* sacrifices to God. The basic rites associated with this sacrifice are set forth in chapter 3, in 7:11–34, and in 22:21, where there are further provisions for making the offering. This abundance of information is not without problems, however. According to 7:11–34, the *shelamim* could be used for three purposes: as a votive offering (*neder*), as a voluntary offering (*nedavah*), and as a thanksgiving offering (*todah*). When we examine the provisions of 7:11–34 more closely we discover, however, that the thanksgiving offering is distinct from the other two. It is accompanied by two kinds of grain offerings, one of which is made from leavened dough. Furthermore, the flesh of the *todah* could be consumed by priests and donors only on the same day as its presentation, whereas in the other two types of *shelamim,* the flesh could be consumed until the morning of the third day. There is also the difference that in 22:21–25 the *todah* is separated from the other types of *shelamim.*

In summary, the *todah* retained distinctive features even after being incorporated in the general category of *shelamim* sacrifices. The code of 7:11–34 appears to represent the outcome of a process of development and change. Our code and that of 22:21f. represent an earlier stage and do not subsume the *todah* under the category of *shelamim* offerings. This is so because the codes of Leviticus were arranged according to a topical order that was not meant to reflect the inner development of ritual but, rather, to instruct the priesthood and the Israelites on proper procedures. It is therefore quite understandable that in the later chapters of Leviticus one may find statements that reflect earlier stages of cultic development.

so that it may be accepted on your behalf On the sense of Hebrew *li-rtsonkhem,* "on your behalf," see Comment to 1:3.

6. It shall be eaten on the day you sacrifice it For similar procedures and terminology, see 7:15–18 and Comments to those verses.

8. And he who eats of it shall bear his guilt See Comment to 5:1.

for he has profaned what is sacred to the LORD . . . Hebrew *kodesh,* "sacred," and the plural *kodashim* often have the sense of "sacred offering(s)."[5] The Hebrew verb *ḥillel,* "to render profane, impure," is related to the noun *ḥol,* "unsanctified, profane."[6]

The penalty of being "cut off" (*karet*) is added to the admonition here. In 7:18, which deals with the same ritual requirements as this passage, no mention is made of it.

9When you reap the harvest of your land, you shall not reap all the way to the edges of your field, or gather the gleanings of your harvest. 10You shall not pick your vineyard bare, or gather the fallen fruit of your vineyard; you shall leave them for the poor and the stranger: I the LORD am your God.

11You shall not steal; you shall not deal deceitfully or falsely with one another. 12You shall not swear falsely by My name, profaning the name of your God: I am the LORD.

הַהִ֖וא מֵעַמֶּֽיהָ׃ 9 וּֽבְקֻצְרְכֶם֙ אֶת־קְצִ֣יר אַרְצְכֶ֔ם לֹ֧א
תְכַלֶּ֛ה פְּאַ֥ת שָׂדְךָ֖ לִקְצֹ֑ר וְלֶ֥קֶט קְצִֽירְךָ֖ לֹ֥א
תְלַקֵּֽט׃ 10 וְכַרְמְךָ֙ לֹ֣א תְעוֹלֵ֔ל וּפֶ֥רֶט כַּרְמְךָ֖ לֹ֣א
תְלַקֵּ֑ט לֶֽעָנִ֤י וְלַגֵּר֙ תַּעֲזֹ֣ב אֹתָ֔ם אֲנִ֖י יְהוָ֥ה אֱלֹהֵיכֶֽם׃
11 לֹ֖א תִּגְנֹ֑בוּ וְלֹא־תְכַחֲשׁ֥וּ וְלֹֽא־תְשַׁקְּר֖וּ אִ֥ישׁ
בַּעֲמִיתֽוֹ׃ 12 וְלֹֽא־תִשָּׁבְע֥וּ בִשְׁמִ֖י לַשָּׁ֑קֶר וְחִלַּלְתָּ֛
אֶת־שֵׁ֥ם אֱלֹהֶ֖יךָ אֲנִ֥י יְהוָֽה׃ 13 לֹֽא־תַעֲשֹׁ֥ק אֶת־

9. When you reap the harvest of your land Verses 9–10 require that some produce from the harvest of field and vineyard be given to the poor and the stranger. In all, four types of gifts are specified: two from the grain harvest and the corresponding two from the vineyards. The two allocations of grain are *pe'ah* and *leket.*

Regarding *pe'ah,* "the corner, edge" of the field, there is no limit or minimum as to the space or quantity to be left unharvested in the corners of the field. Tradition set the minimum at one-sixtieth of the yield, according to the Mishnah Pe'ah 1:1–2. The Mishnah recommends taking into consideration several factors, such as the abundance of the yield, the overall resources of the owner of the field, and the current needs of the poor.

Leket, "gleanings," is a collective noun. Mishnah Pe'ah 4:10 defines *leket* as that which falls to the ground during reaping. It was the practice in ancient Israel, as in the ancient Near East generally, to cut the stalks of grain with one hand while catching what was reaped with the other. This technique is alluded to in Psalms 129:6–7: "Let them be like grass on roofs . . . that affords no handful for the reaper." Whatever the reaper failed to catch in his other hand fell to the ground. This is what is known as *leket,* to be left ungathered. A description of gleaning by the poor in ancient Israel is preserved in the Book of Ruth 2:3,7. There it is told how the poor of Bethlehem, Ruth among them, followed along in the rows of grain after the reapers.

10. You shall not pick your vineyard bare, or gather the fallen fruit The two allocations to the poor and the stranger from the vineyards are: *ʿolelot* and *peret. ʿOlelot,* "grape clusters not fully grown," are defined according to Mishnah Pe'ah 7:4 as grapes that have neither *katef,* "the developed top of the cluster," having small stems branching out from the main stem, nor *natef,* "the developed bottom part of the cluster." Such underdeveloped growths cannot properly be termed *'eshkol,* "a cluster," and must consequently be left unpicked until they mature. At that time, only the poor and the stranger may pick them. *Peret* is "fruit that falls to the ground during picking," as defined in Mishnah Pe'ah 7:3. Such fruit is to be left ungathered.

for the poor and the stranger On the term *ger,* "stranger," see Comments to verse 33 and to 17:8. In 23:20 we find a similar law. The term *ʿani,* one of several used in biblical Hebrew to characterize the poor, expresses the suffering, deprivation, and miserable state of the poor.

11. You shall not steal This parallels the Eighth Commandment.

you shall not deal deceitfully or falsely with one another This approximates the import of the Ninth Commandment: "You shall not bear false witness against your neighbor." Here the verb *lo' teshakkeru,* literally "You shall not lie," is used, and in the Ninth Commandment, the noun *sheker* in the designation *ʿed shaker,* "a false witness."[7] The law of 5:21–24 prescribes the expiation, restitution, and penalties required of one who acts deceitfully in this way.

12. You shall not swear falsely by My name Both the Mishnah and the Sifra assume that our passage and the Third Commandment are parallels. A comparison of the two passages is instructive. Both employ the verb *nishbaʿ,* "to swear, take an oath." But the Third Commandment uses the adverbial *la-shav',* whose meaning is not completely clear, whereas our passage uses the adverbial *la-shaker,* "falsely," whose meaning is precise. Mishnah Shevuʿot 3:8f. defines *shav'* as that which differs from what is generally accepted as true, which contradicts fact or reality, or which projects an impossibility. Thus, *shav'* is an aspect of falsehood.

13You shall not defraud your fellow. You shall not commit robbery. The wages of a laborer shall not remain with you until morning.

14You shall not insult the deaf, or place a stumbling block before the blind. You shall fear your God: I am the LORD.

15You shall not render an unfair decision: do not favor the poor or show deference to the rich; judge your kinsman

רֵעֲךָ֖ וְלֹ֣א תִגְזֹ֑ל לֹֽא־תָלִ֞ין פְּעֻלַּ֥ת שָׂכִ֛יר אִתְּךָ֖ עַד־
בֹּֽקֶר׃ 14 לֹא־תְקַלֵּ֣ל חֵרֵ֔שׁ וְלִפְנֵ֣י עִוֵּ֔ר לֹ֥א תִתֵּ֖ן
מִכְשֹׁ֑ל וְיָרֵ֥אתָ מֵּאֱלֹהֶ֖יךָ אֲנִ֥י יְהוָֽה׃ שני [חמישי
כשהן מחוברות] 15 לֹא־תַעֲשׂ֥וּ עָ֙וֶל֙ בַּמִּשְׁפָּ֔ט
לֹא־תִשָּׂ֣א פְנֵי־דָ֔ל וְלֹ֥א תֶהְדַּ֖ר פְּנֵ֣י גָד֑וֹל בְּצֶ֖דֶק
תִּשְׁפֹּ֥ט עֲמִיתֶֽךָ׃ 16 לֹא־תֵלֵ֤ךְ רָכִיל֙ בְּעַמֶּ֔יךָ לֹ֥א

profaning the name of your God Oaths are sworn in God's name, and one who swears falsely treats God's name as if it were *not* holy. This is the sense of the verb *ve-ḥillalta,* literally "you will profane," in our verse. God's "name," or renown, and the awe in which He is held are diminished by those who fail to revere Him. Profanation of God's name occurs as a result of false oaths and also as a result of improper sacrifice, the neglect of purity, and the practice of idolatry, the latter being an extreme affront to God. Conversely, obedience to God's laws sanctifies His name. In later Jewish literature we encounter the notion of *ḥillul ha-shem,* "the desecration of God's name," which refers to acts that bring dishonor on God's people, Israel, or upon His Torah.[8]

13. You shall not defraud your fellow. The terms *ʿoshek,* "fraud," and *gazel,* "robbery," are explained in the Comment to 5:22.

The wages of a laborer shall not remain with you until morning Hebrew *peʿullah,* "wages," actually connotes both the effort and its reward, both labor and the compensation paid for labor.[9] Hebrew *sakhir,* "hired worker," is usually one paid for a particular job or for his time.[10]

14. You shall not insult the deaf The Hebrew verb *killel,* "to insult," literally "to treat lightly," reflects the adjective *kall,* "slight, of little importance." It is often used in contrast to *kibbed,* "to honor, treat with respect," and *barekh,* "to bless."[11] What is "light" is worth less than what is "heavy." In Hebrew to be "heavy" and to be "honored" are related concepts. Elsewhere the verb *killel* may have the more severe connotation "to curse, blaspheme," as in 24:14. Speaking ill of the deaf is especially reprehensible because it is taking unfair advantage of another's disability.

or place a stumbling block before the blind Compare Deuteronomy 27:18: "Cursed be he who misdirects a blind person on his way."

Later Jewish tradition interpreted the prohibition of placing a stumbling block before the blind as embodying a general norm of behavior. One should not tempt another person by preying on his weakness, his "blindness," so to speak, or mislead one who cannot properly "perceive" the facts of a situation.[12]

You shall fear your God This admonition seems especially appropriate for offenses that cannot be detected and that, therefore, are readily concealed. The deaf cannot hear what is being said about them, and the blind cannot see who causes them to stumble. But God sees and hears on their behalf and will punish their tormentors.

15. You shall not render an unfair decision The several commandments stated together in the verse represent still another instance of "the general followed by the specific." In other words, favoring the poor in judgment and giving preferential treatment to the rich are specific examples of the general category of unfair judgment.

Hebrew *loʾ taʿaseh ʿavel* literally means "Do not commit an injustice." Hebrew *ʿavel* is synonymous with *reshaʿ,* "wickedness," *mirmah,* "deceit," and *ḥamas,* "violence." Its antonyms are *ʾemunnah,* "trustworthiness," and *mishpat,* "justice."[13]

do not favor the poor In the pursuit of justice there can be no favoritism, even toward those for whom we have instinctive sympathy and who are otherwise deserving of our aid. This is stated in Exodus 23:3: "nor shall you show deference to a poor man in his dispute."

The Hebrew idiom *loʾ tissaʾ penei* literally means "Do not lift up the face of." An honored leader

fairly. 16Do not deal basely with your countrymen. Do not
profit by the blood of your fellow: I am the LORD.
17You shall not hate your kinsfolk in your heart. Reprove
your kinsman but incur no guilt because of him. 18You

תַעֲמֹד עַל־דַּם רֵעֶךָ אֲנִי יְהוָה׃ 17 לֹא־תִשְׂנָא
אֶת־אָחִיךָ בִּלְבָבֶךָ הוֹכֵחַ תּוֹכִיחַ אֶת־עֲמִיתֶךָ
וְלֹא־תִשָּׂא עָלָיו חֵטְא׃ 18 לֹא־תִקֹּם וְלֹא־תִטֹּר

may be known as *nesuʾ panim,* literally "one whose face is uplifted," or *nasiʾ,* literally "one elevated, raised above others," hence "a prince."[14]

or show deference to the rich Hebrew *gadol* means "a great person," but the context favors translating "rich" in contrast to *dall,* literally "one lacking in resources, poor."

judge your kinsman fairly On the sense of Hebrew *ʿamit,* "neighbor," see Comment to 18:20.

16. Do not deal basely with your countrymen Rather, "Do not act as a merchant toward your own kinsmen." This dictum remains ambiguous. Hebrew *rakhil* has usually been related to *rokhel,* "merchant."[15] The idiom *loʾ telekh rakhil* has been interpreted to mean that one should not move about in the manner of a merchant, who is presumed to be privy to secret dealings and gossip. This is how the sense of talebearing developed in postbiblical Hebrew.

In Jeremiah 6:28 and Ezekiel 22:9, *rakhil* is equated with acts of corruption and betrayal, even with murder.[16] As a consequence, many traditional commentators, among them Ibn Ezra, Ramban, Rashbam, and Rashi, relate the verbal root *r-kh-l* to *r-g-l,* "to spy."

The Sifra preserves the following interpretation: "That you not act as a merchant who merely loads up his horse and departs."[17] Now, Hebrew *be-ʿammekha* means "among, with your kinsmen." Perhaps the sense is that in dealing with one's own kinsmen one should not be "all business," interested solely in profit, but, rather, considerate and friendly. Merchants were often foreigners who felt no close ties to those with whom they did business. The passage, nevertheless, remains problematic.

Do not profit by the blood of your fellow This part of the verse is also difficult to interpret because of the problems in ascertaining the sense of the Hebrew idiom *loʾ taʿamod ʿal,* literally "do not stand over, by, near."

There have been three principal suggestions. The first, "to stand aside, to stand by," has the sense that one ought not to stand by inactively when one's neighbor's life is in danger. This is the interpretation of the Sifra, followed by Rashi and others. Targum Yerushalmi understands this statement in a similar way: "Do not be silent concerning the 'blood' of your comrade when you know the truth in a legal case." The second suggestion takes the Hebrew to mean "to conspire against, act against." Thus, Targum Onkelos reads: "Do not rise up against the life of your comrade" (Aram. *laʾ tekum ʿal damaʾ de-ḥavrakh*). This is similar to the interpretation of Ibn Ezra: "One ought not to join forces with murderers." "To stand over" has this sense in several biblical passages. The third explanation of the Hebrew is "to survive by means of, subsist, rely on." Ehrlich compares Ezekiel 33:26: *ʿamadta ʿal ḥarbekha,* "You have relied upon your sword for survival," with Genesis 27:40: *ʿal ḥarbekha tiḥyeh,* "Yet by your sword shall you live."[18] This last interpretation is the one expressed in the translation, and it best fits the immediate context. One ought not pursue one's own livelihood in a manner that endangers another or at the expense of another's well-being.

17. You shall not hate your kinsfolk in your heart Verses 17–18 constitute a unit. The context suggests the interpretation that an individual should not allow ill feelings to fester; rather, he should confront his kinsman and admonish him directly, in this way avoiding grudges and vengeance that breed hatred. Moreover, a proper attitude promotes love for one's neighbor. The opening statement (v. 17) contrasts with the conclusion (v. 18) as hate contrasts with love.

Reprove your kinsman but incur no guilt because of him Rather, "Reprove your neighbor so that you will not incur guilt on his account." As the sages put it: "Woe unto the wicked person, and woe unto his neighbor!" One may eventually suffer by being closely involved with wrongdoers, and it becomes necessary to protect oneself when close associates go astray. There is also the suggestion that, beyond self-interest, civic responsibility requires a person to admonish others out of concern for others and for the community as a whole. This line of interpretation is adopted by

shall not take vengeance or bear a grudge against your countrymen. Love your fellow as yourself: I am the LORD.

19You shall observe My laws.

You shall not let your cattle mate with a different kind; you shall not sow your field with two kinds of seed; you shall not put on cloth from a mixture of two kinds of material.

20If a man has carnal relations with a woman who is a slave and has been designated for another man, but has not been redeemed or given her freedom, there shall be an indemnity; they shall not, however, be put to death, since she has not been freed. 21But he must bring to the entrance

אֶת־בְּנֵי עַמֶּךָ וְאָהַבְתָּ לְרֵעֲךָ כָּמוֹךָ אֲנִי יְהוָה׃
19 אֶת־חֻקֹּתַי תִּשְׁמֹרוּ בְּהֶמְתְּךָ לֹא־תַרְבִּיעַ
כִּלְאַיִם שָׂדְךָ לֹא־תִזְרַע כִּלְאָיִם וּבֶגֶד כִּלְאַיִם
שַׁעַטְנֵז לֹא יַעֲלֶה עָלֶיךָ׃ פ 20 וְאִישׁ כִּי־
יִשְׁכַּב אֶת־אִשָּׁה שִׁכְבַת־זֶרַע וְהִוא שִׁפְחָה
נֶחֱרֶפֶת לְאִישׁ וְהָפְדֵּה לֹא נִפְדָּתָה אוֹ חֻפְשָׁה לֹא
נִתַּן־לָהּ בִּקֹּרֶת תִּהְיֶה לֹא יוּמְתוּ כִּי־לֹא חֻפָּשָׁה׃
21 וְהֵבִיא אֶת־אֲשָׁמוֹ לַיהוָה אֶל־פֶּתַח אֹהֶל מוֹעֵד

Ramban and is most often cited by the ancient sages. In the *Damascus Covenant,* one of the compositions known as The Dead Sea Scrolls, the duty to admonish fellow members of the community went so far as to require one to report wrongdoing on the part of others to a special examiner.[19]

18. *You shall not take vengeance or bear a grudge against your countrymen* Hebrew *tikkom* derives from the verb *n-k-m,* "to take vengeance," and *tittor* from *n-t-r,* "to keep, guard, retain." The sense is that one ought not to keep alive the memory of another's offense against him.[20]

Love your fellow as yourself The prefixed *lamed* in *le-reʿakha* indicates the direct object.[21] The sage Hillel paraphrased this commandment in a negative formulation: "What is hateful to you, do not do to your comrade."[22] Rabbi Akiba, quoted in the Sifra, once commented as follows on "Love your fellow as yourself" that "this is a central principle in the Torah" (*zeh kelal gadol ba-torah*).

19. *You shall observe My laws* On the meaning of Hebrew *ḥok,* "law," see Comment to 18:4. This statement introduces the particular laws that follow.

You shall not let your cattle mate with a different kind Hebrew *tarbiʿa* is from the root *r-b-ʿ,* "to crouch, lie down." The Hifil form used here means "to cause to crouch, to allow to lie down," hence "to mate."

Hebrew *kilʾayim* has been variously explained. It is most probably cognate with Ugaritic *klʾat,* "both," said of both hands, and with Akkadian *kilallan,* "both, a pair." On this basis, Hebrew *kilʾayim* would mean "two kinds (together)." It is used of animals, plants, grain, and cloth.[23]

The etymology of Hebrew *shaʿatnez,* "mixture," is not known. In Deuteronomy 22:11, it is defined as a fabric woven of linen and wool. The specifics of rabbinic law on this verse are treated extensively in the tractate Kilayim of the Mishnah.

20. *If a man has carnal relations with a woman who is a slave* The law of verses 20–22 is topically related to the Seventh Commandment because it hinges on the legalities of adultery, even though adultery is not actually involved here.

On the sense of Hebrew *shikhvat zeraʿ,* here rendered "carnal relations," see Comment to 18:20.

and has been designated for another man Rather, "and has been assigned in advance to another man." The Hebrew adjective *neḥrefet* can now be explained precisely. It is cognate with Akkadian *ḫarāpu,* "to be early, arrive early." On this basis *neḥrefet* would mean "assigned in advance," that is, in advance of redemption or manumission.[24] Compare Judges 5:18, literally "Zebulun is a tribe that precipitously exposed itself to death" (*ḥeref nafsho la-mut*). This verb is unrelated to the more frequent Hebrew verb *ḥeref,* "to blaspheme, slander."

there shall be an indemnity The term *bikkoret,* "indemnity," occurs only here in the Hebrew Bible. It is probably cognate with the Akkadian verb *baqāru,* "to make good on a claim, to indemnify." Biblical *bikkoret* is therefore also related to mishnaic *hevker,* "property over which one has relinquished his claim." In our verse, the term *bikkoret* designates the actual payment imposed on the responsible party.[25]

of the Tent of Meeting, as his guilt offering to the LORD, a ram of guilt offering. [22]With the ram of guilt offering the priest shall make expiation for him before the LORD for the sin that he committed; and the sin that he committed will be forgiven him.

[23]When you enter the land and plant any tree for food, you shall regard its fruit as forbidden. Three years it shall be forbidden for you, not to be eaten. [24]In the fourth year all

אֵיל אָשָׁם׃ 22 וְכִפֶּר עָלָיו הַכֹּהֵן בְּאֵיל הָאָשָׁם
לִפְנֵי יְהוָה עַל־חַטָּאתוֹ אֲשֶׁר חָטָא וְנִסְלַח לוֹ
מֵחַטָּאתוֹ אֲשֶׁר חָטָא׃ פ שלישי 23 וְכִי־
תָבֹאוּ אֶל־הָאָרֶץ וּנְטַעְתֶּם כָּל־עֵץ מַאֲכָל
וַעֲרַלְתֶּם עָרְלָתוֹ אֶת־פִּרְיוֹ שָׁלֹשׁ שָׁנִים יִהְיֶה לָכֶם
עֲרֵלִים לֹא יֵאָכֵל׃ 24 וּבַשָּׁנָה הָרְבִיעִת יִהְיֶה כָּל־

Some legal background is required by way of explanation. The law of Exodus 21:7–11 allows a father to sell his preadolescent daughter as a slave to another Israelite. This was usually done out of extreme deprivation or indebtedness. When the slave girl reached marriageable age, her master was required to do one of three things: marry her himself, designate her as his son's wife, or allow her to be redeemed. This last option was interpreted to mean that the master could pledge the girl to another Israelite. Although Exodus 21:8 prohibits the master from selling the girl to a non-Israelite, it does not prohibit such arrangements as would involve another Israelite man. The latter would redeem the girl by a payment to her master and take her as his wife.

The situation projected in our passage is as follows: An Israelite slave girl, here called *shifḥah,* was pledged by her master to another Israelite man. The designation had already been made, but had not been finalized by payment to the girl's master or, possibly, the man had not yet claimed his bride. Legally, the girl was still a slave and unmarried. If at this point, an outsider had carnal relations with her, he would have caused a loss to her master because, no longer a virgin, she would be less desirable as a wife, and the prospective husband would undoubtedly cancel the proposed marriage.

In parallel circumstances, Exodus 22:15–17 stipulates that one who seduced a free maiden who was not yet pledged as a wife had either to marry her himself or pay her father the equivalent of the marriage price (*mohar*). In our case, the option of marriage was ruled out because the girl had been pledged to another man—leaving only one way to deal with the situation. The man who had had carnal relations with the girl had to pay an indemnity to her master to compensate him for his loss. Presumably, since the marriage was called off, and the young woman rendered undesirable, the owner would have to continue maintaining her in his household.

21. *But he must bring . . . as his guilt offering to the LORD* An *'asham,* "guilt offering," is required here in addition to the indemnity because an act of defilement had been committed: a violation of holiness. The woman had been promised to another, and even though the union was not adulterous, it was, legally speaking, more than merely an act of seduction. In rabbinic sources, this guilt offering is known as *'asham shifḥah ḥarufah,* "the guilt offering of the *predesignated* slave woman."[26]

22. *shall make expiation for him* On the meaning of the verb *kipper,* "to expiate," see Comment to 4:20.

23. *When you enter the land* Verses 23–25 represent yet another casuistic passage, projected into the future.

and plant any tree for food On Hebrew *le-ma'akhal,* literally "for eating," cf. Genesis 2:9, 3:6, and so forth.

you shall regard its fruit as forbidden Rather, "You shall trim its fruit in the manner of a foreskin." The syntax is unusual. Literally, this clause would read: "You shall trim its foreskin as foreskin (*va-'araltem 'et 'orlato*). Here, we have a cognate accusative, that is, the verb and the object derive from the same root. Later on in the passage we find the masculine plural noun *'arelim,* "in a state of uncircumcision." Is this formula to be understood graphically, as involving physical acts, or figuratively, as the JPS translation conveys?

In biblical usage, the adjective *'arel* and the noun *'orlah* usually connote physical conditions that may have moral or religious ramifications. They may describe "thickening about your heart," which prevents the heart from experiencing proper attitudes, as in Deuteronomy 10:16. The metaphor is based on a real physical condition. Or, one may say, as in Jeremiah 6:10, that the ear is "blocked" by

its fruit shall be set aside for jubilation before the LORD;
25and only in the fifth year may you use its fruit—that its
yield to you may be increased: I the LORD am your God.
26You shall not eat anything with its blood. You shall not
practice divination or soothsaying. 27You shall not round

פִּרְי֑וֹ קֹ֥דֶשׁ הִלּוּלִ֖ים לַיהוָֽה׃ 25 וּבַשָּׁנָ֣ה הַחֲמִישִׁ֗ת
תֹּֽאכְלוּ֙ אֶת־פִּרְי֔וֹ לְהוֹסִ֥יף לָכֶ֖ם תְּבוּאָת֑וֹ אֲנִ֖י
יְהוָ֥ה אֱלֹהֵיכֶֽם׃ 26 לֹ֥א תֹאכְל֖וּ עַל־הַדָּ֑ם לֹ֥א
תְנַחֲשׁ֖וּ וְלֹ֥א תְעוֹנֵֽנוּ׃ 27 לֹ֣א תַקִּ֔פוּ פְּאַ֖ת רֹאשְׁכֶ֑ם

the earlobe, so that one is prevented from hearing God's words. Exodus 6:12,30 speaks of "uncircumcised" lips that make articulate speech difficult. In these cases, as well, the metaphor has its origin in a physical condition.

In applying the above usages to the fruit of trees and vines, the sense is to "trim" or "remove" certain growths. A good case can be made for understanding the law as requiring the trimming of trees and vines. Targum Onkelos merely reflects later interpretation in translating "You shall remove its fruit" in the same way that it renders the noun *ʿarelim,* later on in the verse, as "fruit removed for destruction." As a matter of law, rabbinic exegesis taught that fruit of the first three years be burned.[27] Trimming may have been the actual intent of biblical law.

24. *set aside for jubilation* The functional sense of Hebrew ***kodesh*** is "devoted, set aside." Hebrew ***hillulim,*** "jubilation," occurs in only one other biblical passage, Judges 9:27: "They [the Shechemites] went out into the fields, gathered and trod out the vintage of their vineyards, and [literally] celebrated rites of jubilation (*va-yaʿasu hillulim*). They entered the temple of their god . . . they ate and drank."

The noun ***hillulim*** derives from the same root as ***hillel,*** "to praise," but this verb has differentiated meanings, some positive and others decidedly negative. Thus, ***holelot*** means "revelry" as an improper pursuit.[28] These various forms of the same root share in common the onomatopoetic quality of *"h-l-l,"* which actually transmits a sound.[29] On that basis, the jubilant shouting at the time of the grape harvest is called ***hillulim.*** However, out of context this term does not inform us of the propriety of the celebration. So, ***hillulim*** in Judges 9:24 connotes a pagan rite, whereas the code in Leviticus obviously enjoins the Israelites to rejoice before the Lord, as they devote the fruits of the fourth year.

A similar celebration was envisioned by a prophet of the exile. God would soon restore Jerusalem and no longer permit Israel's enemies to eat up her grain or drink her wine. Thus, Isaiah 62:9: "But those who harvest it shall eat it, and [literally] celebrate jubilantly (*ve-hillelu*) before the LORD, and those who gather it shall drink it in My sacred courts."

25. *that its yield to you may be increased* Increase of yield is God's blessing.

26. *You shall not eat anything with its blood* Verses 26–28 contain several prohibitions against practices characteristic of the pagan Canaanites and other idolators. Hebrew ***loʾ toʾkhlu ʿal ha-dam,*** "You shall not eat anything with its blood in it," is a rare formulation occurring only here, in 1 Samuel 14:32–34, and in Ezekiel 33:25, which is reminiscent of our verse. It represents an alternate way of stating the prohibition of blood consumption, which we have already encountered several times in Leviticus.[30] The preposition ***ʿal*** means "together with," which is often its meaning in the ritual texts.[31]

Commentators, traditional and modern, have generally realized that the account in 1 Samuel 14 was basic for a proper understanding of our verse. During one of the Philistine wars, the Israelites suffered a setback (1 Sam. 14:24). King Saul, leader of the Israelites, hoping to turn the unfavorable tide of battle, adjured the people by a vow not to partake of the spoils taken from the enemy until nightfall, as an act of expiation. The people, weak and exhausted by combat, and unaware of Saul's ban against eating spoils, followed the example of Saul's own son, Jonathan, and began to slaughter cattle taken in battle: ***va-yoʾhklu ha-ʿam ʿal ha-dam,*** "The people ate [the meat] with its blood in it" (v. 32). They slaughtered the cattle on the bare ground, without recourse to an altar and without draining the blood.

To prevent more consumption of blood, Saul, following very ancient customs, used a local rock as an altar. He ordered that animals be brought to that spot for proper slaughter and, in this way, reminded the people that the blood of animals was to be dashed on the altar and drained from them before the flesh could be eaten. The account in 1 Samuel 14 thus describes quite vividly what is meant

off the side-growth on your head, or destroy the side-growth of your beard. 28 You shall not make gashes in your flesh for the dead, or incise any marks on yourselves: I am the LORD.

29 Do not degrade your daughter and make her a harlot, lest the land fall into harlotry and the land be filled with depravity. 30 You shall keep My sabbaths and venerate My sanctuary: I am the LORD.

וְלֹ֣א תַשְׁחִ֔ית אֵ֖ת פְּאַ֥ת זְקָנֶֽךָ׃ 28 וְשֶׂ֣רֶט לָנֶ֗פֶשׁ
לֹ֤א תִתְּנוּ֙ בִּבְשַׂרְכֶ֔ם וּכְתֹ֣בֶת קַֽעֲקַ֔ע לֹ֥א תִתְּנ֖וּ
בָּכֶ֑ם אֲנִ֖י יְהוָֽה׃ 29 אַל־תְּחַלֵּ֥ל אֶת־בִּתְּךָ֖ לְהַזְנוֹתָ֑הּ
וְלֹא־תִזְנֶ֣ה הָאָ֔רֶץ וּמָלְאָ֥ה הָאָ֖רֶץ זִמָּֽה׃ 30 אֶת־
שַׁבְּתֹתַ֣י תִּשְׁמֹ֔רוּ וּמִקְדָּשִׁ֖י תִּירָ֑אוּ אֲנִ֖י יְהוָֽה׃

by eating meat with its blood in it. In our verse, the prohibition against eating blood is formulated apodictically, leaving no room for exceptions and providing no explanations, such as are found elsewhere in chapter 17 and in Deuteronomy 12.

Some commentators, including Ramban, express the view that eating blood was a magical act, on the order of the other magical practices prohibited in verses 26–28.

You shall not practice divination or soothsaying Some have interpreted Hebrew *lo' tenaḥashu* as reflecting a denominative verb based on *naḥash,* "snake," since snakes were employed in pronouncing charms. More likely, however, the verb *niḥesh* is related to the verb *l-ḥ-sh,* "to whisper, pronounce an incantation." In Hebrew, *nun* and *lamed* can interchange phonetically. All we know from the Bible about the manner of pronouncing incantations is that goblets were used in the process.[32]

Hebrew *ve-lo' teʿonenu,* "and do not practice soothsaying," may be related to reading the omens of the clouds, since in Hebrew, the word for cloud is *ʿanan.* We possess extensive information on the ominous role of clouds in ancient Near Eastern divination. The forms of clouds, their times of appearance, their movements and positions, and the heavenly bodies they obscure were all factors in interpreting omens.[33] Isaiah 2:6 refers to Philistines as engaging in such practices.[34]

27. ***You shall not round off the side-growth on your head*** Hebrew *pe'ah,* "side-growth," is the same word used in verse 9 to designate the corner, or edge, of a field. Hebrew *lo' takkifu,* "you shall not round off," derives from the verb *n-k-f,* "to encircle." Certain peoples who inhabited desert areas are referred to as *ketsutsei pe'ah,* "men with their side-growth cut off."[35]

or destroy the side-growth of your beard Tearing out the hair of one's beard, as well as of the head, was a custom associated with mourning over the dead.[36]

28. ***You shall not make gashes in your flesh for the dead*** In Elijah's contest with the cult prophets of Baal, recounted in 1 Kings 18, we read that the pagan priests gashed themselves as they called upon Baal to answer their prayers. Hebrew *nefesh* may connote a dead body as well as a living person.[37]

or incise any marks Hebrew *kaʿkaʿ* remains unexplained, though its meaning is clear in context. Hebrew *ketovet* incorporates the verb *k-t-v,* "to write," which is also said of incising on stone, so that it could designate some form of tattoo.[38]

29. ***Do not degrade your daughter and make her a harlot*** The verb *ḥillel,* earlier encountered in verse 11, means "to defile, profane." Harlotry was a violation of holiness that resulted in a status similar, for example, to cultic defilement of sacred objects. The verb *zanah* has many connotations, and although harlotry is not necessarily tantamount to adultery, an adulteress may be referred to as *zonah,* thus characterizing her infidelity as being similar to the promiscuity of a harlot.

lest the land fall into harlotry and the land be filled with depravity In biblical idiom "land" may connote the people of the land, as is the intent here. On the sense of Hebrew *zimmah,* "depravity," see Comment to 18:17.[39]

30. ***You shall keep My sabbaths and venerate My sanctuary*** See above, in verse 3, and the restatement in 26:2. In Ezekiel 22:8, "My sabbaths" is paralleled by *kodashai,* "My sacred things," namely, sacred offerings.[40]

³¹Do not turn to ghosts and do not inquire of familiar spirits, to be defiled by them: I the LORD am your God.

³²You shall rise before the aged and show deference to the old; you shall fear your God: I am the LORD.

³³When a stranger resides with you in your land, you shall not wrong him. ³⁴The stranger who resides with you shall be to you as one of your citizens; you shall love him as yourself, for you were strangers in the land of Egypt: I the LORD am your God. ³⁵You shall not falsify measures of length, weight, or capacity. ³⁶You shall have an honest

³¹ אַל־תִּפְנ֤וּ אֶל־הָֽאֹבֹת֙ וְאֶל־הַיִּדְּעֹנִ֔ים אַל־תְּבַקְשׁ֖וּ לְטׇמְאָ֣ה בָהֶ֑ם אֲנִ֖י יְהֹוָ֥ה אֱלֹהֵיכֶֽם׃ ³² מִפְּנֵ֤י שֵׂיבָה֙ תָּק֔וּם וְהָדַרְתָּ֖ פְּנֵ֣י זָקֵ֑ן וְיָרֵ֥אתָ מֵּאֱלֹהֶ֖יךָ אֲנִ֥י יְהֹוָֽה׃ פ   רביעי   [ששי

כשהן מחוברות] ³³ וְכִֽי־יָג֧וּר אִתְּךָ֛ גֵּ֖ר בְּאַרְצְכֶ֑ם לֹ֥א תוֹנ֖וּ אֹתֽוֹ׃ ³⁴ כְּאֶזְרָ֣ח מִכֶּ֗ם יִהְיֶ֤ה לָכֶם֙ הַגֵּ֣ר ׀ הַגָּ֣ר אִתְּכֶ֔ם וְאָהַבְתָּ֥ לוֹ֙ כָּמ֔וֹךָ כִּֽי־גֵרִ֥ים הֱיִיתֶ֖ם בְּאֶ֣רֶץ מִצְרָ֑יִם אֲנִ֖י יְהֹוָ֥ה אֱלֹהֵיכֶֽם׃ ³⁵ לֹא־תַעֲשׂ֥וּ עָ֙וֶל֙ בַּמִּשְׁפָּ֔ט בַּמִּדָּ֕ה בַּמִּשְׁקָ֖ל וּבַמְּשׂוּרָֽה׃

---

31. *Do not turn to ghosts and do not inquire of familiar spirits* On the sense of Hebrew *'al tifnu 'el,* "do not turn to," see verse 4. Hebrew *'ov* is of uncertain origin.⁴¹ It was a part of the magic known to the pagans of Canaan. In 1 Samuel 28:3f., it is related that King Saul, after having outlawed recourse to mediums, actually consulted a woman known as *ba'alat 'ov,* "a sorceress," who conjured up the ghost of the prophet Samuel from the earth. In Isaiah 29:4, we read: "Your speech shall sound like a ghost's *(ke-'ov)* from the ground." Reference is to spiritualist communication with the dead in the netherworld. Hebrew *yid'oni* is usually thought to derive from the verb *y-d-',* "to know, be familiar with," which yields the translation "familiar spirit," namely, the spirits of deceased relatives or intimates.

The verb *tevakkeshu,* "inquire of," suggests that we are dealing with oracular inquiry or augury. Elsewhere we also find the verbs *d-r-sh* and *sh-'-l,* "to inquire of," used in connection with the *'ov* and *yid'oni.*⁴²

to be defiled by them Recourse to such magical practices, typical of idolatrous religions, renders one figuratively impure.⁴³

32. *You shall rise before the aged and show deference to the old* On the sense of the Hebrew verb *h-d-r,* "to show deference," see verse 15. According to later rabbinic law, one was required to show deference to the elderly by caring for them.⁴⁴

you shall fear your God See Comment to verse 14. Respect for the elderly is the sign of a decent society; in a society where proper behavior has broken down, the young fail to respect their elders.⁴⁵

33. *When a stranger resides with you in your land, you shall not wrong him* The Torah, and the Bible generally, emphasize the duty to treat resident foreigners as fairly as one is commanded to treat a citizen.⁴⁶ Verse 10 includes the *ger,* "stranger," among those entitled to the leftovers of the harvest. The *ger* referred to in the Bible was most often a foreign merchant or craftsman or a mercenary soldier. This term never refers to the prior inhabitants of the land; those are identified by ethnological groupings, such as Canaanites and Amorites, or by other specific terms of reference.

In the biblical ethos, the importance of being considerate to foreign residents drew added impetus from the memory of the Israelite sojourn in Egypt—Israelites should be able to empathize with the alien.⁴⁷ In fact, because of xenophobic attitudes, which could lead to extreme acts of violence against strangers, most ancient societies had laws protecting foreign merchants, officials, and others.

Hebrew *lo' tonu,* "do not wrong," usually connotes economic exploitation, the deprivation of property, or denial of legal rights.⁴⁸ It was used with particular reference to those who suffered from lack of legal redress, such as the poor, the widow and the orphan, along with the foreigner.

34. *as one of your citizens* Hebrew *'ezrah,* and the fuller designation *'ezrah ha-'arets,* "the permanent resident of the land," are terms of uncertain etymology. It has been suggested that *'ezrah* was originally a botanical term for a tree or plant that is well rooted in the soil. We read in Psalms 37:35: "well-rooted like a robust native tree" *(ke'ezrah ra'anan).* If this derivation is correct, an *'ezrah* is one whose lineage has "roots" in the land, one who belongs to the group that possesses the land.⁴⁹ However, the term *'ezrah* is never applied to the prior inhabitants of Canaan.

balance, honest weights, an honest *ephah*, and an honest *hin*.

I the LORD am your God who freed you from the land of Egypt. 37You shall faithfully observe all My laws and all My rules: I am the LORD.

36 מֹאזְנֵ֤י צֶ֙דֶק֙ אַבְנֵי־צֶ֔דֶק אֵ֥יפַת צֶ֛דֶק וְהִ֥ין צֶ֖דֶק
יִהְיֶ֣ה לָכֶ֑ם אֲנִי֙ יְהוָ֣ה אֱלֹֽהֵיכֶ֔ם אֲשֶׁר־הוֹצֵ֥אתִי
אֶתְכֶ֖ם מֵאֶ֥רֶץ מִצְרָֽיִם׃ 37 וּשְׁמַרְתֶּ֤ם אֶת־כָּל־
חֻקֹּתַי֙ וְאֶת־כָּל־מִשְׁפָּטַ֔י וַעֲשִׂיתֶ֖ם אֹתָ֑ם אֲנִ֖י יְהוָֽה׃
פ חמישי

*35. **You shall not falsify measures*** The Hebrew reads: "You shall not commit an injustice." See Comment to verse 15.

of length, weight, or capacity Hebrew *middah* is a general term for all sorts of measurements. Here it refers to surface, area, measurement, whereas *mesurah* is a term for liquid capacity.[50]

*36. **You shall have an honest balance . . .*** Similar admonitions occur in Deuteronomy 25:14–15 and Ezekiel 45:10. The ancient scales (*mo'znayim*) had an upright, on which two cups or plates were balanced. In one was a stone or iron weight (*'even*), and the other held the goods to be weighed. Hebrew *'efah,* as a dry measure of capacity, was equal to one-tenth of a *ḥomer;* and, as a liquid measure of capacity, was equal to the *bat,* which contained approximately twenty-two liters. Hebrew *hin* was a liquid measure equal to one-sixth of a *bat,* or approximately 3.6 liters.[51] These are merely specific examples of weights and measures, intended to illustrate the general rule requiring honesty.

I the LORD am your God . . . This statement resembles the First Commandment in its emphasis on the liberation from Egypt.[52]

*37. **You shall faithfully observe*** The two Hebrew verbs *u-shemartem va-ʿasitem* do not refer to two separate acts but rather reinforce each other: "You shall take care to perform."

CHAPTER 20

The Family in Religious Context

Chapter 20 reformulates the essential content of chapter 18 on the subject of incest and forbidden sexual activity. It also reflects certain themes known from chapter 19. There are, however, two main differences between chapters 18 and 20.

In the first instance, the contents of chapter 18 are for the most part formulated apodictically, as categorical imperatives ("Do not . . . ," "You shall . . . ," etc.). As is normally true of apodictic texts, a penalty is not specified for each offense. There is only a collective penalty, formulated within the overall framework of the admonition against pagan worship. Chapter 20, on the other hand, is formulated casuistically in the form of case law ("If . . . ," "When . . . ," etc.). Thus, in addition to an overall admonition, it provides specific penalties, often of a capital nature, for each offense.

The second, major difference between chapters 18 and 20 concerns their characterizations of pagan religions. Chapter 18 speaks out, in verses 1–3, against the ways of the Canaanites and Egyptians, a theme referred to only briefly in chapter 20, in verse 26. Chapter 20 opens with a major statement against the cult of Molech (vv. 1–5), a subject that had been only mentioned once before, in 18:21. The introductory statement is followed in verse 6 by a prohibition against necromancy, a theme addressed again in verse 27. The chapters' distinctive perspective must surely reflect their different historical background. What is common to both chapters is the assumed connection between pagan worship and sexual degeneracy—both are regarded as the causes of exile.

The grouping of the laws in chapter 20 reflects legal distinctions. Verses 1–16 deal with capital offenses, whereas verses 17–21 concern violations for which the penalty is being "cut off" from the Israelite community. This penalty is imposed for certain marital violations that were not considered sufficiently severe to warrant punishment by death.[1] These included marriage with half sisters (v. 17), with aunts (v. 19), and with any woman who had once been married to one's brother (v. 21).

20 And the LORD spoke to Moses: ²Say further to the Israelite people:

Anyone among the Israelites, or among the strangers residing in Israel, who gives any of his offspring to Molech, shall be put to death; the people of the land shall pelt him with stones. ³And I will set My face against that man and will cut him off from among his people, because he gave of his offspring to Molech and so defiled My sanctuary and profaned My holy name. ⁴And if the people of the land

ב וַיְדַבֵּ֥ר יְהֹוָ֖ה אֶל־מֹשֶׁ֥ה לֵּאמֹֽר: 2 וְאֶל־בְּנֵ֨י יִשְׂרָאֵ֜ל תֹּאמַ֗ר אִ֣ישׁ אִישׁ֩ מִבְּנֵ֨י יִשְׂרָאֵ֜ל וּמִן־הַגֵּ֣ר ׀ הַגָּ֣ר בְּיִשְׂרָאֵ֗ל אֲשֶׁ֨ר יִתֵּ֤ן מִזַּרְעוֹ֙ לַמֹּ֔לֶךְ מ֣וֹת יוּמָ֑ת עַ֥ם הָאָ֖רֶץ יִרְגְּמֻ֥הוּ בָאָֽבֶן: 3 וַאֲנִ֞י אֶתֵּ֤ן אֶת־פָּנַי֙ בָּאִ֣ישׁ הַה֔וּא וְהִכְרַתִּ֥י אֹת֖וֹ מִקֶּ֣רֶב עַמּ֑וֹ כִּ֤י מִזַּרְעוֹ֙ נָתַ֣ן לַמֹּ֔לֶךְ לְמַ֗עַן טַמֵּא֙ אֶת־מִקְדָּשִׁ֔י וּלְחַלֵּ֖ל אֶת־שֵׁ֥ם קׇדְשִֽׁי: 4 וְאִ֡ם הַעְלֵ֣ם יַעְלִ֩ימוּ֩ עַ֨ם הָאָ֜רֶץ אֶת־

2. ***Say further to the Israelite people*** Literally, "And to the Israelite people say." The inverted syntax is for emphasis, to reinforce the idea that what follows is addressed to the entire people. The initial, prefixed *vav*, "And," suggests that the provisions of this chapter are additions to what had already been stated in chapter 18.

Anyone among the Israelites The Hebrew reads *mi-benei yisra'el*, "from among the Israelites," rather than *mi-beit yisra'el*, "from the household of Israel," as in 17:3,8. These two terms are virtually synonymous in priestly literature, although each has a history of its own. On the formulation *'ish 'ish*, "any man," see comment to 17:3.

or among the strangers residing in Israel See Comments to 16:9 and 17:8 on the matter of resident aliens and their legal status. The worship of other gods was forbidden to all who resided in the Land of Israel, whether or not they were Israelites.

who gives any of his offspring to Molech On the name Molech (or Moloch) see Comment to 18:21 and Excursus 7. In 18:21, we find a similar injunction, formulated as *lo' titten le-ha'avir*, "you shall not devote for handing over." The verb *n-t-n* more precisely connotes *devotion* to a god in both passages.[2]

shall be put to death; the people of the land shall pelt him with stones The Hofal form of the verb, *yummat*, "he shall be put to death," means execution by human hands.[3] The Hebrew term *'am ha-'arets*, "people of the land," is explained in the Comment to 4:27. It usually refers to those citizens who have a voice in the affairs of the community. The Hebrew verb *r-g-m* is used specifically to describe what is done with stones; they are either thrown or hurled with a slingshot.[4] Elsewhere, stoning is the penalty for blasphemy as well.[5] The question arises as to how the sentence was to be carried out. In Deuteronomy 17:1–7 we also read that one convicted of worshiping other gods is to be stoned. There it is stipulated that the witnesses for the prosecution should cast the first stones, to be followed by others of the community. This suggests that the execution took place subsequent to a trial and was under judicial control.

3. ***And I will set My face against that man and will cut him off*** The Hebrew idiom *ve-nattati panai be-*, "I will set My face against," expresses the intent to punish. In the Hebrew Bible, it is said only of God Himself, and it incorporates the notion of God's "face" or "presence" as a potent force that can either assist or punish.[6] Here, the "cutting off" of the offender is expressed by an active transitive form of the verb, *ve-hikhratti*, "I will cut off." God is the subject who "cuts off." This provides further support for what has already been said, that the penalty known as *karet* was complex and could be understood both as a divine punishment and as an action taken by the community.[7] In the case before us, the punitive process is twofold. The community is commanded to put the offender to death. Should it fail to do its duty, God will punish the offender in His own way. This dynamic is further clarified by the provisions of verses 4–6 below.

and so defiled My sanctuary and profaned My holy name The profanation of God's name is explained in the Comment to 19:12. A central doctrine of the ritual legislation is that pagan worship, however manifested, rendered the sanctuary impure. Such practices usually involved either the introduction of pagan cult objects into the sanctuary or their installation near it.[8] This obviously polluted the sanctuary. But, even in the absence of actual physical intrusion, the very act of disobedience to God by members of the community effectively defiled the sanctuary, which stood

should shut their eyes to that man when he gives of his offspring to Molech, and should not put him to death, [5]I Myself will set My face against that man and his kin, and will cut off from among their people both him and all who follow him in going astray after Molech. [6]And if any person turns to ghosts and familiar spirits and goes astray after them, I will set My face against that person and cut him off from among his people.

[7]You shall sanctify yourselves and be holy, for I the LORD am your God. [8]You shall faithfully observe My laws: I the LORD make you holy.

[9]If anyone insults his father or his mother, he shall be put to death; he has insulted his father and his mother—his bloodguilt is upon him.

[10]If a man commits adultery with a married woman, committing adultery with another man's wife, the adulterer and the adulteress shall be put to death. [11]If a man lies with his father's wife, it is the nakedness of his father that he has uncovered; the two shall be put to death—their bloodguilt is upon them. [12]If a man lies with his daughter-in-law,

עֵֽינֵיהֶם֙ מִן־הָאִ֣ישׁ הַה֔וּא בְּתִתּ֥וֹ מִזַּרְע֖וֹ לַמֹּ֑לֶךְ לְבִלְתִּ֖י הָמִ֥ית אֹתֽוֹ: 5 וְשַׂמְתִּ֨י אֲנִ֜י אֶת־פָּנַ֗י בָּאִ֤ישׁ הַהוּא֙ וּבְמִשְׁפַּחְתּ֔וֹ וְהִכְרַתִּ֣י אֹת֗וֹ וְאֵ֧ת ׀ כָּל־הַזֹּנִ֛ים אַחֲרָ֖יו לִזְנ֣וֹת אַחֲרֵ֣י הַמֹּ֑לֶךְ מִקֶּ֖רֶב עַמָּֽם: 6 וְהַנֶּ֗פֶשׁ אֲשֶׁ֨ר תִּפְנֶ֤ה אֶל־הָֽאֹבֹת֙ וְאֶל־הַיִּדְּעֹנִ֔ים לִזְנ֖וֹת אַחֲרֵיהֶ֑ם וְנָתַתִּ֤י אֶת־פָּנַי֙ בַּנֶּ֣פֶשׁ הַה֔וּא וְהִכְרַתִּ֥י אֹת֖וֹ מִקֶּ֥רֶב עַמּֽוֹ: 7 וְהִ֨תְקַדִּשְׁתֶּ֔ם וִהְיִיתֶ֖ם קְדֹשִׁ֑ים כִּ֛י אֲנִ֥י יְהֹוָ֖ה אֱלֹהֵיכֶֽם: שׁשׁי [שְׁביעי כשהן מחוברות] 8 וּשְׁמַרְתֶּם֙ אֶת־חֻקֹּתַ֔י וַעֲשִׂיתֶ֖ם אֹתָ֑ם אֲנִ֥י יְהֹוָ֖ה מְקַדִּשְׁכֶֽם: 9 כִּֽי־אִ֣ישׁ אִ֗ישׁ אֲשֶׁ֨ר יְקַלֵּ֧ל אֶת־אָבִ֛יו וְאֶת־אִמּ֖וֹ מ֣וֹת יוּמָ֑ת אָבִ֧יו וְאִמּ֛וֹ קִלֵּ֖ל דָּמָ֥יו בּֽוֹ: 10 וְאִ֗ישׁ אֲשֶׁ֤ר יִנְאַף֙ אֶת־אֵ֣שֶׁת אִ֔ישׁ אֲשֶׁ֥ר יִנְאַ֖ף אֶת־אֵ֣שֶׁת רֵעֵ֑הוּ מֽוֹת־יוּמַ֥ת הַנֹּאֵ֖ף וְהַנֹּאָֽפֶת: 11 וְאִ֗ישׁ אֲשֶׁ֤ר יִשְׁכַּב֙ אֶת־אֵ֣שֶׁת אָבִ֔יו עֶרְוַ֥ת אָבִ֖יו גִּלָּ֑ה מֽוֹת־יֽוּמְת֥וּ שְׁנֵיהֶ֖ם דְּמֵיהֶ֥ם בָּֽם: 12 וְאִ֗ישׁ אֲשֶׁ֤ר יִשְׁכַּב֙ אֶת־כַּלָּת֔וֹ מ֥וֹת יֽוּמְת֖וּ

within the settlement. The purity of the sanctuary, which was not only a function of physical condition, was endangered by any actions that aroused God's wrath, whether or not actual contact had occurred.

     4. ***should shut their eyes***   What the community neglects to do, God will do! The verb *he'elim*, "to shut [the eye]," is idiomatic for negligence.[9]

     5. ***Against . . . his kin . . . in going astray after Molech***   Hebrew *mishpahah*, "clan" ("kin"), designates the basic sociological unit in ancient Israelite society.[10] It is presumed that the clan tends to act together in matters of worship, following the way of its leaders. The verb *z-n-h*, "to go astray," essentially connotes sexual waywardness and is proverbial as a metaphor for the worship of other gods.[11]

     6. ***And if any person turns to ghosts***   This verse restates casuistically what has been commanded in 19:4, where the term *'ov*, "ghost," is explained. Although the death penalty is not stipulated in this verse, it is stated in verse 27, as though in retrospect. This law is part of the section (vv. 1–16) that deals with capital offenses. According to the Mishnah Sanhedrin 7:4, the necromancer is liable to the death penalty. Furthermore, verses 2–4, which deal with similar offenses, also stipulate the death penalty. It is likely, therefore, that verse 6 is abbreviated.

     7. ***You shall sanctify yourselves and be holy***   This verse restates 19:2, and its command is repeated, for emphasis, in verse 26.

FORBIDDEN SEXUAL UNIONS   (vv. 8–21)

     8. ***You shall faithfully observe My laws***   Compare 18:20 and 19:37 for similar statements.

     I the LORD make you holy   See Comment to 11:44, where this statement is discussed.

     9. ***If anyone insults his father or his mother***   See Comment to 19:14.

     his bloodguilt is upon him   Hebrew *dam*, "blood," and the plural *damim* often connote the death penalty. (See further in vv. 11–13,16,27.)[12] In Deuteronomy 18:18, a case involving murder is referred to simply as *dam*.

both of them shall be put to death; they have committed incest—their bloodguilt is upon them. [13]If a man lies with a male as one lies with a woman, the two of them have done an abhorrent thing; they shall be put to death—their bloodguilt is upon them. [14]If a man marries a woman and her mother, it is depravity; both he and they shall be put to the fire, that there be no depravity among you. [15]If a man has carnal relations with a beast, he shall be put to death; and you shall kill the beast. [16]If a woman approaches any beast to mate with it, you shall kill the woman and the beast; they shall be put to death—their bloodguilt is upon them.

[17]If a man marries his sister, the daughter of either his father or his mother, so that he sees her nakedness and she sees his nakedness, it is a disgrace; they shall be excommunicated in the sight of their kinsfolk. He has uncovered the nakedness of his sister, he shall bear his guilt. [18]If a man

שְׁנֵיהֶם תֶּבֶל עָשׂוּ דְּמֵיהֶם בָּם׃ 13 וְאִישׁ אֲשֶׁר
יִשְׁכַּב אֶת־זָכָר מִשְׁכְּבֵי אִשָּׁה תּוֹעֵבָה עָשׂוּ
שְׁנֵיהֶם מוֹת יוּמָתוּ דְּמֵיהֶם בָּם׃ 14 וְאִישׁ אֲשֶׁר
יִקַּח אֶת־אִשָּׁה וְאֶת־אִמָּהּ זִמָּה הִוא בָּאֵשׁ יִשְׂרְפוּ
אֹתוֹ וְאֶתְהֶן וְלֹא־תִהְיֶה זִמָּה בְּתוֹכְכֶם׃ 15 וְאִישׁ
אֲשֶׁר יִתֵּן שְׁכָבְתּוֹ בִּבְהֵמָה מוֹת יוּמָת וְאֶת־
הַבְּהֵמָה תַּהֲרֹגוּ׃ 16 וְאִשָּׁה אֲשֶׁר תִּקְרַב אֶל־כָּל־
בְּהֵמָה לְרִבְעָה אֹתָהּ וְהָרַגְתָּ אֶת־הָאִשָּׁה וְאֶת־
הַבְּהֵמָה מוֹת יוּמָתוּ דְּמֵיהֶם בָּם׃ 17 וְאִישׁ אֲשֶׁר־
יִקַּח אֶת־אֲחֹתוֹ בַּת־אָבִיו אוֹ בַת־אִמּוֹ וְרָאָה אֶת־
עֶרְוָתָהּ וְהִיא־תִרְאֶה אֶת־עֶרְוָתוֹ חֶסֶד הוּא
וְנִכְרְתוּ לְעֵינֵי בְּנֵי עַמָּם עֶרְוַת אֲחֹתוֹ גִּלָּה עֲוֺנוֹ
יִשָּׂא׃ 18 וְאִישׁ אֲשֶׁר־יִשְׁכַּב אֶת־אִשָּׁה דָּוָה וְגִלָּה

14. ***If a man marries a woman and her mother*** Compare 18:17.

both he and they shall be put to the fire The unusual feminine object pronoun *'ethen,* "them," occurs thirteen times in the Hebrew Bible. The usual form is *'otan.*

Death by fire bore a special relationship to forbidden sexual behavior. According to 21:9, the daughter of a priest who degrades herself by harlotry is to be punished in this manner. And in the account of Genesis 38:24, Judah threatened his daughter-in-law Tamar with death by fire when he learned that she had become pregnant while awaiting levirate marriage, an offense tantamount to adultery.

15–16. ***If a man has carnal relations with a beast . . . If a woman approaches any beast*** Compare 18:23, where the commandment concerns a woman who has sexual relations with a beast.

and you shall kill the beast In the law of Exodus 21:28–29, it is ordained that a bull who has gored a man to death must be put to death. Here, however, the danger is not of the same sort; the punishment in this case derives from the notion that animals, like humans, also bear guilt. As we are told in Jonah 3:7–8, the herds and flocks of Nineveh participated in the repentance of the city, along with the king and citizenry. The same attribution of moral norms to the animal kingdom is expressed in the Flood stories of Genesis 6:7 and 9:5. Mishnah Sanhedrin 7:4 explains that it would be unseemly to allow an animal that had been involved in the corruption of a human being to be seen walking about. This theme is also discussed in Excursus 2, "The Meaning of the Dietary Laws."

17. ***If a man marries his sister*** Compare Leviticus 18:9,11 and Deuteronomy 27:22. The verb *l-k-ḥ,* "to acquire" as a wife, is a legal term for marriage.[13] In 18:9,11, the prohibition is expressed in terms of sexual access rather than legality, as it is here.

it is a disgrace Hebrew *ḥesed,* as it is used here, is unrelated to the noun *ḥesed,* "steadfast love, kindness," found so frequently in the Bible. This is an instance of homonyms, two words written alike and that sound alike, but that have no etymological connection. In this verse, *ḥesed* is cognate with Aramaic *ḥasda'* and Syriac *ḥesda',* "ignominy, disgrace." In Genesis 30:23, Targum Onkelos renders Hebrew *ḥerpah,* "shame," as *ḥasda'*.

they shall be excommunicated in the sight of their kinsfolk This is a way of expressing banishment.[14]

18. ***If a man lies with a woman in her infirmity*** Intercourse with a menstruating woman is forbidden, as stated in 18:19. Hebrew *davah* means "ill, infirm."[15] In the continuation of this verse,

lies with a woman in her infirmity and uncovers her nakedness, he has laid bare her flow and she has exposed her blood flow; both of them shall be cut off from among their people. ¹⁹You shall not uncover the nakedness of your mother's sister or of your father's sister, for that is laying bare one's own flesh; they shall bear their guilt. ²⁰If a man lies with his uncle's wife, it is his uncle's nakedness that he has uncovered. They shall bear their guilt: they shall die childless. ²¹If a man marries the wife of his brother, it is indecency. It is the nakedness of his brother that he has uncovered; they shall remain childless.

²²You shall faithfully observe all My laws and all My regulations, lest the land to which I bring you to settle in spew you out. ²³You shall not follow the practices of the nation that I am driving out before you. For it is because they did all these things that I abhorred them ²⁴and said to you: You shall possess their land, for I will give it to you to possess, a land flowing with milk and honey. I the LORD am your God who has set you apart from other peoples. ²⁵So

אֶת־עֶרְוָתָהּ֙ אֶת־מְקֹרָ֣הּ הֶֽעֱרָ֔ה וְהִ֕יא גִּלְּתָ֖ה אֶת־
מְק֣וֹר דָּמֶ֑יהָ וְנִכְרְת֥וּ שְׁנֵיהֶ֖ם מִקֶּ֥רֶב עַמָּֽם׃
¹⁹ וְעֶרְוַ֨ת אֲח֧וֹת אִמְּךָ֛ וַאֲח֥וֹת אָבִ֖יךָ לֹ֣א תְגַלֵּ֑ה כִּ֧י
אֶת־שְׁאֵר֛וֹ הֶעֱרָ֖ה עֲוֺנָ֥ם יִשָּֽׂאוּ׃ ²⁰ וְאִ֗ישׁ אֲשֶׁ֤ר
יִשְׁכַּב֙ אֶת־דֹּ֣דָת֔וֹ עֶרְוַ֥ת דֹּד֖וֹ גִּלָּ֑ה חֶטְאָ֣ם יִשָּׂ֔אוּ
עֲרִירִ֖ים יָמֻֽתוּ׃ ²¹ וְאִ֕ישׁ אֲשֶׁ֥ר יִקַּ֖ח אֶת־אֵ֣שֶׁת
אָחִ֑יו נִדָּ֣ה הִ֔וא עֶרְוַ֥ת אָחִ֛יו גִּלָּ֖ה עֲרִירִ֥ים יִהְיֽוּ׃
²² וּשְׁמַרְתֶּ֤ם אֶת־כׇּל־חֻקֹּתַי֙ וְאֶת־כׇּל־מִשְׁפָּטַ֔י
וַעֲשִׂיתֶ֖ם אֹתָ֑ם וְלֹא־תָקִ֤יא אֶתְכֶם֙ הָאָ֔רֶץ אֲשֶׁ֨ר
אֲנִ֜י מֵבִ֧יא אֶתְכֶ֛ם שָׁ֖מָּה לָשֶׁ֥בֶת בָּֽהּ׃ שביעי
²³ וְלֹ֤א תֵֽלְכוּ֙ בְּחֻקֹּ֣ת הַגּ֔וֹי אֲשֶׁר־אֲנִ֥י מְשַׁלֵּ֖חַ
מִפְּנֵיכֶ֑ם כִּ֤י אֶת־כׇּל־אֵ֙לֶּה֙ עָשׂ֔וּ וָאָקֻ֖ץ בָּֽם׃
²⁴ וָאֹמַ֣ר לָכֶ֗ם אַתֶּם֮ תִּֽירְשׁ֣וּ אֶת־אַדְמָתָם֒ וַאֲנִ֞י
אֶתְּנֶ֤נָּה לָכֶם֙ לָרֶ֣שֶׁת אֹתָ֔הּ אֶ֛רֶץ זָבַ֥ת חָלָ֖ב וּדְבָ֑שׁ
אֲנִי֙ יְהֹוָ֣ה אֱלֹֽהֵיכֶ֔ם אֲשֶׁר־הִבְדַּ֥לְתִּי אֶתְכֶ֖ם מִן־
הָֽעַמִּֽים׃ מפטיר ²⁵ וְהִבְדַּלְתֶּ֞ם בֵּֽין־הַבְּהֵמָ֤ה

we encounter several other Hebrew terms that require explanation. The noun *makor,* "source, spring," also refers to the source of the blood flow in the case of a menstruating woman, as is explained in the Comment to 12:7. The verb *heʿerah,* "he uncovered," is related to *ʿervah,* "nakedness."

   19.   *You shall not uncover the nakedness of your mother's sister*   Compare 18:6, 13–14.

   20.   *If a man lies with his uncle's wife . . . they shall die childless*   Compare 18:13–14. The association between childlessness and being "cut off" from the community is explained in Excursus 1.

   21.   *If a man marries the wife of his brother, it is indecency*   Compare 18:16. Hebrew *niddah* means "menstruation, a menstruating woman." Here this term is extended to mean "disgrace, indecency." The application of this image to socioreligious situations derives from the widespread metaphaor of Israel as a faithless bride.[16]

POSSESSION OF THE LAND   (vv. 21–27)

   22.   *You shall faithfully observe all My laws*   This statement introduces the closing admonition of verses 22–26, which is only loosely connected to the specifics of the rest of the chapter. Similar language is to be found in 18:24–28.

   23.   *I abhorred them*   The Hebrew verb used here is *kuts,* "to abhor," which elsewhere conveys the sense of extreme frustration and dislike.[17]

   24.   *You shall possess their land*   The Hebrew verb *y-r-sh,* "to possess," belongs to the ancient vocabulary expressing the collective rights of the Israelites to the land of Canaan. Although the verb eventually appropriated the additional meaning of "inherit," its primary sense had nothing necessarily to do with inheritance.[18] Thus, God allotted the land of Canaan to the people of Israel, "to possess" as its estate, and it was then divided, clan by clan; only once this process was under way did inheritance become a factor.

   a land flowing with milk and honey   This is a well-known characterization of the land of Canaan in biblical literature.[19] Hebrew *devash,* "honey," usually refers to the nectar of trees.[20] As such, this depiction projects a land with plentiful, milk-producing herds and flocks and abounding in fruit trees, especially the date palm.

you shall set apart the clean beast from the unclean, the unclean bird from the clean. You shall not draw abomination upon yourselves through beast or bird or anything with which the ground is alive, which I have set apart for you to treat as unclean. 26You shall be holy to Me, for I the Lord am holy, and I have set you apart from other peoples to be Mine.

27A man or a woman who has a ghost or a familiar spirit shall be put to death; they shall be pelted with stones— their bloodguilt shall be upon them.

הַטְּהֹרָה֙ לַטְּמֵאָ֔ה וּבֵין־הָע֥וֹף הַטָּמֵ֖א לַטָּהֹ֑ר וְלֹֽא־
תְשַׁקְּצ֨וּ אֶת־נַפְשֹֽׁתֵיכֶ֜ם בַּבְּהֵמָ֣ה וּבָע֗וֹף וּבְכֹל֙
אֲשֶׁ֣ר תִּרְמֹ֣שׂ הָֽאֲדָמָ֔ה אֲשֶׁר־הִבְדַּ֥לְתִּי לָכֶ֖ם
לְטַמֵּֽא׃ 26 וִהְיִ֤יתֶם לִי֙ קְדֹשִׁ֔ים כִּ֥י קָד֖וֹשׁ אֲנִ֣י יְהוָ֑ה
וָאַבְדִּ֥ל אֶתְכֶ֛ם מִן־הָֽעַמִּ֖ים לִֽהְי֥וֹת לִֽי׃ 27 וְאִ֣ישׁ
אֽוֹ־אִשָּׁ֗ה כִּֽי־יִהְיֶ֨ה בָהֶ֥ם א֛וֹב א֥וֹ יִדְּעֹנִ֖י מ֣וֹת יוּמָ֑תוּ
בָּאֶ֛בֶן יִרְגְּמ֥וּ אֹתָ֖ם דְּמֵיהֶ֥ם בָּֽם׃ פ

who has set you apart from other peoples Although the distinctiveness of Israel is a major theme in biblical literature, it is rare to read that God actively "separates" Israel, a notion conveyed by the Hifil verb *hivdil,* "to divide, separate." In the following verses, the separateness of Israel, involving their duty to live differently from other nations, is the stated rationale for the requirement to observe the dietary laws, which are the subject of chapter 11.[21]

25. So you shall set apart the clean beast from the unclean As has generally been advocated, it is more precise to render the Hebrew terms *tahor* and *tame'* as "pure" and "impure," respectively, rather than as "clean" and "unclean." The conditions described by these terms are defined by the laws of purity, not by any specific notion of hygiene or physical cleanliness. In this instance, the Israelites must carefully differentiate between the pure and the impure, in emulation of God's ways. He had set them apart; they must do likewise.

You shall not draw abomination upon yourselves The Hebrew verb *shikkets* means "to make something unfit, to consider it unfit."[22]

26. You shall be holy . . . See verse 7.

27. A man or woman who has a ghost or a familiar spirit The insertion of this verse at the conclusion of chapter 20 is rather puzzling, since it seems to be an afterthought. Its addition here may have been occasioned by the omission of the death penalty from the earlier reference to this subject in verse 6.

Laws Governing the Priesthood　　　(21:1–22:33)

Emor　　Chapters 21 and 22 of Leviticus differ significantly from the rest of the Holiness Code (chaps. 17–26) in that they are addressed primarily to the priesthood, not to the Israelite people as a whole.[1] This orientation reflects the special content of these two chapters. They deal with the following subjects: (1) laws of purity, which prohibit priests from having contact with the dead; (2) marital restrictions imposed on the priests; (3) the requirement of physical soundness for the officiating priesthood; and (4) the prerequisites for partaking of "sacred donations" allocated to the priests as their food. In addition, paralleling the requirement of physical soundness for priests is the requirement that sacrificial animals also be free of physical defects.

The varied laws of chapters 21 and 22 are organized as follows: Both the code for ordinary priests (21:1–9) and the code for the High Priest (21:10–15) begin with funerary regulations and conclude with marital restrictions. This establishes a symmetry. Logical sequence is evident in subsequent sections of these two chapters, as well. Thus, 21:16–24 enumerates the bodily defects that render a priest unfit to officiate in the sacrificial cult, whereas 22:1–9, immediately following, deals with priests who become impure, but whose unfitness is only temporary. Finally, 22:10–16 states the privileges of the priesthood. Only they, not lay Israelites, may partake of "sacred donations." Taken as a whole, the section from 21:16 to 22:16 addresses the two basic issues of who may officiate in the sacrificial cult and who may partake of sacred donations.

In 22:17–33, the remaining section of this unit, we find a collection of diverse ordinances applicable to Israelites who participate in religious life by donating sacrificial offerings. All sacrificial animals must be complete (possessing all limbs and organs) and without blemish (22:17–25); newborn animals may not be sacrificed until they are eight days old; and an animal may not be sacrificed on the same day as its mother (22:26–28). In conclusion, 22:29–33 prescribes special regulations governing the thanksgiving offering (*todah*), which was a sacrifice frequently donated by individual Israelites.

Three subjects discussed in chapters 21–22 deserve special comment: the office of the High Priest, the marital and funerary restrictions imposed on the priesthood, and the general requirement of physical soundness, for priests and sacrificial offerings alike.

Both the funerary and the marital restrictions express the concern that priests preserve the purity of their persons. Priestly impurity, which resulted from contact with the dead and from impure marriages, could, in turn, render the sanctuary itself impure. Although the impurity of corpses affected everyone, it was permissible for an Israelite to become impure, when necessary; such an individual could then be restored to purity by following the proper procedures.[2] Priests, by exception, were not similarly permitted, except in the case of an ordinary priest, who was granted a dispensation when one of his close relatives died. The High Priest, however, was prevented from attending even the burial of his own parents. In effect, this law eliminated a funerary role for the Israelite priesthood. There can be little doubt that this fact, resulting from the attribution of extreme impurity to the human corpse, reflects the abhorrence felt in ancient Israel toward the cult of the dead. Worship of the dead was a widespread phenomenon in the ancient Near East, as it was elsewhere; and priests, as officiants in religious cults, usually had a prominent funerary role—as was not the case in the monotheistic religion of ancient Israel.[3]

The marital restrictions imposed on the priesthood set an ideal standard for a wife: a virgin, usually from one's own patrilineal clan or tribe. Although mandated for the High Priest, a dispensation was granted to the ordinary priest to marry a widow, but not a divorcée or harlot. This last restriction must be explained, especially as regards the divorcée. (The prohibition against marrying a harlot requires no explanation.) In Mosaic law, summarized in Deuteronomy 24:1f., the only clear grounds for divorce was serious sexual misconduct, as explained in the Comment to verse 7. Sexual immorality was a religious sin, an offense against God, in addition to its obvious interpersonal offensiveness. Consequently, a divorced woman was stigmatized and considered unfit for marriage to a priest.

The last subject of these chapters, the insistence on physical soundness, both for officiating priests and for sacrificial victims, reflects the notion that God, demanding the very best, would be offended were any blemished or imperfect person or animal to come unto His immediate presence. Nevertheless, even though a disfigured priest could not officiate in the cult, he was not denied his priestly emoluments. There is a marked correspondence between the physical defects that render a priest unfit to officiate and those that render a sacrificial animal unacceptable, as this chart illustrates.

Priest	***Sacrificial Animal***
Blindness	Blindness
A broken arm or leg	One injured or maimed
Scurvy	Scurvy
A boil-scar	A boil or scar
A limb too short or too long	A limb extended or contracted
Crushed testes	Crushed, bruised, torn, or cut testes
A growth in the eye	A wen[4]

The code for the priesthood presented in chapter 21, in particular, bears a striking correspondence to Ezekiel 44. Specific similarities are noted in Comments to the relevant verses.[5]

EMOR

21 The LORD said to Moses: Speak to the priests, the sons of Aaron, and say to them:

None shall defile himself for any [dead] person among his kin, [2]except for the relatives that are closest to him: his mother, his father, his son, his daughter, and his brother; [3]also for a virgin sister, close to him because she has not married, for her he may defile himself. [4]But he shall not defile himself as a kinsman by marriage, and so profane himself.

אמר

כ״א וַיֹּאמֶר יְהֹוָה אֶל־מֹשֶׁה אֱמֹר אֶל־הַכֹּהֲנִים
בְּנֵי אַהֲרֹן וְאָמַרְתָּ אֲלֵהֶם לְנֶפֶשׁ לֹא־יִטַּמָּא
בְּעַמָּיו: 2 כִּי אִם־לִשְׁאֵרוֹ הַקָּרֹב אֵלָיו לְאִמּוֹ
וּלְאָבִיו וְלִבְנוֹ וּלְבִתּוֹ וּלְאָחִיו: 3 וְלַאֲחֹתוֹ הַבְּתוּלָה
הַקְּרוֹבָה אֵלָיו אֲשֶׁר לֹא־הָיְתָה לְאִישׁ לָהּ יִטַּמָּא:
4 לֹא יִטַּמָּא בַּעַל בְּעַמָּיו לְהֵחַלּוֹ: 5 לֹא־יקרחה

v. 5. יִקְרְחוּ ק׳

CHAPTER 21 RESTRICTIONS AND LIMITATIONS (vv. 1–24)

1. *None shall defile himself for any [dead] person among his kin* Similar provisions occur in Ezekiel 44:25: "[A priest] shall not defile himself by entering [a house] where there is a dead person. He shall defile himself only for father or mother, son or daughter, brother or unmarried sister." The term *nefesh,* "[dead] person," occurs in a more explicit form in verse 11 as *nefesh met,* "a dead body."[6]

The precise sense of Hebrew *ʿam* is crucial for understanding the provisions of this chapter. It can designate an entire people or a more limited group.[7] In chapter 21, its consistent meaning is "kin." In verses 1–4, the social context is the clan. As a general rule, an ordinary priest may not become defiled by contact with the dead of his own clan, but he may for those members of his clan who are most closely related to him. Attending to the burial of clan relatives was a traditional duty.

2. *except for the relatives that are closest to him* Alternatively, "Except for his 'flesh' relatives, who are closest to him." The meaning of Hebrew *sheʾer,* "flesh," as a kinship term is explained in the introductory Comment to chapter 18.

The adjective *karov,* "near," can function as a noun with the meaning of "relative." Originally, it expressed physical proximity as well as familial closeness, since extended families often lived together. Thus, according to verse 3, a sister who marries and leaves the family domicile is no longer "close" because she belongs to another family. Note that here, mother precedes father in the list of *sheʾer* relatives, as is true in 19:3, in the commandment to revere one's parents.

3. *also for a virgin sister, close to him because she has not married* The sister is "close" until she marries and goes to live with her husband's family. Then, presumably, there would be others to attend to her burial. According to the Sifra, even a betrothed woman who still resides in her father's household is considered "close." The idiom *ʾasher loʾ hayetah le-ʾish,* "who has never 'belonged' to a man" refers to the legal status of a woman in marriage and to sexual union in marriage.[8]

4. *But he shall not defile himself as a kinsman by marriage* Hebrew *baʿal be-ʿammav,* literally "a husband as one among his kin," is difficult and has been so regarded since late antiquity. The simple sense is that a priest, in the role of husband, is not permitted to attend to the burial of his wife. A man's wife is not his consanguineal relative, but his affinal relative, that is, she is related to him through marriage. All six relatives at whose death a priest may render himself impure are "flesh" relatives—his parents, his brother and sister (under certain conditions), and his son and daughter. Rashbam explains this statement as follows: "No husband (*baʿal*) from among the 'kinship' [of the priesthood] (*be-ʿammav*) may defile himself for his wife." This is, however, a forced explanation.

We can presume that normally an Israelite was responsible for attending to his wife's burial. A rabbinic tradition cites Genesis 2:24 in this regard: "Hence a man leaves his father and his mother and clings to his wife, so that they become one flesh (*basar ʾeḥad*)."[9] This was taken to mean that a man's wife was to be treated as a "flesh" relative in certain respects. Both Abraham and Jacob personally attended to their wives' burials, which suggests that it was a husband's duty to do so.[10] But in the case of a priest, purity took precedence and could be set aside only for attending to strictly consanguineal

5 They shall not shave smooth any part of their heads, or cut the side-growth of their beards, or make gashes in their flesh. 6 They shall be holy to their God and not profane the name of their God; for they offer the LORD's offerings by fire, the food of their God, and so must be holy.

7 They shall not marry a woman defiled by harlotry, nor shall they marry one divorced from her husband. For they are holy to their God 8 and you must treat them as holy,

קָרְחָה בְּרֹאשָׁם וּפְאַת זְקָנָם לֹא יְגַלֵּחוּ וּבִבְשָׂרָם
לֹא יִשְׂרְטוּ שָׂרָטֶת׃ 6 קְדֹשִׁים יִהְיוּ לֵאלֹהֵיהֶם
וְלֹא יְחַלְּלוּ שֵׁם אֱלֹהֵיהֶם כִּי אֶת־אִשֵּׁי יְהוָה לֶחֶם
אֱלֹהֵיהֶם הֵם מַקְרִיבִם וְהָיוּ קֹדֶשׁ׃ 7 אִשָּׁה זֹנָה
וַחֲלָלָה לֹא יִקָּחוּ וְאִשָּׁה גְּרוּשָׁה מֵאִישָׁהּ לֹא יִקָּחוּ
כִּי־קָדֹשׁ הוּא לֵאלֹהָיו׃ 8 וְקִדַּשְׁתּוֹ כִּי־אֶת־לֶחֶם

relatives. At a later period, a basis was found in the law to allow the involvement of a priest in his wife's burial. As Maimonides explains: "As regards the wife of a priest—one must render himself impure, even against his will; but the duty to render himself impure is only by enactment of the Scribes. They (the Scribes) gave her (the wife of a priest) the status of 'a dead person whom one is commanded to bury' (*met mitsvah*)."[11] This means that this duty is not ordained in the Torah. It was reasoned by the sages that situations might arise where such a woman's only heir would be her husband, and if he failed to attend to her burial, there would be no one else to do so.

and so profane himself The Hebrew verbal form *le-heḥallo,* "to profane himself," is rare. It derives from the root *ḥ-l-l,* "to profane, render unfit." It is a Nifal form with reflexive force, which means, as Ibn Ezra observes, that the action is projected onto oneself.

5. ***They shall not shave smooth*** A similar prohibition is stated in Ezekiel 44:20. The verb *k-r-ḥ,* "to make one's head bald," derives from the noun ***korḥah,*** "baldness, bald spot," and the adjective ***kereaḥ,*** "bald." It connotes the removal of all hair from the pate or from a section of it, either by shaving or by pulling out the hair at its roots. Deuteronomy 14:1 prohibits all Israelites from doing this, but it is understandable that this code should emphasize this prohibition with respect to the priests. Like gashing, shaving the hair and pulling it out were rites of mourning in ancient Canaan that Israelite religious leaders sought to prevent.[12]

6. ***They shall be holy to their God*** See Comments to 18:21 and 19:12; and see 22:32 for comparable statements.

offerings by fire On the sense of Hebrew *'isheh,* "offering by fire," see Comment to 1:9.

the food of their God, and so must be holy Sacrificial offerings are often called *leḥem,* "food," and at least in a symbolic sense are considered food for God.[13] The priests must observe strict codes of purity because they are the ones charged with performance of the rites of the sacred cult.

7. ***defiled by harlotry*** The translation takes the Hebrew ***zonah va-ḥalalah*** as a hendiadys, the use of two words to express a single concept, hence, "degraded by harlotry." This corresponds to the wording in verse 11, where we read *zonah ḥalalah,* "a degraded harlot."

The later tradition created a category of unfit priests called *ḥalalim,* "degraded priests," which also included the sons and daughters of priests who had violated certain rules of the priesthood. This is not explicitly provided for in the laws of the Torah. However, it may be suggested by verse 15, where it is said, apropos of the High Priest, "that he may not profane (*ve-lo' yeḥallel*) his offspring."

The rabbinic tradition also provides various definitions of ***zonah,*** "harlot." This term is most often applied to a woman habitually given to harlotry, not to one who may have lapsed on a particular occasion.[14]

nor . . . one divorced from her husband The law prohibiting priests from marrying divorced women persisted into later Judaism. It was adopted by the Christian church for its clergy, who were consecrated; and was also applied to Christian kings. There is a specific reason for this ban, which explains why the divorcée and the harlot are mentioned together. Hoffmann explains that this priestly ban helps to clarify the view of the House of Shammai as to the grounds for divorce. In the law of Deuteronomy 24:1, it is stipulated that a man may divorce his wife if he discovers in her behavior literally "some matter that was sexually improper" (*'ervat davar*), which was taken to mean that only the presumption of marital infidelity constituted legal grounds for initiating divorce. In an effort to

since they offer the food of your God; they shall be holy to you, for I the LORD who sanctify you am holy.

9 When the daughter of a priest defiles herself through harlotry, it is her father whom she defiles; she shall be put to the fire.

10 The priest who is exalted above his fellows, on whose head the anointing oil has been poured and who has been ordained to wear the vestments, shall not bare his head or rend his vestments. 11 He shall not go in where there is any dead body; he shall not defile himself even for his father or mother. 12 He shall not go outside the sanctuary and pro-

אֱלֹהֶיךָ הוּא מַקְרִיב קָדֹשׁ יִהְיֶה־לָּךְ כִּי קָדוֹשׁ אֲנִי
יְהוָה מְקַדִּשְׁכֶם: 9 וּבַת אִישׁ כֹּהֵן כִּי תֵחֵל לִזְנוֹת
אֶת־אָבִיהָ הִיא מְחַלֶּלֶת בָּאֵשׁ תִּשָּׂרֵף: ס
10 וְהַכֹּהֵן הַגָּדוֹל מֵאֶחָיו אֲשֶׁר־יוּצַק עַל־רֹאשׁוֹ׀
שֶׁמֶן הַמִּשְׁחָה וּמִלֵּא אֶת־יָדוֹ לִלְבֹּשׁ אֶת־הַבְּגָדִים
אֶת־רֹאשׁוֹ לֹא יִפְרָע וּבְגָדָיו לֹא יִפְרֹם: 11 וְעַל
כָּל־נַפְשֹׁת מֵת לֹא יָבֹא לְאָבִיו וּלְאִמּוֹ לֹא יִטַּמָּא:
12 וּמִן־הַמִּקְדָּשׁ לֹא יֵצֵא וְלֹא יְחַלֵּל אֵת מִקְדַּשׁ

broaden the grounds for divorce, the House of Hillel, whose view is reported in Gittin 90a, departed from the original sense of *ʿervat davar* in maintaining that *ʿervah*, "nakedness, sexuality," was not the only "matter" (*davar*) that could serve as grounds for divorce. So, although this wider interpretation became normative in later Judaism, it was not originally envisioned in the laws of the Torah. In biblical times, it is likely that divorce always involved a charge of infidelity by the husband. If that charge was made when the marriage was first consummated, the husband had to substantiate it in accordance with the law of Deuteronomy 22:13–14. At other times, a husband could subject his wife to an ordeal if he suspected that she was pregnant by another man, as we read in Numbers 5:11–31. If there was adequate testimony to prove adultery on the wife's part, she was subject to the death penalty under the law of Deuteronomy 22:23–24. In most cases, however, there was insufficient evidence to condemn a woman under this law. There was, however, sufficient motivation for a husband to charge his wife with adultery, thereby accomplishing what he truly sought—divorce.

9. defiles herself through harlotry The verb *teḥel* literally means "to perform a degrading act, to cause defilement." It derives from the same root as *le-heḥallo*, "to profane himself," in verse 4.[15]

it is her father whom she defiles; she shall be put to the fire The behavior of a priest's daughter reflects on her father's sacral office. Death by fire indicates the seriousness of the offense. When Jacob's son Judah learned that Tamar, his daughter-in-law, was pregnant at a time when she was awaiting levirate marriage, he said: "Bring her out . . . and let her be burned" (Gen. 38:24). It seems, therefore, that it was the custom to impose death by burning in the case of serious sexual offenses.

10. The priest who is exalted above his fellows According to Hoffmann, the full title *ha-kohen ha-gadol me-ʾeḥav*, "the priest who is 'greater' than his brothers," is abbreviated as *ha-kohen ha-gadol*, "the chief priest." The full title helps to define the status of the High Priest, so-called, whose distinction derives from two factors. He is the only priest to receive unction with the "oil of anointing," according to the primary laws of Leviticus, and he wears unique vestments.[16]

and who has been ordained On the sense of the technical idiom "to fill the hand," see Comments to 8:28,33.

shall not bare his head or rend his vestments A similar prohibition against baring the head appears in Ezekiel 44:20. On the meaning of the two verbs *paraʿ*, "to bare the head, dishevel the hair," and *param*, "to tear," see Comment to 10:6, where these traditional signs of mourning are explained.[17]

11. He shall not go in where there is any dead body The wording of this verse is strange. Usually, the Hebrew construction *baʾ ʿal* means "to advance against," or "to befall" a person, or even "to appear" at a particular time.[18] In Ezekiel 44:25, which contains the same law, the usage is slightly different, namely, *baʾ ʾel*, "to enter, go in." The two Hebrew prepositions *ʾel* and *ʿal* are often interchangeable, however, and the same meaning may be intended in both statements, here and in Ezekiel. On the other hand, the preposition *ʿal* can mean "on account of, because of," in which

fane the sanctuary of his God, for upon him is the distinction of the anointing oil of his God, Mine the LORD's. 13He
may marry only a woman who is a virgin. 14A widow, or a
divorced woman, or one who is degraded by harlotry—
such he may not marry. Only a virgin of his own kin may he
take to wife—15that he may not profane his offspring
among his kin, for I the LORD have sanctified him.
16The LORD spoke further to Moses: 17Speak to Aaron and
say: No man of your offspring throughout the ages who has
a defect shall be qualified to offer the food of his God. 18No
one at all who has a defect shall be qualified: no man who is
blind, or lame, or has a limb too short or too long; 19no

אֱלֹהָיו כִּי נֵזֶר שֶׁמֶן מִשְׁחַת אֱלֹהָיו עָלָיו אֲנִי
יְהוָה׃ 13 וְהוּא אִשָּׁה בִבְתוּלֶיהָ יִקָּח׃ 14 אַלְמָנָה
וּגְרוּשָׁה וַחֲלָלָה זֹנָה אֶת־אֵלֶּה לֹא יִקָּח כִּי אִם־
בְּתוּלָה מֵעַמָּיו יִקַּח אִשָּׁה׃ 15 וְלֹא־יְחַלֵּל זַרְעוֹ
בְּעַמָּיו כִּי אֲנִי יְהוָה מְקַדְּשׁוֹ׃ פ שני
16 וַיְדַבֵּר יְהוָה אֶל־מֹשֶׁה לֵּאמֹר׃ 17 דַּבֵּר אֶל־
אַהֲרֹן לֵאמֹר אִישׁ מִזַּרְעֲךָ לְדֹרֹתָם אֲשֶׁר יִהְיֶה בוֹ
מוּם לֹא יִקְרַב לְהַקְרִיב לֶחֶם אֱלֹהָיו׃ 18 כִּי כָל־
אִישׁ אֲשֶׁר־בּוֹ מוּם לֹא יִקְרָב אִישׁ עִוֵּר אוֹ פִסֵּחַ
אוֹ חָרֻם אוֹ שָׂרוּעַ׃ 19 אוֹ אִישׁ אֲשֶׁר־יִהְיֶה בוֹ

case this verse could be rendered: "He shall not enter [anywhere] *on account of* a dead body," namely, to attend to a dead body.[19]

he shall not defile himself even for his father or mother In the Hebrew, the word order is inverted for emphasis. The indirect object precedes the verb: "Even for his father or mother he shall not defile himself."

12. ***He shall not go outside the sanctuary*** The High Priest may not leave the sanctuary even for the purpose of attending to the burial of close relatives, including his own parents. The impurity that would result from his contact with the dead would defile the sanctuary upon his return. In effect, he could never purify himself so completely as to avoid the danger of contaminating the Holy of Holies. Hebrew ***mikdash,*** "holy place, sanctuary," is a basic term for a building that served as a sanctuary.[20]

for upon him is the distinction of the anointing oil of his God The translation "distinction" for Hebrew ***nezer*** precisely reflects the etymology of this word. The Hebrew verb ***nazar*** means "to set apart, devote," from which we have ***nazir,*** "one who has vowed to abstain from, to avoid" certain foodstuffs or activities or "one who is distinguished, set apart from others" by position.[21] Once before, in 8:9, the Hebrew term ***nezer ha-kodesh*** was translated "the holy diadem." In that context, reference is to the frontlet of gold worn by the High Priest on certain occasions. Functionally, ***nezer*** can connote a crown or diadem, which is a symbol of distinction, but that is not the derivation of the term itself.

13–14. ***He may marry only a woman who is a virgin. . . . Only a virgin of his own kin may he take to wife*** Again, the term ***ʿam,*** "kin," refers specifically to the priestly clan, as was true in verses 1 and 4. This means that the High Priest must marry a virgin from a priestly family. Verse 15 reasons that if he were to marry outside the priestly kinship, he would profane "his offspring among his kin" (***zarʿo be-ʿamav***). They would be unfit to serve as priests. Ezekiel 44:22, in a similar law, permits the High Priest to marry any virgin "from the offspring of Israel" (***mi-zeraʿ yisraʾel***).

17. ***No man of your offspring throughout the ages who has a defect*** Hebrew ***mum,*** "defect, blemish," is used with respect to both humans and animals. A ***mum*** may be the result of an injury, as is indicated in 24:19–20.

shall be qualified to offer the food of his God On the sense of Hebrew ***leḥem,*** "food," as a way of referring to sacrificial offerings, see Comment to verse 6. Priests who are physically unsound are deprived only of the right to officiate in the cult, not of their emoluments, since it is through no fault of their own that they suffer from such defects.

18. ***no man who is blind, or lame*** The Hebrew adjective ***ʿivver,*** "blind," may refer to a person who has only one good eye or who has lost one eye; it does not necessarily connote total blindness. The adjective ***pisseaḥ,*** "lame," refers to one who cannot walk properly, who cannot "straddle." It can refer to a person who is lame in one leg.[22] Custom frowned on the entry of anyone who was crippled into the sacred precincts of the sanctuary.[23]

man who has a broken leg or a broken arm; [20]or who is a
hunchback, or a dwarf, or who has a growth in his eye, or
who has a boilscar, or scurvy, or crushed testes. [21]No man
among the offspring of Aaron the priest who has a defect
shall be qualified to offer the LORD's offering by fire; having
a defect, he shall not be qualified to offer the food of his
God. [22]He may eat of the food of his God, of the most holy
well as of the holy; [23]but he shall not enter behind the curtain or come near the altar, for he has a defect. He shall
not profane these places sacred to Me, for I the LORD
have sanctified them.

[24]Thus Moses spoke to Aaron and his sons and to all the
Israelites.

שֶׁבֶר רָגֶל אוֹ שֶׁבֶר יָד: 20 אוֹ־גִבֵּן אוֹ־דַק אוֹ
תְּבַלֻּל בְּעֵינוֹ אוֹ גָרָב אוֹ יַלֶּפֶת אוֹ מְרוֹחַ אָשֶׁךְ:
21 כָּל־אִישׁ אֲשֶׁר־בּוֹ מוּם מִזֶּרַע אַהֲרֹן הַכֹּהֵן לֹא
יִגַּשׁ לְהַקְרִיב אֶת־אִשֵּׁי יְהוָה מוּם בּוֹ אֵת לֶחֶם
אֱלֹהָיו לֹא יִגַּשׁ לְהַקְרִיב: 22 לֶחֶם אֱלֹהָיו מִקָּדְשֵׁי
הַקֳּדָשִׁים וּמִן־הַקֳּדָשִׁים יֹאכֵל: 23 אַךְ אֶל־הַפָּרֹכֶת
לֹא יָבֹא וְאֶל־הַמִּזְבֵּחַ לֹא יִגַּשׁ כִּי־מוּם בּוֹ וְלֹא
יְחַלֵּל אֶת־מִקְדָּשַׁי כִּי אֲנִי יְהוָה מְקַדְּשָׁם:
24 וַיְדַבֵּר מֹשֶׁה אֶל־אַהֲרֹן וְאֶל־בָּנָיו וְאֶל־כָּל־בְּנֵי
יִשְׂרָאֵל: פ

or has a limb too short or too long The pair of adjectives *ḥarum ʾo saruʿa* has been interpreted variously. Hebrew *saruʿa* clearly means "extended, raised" according to the Sifra.[24] If a contrast was intended, *ḥarum* should mean "adumbrated, shortened." The Akkadian verb *arāmu* (also written *ḫarāmu*) means "to cover, stretch over," as by a membrane or by flesh. It is used in medical texts to describe birth defects.[25] On this basis, Hebrew *ḥarum* may designate one whose skin was stretched over an unnaturally short limb.

19. ***a broken leg or a broken arm*** Normally, such injuries would be permanent because broken limbs were not set properly in ancient times.

20. ***or who is a hunchback, or a dwarf*** The adjective *gibben,* "hunchback," is related to the noun *gavnunnim,* "crass, rocky terrain," which occurs in Psalms 68:17–18, and also to Late Hebrew *gabbenet,* "a hunch" on the back.[26] The Hebrew adjective *dak* most often means "thin," but on the basis of Akkadian cognates, we know that its basic meaning is "small," which is its sense here.[27]

or who has a growth in his eye, or who has a boil-scar, or scurvy Hebrew *tevallul* is explained in Bekhorot 28b as "a white line in the pupil of the eye." This term derives from the root *b-l-l,* "to mix, pour over," and in Akkadian the cognate *balālu* may mean "to be spotted." It is so used in omens, with reference to the color of animals and humans.[28]

Hebrew *garav,* "boil-scar," is cognate with Akkadian *garabu,* a kind of eczema or scab, perhaps a form of dermatitis.[29] The noun *yallefet* is explained in Bekhorot 41a as "flaky skin," a condition reported as prevalent in Egypt.[30]

or crushed testes Hebrew *meroaḥ ʾeshekh* literally means "one whose testicles are rubbed, crushed." The noun *ʾeshekh* occurs only here in the Hebrew Bible, but it is cognate with Akkadian *išku* and Ugaritic *ušk.*[31] Deuteronomy 23:2 forbids a man with this condition to marry within the Israelite fold because he would be unable to beget children.

21. ***No man . . . shall be qualified to offer the LORD's offering by fire*** Literally, "No man shall *approach* so as to offer. . . ."

22. ***He may eat of the food of his God*** A physically defective priest was prohibited only from officiating; he was not denied his emoluments. The intent was to prevent his presence in the holy precincts where sacrifices were offered—at the altar of sacrifice or inside the Shrine proper.

23. ***He shall not profane these places sacred to Me*** The plural *mikdashai,* "My holy places," is somewhat unusual, but we can compare Jeremiah 51:51: *mikdeshei beit YHVH,* "the sacred areas of the LORD's House," as well as Psalms 68:36: *mi-mikdasheikha,* "in your holy places." This rendering underscores the spatial factor, the question of where the defective priests would have been stationed were they officiating in the cult.[32]

24. ***Thus Moses spoke to Aaron and his sons and to all the Israelites.*** We are not told what Moses said because the verb has no object. This verse, a postscript, serves to link the special provisions of chapter 21 with the rest of the Holiness Code. In stating that these laws are addressed to all the

22 The LORD spoke to Moses, saying: [2]Instruct Aaron and
his sons to be scrupulous about the sacred donations that
the Israelite people consecrate to Me, lest they profane My
holy name, Mine the LORD's. [3]Say to them:
Throughout the ages, if any man among your offspring,
while in a state of uncleanness, partakes of any sacred
donation that the Israelite people may consecrate to the
LORD, that person shall be cut off from before Me: I am the
LORD. [4]No man of Aaron's offspring who has an eruption or
a discharge shall eat of the sacred donations until he is
clean. If one touches anything made unclean by a corpse, or
if a man has an emission of semen, [5]or if a man touches any

כ״ב וַיְדַבֵּר יְהוָה אֶל־מֹשֶׁה לֵּאמֹר: 2 דַּבֵּר אֶל־
אַהֲרֹן וְאֶל־בָּנָיו וְיִנָּזְרוּ מִקָּדְשֵׁי בְנֵי־יִשְׂרָאֵל וְלֹא
יְחַלְּלוּ אֶת־שֵׁם קָדְשִׁי אֲשֶׁר הֵם מַקְדִּשִׁים לִי אֲנִי
יְהוָה: 3 אֱמֹר אֲלֵהֶם לְדֹרֹתֵיכֶם כָּל־אִישׁ ׀ אֲשֶׁר־
יִקְרַב מִכָּל־זַרְעֲכֶם אֶל־הַקֳּדָשִׁים אֲשֶׁר יַקְדִּישׁוּ
בְנֵי־יִשְׂרָאֵל לַיהוָה וְטֻמְאָתוֹ עָלָיו וְנִכְרְתָה הַנֶּפֶשׁ
הַהִוא מִלְּפָנַי אֲנִי יְהוָה: 4 אִישׁ אִישׁ מִזֶּרַע אַהֲרֹן
וְהוּא צָרוּעַ אוֹ זָב בַּקֳּדָשִׁים לֹא יֹאכַל עַד אֲשֶׁר
יִטְהָר וְהַנֹּגֵעַ בְּכָל־טְמֵא־נֶפֶשׁ אוֹ אִישׁ אֲשֶׁר־תֵּצֵא
מִמֶּנּוּ שִׁכְבַת־זָרַע: 5 אוֹ־אִישׁ אֲשֶׁר יִגַּע בְּכָל־

Israelites, the spirit of inclusiveness so characteristic of the Holiness Code is retained, even though chapter 21 deals with matters of specific concern to the priesthood.[33]

CHAPTER 22 SACRED DONATIONS (vv. 1–33)

2. *Instruct Aaron and his sons to be scrupulous about the sacred donations . . . lest they profane My holy name* The Hebrew is unusual. Literally, the verse reads: "Instruct Aaron and his sons to separate themselves from the sacred donations of the Israelite people (lest they profane My holy name) which they consecrate to Me." For a smoother reading, the translation shifts the parenthetical clause, which intrudes on the normal sentence structure, to the end of the verse.

The verb *ve-yinnazru* literally means "and let them separate themselves." Rashi and Ibn Ezra both compare this verse with 15:31 *ve-hizzartem 'et benei yisra'el,* literally "You shall cause the Israelite people to avoid."

The verses that follow provide the details of what such avoidance entails. The first rule is that impure priests may not come into contact with sacred donations.

3. *while in a state of uncleanness* The Hebrew reads *ve-tum'ato 'alav,* "his uncleanness being upon him." The sense is circumstantial.

partakes of any sacred donation Rather, "who shall approach any sacred donation." The verb *yikrav,* used in this statement, means "to approach," and it is preferable to retain the literal sense of the original Hebrew. The purpose of this law was to prevent impure priests from having physical contact with consecrated offerings, lest they defile them. In fact, that is why impure priests are not allowed to partake of them in the first place.

that person shall be cut off from before Me The wording differs from the usual formulation. Normally, one is "cut off" from his kin or people. Here, the idea is that God directly objects to the nearness of impure priests and does not wish them to stand in His presence.[1]

I am the LORD This frequent refrain in the Holiness Code often concludes a section of laws or commandments.

4a. *No man of Aaron's offspring . . . shall eat* The formulation *'ish 'ish* often introduces the positive statement "any man." It may, however, imply negation when the verb in the main clause is negative, as it is here: *lo' yo'khal,* "shall not eat." The negative formulation makes this statement apodictic; it issues an unconditional command.

who has an eruption or a discharge Verse 4a begins a sequence of impurities, ordered from most to least severe, that continues through verse 5. The Hebrew adjective *tsaru'a* (or *metsora'*) describes a person who suffers from a skin ailment known as *tsara'at,* usually rendered "leprosy." The symptoms and purification of this ailment are the subjects of chapters 13 and 14. Hebrew *zav* describes

שֶׁרֶץ אֲשֶׁר יִטְמָא־לוֹ אוֹ בְאָדָם אֲשֶׁר יִטְמָא־לוֹ
לְכֹל טֻמְאָתוֹ׃ 6 נֶפֶשׁ אֲשֶׁר תִּגַּע־בּוֹ וְטָמְאָה עַד־
הָעָרֶב וְלֹא יֹאכַל מִן־הַקֳּדָשִׁים כִּי אִם־רָחַץ בְּשָׂרוֹ
בַּמָּיִם׃ 7 וּבָא הַשֶּׁמֶשׁ וְטָהֵר וְאַחַר יֹאכַל מִן־
הַקֳּדָשִׁים כִּי לַחְמוֹ הוּא׃ 8 נְבֵלָה וּטְרֵפָה לֹא
יֹאכַל לְטָמְאָה־בָהּ אֲנִי יְהוָה׃ 9 וְשָׁמְרוּ אֶת־

swarming thing by which he is made unclean or any human being by whom he is made unclean—whatever his uncleanness—[6]the person who touches such shall be unclean until evening and shall not eat of the sacred donations unless he has washed his body in water. [7]As soon as the sun sets, he shall be clean; and afterward he may eat of the sacred donations, for they are his food. [8]He shall not eat anything that died or was torn by beasts, thereby becoming unclean: I am the LORD. [9]They shall keep My charge, lest they incur

a person who has experienced a bodily discharge. The verb *zav* means "to flow." Procedures relevant to such conditions are set forth in chapter 15.

of the sacred donations until he is clean This section poses two related problems of interpretation. We must first determine the precise meaning of *kodashim,* "sacred donations," a term that can apply to various types of offerings of greater and lesser sanctity. Then, too, we must clarify the meaning of the verb *yithar,* "he shall become pure." This verb is variously used to refer to progressive stages in the cycle of purification. Here, *kodashim* designates sacrificial offerings of which a priest may partake only when he is pure. Therefore, the verb *yithar* must refer to the final purification of an afflicted priest, which occurs only after sacrifices are offered on the eighth day. Hoffmann points out that this requirement is made explicit in 14:20 and 15:13–15, with respect to both the *tsaruʿa* and the *zav.* After the seven-day cycle, the sufferer is called, in the terminology of the Mishnah, *meḥussar kippurim,* "one who lacks expiation." The period of impurity is over, if the ailment has healed, but rites of purification have yet to be performed.[2]

4b–5. If one touches anything made unclean by a corpse A person who comes into contact with the corpse of another Israelite is known as *teme' met,* "one impure because of a corpse."[3] This impurity is so severe that even a vessel that comes into contact with a corpse is rendered impure. According to Numbers 19:10–12, anyone, priest or lay Israelite, who has contact with a person impure in this way, in turn, becomes impure as well.

or if a man has an emission of semen This law is explained in the Comments to 15:15–18.

or if a man touches any swarming thing This type of impurity is explained in the Comments to 11:24,29–30.

or any human being by whom he is made unclean—whatever his uncleanness This law concerns a person, in this case a priest, who touches another person who is in a state of impurity for any of a variety of reasons, including the impurity of a *tsaruʿa* or a *zav.* Whereas verse 4a concerns persons who are themselves the source of impurity, verses 4b–5 concern persons whose impurity is transmitted to them by contact with others who are impure.

6. the person who touches such A priest who touches persons and vessels that are impure, but who was not initially impure himself, needs only to bathe and wait until after sunset in order to be restored to a pure state. In Mishnah Zevaḥim 12:1, such a priest is known as *tevul yom,* "one who immerses on the same day."[4]

unless he has washed his body On the procedure involved, see Comment to 8:6.

7. As soon as the sun sets Hebrew *u-va' ha-shemesh* is circumstantial: "the sun having entered." The "entering" of the sun reflects the ancient cosmology, wherein the sun enters its house of the night and passes through to the East; from there it "goes forth" at dawn. This is expressed in Ecclesiastes 1:5: "The sun rises, and the sun sets—/And glides back to where it rises." The time of the entrance of the sun is usually understood as the time when darkness falls.

for they are his food It would be unfair to deprive priests of their "daily bread" any longer than absolutely necessary. Furthermore, partaking of sacrifices by the priests, especially expiatory offerings, was considered indispensable to the efficacy of these offerings.[5]

guilt thereby and die for it, having committed profanation: I the LORD consecrate them.

[10]No lay person shall eat of the sacred donations. No bound or hired laborer of a priest shall eat of the sacred donations; [11]but a person who is a priest's property by purchase may eat of them; and those that are born into his household may eat of his food. [12]If a priest's daughter marries a layman, she may not eat of the sacred gifts; [13]but

מִשְׁמַרְתִּ֗י וְלֹֽא־יִשְׂא֤וּ עָלָיו֙ חֵ֔טְא וּמֵ֥תוּ ב֖וֹ כִּ֣י
יְחַלְּלֻ֑הוּ אֲנִ֥י יְהוָ֖ה מְקַדְּשָֽׁם׃ 10 וְכָל־זָ֖ר לֹא־יֹ֣אכַל
קֹ֑דֶשׁ תּוֹשַׁ֥ב כֹּהֵ֛ן וְשָׂכִ֖יר לֹא־יֹ֥אכַל קֹֽדֶשׁ׃ 11 וְכֹהֵ֗ן
כִּֽי־יִקְנֶ֥ה נֶ֙פֶשׁ֙ קִנְיַ֣ן כַּסְפּ֔וֹ ה֖וּא יֹ֣אכַל בּ֑וֹ וִילִ֣יד
בֵּית֔וֹ הֵ֖ם יֹאכְל֥וּ בְלַחְמֽוֹ׃ 12 וּבַת־כֹּהֵ֔ן כִּ֥י תִהְיֶ֖ה
לְאִ֣ישׁ זָ֑ר הִ֕וא בִּתְרוּמַ֥ת הַקֳּדָשִׁ֖ים לֹ֥א תֹאכֵֽל׃

8. He shall not eat anything that died or was torn by beasts A similar statement occurs in Ezekiel 44:31: "Priests shall not eat anything, whether bird or animal, that died or was torn by beasts." In 17:15, this same prohibition is addressed to all Israelites, and similar commandments are addressed to the Israelite people in Exodus 22:30 and Deuteronomy 14:21. It is likely, therefore, that this very ancient prohibition was repeated for emphasis in the laws addressed specifically to the priests. There is no basis for concluding that they once applied only to priests and were later extended to all Israelites, as some modern students of biblical religion maintain.

9. They shall keep My charge The Hebrew term *mishmeret,* "charge," is explained in the Comment to 8:35.

lest they incur guilt thereby and die for it Rather, "lest they bear the punishment of the offense, on that account, and die for it." The sense of "bearing punishment" is discussed in the Comment to 5:1, where it is explained that the same term that describes the offense itself may also convey the punishment incurred. In 5:1 the term for "offense" is *'avon,* whereas here it is *ḥet',* but the meaning is the same.

10. No lay person shall eat of the sacred donations. Hebrew *zar,* here translated "lay person," is a relative term, whose precise meaning depends on context. The basic sense is "outsider, stranger, one who is hated."[6] It may refer to a nonpriest, as is the case here, to a non-Levite, or a non-Israelite.[7]

The singular *kodesh* functions as a collective noun: "sacred donations," and is interchangeable with the plural *kodashim,* used in preceding verses.

No bound or hired laborer of a priest shall eat of the sacred donations Essentially, the Hebrew term *toshav* means "resident" and it may refer to foreign residents, as well.[8] It is, however, a term having diverse socioeconomic connotations. In 25:35f., 47f., the *toshav* is one who was seized in default of debt and then compelled to "reside" in the home of the creditor until he worked off his obligation. This explains the translation "bound laborer." Hebrew *sakhir* merely designates a "hired" laborer, one who works for wages, as is explained in the Comment to 19:13.

Only one who is a priest's property or a member of his immediate family may eat of the sacred donations that were apportioned to the priests. The *toshav* of a priest was not his property, but more like an indentured servant; and one's hired laborer was also an employee, not a slave.

11. but a person who is a priest's property by purchase . . . and those that are born into his household may eat of his food Hebrew *kinyan kaspo,* "one purchased by his silver," is a way of referring to slaves, whereas *yelid beito,* "born into his household," designates the children of one's slaves.[9] By definition, these terms refer to non-Israelites, because Israelites could not be owned as slaves by other Israelites, according to the law of 25:42–46.

12. If a priest's daughter marries a layman A priest's daughter derives the privilege of partaking of the priests' food from her father, who is responsible for her care so long as she resides in his domicile. If she marries a member of the priesthood, her entitlement then derives from her husband. But if she marries outside the priesthood, there is no basis for her enjoying this privilege. As in verse 10, Hebrew *zar* here designates a nonpriest.

she may not eat of the sacred gifts Hebrew *terumat ha-kodashim* is a unique combination of terms and requires clarification. The term *terumah* means "levy, collected donation, what is raised." It

if the priest's daughter is widowed or divorced and without offspring, and is back in her father's house as in her youth, she may eat of her father's food. No lay person may eat of it: 14 but if a man eats of a sacred donation unwittingly, he shall pay the priest for the sacred donation, adding one-fifth of its value. 15 But [the priests] must not allow the Israelites to profane the sacred donations that they set aside for the LORD, 16 or to incur guilt requiring a penalty payment, by eating such sacred donations: for it is I the LORD who make them sacred.

17 The LORD spoke to Moses, saying: 18 Speak to Aaron and his sons, and to all the Israelite people, and say to them:

13 וּבַת־כֹּהֵן כִּי תִהְיֶה אַלְמָנָה וּגְרוּשָׁה וְזֶרַע אֵין
לָהּ וְשָׁבָה אֶל־בֵּית אָבִיהָ כִּנְעוּרֶיהָ מִלֶּחֶם אָבִיהָ
תֹּאכֵל וְכָל־זָר לֹא־יֹאכַל בּוֹ׃ ס 14 וְאִישׁ
כִּי־יֹאכַל קֹדֶשׁ בִּשְׁגָגָה וְיָסַף חֲמִשִׁיתוֹ עָלָיו וְנָתַן
לַכֹּהֵן אֶת־הַקֹּדֶשׁ׃ 15 וְלֹא יְחַלְּלוּ אֶת־קָדְשֵׁי בְּנֵי
יִשְׂרָאֵל אֵת אֲשֶׁר־יָרִימוּ לַיהוָה׃ 16 וְהִשִּׂיאוּ אוֹתָם
עֲוֺן אַשְׁמָה בְּאָכְלָם אֶת־קָדְשֵׁיהֶם כִּי אֲנִי יְהוָה
מְקַדְּשָׁם׃ פ שלישי 17 וַיְדַבֵּר יְהוָה אֶל־
מֹשֶׁה לֵּאמֹר׃ 18 דַּבֵּר אֶל־אַהֲרֹן וְאֶל־בָּנָיו וְאֶל

may refer to voluntary contributions or to obligatory levies.[10] The term itself informs us that the sacred materials had been "raised"; the context determines on what basis. Here, *terumat ha-kodashim* refers to priestly emoluments having the status of "lesser sanctity." Most sacrificial offerings were restricted to the priests themselves and were to be eaten only in sacred precincts. They could not be shared with other members of the priestly families. This is not the sense here.[11]

13. ***and without offspring, and is back in her father's house as in her youth*** Rather, "she may return to her father's house." According to biblical law, a widow or a divorcée without children was compelled to rely on her father or her brothers for support. A widow did not inherit her husband's estate; his sons or, if he had no sons, his daughters fell heir to it. Similarly, a childless, divorced woman had no claim on her husband's estate. (In later Judaism, the settlement contained in the *ketubbah,* "writ of marriage," protected women in such circumstances.)[12] This verse ordains, therefore, that the daughter of a priest who had been married to a nonpriest could regain her privileges within her original, priestly family. Once returned, she partakes of the priestly emoluments as she had done before her marriage, according to Hoffmann.[13]

14. ***if a man eats of a sacred donation unwittingly*** This law refers to an ordinary Israelite who inadvertently partakes of what properly belongs only to the priesthood. This law is structured along the lines of the law of *ma'al* set forth in 5:14–16.

he shall pay the priest for the sacred donation The entire payment, including the penalty of one-fifth of the estimated value of the misappropriated property, is referred to as *ha-kodesh,* "the sacred donation." Once remitted, it all became the property of the priest. In ritual texts, "the priest" (*ha-kohen*) usually refers to the priest in charge at the time. Rabbinic law introduced the principle of *tovat hana'ah,* "the right to provide a benefit." In many cases, the Israelite in question could select the priest to whom the required payment would be remitted.[14]

15. ***But [the priests] must not allow the Israelites . . .*** Rather, "For the priests must not profane the sacred donations of the Israelites, which they collect for the LORD, by bringing upon them (the Israelites) the punishment for eating such sacred donations." Rashi understands this as an admonition to the priesthood not to allow ordinary Israelites to partake of sacred donations. The priests, responsible for maintaining proper storage and accurate accounting procedures, were to police themselves in order to prevent priests, who might be so tempted, from dealing in sacred donations to their own advantage. Such individuals would have to be punished appropriately.

Hebrew *'avon 'ashmah* is a unique combination of terms. In the Comment to 4:3 it is explained that *'ashmah* may connote "blame" or "punishment" for a forbidden act as well as the act itself.

The verb *ve-hissi'u,* "they bring upon," derives from the root *nasa',* "to bear, carry." The offender "bears" the punishment for his acts, but when others neglect their responsibility, they *cause* Israelites to bear such punishment.

16. ***for it is I the LORD who make them sacred*** This postscript can be interpreted in two ways: (1) It is God who ordained that the priests are sacred or (2) it is God who declared that the donations are sacred.

When any man of the house of Israel or of the strangers
in Israel presents a burnt offering as his offering for any of
the votive or any of the freewill offerings that they offer to
the LORD, 19 it must, to be acceptable in your favor, be a
male without blemish, from cattle or sheep or goats. 20 You
shall not offer any that has a defect, for it will not be
accepted in your favor.

21 And when a man offers, from the herd or the flock, a
sacrifice of well-being to the LORD for an explicit vow or as a
freewill offering, it must, to be acceptable, be without
blemish; there must be no defect in it. 22 Anything blind, or
injured, or maimed, or with a wen, boil-scar, or scurvy—
such you shall not offer to the LORD; you shall not put any
of them on the altar as offerings by fire to the LORD. 23 You
may, however, present as a freewill offering an ox or a sheep
with a limb extended or contracted; but it will not be

כָּל־בְּנֵי יִשְׂרָאֵל וְאָמַרְתָּ אֲלֵהֶם אִישׁ אִישׁ מִבֵּית
יִשְׂרָאֵל וּמִן־הַגֵּר בְּיִשְׂרָאֵל אֲשֶׁר יַקְרִיב קָרְבָּנוֹ
לְכָל־נִדְרֵיהֶם וּלְכָל־נִדְבוֹתָם אֲשֶׁר־יַקְרִיבוּ לַיהוָה
לְעֹלָה׃ 19 לִרְצֹנְכֶם תָּמִים זָכָר בַּבָּקָר בַּכְּשָׂבִים
וּבָעִזִּים׃ 20 כֹּל אֲשֶׁר־בּוֹ מוּם לֹא תַקְרִיבוּ כִּי־לֹא
לְרָצוֹן יִהְיֶה לָכֶם׃ 21 וְאִישׁ כִּי־יַקְרִיב זֶבַח־
שְׁלָמִים לַיהוָה לְפַלֵּא־נֶדֶר אוֹ לִנְדָבָה בַּבָּקָר אוֹ
בַצֹּאן תָּמִים יִהְיֶה לְרָצוֹן כָּל־מוּם לֹא יִהְיֶה־בּוֹ׃
22 עַוֶּרֶת אוֹ שָׁבוּר אוֹ־חָרוּץ אוֹ־יַבֶּלֶת אוֹ גָרָב אוֹ
יַלֶּפֶת לֹא־תַקְרִיבוּ אֵלֶּה לַיהוָה וְאִשֶּׁה לֹא־תִתְּנוּ
מֵהֶם עַל־הַמִּזְבֵּחַ לַיהוָה׃ 23 וְשׁוֹר וָשֶׂה שָׂרוּעַ
וְקָלוּט נְדָבָה תַּעֲשֶׂה אֹתוֹ וּלְנֵדֶר לֹא יֵרָצֶה׃

18. When any man of the house of Israel The character of the formula *'ish 'ish,* "any man," is explained in the Comment to verse 4.

or of the strangers in Israel Non-Israelites also donated sacrificial offerings to the God of Israel. In the ancient Near East, it was customary to pay respect to the god of the host country. Solomon's prayer, preserved in 1 Kings 8:41–43, refers to the stranger from a distant land who, impressed with the renown of the God of Israel, wishes to worship Him in Jerusalem.

a burnt offering as his offering for any of the votive or any of the freewill offerings The burnt offering (*'olah*), in addition to being the mainstay of the public cult, also served as an individual sacrifice, often brought as a votive, or freewill, offering. The terms *neder,* "votive offering," and *nedavah,* "freewill offering," are explained in the Comment to 7:16.

19. it must, to be acceptable in your favor Hebrew *le-ratson,* "for acceptance," is explained in the Comment to 1:3.

a male without blemish, from cattle or sheep or goats The sense is alternative—either large or small cattle. Compare the formulation further on, in verse 27.

20. You shall not offer any that has a defect Deuteronomy 17:1 states the same requirement: "You shall not sacrifice to the LORD your God an ox or a sheep that has any defect of a serious kind."

21. And when a man offers, from the herd or flock, a sacrifice of well-being Rather, "a sacred gift of greeting." Verses 21–25 specify that a sacred gift of greeting (*shelamim*) may not have defects. The disqualifying defects are then enumerated in detail.

for an explicit vow Rather, "to set aside a votive." The Hebrew verb *le-falle'* means "to set aside" and is explained in the Comment to 27:2, where its importance in the votive system is discussed.

22. Anything blind, or injured, or maimed In the introductory Comment to chapters 21–22, the correspondences between those physical defects that render a priest unfit to officiate in the cult and those that render a sacrificial animal unfit are tabulated in detail. Only terms that do not occur in chapter 21 are explained here.

Hebrew *shavur* means "broken," and *ḥaruts* means "cut off, incised," hence, "maimed."[15] Hebrew *yabbelet* is related to *tevallul,* "wen, a growth in the eye," in 21:20.

23. You may, however, present as a freewill offering an ox or a sheep with a limb extended or contracted . . . Hebrew *kalut* literally means "drawn in."[16] The provisions of verse 23 are

accepted for a vow. ²⁴You shall not offer to the Lᴏʀᴅ anything [with its testes] bruised or crushed or torn or cut. You shall have no such practices in your own land, ²⁵nor shall you accept such [animals] from a foreigner for offering as food for your God, for they are mutilated, they have a defect; they shall not be accepted in your favor.

²⁶The Lᴏʀᴅ spoke to Moses, saying: ²⁷When an ox or a sheep or a goat is born, it shall stay seven days with its mother, and from the eighth day on it shall be acceptable as an offering by fire to the Lᴏʀᴅ. ²⁸However, no animal from the herd or from the flock shall be slaughtered on the same day with its young.

24 וּמָע֤וּךְ וְכָתוּת֙ וְנָת֣וּק וְכָר֔וּת לֹ֥א תַקְרִ֖יבוּ
לַֽיהוָ֑ה וּֽבְאַרְצְכֶ֖ם לֹ֥א תַעֲשֽׂוּ: 25 וּמִיַּ֣ד בֶּן־נֵכָ֗ר לֹ֥א
תַקְרִ֛יבוּ אֶת־לֶ֥חֶם אֱלֹֽהֵיכֶ֖ם מִכָּל־אֵ֑לֶּה כִּ֣י
מָשְׁחָתָ֤ם בָּהֶם֙ מ֣וּם בָּ֔ם לֹ֥א יֵרָצ֖וּ לָכֶֽם: פ

26 וַיְדַבֵּ֥ר יְהוָ֖ה אֶל־מֹשֶׁ֥ה לֵּאמֹֽר: 27 שׁ֣וֹר אוֹ־כֶ֤שֶׂב
אוֹ־עֵז֙ כִּ֣י יִוָּלֵ֔ד וְהָיָ֛ה שִׁבְעַ֥ת יָמִ֖ים תַּ֣חַת אִמּ֑וֹ
וּמִיּ֤וֹם הַשְּׁמִינִי֙ וָהָ֔לְאָה יֵרָצֶ֕ה לְקָרְבַּ֥ן אִשֶּׁ֖ה לַֽיהוָֽה:

28 וְשׁ֖וֹר אוֹ־שֶׂ֑ה אֹת֣וֹ וְאֶת־בְּנ֔וֹ לֹ֥א תִשְׁחֲט֖וּ בְּי֥וֹם

exceptional in that they distinguish between the requirements for a freewill offering and those applicable to a votive, which are more stringent. Elsewhere no such distinction is made. This disparity is understandably troubling to traditional commentators. Ramban interprets the term *nedavah* loosely to mean a voluntary contribution to the sanctuary, *not* intended for use as a sacrificial offering on the altar. For this reason, the requirements of soundness were eased. More likely, however, the less stringent requirements in the case of the *nedavah* had to do with the entirely voluntary character of this offering. It was not obligated by any prior commitment, as was the votive pledge (the *neder*), nor was it even occasioned by the duty to thank God for something He had done for the worshiper.

The language of this law is also somewhat distinctive. The Hebrew reads *nedavah taʿaseh ʾoto,* "You shall make of it a freewill offering." But in such contexts Hebrew ʿasah may mean "to perform a rite, offer a sacrifice." This is so in Exodus 12:48, where *ve-ʿasah pesaḥ* means "and he performs the paschal sacrifice." Compare, for example, Leviticus 14:19; 16:24. On this basis we should translate: "You shall perform it as a freewill offering."

24. *[with its testes] bruised or crushed or torn or cut*　The substance of this law does not differ appreciably from that of 21:20, but the terminology is different. Hebrew *maʿukh* means "rubbed, crushed" and is synonymous with *meroaḥ ʾashakh,* "with crushed testes," in 21:20. Hebrew *katut* means "pounded, pulverized, crushed,"[17] and *natuk* means "detached, torn off."[18] Hebrew *karut* literally means "cut off," hence, "castrated."[19]

You shall have no such practices in your own land　The new JPS translation joins verse 24b to what follows, implying a general prohibition of abhorrent practices that applied to all the defects enumerated in verses 22–24. It is more likely that reference here is specifically to the conditions listed in verse 24a, namely, genital mutilation, or gelding, of animals—things one "does" to an animal. By contrast, the defects listed in verses 22–23 are more likely congenital in nature or the result of injury.

25. *nor shall you accept such [animals] from a foreigner*　Verse 25 concludes this section of the legislation and refers to all the defects listed in verses 22–24. Resident non-Israelites might want to sell animals to Israelites or contribute them as their own offerings. Such animals are subject to the same regulations as those originally belonging to Israelites.

for they are mutilated, they have a defect　Hebrew *moshḥatam bam* literally means "their mutilation is in them." This connotes a distortion of normal physical form. The postexilic prophet Malachi (1:14) states the matter as follows: "A curse on the cheat who has an [unblemished] male in his flock, but for his vow sacrifices a blemished animal to the Lᴏʀᴅ!"

27. *When an ox or a sheep or a goat*　For another instance of this unusual combination see 17:3. Newborn animals may not be sacrificed until the eighth day after birth.

28. *no animal . . . shall be slaughtered on the same day with its young*　The law forbids such sacrifice even after eight days. Traditionally, this prohibition has been explained as expressing compassion for living creatures. It has been understood to apply only to female animals, "mothers," and their male offspring (Heb. *beno,* [literally] "its son"). Practically speaking, male animals account for the majority of sacrifices. This interpretation is cited by Rashi, Maimonides, and others.

29 When you sacrifice a thanksgiving offering to the LORD, sacrifice it so that it may be acceptable in your favor. 30 It shall be eaten on the same day; you shall not leave any of it until morning: I am the LORD.

31 You shall faithfully observe My commandments: I am the LORD. 32 You shall not profane My holy name, that I may be sanctified in the midst of the Israelite people—I the LORD who sanctify you, 33 I who brought you out of the land of Egypt to be your God, I the LORD.

אֶחָד׃ 29 וְכִֽי־תִזְבְּחוּ זֶֽבַח־תּוֹדָה לַיהוָה לִֽרְצֹנְכֶם
תִּזְבָּֽחוּ׃ 30 בַּיּוֹם הַהוּא יֵֽאָכֵל לֹֽא־תוֹתִירוּ מִמֶּנּוּ
עַד־בֹּקֶר אֲנִי יְהוָה׃ 31 וּשְׁמַרְתֶּם מִצְוֺתַי וַעֲשִׂיתֶם
אֹתָם אֲנִי יְהוָה׃ 32 וְלֹא תְחַלְּלוּ אֶת־שֵׁם קָדְשִׁי
וְנִקְדַּשְׁתִּי בְּתוֹךְ בְּנֵי יִשְׂרָאֵל אֲנִי יְהוָה מְקַדִּשְׁכֶם׃
33 הַמּוֹצִיא אֶתְכֶם מֵאֶרֶץ מִצְרַיִם לִהְיוֹת לָכֶם
לֵאלֹהִים אֲנִי יְהוָה׃ פ רביעי

29. sacrifice it so that it may be acceptable Verses 29–30 present a separate law for the thanksgiving offering, which is here treated as distinct from the *shelamim.*

30. It shall be eaten on the same day In the Comments to 19:5–8, it is explained that the thanksgiving offering is subject to different rules.

31. You shall faithfully observe My commandments This concluding statement is typical of ritual legislation in the Torah.[20]

32. You shall not profane My holy name In verse 2 above, the laws began with the same admonition.

33. I who brought you out of the land of Egypt As in 19:36, reference is made, at the conclusion of ritual legislation, to God's act of liberating the Israelites from Egyptian bondage—the basis of His demand for obedience to His laws and commandments.

CHAPTER 23

The Calendar of Sacred Time

Leviticus 23 is a calendar of the annual festivals celebrated in biblical times. As such, it represents the primary statement on the religious festivals in the priestly tradition and, hence, is a highly important source. In conformance with biblical tradition, this calendar also includes the Sabbath, even though it is not, technically speaking, a calendrical festival.

Actually, the Torah preserves three calendrical traditions, corresponding to its three principal collections of laws: the Book of the Covenant, Deuteronomy, and the ritual legislation. Each expresses its own distinctive concept of the festivals, usually conveyed by the precise name given to each occasion. The calendar of Exodus 23:12–19, part of the Book of the Covenant, focuses on the Sabbath and on the three pilgrimage festivals: *ḥag ha-matsot,* "the Pilgrimage Fast of Unleavened Bread"; *ḥag ha-katsir,* "the Spring Harvest Pilgrimage"; and *ḥag ha-'asif,* "the Pilgrimage of Ingathering." The calendar of Deuteronomy 16:1–17 names the *pesaḥ; ḥag ha-shavu'ot,* "the Pilgrimage Festival of Weeks" in the late spring; and *ḥag ha-sukkot,* "the Pilgrimage Festival of Booths" in the autumn. Chapter 23 includes the daily and Sabbath celebrations and those for the New Moon and all the festivals and holy days. The present chapter and Numbers 28–29 together constitute a detailed register of the sacrifices required throughout the year. In addition, Exodus 34:17–26 preserves a brief calendar that is related in form and content to Exodus 23:12–19.

The contents of chapter 23 may be outlined as follows:

A superscription, or title (vv. 1–2)

The Sabbath (v. 3)

A second superscription (v. 4)

The paschal sacrifice and the *matsot* festival (vv. 5–8)

Offerings from the new grain crop, during a seven-week period of counting (vv. 9–22)

23 The Lord spoke to Moses, saying: ²Speak to the Israelite people and say to them:

These are My fixed times, the fixed times of the Lord, which you shall proclaim as sacred occasions.

כ״ג וַיְדַבֵּ֥ר יְהוָ֖ה אֶל־מֹשֶׁ֥ה לֵּאמֹֽר: ² דַּבֵּ֞ר אֶל־
בְּנֵ֤י יִשְׂרָאֵל֙ וְאָמַרְתָּ֣ אֲלֵהֶ֔ם מוֹעֲדֵ֣י יְהוָ֔ה אֲשֶׁר־
תִּקְרְא֥וּ אֹתָ֖ם מִקְרָאֵ֣י קֹ֑דֶשׁ אֵ֥לֶּה הֵ֖ם מוֹעֲדָֽי:

The first day of the seventh month, a day of commemoration with loud blasts of the shofar (vv. 23–25)

The tenth of the seventh month, the Day of Atonement (vv. 26–32)

The Sukkot festival beginning on the fifteenth day of the seventh month (vv. 33–36)

A summary statement (vv. 37–38)

Further laws for the Sukkot festival (vv. 39–43)

A postscript (v. 44)

The above outline, especially the two superscriptions, shows the composite character of chapter 23. The Sabbath law has been appended to the beginning of the calendar proper, and verses 39–43 have been similarly added at the end, after it seemed that the calendar was complete. This latter passage provides additional regulations about the Sukkot festival, including the only statement preserved in the Torah explaining the requirements to dwell in booths during the festival of ingathering and to use greenery in its celebration.

Verses 9–22 are also highly significant, for they ordain detailed offerings from the new grain crop. They also highlight the importance of the Sabbath day in calculating time.

THE SABBATH (vv. 1–3)

2. Speak to the Israelite people The sacred occasions, the Sabbaths and festivals, are to be observed by all the people; they are not merely of concern to the priesthood nor relevant solely to the sacrificial cult of the sanctuary. This introductory statement sets the tone for the entire chapter, whose provisions inform the people, as well as the priests, about how the Sabbath and festivals are to be observed.

These are My fixed times, the fixed times of the Lord, which you shall proclaim as sacred occasions The Hebrew term *mo'ed,* "set time," derives from the root *y-'-d,* "to set, designate" a time or place.[1] The dates of the festivals and the regularity of a Sabbath every seventh day were set by God, and yet the Israelites are also commanded to proclaim them as sacred. These two acts are not contradictory but, rather, complementary. The sanctity of the Sabbath and festivals is not achieved by God's act alone. It requires a combination of divine and human action.[2]

There is, however, a problem in using the term *mo'ed* with reference to the Sabbath. Elsewhere in the ritual legislation it usually designates an annual occurrence.[3] A *mo'ed* occurs at the same time each year; its annual date must be "fixed." There is, however, no need to "fix" the time of the Sabbath, which is not, strictly speaking, a calendrical phenomenon, as Rashi has pointed out. Furthermore, biblical usage regularly differentiates between *shabbat,* "the Sabbath," and *mo'ed,* as in verses 37–38 of our chapter, which speak of the "set times of the Lord" as being "apart from the sabbaths of the Lord." Accordingly, the use of *mo'ed* for the Sabbath is most likely to be explained by the influence of the langauge of verse 4 upon that of verse 2.

Hebrew *mikra' kodesh,* here rendered "sacred occasion," is a somewhat ambiguous term original to the Holiness Code. The verb *k-r-'* may mean "to proclaim" or "to summon, invite."[4] Accordingly, one could render *mikra' kodesh* as "a sacred assembly, convocation," indicating that on an occasion so designated, the community is summoned for common worship and celebration.

3 On six days work may be done, but on the seventh day
there shall be a sabbath of complete rest, a sacred occasion.
You shall do no work; it shall be a sabbath of the LORD
throughout your settlements.
4 These are the set times of the LORD, the sacred occasions,
which you shall celebrate each at its appointed time: 5 In the

3 שֵׁ֣שֶׁת יָמִים֮ תֵּעָשֶׂ֣ה מְלָאכָה֒ וּבַיּ֣וֹם הַשְּׁבִיעִ֗י
שַׁבַּ֤ת שַׁבָּתוֹן֙ מִקְרָא־קֹ֔דֶשׁ כָּל־מְלָאכָ֖ה לֹ֣א
תַעֲשׂ֑וּ שַׁבָּ֥ת הִוא֙ לַיהוָ֔ה בְּכֹ֖ל מוֹשְׁבֹתֵיכֶֽם׃
פ 4 אֵ֚לֶּה מוֹעֲדֵ֣י יְהוָ֔ה מִקְרָאֵ֖י קֹ֑דֶשׁ אֲשֶׁר־
תִּקְרְא֥וּ אֹתָ֖ם בְּמוֹעֲדָֽם׃ 5 בַּחֹ֣דֶשׁ הָרִאשׁ֗וֹן

3. ***On six days work may be done*** This statement emphasizes three norms of conduct basic to the observance of the Sabbath: (1) the prohibition of *mela'khah,* "work," (2) the sanctity of the Sabbath, and (3) the requirement that the Sabbath be observed in all Israelite settlements. The formulation of verse 3, especially use of the passive verb *te'aseh,* "may be done," closely resembles similar statements in Exodus 12:26; 31:5; and 35:2. The active formulation *ta'aseh,* "you shall do," is more common.[5]

Hebrew *mela'khah,* "work," derives from the root *l-'-k,* "to send, dispatch, assign," now attested in Ugaritic.[6] The noun *mal'akh,* "messenger, angel," also derives from this root. On this basis, *mela'khah* is best translated "assigned tasks, what one is sent to do." The main object of the Sabbath law, in this respect, is to avoid performing one's daily tasks on the Sabbath.

a sabbath of complete rest Hebrew *shabbat shabbaton* is superlative, literally "the most restful cessation" from assigned tasks. The Sabbath is to be observed by a greater abstinence from daily tasks than is required on the festivals. On seasonal festivals, one refrains from work primarily to be free to celebrate, whereas on the Sabbath, the very object is rest.

The term *shabbat* means "to desist, cease, be idle."[7] The Sabbath day is, consequently, a hiatus in the regular progression of daily labor. It enables a person literally to "catch his breath" (*hinnafesh*), the verb used to describe God's rest on the Sabbath of Creation.[8]

In other contexts, the term *shabbat* may connote a "sabbath," namely, an occasion that resembles the Sabbath, such as the last year in the seven-year sabbatical cycle or a week, which ends on the Sabbath day. Hebrew *shabbaton* expresses that which is like the Sabbath and as such designates the Day of Atonement and other occasions, including the first and seventh days of festivals.[9]

it shall be a sabbath of the LORD The translation conveys the sense of prepositional *lamed,* which connotes possession: "a Sabbath belonging to the LORD." The Sabbath belongs to God, just as festivals are said to be *ḥag le-YHVH*, "a pilgrimage festival belonging to the LORD."[10] On such occasions, one should not pursue his own affairs but should devote himself to spiritual matters. This is stated most clearly in Isaiah 58:13–14: "If you refrain from trampling the sabbath,/ From pursuing your affairs on My holy day;/ If you call the Sabbath 'delight,'/ The LORD's holy day 'honored';/ And if you honor it and go not your ways/ Nor look to your affairs, nor strike bargains—/ Then you can seek the favor of the LORD." There is the subtle implication that on the Sabbath one is to worship God in special ways, though nothing in the way of special sacrificial rites is specifically ordained here.

throughout your settlements This stipulation occurs frequently in the ritual legislation. It emphasizes the fact that the Sabbath is to be observed by the community of Israelites in their houses and is not solely a celebration to take place in the sanctuary.[11]

THE FEAST OF UNLEAVENED BREAD (vv. 4–8)

This section of the calendar ordains that the paschal sacrifice is to be offered on the fourteenth day of the first month, in the early evening. The Feast of Unleavened Bread begins on the fifteenth day and lasts seven days. The first and seventh days are designated sacred assemblies, when work is forbidden. There is mention of an offering by fire on each of the seven days, but no details about it are provided. Unleavened bread is to be eaten, and all leaven avoided for seven days, beginning at the time of the paschal sacrifice.

4. ***These are the set times of the LORD . . . each at its appointed time*** Each festival is to occur at the same time every year.

first month, on the fourteenth day of the month, at twilight, there shall be a passover offering to the LORD, [6]and on the fifteenth day of that month the LORD's Feast of Unleavened Bread. You shall eat unleavened bread for seven days.

בְּאַרְבָּעָה עָשָׂר לַחֹדֶשׁ בֵּין הָעַרְבָּיִם פֶּסַח לַיהוָה׃
6 וּבַחֲמִשָּׁה עָשָׂר יוֹם לַחֹדֶשׁ הַזֶּה חַג הַמַּצּוֹת
לַיהוָה שִׁבְעַת יָמִים מַצּוֹת תֹּאכֵלוּ׃ 7 בַּיּוֹם

5. ***In the first month, on the fourteenth day of the month*** This is the dating system that was in use during much of the biblical period, especially in the formulation of official records and laws. The operative unit of time was the lunar month (*ḥodesh*), not the week; and the months of the year were designated by ordinal numbers: the first month, . . . the seventh month, and so forth. The counting began in the spring of the year. There is both biblical and extrabiblical evidence that other calendrical systems were also in use during the biblical period, but Leviticus 23 does not refer to them. For further discussion of the month names in the various systems of recording time in biblical Israel, see Excursus 8.

at twilight Hebrew *bein ha-ʿarbayim* is ambiguous. The translation "twilight" understands it as designating the period of time between sunset and nightfall, approximately one and one-third hours in duration. As a dual form *ʿarbayim* expresses two "settings": sunset and a later "setting" that follows—nightfall.[12] Mekhilta Bo' 5 presents the view of Rabbi Nathan that *bein ha-ʿarbayim* is the time after the sun begins to incline toward the west, after the sixth hour of the day. In a hypothetical twelve-hour day that begins at 6:00 A.M. and concludes at 6:00 P.M., this would mean that the time period called *bein ha-ʿarbayim* begins at noon. Mishnah Pesaḥim 5:1 tells us that during the period of the Second Temple, the paschal sacrifice was offered on the altar at approximately nine and a half hours into the day, immediately following the second daily offering (*tamid*), which was scheduled earlier on Passover eve. This was near the midpoint of the second half of the ideal twelve-hour day that begins at 6:00 A.M. and concludes at 6:00 P.M. Again, this is before twilight. There is no similar information available about practices in earlier periods of antiquity.

Here, the term *pesaḥ* refers to the sacrifice not to the festival. Actually, the accepted name "Passover" is a misnomer because the verb *pasaḥ* in the Kal stem does not mean "to pass over, skip over," but rather "to straddle, hedge." Thus, we read in 1 Kings 18:21, [literally] "How long will you keep on straddling (*posḥim*) the two branches?" In other words, *pasaḥ* means to stand with one leg on one branch and the second leg on the other.[13] In the notes to Exodus 12:11,23, the new JPS translation cites this interpretation as an alternative to "passover offering" for Hebrew *pesaḥ*. It notes the rendering "protective offering." Thus, we also read in Exodus 12:23: "For when the LORD goes through to smite the Egyptians, He will see the blood on the lintel and the two doorposts, and the LORD will *protect* the door and not let the Destroyer enter and smite your home."

Mekhilta Bo' 7 cites Isaiah 31:5: "Like the birds that fly, even so will the LORD of Hosts shield Jerusalem, shielding and saving, protecting (*pasoaḥ*) and rescuing." In such terms, the paschal sacrifice commemorates God's protection of the Israelites. The details of the paschal sacrifice are presented in Exodus 12–13.

6. ***and on the fifteenth day of that month the LORD's Feast of Unleavened Bread*** Rather, "the Pilgrimage Feast of Unleavened Bread of the LORD." The Hebrew term *ḥag* is crucial for a proper understanding of the biblical festivals and their development. *Ḥag* means "pilgrimage," and wherever this term is used to characterize a festival, it refers to an actual pilgrimage, either to a nearby or to a faraway cult site. The duty to undertake a pilgrimage is known in a number of other religions, most notably in Islam, where the Arabic term *ḥajatun,* cognate with Hebrew *ḥag,* designates a holy pilgrimage. This means that any festival called *ḥag* could not be fully celebrated at one's home, but required one's presence at a cult site. In earlier times, the pilgrimage might have brought a family to a nearby altar, but subsequently Deuteronomy ordained that all sacrificial offerings were to be brought to one, central Temple, which necessitated a much longer pilgrimage for most Israelites.[14]

There is some ambiguity as to how long the pilgrimage, itself, was to last. In the case of the autumn festival the formulation is clear: verse 34 explicitly states that the pilgrimage is to last for seven days. The same is to be understood here. The pilgrimage lasted for as long as unleavened bread was eaten, namely, for seven days.

The meaning of Hebrew *matsot,* "unleavened bread," is explained in the Comment to 2:4.

7 On the first day you shall celebrate a sacred occasion: you
shall not work at your occupations. 8 Seven days you shall
make offerings by fire to the LORD. The seventh day shall be
a sacred occasion: you shall not work at your occupations.
9 The LORD spoke to Moses, saying: 10 Speak to the Israelite people and say to them:
When you enter the land that I am giving to you and you
reap its harvest, you shall bring the first sheaf of your
harvest to the priest. 11 He shall elevate the sheaf before the
LORD for acceptance in your behalf; the priest shall elevate it
on the day after the sabbath. 12 On the day that you elevate

הָרִאשׁוֹן מִקְרָא־קֹדֶשׁ יִהְיֶה לָכֶם כָּל־מְלֶאכֶת
עֲבֹדָה לֹא תַעֲשׂוּ׃ 8 וְהִקְרַבְתֶּם אִשֶּׁה לַיהוָה
שִׁבְעַת יָמִים בַּיּוֹם הַשְּׁבִיעִי מִקְרָא־קֹדֶשׁ כָּל־
מְלֶאכֶת עֲבֹדָה לֹא תַעֲשׂוּ׃ פ 9 וַיְדַבֵּר יְהוָה
אֶל־מֹשֶׁה לֵּאמֹר׃ 10 דַּבֵּר אֶל־בְּנֵי יִשְׂרָאֵל
וְאָמַרְתָּ אֲלֵהֶם כִּי־תָבֹאוּ אֶל־הָאָרֶץ אֲשֶׁר אֲנִי
נֹתֵן לָכֶם וּקְצַרְתֶּם אֶת־קְצִירָהּ וַהֲבֵאתֶם אֶת־
עֹמֶר רֵאשִׁית קְצִירְכֶם אֶל־הַכֹּהֵן׃ 11 וְהֵנִיף אֶת־
הָעֹמֶר לִפְנֵי יְהוָה לִרְצֹנְכֶם מִמָּחֳרַת הַשַּׁבָּת יְנִיפֶנּוּ

7. *the first day you shall celebrate a sacred occasion* Rather, "a sacred assembly." (See Comment to verse 3.) On the first and seventh, or last, day of the festival, work is forbidden. The community celebrates together. On the intervening days, normal work may be carried on, if necessary, although the celebration continues.

you shall not work at your occupations The composite term *mele'khet 'avodah,* literally "assignment of labor," is somewhat redundant.[15]

8. *Seven days you shall make offerings by fire to the LORD* The Hebrew term *'isheh,* "offering by fire," is explained in the Comment to 1:9. Here, the precise character of the offerings by fire is not specified. The same general reference occurs in the laws for the celebrations of the seventh month. These sacrifices are to be offered on the sanctuary altar. The laws of Numbers 28–29 enumerate which offerings are to be brought on each occasion. This is the import of the introductory statement in Numbers 28:3: "These are the offerings by fire that you are to present to the LORD."

OFFERINGS FROM THE NEW GRAIN CROP (vv. 9–14)

In this section, two offerings taken from the new crop are prescribed: *'omer* and *bikkurim.* The first, *'omer,* is the offering of a "sheaf" of new barley. As originally intended, the priest was to offer it on the morrow of the first Sabbath subsequent to the seven-day festival. New grain could not be eaten until this offering was made. It constituted desacralization, a rite that gives to God the first of the new crop, thus releasing the rest of it for ordinary human use.

Beginning on the day of this offering, a period of counting is initiated. Seven full "sabbaths," or weeks, are counted off. On the fiftieth day, the second offering of meal of new wheat, baked into leavened loaves, is offered in the sanctuary as *bikkurim,* "first fruits." It consists of grain furnished by the Israelite settlements. That day is a sacred assembly on which work is forbidden. Here, it is not designated *ḥag,* "pilgrimage," as it is in Deuteronomy 16:10, a significant difference.

This section concludes with a paraphrase of 19:9–10, requiring Israelites to leave the edges of their fields and their gleanings from the grain harvests for the poor and the stranger.

10. *When you enter the land* Compare such introductory statements as 14:34; 19:23; etc.

you shall bring the first sheaf of your harvest to the priest Hebrew *'omer* means a bundle of stalks, bound together after reaping.[16] Reference is to a sheaf of barley, which is the first grain to ripen in the spring. This sheaf is to be brought to "*the* priest," that is, the particular priest who officiates at the rite in the sanctuary.

11. *He shall elevate the sheaf* Mishnah Menaḥot 5:1 describes the procedure employed in the days of the Second Temple as follows: "How is one to do this? He inserts his two hands underneath the objects being offered and carries them to and fro. He lifts them up and lowers them."[17] The purpose of such rites was to show the offering to God, so that it might be accepted.

the sheaf, you shall offer as a burnt offering to the LORD a lamb of the first year without blemish. [13]The meal offering with it shall be two-tenths of a measure of choice flour with oil mixed in, an offering by fire of pleasing odor to the LORD; and the libation with it shall be of wine, a quarter of a *hin*. [14]Until that very day, until you have brought the offering of your God, you shall eat no bread or parched grain or fresh ears; it is a law for all time throughout the ages in all your settlements.

[15]And from the day on which you bring the sheaf of elevation offering—the day after the sabbath—you shall count off seven weeks. They must be complete: [16]you must

הַכֹּהֵן׃ 12 וַעֲשִׂיתֶם בְּיוֹם הֲנִיפְכֶם אֶת־הָעֹמֶר כֶּבֶשׂ
תָּמִים בֶּן־שְׁנָתוֹ לְעֹלָה לַיהוָה׃ 13 וּמִנְחָתוֹ שְׁנֵי
עֶשְׂרֹנִים סֹלֶת בְּלוּלָה בַשֶּׁמֶן אִשֶּׁה לַיהוָה רֵיחַ
נִיחֹחַ ונסכה יַיִן רְבִיעִת הַהִין׃ 14 וְלֶחֶם וְקָלִי
וְכַרְמֶל לֹא תֹאכְלוּ עַד־עֶצֶם הַיּוֹם הַזֶּה עַד
הֲבִיאֲכֶם אֶת־קָרְבַּן אֱלֹהֵיכֶם חֻקַּת עוֹלָם
לְדֹרֹתֵיכֶם בְּכֹל מֹשְׁבֹתֵיכֶם׃ ס 15 וּסְפַרְתֶּם
לָכֶם מִמָּחֳרַת הַשַּׁבָּת מִיּוֹם הֲבִיאֲכֶם אֶת־עֹמֶר
הַתְּנוּפָה שֶׁבַע שַׁבָּתוֹת תְּמִימֹת תִּהְיֶינָה׃ 16 עַד

v. 13. וְנִסְכּוֹ ק׳

on the day after the sabbath The Hebrew words *mi-moḥorat ha-shabbat,* repeated in verse 15a, are problematic because it is not specified which Sabbath is intended. The accepted rabbinic interpretation is that here *shabbat* does not refer to the Sabbath day but means something similar to *shabbaton* in verse 39, that is, a time of resting. This characterization applies both to the Sabbath and to festivals. This interpretation is explained in the Sifra ʾEmor 23:11,15: *mi-moḥorat ha-shabbat—mi-moḥorat yom tov,* "on the morrow of the Sabbath—on the morrow of the festival." Targum Onkelos explains *mi-moḥorat ha-shabbat* in the same way, as does the Septuagint to 23:11: *tê epaurion tês prōtēs,* "on the morrow of the first day (i.e., the first day of the festival)."[18] Although this interpretation resolves a difficulty in the text, it does not convey its simple sense. It has been suggested that the words *mi-moḥorat ha-shabbat* in verse 11 and in verse 15a represent an abbreviation of the phrase *mi-moḥorat ha-shabbat ha-sheviʿit,* literally "until the morrow of the seventh 'sabbath' of days" in verse 16 below. Verses 15–16 use the term *shabbat* in the sense of "week"; verse 11 uses the abbreviation *shabbat* in its normal sense of a particular day, the Sabbath. It is therefore suggested that the words *mi-moḥorat ha-shabbat* here and in verse 15a were glosses inserted to ensure that the period of counting the seven weeks would begin on the day after the Sabbath. This would require that seven "sabbaths" of days (*shabbatot*) would pass during the period of fifty days. If this analysis is accurate, the text of verse 11 should probably read as follows: *vehenif ʾet ha-ʿomer lifnei YHVH li-rtsonkhem yenifennu ha-kohen,* "He shall present the sheaf before the LORD; for acceptance on your behalf the priest shall present it."[19]

12–13. On the day that you elevate the sheaf The burnt offering (*ʿolah*) was often accompanied by a grain offering (*minḥah*) and a libation (*nesekh*), as prescribed here.[20] The measure of grain required here is twice the usual amount, perhaps to emphasize the signal importance of grain in this celebration.

14. Until that very day . . . you shall eat no bread Hebrew *ʿetsem,* "bone," may mean "the thing, itself; the essence." With prefixed *bet, be-ʿetsem* means "in the same, in the very." For the meaning of Hebrew *kali,* "parched grain," and *karmel,* "fresh ears," see Comment to 2:14. Until God receives a share of the new grain crop, none of it may be used by humans.

throughout the ages in all your settlements Compare verse 3 above and verse 31 below.

THE SHAVUOT FESTIVAL (vv. 15–22)

15–16. And from the day on which you bring the sheaf . . . the day after the sabbath Referring to the Comment to verse 11 above, it should be repeated here that the words *mi-moḥorat ha-shabbat* may be a gloss. The original text may have read: *u-sefartem lakhem mi-yom haviʾakhem,* "And you shall count off, from the day on which you bring." This is how the text of the Temple Scroll from Qumran reads. The offering is known as *ʿomer ha-tenufah,* "the sheaf for the presentation." In biblical usage, when the term *shabbat* refers to a week and not an occasion it probably always connotes a sabbatical week.[21] This is certain in chapter 23 and in the Holiness Code generally. In 25:8 *shevaʿ shabbetot shanim* means "seven septenaries," namely, seven cycles of seven years, each of which ends

count until the day after the seventh week—fifty days; then you shall bring an offering of new grain to the LORD. [17]You shall bring from your settlements two loaves of bread as an elevation offering; each shall be made of two-tenths of a measure of choice flour, baked after leavening, as first fruits to the LORD. [18]With the bread you shall present, as burnt offerings to the LORD, seven yearling lambs without blemish, one bull of the herd, and two rams, with their meal offerings and libations, an offering by fire of pleasing odor to the LORD. [19]You shall also offer one he-goat as a sin offering and two yearling lambs as a sacrifice of well-being. [20]The priest shall elevate these—the two lambs—together with the bread of first fruits as an elevation offering before the LORD; they shall be holy to the LORD, for the priest. [21]On

מִמָּחֳרַת הַשַּׁבָּת הַשְּׁבִיעִת תִּסְפְּרוּ חֲמִשִּׁים יוֹם
וְהִקְרַבְתֶּם מִנְחָה חֲדָשָׁה לַיהוָה׃ 17 מִמּוֹשְׁבֹתֵיכֶם
תָּבִיאּוּ* ׀ לֶחֶם תְּנוּפָה שְׁתַּיִם שְׁנֵי עֶשְׂרֹנִים סֹלֶת
תִּהְיֶינָה חָמֵץ תֵּאָפֶינָה בִּכּוּרִים לַיהוָה׃
18 וְהִקְרַבְתֶּם עַל־הַלֶּחֶם שִׁבְעַת כְּבָשִׂים תְּמִימִם
בְּנֵי שָׁנָה וּפַר בֶּן־בָּקָר לְעָנֶי אֶחָד וְאֵילִם שְׁנָיִם יִהְיוּ
עֹלָה לַיהוָה וּמִנְחָתָם וְנִסְכֵּיהֶם אִשֵּׁה רֵיחַ־נִיחֹחַ
לַיהוָה׃ 19 וַעֲשִׂיתֶם שְׂעִיר־עִזִּים אֶחָד לְחַטָּאת
וּשְׁנֵי כְבָשִׂים בְּנֵי שָׁנָה לְזֶבַח שְׁלָמִים׃ 20 וְהֵנִיף
הַכֹּהֵן ׀ אֹתָם עַל לֶחֶם הַבִּכּוּרִים תְּנוּפָה לִפְנֵי
יְהוָה עַל־שְׁנֵי כְּבָשִׂים קֹדֶשׁ יִהְיוּ לַיהוָה לַכֹּהֵן׃

v. 17. א׳ דגושה

with a sabbatical year, when no planting or harvesting may be done. On this basis, *sheva' shabbatot* in verse 15 must mean "seven *weeks* of days." This indicates, in effect, that the period of counting begins on the day after the first Sabbath, the first Sunday subsequent to the beginning of the festival.[22]

an offering of new grain In the Comment to 2:13 it is explained that this offering of new grain (*minḥah ḥadashah*) is distinct from the grain offering, also of the new harvest, brought by individual Israelites. Both offerings, however, are to be of the best semolina wheat.

17. ***You shall bring from your settlements two loaves*** On the use of unleavened bread in altar offerings, see Comment to 7:13. The rule is that no leaven could ascend the altar. Since no part of the offering ordained here—presented before God to be viewed and accepted—ascends the altar, it was made of *ḥamets,* "leavened dough."[23]

18. ***With the bread you shall present*** Here, the preposition *'al* means "together with, in addition to." The offerings prescribed in verses 18–20 are typical of those included in composite public rites, where several different sacrifices are offered together to constitute a more elaborate celebration. The animals, both small and large, are to be offered as burnt offerings and are accompanied by the grain offerings and libations.[24]

19. ***You shall also offer one he-goat as a sin offering and two yearling lambs as a sacrifice of well-being.*** The various types of sin offerings are discussed in the introductory Comment to chapters 4–5. An explanation of the *shelamim* sacrifice, preferably rendered "sacred gift of greeting," is provided in the Comment to 3:1. The reason a *ḥatta't,* "sin offering," is required on this occasion is unclear. It may perhaps be related to the periodic need to restore the people to a state of cultic purity. This is the only occasion on which the *shelamim* sacrifice is offered on a scheduled basis, as part of the public cult.

20. ***The priest shall elevate these—the two lambs—*** The object pronoun *'otam,* "them," refers to the two yearling lambs of verse 19.

they shall be holy to the LORD, for the priest In the first instance, these offerings are the Lord's, but He commands that they be allotted to the priests. As the Talmud states: "The Lord has acquired it and has given it to the priests."[25] Sections of the *shelamim* are usually reserved for the donors of the sacrifice as well. That is the rule of 7:28f., but it applies only to private offerings. Our law represents the only instance of the *shelamim* as part of the public cult. For this reason, all sections not burned on the altar are designated for the priests. One could say that this unique *shelamim* is treated by the law as a most sacred offering.[26]

The essential offerings set forth in verses 9–22, in celebration of the new grain crop, reflect a widely known mode of worship in which burnt offerings played no part. Sacrifice is, instead, by presentation, the object being that God views the sacrifice, and in that way accepts it. (In the burnt offering, God, so to speak, "breathes in the smoke" that rises from the fire.)[27] It is likely, furthermore, that verses 12–13 and 18–20, which specify certain burnt offerings in addition to the presentation

that same day you shall hold a celebration; it shall be a
sacred occasion for you; you shall not work at your occupations. This is a law for all time in all your settlements,
throughout the ages.
22And when you reap the harvest of your land, you shall
not reap all the way to the edges of your field, or gather the
gleanings of your harvest; you shall leave them for the poor
and the stranger: I the LORD am your God.
23The LORD spoke to Moses, saying: 24Speak to the Israelite people thus: In the seventh month, on the first day of the
month, you shall observe complete rest, a sacred occasion
commemorated with loud blasts. 25You shall not work at
your occupations; and you shall bring an offering by fire to
the LORD.

21 וּקְרָאתֶ֞ם בְּעֶ֣צֶם׀ הַיּ֣וֹם הַזֶּ֗ה מִֽקְרָא־קֹ֙דֶשׁ֙ יִהְיֶ֣ה
לָכֶ֔ם כָּל־מְלֶ֥אכֶת עֲבֹדָ֖ה לֹ֣א תַעֲשׂ֑וּ חֻקַּ֥ת עוֹלָ֛ם
בְּכָל־מוֹשְׁבֹתֵיכֶ֖ם לְדֹרֹתֵיכֶֽם׃ 22 וּֽבְקֻצְרְכֶ֞ם אֶת־
קְצִ֣יר אַרְצְכֶ֗ם לֹֽא־תְכַלֶּ֞ה פְּאַ֤ת שָׂדְךָ֙ בְּקֻצְרֶ֔ךָ
וְלֶ֥קֶט קְצִֽירְךָ֖ לֹ֣א תְלַקֵּ֑ט לֶֽעָנִ֤י וְלַגֵּר֙ תַּעֲזֹ֣ב אֹתָ֔ם
אֲנִ֖י יְהוָ֥ה אֱלֹהֵיכֶֽם׃ ס חמישי 23 וַיְדַבֵּ֥ר
יְהוָ֖ה אֶל־מֹשֶׁ֥ה לֵּאמֹֽר׃ 24 דַּבֵּ֛ר אֶל־בְּנֵ֥י יִשְׂרָאֵ֖ל
לֵאמֹ֑ר בַּחֹ֣דֶשׁ הַשְּׁבִיעִ֗י בְּאֶחָ֣ד לַחֹ֘דֶשׁ֒ יִהְיֶ֤ה לָכֶם֙
שַׁבָּת֔וֹן זִכְר֥וֹן תְּרוּעָ֖ה מִקְרָא־קֹֽדֶשׁ׃ 25 כָּל־
מְלֶ֥אכֶת עֲבֹדָ֖ה לֹ֣א תַעֲשׂ֑וּ וְהִקְרַבְתֶּ֥ם אִשֶּׁ֖ה
לַיהוָֽה׃ ס 26 וַיְדַבֵּ֥ר יְהוָ֖ה אֶל־מֹשֶׁ֥ה לֵּאמֹֽר׃

offerings for the initial and final celebrations of the new grain crop, are later developments. They do not represent the earliest form of celebrating these occasions and may have been added in order to bring the code of verses 9–22 into conformity with what subsequently became the full regimen of offerings.

21. On that same day you shall hold a celebration In this verse, the Hebrew verb *u-kera'tem* is derived from the noun *mikra',* "assembly," and means literally "you shall proclaim an assembly." This interpretation is required by the syntax of the Hebrew, which would not be balanced if the verb *k-r-'* were understood in its usual sense of "to proclaim."

22. And when you reap the harvest of your land This verse paraphrases 19:9–10. It is appended here because of its topical connection with the harvest.

THE FIRST DAY OF THE SEVENTH MONTH (vv. 23–25)

This section ordains the celebration of three major sacred occasions occurring during the seventh month: (1) the first day of the seventh month (which in the later tradition becomes the Jewish New Year); (2) the Day of Atonement; and (3) the Sukkot festival.

24. In the seventh month, on the first day of the month . . . a sacred occasion commemorated with loud blasts. Note the same system of dating in verse 5 above and subsequently in verses 27, 33, and 39. Hebrew *zikhron teru'ah* means literally "commemoration by blasting" the shofar. The same designation of this occasion occurs in Numbers 29:1. The sounding of horns had various functions in ancient Israel, as well as elsewhere in the ancient Near East. Usually, it was a method of assembling the people before moving on to a new location or of mustering troops for battle.[28] There were cultic uses as well. Horns were blasted when sacrifices were offered, and they were used by Temple musicians.[29] In our text, the horn was blasted to announce the forthcoming pilgrimage festival, which occurred two weeks after the first day of the month. Thus we read in Psalms 81:4 literally, "Blow the horn on the New Moon,/ on the full moon for the day of our pilgrimage festival." Chapter 23 presents this occasion as a day of rest and of sacred assembly. It is not conceived of as a New Year at this stage, but, rather, as an occasion preliminary to the Sukkot festival.

²⁶The LORD spoke to Moses, saying: ²⁷Mark, the tenth day of this seventh month is the Day of Atonement. It shall be a sacred occasion for you: you shall practice self-denial, and you shall bring an offering by fire to the LORD; ²⁸you shall do no work throughout that day. For it is a Day of Atonement, on which expiation is made on your behalf before the LORD your God. ²⁹Indeed, any person who does not practice self-denial throughout that day shall be cut off from his kin; ³⁰and whoever does any work throughout that day, I will cause that person to perish from among his people. ³¹Do no work whatever; it is a law for all time, throughout the ages in all your settlements. ³²It shall be a sabbath of complete rest for you, and you shall practice self-

²⁷ אַ֡ךְ בֶּעָשׂ֣וֹר לַחֹדֶשׁ֩ הַשְּׁבִיעִ֨י הַזֶּ֜ה י֣וֹם הַכִּפֻּרִ֗ים ה֤וּא מִֽקְרָא־קֹ֙דֶשׁ֙ יִהְיֶ֣ה לָכֶ֔ם וְעִנִּיתֶ֖ם אֶת־נַפְשֹׁתֵיכֶ֑ם וְהִקְרַבְתֶּ֥ם אִשֶּׁ֖ה לַיהוָֽה: ²⁸ וְכָל־מְלָאכָה֙ לֹ֣א תַעֲשׂ֔וּ בְּעֶ֖צֶם הַיּ֣וֹם הַזֶּ֑ה כִּ֣י י֤וֹם כִּפֻּרִים֙ ה֔וּא לְכַפֵּ֣ר עֲלֵיכֶ֔ם לִפְנֵ֖י יְהוָ֥ה אֱלֹהֵיכֶֽם: ²⁹ כִּ֤י כָל־הַנֶּ֙פֶשׁ֙ אֲשֶׁ֣ר לֹֽא־תְעֻנֶּ֔ה בְּעֶ֖צֶם הַיּ֣וֹם הַזֶּ֑ה וְנִכְרְתָ֖ה מֵֽעַמֶּֽיהָ: ³⁰ וְכָל־הַנֶּ֗פֶשׁ אֲשֶׁ֤ר תַּֽעֲשֶׂה֙ כָּל־מְלָאכָ֔ה בְּעֶ֖צֶם הַיּ֣וֹם הַזֶּ֑ה וְהַֽאֲבַדְתִּ֛י אֶת־הַנֶּ֥פֶשׁ הַהִ֖וא מִקֶּ֥רֶב עַמָּֽהּ: ³¹ כָּל־מְלָאכָ֖ה לֹ֣א תַעֲשׂ֑וּ חֻקַּ֤ת עוֹלָם֙ לְדֹרֹ֣תֵיכֶ֔ם בְּכֹ֖ל מֹֽשְׁבֹֽתֵיכֶֽם: ³² שַׁבַּ֨ת שַׁבָּת֥וֹן הוּא֙ לָכֶ֔ם וְעִנִּיתֶ֖ם אֶת־

DAY OF ATONEMENT (vv. 26–32)

The Commentary to 16:29–34 presents a detailed discussion of the rites ordained for this occasion. The introductory Comment to chapters 4–5 contains further clarification of the Hebrew verb *kipper*, "to expiate, atone," and the noun *kippurim*, "expiation, atonement."

27. *Mark, the tenth day of this seventh month* Hebrew ʾakh, "moreover," here translated "Mark," is often used in the ritual laws for emphasis. Compare verse 39 below.

you shall practice self-denial As explained in the Comment to 16:31, self-denial refers to fasting.

28. *you shall do no work* The prohibition of labor is repeated for emphasis in verse 30 below.

29–30. *shall be cut off... I will cause that person to perish* This is the only instance in the priestly codes of the Torah where God is said *to cause* the offender to perish. The closest we come to this notion is in 17:10 and in 20:3–6, where God is said to cut off the offender from the community.[30]

32. *It shall be a sabbath of complete rest for you* See Comment to verse 3 above.

from evening to evening, you shall observe this your sabbath The phrase *me-ʿerev ʿad ʿerev*, "from evening to evening," appears only in this verse; it is not said of any other sacred occasion, even the regular Sabbath. Indeed, it is uncertain as to whether in biblical times the Sabbath and the festivals began on the prior evening, as became the custom in later Judaism. In the laws of Passover and the *matsot* festival (vv. 5–8), the paschal sacrifice is indeed offered on the eve of the fifteenth day, and that event effectively marks the beginning of the festival as a whole. But the paschal offering was, after all, unusual in this very respect, for sacrifices in celebration of sacred occasions were typically offered in the morning.

Traditionally this verse has been interpreted as setting the norm for the entire gamut of festivals in the Jewish religious calendar, namely, that the celebration commences the previous evening. This fact notwithstanding, the uniqueness of the provision "from evening to evening" in connection with the Day of Atonement might suggest that the practice in this case was exceptional. The issue revolves around the definition of *yom*, "day," in Genesis 1. The repeated phrase "there was evening and there was morning" regarding the days of Creation could be taken to mean that where ritual legislation refers to a particular "day" of the month, it means a day extending from evening to evening. Rashbam notes, however, that this formula could be taken to mean that the second day and those following it began at dawn.[31] In fact, his view has much to recommend it because there are many indications that in biblical Hebrew usage *yom*, "day," meant the daylight hours.[32] On this basis the requirement regarding the Day of Atonement was probably unique, and it is likely that, except for Passover, all other festivals, even the Sabbath, began at dawn in biblical times. Rabbinic halakhot clearly determined that the Sabbath and festivals commence with the evening.

נַפְשֹׁתֵיכֶם בְּתִשְׁעָה לַחֹדֶשׁ בָּעֶרֶב מֵעֶרֶב עַד־
עֶרֶב תִּשְׁבְּתוּ שַׁבַּתְּכֶם׃ פ ששי 33 וַיְדַבֵּר
יְהוָה אֶל־מֹשֶׁה לֵּאמֹר׃ 34 דַּבֵּר אֶל־בְּנֵי יִשְׂרָאֵל
לֵאמֹר בַּחֲמִשָּׁה עָשָׂר יוֹם לַחֹדֶשׁ הַשְּׁבִיעִי הַזֶּה
חַג הַסֻּכּוֹת שִׁבְעַת יָמִים לַיהוָה׃ 35 בַּיּוֹם הָרִאשׁוֹן
מִקְרָא־קֹדֶשׁ כָּל־מְלֶאכֶת עֲבֹדָה לֹא תַעֲשׂוּ׃
36 שִׁבְעַת יָמִים תַּקְרִיבוּ אִשֶּׁה לַיהוָה בַּיּוֹם
הַשְּׁמִינִי מִקְרָא־קֹדֶשׁ יִהְיֶה לָכֶם וְהִקְרַבְתֶּם אִשֶּׁה
לַיהוָה עֲצֶרֶת הִוא כָּל־מְלֶאכֶת עֲבֹדָה לֹא תַעֲשׂוּ׃
37 אֵלֶּה מוֹעֲדֵי יְהוָה אֲשֶׁר־תִּקְרְאוּ אֹתָם מִקְרָאֵי
קֹדֶשׁ לְהַקְרִיב אִשֶּׁה לַיהוָה עֹלָה וּמִנְחָה זֶבַח
וּנְסָכִים דְּבַר־יוֹם בְּיוֹמוֹ׃ 38 מִלְּבַד שַׁבְּתֹת יְהוָה

denial; on the ninth day of the month at evening, from evening to evening, you shall observe this your sabbath.
33The Lord spoke to Moses, saying: 34Say to the Israelite people:

On the fifteenth day of this seventh month there shall be the Feast of Booths to the Lord, [to last] seven days. 35The first day shall be a sacred occasion: you shall not work at your occupations; 36seven days you shall bring offerings by fire to the Lord. On the eighth day you shall observe a sacred occasion and bring an offering by fire to the Lord; it is a solemn gathering: you shall not work at your occupations.

37Those are the set times of the Lord that you shall celebrate as sacred occasions, bringing offerings by fire to the Lord—burnt offerings, meal offerings, sacrifices, and libations, on each day what is proper to it—38apart from

Chapter 23 thus represents the Day of Atonement as a day of complete rest, a Sabbath in that respect, on which an offering by fire was presented and on which Israelites were to fast and otherwise deprive themselves, the object being to secure expiation of sins. Recalling the complex legislation of chapter 16, it is worth repeating here that the tenth day of the seventh month was essentially a day on which the sanctuary was purified, and all violations of its purity expiated through various religious rites. Undoubtedly, scheduling this occasion only a few days prior to the major pilgrimage festival of the year ensured that the sanctuary and, hence, the people would be restored to a state of fitness in time for the celebration of the autumn Sukkot festival.

THE SUKKOT FESTIVAL (vv. 33–44)

This section combines two laws for the Sukkot festival: a seven-day observance and a concluding celebration on the eighth day. Like the *matsot* festival in the spring of the year, the first and seventh days of Sukkot are sacred assemblies on which work is forbidden. Offerings by fire are ordained for *each* of the seven days. Verses 39–43 provide further features: Greenery is to be used in the celebration, and the Israelites are to dwell in booths. Although Deuteronomy 16:13 also calls this occasion "the Feast of Booths," it does not provide any rationale for the name of the festival or for the related commemorative practice, such as is given here.

*34. **On the fifteenth day of this seventh month there shall be the Feast of Booths to the Lord*** Hebrew *sukkah,* "booth," derives from the verb *s-kh-kh,* "to cover over," as would be said of branches. It designates a small, often impermanent structure that is covered on top, but that may be only partially enclosed on its sides. In Genesis 33:17 there is reference to a "booth" used as a stall for livestock, and in Isaiah 1:8, to a "booth" for watchmen in a vineyard.[33]

*36. **On the eighth day . . . it is a solemn gathering*** Hebrew *ʿatseret,* "solemn gathering," is a variation of *ʿatsarah,* a term that designates religious gatherings, such as public fasts.[34] According to Deuteronomy 16:8, as well as the ritual legislation, the *ʿatseret* consistently comes at the conclusion of a prolonged celebration. This undoubtedly prompted the Septuagint to render it by Greek *exodion,* "finale, recessional." Etymologically, this term derives from the verb *ʿatsar,* "to detain, restrain, confine," and may refer to the fact that the people are kept together for an additional day.

*37. **Those are the set of times of the Lord . . . on each day what is proper*** Hebrew *devar yom be-yomo,* "on each day what is proper," is an administrative formula, originally employed in delineating disbursements of food and other materials. It is also appropriate for listing offerings prescribed for particular occasions.[35]

the sabbaths of the LORD, and apart from your gifts and from all your votive offerings and from all your freewill offerings that you give to the LORD.

³⁹Mark, on the fifteenth day of the seventh month, when you have gathered in the yield of your land, you shall observe the festival of the LORD [to last] seven days: a complete rest on the first day, and a complete rest on the eighth day. ⁴⁰On the first day you shall take the product of *hadar* trees, branches of palm trees, boughs of leafy trees, and willows of the brook, and you shall rejoice before the LORD your God seven days. ⁴¹You shall observe it as a festival of the LORD for seven days in the year; you shall observe it in the seventh month as a law for all time, throughout the ages. ⁴²You shall live in booths seven days; all citizens in Israel shall live in booths, ⁴³in order that future generations may know that I made the Israelite people live in booths when I brought them out of the land of Egypt, I the LORD your God.

⁴⁴So Moses declared to the Israelites the set times of the LORD.

וּמִלְּבַ֣ד מַתְּנֽוֹתֵיכֶ֗ם וּמִלְּבַ֤ד כָּל־נִדְרֵיכֶם֙ וּמִלְּבַד֙
כָּל־נִדְבֽוֹתֵיכֶ֔ם אֲשֶׁ֥ר תִּתְּנ֖וּ לַיהוָֽה: 39 אַ֡ךְ
בַּחֲמִשָּׁה֩ עָשָׂ֨ר י֜וֹם לַחֹ֣דֶשׁ הַשְּׁבִיעִ֗י בְּאָסְפְּכֶם֙
אֶת־תְּבוּאַ֣ת הָאָ֔רֶץ תָּחֹ֥גּוּ אֶת־חַג־יְהוָ֖ה שִׁבְעַ֣ת
יָמִ֑ים בַּיּ֤וֹם הָֽרִאשׁוֹן֙ שַׁבָּת֔וֹן וּבַיּ֥וֹם הַשְּׁמִינִ֖י
שַׁבָּתֽוֹן: 40 וּלְקַחְתֶּ֨ם לָכֶ֜ם בַּיּ֣וֹם הָרִאשׁ֗וֹן פְּרִ֨י עֵ֤ץ
הָדָר֙ כַּפֹּ֣ת תְּמָרִ֔ים וַעֲנַ֥ף עֵץ־עָבֹ֖ת וְעַרְבֵי־נָ֑חַל
וּשְׂמַחְתֶּ֗ם לִפְנֵ֛י יְהוָ֥ה אֱלֹהֵיכֶ֖ם שִׁבְעַ֥ת יָמִֽים:
41 וְחַגֹּתֶ֤ם אֹתוֹ֙ חַ֣ג לַֽיהוָ֔ה שִׁבְעַ֥ת יָמִ֖ים בַּשָּׁנָ֑ה
חֻקַּ֤ת עוֹלָם֙ לְדֹרֹ֣תֵיכֶ֔ם בַּחֹ֥דֶשׁ הַשְּׁבִיעִ֖י תָּחֹ֥גּוּ
אֹתֽוֹ: 42 בַּסֻּכֹּ֥ת תֵּשְׁב֖וּ שִׁבְעַ֣ת יָמִ֑ים כָּל־הָֽאֶזְרָח֙
בְּיִשְׂרָאֵ֔ל יֵשְׁב֖וּ בַּסֻּכֹּֽת: 43 לְמַ֘עַן֮ יֵדְע֣וּ דֹרֹֽתֵיכֶם֒
כִּ֣י בַסֻּכּ֗וֹת הוֹשַׁ֙בְתִּי֙ אֶת־בְּנֵ֣י יִשְׂרָאֵ֔ל בְּהוֹצִיאִ֥י
אוֹתָ֖ם מֵאֶ֣רֶץ מִצְרָ֑יִם אֲנִ֖י יְהוָ֥ה אֱלֹהֵיכֶֽם:
44 וַיְדַבֵּ֣ר מֹשֶׁ֔ה אֶת־מֹעֲדֵ֖י יְהוָ֑ה אֶל־בְּנֵ֖י יִשְׂרָאֵֽל:

פ   שביעי

38. ***apart from the sabbaths of the LORD, and apart from your gifts*** Hebrew *mattanah*, "gift," usually indicates a voluntary presentation. The formulation here resembles that in several of the laws of Deuteronomy.³⁶

39. ***when you have gathered in the yield of your land*** This is the basis for the older name of the festival, used in Exodus 23:16 and 34:22: *ḥag ha-'asif*, "the Pilgrimage Festival of Ingathering."

40. ***The product of*** hadar ***trees*** There is no positive horticultural identification of a tree, or a type of tree, called *hadar*. Words probably related etymologically to *hadar* connote beauty and majesty. Hebrew *'ets hadar*, "hadar trees," is a general category that is followed by the specification of three beautiful trees: (1) *kappot temarim*, "palm branches," (2) *'anaf 'ets 'avot*, "branches of leafy trees," and (3) *'arvei naḥal*, "willows of the brook."³⁷ This greenery symbolizes the abundance of water and oases and the beauty of the Land of Israel.³⁸ Traditionally, the "fruit of the tree" has been taken to be the citron (*'etrog*).³⁹ It is a much later addition to the Sukkot celebration.

you shall rejoice before the LORD your God This is the only festival prescribed in chapter 23 on which rejoicing is explicitly commanded. In the festival calendar of Deuteronomy 16, rejoicing is also mentioned in connection with the Feast of Weeks (v. 11). Elsewhere we read that sacrificial worship in the Temple is an occasion for rejoicing. It is not clear just why the Sukkot festival is singled out here, although it may be because Sukkot was the most prominent of the ancient pilgrimage festivals.⁴⁰

41. ***You shall observe it as a festival of the LORD*** Rather, "you shall observe it as a *pilgrimage* festival of the LORD." The pilgrimage is to last seven days.

42. ***all citizens in Israel*** Hebrew *'ezraḥ*, "citizen," is explained in the Comment to 16:29.

43. ***that I made the Israelite people live in booths*** According to Exodus 12:37, Sukkot is the name of the first stop on the exodus route from Egypt. A double entendre may have been intended: God brought the Israelites to Sukkot when He led them out of Egypt, and He also made them dwell in *sukkot*, "booths," at that time.

44. ***So Moses declared*** Rather, "He commanded." As the leader of the people, Moses ordered that the Israelites observe the set times of the Lord. The two passages dealing with the Sukkot

24 The LORD spoke to Moses, saying:

²Command the Israelite people to bring you clear oil of beaten olives for lighting, for kindling lamps regularly. ³Aaron shall set them up in the Tent of Meeting outside the curtain of the Pact [to burn] from evening to morning before the LORD regularly; it is a law for all time throughout

כ״ד וַיְדַבֵּ֥ר יְהוָ֖ה אֶל־מֹשֶׁ֥ה לֵּאמֹֽר: ² צַ֣ו אֶת־
בְּנֵ֣י יִשְׂרָאֵ֗ל וְיִקְח֣וּ אֵלֶ֜יךָ שֶׁ֣מֶן זַ֥יִת זָ֛ךְ כָּתִ֖ית
לַמָּא֑וֹר לְהַעֲלֹ֥ת נֵ֖ר תָּמִֽיד: ³ מִח֡וּץ לְפָרֹ֣כֶת
הָעֵדֻ֡ת בְּאֹ֩הֶל֩ מוֹעֵ֨ד יַעֲרֹ֣ךְ אֹת֩וֹ אַהֲרֹ֜ן מֵעֶ֤רֶב עַד־
בֹּ֙קֶר֙ לִפְנֵ֣י יְהוָ֖ה תָּמִ֑יד חֻקַּ֥ת עוֹלָ֖ם לְדֹרֹֽתֵיכֶֽם:

festival, verses 33–38 and verses 39–44, may be differentiated according to their content. The former passage deals with the public celebration of the festival in the sanctuary in the manner of the statements regarding the Passover, the first day of the seventh month, and the Day of Atonement. The latter passage addresses the Israelite families and commands them to provide themselves with certain kinds of greenery and to dwell in booths.

CHAPTER 24

A Collection of Laws

Chapter 24 is a brief collection of diverse religious laws concerning the kindling of lamps in the sanctuary, the rows of bread displayed before God in the sanctuary, and laws governing blasphemy and other serious crimes. A number of other features of this chapter warrant special comment. There is, first of all, a statement on the "law of retaliation" (lex talionis), similar to what we find in Exodus 21:23–25 and Deuteronomy 19:21. This subject is discussed in Excursus 9. In addition, verses 10–12 preserve a didactic narrative about an incident of blasphemy, which serves as a background to the legislation on the subject. This recorded incident occasions two further items of interest: a reference to incarceration as a form of detention; and a divine revelation that was needed for an immediate purpose.

THE KINDLING OF THE MENORAH (vv. 1–4)

Command the Israelite people . . . clear oil of beaten olives The Hebrew adjective *zakh*, "clear, pure," is used to indicate the purity of ingredients.[1] The verb *k-t-t* means "to pulverize, crush, grind," and the particular form *katit* is passive: "beaten."[2] In the Rashi to Mishnah Menaḥot 8:4, it is explained that olive oil from the first of three pressings was called *zakh* in the period of the Second Temple. This same law regarding the kindling of the lamps is restated in Exodus 27:20–21. The traditional commentaries were understandably troubled by the precise repetition. Rashi explains that our passage represents the essential statement of the specific law, whereas the Exodus passage is part of the monumental general description of the Tabernacle.

for kindling lamps regularly The Hebrew word *tamid*, whether used as an adjective or as an adverb (cf. in v. 3), has the sense of regularity. It does not mean "forever, always." In practice, the lamp in the sanctuary burned only from evening to morning, as verse 3 states explicitly. The requirement that the lamp be lit in all generations is not conveyed by the word *tamid*, but by the formula *ḥukkat ʿolam le-doroteikhem,* "It is a law for all time throughout the ages."[3]

3. the curtain of the Pact The composite term *parokhet ha-ʿedut* is best translated "the curtain of [the Ark of] the Pact." The term *parokhet* is explained in the Comment to 1:12. In its portrayal of the sanctuary, priestly literature clearly differentiates between the inner and outer sections of the enclosed sanctuary. Behind the *parokhet* stood the Ark, known in some texts as the "Ark of the Pact" (*ʾaron ha-ʿedut,* or simply *ha-ʿedut*), in which rested the "Tablets of the Pact" (*luḥot ha-ʿedut*).[4]

4. He shall set up the lamps on the pure lampstand The actual instructions for fashioning of the lampstand are ordained in Exodus 25:31–39. It was to be made of pure gold, of one solid piece

the ages. 4 He shall set up the lamps on the pure lampstand before the LORD [to burn] regularly.

5 You shall take choice flour and bake of it twelve loaves, two-tenths of a measure for each loaf. 6 Place them on the pure table before the LORD in two rows, six to a row. 7 With each row you shall place pure frankincense, which is to be a token offering for the bread, as an offering by fire to the LORD. 8 He shall arrange them before the LORD regularly

4 עַל הַמְּנֹרָה הַטְּהֹרָה יַעֲרֹךְ אֶת־הַנֵּרוֹת לִפְנֵי
יְהוָה תָּמִיד׃ פ 5 וְלָקַחְתָּ סֹלֶת וְאָפִיתָ אֹתָהּ
שְׁתֵּים עֶשְׂרֵה חַלּוֹת שְׁנֵי עֶשְׂרֹנִים יִהְיֶה הַחַלָּה
הָאֶחָת׃ 6 וְשַׂמְתָּ אוֹתָם שְׁתַּיִם מַעֲרָכוֹת שֵׁשׁ
הַמַּעֲרָכֶת עַל הַשֻּׁלְחָן הַטָּהֹר לִפְנֵי יְהוָה׃ 7 וְנָתַתָּ
עַל־הַמַּעֲרֶכֶת לְבֹנָה זַכָּה וְהָיְתָה לַלֶּחֶם לְאַזְכָּרָה
אִשֶּׁה לַיהוָה׃ 8 בְּיוֹם הַשַּׁבָּת בְּיוֹם הַשַּׁבָּת יַעַרְכֶנּוּ

that was hammered into shape. It had seven branches. According to 1 Kings 7:49 there were ten lampstands in the Solomonic Temple. They stood in two rows in front of the inner sanctum, which was called *devir.* This corresponded to the position of the one lampstand in the sanctuary.[5]

The noun *menorah* derives from *ner,* "a light," and its form suggests that its basic meaning is "the place of light," hence, "lampstand." Whatever details are known about the menorah of biblical times come from textual descriptions. Artifacts unearthed in archaeological excavations represent the later models of the menorah that ultimately became prominent graphic symbols of Judaism and of the Jewish people.[6]

THE ROWS OF BREAD (vv. 5–9)

5. ***You shall take choice flour*** Rather, "semolina flour." The bread presented as an offering on a table inside the sanctuary is elsewhere known as *leḥem ha-panim,* "the bread of display," or as *leḥem ha-tamid,* "the regularly [offered] bread."[7] As explained in the Comment to 2:4, Hebrew *ḥallah* means "a round loaf." The amount of flour used for each loaf was two-tenths of an *ʾefah,* or about 2.2 liters.[8]

The practice of displaying bread in the sanctuary is very ancient. There is a reference to this offering in an account from the early career of David. While fleeing from Saul, David and his men arrived at the sanctuary of Nob and were given some of the bread of display to eat.[9] According to ritual legislation, only priests were permitted to partake of these consecrated loaves and, then, only within sacred precincts. In the aforementioned story, the priest at Nob had to be assured that David's fighting men were pure before he permitted them to eat of the bread of display.

As noted by Ibn Ezra, the twelve loaves clearly represent the Twelve Tribes of Israel.

6. ***Place them on the pure table . . . in two rows*** Hebrew *maʿarekhet,* "set, row," led to the designations of the bread of display as *leḥem ha-maʿarekhet,* "the bread of the row," and *ʿerekh leḥem,* "a row of bread."[10] The same terminology is used to designate a battle line.

7. ***With each row you shall place pure frankincense*** Frankincense (*levonah*) was also an ingredient of the incense. Here, its function was that of a "token portion" (*ʾazkarah*).[11] In most of the grain offerings prescribed in priestly legislation, a small amount of flour was scooped up by the officiating priest and then placed on the altar to burn. That constituted the "token portion." This case is exceptional, as Rashi comments, "for none of the bread went to the 'Most High,' but rather, the frankincense was burned when they removed it (the bread) each sabbath."

In effect, two different modes of sacrifice are reflected in the prescribed manner of offering the bread of display. The loaves themselves were a presentation to God for which no altar of burnt offerings was used. The bread was viewed by God and, by this means, accepted by Him. Subsequently, the loaves were apportioned to the priests. In an effort to adapt this widespread mode of sacrifice to the more distinctive method of burning offerings on the altar, frankincense was to be burned near the loaves of bread; just as with other offerings of grain, a small amount of flour was burned on the altar. God was pictured as inhaling the aroma of the burning frankincense, which served as "an offering by fire."

every sabbath day—it is a commitment for all time on the part of the Israelites. [9]They shall belong to Aaron and his sons, who shall eat them in the sacred precinct; for they are his as most holy things from the LORD's offerings by fire, a due for all time.

[10]There came out among the Israelites one whose mother was Israelite and whose father was Egyptian. And a fight broke out in the camp between that half-Israelite and a certain Israelite. [11]The son of the Israelite woman pronounced the Name in blasphemy, and he was brought to Moses—now his mother's name was Shelomith daughter of Dibri of the tribe of Dan—[12]and he was placed in

לִפְנֵי יְהוָה תָּמִיד מֵאֵת בְּנֵי־יִשְׂרָאֵל בְּרִית עוֹלָם׃
9 וְהָיְתָה לְאַהֲרֹן וּלְבָנָיו וַאֲכָלֻהוּ בְּמָקוֹם קָדֹשׁ כִּי
קֹדֶשׁ קֳדָשִׁים הוּא לוֹ מֵאִשֵּׁי יְהוָה חָק־עוֹלָם׃
ס 10 וַיֵּצֵא בֶּן־אִשָּׁה יִשְׂרְאֵלִית וְהוּא בֶּן־
אִישׁ מִצְרִי בְּתוֹךְ בְּנֵי יִשְׂרָאֵל וַיִּנָּצוּ בַּמַּחֲנֶה בֶּן
הַיִּשְׂרְאֵלִית וְאִישׁ הַיִּשְׂרְאֵלִי׃ 11 וַיִּקֹּב בֶּן־הָאִשָּׁה
הַיִּשְׂרְאֵלִית אֶת־הַשֵּׁם וַיְקַלֵּל וַיָּבִיאוּ אֹתוֹ אֶל־
מֹשֶׁה וְשֵׁם אִמּוֹ שְׁלֹמִית בַּת־דִּבְרִי לְמַטֵּה־דָן׃

The preposition *ʿal* means "near, together with," not "on, upon." In Mishnah Menaḥot 11:5, we are told how the frankincense was burned during the period of the Second Temple. Two containers (*bazikhin*) were placed near the rows of loaves for this purpose.

8. *He shall arrange them before the LORD regularly every sabbath day* In Hebrew, repetition is a way of expressing regularity. Thus, *be-yom ha-shabbat, be-yom ha-shabbat,* "on the Sabbath day, on the Sabbath day," means "every Sabbath," just as *ba-boker, ba-boker,* "in the morning, in the morning," means "every morning" in Exodus 29:39. Note that here, *tamid* designates a weekly, not a daily procedure, which was the case in 6:13.

9. *for they are his as most holy things from the LORD's offerings* See Comment to 2:3.

LAWS GOVERNING BLASPHEMY AND OTHER SERIOUS CRIMES (vv. 10–22)

10. *There came out among the Israelites* This begins a brief narrative that serves to introduce the law governing the crime of blasphemy in verse 13. The point is made that the blasphemer was not a full-fledged Israelite, but was of mixed parentage, in contrast to the person with whom he fought, "the Israelite man." Hebrew *va-yinnatsu* connotes physical fighting.[12] In the heat of the fight, the man of mixed parentage blasphemed.

11. *pronounced the Name in blasphemy* The Hebrew verb *n-k-v,* which also occurs in verse 15, literally means "to pierce," and by extension, "to specify, pronounce explicitly, identify."[13] Targum Onkelos renders it in Aramaic as *u-faresh,* "he pronounced explicitly." The force of the two verbs taken together—*va-yikov . . . va-yekallel,* literally "he pronounced . . . he cursed"—is to make of the later verb an adverbial phrase: "he pronounced by cursing blasphemously." Hebrew *ha-shem,* "the Name," is an abbreviation of *shem YHVH,* "the name of the LORD," as it appears in verse 15. This implicit way of referring to God as "the Name" became proverbial in later Jewish literature.[14]

The genealogy of the blasphemer in this incident is certainly significant. His Israelite mother came from the tribe of Dan, associated with the northern cult at the temple of Dan, which the Jerusalemite priesthood considered illegitimate.[15]

A prohibition against blasphemy is preserved in the Book of the Covenant (Exod. 22:27). That the penalty for blasphemy is death, as stated in biblical law, is intimated in Job 2:9, where we read that Job's wife urged him to end his life, which had become insufferable, by committing blasphemy.

This section, which continues through verse 12, recounts a rare instance of incarceration, similar to what is recorded in Numbers 15:34. In both passages, the term *mishmar,* "guardhouse," is used; and in both instances, detention was necessary until God provided a specific communication regarding the appropriate penalty, an act conveyed by the verb *p-r-sh,* "to state clearly, specify." The specific communication from God specifying the penalty to be imposed on the blasphemer serves to dramatize the concept, basic to priestly literature, that all the particulars of religious law were communicated by God to Moses. In another instance, Moses was urged to detain two persons, but he refused to do so.[16]

custody, until the decision of the LORD should be made clear to them.

[13]And the LORD spoke to Moses, saying: [14]Take the blasphemer outside the camp; and let all who were within hearing lay their hands upon his head, and let the whole community stone him.

[15]And to the Israelite people speak thus: Anyone who blasphemes his God shall bear his guilt; [16]if he also pronounces the name LORD, he shall be put to death. The whole community shall stone him; stranger or citizen, if he has thus pronounced the Name, he shall be put to death.

[17]If anyone kills any human being, he shall be put to death. [18]One who kills a beast shall make restitution for it: life for life. [19]If anyone maims his fellow, as he has done so

12 וַיַּנִּיחֻהוּ בַּמִּשְׁמָר לִפְרֹשׁ לָהֶם עַל־פִּי יְהוָה׃
פ 13 וַיְדַבֵּר יְהוָה אֶל־מֹשֶׁה לֵּאמֹר׃
14 הוֹצֵא אֶת־הַמְקַלֵּל אֶל־מִחוּץ לַמַּחֲנֶה וְסָמְכוּ
כָל־הַשֹּׁמְעִים אֶת־יְדֵיהֶם עַל־רֹאשׁוֹ וְרָגְמוּ אֹתוֹ
כָּל־הָעֵדָה׃ 15 וְאֶל־בְּנֵי יִשְׂרָאֵל תְּדַבֵּר לֵאמֹר
אִישׁ אִישׁ כִּי־יְקַלֵּל אֱלֹהָיו וְנָשָׂא חֶטְאוֹ׃ 16 וְנֹקֵב
שֵׁם־יְהוָה מוֹת יוּמָת רָגוֹם יִרְגְּמוּ־בוֹ כָּל־הָעֵדָה
כַּגֵּר כָּאֶזְרָח בְּנָקְבוֹ־שֵׁם יוּמָת׃ 17 וְאִישׁ כִּי יַכֶּה
כָּל־נֶפֶשׁ אָדָם מוֹת יוּמָת׃ 18 וּמַכֵּה נֶפֶשׁ־בְּהֵמָה
יְשַׁלְּמֶנָּה נֶפֶשׁ תַּחַת נָפֶשׁ׃ 19 וְאִישׁ כִּי־יִתֵּן מוּם

Penal incarceration as the actual punishment for a crime was seldom the norm in the ancient Near East. There were, however, debtors' prisons and those where slaves were held, often on the estates of large landowners and kings. These guarded facilities served as living quarters from which escape was difficult.[17]

14. Take the blasphemer outside the camp Capital sentences were executed outside the area of settlement. This was due, at least in part, to the impurity attached to a corpse. It was also because the taking of a human life, even though by judicial process and required by law, was regarded as a horrendous act. In the laws of Deuteronomy (17:5), one convicted of a capital offense was to be taken to the gates of the city to be executed. Naboth the Jezreelite, who had been wrongly condemned to die, was nevertheless executed outside the city, according to custom.[18]

and let all who were within hearing lay their hands upon his head Biblical law considers hearing, not only seeing, to be a form of witnessing, especially where the act involved consists primarily of speaking audibly, as with blasphemy. On the same basis, one attests to hearing the pronouncement of vows. Conversely, one who has not actually heard an oath is not bound by it. When two parties to a contract make mutual commitments, God hears them and holds them responsible.[19]

The entire community has a responsibility to root out blasphemy because it adversely affects everyone, even if it is committed by a single individual. Such a direct affront to God awakens His anger.

The laying on of hands, as explained in the Comment to 1:4, symbolizes the transfer of authority and has both cultic and legal functions.

15. Anyone who blasphemes his God shall bear his guilt The formulation *'ish 'ish,* "anyone, any man," is characteristic of the Holiness Code. The idiom *nasa' ḥet'* is synonymous with *nasa' 'avon,* "to bear the punishment of a sin, or offense."[20]

16. The whole community shall stone him; stranger or citizen Non-Israelites are responsible for acts considered vital to maintaining the religious character of the community.[21] Therefore, offenses that threaten that overall religious character are punishable, even when committed by non-Israelite residents.

17. If anyone kills any human being, he shall be put to death. Similar laws involving precise retaliation for murder and bodily injury occur in Exodus 21:23–25 and Deuteronomy 19:21. They are stated here because of their legal relationship to the death penalty imposed for blasphemy. One who kills a human being intentionally must pay with his life. The law code of Numbers 35:9–34 stipulates exceptions to this rule, for cases of accidental manslaughter.

18. One who kills a beast shall make restitution for it Biblical criminal law consistently differentiates between human life and the life of animals. Restitution can be made for destruction of livestock, even if intentional. This is stated most explicitly in verse 21.

shall it be done to him: [20]fracture for fracture, eye for eye, tooth for tooth. The injury he inflicted on another shall be inflicted on him. [21]One who kills a beast shall make restitution for it; but one who kills a human being shall be put to death. [22]You shall have one standard for stranger and citizen alike: for I the LORD am your God.

בַּעֲמִיתוֹ כַּאֲשֶׁר עָשָׂה כֵּן יֵעָשֶׂה לּוֹ׃ 20 שֶׁבֶר
תַּחַת שֶׁבֶר עַיִן תַּחַת עַיִן שֵׁן תַּחַת שֵׁן כַּאֲשֶׁר
יִתֵּן מוּם בָּאָדָם כֵּן יִנָּתֶן בּוֹ׃ מפטיר 21 וּמַכֵּה
בְהֵמָה יְשַׁלְּמֶנָּה וּמַכֵּה אָדָם יוּמָת׃ 22 מִשְׁפַּט
אֶחָד יִהְיֶה לָכֶם כַּגֵּר כָּאֶזְרָח יִהְיֶה כִּי אֲנִי יְהוָה
אֱלֹהֵיכֶם׃ 23 וַיְדַבֵּר מֹשֶׁה אֶל־בְּנֵי יִשְׂרָאֵל

life for life That is to say, the assessed value of the animal destroyed or of another animal provided in place of the one killed.

19. ***If anyone maims his fellow*** Hebrew *mum,* "blemish, injury," here refers to a permanent condition—the loss of a limb, an eye—or a break that does not mend, as is specified in the following verses. The same term, *mum*, is used in 21:17 and 22:20f. to describe disqualifying defects in priests and sacrificial animals.

20. ***fracture for fracture, . . . The injury he inflicted on another shall be inflicted on him*** The full implications of retaliatory punishment for injuries are explored in Excursus 9.[22]

22. ***You shall have one standard for stranger and citizen alike*** The Hebrew term *mishpat* means "norm of justice, standard." The same rules apply whether the offender or the victim are Israelites or resident non-Israelites. This stipulation must be made explicit because of the practice, in certain legal systems, of judging resident aliens by a different law. Extraterritoriality was not endorsed by biblical law in cases of killing or bodily injury, nor in cases of blasphemy.

23. ***Moses spoke thus to the Israelites*** It was important to record the actual compliance of the Israelites with God's command.[23]

The Principles of Land Tenure (25:1–26:2)

Be-har

Chapter 25 of Leviticus is the only code of practice on the subject of land tenure in ancient Israel that is preserved in the Torah. This unique collection of laws and commandments governs the permanent rights of landowners and the legalities of the sale and mortgaging of land. There are also laws regarding indebtedness and indenture, a system of repaying debts through one's labors. In chapter 25, the seventh year, when fields are to lie fallow, is called the "Sabbatical year"; and after a cycle of seven Sabbatical years—every half century—there is to be a Jubilee year.

The basic biblical theory of land tenure is expressed in verses 23–24: "But the land must not be sold beyond reclaim, for the land is Mine; you are but strangers resident with Me. Throughout the land that you hold, you must provide for the redemption of the land." Its fundamental tenet is that the land of Canaan belongs to God, who had granted it to the Israelites as an *'aḥuzzah,* "tenured land, land holding." It is not theirs to dispose of as they wish; it could not be permanently alienated. Israelite landowners who were compelled by circumstances to sell their land or to mortgage it to pay their debts retained the right to redeem, or retrieve, it. If the original owner raised the necessary funds, the creditor or purchaser was required to restore it to him; and, as a last resort, the land reverted to the original owner on the Jubilee. In effect, all transfers of land designated as *'aḥuzzah* became long-term leases and were not to be considered final sales.

Chapter 25 guarantees the rights of individual landowners in contrast to the more ancient system of *ge'ullah,* "redemption," that sought to retain ancestral land within the clan. According to that system, the redeemer, a relative within the clan, gained title to the land he had redeemed out of his own resources, for preventing loss of land to the clan as a whole was deemed more important than protecting the rights of any individual owner. Chapter 25 represents a significant adaptation of the ancient system of redemption. The redeemer from the same clan was commanded to restore the land to its original owner, as concern shifts from the clan to the individual owner.

23Moses spoke thus to the Israelites. And they took the blasphemer outside the camp and pelted him with stones. The Israelites did as the Lord had commanded Moses.

וַיּוֹצִ֣יאוּ אֶת־הַֽמְקַלֵּ֗ל אֶל־מִחוּץ֙ לַֽמַּחֲנֶ֔ה וַיִּרְגְּמ֥וּ אֹת֖וֹ אָ֑בֶן וּבְנֵֽי־יִשְׂרָאֵ֣ל עָשׂ֔וּ כַּֽאֲשֶׁ֛ר צִוָּ֥ה יְהֹוָ֖ה אֶת־מֹשֶֽׁה׃ פ

25 BE-HAR
The Lord spoke to Moses on Mount Sinai: **2**Speak to the Israelite people and say to them:

When you enter the land that I assign to you, the land shall observe a sabbath of the Lord. **3**Six years you may sow

בהר
כ״ה וַיְדַבֵּ֤ר יְהֹוָה֙ אֶל־מֹשֶׁ֔ה בְּהַ֥ר סִינַ֖י לֵאמֹֽר׃ **2** דַּבֵּ֞ר אֶל־בְּנֵ֤י יִשְׂרָאֵל֙ וְאָֽמַרְתָּ֣ אֲלֵהֶ֔ם כִּ֤י תָבֹ֨אוּ֙ אֶל־הָאָ֔רֶץ אֲשֶׁ֥ר אֲנִ֖י נֹתֵ֣ן לָכֶ֑ם וְשָֽׁבְתָ֣ה הָאָ֔רֶץ שַׁבָּ֖ת לַֽיהֹוָֽה׃ **3** שֵׁ֤שׁ שָׁנִים֙ תִּזְרַ֣ע שָׂדֶ֔ךָ וְשֵׁ֥שׁ

Indeed, land tenure is at the heart of the chapter, which does not provide for a moratorium on debts every seventh year, as does the law of Deuteronomy 15; nor does it require the release of indentured servants every seventh year, as do both Deuteronomy 15 and Exodus 21. Both of the latter chapters are primarily concerned with the alleviation of poverty. By contrast, according to the system embodied in chapter 25, a maximum of fifty years could elapse until relief was forthcoming. Undoubtedly, it was expected that by rendering sales and mortgages of land conditional and of limited duration and by guaranteeing the right of retrieval by original owners, the debilitating process of disenfranchisement could be stemmed.

In the agrarian societies of the past, virtually all indebtedness was associated with the land. One borrowed for the purpose of securing seed, implements, or work animals and to defray the cost of hiring laborers. The loan was to be repaid after the harvest. If the crop failed, or if the borrower, for whatever other reason, found himself unable to repay his debt, the next step was mortgaging or selling land. And, as a consequence, one who no longer had land to pledge or sell was often forced to indenture himself or his children in order to work off the debt. Hence the strong admonitions in chapter 25 against the abuse of fellow Israelites who had been indentured. If an Israelite became indentured to another Israelite and no redeemer came to his assistance and he, himself, could not repay his debt, there was no recourse except to await the Jubilee, when a general "release" was declared. The only exception stated in verses 47f. was when an Israelite became indentured to a non-Israelite. In that event, an additional effort was to be made on the part of his entire clan to redeem him.

Excursus 9 considers exactly how the legislation of this chapter fits into the historical development of economic institutions in biblical Israel, as seen against the background of the ancient Near East.

CHAPTER 25   THE SABBATICAL YEAR AND THE JUBILEE   (25:1–23)

The seventh year in a continuous cycle of years is called the sabbatical year (just as the seventh day is the Sabbath). In that year, the sowing and reaping of fields, as well as the pruning and picking of vines, are prohibited. What grows naturally is for the taking, by man and beast (vv. 1–7).

Every fiftieth year, a Jubilee (*yovel*) is proclaimed. On that occasion there is to be "release" (*deror*), by which all tenured land reverts to its original owners, and all indentured Israelites return to their homes. The agricultural prohibitions of the sabbatical year also apply (vv. 8–12).

All sales of land are to be considered leases, not final sales. The cost of the lease, for any who desired to "buy it out," is to be computed in terms of crop years, namely, the number of crop years remaining until the next Jubilee. This section concludes with an additional admonition against violating the laws of the sabbatical year; it emphasizes the rewards of obedience to the law (vv. 13–22).

2. When you enter the land . . . the land shall observe a sabbath of the Lord   Exodus 23:10–11 also commands the abandonment of agricultural land every seventh year, in somewhat the same terms.[1] The salient difference is that only in the Holiness Code is the seventh year called a sabbath. (As well, only here is the fiftieth year, the Jubilee, called a sabbath.) The application of the sabbatical idea to measuring time is basic to chapter 23, where, in verses 15–16, the seven weeks of

your field and six years you may prune your vineyard and
gather in the yield. [4]But in the seventh year the land shall
have a sabbath of complete rest, a sabbath of the LORD: you
shall not sow your field or prune your vineyard. [5]You shall
not reap the aftergrowth of your harvest or gather the
grapes of your untrimmed vines; it shall be a year of complete rest for the land. [6]But you may eat whatever the land
during its sabbath will produce—you, your male and
female slaves, the hired and bound laborers who live with
you, [7]and your cattle and the beasts in your land may eat all
its yield.

שָׁנִים תִּזְמֹר כַּרְמֶךָ וְאָסַפְתָּ אֶת־תְּבוּאָתָהּ׃
4 וּבַשָּׁנָה הַשְּׁבִיעִת שַׁבַּת שַׁבָּתוֹן יִהְיֶה לָאָרֶץ
שַׁבָּת לַיהוָה שָׂדְךָ לֹא תִזְרָע וְכַרְמְךָ לֹא תִזְמֹר׃
5 אֵת סְפִיחַ קְצִירְךָ לֹא תִקְצוֹר וְאֶת־עִנְּבֵי נְזִירֶךָ
לֹא תִבְצֹר שְׁנַת שַׁבָּתוֹן יִהְיֶה לָאָרֶץ׃ 6 וְהָיְתָה
שַׁבַּת הָאָרֶץ לָכֶם לְאָכְלָה לְךָ וּלְעַבְדְּךָ וְלַאֲמָתֶךָ
וְלִשְׂכִירְךָ וּלְתוֹשָׁבְךָ הַגָּרִים עִמָּךְ׃ 7 וְלִבְהֶמְתְּךָ
וְלַחַיָּה אֲשֶׁר בְּאַרְצֶךָ תִּהְיֶה כָל־תְּבוּאָתָהּ לֶאֱכֹל׃

counting prior to Shavuot are called *shabbatot,* "sabbaths." Those are weeks of days, whereas here we are speaking of weeks of years, of seven-year cycles. The land is personified—it, too, tires and requires rest.[2]

3. *Six years you may sow your field* Compare the wording in Exodus 23:10: "Six years you shall sow your land. . . ."

and six years you may prune your vineyard Hebrew *kerem,* "vineyard," is a term that may also designate olive groves, although in Exodus 23:11 olive groves and vineyards are listed as two items.

Pruning was essential for assuring the growth of the grapes. There were two prunings each year, one in the winter, or rainy season, when the shoots that had not produced grapes the previous year were snipped off, and a second in June or July, when the new blossoms had already appeared.[3]

This latter trimming is precisely described in Isaiah 18:4–10: "For before the vintage, yet after the budding,/ When the blossom has hardened into berries,/ He will trim away the twigs with pruning hooks,/ And lop off the trailing branches."

and gather in the yield That is, the yield of "the land" (*ha-'arets*) in verse 2.

4. *the land shall have a sabbath of complete rest* On the composite term *shabbat shabbaton,* "a sabbath of complete rest," see Comments to 16:31 and to 23:3.

Allowing the land to lie fallow every seventh year helped to reduce the amount of sodium in the soil, especially where irrigation was employed. This subject is treated in Excursus 10.

5. *You shall not reap the aftergrowth of your harvest* Hebrew *safiaḥ,* "aftergrowth," refers to what grows naturally the following season from seeds that had fallen to the ground during reaping. Maimonides clearly explains this in his commentary to Mishnah Kilayim 2:5: "At times, some of the plant grows a second and even a third time after reaping. That which grows a second time is called *safiaḥ,* and after a third time, *shaḥis.* This is described in Isaiah 37:30: 'This year you eat what grows of itself (*safiaḥ*), and the next year, what springs from that (*shaḥis*), and in the third year sow and reap and plant vineyards and eat their fruit.'"[4]

the grapes of your untrimmed vines Rather, "the grapes of your forbidden vines."

Hebrew *'invei nezirekha* occurs only here. The translation "untrimmed vines" is correct, functionally speaking, because vines were not to be trimmed during the Sabbatical year. Underlying this strange idiom is the law of the Nazirite (*nazir*) in Numbers 2:11–12. The Nazirite may not partake of anything that grows on the vine, probably a very ancient prohibition. Samson's mother is instructed that her son is not to drink intoxicants, for he is to be a Nazirite of God (Judg. 13:7), and the prophet Amos (2:11–12) castigates the people for giving Nazirites wine to drink. It may have been proverbial in ancient Israel to refer to grapes that grew naturally during the Sabbatical year as "Nazirite" grapes. This may be implied in the comment of Ramban: "And the vine which was not worked was called *nazir,* because one is to set it aside, and separate it from himself, as if it were not his own."

6. *the hired and bound laborers who live with you* Both terms, *sakhir* and *toshav,* are subject to varying interpretations, according to context. Hebrew *sakhir* usually refers to a laborer who works for wages, whereas *toshav* often designates a foreign "resident," a merchant or laborer. This is

[8]You shall count off seven weeks of years—seven times seven years—so that the period of seven weeks of years gives you a total of forty-nine years. [9]Then you shall sound the horn loud; in the seventh month, on the tenth day of the month—the Day of Atonement—you shall have the horn sounded throughout your land [10]and you shall hallow the fiftieth year. You shall proclaim release throughout the land for all its inhabitants. It shall be a jubilee for you: each of you shall return to his holding and each of you shall

ס 8 וְסָפַרְתָּ֣ לְךָ֗ שֶׁ֚בַע שַׁבְּתֹ֣ת שָׁנִ֔ים שֶׁ֥בַע
שָׁנִ֖ים שֶׁ֣בַע פְּעָמִ֑ים וְהָי֣וּ לְךָ֗ יְמֵי֙ שֶׁ֚בַע שַׁבְּתֹ֣ת
הַשָּׁנִ֔ים תֵּ֥שַׁע וְאַרְבָּעִ֖ים שָׁנָֽה׃ 9 וְהַֽעֲבַרְתָּ֞ שׁוֹפַ֤ר
תְּרוּעָה֙ בַּחֹ֣דֶשׁ הַשְּׁבִעִ֔י בֶּעָשׂ֖וֹר לַחֹ֑דֶשׁ בְּיוֹם֙
הַכִּפֻּרִ֔ים תַּעֲבִ֥ירוּ שׁוֹפָ֖ר בְּכָל־אַרְצְכֶֽם׃
10 וְקִדַּשְׁתֶּ֗ם אֵ֣ת שְׁנַ֤ת הַחֲמִשִּׁים֙ שָׁנָ֔ה וּקְרָאתֶ֥ם
דְּר֛וֹר בָּאָ֖רֶץ לְכָל־יֹשְׁבֶ֑יהָ יוֹבֵ֥ל הִוא֙ תִּהְיֶ֣ה לָכֶ֔ם
וְשַׁבְתֶּ֗ם אִ֚ישׁ אֶל־אֲחֻזָּת֔וֹ וְאִ֥ישׁ אֶל־מִשְׁפַּחְתּ֖וֹ

suggested here by the words *ha-garim ʿimmakh,* "who live with you." In the ancient Near East, as in other parts of the world, laborers were often billeted on the estates of their employers, and this was especially true of foreign laborers. This practice also helps to explain the translation "bound laborer" for Hebrew *toshav.* In verse 35 we read of one Israelite "holding" another as one would a "foreign resident" (*ger toshav*).[5]

Verse 6 states that one's hired and bound laborers are entitled to join in gathering what grows naturally during the Sabbatical year, just as are one's slaves. The owner of a field, grove, or vineyard may also gather in this way, so long as he does not act as an owner, but just as another Israelite, taking his turn.

7. and your cattle and the beasts in your land may eat all its yield Verses 6–7 recall Exodus 23:11, where we read that owners of fields must leave the natural growth of the land for the needy among the Israelites and for the beasts, as well. The reference to beasts symbolizes the freedom characteristic of the Sabbatical year: Man and beast are free to roam about and gather their sustenance.

8. You shall count off seven weeks of years This mirrors the wording of 23:15–16, where we read of seven weeks of *days.*

gives you a total of forty-nine years The Hebrew idiom *ve-hayu lekha* literally means "they shall be for you," but the sense is "they shall total, amount to."[6]

9. Then you shall sound the horn loud Hebrew *teruʿah* is the term for the sustained, loud blast of the shofar.[7]

in the seventh month, on the tenth day of the month The sounding of the shofar five days before the autumn harvest festival of Sukkot served to proclaim the advent of the Jubilee. According to 23:27 (and 16:29) this was the day of Yom Kippur. There is an obvious problem in this statement: The year of the Jubilee is said to begin in the seventh month of the year. Two calendars, each with its own history, are reflected in this verse.[8] The year of the Jubilee began in the autumn, whereas the calendar in regular use numbered the months from the springtime, as prescribed in Exodus 12:1–2.

10. and you shall hallow the fiftieth year. The Jubilee year is to be hallowed just as the Sabbath day is hallowed. The verb *kiddesh,* "to sanctify, hallow," is customarily used to convey the sanctification of the Sabbath; by using this verb in connection with the Jubilee, a parallelism between the two occasions is created.[9]

You shall proclaim release throughout the land for all its inhabitants The Hebrew term *deror* has conventionally been rendered "freedom, liberty." More has been learned about it in recent years, however. Hebrew *deror* is cognate with Akkadian *andurāru,* which designates an edict of release issued by the Old Babylonian kings and some of their successors. This edict was often issued by a king upon ascending the throne and was a feature of a more extensive legal institution known as *mesharum,* a moratorium declared on debts and indenture.[10] The Akkadian verb *darāru,* like Hebrew *d-r-r,* means "to move about freely," referring in this instance to the freedom granted those bound by servitude.[11] In Jeremiah 34:15, we read that, as the Chaldeans approached Jerusalem, King Zedekiah ordered the people to release their indentured servants, to proclaim a *deror,* "release." In Isaiah 61:1,

return to his family. 11That fiftieth year shall be a jubilee for
you: you shall not sow, neither shall you reap the aftergrowth or harvest the untrimmed vines, 12for it is a jubilee.
It shall be holy to you: you may only eat the growth direct
from the field.

13In this year of jubilee, each of you shall return to his
holding. 14When you sell property to your neighbor, or buy
any from your neighbor, you shall not wrong one another.

תָּשֻׁבוּ׃ 11 יוֹבֵל הִוא שְׁנַת הַחֲמִשִּׁים שָׁנָה תִּהְיֶה
לָכֶם לֹא תִזְרָעוּ וְלֹא תִקְצְרוּ אֶת־סְפִיחֶיהָ וְלֹא
תִבְצְרוּ אֶת־נְזִרֶיהָ׃ 12 כִּי יוֹבֵל הִוא קֹדֶשׁ תִּהְיֶה
לָכֶם מִן־הַשָּׂדֶה תֹּאכְלוּ אֶת־תְּבוּאָתָהּ׃ 13 בִּשְׁנַת
הַיּוֹבֵל הַזֹּאת תָּשֻׁבוּ אִישׁ אֶל־אֲחֻזָּתוֹ׃ שני
14 וְכִי־תִמְכְּרוּ מִמְכָּר לַעֲמִיתֶךָ אוֹ קָנֹה מִיַּד
עֲמִיתֶךָ אַל־תּוֹנוּ אִישׁ אֶת־אָחִיו׃ 15 בְּמִסְפַּר

the Judeans exiled in Babylonia are to be freed under terms of a *deror* as they are restored to their land. The biblical laws of the Jubilee year thus incorporate Near Eastern legal institutions of great antiquity.

It shall be a jubilee for you Hebrew *yovel* means both "ram" and "ram's horn."[12] The fiftieth year is called "Jubilee" because its advent is proclaimed by sounding the ram's horn.

each of you shall return to his holding This refers primarily to families who were evicted from their homes and farms due to foreclosure and who had been unable to repay their loans. This situation is clearly projected in verses 13–17 and, again, in verses 25–28.

The term *'aḥuzzah,* "tenured land, land holding," is the key to a proper understanding of chapter 25 as a whole. It receives considerable attention in Excursus 10. Here, it suffices to emphasize the rule that an *'aḥuzzah* is settled and worked by permission of the rulers of the land. Verse 23 states: "For the land is Mine," namely, the Lord's. God granted the Israelite people the land of Canaan as its *'aḥuzzah.* The Israelites are God's tenants, so to speak. They do not possess or rule the land as a result of conquest, and they do not have the right to dispose of it as if it were entirely their own. This is the basic theory of land tenure expressed in the legislation of chapter 25, and it is the foundation for the laws governing sale and purchase of most real estate owned, in the usual sense, by Israelites.

and each of you shall return to his family Rather, "to his clan." The Hebrew term *mishpaḥah* designates the basic socioeconomic unit in ancient Israel. It was more inclusive than the immediate family, which is the unit whose parameters are reflected in the incest laws of chapters 18 and 20.[13]

Understood in terms of Exodus 21:2f. and Deuteronomy 15:12f., this means that indentured Israelites, compelled to live on the estates of their creditors, would be free to return to their own homes. In those other legal statements we read of the master "dismissing, freeing" his indentured servants, allowing them to return home.[14] In 2 Kings 4:1f. we are told how a certain creditor sought to take a woman's son away from home to work as an indentured servant.

11. ***That fiftieth year shall be a jubilee for you*** The syntax of the Hebrew is somewhat unusual. Literally, it reads: "It is a Jubilee, the fiftieth year—it shall be for you."

you shall not sow See Comments to verses 4–5 regarding the formulation of this commandment.

12. ***you may only eat the growth direct from the field*** This is the sense of *min ha-sadeh,* "from the field." The same wording occurs in Exodus 23:16, in the context of harvesting directly from the field. Here, the owner of fields and groves is forbidden to harvest his yield in the usual way, but must leave it for all to eat. He may, of course, join in with others to gather food, but not in the status of an owner.

13. ***In this year of jubilee, each of you shall return to his holding*** This is a general, introductory statement. It is followed by a delineation of the specific conditions under which a person was likely to lose possession of his land in the first place.

14. ***When you sell property to your neighbor*** The verb *timkeru,* "you sell," is in the plural, whereas *la-'amitekha* has a singular suffix. Such fluctuations of syntax occasionally occur in biblical Hebrew.[15] The term *'amit,* "neighbor," refers to a fellow Israelite and would not be used to designate a non-Israelite. This law only applies to transfers of property among Israelites.[16]

15In buying from your neighbor, you shall deduct only for
the number of years since the jubilee; and in selling to you,
he shall charge you only for the remaining crop years: 16the
more such years, the higher the price you pay; the fewer
such years, the lower the price; for what he is selling you is a
number of harvests. 17Do not wrong one another, but fear
your God; for I the LORD am your God.

18You shall observe My laws and faithfully keep My rules,
that you may live upon the land in security; 19the land shall
yield its fruit and you shall eat your fill, and you shall live

שָׁנִים אַחַר הַיּוֹבֵל תִּקְנֶה מֵאֵת עֲמִיתֶךָ בְּמִסְפַּר
שְׁנֵי־תְבוּאֹת יִמְכָּר־לָךְ׃ 16 לְפִי רֹב הַשָּׁנִים
תַּרְבֶּה מִקְנָתוֹ וּלְפִי מְעֹט הַשָּׁנִים תַּמְעִיט מִקְנָתוֹ
כִּי מִסְפַּר תְּבוּאֹת הוּא מֹכֵר לָךְ׃ 17 וְלֹא תוֹנוּ
אִישׁ אֶת־עֲמִיתוֹ וְיָרֵאתָ מֵאֱלֹהֶיךָ כִּי אֲנִי יְהֹוָה
אֱלֹהֵיכֶם׃ 18 וַעֲשִׂיתֶם אֶת־חֻקֹּתַי וְאֶת־מִשְׁפָּטַי
תִּשְׁמְרוּ וַעֲשִׂיתֶם אֹתָם וִישַׁבְתֶּם עַל־הָאָרֶץ
לָבֶטַח׃ שלישי [שני כשהן מחוברות]
19 וְנָתְנָה הָאָרֶץ פִּרְיָהּ וַאֲכַלְתֶּם לָשֹׂבַע וִישַׁבְתֶּם

Hebrew *mimkar* literally means "what is sold," namely, "possessions, property." Compare Ezekiel 7:13: "For the seller shall not return to what he sold (*ha-mimkar*)."

you shall not wrong one another The verb *honah* connotes economic oppression or fraud, as is explained in the Comment to 19:33. Ezekiel (45:9f.) admonishes the princes of Israel not to "oppress" the people in matters of land and currency. How to avoid fraud in land transfers is explained in the following verses.

15. In buying from your neighbor The value of leases on the land was to be computed in terms of crop years. Since all land that was "sold" would revert to its original owners at the next Jubilee, the price was to be equivalent to the number of crops the purchaser would realize from the land before that occasion. The same principle operated in the case of indentured Israelites, as we read in verse 50, regarding the period of time they would continue to serve. Thus, if at the time of the sale only a few years remained, the cost of the lease would be relatively small.

16. the more such years, the higher the price you pay . . . Rather, "The more the [remaining] years, the higher you may fix its purchase price, and the less the [remaining] years, the lower its purchase price. For he is actually selling you a number of crop years." The term *miknah,* "purchase, what is purchased," is known from Jeremiah 32:11, where we find *sefer ha-miknah,* "the deed of purchase."[17] Our verse restates the rule set forth in verse 15 that "sales" of agricultural land held as an *'aḥuzzah* are, legally speaking, leases.

17. Do not wrong one another, but fear your God This repeats, for emphasis, the statement of verse 14. It is characteristic of the Holiness Code to exhort the Israelite people to act out of fear of God, especially in matters that do not lend themselves easily to enforcement. Only those who realize that God sees all and will punish even secret transgressions of His laws will resist the temptation to try to get away with their sins and their crimes.

18. You shall observe My laws Verses 18–22 interrupt the continuity of the legislation governing the Sabbatical year and the Jubilee year. This subject is resumed in verse 23, which then concludes this section of chapter 25. Verse 23 takes up where verse 17 leaves off: After stipulating the rules for the sale of land, verse 23 reemphasizes the point that such sales are not final. Verses 18–22 constitute, therefore, an exhortation to obey God's laws and commandments, with the promise of security and abundance as a reward for such obedience.

that you may live upon the land in security Here, and in verse 19, Hebrew *la-vetaḥ,* "in security," describes a situation in which a people is safe from attack and need not fear invasions. It is customarily a feature of the covenantal promise to Israel, expressed most emphatically in the Book of Deuteronomy. In Judges 18:7f. we find a description of a people living "securely." The residents of Laish in southern Phoenicia never expected an inland attack and consequently were overwhelmed by the tribe of Dan without recourse to fighting. The Israelite people will subdue its enemies all around, so that they may live securely, without fear, as we read in Deuteronomy 12:10: "When you cross the Jordan and settle in the land that the LORD your God is allotting to you, and He grants you safety from all your enemies around you and you live in security (*betaḥ*)."[18]

upon it in security. 20And should you ask, "What are we to eat in the seventh year, if we may neither sow nor gather in our crops?" 21I will ordain My blessing for you in the sixth year, so that it shall yield a crop sufficient for three years. 22When you sow in the eighth year, you will still be eating old grain of that crop; you will be eating the old until the ninth year, until its crops come in.

23But the land must not be sold beyond reclaim, for the land is Mine; you are but strangers resident with Me.

לָבֶ֖טַח עָלֶֽיהָ׃ 20 וְכִ֣י תֹאמְר֔וּ מַה־נֹּאכַ֖ל בַּשָּׁנָ֣ה
הַשְּׁבִיעִ֑ת הֵ֚ן לֹ֣א נִזְרָ֔ע וְלֹ֥א נֶאֱסֹ֖ף אֶת־תְּבוּאָתֵֽנוּ׃
21 וְצִוִּ֤יתִי אֶת־בִּרְכָתִי֙ לָכֶ֔ם בַּשָּׁנָ֖ה הַשִּׁשִּׁ֑ית
וְעָשָׂת֙ אֶת־הַתְּבוּאָ֔ה לִשְׁלֹ֖שׁ הַשָּׁנִֽים׃ 22 וּזְרַעְתֶּ֗ם
אֵ֚ת הַשָּׁנָ֣ה הַשְּׁמִינִ֔ת וַאֲכַלְתֶּ֖ם מִן־הַתְּבוּאָ֣ה יָשָׁ֑ן
עַ֣ד ׀ הַשָּׁנָ֣ה הַתְּשִׁיעִ֗ת עַד־בּוֹא֙ תְּב֣וּאָתָ֔הּ תֹּאכְל֖וּ
יָשָֽׁן׃ 23 וְהָאָ֗רֶץ לֹ֤א תִמָּכֵר֙ לִצְמִתֻ֔ת כִּי־לִ֖י הָאָ֑רֶץ
כִּֽי־גֵרִ֧ים וְתוֹשָׁבִ֛ים אַתֶּ֖ם עִמָּדִֽי׃ 24 וּבְכֹ֖ל אֶ֣רֶץ

19. the land shall yield its fruit and you shall eat your fill Along with security will come fertility and abundance. Hebrew *sovaʿ*, "plenty, satiety," is a term with an interesting history in the ancient Near East. It occurs in royal inscriptions relating the achievements of kings who provided well for their peoples. In the Hebrew Bible, it frequently pertains to God's promise of blessing, since God is the ultimate provider of His people.[19] This reference to abundant fertility links verse 19 to verses 20–22, which pertain to the Sabbatical year rather than to the Jubilee itself. Verses 20–22 take their cue from the theme of abundance.

20. "What are we to eat in the seventh year, if we may neither sow nor gather in our crops?" Hebrew *hen,* "if," is merely a different form of the conditional particle *ʾim.*[20] This verse projects the anxiety of the people. They are assured that the crop of the sixth year will be so abundant that it will last beyond the end of the seventh year, when they would normally rely on a new crop. The sense is: "What are we to eat at the end of the seventh year and well into the eighth year?"

21. I will ordain My blessing This and verse 22 are the response. Until the crop of the eighth year is harvested, you will have sufficient food from the "old" crop, namely, that of the sixth year. The language recalls Deuteronomy 28:8: "The Lord will ordain blessings for you." The Hebrew verb *tsivvah,* "to command, ordain," has as its primary sense "to dispatch, send." God employs the forces of nature, which are under His control, to provide for His people.[21]

so that it shall yield a crop sufficient for three years The verb *ʿasah* may connote "producing" crops or fruit. Compare Psalms 107:37: *va-yaʿasu peri tevuʾah,* "that yield a fruitful harvest."[22]

22. you will still be eating old grain Compare 26:10, where Hebrew *yashan*, "old grain," contrasts with *ḥadash,* "new grain."[23]

23. But the land must not be sold beyond reclaim The text returns to its principal subject: the status of *ʾaḥuzzah* land as inalienable. Hebrew *li-tsemitut* does not mean "in perpetuity." We now know its precise meaning from the Akkadian contracts discovered at Ugarit. In these documents, the descriptive term *tsamit* (or *tsamat*) means "finally handed over." This term establishes that the sale recorded is final and that the property sold is irretrievable. A clause will often read *tsamit adi dāriti,* "finally handed over to all generations." The sale is permanent, because it is final and concluded at the full price. This clause corresponds to the formula appearing in verse 30 of our chapter. That formula deals with sales of urban dwellings that become final if not redeemed within one year: *li-tsemitut la-koneh ʾoto le-dorotav,* literally "finally handed over to the one who purchases it, to his generations."[24] One verse states that sales of *ʾaḥuzzah* land are not of that status; they are not *li-tsemitut.*

As was true of the institution of "release" (*deror*), prescribed in verse 10, we find in the term *tsemitut* another instance of very ancient terminology in chapter 25. The repeated emphasis in our legislation on computing the price of the land in terms of crop years also relates to the fact that in the Akkadian contracts from Ugarit, property "finally handed over" is at the full price. Not so *ʾaḥuzzah* land.[25]

you are but strangers resident with Me The Israelites—merely God's tenants in the land of Canaan—do not have the right to alienate the land.

24Throughout the land that you hold, you must provide for
the redemption of the land.
25If your kinsman is in straits and has to sell part of his
holding, his nearest redeemer shall come and redeem what
his kinsman has sold. 26If a man has no one to redeem for
him, but prospers and acquires enough to redeem with,

אֲחֻזַּתְכֶם גְּאֻלָּה תִּתְּנוּ לָאָרֶץ׃ ס רביעי
25 כִּי־יָמוּךְ אָחִיךָ וּמָכַר מֵאֲחֻזָּתוֹ וּבָא גֹאֲלוֹ
הַקָּרֹב אֵלָיו וְגָאַל אֵת מִמְכַּר אָחִיו׃ 26 וְאִישׁ כִּי
לֹא יִהְיֶה־לּוֹ גֹּאֵל וְהִשִּׂיגָה יָדוֹ וּמָצָא כְּדֵי גְאֻלָּתוֹ׃

ADDITIONAL LAWS REGARDING LAND TENURE AND INDENTURE (25:24–55)

As we have seen, the permanent alienation of land classified as *'aḥuzzah,* "tenured land," is prohibited. It is stressed here that clan relatives are obligated to redeem the lands of their relatives in the event of sale or foreclosure. One whose own fortunes improved was then duty-bound to redeem his own land by paying off the remainder of the creditor's, or purchaser's, lease. But even if no redemption was possible, the land reverted to its original owner at the Jubilee (vv. 23–28).

Urban real estate, located within city walls, was exempt from the general rule. It could be redeemed for only one year after its sale; afterward it was considered permanently alienated. Two other, related provisions are included in the legislation. Village dwellings, where no walls encompass the settlement, were subject to the general rule, and could still be redeemed after one year; they reverted on the Jubilee, just like agricultural land. As regards the holdings of the Levites, property within the Levitical cities could be redeemed indefinitely, but the enclosed areas adjacent to the Levitical cities could never be sold in the first instance. They were effectively removed from the sphere of economic activity (vv. 29–34) and held in trust for the Levites.

We then encounter three related laws governing indebtedness and indenture. (1) If one Israelite becomes indebted to another, he may not be charged any form of interest on his debt. (2) If one Israelite becomes indentured to another, he may not be treated as a slave and must be given his freedom in the Jubilee year, at the latest. (3) If an Israelite becomes indentured to a non-Israelite, efforts must be undertaken by the entire clan to redeem him as soon as possible. If not redeemed, such an indentured Israelite gains his freedom at the next Jubilee, along with his wife and children (vv. 35–55).

This section of Leviticus concludes with a series of commandments, prohibiting idolatry of various sorts and enjoining the Israelites to observe the Sabbath and show respect for what is sacred (26:1–2).

24. you must provide for the redemption of the land After stipulating the basis for computing sales of *'aḥuzzah* land, the legislation now deals with the law of redemption, an alternative that is preferable to the Jubilee. Land should be retrieved as soon as it is financially feasible. The effect of this law is to obligate the purchaser to accept the redemption payment of the original owner. He may not refuse to do so. Verse 24 is a general statement that is followed by a series of situations in which the rule applies.

25. If your kinsman is in straits The Hebrew verb *m-w-kh,* which occurs only in this chapter and in 27:8, is probably related to the root *m-k-k,* "to collapse." In Late Hebrew we find the form *namokh,* "low." The sense is that of "reduction" to poverty.[26]

his nearest redeemer It is preferable to understand Hebrew *karov* as "relative, one closely related," within the clan, as is explained in the Comment to 21:2. The order of relatedness is delineated below in verses 48–49. An actual redemption of this kind is recorded in Jeremiah 32:6–14, although the legalities of that act differ somewhat from the law set forth in this chapter. Here, the object of redemption is to restore the property to one's relative, who would retain possession of his land within the clan. The redeemer would not possess the land himself.

26. but prospers and acquires enough to redeem with The Hebrew idiom *ve-hissigah yado* literally means "his hand reaches," which is to say that he has the means "at hand." The idiom

27he shall compute the years since its sale, refund the difference to the man to whom he sold it, and return to his holding. 28If he lacks sufficient means to recover it, what he sold shall remain with the purchaser until the jubilee; in the jubilee year it shall be released, and he shall return to his holding.

29If a man sells a dwelling house in a walled city, it may be redeemed until a year has elapsed since its sale; the redemption period shall be a year. 30If it is not redeemed before a full year has elapsed, the house in the walled city shall pass to the purchaser beyond reclaim throughout the ages; it shall not be released in the jubilee. 31But houses in

27 וְחִשַּׁב֙ אֶת־שְׁנֵ֣י מִמְכָּר֔וֹ וְהֵשִׁיב֙ אֶת־הָ֣עֹדֵ֔ף לָאִ֕ישׁ אֲשֶׁ֥ר מָֽכַר־ל֖וֹ וְשָׁ֥ב לַאֲחֻזָּתֽוֹ: 28 וְאִם־לֹ֨א מָֽצְאָ֜ה יָד֗וֹ דֵּי֮ הָשִׁ֣יב לוֹ֒ וְהָיָ֣ה מִמְכָּר֗וֹ בְּיַד֙ הַקֹּנֶ֣ה אֹת֔וֹ עַ֖ד שְׁנַ֣ת הַיּוֹבֵ֑ל וְיָצָא֙ בַּיֹּבֵ֔ל וְשָׁ֖ב לַאֲחֻזָּתֽוֹ: 29 וְאִ֗ישׁ כִּֽי־יִמְכֹּ֤ר בֵּית־מוֹשַׁב֙ עִ֣יר חוֹמָ֔ה וְהָיְתָ֣ה גְּאֻלָּת֔וֹ עַד־תֹּ֖ם שְׁנַ֣ת מִמְכָּר֑וֹ יָמִ֖ים תִּהְיֶ֥ה גְאֻלָּתֽוֹ: 30 וְאִ֣ם לֹֽא־יִגָּאֵ֡ל עַד־מְלֹ֣את לוֹ֩ שָׁנָ֨ה תְמִימָ֜ה וְ֠קָם הַבַּ֨יִת אֲשֶׁר־בָּעִ֜יר אֲשֶׁר־לֹ֣א חֹמָ֗ה לַצְּמִיתֻ֛ת לַקֹּנֶ֥ה אֹת֖וֹ לְדֹֽרֹתָ֑יו לֹ֥א יֵצֵ֖א בַּיֹּבֵֽל: 31 וּבָתֵּ֣י

חמישי [שלישי כשהן מחוברות]

ק לֽוֹ v. 30.

mats'ah yado has the slightly different meaning "he is able," literally "his hand has overtaken." The idiomatic formulation creates a practical sequence: A person acquires the means and is therefore able to redeem his land.27

27. **he shall compute the years since its sale** Hebrew *ḥishev,* "to record, keep on account," occurs in 2 Kings 12:16, literally, "But they do not keep an accounting of the men to whom the silver is remitted for paying the workers, for they work on trust." This connotation is an extension of the sense of calculating. Ecclesiastes preserves the related forms *ḥishavon* and *ḥeshbon,* "calculation."28

refund the difference Two other usages bear explanation. Hebrew *'odef,* "surplus, excess," is an ancient accounting term, and the verb *heshiv,* normally "to bring back, return," may mean "to pay, to refund," as it does here.29 The procedure was that one who wished to redeem land he had sold had to pay the purchaser the value of the rest of his lease; that is, he deducted from the price the value of the years the purchaser had already benefited from the land.

28. **it shall be released** The Hebrew verb *yatsa'* used here, which simply means "to go out, depart," may have the specialized connotation of gaining one's freedom, changing status, or being released. An indentured servant "departs" from his master's estate, which means that he gains release. Cognates of Hebrew *yatsa'* in other Semitic languages, such as Akkadian *atsû,* may also have this connotation.30

To summarize the preceding verses: An owner of land who had sold it under economic stress could redeem it at any time, either through his own resources or those of a clan relative. Implicit in the law is the fact that the purchaser could not refuse the right of redemption.

29. **If a man sells a dwelling house in a walled city** The law of redemption is limited in the case of urban dwellings. A town, defined as an area surrounded by a wall, is excluded from the tenure system applicable to agricultural land held as an *'aḥuzzah.* In the ancient Near East, towns and cities had a special status as regards tax exemptions and legal prerogatives. In agrarian societies arable land and, to a degree, pastureland as well were the mainstay of the economy. They accounted for most of the employment in addition to their value as the source of food. In the towns lived the artisans, and those we would today call members of the service professions, which often included members of priestly families. The implications of these realities are discussed in Excursus 10.

the redemption period shall be a year Literally, "for days." Hebrew *yamim,* "days," when used in certain contexts, is a way of indicating a year of days. This is clarified by verse 30, as though by way of explanation: "before a full year has elapsed." Similarly, in 1 Samuel 1:21, *zevaḥ ha-yamim* is best rendered "the annual sacrifice."

30. **shall pass to the purchaser beyond reclaim throughout the ages** Rather, "shall legally become the property of the purchaser." Here, the sense of Hebrew *ve-kam,* literally "to stand," is "to belong to, become the property of." Compare Genesis 23:20, literally, "And the field and the cave within it became the property (*va-yakom*) of Abraham." This meaning is rare, but precise, when it occurs.31

villages that have no encircling walls shall be classed as
open country: they may be redeemed, and they shall be
released through the jubilee. 32As for the cities of the
Levites, the houses in the cities they hold—the Levites shall
forever have the right of redemption. 33Such property as
may be redeemed from the Levites—houses sold in a city
they hold—shall be released through the jubilee; for the
houses in the cities of the Levites are their holding among
the Israelites. 34But the unenclosed land about their cities
cannot be sold, for that is their holding for all time.

הַחֲצֵרִים אֲשֶׁר אֵין־לָהֶם חֹמָה סָבִיב עַל־שְׂדֵה
הָאָרֶץ יֵחָשֵׁב גְּאֻלָּה תִּהְיֶה־לּוֹ וּבַיֹּבֵל יֵצֵא׃
32 וְעָרֵי הַלְוִיִּם בָּתֵּי עָרֵי אֲחֻזָּתָם גְּאֻלַּת עוֹלָם
תִּהְיֶה לַלְוִיִּם׃ 33 וַאֲשֶׁר יִגְאַל מִן־הַלְוִיִּם וְיָצָא
מִמְכַּר־בַּיִת וְעִיר אֲחֻזָּתוֹ בַּיֹּבֵל כִּי בָתֵּי עָרֵי
הַלְוִיִּם הִוא אֲחֻזָּתָם בְּתוֹךְ בְּנֵי יִשְׂרָאֵל׃ 34 וּשְׂדֵה
מִגְרַשׁ עָרֵיהֶם לֹא יִמָּכֵר כִּי־אֲחֻזַּת עוֹלָם הוּא
לָהֶם׃ ס 35 וְכִי־יָמוּךְ אָחִיךָ וּמָטָה יָדוֹ עִמָּךְ

31. *But houses in villages that have no encircling walls* The term used here for "villages," Hebrew *ḥatserim,* has an interesting history. It was originally a pastoral term, synonymous with "tents." Deuteronomy 2:23 relates that the land of the Ammonites in Transjordan was once populated by a people who lived in *ḥatserim.* According to Isaiah 42:11, the Kedemite tribes lived in such encampments in the vicinity of Petra. In the genealogy of Genesis 25:13ff., the clans of Ishmael, who were related to the Kedemites, lived in *ḥatserim* and *tirot,* "circular encampments."[32] Here, reference is primarily to agricultural villages, where there were houses, not tents, and fields, not pastureland.

shall be classed as open country Rather, "Shall be classed as arable land." The sense of the Hebrew verb *yeḥashev* is "to be counted among, considered part of."[33] Dwellings located in unwalled towns are considered part of the *ʾaḥuzzah* of the Israelites and therefore are subject to the general rule governing such lands. They are different from urban dwellings, in general. Hebrew *sedeh ha-ʾarets,* literally "the field of the land," means, in effect, agricultural land.

32. *As for the cities of the Levites, the houses in the cities they hold* The urban dwellings of the Levites within their cities are to be released on the Jubilee and are redeemable, unlike other urban dwellings, which are subject to a different law, according to verse 31. In Numbers 35:1–18, we read that the Levites are to be given forty-eight towns, inclusive of the six "cities of asylum" established by the legislation of Deuteronomy 19:2–9. These towns are to be considered a surrogate *ʾaḥuzzah,* in place of agricultural land. Verse 34 adds that the areas adjacent to the Levitical towns are included in this surrogate *ʾaḥuzzah,* an arrangement necessitated by the fact that the Levites were not assigned a territory, as were the other tribes of Israel, as we learn from Deuteronomy 18:1–2.

33. *Such property as may be redeemed from the Levites—houses sold in a city they hold—shall be released through the jubilee* The parenthetical comment, separated by dashes in the translation, may be a gloss inserted by a later writer to explain the anomalous usage of the verb *gaʾal* in this verse. It usually means "to redeem," reflecting the system of clan responsibility for assisting needy relatives; but that meaning does not work here because this verse concerns urban dwellings sold or mortgaged *by* Levites who found themselves in difficult financial straits. The clause *ʾasher yigʾal min ha-leviʾim* should, therefore, be understood to mean "which is appropriated from the Levites," namely, by those who had either purchased it or held it as security for debts.[34] Since the Levitical towns are the surrogate *ʾaḥuzzah* of the Levites, properties within them come under the provisions of the *ʾaḥuzzah.* As in verse 28, usage of the verb *yatsaʾ,* "to depart," is legal: "to be released, to go free."

34. *But the unenclosed land about their cities cannot be sold* The term translated "unenclosed land (*migrash*)" originally designated an area for livestock. Like the term *ḥatserim* encountered in verse 31 it came to designate an area used primarily for gardening or agriculture, although the Levites may also have kept their livestock there.[35] Such areas, immediately outside the towns, could not be sold under any circumstances, no matter how severe the economic situation of the Levites. Held in trust for the Levites, they were effectively removed from the context of indebtedness. Perhaps the reason for this exceptional restriction was related to the sustenance that the Levites derived from such plots of land, the only ones they possessed.

for that is their holding for all time The composite term *ʾaḥuzzat ʿolam,* "a holding for all time," is best known from the covenantal promises to the patriarchs and to other leaders of the

35 If your kinsman, being in straits, comes under your authority, and you hold him as though a resident alien, let him live by your side: 36 do not exact from him advance or accrued interest, but fear your God. Let him live by your side as your kinsman. 37 Do not lend him money at advance interest, or give him your food at accrued interest. 38 I the LORD am your God, who brought you out of the land of Egypt, to give you the land of Canaan, to be your God.

39 If your kinsman under you continues in straits and must give himself over to you, do not subject him to the

וְהֶחֱזַ֣קְתָּ בּ֔וֹ גֵּ֥ר וְתוֹשָׁ֖ב וָחַ֥י עִמָּֽךְ׃ 36 אַל־תִּקַּ֤ח
מֵֽאִתּוֹ֙ נֶ֣שֶׁךְ וְתַרְבִּ֔ית וְיָרֵ֖אתָ מֵּֽאֱלֹהֶ֑יךָ וְחֵ֥י אָחִ֖יךָ
עִמָּֽךְ׃ 37 אֶ֨ת־כַּסְפְּךָ֔ לֹֽא־תִתֵּ֥ן ל֖וֹ בְּנֶ֑שֶׁךְ וּבְמַרְבִּ֖ית
לֹא־תִתֵּ֥ן אָכְלֶֽךָ׃ 38 אֲנִ֗י יְהוָה֙ אֱלֹ֣הֵיכֶ֔ם אֲשֶׁר־
הוֹצֵ֥אתִי אֶתְכֶ֖ם מֵאֶ֣רֶץ מִצְרָ֑יִם לָתֵ֤ת לָכֶם֙ אֶת־
אֶ֣רֶץ כְּנַ֔עַן לִהְי֥וֹת לָכֶ֖ם לֵאלֹהִֽים׃ ס ששי
[רביעי כשהן מחוברות] 39 וְכִֽי־יָמ֥וּךְ אָחִ֛יךָ
עִמָּ֖ךְ וְנִמְכַּר־לָ֑ךְ לֹא־תַעֲבֹ֥ד בּ֖וֹ עֲבֹ֥דַת עָֽבֶד׃

Israelites.[36] In such contexts, the sense is that the rights conferred by God to the Israelites over the land are permanent, for all time. In verse 46, non-Israelite slaves may be owned by Israelites as "property for all time (*'aḥuzzah le-'olam*)." Like the land itself, the non-Israelite population of Canaan and the foreigners from surrounding lands were subdued. In our verse, however, *'aḥuzzat 'olam* is a specific legal term. It is a way of stating that the plots (*migrash*) of the Levites are protected from liability and remain continuously in the possession of the Levites.

35. *If your kinsman, being in straits, comes under your authority* Verses 35–38 deal with indebtedness, just as further on, verses 39–41 deal with indenture, which is a more severe set of circumstances. The crucial difference between them is that one who possesses property that he can sell or mortgage is still free, but one who has no assets must work off his debts as an indentured servant.

The sense of Hebrew *ki yamukh* is "if he is reduced," as is explained in the Comment to verse 25. The idiom *u-matah yado* occurs only here. Literally it means "if his hand stumbles, buckles." This image is usually applied to stumbling feet. Here, the sense is not physically graphic, but rather situational: *u-matah yado 'immakh,* literally "if he lost his means in dealing with you," that is, if he became indebted to you. This usage expresses the opposite of *ve-hissigah yado,* literally "his hand reaches," in verse 25, or *mats'ah yado,* "his hand overtakes," in verse 28. Both of those idioms indicate adequate means, whereas *matah yado* indicates inadequate means.

and you hold him as though a resident alien On the composite term *ger toshav,* "resident alien," see Comment to verse 6. One who mortgaged his land or sold it to another became, in a real sense, a tenant on his own land.

let him live by your side The same idiom, slightly expanded, occurs in the next verse: *ve-ḥai 'aḥikha 'immakh,* "let him live by your side, as your brother." The precise sense of this idiom is hard to determine. It could be taken to mean that the person involved may not be evicted from his land, but he must be allowed to continue to reside at your side as a member of the community.[37]

36. *do not exact from him advance or accrued interest* Literally, Hebrew *neshekh* means "a bite," and *tarbit* means "increment, profit" on a loan, as noted by Ramban. An alternate form, in verse 37, is *marbit.* In Exodus 22:24, we read: "Exact no interest (*neshekh*) from them" and in Deuteronomy 23:20: "You shall not deduct interest (*neshekh*) from loans to your countrymen." In late Hebrew we encounter the term *ribbit* based on the same root as *tarbit* and *marbit.* All of these three terms are cognate with Aramaic *marbitha'*, and probably as well with Akkadian *ribbatum,* which means "back payment, arrears."[38] If so, the sense would be the additional payment one owed from the time he borrowed. The fact that in verse 37 *neshekh* is used with reference to silver and *marbit* with reference to foodstuffs led Mishnah Bava Metsia 5:1 to define *neshekh* as a demand for payment in excess of what was lent, and *tarbit* or *marbit* as the demand for more grain or foodstuffs than were provided to the borrower. The Mishnah deals extensively with fluctuations in market prices for commodities, from one season of the year to the next. Typically, one went into debt at the time of planting, with the expectation of repaying the debt after the harvest.

38. *I the LORD am your God* The God who gave the Israelites a land of their own and freed them from the servitude of Egypt now commands them, in turn, to prevent conditions of servitude among their own people.

treatment of a slave. 40He shall remain with you as a hired or bound laborer; he shall serve with you only until the jubilee year. 41Then he and his children with him shall be free of your authority; he shall go back to his family and return to his ancestral holding.—42For they are My servants, whom I freed from the land of Egypt; they may not give themselves over into servitude.—43You shall not rule over him ruthlessly; you shall fear your God. 44Such male

40 כְּשָׂכִיר כְּתוֹשָׁב יִהְיֶה עִמָּךְ עַד־שְׁנַת הַיֹּבֵל
יַעֲבֹד עִמָּךְ׃ 41 וְיָצָא מֵעִמָּךְ הוּא וּבָנָיו עִמּוֹ וְשָׁב
אֶל־מִשְׁפַּחְתּוֹ וְאֶל־אֲחֻזַּת אֲבֹתָיו יָשׁוּב׃ 42 כִּי־
עֲבָדַי הֵם אֲשֶׁר־הוֹצֵאתִי אֹתָם מֵאֶרֶץ מִצְרָיִם לֹא
יִמָּכְרוּ מִמְכֶּרֶת עָבֶד׃ 43 לֹא־תִרְדֶּה בוֹ בְּפָרֶךְ
וְיָרֵאתָ מֵאֱלֹהֶיךָ׃ 44 וְעַבְדְּךָ וַאֲמָתְךָ אֲשֶׁר יִהְיוּ־

39. *If your kinsman . . . must give himself over to you* Verses 39–46 deal with indenture. An Israelite indentured to another must not be treated as a slave. He may not be overworked, and he must be granted release in the Jubilee year. Hebrew *ve-nimkar,* "to be sold," must be understood as being handed over to indenture.

do not subject him to the treatment of a slave Hebrew *ʿeved* has many connotations, all expressive of "serving." Here, it refers to indenture, not to slavery in the full economic sense of the term.

40. *He shall remain with you as a hired or bound laborer* For this terminology, see Comments to verses 6, 23, and 35. The legal status of the indentured Israelite is that of an employee.

he shall serve with you only until the jubilee year This provision differs from the laws of Exodus 21:1–6 and Deuteronomy 15:12–18, both of which set the limit of service at six years. According to our legislation, indenture may last as long as fifty years. If contrasted with actual slavery, or with serfdom, which continue through the generations, our law is relatively lenient; but compared with the other laws of the Torah, it is most severe and allows for almost lifelong indenture. This could, of course, occur under the laws of Exodus 21 and Deuteronomy 15, in cases where the indentured servant insists on remaining with his master for any of a variety of reasons.

41. *Then he and his children with him shall be free of your authority* Again, the verb *yatsaʾ,* "to depart," connotes release, freedom. The reference here to the release of the children of an indentured Israelite is significant. Jubilee is all-inclusive and undoubtedly applies to one's wife and children as well. The law of Exodus 21:1–6, in contradistinction, requires that the wife and children of an indentured Israelite, if he married while indentured, would not be released, but would remain with the master. So, our legislation, while allowing for indenture for as long as fifty years, removes all restrictions on the freedom of the indentured person and his family once that period is over. It is noteworthy that the Sifra interprets the following two terms—*va-ʿavado le-ʿolam,* "he shall then remain his slave for life," in Exodus 21:6 and *ʿeved ʿolam,* "slave in perpetuity," in Deuteronomy 15:17—both to mean until the Jubilee, not actually forever. This serves to reconcile the differences between the various laws of the Torah.

he shall go back to his family and return to his ancestral holding Indentured servants often lived on the estates of their masters. With the Jubilee, land was restored to its original owners, and indentured servants were released. So, an indentured Israelite had a home, once again, to which he could return.

42. *For they are My servants* God acquired the Israelites as His "slaves," by redeeming them from Egyptian bondage. His claim has priority. Israelites, however, should not hold other Israelites in slavery, because they were once slaves themselves.

Hebrew *mimkeret,* "sale," is a feminine form of *mimkar,* which occurs in verse 14.

43. *You shall not rule over him ruthlessly* Hebrew *be-farekh*, here translated "ruthlessly," literally means "with backbreaking labor," as Rashi notes. This idiom also evokes the Egyptian bondage: "The Egyptians ruthlessly imposed upon the Israelites the various labors that they made them perform" (Exod. 1:13–14). What the Egyptians did to the Israelites, Israelites ought not to do to one another. Fear of God should assure compliance with His commandments in this regard.

44. *Such male and female slaves as you may have* Israelites may own non-Israelite slaves. These may come from either non-Israelite residents of Canaan or from neighboring peoples.

and female slaves as you may have—it is from the nations round about you that you may acquire male and female slaves. ⁴⁵You may also buy them from among the children of aliens resident among you, or from their families that are among you, whom they begot in your land. These shall become your property: ⁴⁶you may keep them as a possession for your children after you, for them to inherit as property for all time. Such you may treat as slaves. But as for your Israelite kinsmen, no one shall rule ruthlessly over the other.

⁴⁷If a resident alien among you has prospered, and your kinsman being in straits, comes under his authority and gives himself over to the resident alien among you, or to an offshoot of an alien's family, ⁴⁸he shall have the right of redemption even after he has given himself over. One of his kinsmen shall redeem him, ⁴⁹or his uncle or his uncle's son shall redeem him, or anyone of his family who is of his own flesh shall redeem him; or, if he prospers, he may redeem himself. ⁵⁰He shall compute with his purchaser the total

לָכֶ֞ם מֵאֵ֣ת הַגּוֹיִ֗ם אֲשֶׁר֙ סְבִיבֹ֣תֵיכֶ֔ם מֵהֶ֥ם תִּקְנ֖וּ עֶ֥בֶד וְאָמָֽה: 45 וְ֠גַם מִבְּנֵ֨י הַתּוֹשָׁבִ֜ים הַגָּרִ֤ים עִמָּכֶם֙ מֵהֶ֣ם תִּקְנ֔וּ וּמִמִּשְׁפַּחְתָּם֙ אֲשֶׁ֣ר עִמָּכֶ֔ם אֲשֶׁ֥ר הוֹלִ֖ידוּ בְּאַרְצְכֶ֑ם וְהָי֥וּ לָכֶ֖ם לַאֲחֻזָּֽה: 46 וְהִתְנַחַלְתֶּ֨ם אֹתָ֜ם לִבְנֵיכֶ֤ם אַחֲרֵיכֶם֙ לָרֶ֣שֶׁת אֲחֻזָּ֔ה לְעֹלָ֖ם בָּהֶ֣ם תַּעֲבֹ֑דוּ וּבְאַ֨חֵיכֶ֤ם בְּנֵֽי־יִשְׂרָאֵל֙ אִ֣ישׁ בְּאָחִ֔יו לֹא־תִרְדֶּ֥ה ב֖וֹ בְּפָֽרֶךְ: ס

47 וְכִ֣י תַשִּׂ֗יג יַ֣ד גֵּ֤ר וְתוֹשָׁב֙ עִמָּ֔ךְ וּמָ֥ךְ אָחִ֖יךָ עִמּ֑וֹ וְנִמְכַּ֗ר לְגֵ֤ר תּוֹשָׁב֙ עִמָּ֔ךְ א֥וֹ לְעֵ֖קֶר מִשְׁפַּ֥חַת גֵּֽר: 48 אַחֲרֵ֣י נִמְכַּ֔ר גְּאֻלָּ֖ה תִּהְיֶה־לּ֑וֹ אֶחָ֥ד מֵאֶחָ֖יו יִגְאָלֶֽנּוּ: 49 אוֹ־דֹד֞וֹ א֤וֹ בֶן־דֹּדוֹ֙ יִגְאָלֶ֔נּוּ אֽוֹ־מִשְּׁאֵ֧ר בְּשָׂר֛וֹ מִמִּשְׁפַּחְתּ֖וֹ יִגְאָלֶ֑נּוּ אֽוֹ־הִשִּׂ֥יגָה יָד֖וֹ וְנִגְאָֽל: 50 וְחִשַּׁב֙ עִם־קֹנֵ֔הוּ מִשְּׁנַת֙

---

45. *These shall become your property* In ancient law, slaves were often regarded as having a legal status parallel to that of land. Just as the land was a "holding" (*'aḥuzzah*) to be handed down within families, so were slaves.

46. *you may keep them as a possession for your children after you* Hebrew *ve-hitnaḥaltem* means "to receive as a possession, to be assigned as a possession" and most frequently applies to land.[39] Here, a form of the verb *naḥal*, "to receive as a possession," combines with the term *'aḥuzzah* and with the verb *la-reshet*, "to appropriate as a possession." These three terms have independent histories but are here used synonymously.[40] The rights Israelites were granted over their non-Israelite slaves, like those they had over the land, were permanent.

such you may treat as slaves. But as for your Israelite kinsmen A contrast is drawn between Israelites and non-Israelites. Israelites are bound together by kinship and cannot be held as slaves by one another. That is the force of the term *'aḥ,* "brother," which occurs twice in verse 46.

47. *If a resident alien among you has prospered* Verses 47–54 deal with a situation in which an Israelite becomes indentured to a non-Israelite. The vocabulary echoes that of verse 25, where the relevant idioms are explained.

or to an offshoot of an alien's family Hebrew *'eker*, "offshoot," occurs only here in the Bible. It is related to *'ikkar,* "root." Hebrew *'eker* is cognate with Aramaic *'qr,* a term known from the Aramaic inscriptions of Sfire, in Syria; it is a relatively old term governing family relationships.[41]

48. *he shall have the right of redemption* The clan of the Israelite indentured to a non-Israelite bears the responsibility for redeeming their kinsman.

One of his kinsmen shall redeem him The order of obligation to redeem kinsmen within the clan correlates, in a general way, with the law of inheritance set forth in the account of Zelophehad's daughters, in Numbers 27:8–11. First come brothers, then uncles and cousins, then other consanguineal relatives. These could even include grandchildren, also considered consanguineal relatives in the laws of Leviticus 18:10.

49. *or anyone of his family who is of his own flesh* Not all relatives within the clan are consanguineal. The clan (*mishpaḥah*) usually designates a fairly large unit.[42]

from the year he gave himself over to him until the jubilee
year; the price of his sale shall be applied to the number of
years, as though it were for a term as a hired laborer under
the other's authority. 51 If many years remain, he shall pay
back for his redemption in proportion to his purchase
price; 52 and if few years remain until the jubilee year, he
shall so compute: he shall make payment for his redemption according to the years involved. 53 He shall be under
his authority as a laborer hired by the year; he shall not rule
ruthlessly over him in your sight. 54 If he has not been
redeemed in any of those ways, he and his children with
him shall go free in the jubilee year. 55 For it is to Me that the
Israelites are servants: they are My servants, whom I freed
from the land of Egypt, I the LORD your God.

הַמָּכְרוֹ לוֹ עַד שְׁנַת הַיֹּבֵל וְהָיָה כֶּסֶף מִמְכָּרוֹ
בְּמִסְפַּר שָׁנִים כִּימֵי שָׂכִיר יִהְיֶה עִמּוֹ׃ 51 אִם־עוֹד
רַבּוֹת בַּשָּׁנִים לְפִיהֶן יָשִׁיב גְּאֻלָּתוֹ מִכֶּסֶף מִקְנָתוֹ׃
52 וְאִם־מְעַט נִשְׁאַר בַּשָּׁנִים עַד־שְׁנַת הַיֹּבֵל
וְחִשַּׁב־לוֹ כְּפִי שָׁנָיו יָשִׁיב אֶת־גְּאֻלָּתוֹ׃ 53 כִּשְׂכִיר
שָׁנָה בְּשָׁנָה יִהְיֶה עִמּוֹ לֹא־יִרְדֶּנּוּ בְּפֶרֶךְ לְעֵינֶיךָ׃
54 וְאִם־לֹא יִגָּאֵל בְּאֵלֶּה וְיָצָא בִּשְׁנַת הַיֹּבֵל הוּא
וּבָנָיו עִמּוֹ׃ מפטיר 55 כִּי־לִי בְנֵי־יִשְׂרָאֵל עֲבָדִים
עֲבָדַי הֵם אֲשֶׁר־הוֹצֵאתִי אוֹתָם מֵאֶרֶץ מִצְרָיִם
אֲנִי יְהוָה אֱלֹהֵיכֶם׃

26 You shall not make idols for yourselves, or set up for
yourselves carved images or pillars, or place figured stones
in your land to worship upon, for I the LORD am your God.
2 You shall keep My sabbaths and venerate My sanctuary,
Mine, the LORD's.

כ״ו לֹא־תַעֲשׂוּ לָכֶם אֱלִילִם וּפֶסֶל וּמַצֵּבָה לֹא־
תָקִימוּ לָכֶם וְאֶבֶן מַשְׂכִּית לֹא תִתְּנוּ בְּאַרְצְכֶם
לְהִשְׁתַּחֲוֹת עָלֶיהָ כִּי אֲנִי יְהוָה אֱלֹהֵיכֶם׃ 2 אֶת־
שַׁבְּתֹתַי תִּשְׁמֹרוּ וּמִקְדָּשִׁי תִּירָאוּ אֲנִי יְהוָה׃

50. *He shall compute with his purchaser* The dynamics of this system are clarified in the Comments to verses 15–16, 27, and 40; they parallel the system employed in determining the value of real estate being redeemed. The computation is in terms of wages (over a period of years) instead of crop years, as is the case in long-term leases.

53. *he shall not rule ruthlessly over him in your sight* The duty to redeem an Israelite relative indentured to a non-Israelite is exceptional. To allow a fellow Israelite to remain indentured to a gentile would be a cruel humiliation; and one was not permitted to remain indifferent in such a situation, which could lead to forfeiture of land mortgaged to debts and its seizure by non-Israelites.

54. *If he has not been redeemed in any of those ways* The last recourse is the Jubilee, if all other efforts have failed.

55. *For it is to Me that the Israelites are servants* This repeats the statement of verse 42.

CHAPTER 26

26:1. *You shall not make idols for yourselves* In 19:4, the term *'elil* is explained as "an object of naught." Hebrew *pesel* is a sculptured object, usually representational.[43] The term *matsevah*, translated "pillars," is the usual term for stele, usually a stone object, standing upright, and often bearing an inscription.[44]

Hebrew *'even maskit* is difficult to explain precisely. The term *maskit* occurs in Numbers 33:52, with reference to the pagan iconography of the Canaanites, which the Israelites are commanded to destroy. The Sifra derives *maskit* from the verb *sakhakh,* "to cover over," and explains it as designating a paved area outside a temple, where it was customary to prostrate oneself. Targum Onkelos translates *'even segida'* as "a stone for worshiping." Targum Jonathan renders *'even metsayar* as "a decorated stone, one with figures drawn on it," deriving *maskit* from the verb *sakhah,* "to gaze upon, view." From Ezekiel 8:10–12, we could conclude that, indeed, the *maskit* involved drawn figures—in that case, figures drawn on the walls of temple chambers. Proverbs 25:11 would imply that *maskit* refers to decorated metal objects. NEB and NJPS have: "silver showpieces." Despite the uncertainty, clearly the intent of this verse is to forbid pagan cult objects of various sorts. Such are incompatible with the worship of the God of Israel.

2. *You shall keep My sabbaths and venerate My sanctuary* This restates numerous commandments on the observance of the Sabbath. The Masoretic vocalization *mikdashi,* "My sanc-

BE-ḤUKKOTAI

[3]If you follow My laws and faithfully observe My commandments, [4]I will grant your rains in their season, so that

בחקתי
3 אִם־בְּחֻקֹּתַ֖י תֵּלֵ֑כוּ וְאֶת־מִצְוֺתַ֣י תִּשְׁמְר֔וּ
וַעֲשִׂיתֶ֖ם אֹתָֽם׃ 4 וְנָתַתִּ֥י גִשְׁמֵיכֶ֖ם בְּעִתָּ֑ם וְנָתְנָ֤ה

tuary," is not really problematic. Instead of worshiping improperly, Israelites should attend God's legitimate sanctuary. Nevertheless, it is tempting to vocalize *mekuddashai,* "My sacred occasions." Compare Ezra 3:5: *u-le-khol moʿadei YHVH ha-mekuddashim,* "for all the sacred fixed times of the LORD." This would tie in well with the emphasis on the Sabbath.[45]

Epilogue to the Holiness Code (26:3–46)

Be-ḥukkotai The Epilogue to the Holiness Code is the only composition within the Book of Leviticus that is neither legal nor ritual in character. For the rest, Leviticus is made up of collections of religious law and descriptions of ritual celebrations, all of which are written in formulaic language. In both form and function, the Epilogue is the counterpart of Deuteronomy 28–30. Each composition appears after a collection of laws and seems to reinforce the sanction of those laws. Two major principles of biblical religion find expression in these Epilogues: the concept of free will and the doctrine of reward and punishment. Obedience to God's will brings reward; disobedience brings dire punishment. The choice rests with the people of Israel and its leaders.

The Epilogue may be divided into three sections. (1) The Blessing (vv. 3–13): God promises Israel that if His laws and commandments are properly obeyed He will bring peace and prosperity to the land and provide safety from wild beasts. He will enable the population to increase and assure the people of victory over all their enemies. The land will be abundantly productive and free from the ravages of war. The Blessing concludes with God's commitment to an enduring covenantal relation with the people of Israel. God's redemptive power, demonstrated at the Exodus, will be reaffirmed: Israel will be free of oppression. (2) The Execration (vv. 14–45): As in Deuteronomy, more space is devoted to the punishments that will befall Israel and the land, should Israel violate or disregard God's commandments, than is devoted to the Blessing. The Execration is composed in an escalating scale with admonition heaped upon admonition. If the Israelites do not return to God after one series of tragic circumstances, then even more horrible punishments will ensue. Defeat and disease will be followed by natural disasters that threaten the fertility of the land. Wild beasts will prey on the populace and ravage the livestock. These adversities will be followed by invasion, famine, and pestilence. Towns and holy places will be made desolate; human beings will eat the flesh of their children who died of hunger. The ultimate punishment will be prolonged exile in foreign lands and the danger of collective extinction. At this point, a new theme is suddenly introduced: expiation of the sins of the people through the suffering of exile and the anguish of the desolate land. A door is opened to divine mercy and forgiveness. A contrite people of Israel will confess its sins, and, in response, God will remember His covenant and the land. The Epilogue ends with a promise of restoration.[1] (3) A Postscript (v. 46): Verse 46 serves as the conclusion to the entire Holiness Code, which begins in chapter 17.

THE BLESSING (vv. 3–13)

3. ***If you follow My laws*** The Hebrew idiom *ʾim be-ḥukkotai telekhu,* literally "if you walk in My laws," conceives of God's laws and commandments as the right "path" of life, a frequent theme in biblical literature.[2] This statement sets the tone for the entire Blessing.

and faithfully observe My commandments Literally, "observe and do My commandments." The two verbs reinforce one another, yielding the sense of thoroughgoing observance.

the earth shall yield its produce and the trees of the field
their fruit. 5Your threshing shall overtake the vintage, and
your vintage shall overtake the sowing; you shall eat your
fill of bread and dwell securely in your land.
6I will grant peace in the land, and you shall lie down
untroubled by anyone; I will give the land respite from
vicious beasts, and no sword shall cross your land. 7You
shall give chase to your enemies, and they shall fall before
you by the sword. 8Five of you shall give chase to a hundred, and a hundred of you shall give chase to ten thousand; your enemies shall fall before you by the sword.
9I will look with favor upon you, and make you fertile
and multiply you; and I will maintain My covenant with

הָאָרֶץ יְבוּלָהּ וְעֵץ הַשָּׂדֶה יִתֵּן פִּרְיוֹ: 5 וְהִשִּׂיג לָכֶם
דַּיִשׁ אֶת־בָּצִיר וּבָצִיר יַשִּׂיג אֶת־זָרַע וַאֲכַלְתֶּם
לַחְמְכֶם לָשֹׂבַע וִישַׁבְתֶּם לָבֶטַח בְּאַרְצְכֶם: שני
6 וְנָתַתִּי שָׁלוֹם בָּאָרֶץ וּשְׁכַבְתֶּם וְאֵין מַחֲרִיד
וְהִשְׁבַּתִּי חַיָּה רָעָה מִן־הָאָרֶץ וְחֶרֶב לֹא־תַעֲבֹר
בְּאַרְצְכֶם: 7 וּרְדַפְתֶּם אֶת־אֹיְבֵיכֶם וְנָפְלוּ לִפְנֵיכֶם
לֶחָרֶב: 8 וְרָדְפוּ מִכֶּם חֲמִשָּׁה מֵאָה וּמֵאָה מִכֶּם
רְבָבָה יִרְדֹּפוּ וְנָפְלוּ אֹיְבֵיכֶם לִפְנֵיכֶם לֶחָרֶב:
9 וּפָנִיתִי אֲלֵיכֶם וְהִפְרֵיתִי אֶתְכֶם וְהִרְבֵּיתִי
אֶתְכֶם וַהֲקִימֹתִי אֶת־בְּרִיתִי אִתְּכֶם: שלישי

4. ***I will grant your rains in their season*** In the Land of Israel, as in adjacent areas, rainfall is limited to a fixed season of the year. At other times, there is no rain for months on end. If sufficient rain does not fall at the expected time, the results are more harmful than in temperate climates. This explains the repeated emphasis on "rains in their season."[3]

the earth shall yield its produce Hebrew *yevul* refers to all that the earth produces, that comes forth from the earth.[4] The noun *yevul* derives from the verb *y-b-l* (or *w-b-l*), which is most often expressed in the Hifil form "to bring."

5. ***Your threshing shall overtake the vintage*** There will be so much grain to thresh that the threshing will continue into late summer when the vines are picked, an activity called *batsir*. Although the verb *dush*, "to thresh," is well attested in biblical Hebrew, the noun *dayish* is unique to this verse. The closest we come to it is in Deuteronomy 25:4: "You shall not muzzle an ox while it is threshing (*be-disho*)."[5]

You shall eat your fill of bread and dwell securely in your land Hebrew *la-sova'*, "to satiety," and the noun *sava'*, "abundance," are proverbial for the blessings of fertility, especially abundant grain. The assurance of security conveyed by Hebrew *betaḥ* or *la-vetaḥ* is also common to many biblical blessings. In 25:18–19 we read that proper observance of the Sabbatical year will also be rewarded by domestic security.

6. ***I will grant peace in the land*** This promise, and all the others included in verses 4–6, are closely paralleled in Ezekiel 34:25–28.

and no sword shall cross your land The image of a sword "crossing" (*'avar*) is a rare way of depicting the ravages of war. Its only other occurrence is in Ezekiel 14:17: "Or, if I were to bring the sword upon that land and say, 'Let a sword sweep through (*ta'avor*) the land.'"

7. ***You shall give chase to your enemies, and they shall fall before you by the sword*** This statement reinforces the promises that immediately precede it: You shall not suffer from war, but your enemies will.[6]

8. ***Five of you shall give chase to a hundred*** In the poetry of Deuteronomy 32:29, we read: "Were they wise, they would think upon this,/ Gain insight into their future:/ 'How could one have routed a thousand,/ Or two put ten thousand to flight,/ Unless their Rock had sold them,/ The LORD had given them up?'"[7] This is echoed in Joshua 23:10.

9. ***I will look with favor upon you*** When God turns toward His people, they are blessed with victory and prosperity, but when He turns away from them, or turns against them, the result is disaster. We read of this again, in verse 17 of the Execration.[8]

and I will maintain My covenant with you The Hebrew verb *hekim* may refer to the initial making of a covenant, or to maintaining in force an already established covenant, or even to fulfilling

you. [10]You shall eat old grain long stored, and you shall
have to clear out the old to make room for the new.
[11]I will establish My abode in your midst, and I will not
spurn you. [12]I will be ever present in your midst: I will be
your God, and you shall be My people. [13]I the LORD am
your God who brought you out from the land of the
Egyptians to be their slaves no more, who broke the bars of
your yoke and made you walk erect.

[חמישי כשהן מחוברות] 10 וַאֲכַלְתֶּם יָשָׁן
נוֹשָׁן וְיָשָׁן מִפְּנֵי חָדָשׁ תּוֹצִיאוּ׃ 11 וְנָתַתִּי מִשְׁכָּנִי
בְּתוֹכְכֶם וְלֹא־תִגְעַל נַפְשִׁי אֶתְכֶם׃ 12 וְהִתְהַלַּכְתִּי
בְּתוֹכְכֶם וְהָיִיתִי לָכֶם לֵאלֹהִים וְאַתֶּם תִּהְיוּ־לִי
לְעָם׃ 13 אֲנִי יְהוָה אֱלֹהֵיכֶם אֲשֶׁר הוֹצֵאתִי אֶתְכֶם
מֵאֶרֶץ מִצְרַיִם מִהְיֹת לָהֶם עֲבָדִים וָאֶשְׁבֹּר מֹטֹת
עֻלְּכֶם וָאוֹלֵךְ אֶתְכֶם קוֹמְמִיּוּת׃ פ 14 וְאִם־

it. The second sense is the connotation here, where *hekim* stands in contrast to *hefer*, "to nullify, abrogate," in verse 15. The same contrast occurs in Ezekiel 16:59–62; it occurs in legal contexts and is also appropriate for describing the commitments of a covenant. In Numbers 30, the same terms are used in defining the obligations of a father to his daughter and of a husband to his wife as regards vows. Depending on the circumstances, a father either "affirms, maintains in force" (*hekim*) his daughter's vows or "annuls" (*hefer*) them. The same is true of a husband.

10. You shall eat old grain long stored The Hebrew reads *yashan noshan*, literally "very old." A similar thought is expressed in 25:22 with respect to the Sabbatical year. Its observance, including the special provisions for the poor, will result in the reward of an abundance of grain.

11. I will establish My abode in your midst Hebrew *mishkan* often refers specifically to the Tabernacle, as in 8:10; but here it has the more general sense of "residence."[9]

I will not spurn you The verb *g-ʿ-l* is relatively rare in the Hebrew Bible and, when used together with *nefesh*, has the sense of intense feelings of abhorrence. This is expressed further on in verses 43–44, where *g-ʿ-l* is synonymous with *m-ʾ-s*, "to despise." The primary image seems to be that of physical spoilage, or filth.

12. I will be ever present in your midst This is a loose rendering of Hebrew *ve-hithallakhti be-tokhekhem*, literally "I will walk about in your midst." In a religious society, the presence and nearness of God are of vital concern and are contingent on the behavior of the people.[10] The notion that God "walks about" is also conveyed in Nathan's oracle addressed to David, as we read in 2 Samuel 7:6–7: "From the day that I brought the people of Israel out of Egypt to this day I have not dwelt in a house, but have moved about (*va-ʾehyeh mithallekh*) in Tent and Tabernacle. As I moved about (*ʾasher hithallakhti*) wherever the Israelites went. . . ."

I will be your God, and you shall be My people This formal statement defines the covenantal relationship between God and Israel and serves as the legal terms of adoption. Thus we read once again in Nathan's oracle, in 2 Samuel 7:14: "I will be a father to him [the Davidic king], and he shall be a son to Me." The reverse of this pledge of adoption, expressing disapproval and rejection of Israel, is found in Hosea 1:9: "For you are not My people, and I will not be your [God]."[11]

13. who broke the bars of your yoke The bars (*motot*) of the yoke (*ʿol*) were tied to the neck of a work animal by means of thongs (*moserot*). Jeremiah 28:10–13 provides a graphic description of a yoke on a human being; breaking the yoke is a metaphor for liberation.[12] The bars of Jeremiah's yoke are broken and thereby set him free. Yokes are still used in many parts of the Near East today and have not changed much since antiquity.[13] The aptness of the biblical metaphor is apparent. A person who is subjugated, upon whom a yoke is placed, is bent over. Once the bars of the yoke are broken, he can stand at full stature, a position conveyed by the unique word **komamiyyut**, "in an upright position." We find a later echo of this verse in the Grace after Meals: "May the All Merciful One break off the yoke of exile from our necks and allow us to walk at full stature to our land."

14 But if you do not obey Me and do not observe all these
commandments, 15 if you reject My laws and spurn My
rules, so that you do not observe all My commandments
and you break My covenant, 16 I in turn will do this to you: I
will wreak misery upon you—consumption and fever,
which cause the eyes to pine and the body to languish; you
shall sow your seed to no purpose, for your enemies shall
eat it. 17 I will set My face against you: you shall be routed by
your enemies, and your foes shall dominate you. You shall
flee though none pursues.

לֹא תִשְׁמְעוּ לִי וְלֹא תַעֲשׂוּ אֵת כָּל־הַמִּצְוֺת
הָאֵלֶּה׃ 15 וְאִם־בְּחֻקֹּתַי תִּמְאָסוּ וְאִם אֶת־מִשְׁפָּטַי
תִּגְעַל נַפְשְׁכֶם לְבִלְתִּי עֲשׂוֹת אֶת־כָּל־מִצְוֺתַי
לְהַפְרְכֶם אֶת־בְּרִיתִי׃ 16 אַף־אֲנִי אֶעֱשֶׂה־זֹּאת
לָכֶם וְהִפְקַדְתִּי עֲלֵיכֶם בֶּהָלָה אֶת־הַשַּׁחֶפֶת וְאֶת־
הַקַּדַּחַת מְכַלּוֹת עֵינַיִם וּמְדִיבֹת נָפֶשׁ וּזְרַעְתֶּם
לָרִיק זַרְעֲכֶם וַאֲכָלֻהוּ אֹיְבֵיכֶם׃ 17 וְנָתַתִּי פָנַי
בָּכֶם וְנִגַּפְתֶּם לִפְנֵי אֹיְבֵיכֶם וְרָדוּ בָכֶם שֹׂנְאֵיכֶם
וְנַסְתֶּם וְאֵין־רֹדֵף אֶתְכֶם׃ ס 18 וְאִם־עַד־

THE EXECRATION (vv. 14–45)

The Execration often employs the terms and idioms of the Blessing to state the reverse, a literary technique that heightens the opposition of obedience and disobedience. See Excursus 10 for a list of examples.

15. If you reject My laws It is Israel who creates the unfavorable situation, not God. He promised not to reject His people as long as they remained obedient.

16. I will wreak misery upon you The Hebrew clause *ve-hifkadti ʿaleikhem* literally means "I shall assign to you, bring upon you by command."[14] The sense is that God will unleash destruction against His people. As for Hebrew *behalah,* it is better rendered "shock, convulsions," since the verb *b-h-l* describes physical movement.[15]

consumption and fever The two medical terms *shaḥefet* and *kadaḥat* occur elsewhere only in Deuteronomy 28:22. Hebrew *kadaḥat* derives from the verb *k-d-ḥ,* "to burn, flare," said of fire and of "fuming" rage, as, for example, in Deuteronomy 32:22 and Jeremiah 15:14. Hence, "fever." Hebrew *shaḥefet* is rendered "consumption" on the basis of the Arabic cognate, *saḥafa,* "to flay, remove the fat," such as the fat of an animal.[16]

which cause the eyes to pine Hebrew *mekhallot ʿeinayim* literally means "which exhaust the eyes" so that the eyes can no longer see. They will have been worn out by anxious expectation. Similarly, *medivot nefesh* means "that cause despair, depression." The form *medivot* is an abbreviation of *madʾivot.*[17] Prolonged illness causes one to despair of ever being healed. Hebrew *nefesh* often refers to the physical body, or to parts of it, as well as to emotional states.[18]

you shall sow your seed to no purpose Hebrew *la-rik* means "in emptiness." Its usual synonyms are *hevel,* "vapor, nothingness," and *tohu,* "formlessness."[19]

Your enemies shall eat it In a situation of blessing, one enjoys the fruits of one's labors. It is tragic, however, to witness a people deprived of its crops by conquering hordes. The same situation is projected in the Execration of Deuteronomy 28:37,51.

17. I will set My face against you This is the reverse of verse 9 of the Blessing.[20]

you shall be routed by your enemies The same dire prediction is found in the Execration of Deuteronomy 28:25. The Hebrew verb *n-g-f* means "to throw back, batter." In Solomon's prayer at the dedication of the Temple in Jerusalem (1 Kings 8:33–34) the hope is expressed that if Israel is ever routed by its enemies as a consequence of its sins, the people will be able to plead for forgiveness in the Temple.[21]

and your foes shall dominate you The Hebrew verb *r-d-h* means "to exercise rule." The same thought is echoed in verses 36–37.[22]

You shall flee though none pursues This is the height of anxiety: the terror of being pursued.

18 And if, for all that, you do not obey Me, I will go on to discipline you sevenfold for your sins, 19 and I will break your proud glory. I will make your skies like iron and your earth like copper, 20 so that your strength shall be spent to no purpose. Your land shall not yield its produce, nor shall the trees of the land yield their fruit.

21 And if you remain hostile toward Me and refuse to obey Me, I will go on smiting you sevenfold for your sins. 22 I will loose wild beasts against you, and they shall bereave you of your children and wipe out your cattle. They shall decimate you, and your roads shall be deserted.

אֵלֶּה לֹא תִשְׁמְעוּ לִי וְיָסַפְתִּי לְיַסְּרָה אֶתְכֶם
שֶׁבַע עַל־חַטֹּאתֵיכֶם׃ 19 וְשָׁבַרְתִּי אֶת־גְּאוֹן עֻזְּכֶם
וְנָתַתִּי אֶת־שְׁמֵיכֶם כַּבַּרְזֶל וְאֶת־אַרְצְכֶם כַּנְּחֻשָׁה׃
20 וְתַם לָרִיק כֹּחֲכֶם וְלֹא־תִתֵּן אַרְצְכֶם אֶת־
יְבוּלָהּ וְעֵץ הָאָרֶץ לֹא יִתֵּן פִּרְיוֹ׃ 21 וְאִם־תֵּלְכוּ
עִמִּי קֶרִי וְלֹא תֹאבוּ לִשְׁמֹעַ לִי וְיָסַפְתִּי עֲלֵיכֶם
מַכָּה שֶׁבַע כְּחַטֹּאתֵיכֶם׃ 22 וְהִשְׁלַחְתִּי בָכֶם אֶת־
חַיַּת הַשָּׂדֶה וְשִׁכְּלָה אֶתְכֶם וְהִכְרִיתָה אֶת־
בְּהֶמְתְּכֶם וְהִמְעִיטָה אֶתְכֶם וְנָשַׁמּוּ דַּרְכֵיכֶם׃

18. *And if, for all that, you do not obey Me* This introduces a point of transition in the Execration. We find similar transitions in verses 27, 33, and 37. The conditional formulation brings home the point that God would cause an end to the suffering of the people and the land whenever the people overcame its disobedience and confessed its sins. This was not to occur, however, until after the suffering brought on by a prolonged exile.

I will go on to discipline you sevenfold for all your sins The infinitive *le-yasserah* means "to rebuke, censure" but also conveys the nuance of imposing punishment.[23] The notion of sevenfold is proverbial in biblical literature and is usually expressed by the adverb *shivʿatayim,* "seven times."[24]

19. *and I will break your proud glory* The same image is expressed in Ezekiel 24:21; 33:28, and elsewhere. Hebrew *ʿoz* means "power, might," and the combination *geʾon ʿoz* means "powerful pride," the pride that comes from having power. The sense is that the land, which was "the pride" of the people, will be destroyed. This theme is expanded in the following verses.[25]

I will make your skies like iron The same statement occurs in the Execration of Deuteronomy 28:33 and in the treaties of King Esarhaddon of Assyria, who ruled in the seventh century B.C.E. In these treaties, the king's vassals are warned that they will be severely punished by the gods of the empire for any violations of the treaties.[26] The sense of the statement is that the rains will cease and the artesian springs of the earth will become dry.

20. *so that your strength shall be spent to no purpose* This restates the thoughts expressed in verse 16.

21. *And if you remain hostile toward Me* Here, again, is a transition, where the conditions for God's forgiveness are stated.

Hebrew *keri,* "hostility," and the idiom *halakh ʿim . . . be-keri,* "to walk with . . . in hostility," are unique to this chapter. Targum Onkelos translates *be-kashyu,* "with hardness, obstinacy," deriving *keri* from the root *k-r-r,* "to be cold." Compare the noun form *karah,* "cold wave," in Nahum 3:17, and *mekerah,* "cool chamber," in Judges 3:24. The reverse of "walking in hostility" is "agreeing to obey" (*ʾavah le-shmora*) suggesting that *keri* is synonymous with *meri,* "rebelliousness." Note the contrast in Isaiah 1:19–20: "If, then, you agree and give heed,/ You will eat the good things of the earth;/ But if you refuse and disobey (*u-meritem*),/ You will be devoured by the sword." The notion of *meri* as "rebelliousness" is a major theme in the prophecies of Ezekiel, but the term *keri* occurs nowhere else in the Bible; hence its meaning remains uncertain.[27]

22. *I will loose wild beasts against you* The Hifil form used here, *ve-hishlaḥti,* is rare in biblical Hebrew. It conveys the sense of "driving" the beasts through the land. This threat is the reverse of the Blessing stated in verse 6.[28]

and they shall bereave you of your children The verb *sh-kh-l* is used specifically to connote the loss of children or with respect to animals, the loss of young. The parallel word, both in Hebrew and in Ugaritic, is *ʾulmān,* "widowhood." Thus we read in Isaiah 47:8–9: "I shall not become a widow/ Or know loss of children. . . ."[29]

[23]And if these things fail to discipline you for Me, and
you remain hostile to Me, [24]I too will remain hostile to you:
I in turn will smite you sevenfold for your sins. [25]I will
bring a sword against you to wreak vengeance for the
covenant; and if you withdraw into your cities, I will send
pestilence among you, and you shall be delivered into
enemy hands. [26]When I break your staff of bread, ten
women shall bake your bread in a single oven; they shall
dole out your bread by weight, and though you eat, you
shall not be satisfied.

[27]But if, despite this, you disobey Me and remain hostile
to Me, [28]I will act against you in wrathful hostility; I, for
My part, will discipline you sevenfold for your sins. [29]You

23 וְאִם־בְּאֵלֶּה לֹא תִוָּסְרוּ לִי וַהֲלַכְתֶּם עִמִּי קֶרִי׃
24 וְהָלַכְתִּי אַף־אֲנִי עִמָּכֶם בְּקֶרִי וְהִכֵּיתִי אֶתְכֶם
גַּם־אָנִי שֶׁבַע עַל־חַטֹּאתֵיכֶם׃ 25 וְהֵבֵאתִי עֲלֵיכֶם
חֶרֶב נֹקֶמֶת נְקַם־בְּרִית וְנֶאֱסַפְתֶּם אֶל־עָרֵיכֶם
וְשִׁלַּחְתִּי דֶבֶר בְּתוֹכְכֶם וְנִתַּתֶּם בְּיַד־אוֹיֵב׃
26 בְּשִׁבְרִי לָכֶם מַטֵּה־לֶחֶם וְאָפוּ עֶשֶׂר נָשִׁים
לַחְמְכֶם בְּתַנּוּר אֶחָד וְהֵשִׁיבוּ לַחְמְכֶם בַּמִּשְׁקָל
וַאֲכַלְתֶּם וְלֹא תִשְׂבָּעוּ׃ ס 27 וְאִם־בְּזֹאת
לֹא תִשְׁמְעוּ לִי וַהֲלַכְתֶּם עִמִּי בְּקֶרִי׃ 28 וְהָלַכְתִּי
עִמָּכֶם בַּחֲמַת־קֶרִי וְיִסַּרְתִּי אֶתְכֶם אַף־אָנִי שֶׁבַע
עַל־חַטֹּאתֵיכֶם׃ 29 וַאֲכַלְתֶּם בְּשַׂר בְּנֵיכֶם וּבְשַׂר

They shall decimate you Deserted roads are often depicted as a feature of wars and invasion in biblical literature. Compare Lamentations 1:4: "Zion's roads are in mourning." Similar themes occur in Isaiah 33:8; Ezekiel 30:34; and in Psalms 107:38.

23. ***and if these things fail to discipline you*** Rather, "and if, after these things, you do not submit to my discipline." This is another point of transition. Reference is to verse 18, where the theme of "discipline" was introduced. The discipline consists of the punishments endured by the people and the land. The Nifal form *tivvaseru* means "to be disciplined, to submit to discipline."

25. ***I will bring a sword against you to wreak vengeance for the covenant*** Rather, "a sword enforcing the threats of the covenant."

The unique clause *nokemet nekam berit* uses the verb *n-k-m* and the noun *nakam* in an unusual sense. Usually *nakam* means "vengeance," and the verb occurs in the Nifal meaning "to be avenged" or in the Kal stem, as is the case here, with the meaning "to avenge, wreak vengeance." Translated in the usual way, our clause would mean that God brings against Israel a sword that exacts vengeance for the violation of the covenant (*berit*). Yet, Hebrew *nekam berit* seems to connote some feature of the covenant itself. Commenting on this verse, the Sifra speaks of "*nakam* that is in the covenant and *nakam* that is not in the covenant." It is as though *nakam* refers to the adjurations and admonitions stated in the terms of the covenant. In Deuteronomy 29:20 we read of *'alot ha-berit,* "the oaths of the covenant," which comprise the section in most treaties that states the penalties for violation. Perhaps the sages of the Sifra were thinking of the statement in the Epilogue of Deuteronomy (28:61) where the Israelites are warned that God will bring afflictions upon them that are not even mentioned in the Execration! This suggests that *nakam* in our verse does not mean "vengeance," in the usual sense, but rather the threat of punishment.

I will send pestilence among you Seeking refuge in cities will be to no avail because pestilence will spread quickly through the crowded towns under siege. The same thought is expressed in Deuteronomy 28:21.[30]

26. ***When I break your staff of bread*** The idiom *matteh leḥem,* "staff of bread," occurs several times in the prophecies of Ezekiel. It is synonymous with *mishʿan leḥem,* "support of bread," in Isaiah 3:1. This is the origin of the aphorism "Bread is the staff of life."[31]

They shall dole out your bread by weight The same thought is expressed in Ezekiel 4:16: "O mortal, I am going to break the staff of bread in Jerusalem, and they shall eat bread by weight, in anxiety, and drink water by measure, in horror."

The verb *ve-heshivu,* literally "they shall return," conveys the sense of "paying, allocating." Compare Numbers 5:7: "He shall make restitution (*ve-heshiv 'et 'ashamo*)"; and see 25:27.

27. ***But if, despite this*** This is yet another transition, leading into the final round of admonitions.

shall eat the flesh of your sons and the flesh of your daughters.
30 I will destroy your cult places and cut down your incense stands, and I will heap your carcasses upon your lifeless fetishes.

בְּנֹתֵיכֶם תֹּאכֵלוּ׃ 30 וְהִשְׁמַדְתִּי אֶת־בָּמֹתֵיכֶם
וְהִכְרַתִּי אֶת־חַמָּנֵיכֶם וְנָתַתִּי אֶת־פִּגְרֵיכֶם עַל־
פִּגְרֵי גִּלּוּלֵיכֶם וְגָעֲלָה נַפְשִׁי אֶתְכֶם׃ 31 וְנָתַתִּי

29. ***You shall eat the flesh of your sons and the flesh of your daughters*** The same horror is depicted in Deuteronomy 28:53f. and in Lamentations 2:20. Similar descriptions are found in the Assyrian vassal treaties, as is explained in Excursus 11.

30. ***I will destroy your cult places*** Verses 30–31 closely parallel the oracle of Ezekiel 6:3f. This is a cruelly ironic statement: The Israelite warriors and citizenry will be slain at the very altars and cult centers where they offended God by their worship of foreign gods and idols.

The verses contain several archaeological terms of interest. Hebrew *bamah,* a term for various cult installations, means "back," as we now know from Ugaritic, where we find *bmt pḫl,* "the back of a mare," on which goods are loaded. Hebrew *bamah* has, therefore, two connotations. (1) Topographically, it refers to the high ridges or peaks of mountains, as in Amos 4:13 or in Deuteronomy 32:13. This parallels the sense of the "shoulder" of a mountain, as in Joshua 15:10. (2) Architecturally, it refers to a raised platform or structure, as is the meaning here. The Books of Kings often refer to the *bamot,* which were tolerated by most kings, but condemned by pious monotheists. Both usages reflect a semantic process whereby the physiognomy of humans and animals is transferred to the inanimate natural world as well as to architecture.[32]

The term *ḥammanim* is translated "incense altars." An Aramaic altar inscription from Palmyra contains the words *ḥmn' dnh w'lt' dnh,* "this *ḥamman* and this altar." On the reverse side of the altar there is a relief depicting two standing men with an incense stand, or altar, placed between them. This would seem to mean that the *ḥamman* was the incense altar itself. In still another Palmyrene inscription we read that someone dedicated *ḥmn' klh hw w'trh w'p ṭll 'drwn' klh,* "the complete *ḥamman,* with its installation, and even covered the entire chamber with a roof." This suggests that the *ḥamman* was located within a chamber. The etymology of *ḥamman* may have actually been confused by this recent evidence. Identifying it as an incense altar implied that *ḥamman* derived from the root *ḥ-m-m,* "to be hot." We are now able to determine that this is not so because a word *ḥmn* is now attested in Ugaritic ritual texts that mention many cultic artifacts. Now, in Ugaritic the verb meaning "to be hot" also occurs, but it is written with a different letter, *ḫēṭ.* (In the Semitic languages, there were originally *both ḥēṭ* and *ḫēṭ,* but over the course of time, certain languages like Hebrew reduced the alphabet, leaving only *ḥet.* As a result, there is often confusion about the derivation of words written with a Hebrew *ḥet.*) As a consequence, Hebrew and Aramaic *ḥamman* probably have nothing to do with the idea of being "hot"; nor is it likely that the Late Hebrew word for "sun" (*ḥammah*) is relevant to the artifact called *ḥamman.* The suggestion that *ḥammanim* were sun disks must also be discarded. We see, instead, on the basis of the Ugaritic evidence, that we are dealing with the name of an artifact or structure that had an independent origin. This is not to say that a *ḥamman,* "altar," could not be dedicated to the sun-god in pagan societies, but only to emphasize that this is not the meaning of the word itself.

In the Ugaritic ritual texts we read of offerings brought "at the *ḥmn.*" The word *ḥmn* also occurs as part of a personal name, which suggests a possible connection between *ḥamman* and the name of the god Baal-Ḥammôn mentioned in a ninth-century B.C.E. Phoenician inscription from ancient Turkey. The same deity was prominent at Carthage. The cult of Baal-Ḥammôn continued over many centuries. Until recently, it was not known as early as the second millennium B.C.E., but the attestation of this name in Ugaritic, if accurate, may push back the date. It seems quite possible, therefore, that the name of a deity is reflected in the word *ḥammanim* and that it means literally "an altar of Ḥammôn." The biblical evidence concerning *ḥammanim* correlates well with that of Ugarit and Palmyra. In 2 Chronicles 14:4 and 34:3 we read that the *ḥamman* was installed "above" altars and *bamot.* Whether the *ḥamman* was uniformly used as an incense altar is not entirely clear. In Isaiah 27:9 we are told that the sin of Jacob can be expiated by destroying improper cultic artifacts: "That he make all the altar-stones/ Like shattered blocks of chalk—/ With no sacred post left standing,/ nor any *ḥammanim.*"[33]

Hebrew *gillulim,* translated "fetishes," always appears in the plural. It is a derisive term used to

I will spurn you. [31]I will lay your cities in ruin and make
your sanctuaries desolate, and I will not savor your pleasing
odors. [32]I will make the land desolate, so that your enemies
who settle in it shall be appalled by it. [33]And you I will
scatter among the nations, and I will unsheath the sword
against you. Your land shall become a desolation and your
cities a ruin.

[34]Then shall the land make up for its sabbath years
throughout the time that it is desolate and you are in the
land of your enemies; then shall the land rest and make up
for its sabbath years. [35]Throughout the time that it is

אֶת־עָרֵיכֶם חָרְבָּה וַהֲשִׁמּוֹתִי אֶת־מִקְדְּשֵׁיכֶם וְלֹא
אָרִיחַ בְּרֵיחַ נִיחֹחֲכֶם׃ 32 וַהֲשִׁמֹּתִי אֲנִי אֶת־הָאָרֶץ
וְשָׁמְמוּ עָלֶיהָ אֹיְבֵיכֶם הַיֹּשְׁבִים בָּהּ׃ 33 וְאֶתְכֶם
אֱזָרֶה בַגּוֹיִם וַהֲרִיקֹתִי אַחֲרֵיכֶם חָרֶב וְהָיְתָה
אַרְצְכֶם שְׁמָמָה וְעָרֵיכֶם יִהְיוּ חָרְבָּה׃ 34 אָז תִּרְצֶה
הָאָרֶץ אֶת־שַׁבְּתֹתֶיהָ כֹּל יְמֵי הָשַּׁמָּה וְאַתֶּם
בְּאֶרֶץ אֹיְבֵיכֶם אָז תִּשְׁבַּת הָאָרֶץ וְהִרְצָת אֶת־
שַׁבְּתֹתֶיהָ׃ 35 כָּל־יְמֵי הָשַּׁמָּה תִּשְׁבֹּת אֵת אֲשֶׁר

characterize pagan statues and probably derives from the root *g-l-l,* "to roll," as to roll a stone. From the same root we have the noun *gal,* "a pile, mound" (also a "wave" of water). Our verse paraphrases Ezekiel 6:4b: "I shall cast your slain before your fetishes (*lifnei gilluleikhem*)." Here we read *ve-natatti pigreikhem ʿal pigrei gilluleikhem,* literally "I shall place your corpses atop the corpses of your fetishes." The problem is that elsewhere Hebrew *peger* refers to the corpse of an animate being and would not apply to a statue or stone object. There is, however, an analogous usage of *nevelah,* "cadaver," also a term usually reserved for animate creatures. In Jeremiah 16:18 we read: "Because they have defiled My land/ With the corpses of their abominations (*be-nivlat shikkutseihem*)." The lifelessness of pagan statues, and therefore the powerlessness of the would-be deities they represent, is epitomized in Psalms 135:15–17: "The idols of the nations are silver and gold, the work of men's hands. They have mouths, but cannot speak; they have eyes, but cannot see. . . ."[34]

and I will not savor your pleasing odors On the meaning of Hebrew *reaḥ niḥoaḥ,* "pleasing odor," see Comment to 1:9. God will refuse to accept the offerings of those who have angered Him by violating His commandments. This theme, discussed in Excursus 11, is also present in ancient Near Eastern royal inscriptions and treaties.[35]

32. I will make the land desolate The syntax of the Hebrew is emphatic: "I, Myself, will make the land desolate."

so that your enemies . . . shall be appalled by it A degree of sensitivity is attributed even to the enemies of Israel and to the deported peoples who will be settled in the land by the conquerors. Like all other ancient people, they, too, will interpret the desolation as a punishment for some horrible offense committed by the Israelites against their God. A similar projection is found in Deuteronomy 29:21–23: "And later generations will ask—the children who succeed you, and foreigners who come from distant lands . . . all nations will ask, 'Why did the LORD do thus to the land? Wherefore that awful wrath?'"

33. And you I will scatter among the nations The verb *zarah* means "to winnow," and in the Piel stem *zerah* means "to scatter," as one scatters chaff to the winds. This verb is used in the prophecies of Jeremiah, Ezekiel, and Zechariah to describe dispersion.[36]

and I will unsheath the sword against you The verb *herik* used here means "to empty," referring to emptying the sheath as the sword is drawn. The idiom *herik ḥerev* appears only here and in Ezekiel, where it is used repeatedly.[37]

and your cities a ruin Hebrew *ḥorvah* has an abstract sense: "a state of ruin."[38]

34. Then shall the land make up for its sabbath years In its desolation, the land will lie abandoned for a prolonged period as punishment for not having been allowed to lie fallow every seventh year as was commanded in 25:1f. Had the Israelites obeyed the law of the sabbatical year, the land would not be desolate.

In certain contexts, the verb *r-ts-h* means "to expiate, make up." The passive form reflects this meaning in Isaiah 40:2: "that her iniquity is expiated (*ki nirtsah ʿavonah*)." Here, the form *hirtsah* means "to secure expiation, to make up for."

לֹא־שָׁבְתָה בְּשַׁבְּתֹתֵיכֶם בְּשִׁבְתְּכֶם עָלֶיהָ׃
36 וְהַנִּשְׁאָרִים בָּכֶם וְהֵבֵאתִי מֹרֶךְ בִּלְבָבָם
בְּאַרְצֹת אֹיְבֵיהֶם וְרָדַף אֹתָם קוֹל עָלֶה נִדָּף וְנָסוּ
מְנֻסַת־חֶרֶב וְנָפְלוּ וְאֵין רֹדֵף׃ 37 וְכָשְׁלוּ אִישׁ־
בְּאָחִיו כְּמִפְּנֵי־חֶרֶב וְרֹדֵף אָיִן וְלֹא־תִהְיֶה לָכֶם
תְּקוּמָה לִפְנֵי אֹיְבֵיכֶם׃ 38 וַאֲבַדְתֶּם בַּגּוֹיִם וְאָכְלָה
אֶתְכֶם אֶרֶץ אֹיְבֵיכֶם׃ 39 וְהַנִּשְׁאָרִים בָּכֶם יִמַּקּוּ
בַּעֲוֺנָם בְּאַרְצֹת אֹיְבֵיכֶם וְאַף בַּעֲוֺנֹת אֲבֹתָם אִתָּם
יִמָּקּוּ׃ 40 וְהִתְוַדּוּ אֶת־עֲוֺנָם וְאֶת־עֲוֺן אֲבֹתָם
בְּמַעֲלָם אֲשֶׁר מָעֲלוּ־בִי וְאַף אֲשֶׁר־הָלְכוּ עִמִּי
בְּקֶרִי׃ 41 אַף־אֲנִי אֵלֵךְ עִמָּם בְּקֶרִי וְהֵבֵאתִי אֹתָם

desolate, it shall observe the rest that it did not observe in your sabbath years while you were dwelling upon it. 36 As for those of you who survive, I will cast a faintness into their hearts in the land of their enemies. The sound of a driven leaf shall put them to flight. Fleeing as though from the sword, they shall fall though none pursues. 37 With no one pursuing, they shall stumble over one another as before the sword. You shall not be able to stand your ground before your enemies, 38 but shall perish among the nations; and the land of your enemies shall consume you.

39 Those of you who survive shall be heartsick over their iniquity in the land of your enemies; more, they shall be heartsick over the iniquities of their fathers; 40 and they shall confess their iniquity and the iniquity of their fathers, in that they trespassed against Me, yea, were hostile to Me.

36. *I will cast a faintness into their hearts* Hebrew *morekh,* "faintness," occurs only here and is probably derived from the root *r-k-k,* "to be soft." In Deuteronomy 20:8 the cowardly are called literally "the soft of heart" (*rakh ha-levav*) and are considered unfit for military service.

The sound of a driven leaf The "leaf blown away" (the verb *niddaf*) by the wind is a vivid description, also found in Job 13:25. The slightest sound will alarm the people, so great is their fear.

they shall fall though none pursues This repeats the thought expressed in verse 17.

37. *They shall stumble over one another* A similar thought is expressed in Jeremiah 46:12b: "For warrior stumbles against warrior;/ The two fall down together."

You shall not be able to stand your ground Hebrew *tekumah,* unique to this verse, connotes the strength to *withstand,* to remain standing in the face of attack.

and the land of your enemies shall consume you A land may be said to devour its inhabitants in the sense that if it becomes unproductive, its population will perish. Ironically, this is how the spies, at least most of them, described the land of Canaan: "The country that we traversed and scouted is one that devours its settlers." Here, the sense is that the exiled community will be swallowed up by the land of exile and become extinct.

39. *shall be heartsick* Hebrew *yimmakku* means literally "they will waste away, melt." One's eyes may "melt" in their sockets (Zech. 14:12), as we find with the noun *mak,* "rot," in Isaiah 3:24 and 5:24. The root *m-k-k* may be related to *m-g-g,* which also connotes dread in Exodus 15:14 and Ezekiel 21:20. In Ezekiel 4:17 and 24:23 there is the unusual idiom "to waste away because of transgression (*ʿavon*)," which conveys the meaning that the people will experience severe remorse.

over the iniquities of their fathers The text actually reads "over the iniquities of their fathers which are with them (*ʾittam*)." The realization that they are suffering for the cumulative sins of generations is even more distressing to the exiles. In Lamentations 5:7 we find the same reaction on the part of the Judean exiles: "Our fathers sinned and are no more;/ And we must bear their guilt." Elsewhere in biblical literature the opposite view is expressed. Thus, Ezekiel in chapter 18 insists that each generation bears responsibility for its own sins.

40. *and they shall confess their iniquity* For the sense of Hebrew *ve-hitvaddu,* "they shall confess," see Comments to 5:5 and 16:21.[39]

in that they trespassed against Me The noun *maʿal* and the related verb *maʿal* are explained in the Comments to 5:14f. More extended usages, connoting betrayal, occur in Ezekiel 17:20; 18:24; 39:23; and in Ezra 10:2.

41When I, in turn, have been hostile to them and have removed them into the land of their enemies, then at last shall their obdurate heart humble itself, and they shall atone for their iniquity. 42Then will I remember My covenant with Jacob; I will remember also My covenant with Isaac, and also My covenant with Abraham; and I will remember the land.

43For the land shall be forsaken of them, making up for its sabbath years by being desolate of them, while they atone for their iniquity; for the abundant reason that they rejected My rules and spurned My laws. 44Yet, even then, when they are in the land of their enemies, I will not reject them or spurn them so as to destroy them, annulling My

בְּאֶ֖רֶץ אֹֽיְבֵיהֶ֑ם אוֹ־אָ֣ז יִכָּנַ֗ע לְבָבָם֙ הֶֽעָרֵ֔ל וְאָ֖ז
יִרְצ֥וּ אֶת־עֲוֺנָֽם׃ 42 וְזָכַרְתִּ֖י אֶת־בְּרִיתִ֣י יַעֲק֑וֹב
וְאַף֩ אֶת־בְּרִיתִ֨י יִצְחָ֜ק וְאַ֨ף אֶת־בְּרִיתִ֧י אַבְרָהָ֛ם
אֶזְכֹּ֖ר וְהָאָ֥רֶץ אֶזְכֹּֽר׃ 43 וְהָאָ֩רֶץ֩ תֵּעָזֵ֨ב מֵהֶ֜ם וְתִ֣רֶץ
אֶת־שַׁבְּתֹתֶ֗יהָ בָּהְשַׁמָּה֙ מֵהֶ֔ם וְהֵ֖ם יִרְצ֣וּ אֶת־עֲוֺנָ֑ם
יַ֣עַן וּבְיַ֔עַן בְּמִשְׁפָּטַ֣י מָאָ֔סוּ וְאֶת־חֻקֹּתַ֖י גָּעֲלָ֥ה
נַפְשָֽׁם׃ 44 וְאַף־גַּם־זֹ֡את בִּֽהְיוֹתָם֩ בְּאֶ֨רֶץ אֹֽיְבֵיהֶ֜ם
לֹֽא־מְאַסְתִּ֤ים וְלֹֽא־גְעַלְתִּים֙ לְכַלֹּתָ֔ם לְהָפֵ֥ר בְּרִיתִ֖י
אִתָּ֑ם כִּ֛י אֲנִ֥י יְהוָ֖ה אֱלֹהֵיהֶֽם׃ 45 וְזָכַרְתִּ֥י לָהֶ֖ם

41. and have removed them into the land of their enemies Hebrew *ve-heve'ti* does not mean "remove," but "bring," and the use of this verb in the present context is strange. The Septuagint reads *kai apolô,* implying a Hebrew text that reads *ve-he'evadti,* "I have caused to perish." It should be noted that the verb *'avad* is actually used in verse 38 and does not connote complete destruction—for verse 39 speaks of those who survive. To accept the reading *ve-he'evadti* would not contradict verse 44, where it is stated that God did not destroy His people in exile. It seems that the verb *'avad* may describe stages in a process of perishing without implying actual extinction. In fact, certain forms of the verb *'avad* convey the sense of "scattering, dispersing," as in Numbers 24:19 and Jeremiah 23:1; 49:38.

then at last Hebrew *'o 'az,* literally "or then" may be compared with *ki 'az,* "only then, surely then," in Joshua 1:8: "Only then (*ki 'az*) will you prosper . . . and only then (*ve-'az*) will you be successful."

their obdurate heart Hebrew *libbam he'arel* literally means "their uncircumcised heart." This image is best known from Deuteronomy 10:16, Jeremiah 9:25, and Ezekiel 44:7. Its sense is that of a "thickened" heart. Whenever the image of the foreskin (*'orlah*) is employed actual physical thickness seems to be involved. The thickened heart cannot feel or think; one whose earlobe is too thick cannot hear God's words (Jer. 6:10); Moses' thickened lips made it difficult for him to speak articulately (Exod. 6:12). According to the law of Leviticus 19:23, trees and vines classified as *'arelim* are untrimmed.

In exile, the people will submit to God's will, and their contrition will prompt God to remember His covenant. This theme is expressed in Ezekiel 20:43: "There you will recall your ways and all the acts by which you defiled yourselves; and you will loathe yourselves for all the evils that you committed."

42. Then will I remember My covenant This is a familiar theme. We read in Genesis 9:15 that after the Flood God states that whenever He sees the rainbow, He will remember His promise not to bring destruction on the natural world for the sins of mankind. He acts to deliver the Israelites from Egyptian bondage after remembering His covenant with the patriarchs (Exod. 6:5). Perhaps most appropriate is the statement in Ezekiel 16:60: "Nevertheless, I will remember the covenant I made with you in the days of your youth, and I will establish it with you as an everlasting covenant."

and I will remember the land This statement is unique in Scripture. The personification of the land is, in itself, a frequent theme, but nowhere else is it said that God remembers the land.

43. For the land shall be forsaken of them The land and the people must both atone, each in its own way. The land atones through its desolation and the loss of its inhabitants; the people atone through exile.

for the abundant reason that Hebrew *ya'an u-ve-ya'an* is emphatic: "For the very reason that."[40]

covenant with them: for I the LORD am their God. 45I will remember in their favor the covenant with the ancients, whom I freed from the land of Egypt in the sight of the nations to be their God: I, the LORD.

46These are the laws, rules, and instructions that the LORD established, through Moses on Mount Sinai, between Himself and the Israelite people.

בְּרִית רִאשֹׁנִים אֲשֶׁר הוֹצֵאתִי־אֹתָם מֵאֶרֶץ
מִצְרַיִם לְעֵינֵי הַגּוֹיִם לִהְיֹת לָהֶם לֵאלֹהִים אֲנִי
יְהוָה׃ 46 אֵלֶּה הַחֻקִּים וְהַמִּשְׁפָּטִים וְהַתּוֹרֹת אֲשֶׁר
נָתַן יְהוָה בֵּינוֹ וּבֵין בְּנֵי יִשְׂרָאֵל בְּהַר סִינַי בְּיַד־
מֹשֶׁה׃ פ רביעי [ששי כשהן מחוברות]

44. Yet, even then No matter how disloyal the Israelites have been, the Lord remains their God and will restore them.

45. the covenant with the ancients Hebrew *ri'shonim,* "the former ones," refers to Israelites who lived in former generations; in this case, to those who left Egypt.[41]

in the sight of the nations God pledged to redeem the Israelites whom He liberated from Egypt. This He did in the sight of the nations, who witnessed the covenant, so to speak. For this reason, to allow Israel to perish, though the punishment be deserved, would detract from God's renown. Hence, if Israel shows remorse and mends its ways, God will not cause the entire people to perish. The same thoughts are expressed in Isaiah 52:10 and in Ezekiel 20:9,14.

POSTSCRIPT (v. 46)

These are the laws All that is commanded in chapters 17–26, the Holiness Code, comes from the Lord, as transmitted through Moses on Mount Sinai. A similar statement appears at the end of chapter 27, which concludes the Book of Leviticus. From a traditional point of view, it was important to record the source of legislation so that its authority could not be questioned.[42]

CHAPTER 27

Funding the Sanctuary

It is likely that chapter 27 was appended to the Book of Leviticus. From a purely textual perspective, the Epilogue (26:3–46) would seem to be a suitable conclusion to the book. But in order to include in Leviticus a matter of central importance, the funding of the sanctuary, chapter 27 was added. Maintaining the physical plant of the sanctuary was certainly costly, and it was necessary to provide the materials used in public sacrifice and to support the clergy.

The sources of income, as set forth in this chapter, were of the following kinds: (1) votive pledges in fixed amounts of silver (vv. 1–8); (2) votary pledges of animals (vv. 9–13); (3) consecrations of urban property, land holdings, and acquired agricultural land (vv. 14–25); (4) firstlings (vv. 26–27); (5) donations of property that had been acquired under the law of *ḥerem,* "proscription" (vv. 28–29); and (6) tithes of produce and livestock (vv. 30–33).

The actual goal of the system of funding prescribed in chapter 27 was to secure silver for the sanctuary and its related needs, not, for the most part, to secure the actual commodities that were pledged or consecrated. What was donated could be redeemed, and it was the redemption payment that was sought by the sanctuary in most cases. There were exceptions, of course. For certain reasons *ḥerem* property could not be redeemed; and donated animals that were suitable for sacrifice would be retained by the sanctuary. On the whole, however, the sanctuary preferred silver. The legislation of chapter 27, although couched in traditional terms of devotion, actually worked in such a way as to provide silver for the sanctuary.

27 The LORD spoke to Moses, saying:
2Speak to the Israelite people and say to them: When anyone explicitly vows to the LORD the equivalent for a human being, 3the following scale shall apply: If it is a male from twenty to sixty years of age, the equivalent is fifty shekels of silver by the sanctuary weight; 4if it is a female,

כ״ז וַיְדַבֵּר יְהוָה אֶל־מֹשֶׁה לֵּאמֹר: 2 דַּבֵּר אֶל־
בְּנֵי יִשְׂרָאֵל וְאָמַרְתָּ אֲלֵהֶם אִישׁ כִּי יַפְלִא נֶדֶר
בְּעֶרְכְּךָ נְפָשֹׁת לַיהוָה: 3 וְהָיָה עֶרְכְּךָ הַזָּכָר מִבֶּן
עֶשְׂרִים שָׁנָה וְעַד בֶּן־שִׁשִּׁים שָׁנָה וְהָיָה עֶרְכְּךָ
חֲמִשִּׁים שֶׁקֶל כֶּסֶף בְּשֶׁקֶל הַקֹּדֶשׁ: 4 וְאִם־נְקֵבָה

VOTARY PLEDGES IN FIXED AMOUNTS OF SILVER (vv. 1–8)

The custom of pledging one's valuation in silver to the sanctuary harks back to the actual dedication of oneself, or one's child, to Temple service. In 1 Samuel 1 we read that Hannah vowed at the sanctuary of Shiloh that if God granted her a son she would bring him to Shiloh, where he would remain in service all his days. When Samuel was born to her, she, indeed, devoted him in this way. Pledging the equivalent of one's life, according to a scale established by the priesthood, served two ends: the spirit of the ancient tradition was satisfied, and, in practical terms, the sanctuary received necessary funds.

A key source for understanding the system of "equivalents" is 2 Kings 12:5–6. King Jehoash of Judah required funds for Temple repairs and decided to tap several sources of revenue for this purpose (with *kesef* understood to mean "silver"): "Jehoash said to the priests, 'All the silver, current silver, brought into the House of the LORD as sacred donations—any silver a man may pay as the silver equivalent of persons *(kesef nafshot ʿerko),* or any other silver that a man may be minded to bring to the House of the LORD—let the priests receive it, each from his benefactor.'" This is precisely the sort of votary, or sacred pledge, that is the subject of verses 1–8 of our chapter. The term *ʿerekh,* "equivalent," is used in the same way in both sources. Our chapter fixes equivalents for persons of various ages and for both sexes.

2. *When anyone explicitly vows to the LORD the equivalent for a human being* Rather, "When a person vows to set aside a votary offering. . . ." The preferred translation closely approximates the interpretation of Rashi, Ramban, and the Targum Onkelos. The point is that the verb *hipliʾ,* with a final *alef,* is a variant of the verb *palah,* with a final *heh,* a verb whose meaning is clearly known: "to set apart."[1] The term *neder* here refers to the substance of the vow, to what is pledged, not to the original pronouncement of the vow; hence the preferred translation "votary offering."[2] On the unusual form *ʿerekkha,* literally "your equivalent," see Comment to 5:15, where this form is explained.

3. *the following scale shall apply*

Age	*Male*	*Female*
20–60 years of age	50 shekels	30 shekels
5–20 years of age	20 shekels	10 shekels
1 month–5 years of age	5 shekels	3 shekels
over 60 years of age	15 shekels	10 shekels

The silver content of the shekel is specified in verse 25. Some features of this scale are readily explicable. The age factor reflects productive capacity. Elsewhere, in Numbers 4:3,32, we find the age of service in the Tabernacle to be between twenty and fifty years of age, but the principle is the same. At the age of one month, a child was considered viable and likely to survive the perils of infant mortality.[3] That is why, according to Numbers 18:15–16, first-born sons are redeemed according to this same system of equivalents, beginning at the age of one month. First-born sons did not have to be pledged, of course: They already belonged to God. Gender differentiation may be linked to productivity, it being presumed that a male could earn more than a female. The difference in valuations may also reflect a certain attitude toward women. It is worthy of note, nonetheless, that women could participate in the votive system freely, a fact that is indicated by a number of biblical sources.[4]

the equivalent is thirty shekels. 5If the age is from five years
to twenty years, the equivalent is twenty shekels for a male
and ten shekels for a female. 6If the age is from one month
to five years, the equivalent for a male is five shekels of
silver, and the equivalent for a female is three shekels of
silver. 7If the age is sixty years or over, the equivalent is
fifteen shekels in the case of a male and ten shekels for a
female. 8But if one cannot afford the equivalent, he shall be
presented before the priest, and the priest shall assess him;
the priest shall assess him according to what the vower can
afford.

9If [the vow concerns] any animal that may be brought as
an offering to the LORD, any such that may be given to the

הִוא וְהָיָה עֶרְכְּךָ שְׁלֹשִׁים שָׁקֶל׃ 5 וְאִם מִבֶּן־חָמֵשׁ
שָׁנִים וְעַד בֶּן־עֶשְׂרִים שָׁנָה וְהָיָה עֶרְכְּךָ הַזָּכָר
עֶשְׂרִים שְׁקָלִים וְלַנְּקֵבָה עֲשֶׂרֶת שְׁקָלִים׃ 6 וְאִם
מִבֶּן־חֹדֶשׁ וְעַד בֶּן־חָמֵשׁ שָׁנִים וְהָיָה עֶרְכְּךָ הַזָּכָר
חֲמִשָּׁה שְׁקָלִים כָּסֶף וְלַנְּקֵבָה עֶרְכְּךָ שְׁלֹשֶׁת
שְׁקָלִים כָּסֶף׃ 7 וְאִם מִבֶּן־שִׁשִּׁים שָׁנָה וָמַעְלָה
אִם־זָכָר וְהָיָה עֶרְכְּךָ חֲמִשָּׁה עָשָׂר שָׁקֶל וְלַנְּקֵבָה
עֲשָׂרָה שְׁקָלִים׃ 8 וְאִם־מָךְ הוּא מֵעֶרְכֶּךָ וְהֶעֱמִידוֹ
לִפְנֵי הַכֹּהֵן וְהֶעֱרִיךְ אֹתוֹ הַכֹּהֵן עַל־פִּי אֲשֶׁר
תַּשִּׂיג יַד הַנֹּדֵר יַעֲרִיכֶנּוּ הַכֹּהֵן׃ ס 9 וְאִם־
בְּהֵמָה אֲשֶׁר יַקְרִיבוּ מִמֶּנָּה קָרְבָּן לַיהוָה כֹּל אֲשֶׁר

But if one cannot afford the equivalent The verb *mukh,* "to be in straits," is explained in the Comment to 25:25.

he shall be presented before the priest The Hebrew verb *heʿemid* means "to station, present." It is also used to describe the presentation of offerings. See Comments to 14:11 and 16:7.

and the priest shall assess him The Hebrew verb *heʿerikh,* "to evaluate, assess," is part of the administrative vocabulary of ancient Israel. Thus, King Jehoiakim "assessed" the entire land of Judah when levying taxes to pay for the tribute he owed Pharaoh Necho (2 Kings 23:35).

according to what the vower can afford Hebrew *kaʾasher tassig yad ha-noder* literally means "which the hand of the vower can reach."[5] The adjustment of valuations, like the allowance for adjusting certain required sacrifices, is a general feature of priestly administration. Allowance was made for reductions when the inability of an Israelite to afford the standard cost of an offering or donation would deprive him of expiation or, as in this case, preclude the performance of a pious act.

VOTARY PLEDGES OF ANIMALS (vv. 9–13)

One could donate animals to the sanctuary and then redeem them. There was a surcharge of 20 percent over and above the value of the animal, as assessed by the priesthood. These particular laws, and those to follow regarding donations of real property to the sanctuary, point to the administrative functions of the priesthood. The priesthood set the value of the animal, which undoubtedly had an effect on the marketplace as well. All transactions were negotiated in sanctuary weight (v. 25), another factor of economic control.

One who gave of his own property to the sanctuary was held in high esteem. Logically, one should not undo this act by buying back what was devoted. Then, too, what was devoted had already become sacred. Accordingly, a surcharge of 20 percent was imposed on the donor who would seek to recover what had already been consecrated. At the same time, the sanctuary was allowed to profit from the transaction.

9. If [the vow concerns] any animal that may be brought as an offering to the LORD Traditional commentators disputed the legal import of this statement. The crucial factor is the intent of the donor: If it was to devote an actual altar offering, the donation constituted a valid assignment to "the altar." And even though a particular sacrifice was not specified, the law of 22:21f. applied, that is to say, the animal would be accepted as a sacrifice. Once this occurred, no redemption was possible. The contrast between verses 9–10 and verse 11 hinges upon the presumed intent of the donor. It was presumed that one who donated an animal of a species unsuitable for sacrifice intended a contribution of the value of the animal, not of the animal itself. For this reason, redemption was allowed. With Maimonides dissenting, the majority view is that the sacrificial votary is the subject of verses 9–10.[6]

Lord shall be holy. [10]One may not exchange or substitute another for it, either good for bad, or bad for good; if one does substitute one animal for another, the thing vowed and its substitute shall both be holy. [11]If [the vow concerns] any unclean animal that may not be brought as an offering to the Lord, the animal shall be presented before the priest, [12]and the priest shall assess it. Whether high or low, whatever assessment is set by the priest shall stand; [13]and if he wishes to redeem it, he must add one-fifth to its assessment.

[14]If anyone consecrates his house to the Lord, the priest shall assess it. Whether high or low, as the priest assesses it, so it shall stand; [15]and if he who has consecrated his house wishes to redeem it, he must add one-fifth to the sum at which it was assessed, and it shall be his. [16]If anyone conse-

יִתֵּן מִמֶּנּוּ לַיהוָה יִהְיֶה־קֹּדֶשׁ׃ 10 לֹא יַחֲלִיפֶנּוּ
וְלֹא־יָמִיר אֹתוֹ טוֹב בְּרָע אוֹ־רַע בְּטוֹב וְאִם־הָמֵר
יָמִיר בְּהֵמָה בִּבְהֵמָה וְהָיָה־הוּא וּתְמוּרָתוֹ יִהְיֶה־
קֹּדֶשׁ׃ 11 וְאִם כָּל־בְּהֵמָה טְמֵאָה אֲשֶׁר לֹא־
יַקְרִיבוּ מִמֶּנָּה קָרְבָּן לַיהוָה וְהֶעֱמִיד אֶת־הַבְּהֵמָה
לִפְנֵי הַכֹּהֵן׃ 12 וְהֶעֱרִיךְ הַכֹּהֵן אֹתָהּ בֵּין טוֹב וּבֵין
רָע כְּעֶרְכְּךָ הַכֹּהֵן כֵּן יִהְיֶה׃ 13 וְאִם־גָּאֹל יִגְאָלֶנָּה
וְיָסַף חֲמִישִׁתוֹ עַל־עֶרְכֶּךָ׃ 14 וְאִישׁ כִּי־יַקְדִּשׁ אֶת־
בֵּיתוֹ קֹדֶשׁ לַיהוָה וְהֶעֱרִיכוֹ הַכֹּהֵן בֵּין טוֹב וּבֵין
רָע כַּאֲשֶׁר יַעֲרִיךְ אֹתוֹ הַכֹּהֵן כֵּן יָקוּם׃ 15 וְאִם־
הַמַּקְדִּישׁ יִגְאַל אֶת־בֵּיתוֹ וְיָסַף חֲמִישִׁית כֶּסֶף־
עֶרְכְּךָ עָלָיו וְהָיָה לוֹ׃ חמישי [שביעי כשהן

10. *One may not exchange or substitute another for it* The Hebrew verbs *hemir* and *heḥelif* mean essentially the same thing: "to substitute." The nominal term *temurah* is used in barter or exchange.[7]

the thing vowed and its substitute shall both be holy The donor was also at a disadvantage if he sought to substitute another animal for the one donated. It too became sanctuary property.

11. *If [the vow concerns] any unclean animal* An impure animal is unfit for sacrifice. Therefore, the donor is presumed to have intended the assessed value of the animal as his pledge, not a sacrificial votary. By payment of the 20 percent surcharge, he may retrieve it. For a definition of "clean" and "unclean" animals (or, more precisely, of "pure" and "impure" animals) see introductory Comment to chapter 11.

12. *Whether high or low* The assessment of the priest stands, even if it exceeds the market price of the animal.

13. *and if he wishes to redeem it* The law is stated conditionally, although, in actual practice, it was usually expected that the donor would redeem what he had pledged.

CONSECRATIONS (vv. 14–25)

The Hebrew verb *hikdish* means "to consecrate." It enjoys a wide range of connotations, from the devotion of sacrificial offerings as in 22:2f. to the consecration of the first-born in response to God's command.[8] In Nehemiah 12:47, we read of "consecrations" in support of the clergy. In 2 Kings 12:18–19 we read of the donations that kings "consecrated" to the Temple, frequently from the spoils of war. This section of chapter 27 speaks of three specific types of consecrations: (1) urban dwellings, (2) *'aḥuzzah* land, and (3) acquired agricultural land.

14. *If anyone consecrates his house to the Lord* According to 25:29f., urban dwellings are not subject to the Jubilee; if not redeemed within a year, they become the permanent property of the purchaser. Here, nothing is said about a time limit, because consecration differs from an ordinary sale.

so it shall stand In verse 12, the verb employed is *yihyeh,* "it shall be, stand"; here, *yakum* has essentially the same functional meaning: "to be in force, to be legally valid."[9]

15. *he must add one-fifth* The formulaic *ḥamishit kesef ʿerkekha,* "one-fifth of the silver equivalent" (cf. v. 19) replaces *ḥamishito,* "its fifth part" of verses 13,31. The meaning is the same.

and it shall be his Hebrew *ve-hayah lo* connotes possession.

מחוברות] 16 וְאִ֣ם ׀ מִשְּׂדֵ֣ה אֲחֻזָּת֗וֹ יַקְדִּ֥ישׁ אִישׁ֙
לַֽיהוָ֔ה וְהָיָ֥ה עֶרְכְּךָ֖ לְפִ֣י זַרְע֑וֹ זֶ֚רַע חֹ֣מֶר שְׂעֹרִ֔ים
בַּחֲמִשִּׁ֖ים שֶׁ֥קֶל כָּֽסֶף׃ 17 אִם־מִשְּׁנַ֥ת הַיֹּבֵ֖ל יַקְדִּ֣ישׁ
שָׂדֵ֑הוּ כְּעֶרְכְּךָ֖ יָקֽוּם׃ 18 וְאִם־אַחַ֣ר הַיֹּבֵל֮ יַקְדִּ֣ישׁ
שָׂדֵהוּ֒ וְחִשַּׁב־ל֨וֹ הַכֹּהֵ֜ן אֶת־הַכֶּ֗סֶף עַל־פִּ֤י הַשָּׁנִים֙
הַנּ֣וֹתָרֹ֔ת עַ֖ד שְׁנַ֣ת הַיֹּבֵ֑ל וְנִגְרַ֖ע מֵעֶרְכֶּֽךָ׃ 19 וְאִם־
גָּאֹ֤ל יִגְאַל֙ אֶת־הַשָּׂדֶ֔ה הַמַּקְדִּ֖ישׁ אֹת֑וֹ וְ֠יָסַף
חֲמִשִׁ֧ית כֶּֽסֶף־עֶרְכְּךָ֛ עָלָ֖יו וְקָ֥ם לֽוֹ׃ 20 וְאִם־לֹ֤א
יִגְאַל֙ אֶת־הַשָּׂדֶ֔ה וְאִם־מָכַ֥ר אֶת־הַשָּׂדֶ֖ה לְאִ֣ישׁ
אַחֵ֑ר לֹ֥א יִגָּאֵ֖ל עֽוֹד׃ 21 וְהָיָ֨ה הַשָּׂדֶ֜ה בְּצֵאת֣וֹ
בַיֹּבֵ֗ל קֹ֛דֶשׁ לַֽיהוָ֖ה כִּשְׂדֵ֣ה הַחֵ֑רֶם לַכֹּהֵ֖ן תִּהְיֶ֥ה
אֲחֻזָּתֽוֹ׃ ששי 22 וְאִם֙ אֶת־שְׂדֵ֣ה מִקְנָת֔וֹ אֲשֶׁ֕ר

crates to the LORD any land that he holds, its assessment
shall be in accordance with its seed requirement: fifty
shekels of silver to a *homer* of barley seed.
17If he consecrates
his land as of the jubilee year, its assessment stands.
18But if
he consecrates his land after the jubilee, the priest shall
compute the price according to the years that are left until
the jubilee year, and its assessment shall be so reduced;
19and if he who consecrated the land wishes to redeem it, he
must add one-fifth to the sum at which it was assessed, and
it shall pass to him.
20But if he does not redeem the land,
and the land is sold to another, it shall no longer be
redeemable:
21when it is released in the jubilee, the land
shall be holy to the LORD, as land proscribed; it becomes the
priest's holding.

16. If anyone consecrates to the LORD any land that he holds Rather, "any part of his tenured land" (cf. the translation in v. 21, and see vv. 24,28). The legal status of the *'aḥuzzah,* "land holding, tenured land," is explained in the Comment to 25:25 and in Excursus 10. Chapter 27 differentiates between an *'aḥuzzah,* which belongs to an original owner, and acquired land, which had been transferred to someone other than the original owner.

its assessment shall be in accordance with its seed requirement The method of delineating plots of arable land by reference to the quantity of seed required in the planting is common to many ancient Near Eastern societies. The formula used here, *zera' ḥomer,* "a *ḥomer* of seed," means "[an area sown with] a *ḥomer* of seed."[10] The term *ḥomer* literally means "an ass, mule," but the Hebrew term and its cognates in Akkadian and Ugaritic designate a dry measure, equal to the normal load of an ass. Estimates of its bulk vary from 3.8 to 6.5 bushels.[11] According to Ezekiel 45:11f., the most extensive catalogue of weights and measures preserved in the Bible, a *ḥomer* equals ten *'efah*s. It was equivalent to the *kur* (Sum. *gur,* Akk. *kurru*).[12]

17. as of the jubilee year At the Jubilee, *'aḥuzzah* land reverted to its original owners, as mandated in 25:10,13f. All transfers of such property were, in fact, not final sales, but long-term leases that expired at the next Jubilee. What was being consecrated, in our case, was a lease computed in crop years. At the Jubilee, the sanctuary lost its right to the yields of such lands, which then reverted to their owners. As verses 17–18 explain, a full valuation would apply only if the full forty-nine years remained. Anything less would necessitate proportional reductions.

18. shall be so reduced Hebrew *ve-nigra'* is a mathematical term that means "to be subtracted."[13]

20. and the land is sold to another The formulation is ambiguous. It could not mean that the donor sold the land after he had consecrated it, for such a sale would not be binding. The sense must be, therefore, that the priesthood sold the land when it became apparent that its donor did not intend to redeem it. Once this occurred, the donor lost his right to redeem it, ever, according to Rashi and Ramban.

21. when it is released in the jubilee, the land shall be holy to the LORD, as land proscribed If the donor failed to redeem the land prior to the next Jubilee, the initial consecration is considered permanently binding, and the land remains the property of the sanctuary forever: it is holy to the LORD. At the time of the next Jubilee, the sanctuary would be the legal owner. The status of such land is compared to that of *ḥerem* land, land that could never be redeemed. This status is explained in the Comment to verses 28–29. In this way, the sanctuary enjoyed a special privilege. In all other cases, according to 25:14f., sales of *'aḥuzzah* land were never to be final, whereas unredeemed consecrations were. Normally it was guaranteed that land would revert to the original owner at the Jubilee, even if he lacked the means to buy back his land. The legislation of chapter 27 is complex in this regard. On

22 If he consecrates to the LORD land that he purchased, which is not land of his holding, 23 the priest shall compute for him the proportionate assessment up to the jubilee year, and he shall pay the assessment as of that day, a sacred donation to the LORD. 24 In the jubilee year the land shall revert to him from whom it was bought, whose holding the land is. 25 All assessments shall be by the sanctuary weight, the shekel being twenty *gerahs*.

26 A firstling of animals, however, which—as a firstling—is the LORD's, cannot be consecrated by anybody; whether ox or sheep, it is the LORD's. 27 But if it is of unclean animals, it may be ransomed as its assessment, with one-fifth added; if it is not redeemed, it shall be sold at its assessment.

לֹא מִשְּׂדֵה אֲחֻזָּתוֹ יַקְדִּישׁ לַיהוָה׃ 23 וְחִשַּׁב־לוֹ
הַכֹּהֵן אֵת מִכְסַת הָעֶרְכְּךָ עַד שְׁנַת הַיֹּבֵל וְנָתַן
אֶת־הָעֶרְכְּךָ בַּיּוֹם הַהוּא קֹדֶשׁ לַיהוָה׃ 24 בִּשְׁנַת
הַיּוֹבֵל יָשׁוּב הַשָּׂדֶה לַאֲשֶׁר קָנָהוּ מֵאִתּוֹ לַאֲשֶׁר־
לוֹ אֲחֻזַּת הָאָרֶץ׃ 25 וְכָל־עֶרְכְּךָ יִהְיֶה בְּשֶׁקֶל
הַקֹּדֶשׁ עֶשְׂרִים גֵּרָה יִהְיֶה הַשָּׁקֶל׃ ס 26 אַךְ־
בְּכוֹר אֲשֶׁר־יְבֻכַּר לַיהוָה בִּבְהֵמָה לֹא־יַקְדִּישׁ אִישׁ
אֹתוֹ אִם־שׁוֹר אִם־שֶׂה לַיהוָה הוּא׃ 27 וְאִם
בַּבְּהֵמָה הַטְּמֵאָה וּפָדָה בְעֶרְכֶּךָ וְיָסַף חֲמִשִׁתוֹ
עָלָיו וְאִם־לֹא יִגָּאֵל וְנִמְכַּר בְּעֶרְכֶּךָ׃ 28 אַךְ־כָּל־

the one hand, it utilized the Jubilee law in computing the value of the land. On the other hand, the privilege of the sanctuary overrode the rights of the original owner.

it becomes the priest's holding This accords with the law of Numbers 18:14, which grants all *ḥerem* land to the priesthood.

22. ***If he consecrates to the LORD land that he purchased*** This reflects the provisions of 25:25f. If one is compelled to sell any part of his *'aḥuzzah,* it reverts to him at the next Jubilee, even if he has been unable to redeem it in the interim. One who purchased *'aḥuzzah* land on this basis, therefore, was not a full owner. If he subsequently consecrated such acquired land, he had to be prepared to remit its value in silver to the sanctuary at the time of its consecration, plus the surcharge of 20 percent. Otherwise, his consecration would not be accepted in the first place because the field could not be collateral for his donation, as it would have been if it were his true *'aḥuzzah.*

23. ***the proportionate assessment*** Hebrew *mikhsah* means "cut, portion."[14] The sense is that the donor must pay the Temple an appropriate amount in silver, equal to the assessed yield of the crop years remaining until the next Jubilee.

24. ***whose holding the land is*** Rather, "to whom the tenured land belongs." The consecration of the land by one who had purchased it from its original owner does not affect the primary rights of the original owner.

25. ***All assessments shall be by the sanctuary weight*** The standard known as *shekel ha-kodesh,* "sanctuary weight," contained twenty *gerah*s or "grains" of silver.[15] There is mention of a royal standard, called *'even ha-melekh,* "the royal 'stone,'" in 2 Samuel 14:26.

FIRSTLINGS (vv. 26–27)

All Torah traditions know of the idea that the first-born males of man and beast are initially consecrated to God.[16] Although chapter 27 makes no mention of the essential obligation to devote first-born sons, it does deal, as part of its primary concern with Temple funding, with firstlings as a source of such income. Of immediate concern in the chapter is the fact that already at birth, the firstlings of the herds and flocks are sacred. They are not something one can consecrate, for one may consecrate only what he owns.

26. ***A firstling of animals, however, which—as a firstling—is the LORD's*** This refers to pure animals, suitable for sacrifice. (Verse 27 deals with the firstlings of impure animals.) The Hebrew verb *yevukhar* is a denominative based on the noun *bekhor,* "firstling." The sense of *yevukkar* is "to be assigned as a firstling to the Lord." In Deuteronomy 21:16 we find the active form "he may not treat as first-born (*yevakker*) the son of the loved one."

²⁸But of all that anyone owns, be it man or beast or land of his holding, nothing that he has proscribed for the Lᴏʀᴅ may be sold or redeemed; every proscribed thing is totally consecrated to the Lᴏʀᴅ. ²⁹No human being who has been proscribed can be ransomed: he shall be put to death.

חֵ֩רֶם אֲשֶׁ֨ר יַחֲרִ֥ם אִ֛ישׁ לַֽיהֹוָ֖ה מִכָּל־אֲשֶׁר־ל֗וֹ
מֵאָדָ֤ם וּבְהֵמָה֙ וּמִשְּׂדֵ֣ה אֲחֻזָּת֔וֹ לֹ֥א יִמָּכֵ֖ר וְלֹ֣א
יִגָּאֵ֑ל כָּל־חֵ֕רֶם קֹֽדֶשׁ־קׇדָשִׁ֥ים ה֖וּא לַֽיהֹוָֽה׃ שביעי
²⁹ כָּל־חֵ֗רֶם אֲשֶׁ֧ר יׇחֳרַ֛ם מִן־הָאָדָ֖ם לֹ֣א יִפָּדֶ֑ה מ֥וֹת

27. *But if it is of unclean animals* The law is that firstlings of impure animals, unsuitable for sacrifice, may be redeemed on the usual basis. If they are not redeemed, the sanctuary may sell them for silver. No time limit is stipulated. This last provision differs from the law of Exodus 13:13, repeated in Exodus 34:20, requiring that the firstling of an ass (an example of an impure animal) must be either exchanged for a lamb or destroyed. This difference between the two laws regards the legal status of the firstlings of impure animals. According to the legislation of Exodus, the sanctuary administration could not benefit from an impure animal in any way. It could not receive an animal unsuitable for sacrifice. In our legislation, the sanctuary had the right to dispose of impure firstlings profitably. The wording of our law indicates subtly that it reflects the legislation of Exodus. Throughout most of chapter 27, the verb *ga'al*, "to redeem," is used. Only here, and in verse 29, is the verb *padah*, "to redeem," used, precisely because it is the verb that is used in Exodus 13:13 and 34:20 in a similar matter of law.[17]

The difference between the laws of Exodus and Leviticus on the matter of firstlings also reflects differing administrative practices on the part of the priesthood of the sanctuary. As has been stated, our legislation is aimed at securing silver for the sanctuary, and its provisions indicate the extensive use of currency in the economy at large.

PROSCRIBED PROPERTY (vv. 28–29)

28. *But of all that anyone owns . . . nothing that he has proscribed for the Lᴏʀᴅ may be sold or redeemed* In the Comment to verse 21, it is noted that an 'aḥuzzah consecrated to the sanctuary, but not redeemed prior to the next Jubilee year, acquired the status of *ḥerem*, "proscribed property." This verse is the actual statement on the legal status of land and other property that is proscribed; verse 29 gives the law regarding a person condemned under the *ḥerem*.

The verb *ḥ-r-m* means "to set apart, denote, restrict" and, in biblical Hebrew, seems always to have a negative or prohibitive connotation; it describes what is to be avoided, destroyed, or forbidden. Its cognates in certain other Semitic languages can connote the positive aspects of holiness as well as the negative.

To designate something as *ḥerem* may mean either that it is to be destroyed completely or that it is to be reserved exclusively for specific purposes associated with the sanctuary. The institution of the *ḥerem* was variously interpreted in biblical Israel. Historically, it was associated with war. It had been a very ancient, pre-Israelite practice to donate the spoils of war to gods, including conquered cities and territories. At times this involved killing off the army of the enemy and even a population that refused to surrender. This practice is known from Mari, a town in Syria, from documents dating to the eighteenth century B.C.E. It was also operative among some of Israel's contemporary neighbors. King Mesha of Moab, mentioned in 2 Kings 3:4 as a contemporary of Ahab, king of northern Israel in the ninth century B.C.E., records in his royal inscription that he proscribed (Moab. *hḥrm* = Heb. *heḥerim*) conquered towns to Kemosh, the national god of the Moabites.[18]

In biblical law, the institution of the *ḥerem* is carried over into the context of juridical punishment, where the penalty for worshiping other gods is death. Exodus 22:19 ordains that any person who offers sacrifice to another god is to be proscribed, which is to say, condemned to death. A similar punishment is ordained for the town whose inhabitants collectively participate in the worship of other gods, according to Deuteronomy 13:13f.

Whereas these precedents explain verse 29, which concerns a condemned man, there remains a serious difficulty with respect to verse 28. From what we know of the *ḥerem*, it is an imposed condition; one would not speak of voluntarily proscribing a field. Nor did this difficulty go unnoticed by the rabbinic sages and the medieval commentators. Two related explanations are given: First, verse

30All tithes from the land, whether seed from the ground
or fruit from the tree, are the LORD's; they are holy to the
LORD. 31If anyone wishes to redeem any of his tithes, he
must add one-fifth to them. 32All tithes of the herd or
flock—of all that passes under the shepherd's staff, every
tenth one—shall be holy to the LORD. 33He must not look

יוּמָת׃ 30 וְכָל־מַעְשַׂר הָאָרֶץ מִזֶּרַע הָאָרֶץ מִפְּרִי
הָעֵץ לַיהוָה הוּא קֹדֶשׁ לַיהוָה׃ 31 וְאִם־גָּאֹל יִגְאַל
אִישׁ מִמַּעַשְׂרוֹ חֲמִשִׁיתוֹ יֹסֵף עָלָיו׃ מפטיר
32 וְכָל־מַעְשַׂר בָּקָר וָצֹאן כֹּל אֲשֶׁר־יַעֲבֹר תַּחַת
הַשָּׁבֶט הָעֲשִׂירִי יִהְיֶה־קֹּדֶשׁ לַיהוָה׃ 33 לֹא יְבַקֵּר

28 may be speaking of a man who swore to devote his property. Or, second, it may be speaking of one who took an oath in another matter, swearing that if he failed to uphold that oath, his property would be forfeit as *ḥerem.* In either case, the oath, once taken, made of the act of devotion a binding obligation; it was no longer a voluntary act.[19] On this basis, one could translate verse 28 as follows: "But anything that a man (swears) to devote as proscribed property to the LORD *('asher yaḥarim 'ish le-YHVH).*" In late Second Temple times, this was a common practice. One would state: *harei ʿalai be-ḥerem,* "I owe this, under penalty of proscription." Such oaths were called *ḥaramim* because it was stipulated that the penalty for failure to uphold the oath was the proscription, or confiscation, of one's property by the Temple.[20]

Based on the limited information available concerning the *ḥerem* in biblical times, this interpretation is perhaps the closest we can come to resolving the difficulty in verse 28, but it is far from adequate. One has the impression that there is a background to this law that is unknown to us since it diverges decidedly from the norms applicable to the institution of the *ḥerem* as they are known from other biblical sources.

Several additional notes on verse 28: The "man" whom one proscribes is undoubtedly a non-Israelite slave, who is considered the property of his owner. And in verse 21, *sedeh ha-ḥerem* would mean "a field that has acquired the status of *ḥerem.*" Such property, according to verse 28, may not be redeemed by the one who devoted it; nor may the sanctuary ever sell it, although it probably could use the revenue from it.

29. No human being who has been proscribed can be ransomed This law reflects, at least in part, the provisions of Exodus 22:19, which ordain that anyone who worships another god shall be proscribed, that is, condemned to death. (This law is cited here because of its topical relation to v. 28, although it has nothing to do with the subject of income for the sanctuary.) Like the murderer of Numbers 35:31–34 who cannot be ransomed (note the verb *padah,* "to redeem"), one condemned under the law of *ḥerem* must pay with his life.

TITHES (vv. 30–33)

This chapter speaks of two kinds of tithes: a tenth of the yield of the land and a tenth of the flocks and herds.

30. All tithes from the land . . . are the LORD's; they are holy to the LORD In its overall effect, this law is consonant with the provisions of Deuteronomy 14:22f., although the matter is stated differently here. In the legislation of Deuteronomy, Israelites are required to set aside a tithe from the produce of the fields and to bring it each year to the central Temple. There, they are to consume it "in the presence of the Lord" as a sacred meal. Those distant from the Temple were to convert the ritual produce into silver and to use that silver to purchase offerings when they arrived at the Temple, which they would then celebrate in God's presence. This was in addition to the tithe given locally to the Levites. In the later tradition this tithe was called *maʿaser sheni,* "the second tithe." As of the time it was set aside initially, the tithe, and its eventual equivalent in silver, were preassigned. They belonged to the sanctuary and could not be used for any other purpose.[21] Here, the procedures for the tithe follow the general pattern of the legislation of chapter 27. Redemption imposed a surcharge of 20 percent, as is noted in verse 31.

32. All tithes of the herd or flock No other Torah legislation ordains a tithe from the annual increments of the herds and flocks. Yet this statement seems to assume the existence of such a

out for good as against bad, or make substitution for it. If he does not make substitution for it, then it and its substitute shall both be holy: it cannot be redeemed.

34 These are the commandments that the LORD gave Moses for the Israelite people on Mount Sinai.

בֵּין־טוֹב לָרַע וְלֹא יְמִירֶנּוּ וְאִם־הָמֵר יְמִירֶנּוּ וְהָיָה־
הוּא וּתְמוּרָתוֹ יִהְיֶה־קֹּדֶשׁ לֹא יִגָּאֵל׃ 34 אֵלֶּה
הַמִּצְוֺת אֲשֶׁר צִוָּה יְהוָה אֶת־מֹשֶׁה אֶל־בְּנֵי
יִשְׂרָאֵל בְּהַר סִינָי׃

law, just as verse 30 assumes the law of tithes from the yield of the field. There are, indeed, indications of such a law as applied to the herds and flocks. In 1 Samuel 8:15–17, Samuel warns the people of the burdens of a monarchy. Among the prerogatives of a king, he says, is the right to demand a tenth of the livestock as well as of the produce. In that early law, the tithe is regarded as a royal tax of sorts, whereas here, the tithe is a tax payable to the Levites, as it is in Deuteronomy.

There are more subtle indications of tithing the herds and flocks. Thus, Abraham pledged a tenth of all his possessions to the Canaanite priest-king, Melchizedek, and Jacob similarly pledged a tenth of his wealth at Bethel, in Genesis 14:20 and 34:22, respectively. Both patriarchs were known as owners of large herds and flocks.

The annual increment of the herds and flocks was counted under the shepherd's staff. Jeremiah (33:13) prophesies that "sheep shall pass again under the hands of one who counts them," and Ezekiel (20:37) uses the term as metaphor, as God states: "I will make you pass under the shepherd's staff."

*33. **He must not look out for good as against bad*** The actual tenth animal is to be counted as the tithe, whatever its condition. That very animal is preassigned, as of the moment of its designation as "the tenth." It can be neither substituted nor redeemed. Hebrew *yevakker* means "to search out, examine," as a shepherd "seeks out" his livestock to examine them. Thus, we read in Ezekiel 34:11–12: "For thus said the Lord GOD: . . . I am going to take thought for My flock and I will seek them out (*u-vikkartim*). As a shepherd seeks out his flock (*ke-vakkarat roʿeh ʿedro*). . . ."[22]

THE POSTSCRIPT (v. 34)

These are the commandments that the LORD gave Moses . . . on Mount Sinai This postscript reverts to the opening verse of chapter 25: "The LORD spoke to Moses on Mount Sinai." It was customary to state, both at the beginning and at the end of major sections, or books, of the Torah, where and when the revelation from God had occurred. The same kind of postscript occurs in 26:46 and in the closing verse of the Book of Numbers, 36:13.

חזק
סכום הפסוקים של ספר
שמונה מאות
וחמשים ותשעה
טנף
וחציו והנגע בבשר
וסדרים כה

NOTES TO THE COMMENTARY

Chapter 1

1. This principle is clearly stated in Num. 35:9–34, in the context of criminal law. See M. Greenberg, "Certain Postulates of Biblical Criminal Law," in *Yehezkel Kaufmann Jubilee Volume,* ed. M. Haran (Jerusalem: Magnes Press, 1960), 5f.

2. See Comment to 5:20f., where it is explained that in the case of certain crimes involving false oaths, provision was made for ritual atonement, but only after full restitution had been made and the crime confessed.

3. An example of prophetic criticism is found in Isa. 1, where the prophet calls upon the people to "purify" their deeds, not just their physical persons, to deal justly and kindly, not merely to offer sacrifices. Also cf. Jer. 7:3–15; Amos 2:6–8; Hos. 8:11–14.

4. See Lev. 8:10; and cf. Exod. 25:9; Num. 1–10. Note the parallelism of *'ohel,* "tent," and *mishkan* in Num. 24:5.

5. See M. Haran, "The Nature of the ''Ohel Mo'edh' in Pentateuchal Sources," JSS 5 (1960): 50ff., and "Shiloh and Jerusalem: The Origins of the Priestly Tradition in the Pentateuch," JBL 81 (1962): 14ff. The oracular function of *'ohel mo'ed* in priestly literature is prescribed in Exod. 25:32; 29:42–43; 30:6,36; Num. 7:89; 17:9.

6. Cf. usage of *nefesh* in chaps. 2–5; and cf. *'ish,* "person," in chap. 17.

7. See A. Alt, "The Origins of Israelite Law," in *Essays in Old Testament History and Religion,* trans. R. A. Wilson (Oxford: Blackwell, 1966), 79–132, especially 88f.

8. See B. Mazar, *The Excavations in the Old City of Jerusalem* (Jerusalem: Israel Exploration Society, 1969), plate 10, no. 5, for a fragment of a stone vessel with the word *korban* written on it. The object dates from late Second Temple times. Also see J. A. Fitzmyer, "The Aramaic Qorbān Inscriptions . . .," JBL 78 (1959): 60–65.

9. In the introduction to the Sifra (Weiss, 1f.) the thirteen hermeneutic principles of Torah interpretation are presented. One of them (statement no. 7) is explained as follows: "Through the general, followed by the specific. How so? 'From cattle (*behemah*)'—the general; 'From the herd (*bakar*) and from the flock (*tso'n*)'—the specific. The general includes only what is specified" (leaf 2a).

10. For the so-called Tariffs from Marseilles and Carthage, see G. A. Cooke, *A Text-Book of North Semitic Inscriptions* (Oxford: Clarendon Press, 1903), 112–113, and commentary following. Also ANET, pp. 656–657.

11. See B. A. Levine, *In the Presence of the Lord* (Leiden: E. J. Brill, 1974), 6, and n. 5. Cf. Judg. 13:20: "As the flames leaped up (*ba'alot*) from the altar toward the sky." For the Ugar. parallel, wherein one "ascends" in order to offer the sacrifice, see Keret, line 145, and commentary by H. L. Ginsberg, *The Legend of King Keret: A Canaanite Epic of the Bronze Age* (New Haven: American Schools of Oriental Research, 1946), 37f.

12. Levine, *op. cit.,* pp. 22f.

13. Cf. usage of *le-ratson,* "for acceptance in favor of," in Lev. 19:5 and in Isa. 56:7. Regarding unacceptable sacrifices, cf. Lev. 22:19.

14. Cf. 17:1–19, where this requirement is stated.

15. See A. Goetze, *The Hittite Ritual of Tunnawi* (New Haven: American Oriental Society, 1938), 21, and nn. 34–35. Also see D. Wright, "The Gesture of Hand Placement in the Hebrew Bible and in Hittite Literature," JAOS 106 (1986): 433–446.

16. In the Mishnah, we have the formula *shor zeh 'olah,* "This bull is an *'olah,*" in Mish. Ar. 5:6, 8:7; and cf. *'ayil zeh 'olah,* "this ram is an *'olah,*" in Mish. Men. 3:9. Such statements assigned the animal, in a legal sense, to a specific sacrifice.

17. See the discussion in Levine, *op. cit.*, pp. 67–77.

18. See the article by M. Haran, EB (Hebrew), s.v. *mizbeaḥ,* "altar," and photo on p. 779 of the horned altar from Megiddo. Also see A. Biran, "An Israelite Horned Altar at Dan," BA 37 (1974): 106–107, and Y. Aharoni, "The Horned Altar of Beer-sheba," BA 37 (1974): 2–6.

19. In certain rites of riddance, the hide was burned outside the camp. Cf. 4:11–12. In the Marseilles Tariffs (see n. 10, above), we also read that the hides of certain sacrificial animals belonged to the donors of the sacrifice. On usage of *n-t-ḥ,* "to section," see Lev. 8:20; 9:13; and cf. 1 Kings 18:23,33 (Elijah's sacrifice on Mount Carmel).

20. Also cf. Exod. 40:23, where the verb *'-r-kh,* "to set up, arrange," refers to the placing of the bread of display in the sanctuary. Also cf. Lev. 6:5; Num. 23:4. In Pss. 23:5, we read: "You spread (*ta'arokh*) a table before me in the presence of my enemies."

21. See AHW, s.v. *piṭru.* In Lev. 4:9, the same appendage is called *ha-yoteret 'al ha-kaved,* "the covering over the liver." Targ. Onk. translates *peder* by Aram. *ḥatsra',* a known term for this appendage.

22. Cf. Lev. 3:3; Exod. 12:9. For the Akk. forms see AHW, s.v. *qerbu(m)* II, and *qerbītu.*

23. For the Akk. forms see AHW, s.v. *qutru,* "smoke, incense," and *qutrennu,* "incense offering." Also see M. Haran, "The Uses of Incense in the Ancient Israelite Ritual," VT 10 (1960): 113–129.

24. J. Hoftijzer ("Das Sogenannte Feueropfer," VTSup 16 [1967]: 114–134) attempts to relate Heb. *'isheh* to Ugar. *itt,* which he translates "gift of devotion." His understanding of the Ugar. term is questionable, however. It is preferable to stay with the traditional derivation from *'esh,* "fire." Precisely, *'isheh* designates the part of a sacrifice that is burned. This term may therefore be used in connection with various offerings, so long as at least part of them is burned (Hoffmann to 3:5).

25. See *Midrash Ha-Gadol: Leviticus,* ed. E. N. Rabinowitz (New York: The Jewish Theological Seminary of America, 1932), 36, line 10.

26. See A. L. Oppenheim, *Ancient Mesopotamia* (Chicago: University of Chicago Press, 1964), 130 for the practice of fumigation in Mesopotamian temple cults. Also see Maimonides, Guide 3.45 (Ibn Tibbon, 57a).

27. The use of aromatic spices in preparing cakes for grain offerings so as to add to their taste is prescribed in 2:2.

28. See Mish. Zev. 7:5–6.

29. Cf. usage of the verb *matsah,* "to squeeze, drain out," in Judg. 6:38; Isa. 51:17.

30. Note the same system in chap. 5, and see Comment to 12:8, where a comparison is made with the provisions of the Marseilles Tariffs. They also provide for less expensive offerings in the case of donors whose means are inadequate.

Chapter 2

1. See further in Lev. 4:2,27; 5:1. Also cf. Gen. 46:15,18, which refer to the collective *nefesh,* "persons," of Jacob's clan. Also see Comment to 1:2, where the terms referring to persons are discussed.

2. See *The Oxford English Dictionary,* s.v. "meal." In addi-

tion to the fact that "meal" usually excludes wheat, it is a term that refers to the state of the grain as being ground, not to varieties of grain, as such.

3. Cf. usage in Gen. 32:14; 43:11; 1 Kings 10:25; 2 Kings 17:4.

4. Also cf. 1 Sam. 2:17; Pss. 141:2.

5. Cf. 2 Kings 16:15; Pss. 141:2 (*minḥat ʿerev,* "the sacrifice of the evening"); as well as Ezra 9:4; Dan. 9:21.

6. See the article by M. Zahari, EB (Hebrew), s.v. *levonah,* where Hebrew *levonah* is identified as *Boswellia,* especially, *Boswellia carteri birdw.,* of the family of *Burseraceae.* This plant grows primarily in Arabia, Somalia, Ethiopia, and India.

7. See CAD, s.v. *zikru* B, "image, counterpart"; and also G. R. Driver, "Three Technical Terms in the Pentateuch," JSS 1 (1954): 99f.

8. See B. A. Levine, "Notes on Some Technical Terms of the Biblical Cult," *Leshonenu* 30 (1965–1966): 3–11.

9. Cf. Gk. *madza,* "barley cake," derived from the verb *mássô,* "to knead dough." (Liddel-Scott, *Greek-English Lexicon,* s.v. *madza,* and s.v. *mássô*). Gk. *madza* was a barley cake inferior in quality to wheat bread and was normally eaten by slaves and other poor folk.

10. See CAD, s.v. *emṣu* A.

11. Cf. Judg. 14:18–19; 1 Sam. 14:25.

12. See CAD, s.v. *dišpu.*

13. See Maimonides, Guide 3.46 (Ibn Tibbon, 57b).

14. See the Ugar. epic of Keret, line 72, in H. L. Ginsberg, *The Legend of King Keret: A Canaanite Epic of the Bronze Age* (New Haven: American Schools of Oriental Research, 1946).

15. See F. Blome, *Die Opfermaterie in Babylonien und Israel* (Rome: Pontifical Institute, 1934), 298f., for a discussion of the use of honey in Mesopotamian cults and in ancient Israel.

16. See Excursus 8 for a discussion of desacralization, as this process was involved in the offering of the first sheaf, as ordained in 23:11f.

17. Also cf. Ezek. 43:24 on the use of salt in the Temple of Jerusalem.

18. Cf. the view of F. C. Fensham, "Salt as Curse in the Old Testament and the Ancient Near East," BA 25 (1962): 48–50. Also see the articles by H. Eising, TWAT, s.v. *melaḥ,* and by H. Beinart, EB (Hebrew), s.v. *melaḥ.*

19. See B. A. Levine, EncJud, s.v. "Firstborn," and s.v. "First Fruits."

20. See J. Levy, *Wörterbuch über die Talmudim und Midraschim,* s.v. *geris* (pl. *gerisim*).

21. See HALAT, s.v. *kali,* for late form *kelayot,* "roasted kernels," and for cognate forms. Also cf. the Akk. cognate *qalītu,* from the verb *qalû,* "to burn," in CAD, s.v. *qalītu.*

22. On *karmel*, see G. H. Dalman, *Arbeit und Sitte im Palästina,* vol. 3 (Reprints, Hildesheim: Alms, 1964), 266–275.

Chapter 3

1. See Comment to 2:10 on the various classes of sacrifices.

2. This is explained in the Comment to v. 1 of this chap.

3. This interpretation of the term *shelamim* and the function of the offering by that name are presented in B. A. Levine, *In the Presence of the Lord* (Leiden: E. J. Brill, 1974), 3–52.

4. Ibid., pp. 115–117.

5. Also cf. Zeph. 1:7.

6. See Judg. 6:19. In 1 Sam. 2:13–15, we read of the cultic misdeeds of the sons of Eli at Shiloh. There, the fork is called *mazleg,* and it had three "teeth." That passage mentions four different terms for pots used in the preparation of the *zevaḥ.* This is the longest list of such vessels in the Bible, indicating to what extent we learn about material culture from descriptions of the cult.

7. The Ugar. term *šlmm* occurs in the Keret epic, lines 126–136. See H. L. Ginsberg, *The Legend of King Keret: A Canaanite Epic of the Bronze Age* (New Haven: American Schools of Oriental Research, 1946), 17, and comments, 39.

8. See Rashi and Ḥul. 49b.

9. See Comments to vv. 16–17 of this chap.; and cf. Lev. 7:23–25; 1 Sam. 2:15–16; Ezek. 44:7,15. Fat is desired by God. This is reflected in Gen. 4:4; Isa. 1:4; 43:24.

10. See the detailed comparative study of *kesalim,* "tendons," by M. Held, "Studies in Comparative-Semitic Lexicography," in *Studies in Honor of Benno Landsberger* (Chicago: University of Chicago Press, 1965), 401f.

11. See Rashi and the discussion by Hoffmann, p. 118. Also see Comment to 1:8.

12. In Mish. Shab. 5:4, it is related that small carts were used to enable broadtail sheep to walk about because their tails were so heavy. See the discussion in Hoffmann, p. 122.

13. In Arab. *laḥm* means "meat," a point noted by Ibn Janaḥ. See the article by W. Donnerhausen, TWAT, s.v. *leḥem.*

14. See A. L. Oppenheim, *Ancient Mesopotamia* (Chicago: University of Chicago Press, 1964), 183f.

15. See usage in Ezek. 4:1; 23:14; and B. A. Levine, TWAT, s.v. *mitsvah.*

16. Cf. Lev. 6:11; 7:36; and frequently in Num. Also cf. the law of the Passover in Exod. 12.

Chapter 4

1. See introductory Comment to chaps. 1–7 for a discussion of this principle.

2. See Excursus 1.

3. See Mish. Hor. 2:1–2 and Mish. Ker. 4:1f.

4. On the Akk. verb *ḫāṭû,* see CAD, s.v. *ḫāṭû,* and for the adjective, see CAD, s.v. *ḫāṭû.* Also see B. A. Levine, *In the Presence of the Lord* (Leiden: E. J. Brill, 1974), 102f.

5. See Mish. Ker. 7, especially 7:3.

6. According to 7:36, Aaron's sons were also anointed. The two traditions are discussed in the introductory Comment to chaps. 8–9.

7. See further in Comment to v. 12 of this chap.

8. Cf. Exod. 34:6–7.

9. As in Gen. 20:9; 2 Kings 17:21; Pss. 32:1.

10. See Lev. 6:19; 8:15; Ezek. 45:18; 51:9.

11. In 1 Kings 6:31 we read that the innermost section of the Solomonic Temple, the *devir,* was separated from the outer hall, the *heikhal,* by a wooden door. There is no mention of a curtain. In 2 Chron. 3:14, the postexilic author, in his recasting of the passage in 1 Kings, speaks of both a door and a curtain. On the term *parokhet,* see B. A. Levine, EB (Hebrew), s.v. *parokhet.*

12. For archaeological evidence on horned altars see chap. 1, n. 18.

13. See Comment to 1:6; and cf. Ezek. 43:21, on the burning of the bull of the sin offering outside the Temple. This is Ezekiel's way of restating the law of 8:17. See Comment to 8:17.

14. See Comment to 17:11.

15. Cf. Exod. 29:14; Lev. 16:27; Mal. 2:3.

16. See A. E. Cowley, *AP*, papyrus 15, line 26, and E. Kraeling, *Brooklyn Museum Aramaic Papyri* (New Haven: Yale University Press, 1953), papyrus 2, line 7, and papyrus 7, line 21. The standard clause reads: *yqwm bʿdh* (= *yequm baʿedah*), "he arises in the community." Also see C. F. Jean, J. Hoftijzer, *Dictionnaire des inscriptions semitiques de l'ouest* (Leiden; E. J. Brill, 1965), 39, s.v. *bʿḏ,* for relevant literature. In Ugaritic poetry we find reference to *ʿdt ilm,* "the *assembly* of the gods," which recalls *ʿadat ʾel,* "the divine assembly," in Pss. 82:1. See R. E. Whitaker, *A Concordance to the Ugaritic Literature,* s.v. *ʿdt,* for this and additional sources in Ugaritic. See also B. A. Levine, J-M de Tarragon, "Shapshu Cries Out in Heaven: Dealing with Snakebites at Ugarit," *RB,* 1988, 480–517, especially 498, in comments to Pines 117–120. In Judg. 14:8 we read

of an *ʿedah* of bees. The realism of the term *ʿedah* was discussed in the Introduction to Leviticus, in the section entitled "Institutional History: Realistic Functions in Leviticus."

The Sifra, followed by Rashi, understands *ʿedah* as referring here to the high court. Although this is patently a later, imposed interpretation, it does reflect a reality of life in ancient Israel, the need for communal representation. In Num. 35:24–25, it is the *ʿedah* that has the authority to determine the innocence or guilt of an accused murderer, and it is hard to imagine that the entire populace carried out this function. Similarly, Exod. 12:6 states that "all the assembled population of the Israelites shall slaughter it [the paschal sacrifice]," which was correctly interpreted by the sages to mean that representatives acted on behalf of the community (Kid. 41:a–b).

17. This is the view of Rashi, Ibn Ezra, and Hoffmann.

18. Cf. Exod. 18:13; Num. 11:16; 22:4,7; Deut. 31:28. See the discussion by H. Reviv, "Structure of Society," in *The World History of the Jewish People,* vol. 5, *The Age of the Monarchies: Culture and Society,* ed. A. Malamat (New Brunswick, N. J.: Rutgers University Press, 1979), 125–146, on the functions of the *zekenim.*

19. See Ruth 4:2; and cf. 2 Kings 19:2.

20. See Yoma 5a.

21. See the discussion of the verb *kipper* and related forms in Levine, *In the Presence,* pp. 56f., 77f., 123–127.

22. See AHW, s.v. *salāḫu(m)* 1, and the construction *slḥ npš,* "washing of the upper part of the animal," in Ugar. (UT 9.1).

23. Cf. usage of the verb *kahal,* "to assemble," in Exod. 35:1; Num. 20:8; Deut. 31:28. As a term for the Israelites, *kahal* is used in Deut. 23:2–4, for example, and frequently throughout the rest of the Bible.

24. Cf. the early source in Exod. 22:27: "You shall not revile God, nor put a curse upon a chieftain (*nasi'*) among your people." See E. A. Speiser, "Background and Function of the Biblical Nasi'," CBQ 25 (1963): 111–117.

25. Much has been written about the *ʿam ha-'arets* in biblical times. See H. Tadmor, "'The People' and the Kingship in Ancient Israel," *Journal of World History* 11 (1968): 56–58; and the informative note by A. Malamat, "The Last Kings of Judah and the Fall of Jerusalem," IEJ 18 (1968): 140. Also cf. Gen. 23:12–13; 42:6; 2 Kings 11; and especially 21:24; 23:30. The burnt offering of the *ʿam ha-'arets* is actually mentioned in 2 Kings 16:15.

Chapter 5

1. See the introductory Comment to chaps. 1–7.

2. Also cf. Exod. 36:6.

3. TJ Yev. 6, end of halakhah 1.

4. Cf. Num. 5:21–22; Judg. 17:2; Prov. 29:24.

5. Cf. Neh. 10:30.

6. Cf. similar usage in Exod. 28:38,43; Num. 18:1,32; Isa. 53:6; Ezek. 4:4–6.

7. This is epitomized by use of *'elohim,* "God," in Exod. 21:6; 22:7,10; Deut. 1:16–17; and see Comment to v. 20.

8. Also cf. Mish. Shevu. 4:2.

9. There are several laws that prohibit false testimony: Exod. 20:16; 23:1; Deut. 5:17; 19:16–18f. These all speak of an active offense, not of an omission. On the difference between speech and deed, see the comment of Rabad, in his commentary to Sifra Va-yikra' (Weiss, 22b.8). Omission may stand in contrast to *zadon,* "a presumptuous act," defined in Num. 15:30 as one performed *be-yad ramah,* "defiantly, in a high-handed manner." What was not in a high-handed manner could be considered inadvertent, perhaps.

10. See Comment to 1:2 for this type of legal formulation.

11. See the introductory Comment to chap. 11 for rabbinic sources on the various categories of impurity.

12. See Comment to 4:11.

13. In vv. 3–4: *ve-hu' yadaʿ,* "he knew," thus refers to the final knowledge on the part of the offender, which prompted him to undertake expiation; it does *not* refer to his initial knowledge, this according to Hoffmann. See Mish. Shevu. 1.

14. Cf. usage in Gen. 2:17: "But as for the tree of knowledge of good and bad (*tov va-raʿ*)."

15. See the study by M. Greenberg, cited in chap. 1, n. 1.

16. See Mish. Shevu. 3:10, 4:2, Mish. Hor. 2:7, and Mish. Ker. 2:3–4.

17. See sources cited in chap. 1, n. 10. In line 15 of the tariff we read *bkl zbḥ 'š yzbḥ dl mqn',* "as regards any offering which one poor in livestock offers." Also cf. usage of Hebrew *dal,* "poor" (Punic *dl*). See Comment to 14:21.

18. See the discussion of this matter in B. A. Levine, *In the Presence of the Lord* (Leiden: E. J. Brill, 1974), 22f.

19. Cf. similar usage in Exod. 21:21; Lev. 9:16; Num. 15:24; 29:18.

20. See Comment to 2:2.

21. Cf. 26:40; and see Num. 5:6; Josh. 7:1; 22:16; Ezek. 14:13; 18:24.

22. See J. Milgrom, *Cult and Conscience: The Asham and the Priestly Doctrine of Repentance* (Leiden: E. J. Brill, 1976), for a discussion of *maʿal* in comparative perspective.

23. Cf. Gen. 31:39, literally "I wiped it off (that is, made good on the obligation)."

24. See E. A. Speiser, "Leviticus and the Critics," in *Yehezkel Kaufmann Jubilee Volume,* ed. M. Haran (Jerusalem: Magnes Press, 1960), 29f. See also A. Gianto, "Some Notes on the Mulk Inscription from Nebi Yunis," Bib. 63 (1987): 397–401: and see the Comment to 1:3.

25. Also cf. 2 Kings 23:35; Pss. 55:14.

26. In 2 Kings 12:17 we find the designations *kesef 'asham ve-khesef ḥatta'ot,* literally "silver for the guilt offering and silver for the sin offerings." Such remittances to the Temple of Jerusalem were exempt from a royal decree appropriating all contributions brought there for use in repairing it. These designations would seem to indicate that both the *'asham* and the *ḥatta't* were offered by their donors in the form of silver, at certain periods of history.

27. 2 Sam. 14:26 mentions a royal standard, *'even ha-melekh,* "the royal 'stone'"; and in 1 Kings 12:24; 15:18, we read of a royal treasury, separate from the Temple treasury.

28. See the introductory Comment to chap. 27.

29. See Mish. Meʿil. 1. For example, one may have assumed that because sacrificial animals were slaughtered in the wrong place, their meat was no longer sacred; but it was.

30. See Mish. Ker. 6:3.

31. See Mish. BM 4:8.

32. See further in Jer. 5:1–3; Zech. 5:3–4; Mal. 3:5.

33. Cf. Exod. 22:6–13; 23:4; Lev. 19:11–13; Deut. 21:1–13; and see Mish. BK 9:7–8, Mish. Shevu. 8.

34. Cf. 18:20; 25:14.

35. See Mish. Shevu. 5:1, Mish. Zev. 5:5, Mish. Ker. 2:2.

36. For an example, see *AP*, no. 10, line 6 (p. 30), where we read in a loan contract that the borrower must pay "the interest just like the capital" (in Aramaic, *marbitha' ke-re'sha'*). For the comparable Hebrew term, *marbit,* "accrued interest," see Comment to 25:36. See Mish. BK 9:5–6, which stipulates the later law that the capital (*ro'sh*) must be paid immediately, whereas the fine may be deferred in the case of *'asham.*

Chapter 6

1. "The Torah" was a designation later applied to the entirety of the Five Books of Moses. Cf. Neh. 8:18; 2 Chron. 34:14; and see "Leviticus in the Ongoing Jewish Tradition."

2. Cf. Exod. 15:4; 19:13; 2 Kings 13:17. Some dictionaries list the verb *yarah* 1, "to shoot," and *yarah* 2, "to show, indicate," separately, but this differentiation is questionable.

3. Cf. 2 Kings 12:3: "as the priest Jehoiada instructed him (*horahu*)." Also cf. usage in Exod. 4:15; Isa. 28:26.

4. Cf. usage in Exod. 12:49 (the Passover ritual); Lev. 14:5–7; Num. 15:29; 19:2,14 (purification after contact with a dead body). Also cf. Deut. 17:10–11; 24:8; 2 Kings 12:3; Jer. 18:18; Ezek. 44:23. In Ḥag. 2:11f. we read that a specific ruling (*torah*) is sought of the priests of Jerusalem in the postexilic period. There, the formulation is casuistic, and the responses of the priests are binary: "yes" or "no".

5. See the laws governing public sacrifice in Num. 28–29; and cf. the provisions of Exod. 29:38f. on the daily public sacrifices.

6. The priestly *ḥatta't,* as prescribed in 4:1–21, is not included in the legislation of chaps. 6–7. See Comment to 6:23 for a possible explanation of its absence.

7. See Comment to 2:3 for a discussion of the classes of sacrifices.

8. See sources cited in chap. 3, n. 2.

9. Also cf. Exod. 21:4; Num. 35:19; Deut. 31:6.

10. Also cf. Exod. 38:1; Lev. 4:1 for forms of the verb *y-k-d,* "to blaze, burn."

11. See the provisions of Exod. 28:36–43; 33:2–31; Ezek. 44:17–18.

12. On the use of linen in Egypt, see A. Lucas, *Ancient Egyptian Materials and Industries,* rev. J. R. Harris (London: E. Arnold, 1962), 142f.

13. One would have normally expected *mad baddo.*

14. Cf. Exod. 22:5; Num. 21:28; Judg. 7:15,20.

15. See B. A. Levine, "Notes on Some Technical Terms of the Biblical Cult," *Leshonenu* 30 (1965–1966): 5f. for a comparative discussion of the term *tamid.*

16. This factor in the expiatory system was explained to me in a verbal communication by Y. Muffs.

17. Also cf. 22:10–13 regarding the rights of the families of priests to benefit from sacred donations and also the limitations on such rights.

18. For the view of M. Haran, see his study "The Priestly Image of the Tabernacle," HUCA 36 (1965): 216f.

19. See B. A. Levine, "The Descriptive Tabernacle Texts of the Pentateuch," JAOS 85 (1965): 307ff. for a discussion of the differing traditions.

20. Also cf. 1 Sam. 3:3 where we read that little Samuel lay down to sleep in the sanctuary at Shiloh when "the lamp of God had not yet gone out."

21. See AHW, s.v. *rabāku,* and J. Levy, *Wörterbuch über die Talmudim und Midraschim,* s.v. the rare Late Heb. and Aram. form *revikhah/revikha'.*

22. For the tariffs, see sources cited in chap. 1, n. 10, and B. A. Levine, *In the Presence of the Lord* (Leiden: E. J. Brill, 1974), 118f.

23. See further in the Comment to 7:11f. for other implications of this rule.

24. See CAD, s.v. *marāqu,* "to grind, crush," and Levy, *Wörterbuch,* s.v. *marak* for Late Heb. and Aram. forms meaning "to burnish, cleanse."

25. This subject is discussed in the introductory Comment to chaps. 4–5 and noted in the Comments to 5:6,11; 7:15. Also see Comment to v. 9.

Chapter 7

1. See Comments to 6:10–11.

2. See Comment to 4:11 for an explanation of such practices.

3. This class of sacrifices is explained in the Comment to 2:3.

4. Cf. Pss. 50:14–15; 107:21–22; Jon. 2:10 for examples.

5. This combination is suggested by Num. 9:11: "they shall eat *it* [= the paschal sacrifice] with *matsot* and bitter herbs."

6. This connotation of *'al* also occurs in Num. 28:15,24 in similar laws.

7. Cf. Mish. Men. 5:1 for later classification of these offerings.

8. Cf. usage in Num. 31:28; Ezra 8:5. Also cf. further in v. 34, below, for the other more general connotation of *terumah.*

9. This point is made by M. Haran, EB (Hebrew), s.v. *matanot kehunah,* in his discussion of the priestly emoluments.

10. See the discussion of the special place of the thanksgiving offering in "Leviticus in the Ongoing Jewish Tradition."

11. On the original pronouncement of vows, see Gen. 28:20; 31:3; Num. 21:12; 30; Deut. 23:2; Judg. 11:20. For the act of fulfillment, see Lev. 22:21–23; Num. 15:8.

12. Cf. Ezra 1:4; 3:5; 8:28 for postexilic examples of such voluntary contributions.

13. Cf. examples in Lev. 22:21; 23:38; Num. 15:3; 29:29; Deut. 23:24; and cf. Pss. 54:8.

14. See B. A. Levine, EB (Hebrew), s.v. *piggul.*

15. See Lev. 17:15. Carcasses and torn flesh are strictly forbidden. Cf. the laws of Exod. 22:30; Deut. 14:21; Ezek. 44:31.

16. See Excursus 1 on the penalty known as *karet.* Also cf. Lev. 20:17; Num. 19:13. According to the Sifra and Mish. Kelim 25:9, the mere *intention* not to dispose of the sacrificial flesh within permissible time limits rendered the flesh impure.

17. Also cf. 12:2; 15:2,19; 17:15–16; 18:19 for related prohibitions.

18. For creatures termed "abomination" see 11:10–13; and cf. 20:25. See the notations in *Biblia Hebraica Stuttgartensia,* s.v. Lev. 7:21.

19. On the meaning of *ḥelev,* see Comments to 3:16–17.

20. Cf. Exod. 35:3; Lev. 23:3,14,21,31. This locution also appears in the law establishing cities of asylum in Num. 35:29.

21. On the meaning of *tenufah* see J. Milgrom, "The Alleged Wave Offering in Israel and the Ancient Near East," IEJ 22 (1972): 33–38.

22. See Comment to 8:26.

23. See Comment to 8:27.

24. See B. A. Levine, "Research in the Priestly Source: The Linguistic Factor" (Hebrew), *Eretz-Israel* 16 (1982): 125ff. for a full discussion of this term.

25. According to Leviticus 1:1, instructions for the various sacrifices were issued at the Tent of Meeting. In Exod. 29:38–46 and in Num. 28:6, the daily public sacrifices are said to have been ordained at Mount Sinai. According to Exod. 24:12, Moses was shown the blueprint of the Tabernacle at Mount Sinai. Our verse accords with the Exod. traditions in this regard. Also cf. the statements in Lev. 25:1; 26:46; 27:34, and the Comments to those verses. In Num. 36:13, the laws of Numbers are said to have been communicated in the steppes of Moab. It was a matter of importance, in traditional terms, to identify the site of the various revelations. These discrepancies are discussed in the Introduction to Leviticus, in the section entitled "Literary History: Where Leviticus Was Written."

Chapter 8

1. See the discussion about the composition and content of chaps. 8–9 by B. A. Levine, "The Descriptive Tabernacle Texts of the Pentateuch," JAOS 85 (1965): 307ff.

2. Cf. 1 Kings 8:11; Ezek. 43:2–5; 44:4.

3. See Exod. 13:21–22; 33:9–10; Num. 12:5.

4. See Comment to 9:4; and cf. Exod. 40:34–37; Lev. 16:2; Deut. 31:15.

5. The entire people contributed to the Tabernacle, as is stated in Exod. 25:1f.; 30:11–16; and Num. 7, which lists the donations of each of the twelve tribes.

6. For a different view see G. B. Gray, *Sacrifice in the Old Testament* (Oxford, 1925), reissue by Ktav (New York, 1971), 179–270.

7. A photograph of the excavated temple at Tell Arad, showing its different sections, may be found in Y. Aharoni, "Arad: Its Inscriptions and Temple," BA 31 (1968): 2f., and illustrations. On graduated sanctity and prohibitions of access, see M. Haran, "The Priestly Image of the Tabernacle," HUCA 36 (1965): 191–226, and J. Milgrom, *Studies in Levitical Terminology,* vol. 1 (Berkeley: University of California Press, 1970), for a discussion of the role of the Levites.

8. Cf. Ezek. 42:13–14; 44:17–19; 46:1–3,19–24. Also see B. A. Levine, *Encyclopedia of Religion,* ed. Mircea Eliade (1987): vol. 2, s.v. "Biblical Temple."

9. See Mish. Yoma 3:2.

10. Cf. Exod. 30:17f.

11. Cf. 1 Kings 7:23–26, 38–39.

12. See Exod. 28:42; Lev. 6:3; 16:4.

13. Islamic religion still requires removal of one's shoes upon entering a mosque or shrine. Karaites and Samaritans follow the same practice.

14. The *kuttonet,* "tunic," is also mentioned in 16:4 as one of the vestments of the High Priest, to be worn by him on Yom Kippur.

15. See CAD, s.v. *epattu.* A Ugar. cognate of Heb. *'efod, ipd* (pl. *ipdm*), is now also clearly attested in an administrative record from Ras Ibn Hani, a site near the city of Ugarit. The text lists sales of such garments to various persons. See P. Bordreuil, "Découvertes épigraphiques récentes à Ras Ibn Hani et à Ras Shamra, A, RIH 83/24 + 84/2," CRAIBL (1984), 422f. See also R. E. Whitaker, *A Concordance of the Ugaritic Literature,* s.v. *ipd.* Golden garments are also mentioned in Pss. 45:14; Song 3:10. The *'efod,* as a garment, is mentioned in 1 Sam. 2:18,28; 14:3; 22:18; 2 Sam. 6:14. The references to it in 1 Sam. 21:10; 23:6,9 do not make it clear what is being pictured. On the garments of gods, see A. L. Oppenheim, "The Golden Garments of the Gods," JNES 8 (1949): 172–193.

16. See AHW, s.v. *puru(m)* II; and cf. Esther 3:7; 9:24.

17. Cf. the use of lots in Lev. 16:9–10, in the identification of the scapegoat, and in Num. 25:26; 34:54; Josh. 17:14–17; 18:6.

18. See the article by N. H. Tur-Sinai, EB (Hebrew), s.v. *'urim ve-tummim,* and literature cited there.

19. Heb. *mitsnefet* is parallel to *'attarah,* "crown," in Isa. 62:3; Ezek. 21:31.

20. See Mish. Pes. 7:7.

21. Such a vessel dating from the period of the First Temple was found at Beer-sheba with the word *kodesh* written on it. Similar finds are recorded at Hazor. At Arad, two shallow plates were found with a *kof* written on them, which could represent either *kodesh* or *korban,* "offering." See Y. Aharoni, ed., *Beer-Sheba I* (Tel Aviv: Tel Aviv University, 1973), 73; and cf. chap. 1, n. 8 of the Commentary.

22. Cf. relevant sources in Judg. 8:9; 1 Sam. 9:10; 10:1; 2 Sam. 12:7; 1 Kings 1:34; 19:16; Pss. 45:8; 89:21. See the discusssion by J. Liver, EB (Hebrew), s.v. *meshiḥah.*

23. Cf. usage in 4:7.

24. See Comment to 4:3.

25. Also see Comments to 12:6; 14:1–32.

26. Cf. Judg. 17:5,12; 1 Kings 13:33. Also see Exod. 29:9; Lev. 21:10; Ezek. 43:26.

27. The Akk. expression *mullû ana* (sometimes *ina*) *qatê* means "to hand over, assign" is not a precise parallel to Heb. *mille' yad* as has been maintained. See CAD, s.v. *mullû* 9c. To say in Akk. that someone "filled" something *into* another's "hand" is different from saying that someone was, himself, appointed to an office by having his hands filled. The Heb. idiom undoubtedly refers to a symbolic act, which at one time involved placing an actual object in the hand of another. See M. Haran, EB (Hebrew), s.v. *millu'im.*

28. Cf. Lev. 2:13; Num. 25:12–13.

29. See Comment to 6:16.

30. In the second part of v. 30, the Heb. *'et 'aharon 'et begadav* means "Aaron *with* his vestments."

31. This interpretation was brought to my attention by Y. Muffs, in a verbal communication.

32. Cf. the restrictions imposed on the High Priest in 21:10–15.

33. See Sifra, Mekh. De-Millu'im, par. 36.

34. On the sense of the verb *sh-m-r,* "to guard against violations," cf. usage in Lev. 18:30; 22:9; Num. 18:7; Deut. 11:1; Zech. 3:7; Mal. 3:14.

Chapter 9

1. Cf. Pss. 28:2; 63:5; 134:2.

2. See Mish. Ber. 5:4.

Chapter 10

1. Cf. Lev. 16:1–2; Num. 3:4; 26:61.

2. Lev. R. 'Aḥarei Mot 8 (Margaliot, p. 461).

3. See M. Haran, "The Tabernacle: A Graded Taboo of Holiness," in *Sefer Segal,* ed. J. Liver (Jerusalem: Kiriat Sefer, 1964), 33–41.

4. Cf. Lev. 14:4; and also Exod. 29:43. See the comments of Rashi on this verse.

5. Cf. 21:2,10–13 for laws governing priests in their funerary responsibilities.

6. See Num. 19:11f. for laws of impurity related to contact with dead bodies.

7. This is the sense in Num. 21:28; Ezek. 19:13; Amos 1:4.

8. Cf. this usage in Exod. 24:17; Isa. 30:27.

9. Cf. Num. 6:5; Ezek. 44:20.

10. See Mish. Sot. 1:5, Sot. 7a.

11. This subject is discussed in Excursus 1.

12. This is the sense in Num. 1:53; 17:1; 18:5.

13. This is the sense in Gen. 23:2; Deut. 21:3; 2 Sam. 15:30; 19:2.

14. This is implied in Gen. 50:10; 1 Sam. 31:13. This custom persists until the present time.

15. See Comment to 21:2.

16. See Comments to 7:35–38, which reflect the same tradition.

17. Cf. Isa. 5:11; 24:9. Similarly, *nesekh shekhar* in Num. 28:7 does not mean "a libation of beer," but refers to a libation of wine.

Chapter 11

1. See Shevu. 3a, 7a, Ḥul. 71a for similar designations.

2. Cf. usage in Judg. 14:6.

3. See Rashi to v. 26, below.

4. See Comment to 4:16.

5. See the article by H. Rabinowicz, EncJud, s.v. "Dietary Laws," and literature cited.

6. Cf. Pss. 80:14, where *ḥazir* refers to a wild boar.

7. Cf. Lev. 17:15; Deut. 14:21.

8. See AHW, s.v. *sappartu.*

9. Cf. Deut. 14:19; 1 Sam. 17:5; Ezek. 29:14.

10. See AHW, s.v. *šarāṣu,* a rare verb in Akk.

11. See Av. Zar. 39a.

12. Cf. AHW, s.v. *šakāṣu;* and cf. Ezek. 8:10.

13. Cf. Job 38:36, where *sekhvi* may designate a pure bird.

14. Cf. Pss. 84:4.

15. The bird called *raḥam* is listed in the Balaam text from Deir ʿAlla, in a long list of birds of prey. See B. A. Levine, "The Deir ʿAlla Plaster Inscriptions," JAOS 101 (1981): 196f.

16. Cf. 1:9, in the procedures for preparing the burnt offering.

17. See "Leviticus in the Ongoing Jewish Tradition."

18. See Mish. Shab. 7:8, Mish. Kelim 2:4, 7:2 for usage of *beit kibbul.*

19. See further in v. 38 of this chap.

20. See the articles in EB (Hebrew), s.v. *tanur,* and also EB (Hebrew), s.v. *melaʾkhot ha-bayit* (*bishul,* "cooking").

21. On cisterns in the biblical world, see R. W. Hamilton, IDB, s.v. "Water Storage," especially 813f.; and the study by T. J. Jones, *Quelle, Brunnen und Zisterne im alten Testament* (Leipzig: E. Pfeiffer, 1928).

22. See R. J. Williams, "The Passive Qal Theme in Hebrew," in *Essays on the Ancient Semitic World,* ed. J. W. Wevers and D. B. Redford (Toronto: University of Toronto Press, 1970), 43–50.

23. See above, in Comment to v. 8; and cf. other statements of this law in Lev. 17:13–15; Deut. 14:20.

24. In v. 43, we have two forms of the verb *tameʾ,* "to be impure": (1) *tittammeʾu,* "you make yourselves impure," an assimilated Hitpael form (cf. in v. 24, above), and (2) *ve-nitmetem,* "you become impure," a Nifal form, which would normally be written with an *alef: ve-nitmeʾtem.*

25. Also cf. 19:36–37; 20:26; 21:8.

Chapter 12

1. Cf. Gen. 4:1; Judg. 13:5,7; Isa. 7:14.

2. This is actually the translation given in Num. 5:28. See Z. Ben-Hayyim, *The Literary and Oral Tradition of Hebrew and Aramaic Amongst the Samaritans,* vol. 3, pt. 1, *Recitation of the Law* (Jerusalem: Academy of the Hebrew Language, 1961), 56, to Lev. 12:2.

3. Also cf. Lev. 20:18; Isa. 30:22; and the noun *madveh,* "illness," in Deut. 7:15; 28:60.

4. See Comment to 19:23 on the meaning of *ʿorlah.*

5. Also see further in Gen. 17:23–26; 34:14f. and "Leviticus in the Ongoing Jewish Tradition" for literature on the rite of circumcision.

6. The verb *yashav,* usually "to sit, dwell," has the sense of "to await, remain inactive" in Exod. 16:29; Josh. 20:6; Judg. 5:16; 2 Sam. 11:2.

7. Cf. Lev. 22:11f., Yev. 65a, and Mak. 14b.

8. See Comments to 14:19–20; 15:14–15,29–30; also Num. 6:8–11 on the ritual duties of the Nazirite.

9. Cf. usage in Jer. 2:13; 17:13; Hos. 13:15.

10. Cf. the provisions of 5:7–10; 14:21f.; 27:8.

Chapter 13

1. See R. K. Harrison, IDB, s.v. "Leprosy"; and J. Leibowitz, EB (Hebrew), s.v. *tsaraʿat.*

2. For this term, see 13:51–52; 14:44.

3. Cf. Job 37:21 for the adjectival form *bahir,* "bright," and cf. usage of the verbs *bahar* and *bahak* in Late Heb. in E. Ben-Yehudah, *Thesaurus,* s.v. *bahak,* and s.v. *bahar.*

4. See CAD, s.v. *lapātu* 1.a, "to touch," and s.v. the noun *liptu,* "touch," but also "plague, disease, discolored spot."

5. Heb. *tsaraʿat* may reflect a phonetic variant of the verb *saraʿ,* "to extend, spread." Cf. the adjective *saruʿa* in 21:18; 22:23, and the Hitpael *histareʿa,* "to stretch out," in Isa. 28:20.

6. See Comments to 6:20; 11:25f., and throughout chaps. 14–17, 19, and further in this chap., vv. 55–58.

7. Cf. usage in Isa. 11:11; Zech. 4:12.

8. Cf. Deut. 28:35; 2 Sam. 14:25; Job. 2:7.

9. For the Akk. idiom, see CAD, s.v. *qaqqadu* 1.10, and also p. 101, in the lexical section, col. 2.

10. Cf. in the story of the Egyptian plagues, Exod. 9:9–11; in the admonition of Deut. 28:27,35; and also 2 Kings 20:7 paralleled in Isa. 38:21; Job 2:7.

11. The verb *pasah* is limited, in biblical Heb., to this chapter, but it may represent a variant of the root *p-w-sh,* "to move swiftly, to be scattered," as in Jer. 50:11; Nah. 3:18; Hab. 1:8; Mal. 3:20.

12. See the comments of Leibowitz in the article cited in n. 1 to this chap.

13. See Comment to 27:33.

14. This identification is discussed by Leibowitz (see n. 1 to this chap.).

15. See CAD, s.v. *marāṭu,* in Akk.; and J. Levy, *Wörterbuch über die Talmudim und Midraschim,* s.v. *merat.*

16. NJPS translates "in isolated quarters" in 2 Kings 15:5. On the Ugar. designation *bt ḥpṯt,* a place located in the netherworld, see R. E. Whitaker, *A Concordance of the Ugaritic Literature,* s.v. *ḥpṯt: w rd.bt ḥpṯt.arṣ/ tspr.b yrdm.arṣ,* "Descend to the recesses of the earth/Be numbered among those who descend into the earth."

17. See Comment to v. 55 in this chap.

18. See the provisions of Deut. 22:11, and S. Ahituv, EB (Hebrew), s.v. *shaʿtnez.*

19. See L. Bellinger, IDB, s.v. "Cloth."

20. See Levy, *Wörterbuch,* s.v. *peḥat* and related forms.

21. This is a conflate form, combining the Hofal *hukhbas* and the assimilated Hifil *hikkabbes.*

Chapter 14

1. See L. Bellinger, IDB, s.v. "Cloth." Also see I. Ziderman, "The First Identification of Authentic *Tĕkēlet,*" BASOR 265 (1987): 25f. and n. 1.

2. Cf. Gen. 26:19; Num. 19:17; and metaphorically in Jer. 2:13. Also cf. Lev. 15:3.

3. See Comment to 3:5.

4. See Comments to Lev. 16:10,21–22; and cf. Exod. 22:4.

5. Cf. Lev. 17:5; Num. 19:16; 1 Sam. 14:25; and further on, in v. 53.

6. See B. A. Levine, *In the Presence of the Lord* (Leiden: E. J. Brill, 1974), 110f.

7. See Hoffmann's comments on this verse. Also see J. R. Kraemer, "*Šeqʿarūrōt:* A Proposed Solution for an Unexplained Hapax," JNES 25 (1966): 125–129. For a Mesopotamian magical procedure pertaining to fungus in a house, see R. Caplice, *The Akkadian Namburbi Texts: An Introduction* (Los Angeles: Undena, 1974), 18–19, no. 9, and nn.

8. See CAD, s.v. *ḫalāṣu.*

9. See J. Levy, *Wörterbuch über die Talmudim und Midraschim,* s.v. *kataʿ, ketaʿ,* and related forms.

10. Judg. 6:30–32; 8:9; 2 Kings 23:8.

Chapter 15

1. See Comment to v. 18, below.

2. See the article by J. Leibowitz and J. Licht, EB (Hebrew), s.v. *maḥalot u-negaʿim.* A tractate of the Mishnah, in the order Toharot (Purities), is called Zavim, and there the later laws

derived from our chapter are set forth. In v. 19 the menstruating woman is also called *zavah.*

3. Cf. usage in Ezek. 16:26; 23:20.

4. Heb. *rir* is the modern word for "saliva."

5. Cf. Deut. 32:34; Job 14:17; Esther 3:12; 8:8–10.

6. See the later laws of Mish. Kelim 1:1f. for the various kinds of contact and the resultant impurities.

7. This approximates the interpretation of Ramban.

8. This is explained by Hoffmann, in his comments to vv. 13–15.

9. A tractate of the Mishnah, in the order Toharot (Purities), is called Tevul Yom.

10. UT 77 is a mythological rendering of the marriage of the moon-god Yariḥ with his goddess Nikkal. Also see S. N. Kramer, *The Sacred Marriage Rite. Aspects of Faith, Myth, and Ritual in Ancient Sumer* (Bloomington: Indiana University Press, 1969); and T. Jacobsen, *The Treasures of Darkness* (New Haven: Yale University Press, 1976), 23f., especially 32ff., on relevant Sumerian rites.

11. See Excursus 1.

12. See the basic law of the *nazir* in Num. 6.

13. See the introductory Comment to chap. 7 for a discussion of this pattern.

14. See "Leviticus in the Ongoing Jewish Tradition" for the relevant developments in Jewish religious law.

Chapter 16

1. See Excursus 4 for literature and a discussion of the scapegoat theme.

2. See the provisions of Lev. 4:1–12; Num. 18:1f.

3. See Lev. 4:13–21; Num. 19; and B. A. Levine, *In the Presence of the Lord* (Leiden: E. J. Brill, 1974), 77f.

4. See "Leviticus in the Ongoing Jewish Tradition."

5. Cf. Exod. 19:10f. (before the Sinaitic theophany) and Exod. 24:6f. (at the Sinaitic covenant enactment).

6. This is stated in v. 16 of this chap.

7. So in Yoma 53a. Also see Mish. Moʿed (Albeck, p. 215) for discussion of an ancient controversy between the Pharisees and Sadducees on the interpretation of this verse.

8. See further in v. 23 of this chap.

9. This *lamed* is called *lamed auctoris,* and it was studied by H. Cazelles, "La question de *lamed auctoris,*" RB 56 (1949): 93–101. It regularly occurs in seals and stamps, where we may find an inscription that reads "X, servant of Y," or the like. There are many examples. See N. Avigad, "Three Ornamented Hebrew Seals," IEJ 4 (1954): 236.

10. See Levine, *op. cit.,* pp. 67f., 123f., for a discussion of the verb *kipper.*

11. See further in the Comment to v. 30 of this chap.

12. God is so envisioned in 1 Sam. 4:4; 2 Sam. 6:2, etc.

13. See B. A. Levine, "*Kippurim*" (Hebrew), *Eretz-Israel* 9 (1969): 88ff.

14. See the comments of Hoffmann on vv. 12–13.

15. Cf. Lev. 4:6,17; Num. 19:4.

16. Cf. Exod. 19:10; Lev. 13:6; and Jer. 2:22: "Though you wash with natron/And use much lye,/Your guilt is ingrained before Me/—declares the Lord."

17. The use of water in purification of persons is prescribed in Lev. 14:8–9; 15:13; Ezek. 36:25. The purifying powers of fire are reflected in the laws of Num. 31:22–23.

18. Cf. Exod. 24:10: "like the very sky for purity (*la-tohar*)." Also cf., as regards the purity of metals, Exod. 25:11, and as regards the purity of water, Lev. 11:36.

19. Cf. instances in Lev. 8:12; 21:8; 1 Kings 8:64.

20. Cf. usage in Pss. 32:5; Prov. 28:13.

21. The translation is original here, for emphasis.

22. Cf. usage in Exod. 22:4.

23. See Levine, *In the Presence of the Lord,* pp. 22f.

24. See the discussion of the order of the months in Excursus 8.

25. On the calendar, see E. J. Weisenberg, EncJud, s.v. "Calendar," and s.v. "Tishri."

26. Cf. provisions for resident non-Israelites in Lev. 17:8,10; 19:34; 20:2. As regards celebration of the Passover, see Exod. 12:49; Num. 9:14.

27. See "Leviticus in the Ongoing Jewish Tradition."

28. See Comment to 23:32. Note the comments of Rashi, Men. 65b, words beginning *regel u-teḥillat regel.*

29. See the source cited in n. 10 to this chap.

30. See the introductory Comment to chaps. 8–9 for a discussion of compliance formulas, which occur regularly in those chaps.

Chapter 17

1. This name was first used in 1877, but the most convenient reference is in August Klostermann, *Der Pentateuch,* vol. 1 (Leipzig: A. Deichert, 1893), 368, 418. In Leviticus, the theme of holiness is rare outside the Holiness Code, being virtually restricted to 11:44–45. But within the Holiness Code it occurs frequently; cf. 20:7–8; 21:8,15,23; 22:9,16,32.

2. This is true of 17:1; 18:1; 19:2; 20:2; 22:17, etc. The only exception is 21:1–22:16, a section whose content concerns only the priesthood.

3. For a full discussion of this theme see Comment to 26:3–46, and Excursus 11.

4. This type of formula is discussed by B. A. Levine, "The Descriptive Tabernacle Texts of the Pentateuch," JAOS 85 (1965): 307ff.

5. Cf. Jer. 2:4,26; 3:18,20; and Ezek. 3:1,4–5; 4:4–5.

6. Also cf. 7:23, where the same formula occurs.

7. See Mish. Ḥul. 5:1, etc.

8. See Sifra (Weiss, 83b.6).

9. This was the view of Julius Wellhausen, in *Prolegomena to the History of Ancient Israel* (originally appearing in 1883), 3rd ed. (Cleveland and New York: Meridian Books, 1961), 28–51.

10. Also cf. 1:5,11; 4:4,15; 14:13; etc., where the verb *shaḥat* connotes sacrificial slaughters specifically.

11. See Y. Kaufmann, *Toledot ha-ʾemunah ha-yisraʾelit,* vol. 1, 3rd ed. (Jerusalem: Mosad Bialik, 1966), 126f., for an exposition of this point of view.

12. Cf. usage of the formula *le-hakriv korban* in 1:2; 7:12,14; 9:15; 27:9.

13. As an example, various cultic vessels are referred to as *korban* in Num. 7, even including the wagons donated for transporting the dismantled Tabernacle. In Neh. 10:35; 13:31, the wood used on the altar, which was donated by the people for that purpose, is called *korban ha-ʿetsim,* "the offering of wood."

14. This is the sense of *shafakh dam* in Gen. 9:6; Num. 35:33; Deut. 21:7; Pss. 79:10.

15. This contrast is expressed in Num. 19:14–16; Deut. 22:25,27; 38:3,16.

16. Cf. *ha-mizbeaḥ* in 3:2,8,13; 5:11; 8:11; Josh. 22:20,28–29; 2 Kings 23:9.

17. See Mekh. Boʾ 5b:5 (ed. Freedman).

18. This is the meaning of *zanah* in Gen. 34:31; 38:24; Pss. 33:27.

19. This theme is elaborated in Isa. 1:21; Jer. 2:2–3,20f.; 3:1f.; Ezek. 23:30; etc.

20. Cf. similar usage of *zanah* in Lev. 19:29; 20:5–6; Deut. 31:16; Judg. 8:27f.; Ezek. 20:30; etc.

21. Also cf. 6:11,15; 16:29 for the notion of permanence; and see Excursus 1.

22. See further in vv. 10,13.

23. Cf. Lev. 3:17; 7:26–27; 19:25; Deut. 12:16,23–24 on the prohibition of blood.

24. Also cf. Lev. 20:3–6; Ezek. 14:8, where active forms of the verb *karat* also occur.

25. This danger is explained in the Comment to 1:4, and note the literature cited there.

26. See B. A. Levine, *In the Presence of the Lord* (Leiden: E. J. Brill, 1974), 67f.

27. This is discussed in the introductory Comment to chaps. 1–7; and note the literature cited there.

28. See Levine, *op. cit.,* pp. 67f.

29. See the article by H. Rabinowicz, EncJud, s.v. "Dietary Laws," especially 28f.

30. Our legislation emphasizes the proper worship of God and limits itself to sacrificial matters.

31. See CAD, s.v. *napištu.*

32. Examples of *taraf* are found in Gen. 31:39; 37:33; 44:28.

33. Heb. *terefah* and *nevelah* are listed as a pair in Lev. 7:24; 22:8; Exod. 22:30; Deut. 14:21; Ezek. 4:14; 44:31, etc.

34. On laundering one's clothes, see Comment to 11:25, and the introductory Comment to chaps. 13–14. Also cf. Exod. 19:10; Num. 19:7.

Chapter 18

1. Cf. Lev. 19:2–4; 21:23; 22:2,16; 23:22; also Exod. 6:7; 16:2; and Lev. 11:44–45, the only explicit reference in Lev. outside the Holiness Code.

2. This is the context in Deut. 12:1f.,30–31.

3. See Comment to v. 24, below.

4. Cf. Prov. 8:15 on the meaning of the verb *ḥ-k-k,* "to engrave"; and for usage of *mishpat,* see Exod. 21:1; Deut. 1:17; 1 Kings 3:28.

5. Cf. Gen. 18:19; Judg. 2:22; 1 Kings 16:26, etc. Obedience to the norms of justice can also be referred to as "walking on a path," as in 1 Kings 3:14; 9:4; Prov. 2:20.

6. Cf. Deut. 30:19 on the alternatives of life and death.

7. See Targ. Onk., Rashi, Ibn Ezra, and Ramban on this verse.

8. Tosef. Shab. 15:17 (Lieberman, p. 75) and Yoma 85b.

9. See Tosef. Shab. 9:22 (Lieberman, p. 40).

10. This is its sense in Gen. 20:4; Deut. 22:14; Isa. 8:13.

11. See AHW, s.v. *šīru* (also written *šēru*).

12. On the use of Heb. *basar,* "meat, flesh," to characterize close family relationships, see Judg. 9:2; Isa. 58:7. For Ugar. *ṯar* see R. E. Whitaker, *A Concordance of the Ugaritic Literature,* s.v. *ṯar.*

13. Cf. Hab. 3:13; Pss. 137:7; and see CAD, s.v. *erû.* It is tempting to suggest a cognate relationship with the Akk. verb *erû* (also written *arû*), "to be pregnant," that in the causative stem means "to impregnate," just as in Heb.

14. Cf. 20:18–19.

15. See Comment to v. 10, below.

16. See vv. 14–15, below.

17. Cf. Deut. 27:21.

18. This is its sense in Gen. 12:1; 31:8–13; Ruth 2:11, etc.

19. Hoffmann on this verse.

20. See CAD, s.v. *kallatu.*

21. Cf. Isa. 62:5; Jer. 7:34; Joel 2:16.

22. The form *she'erah,* meaning "her food," occurs in Exod. 21:10.

23. Cf. Lev. 19:29; 20:14; Jer. 13:27.

24. Also cf. Gen. 31:50.

25. There may have been some virtue in making it possible for a surviving, unwed sister to be married in this way.

26. See Comment to 20:2.

27. Cf. Deut. 23:18; 1 Kings 14:24; and Job 38:14.

28. This was suggested by W. F. Albright in *From the Stone Age to Christianity* (Baltimore: The Johns Hopkins Press, 1940 and repr.), 423f.

29. See *The Code of Maimonides: The Book of Holiness (Book V),* trans. L. I. Rabinowitz and P. Grossman (New Haven: Yale University Press, 1965), 135 (21.8).

Chapter 19

1. Sifra, introduction to the Kedoshim (Weiss, 86b).

2. Rashi makes this comparison. Also cf. Sifra Kedoshim 1:9 (Weiss, 86b).

3. Cf. further in v. 31, and in Deut. 31:8,20; Isa. 45:22; Hos. 3:1; Pss. 40:5; Job 5:11.

4. See Comment to 3:1, where the alternative translation is explained.

5. See Excursus 6.

6. See Comments to v. 12, below, and to 10:10. Also cf. Exod. 20:25; Ezek. 22:8; Zech. 3:4.

7. Also cf. Exod. 23:7; Deut. 19:16–18f.

8. On profaning the name, see Mish. Avot 4:4, 5:9.

9. This is also the meaning of *pe'ullah* in Pss. 40:10; 62:11.

10. This seems to be the meaning in 25:50; cf. Exod. 22:14; Deut. 15:18; 24:14.

11. Cf. Gen. 12:3; 1 Sam. 2:30; 2 Sam. 6:22; 19:22, etc.

12. On this interpretation of a stumbling block, cf. Sifra Kedoshim 2:14 (Weiss, 88b–89a), and Rashi.

13. Cf. the synonyms of Heb. *'avel* in Isa. 58:3; Hos. 10:13; Pss. 43:1; Job 5:16; 34:10; and its opposites in Deut. 32:4; Isa. 61:8; Ezek. 18:24.

14. For *nesu' panim* cf. 2 Kings 5:1; Isa. 3:3; 9:14, etc. On use of the term *nasi',* "prince," see E. A. Speiser, "The Origins and Functions of the Biblical *Nāśi',*" CBQ 25 (1963): 111–117.

15. Cf. 1 Kings 10:15; Ezek. 17:4; 27:13; Neh. 3:31.

16. Cf. Jer. 6:28; 22:9.

17. See Sifra Kedoshim 4:6 (Weiss, 89a).

18. A. B. Ehrlich, *Mikra' Ki-feshuto,* vol. 2 (New York: Ktav Publishing House, repr. 1969), 231.

19. See C. Rabin, *The Zadokite Documents* (Oxford: Clarendon Press, 1954), 147f., s.v. ix.16f.

20. Cf. for this usage Nah. 1:2; Jer. 3:5,12; Pss. 103:9, Lam. 1:11. Also see G. E. Mendenhall, *The Tenth Generation* (Baltimore: The Johns Hopkins University Press, 1973), 69–104.

21. Cf. the direct object with *lamed* in 2 Sam. 3:30: *hargu le-'avner,* "they have killed Abner" (Ibn Ezra).

22. For Hillel's dictum see Shab. 31a, and cf. Targ. Jon. to this verse.

23. See UT, glossary, no. 1231, s.v. *kl'* 1; and see CAD, s.v. *kilallan.* Also cf. Deut. 22:9,11.

24. See CAD, s.v. *ḫarapu* A, and E. A. Speiser, "Leviticus and the Critics," *Yeḥezkel Kaufmann Jubilee Volume,* ed. M. Haran (Jerusalem: Magnes Press, 1960), 34f.

25. See Speiser, "Leviticus and the Critics," 34.

26. See Mish. Zev. 5:5, and B. A. Levine, *In the Presence of the Lord* (Leiden: E. J. Brill, 1974), 101.

27. See Mish. Ter. 7:5, and Mish. Or. 2.

28. Cf. Pss. 5:6; 77:3; Eccles. 1:17; 7:25.

29. Cf. CAD, s.v. *alālu* B, "to shout *'alala,*!'" and also s.v. the noun *elēlu,* "jubilation."

30. Cf. 3:17; 7:26–27; 17:11 for other statements prohibiting the consumption of blood.

31. Examples are Exod. 12:8; 23:18; 34:25.

32. This emerges from the statement of one of Joseph's attendants to the effect that his master needed the goblet hidden in Benjamin's sack of grain for divination (Gen. 44:5,15).

33. See B. A. Levine, "The Deir ʿAlla Plaster Inscriptions," JAOS 101 (1981): 195ff., and literature cited.

34. Also cf. Isa. 57:3; Jer. 27:9; Mic. 5:11.

35. On cutting the side-growth, cf. Jer. 9:25; 25:23; 49:32.

36. Cf. Lev. 21:5 and Deut. 14:1; Isa. 15:2; 22:12; Jer. 16:6; Amos 8:10.

37. Cf. Lev. 21:1: Num. 5:2; 9:6–7,10.

38. For the sense of incising, cf. Exod. 21:18; 32:15–16; Deut. 9:10; 10:2.

39. Such is intended in Gen. 8:2,9; 27:46; 41:36.

40. Some read *mekuddashai,* "My sacred times," in place of *mikdashi,* "My sanctuary." This would parallel "My Sabbaths." Cf. Ezra 3:5. Both *mikdashi* and *mekuddashai* would be written with the same alphabetic consonants, vocalized differently. See Comment to 26:2. The Masoretic reading *mikdashi,* "My sanctuary," produced the rendering of Targ. Jon.: "and to My temple you shall go with awe."

41. Cf. Lev. 20:6; Deut. 18:11; 2 Kings 21:6; 23:24; Isa. 8:19. For a Hittite etymology, see C. Rabin, "Hittite Words in Hebrew," *Orientalia* 32 (1963): 115f.

42. Cf. Isa. 8:19; 2 Chron. 10:13.

43. This idea of defiling is clearly expressed in Ezek. 22:3–4; Mic. 2:10.

44. See Sifra Kedoshim 7:12–14.

45. Cf. Deut. 28:50; Isa. 3:5; Lam. 4:16; 5:12.

46. Cf. Exod. 22:20; 23:9; Deut. 10:18; 24:17–19; Ezek. 47:22–23.

47. The laws of Exod. 23:9 and Deut. 5:14–15, etc. express the memory of Israelites as strangers.

48. For the use of "wrongdoing," cf. 25:14–17.

49. A parallel semantic transaction is the use of "seed" to connote descendants (Gen. 19:32,34).

50. On the sense of *middah,* "measure," cf. Ezek. 40:20f.; 41:13. On *mesurah,* see Ezek. 4:11,16; 1 Chron. 23:29.

51. A good summary of weights and measures is provided by O. R. Sellers, IDB, s.v. "Weights and Measures."

52. Also cf. 22:33, which exhibits the same emphasis.

Chapter 20

1. See Excursus 7.

2. The verb *natan,* "to give," connotes the devotion of the Levites in Num. 3:9; 8:16; it can also mean "to devote a sacrifice," as in Mic. 6:7. On usage of the verb *heʿevir,* "to hand over, offer," cf. 2 Kings 23:10; Jer. 32:35.

3. Cf. Exod. 21:15–17,29, and the discussion by J. Milgrom, *Studies in Levitical Terminology,* vol. 1 (Berkeley: University of California Press, 1970), 5f.

4. Cf. Lev. 24:14; Num. 15:35–36; 21:21.

5. Cf. Lev. 24:14,16; and Mish. Sanh. 7:1–4.

6. This admonition is repeated in vv. 5–6. The idiom "to set the face against," said of God, occurs in Lev. 15:7; 26:17; Jer. 21:10; 44:11; Ezek. 14:8. Cf. a similar idiom in Jer. 3:12.

7. See Comment to 17:10.

8. Cf. Jer. 7:30; Ezek. 5:11; 2 Chron. 36:14.

9. See Comments to 5:12 and 14:13.

10. See the introductory Comment to chap. 18 and Comment to 25:47.

11. See Comment to 17:4.

12. Also cf. Gen. 42:22; Num. 35:27; Josh. 2:19; Ezek. 3:18; 18:13.

13. Cf. Deut. 22:13; 23:1.

14. See Excursus 1 on the subject of *karet.*

15. See Comment to 12:2; and cf. Lev. 15:33; Deut. 7:15; 28:60; Isa. 30:22; Lam. 1:22, where the term *madveh,* "infirmity, disease," occurs.

16. For similar, extended usage, cf. Ezek. 22:10, within a passage whose overall similarity to our code has already been noted. Also cf. Ezek. 36:17; Lam. 1:8,17; Ezra 9:11, which refer to the impurity of the Israelite people.

17. Cf. Num. 21:5; Isa. 7:16.

18. See B. A. Levine, "Late Language in the Priestly Code: Literary and Historical Ramifications," in *Proceedings of the Eighth World Congress of Jewish Studies* (Jerusalem: World Union of Jewish Studies, 1983).

19. Cf. Exod. 3:8,17; 13:5; Num. 16:14; Deut. 16:14.

20. See Comment to 2:11.

21. See Comments to 10:10; 11:44–47.

22. See Comments to 7:21; 11:10; and cf. Deut. 7:26.

Chapter 21

1. This is evident in 21:1, 16–17; 22:1–2.

2. See Num. 19 for the provisions relative to the impurity of dead bodies.

3. For a salient example of the royal ancestor cult at Ugarit, see the study by B. A. Levine and J.-M. de Tarrgon, "Dead Kings and Rephaim: The Patrons of the Ugaritic Dynasty," JAOS 104 (1984): 649–659. On the *kispum,* or feast for the dead in Syria-Mesopotamia, see M. Bayliss, "The Cult of Dead Kin in Assyria and Babylonia," *Iraq* 35 (1973): 115–125. Also see CAD, s.v. *kispu(m).* On the cult of the dead in Egypt, see A. Erman, H. Ranke, *La civilisation égyptienne* (Paris: Payot, 1963), 385f., especially 400f. Egyptian concepts were somewhat different from those generally operative in the rest of the ancient Near East, but the duty to serve the departed was very important in Egypt, nonetheless.

4. The link between defects that invalidate priests and those that invalidate sacrificial animals is reflected in the language of the respective laws. The unfit priest may not "draw near" (*karav*), according to 21:17–18; in a parallel fashion, Israelites may not "bring near, offer" (the Hifil form *hikriv*) blemished animals, according to 22:20,24.

5. This similarity was duly noted by Hoffmann.

6. The unusual verbal form *yittammaʾ* (יִטַּמָּא) represents the Hitpael.

7. Cf. Lev. 16:33; Num. 11:29.

8. Cf. usage in Deut. 24:2; Ruth 1:12.

9. Sifra and Yev. 22b.

10. Cf. Gen. 23; 48:7; 49:31f.

11. Maimonides, Yad, Hilkhot ʾAvel 2.7. This source is cited by Hoffmann.

12. See Comment to 19:27.

13. See Comment to 3:11,16; cf. Num. 22:24.

14. Rabbinic law preserves various definitions of *zonah,* "harlot." See Yev. 61b.

15. Ibn Ezra takes the form *teḥel* as a Hifil feminine singular imperfect: "she has profaned, defiled."

16. See Comments to 8:7,10f.

17. Often, it is the verb *karaʿ,* "to tear," that is used in the context of mourning. See Num. 14:6; 2 Kings 5:8; Jer. 36:24; 41:15.

18. Cf. usage in Isa. 10:28; 2 Kings 7:6; and, in the sense "to bring upon," in Deut. 28:2; Josh. 23:15.

19. Cf. usage in Deut. 8:3; Isa. 53:9; Jer. 4:28.

20. Cf., in priestly writings, Exod. 25:8; Lev. 12:4; Num. 3:38.

21. Cf. such usage in Gen. 49:26; Deut. 33:16; Lam. 4:7.

22. Cf. usage in Exod. 12:13,23; 2 Sam. 9:13; 1 Kings 21:26; Isa. 31:5.

23. Cf. Deut. 15:21; 2 Sam. 5:8. The postexilic prophet Malachi (1:8) deplored the practice of allowing defective priests to officiate in the Temple cult.

24. See Isa. 28:20.

25. See CAD, s.v. *arāmu.*

26. See Mish. Bek. 7:2 for rabbinic definitions of *gibben.*

27. See CAD, s.v. *daqqaqu.*

28. See CAD, s.v. *balālu.* In form, Heb. *tevallul* resembles *te'ashur,* "cypress tree." This is a rare form, with *tav* preformative (Ibn Ezra).

29. See CAD, s.v. *garābu.*

30. Also cf. 22:22.

31. See CAD, s.v. *išku;* and cf. Ugar. *ušk* in R. E. Whitaker, *A Concordance of the Ugaritic Literature*, s.v. *ušk.*

32. An alternative vocalization, *mekuddashai* instead of *mikdashai,* is suggested by Isa. 13:3, where *mekuddashai* means "my consecrated persons," and by Ezra 3:5, where the same form of the word describes sacred festivals. See Comments to 19:30 and 26:2.

33. Note the similar statement in 22:17.

Chapter 22

1. Cf. 1 Kings 8:25; Isa. 48:19; Jer. 33:18; and see Excursus 1.

2. See Mish. Zev. 2:1.

3. See Mish. Kelim 1:1f. for laws affecting one who becomes impure through contact with a dead body.

4. Also cf. Mish. Kelim 1:1f.

5. See Comments to 10:13–14.

6. See Comment to 10:1 on the meaning of *zar* as an adjective.

7. Reference is to a non-Levite in Num. 18:7 and to a nonpriest in Exod. 30:33; Num. 17:5.

8. On *toshav* as a foreign resident, see Gen. 23:4; Num. 35:15.

9. As in Gen. 17:12–13,23,27; Isa. 2:14.

10. Cf. usage in Exod. 25:2–3; Ezek. 45:13.

11. Cf. the provisions of Num. 18:19, where the rights of daughters to partake of levied donations (*terumah*) are affirmed.

12. See B. A. Levine, "*Mulūgu/Melûg:* The Origins of a Talmudic Legal Institution," JAOS 88 (1968): 271–285; idem, "In Praise of the Israelite *Mispāḥâ:* Legal Themes in the Book of Ruth," in *The Quest for the Kingdom of God,* ed. H. Huffmon et al. (Winona Lake, Ind.: Eisenbrauns, 1983), 95–106.

13. Hoffmann correctly analyzes the verb *ve-shavah* as a perfect form with *vav* consecutive: "She shall/may return."

14. See Mish. Ter. 6:1–2.

15. See the article by E. Kutsch, TWAT, s.v. *ḥrp* II.

16. See A. Kohut, ed., *Aruch Completum* (Hebrew), s.v. *kalut.*

17. On the verb *katat,* "to pound, crush," see Deut. 9:21; 2 Kings 18:4; Isa. 2:4 paralleled in Mic. 4:3.

18. Cf. the term *netek,* translated "scall," which may mean "impetigo" in 13:30f. Also see Josh. 4:18; Jer. 10:20; 33:20; Eccles. 4:12.

19. Cf. usage in Deut. 23:2.

20. For similar formulas, cf. Exod. 16:28; Lev. 26:3; Neh. 1:9.

Chapter 23

1. Cf. usage of the verb *y-'-d* in 2 Sam. 20:5; Amos 3:3.

2. See Excursus 6 for a discussion of this interaction.

3. This is the sense in v. 4 of *be-mo'adam,* "each at its appointed time." Also cf. usage in Gen. 17:21; 18:14.

4. Cf. usage of *kara'* in Num. 10:12; 2 Sam. 9:13; Zeph. 1:7.

5. We find the active formulation in the two versions of the Decalogue, Exod. 20:10; Deut. 5:14.

6. See R. E. Whitaker, *A Concordance of the Ugaritic Literature,* s.v. *lak.*

7. Cf. usage of the verb *shavat,* "to desist," in Exod. 21:19; 23:12; 34:21; Josh. 5:12; Isa. 14:4.

8. Cf. Exod. 31:17, in one of the Sabbath laws.

9. The ending *on,* which developed from *an,* effectively transforms a noun to an adjective. Cf. *ro'sh,* "head," with *ri'shon,* "first, at the head." For usage of *shabbaton,* cf. 16:31; 23:32; 25:4. Also see Exod. 16:23; 31:15. See Rashi on Men. 65b, words beginning *regel u-teḥillat regel.*

10. See further in v. 39 for *ḥag le-YHVH.*

11. Cf. similar stipulations concerning the Sabbath in Exod. 35:3, and in this chapter in vv. 14,21,31, concerning the festivals.

12. See Ibn Ezra to Exod. 12:6 on the meaning of *bein ha-'arbayim.*

13. It is actually the Piel form *pissaḥ* (not the Kal stem) that means "to skip over" as in 1 Kings 18:26. (See the discussion of the name *pesaḥ* in S. Lieberman, *Hellenism in Jewish Palestine* [New York: Jewish Theological Seminary of America, 1950].)

14. For a discussion of the centralization of the cult see Excursus 8 and see Deut. 12.

15. Cf. usage of *mele'khet 'avodah* in Num. 28 passim.

16. Heb. *'omer* is synonymous with *'alummah,* "sheaf" (Gen. 37:7).

17. See literature cited in the Comment to 7:20; and cf. Mish. Men. 5:1.

18. See Sifra (Weiss, 100b).

19. See H. L. Ginsberg, "The Grain Harvest Laws of Lev. 23:9–22 and Num. 28:26–31," PAAJR Jubilee Volume (1980): 141–154. Also see B. A. Levine, "The Temple Scroll: Aspects of Its Historical Provenance and Literary Character," BASOR 232 (1978): 5–23. The absence of the critical words *mi-moḥorat ha-shabbat* from the Scroll's version of 23:15 is discussed.

20. See Comment to 2:1; and cf. Num. 15:4f., for laws governing grain offerings and libations.

21. The only possible exception is in 2 Kings 11:5,7–9, in the designation *ba'ei ha-shabbat . . . yots'ei ha-shabbat,* "those who enter each *shabbat* . . . those who exit each *shabbat,*" where *shabbat* may mean "week," a unit of time that ends on the Sabbath day. See the study by J. Tigay, "Notes on the Development of the Jewish Week," *Eretz-Israel* 14 (1978): 111–121.

22. Thus Ginsberg, "The Grain Harvest Laws."

23. Cf. Mish. Men. 5:1 for the later law governing *ḥamets* in sacrificial offerings.

24. Examples of composite rituals are Num. 28:11f., for the New Moon; 29:2f., for the day of blasting the shofar; 29:8f., for the Day of Atonement; and 29:13f., for the Sabbath.

25. See Men. 45b.

26. See Comment to 2:3 for an explanation of the classes of sacrifices.

27. This phenomenology is explained in the Comments to 1:4 and 2:1f.

28. Cf. Num. 10:3; Judg. 3:27; 6:34. The shofar was also blasted to warn of danger (Ezek. 33:3; Amos 3:6) as well as to announce victory (2 Kings 11:4). The blast of the shofar could create panic among the ranks of the enemy (Josh. 5:8 [at Jericho]; Judg. 7:16; Jer. 4:19). Major announcements or proclamations were also issued with shofar blasts, as was true of the Jubilee year (Lev. 25:9) and at the anointing of a new king (1 Kings 1:34,39).

29. Cf. Num. 10:10 for the use of the shofar at the offering of sacrifices. Temple musicians used horns of various sorts (Pss. 33:3; 95:1f.; 150:2, etc.).

30. See Excursus 1.

31. See the comments of Rashbam to Gen. 1:5.

32. As an example, cf. 7:15: "And the flesh of the thanksgiving sacrifice of well-being shall be eaten on the day that it is offered (*be-yom korbano*); none of it shall be set aside until morning."

33. Cf. usage of the verb *sakhakh* in Nah. 2:6; Job. 40:22. On the term *sukkah* itself, see Isa. 4:6; Jon. 4:5.

34. See Excursus 8; and cf. Isa. 1:13; Joel 1:14; Amos 5:21 on usage of *'atseret* and *'atsarah.*

35. Cf. 2 Kings 25:30; Neh. 11:23 for the administrative formulas.

36. Cf. Deut. 12:6,11; 16:17; and note usage of *mattanah* in Exod. 28:38; Lev. 7:12f.

37. Neh. 8:15 adds *hadas*, "myrtle," to the greenery.

38. This is expressed in Deut. 8:1f., where the land of Canaan is described.

39. There is no mention of the *'etrog* even in Neh. 8:15. The word *'etrog* itself is of Persian origin. It represents a later interpretation of *hadar* as "citrus fruit." See Mish. Suk. 3:1, Targ. Onk., and Rashi for later interpretations.

40. On the theme of rejoicing see Exod. 12:9,48; and frequently in Deut. (12:7; 14:26; 16:14; 26:11).

Chapter 24

1. Cf. Exod. 30:24f.

2. See Comment to 22:24.

3. See Comment to 6:13, where the term *tamid* is explained.

4. Cf. Exod. 25:22; 27:21; 31:18.

5. Also see Exod. 31:8.

6. See C. L. Meyers, *The Tabernacle Menorah: A Synthetic Study of a Symbol from the Biblical Cult* (Missoula, Mont.: Scholars Press, 1976).

7. See Exod. 25:30; 39:36; Num. 4:7; 1 Kings 7:48; and further in v. 6 of this chap.

8. See O. R. Sellers, IDB, s.v. "Weights and Measures."

9. Cf. 1 Sam. 31:7f.

10. Cf. Exod. 40:23; Neh. 10:34; 1 Chron. 23:29; and, as designating a battle array, 1 Sam. 17:8.

11. See Comment to 2:2; and cf. Exod. 30:24.

12. Cf. usage in Exod. 2:13; 21:22; Deut. 25:11; 2 Sam. 14:5.

13. Cf. usage in Num. 1:17; Isa. 62:2; Ezra 8:20.

14. Also cf. Deut. 28:58. The formula *ḥillul ha-shem*, "the desecration of God's name," occurs in Mish. Avot 4:4. See J. Pedersen, *Israel*, vols. 1–2 (London: Cumberlege, repr. 1946), 245ff.; and the article by R. Abba, IDB, s.v. "Name," especially "name and revelation."

15. On the foundation of the cult of Dan, see 1 Kings 12:25f.; 13:33–34.

16. Cf. Num. 11:28f.

17. For the term *mishmar*, "guardhouse," see Gen. 40:3–4 (the Joseph story); 42:17.

18. Cf. 1 Kings 21:13; and also Num. 15:35; 31:19; Deut. 17:5.

19. Cf. the provisions of Num. 30:4–12 on vows heard when they were pronounced; and relevant to oaths, see Judg. 11:10; 1 Sam. 14:27.

20. See Comment to 5:1.

21. Cf. the provisions of Exod. 12:19,48; Lev. 18:15; 19:34; Num. 15:15; and see in v. 22 of this chap.

22. See the article by J. M. Renger, IDBSup, s.v. "Lex Talionis."

23. See Comment to 8:4.

Chapter 25

1. Cf. similar wording in Exod. 12:25; Lev. 14:34; 19:23; 23:10. The relevant laws in each case are to be observed in the land of Canaan.

2. See Comment to 23:3.

3. See G. H. Dalman, *Arbeit und Sitte im Palästina*, vol. 4 (Hildesheim: Alms, repr. 1964), 290f.

4. Cf. Comments to vv. 21–22.

5. See further, in Comments to vv. 10 and 47; and see the Sifra on this verse. Heb. *toshav* also occurs frequently with *ger*, "alien," as in Exod. 12:45; Lev. 22:10. Also cf. Num. 35:15. See the study by B. L. Eichler, *Indenture at Nuzi: The Personal Tidennūtu Contract and its Mesopotamian Analogues* (New Haven: Yale University Press, 1973), for ancient Near Eastern forms of indenture.

6. Cf. usage of *yom*, "day," in genealogical lists (as in Gen. 5:5) as indicating a year of life. Also cf. Gen. 25:7; 47:8; Exod. 13:10.

7. In effect, the Heb. *le-ha'avir shofar teru'ah* means *le-ha'avir teru'at shofar*, "to cause the sound of the shofar blast to be heard." Cf. Jer. 4:19; Zeph. 1:16. Also cf. Josh. 6:5 (the long blasts of the shofar at the walls of Jericho).

8. Cf. the formulation in 16:29; 23:26. The change of calendars reflected in this verse is discussed in Excursus 8, in connection with the scheduling of the annual festivals.

9. Cf. Jer. 19:22 for the same form of the verb occurring here, and also Gen. 2:3; and in the two versions of the Decalogue, Exod. 20:8; Deut. 5:12.

10. See F. R. Kraus, *Ein Edikt des Königs Ammi-ṣaduqa von Babylon* (Leiden: E. J. Brill, 1958); J. J. Finkelstein, "Ammiṣaduqa's Edict and the Babylonian 'Law Codes,'" JCS 15 (1961): 91–104; J. Lewy, "The Biblical Institution of DᵉRÔR in the Light of Akkadian Documents," *Eretz-Israel* 5 (1958): 21–31.

11. See CAD, s.v. *darāru*, and s.v. *andurāru*; and cf. Song 5:5,13: *mor derôr*, literally "free-flowing myrrh." Also note the bird called *derôr* (Pss. 84:4; Prov. 26:2), so called for its freedom in flight.

12. Cf. Exod. 19:13; Josh. 6:4f. This word for "ram" also occurs in the Punic tariffs. See sources cited in chap. 1, n. 10.

13. See further in Comment to v. 49 of this chap.

14. Cf. Exod. 21:2f.; Deut. 15:12f.; 2 Kings 4:1.

15. In the second part of this verse an infinitive absolute, *kanoh*, functions as a finite verb.

16. The term *'amit* occurs in Lev. 5:21; 18:20; 19:15; etc.; and in Zech. 13:7.

17. The contrast "increase-decrease" and similar formulations are known from Exod. 16:17–18, where we read that no one gathered more manna than the next; from Exod. 30:15, with reference to the head tax; and from Num. 11:32f., regarding the gathering of the quail in the wilderness.

18. For use of *betaḥ* in covenantal promises, cf. Deut. 33:8; and also Gen. 34:25; Ezek. 28:26; 34:27.

19. See H. L. Ginsberg, "Ugaritico-Phoenicia," JANESCU 5 (1973): 138, on the combination *všb' vmn'm*, "and new grain and fine food," in the Karatepe inscription.

20. Heb. *hen*, in the sense of "if," has cognates in Ugar. (*hm*), in Aram. (*hn*, *'n*), and in Arab. (*'innah*). It occurs with this meaning quite often in biblical Heb. Cf. Exod. 4:1: *ve-hen lo' ya-'aminu li*, loosely "and what if they do not believe me?" Also cf. Jer. 2:10; 3:21; Hag. 2:12; Job 13:15.

21. Cf. Isa. 5:6; 10:6; Nah. 1:14. See B. A. Levine, TWAT, s.v. *mitsvah*, especially 1090, section IV.

22. The unusual form *ve-'asat* (instead of the usual *ve-'asetah*) is a rare third person feminine perfect. This is its only occurrence in biblical Heb., but it is known in Late Heb.

23. Cf. similar terminology in Mish. Dem. 4:7.

24. Targ. Onk. renders *li-tsemitut* by Aram. *ḥoltana'*, "absolutely, irreversibly." See CAD, s.v. *ṣamātu*.

25. See Y. Muffs, *Studies in the Aramaic Legal Papyri from Elephantine* (Leiden: E. J. Brill, 1969), 20f.

26. Cf. Eccles. 10:8; Pss. 106:43.

27. In the context of being alternately able or unable to afford certain sacrifices, cf. usage in Lev. 5:11; 12:8; 14:22; Ezek. 46:7. Also cf. Lev. 25:28; Judg. 9:33; 1 Sam. 10:7; Isa. 10:10; Pss. 21:9; Eccles. 9:10.

28. See Lev. 25:50,52; Num. 27:18,23; Eccles. 7:27,29, for relevant forms of the verb *ḥishev*, "to figure, compute."

29. On *'odef*, cf. Exod. 16:23 ("leftover"); 26:12–13; Num. 3:46–49. On *heshiv*, "to refund," cf. vv. 51–52 in this chap. The administration of temples required special accounting procedures, and it is to be expected that priestly law should preserve technical accounting terms.

30. For Heb. usage, cf. v. 33 in this chap. and also Exod. 21:2–3,11, on the release of indentured servants; Deut. 24:2. Akk. usage of cognate *aṣû,* "to go out," in legal contexts is the same. See CAD, s.v. *aṣû.*

31. Cf. usage in Num. 30:5 pertaining to vows that are "binding, in force"; see also Deut. 19:15; 25:6; 1 Sam. 24:21; Ruth 4:5.

32. For *tirot,* "circular encampments," cf. Ezek. 25:4; Pss. 69:26; 1 Chron. 1:29. Also cf. usage of *ḥatserim* in Josh. 15, 21; Neh. 11–12. Also see A. Malamat, "*Ḥaṣērîm* in the Bible and Mari," *Yediot* 27 (1963): 181–184.

33. Cf. usage in 2 Sam. 4:2, as it pertains to territory that "belongs" to a town or region.

34. It is also possible that the version of the Vulg. is correct. That version suggests reading *va-'asher lo' yiga' el,* "whatever is *not* redeemed." The sense would be that whatever is *not* redeemed of the property of the Levites would revert to them at the Jubilee, as is true of *'aḥuzzah* land belonging to Israelites generally.

35. Cf. the pastoral context of *migrash* in Num. 35:3; Josh. 14:4; 1 Chron. 14:4.

36. Cf. usage in Gen. 17:8; 48:4, in passages regarded as part of the priestly literature.

37. See Hoffmann on this verse.

38. See AHW, s.v. *ribbetu(m)* for Akk. *ribbātu(m);* F. R. Kraus, *Ein Edikt des Königs Ammi-ṣaduqa von Babylon* (Leiden: E. J. Brill, 1958), 95f.; J. J. Finkelstein, "Ammiṣaduqa's Edict and the Babylonian 'Law Codes,'" p. 95. For Aramaic *marbitha'* see chapter 5, note 36.

39. See Isa. 14:2 for a similar thought; and cf. Num. 32:18; 34:13; 35:54; Ezek. 47:13 for references to allotting the promised land.

40. See source cited in Excursus 10, n. 13.

41. See the discussion by H. R. Cohen, *Biblical Hapax Legomena in the Light of Akkadian and Ugaritic* (Missoula, Mont.: Scholars Press, 1978), 19–20, on the word *'eker,* which occurs in the Aram. treaties from Sefire. See J. Gibson, *Textbooks of Syrian Semitic Inscriptions,* vol. 2 (Oxford: Clarendon Press, 1971), 28, to no. 7, line 3.

42. See Excursus 5 on the structure of the Israelite clans.

43. Cf. the prohibitions of the Decalogue, in Exod. 20:4 = Deut. 5:8; and cf. Deut. 4:16.

44. See the study by M. Ottosson, *Temple and Cult Places in Palestine* (Uppsala: University of Stockholm, 1980). Extensive bibliography may be found in J. Gamberini, TWAT, s.v. *matsevah.* Also cf. Gen. 25:18; 31:45; 35:13; Deut. 15:22; Hos. 3:4.

45. See Comment to 19:30.

Chapter 26

1. The composition of the Epilogue is discussed in Excursus 11.

2. The theme of walking in the way of God's laws and commandments is expressed in Lev. 18:4; 20:23; 25:18. Also cf. 1 Kings 3:3; 2 Kings 17:18–19; Ezek. 20:19.

3. On rains in their season, see Deut. 11:14; Ezek. 34:26–27; Zech. 8:12; Pss. 67:7; 85:18.

4. The term *yevul,* "crop, yield," also occurs in Deut. 32:22 and in Judg. 6:4.

5. The implement used for threshing was a board with iron teeth known as *ḥaruts* or *morag ḥaruts,* "threshing board," in Isa. 28:27–28; 41:5; and cf. 2 Sam. 24:22; Amos 1:3.

6. The idiom *nafal ba-ḥerev,* "to fall by the sword," is frequent in biblical literature. Cf. 1 Sam. 31:8, 2 Sam. 3:29; Jer. 20:4,39:18, etc.

7. Also cf. Josh. 23:10: "A single man of you would put a thousand to flight."

8. We read of God's turning away from Israel in Deut. 31:17–18; Isa. 8:17; Jer. 18:17; Ezek. 39:23–24, 29.

9. Cf. this usage of *mishkan* in Ezek. 37:27.

10. See the discussion by B. A. Levine, "On the Presence of God in Biblical Religion," in *Religions in Antiquity,* ed. J. Neusner (Leiden: E. J. Brill, 1968), 61–87.

11. See NJPS translation of Hos. 1:9 and nn. there. Also cf. Hos. 2:25; and note similar statements in Jer. 24:7; 31:1; 32:38; Ezek. 11:20; Zech. 8:8.

12. For the breaking of the bars of Israel's yoke, also cf. Ezek. 34:27; Nah. 1:13.

13. See G. Dalman, *Arbeit und Sitte im Palästina,* vol. 2 (Hildesheim: Alms, repr. 1964), 99–105, and pls. 18–21b, 29–42, where various yokes are illustrated.

14. The usual idiom is *pakad 'al,* "to visit punishment upon," as in Exod. 32:34; Isa. 13:11.

15. On *bahal* as a verb of motion, see Ezek. 7:7; Pss. 83:16.

16. For the Late Heb. verb *shahaf,* see A. Kohut, ed., *Aruch Completum* (Hebrew), s.v. *sh-ḥ-f* (verb).

17. Cf. the full form *mad'ivot* in Jer. 31:12,55.

18. On use of Heb. *nefesh* in characterizing emotional states, cf. *mar nefesh,* "embittered," in 1 Sam. 22:2; 30:6; and *katsar nefesh,* "to be short of breath, impatient, anxious," in Num. 21:4; and cf. Exod. 6:9.

19. Cf. the combination of *hevel* and *rik* in Isa. 30:7; 49:4.

20. The preposition *bet* in the pronoun *bakhem* expresses opposition: "against you."

21. On the verb *nagaf,* cf. Num. 14:42; Judg. 20:32,39.

22. See usage of *radah* in 1 Kings 5:4; Neh. 9:28.

23. See v. 23; and cf. Jer. 31:18; Pss. 94:10 for usage of the verb *y-s-r.*

24. On "sevenfold," see Gen. 4:24; Pss. 79:12; Prov. 6:31.

25. In Isa. 4:2, the produce of the land is referred to as its "pride."

26. Cf. Deut. 11:27; 28:33; and see M. Weinfeld, "Traces of Assyrian Treaty Formulas in Deuteronomy," Bib. 46 (1965): 417–427. See D. J. Wiseman, "The Vassal Treaties of Esarhaddon," *Iraq* 20 (1958).

27. On *meri,* "rebelliousness," see Ezek. 2:5; 9:25; 12:2; 27:12–13.

28. On the Hifil form of *sh-l-ḥ,* see Exod. 8:17; 2 Kings 15:37; Ezek. 14:13; Amos 8:11.

29. Cf. usage of the verb *shakhal* in Ezek. 5:17; 14:15; Hos. 9:15. See O. Loretz et al., *Die Keilalphabetischen Texte aus Ugarit* (Kevelaer: Butzon und Bercker, 1976), 1.23:8. Speaking of the moribund deity Mot-wa-Shar, the text reads *bdh ḫṯ tkl/ bdh ḫṯ ulmn,* "In his one hand is the rod of bereavement In his other hand is the rod of widowhood."

30. In Judg. 20:11, we read of the populace gathering in towns; cf. 2 Sam. 17:13; Jer. 4:5; 8:14.

31. On "the staff of bread," see Ezek. 5:16; 14:13; Pss. 105:16.

32. See B. A. Levine, EncJud, s.v. "Cult Places, Israelite," for the meaning of *bamah.* For Ugar. usage, see O. Loretz, *Die Keilalphabetischen Texte* 1.4. IV. 14–15, and 1.19.II,10

33. On the term *ḥammanim,* see H. Ingholt, "Le sens du mot *ḥammān,*" *Biblical Archaeology and History* 30 (1939): 795–802; and the articles by K-M Beyse, TWAT, s.v. *ḥmm* III; and the article by H. Beinart in EB (Hebrew), s.v. *ḥamman, ḥammanim,* with photo. Also see H. W. Haussig et al., eds., *Götter und Mythen in Vorderen Orient,* s.v. *Baal-Ḥammôn.*

34. This interpretation was communicated to me by Moshe Greenberg.

35. After the Flood, the Lord savored the sweet aroma of Noah's sacrifice, as we read in Gen. 8:21. Also cf. Amos 8:21.

36. On "scattering," see Jer. 15:7; Ezek. 6:8; 12:15; 22:15; 29:12; 30:33–36; Zech. 3:2–4,24; Pss. 44:12; 106:27.

37. On unsheathing swords, see Ezek. 5:2,12; 12:4; 28:7; 30:11. A similar idiom *herik ḥanit,* "to draw the javelin," occurs in Pss. 35:3.

38. On *ḥorvah,* cf. Isa. 64:10; Jer. 7:34; Ezek. 5:14; 38:8.

39. On confession, see Neh. 1:6; 9:6.

40. The idiom *yaʿan u-ve-yaʿan* also occurs in Ezek. 13:10; 36:3.

41. Cf. references to former generations in Jer. 11:10; Pss. 79:8.

42. Cf. the final verse of the Book of Num. (36:13), where we find a similar postscript.

Chapter 27

1. See Comment to 22:21.

2. Cf. this usage in Pss. 65:2; and see Lev. 22:13; Num. 29:39; Deut. 12:26; 1 Sam. 1:21.

3. Cf. Num. 3:5; 8:14–15.

4. In addition to the narrative of Hannah, Samuel's mother, in 1 Sam. 1:11f., cf. the laws of Num. 30, regarding the vows of a young, unmarried woman living in her father's home.

5. See Comments to 5:11; 14:30; and cf. Ezek. 46:7.

6. For the view of Maimonides, see Yad, Hilkhot ʿArakhin Va-Ḥaramin 5.7, cited by Hoffmann.

7. Cf. usage in Ezek. 48:14; Job 15:31; Ruth 4:7. The term *temurah* carried over into Late Heb. Mish. Tem. deals with the subject of this chapter.

8. Cf. usage in Num. 3:13; Deut. 15:19.

9. Cf. usage of the verb *kum,* "to be in force, binding," in Gen. 23:10 (that the field of Ephron will legally belong to Abraham) and in Num. 30 (on the binding force of vows).

10. This practice is explained by B. A. Levine, "Research in the Priestly Source: The Linguistic Factor" (Hebrew), *Eretz-Israel* 16 (1982): 125ff.

11. See Hos. 3:2; and cf. the catalog of weights and measures in Ezek. 45:11f. Also see source cited in chap. 24, n. 8.

12. See CAD, s.v. *kurru* A (from Sum. *gur*).

13. Cf. Exod. 5:8,19; 21:10; Num. 36:3–4.

14. Cf. usage in Exod. 12:4; and see CAD, s.v. *miksu,* "share of the yield of the field."

15. This is specified in Exod. 30:13; Num. 3:47; Ezek. 45:12.

16. Cf. the laws of Exod. 13:2f.; 22:28–29; 34:19–20; Num. 33:4; Deut. 15:19f.

17. According to the provisions of Deut. 16:21–23, a firstling of a type normally suitable for sacrifice, but which is blemished, could be used for food if the flesh were eaten in a nonsacral manner outside the Temple.

18. Cf. usage in Deut. 3:6; 7:2; 13:16–18; 1 Sam. 15:17f. See the discussion in B. A. Levine, *In the Presence of the Lord* (Leiden: E. J. Brill, 1974), 128f.

19. See Ramban to v. 29. There are indications that failure to obey edicts issued by those in authority may have resulted in the proscription or confiscation of one's property. In Ezra 10:5–8 we read that the entire Judean community was summoned to Jerusalem pursuant to Ezra's order to the chief priests. He had bound them by oath to require all Israelites who had married foreign wives to divorce them, and if any person failed to appear at the appointed time for the imposition of this edict, all his property would be proscribed *(yoḥoram).*

20. See *Biblical Essays,* a collection of studies by A. Malamat (Jerusalem: Hebrew University, 1977), 52–61.

21. See the Mish. Maʿas. Sh. for later laws relevant to this kind of tithe.

22. Cf. usages of Aram. *bakker,* "to search out, investigate," in Ezra 4:15–19; 5:17; 6:1; 7:14.

LEVITICUS IN THE ONGOING JEWISH TRADITION

> Because we have sinned, we and our forefathers, our city lies in ruin, and our Temple is desolate; our Glory has departed, and the Divine Presence has been withdrawn from our "House of Life."
>
> We are, therefore, unable to fulfill our obligations in Your chosen "House," in the great sacred Temple which bears Your name, because of the hand that has been cast against Your sanctuary.[1]

Modern students of ancient religions often find it difficult to identify with the pathos and the sense of deprivation conveyed by such statements as this one, taken from the Jewish liturgy. There is a tendency to regard such pronouncements as little more than disclaimers intended to absolve worshipers of those obligations imposed by the Torah but no longer possible to fulfill. Such a reading of Jewish liturgy would, however, misrepresent the mentality of the Jews of antiquity as well as of their successors, virtually to the modern period. To take such pronouncements less than seriously would be to miss the essence of religious experience itself.

As regards the substance of Leviticus—its laws and rituals—the termination of sacrificial worship subsequent to the destruction of the Second Temple of Jerusalem in 70 C.E. by the invading Romans ultimately rendered obsolete the basic system of sacrifice and purification upon which the priestly regimen of biblical religion rested. One cannot appreciate what became of this Levitical system without first exploring the transformation from sacrificial worship, which reflects the function of sacred space, to the alternative modes of worship and different religious institutions that became vital in later Judaism.

We shall attempt to clarify how historical events, over which Jewish leadership had little control, interacted with internal policy decisions, over which that leadership exercised considerable control, to produce a new Judaism. The priesthood, so central to the Levitical system, ultimately retained only a vestigial role in historic Judaism. This brief treatment cannot presume to provide a comprehensive outline of later Jewish religious observance. The purpose is rather to analyze the methods that were applied to the restructuring of Judaism in late antiquity. In this way, the reader of the Commentary may catch a glimpse of continuity and change and focus attention on the lasting relevance of Leviticus. The reader will be referred to special studies on particular subjects and should consult appropriate religious authorities on questions of practice.

From Sacrifice to Alternative Forms of Worship

Some students of ancient Judaism maintain that what history decreed in the first century C.E. had, in fact, already been decided by the Jewish leadership. Prayers and blessings

had all but replaced sacrifice, so the argument goes, even before the Romans made its continuation impossible. Although there is a degree of validity to this argument, it applies only to certain aspects of historical development in antiquity. Even in the pagan societies of late antiquity, there was opposition to sacrifice among those who had ceased believing in the mythological pantheons and who questioned the efficacy of elaborate cultic celebrations. Within ancient Jewry, alternative modes of worship—all in a monotheistic framework—had been developing for centuries prior to the Roman destruction of Jerusalem, as successive restrictions were placed on the consecration of space. The Jewish leadership, as a result, was not entirely unprepared for the eventual loss of the central Temple in Jerusalem. But no amount of preparation could thoroughly cushion the shock of the Temple's destruction or lessen the challenge of accommodating to a new reality. Indeed, it would be a gross misjudgment of the religious attitudes of the first century, both in the Land of Israel and in the lands of the Diaspora, to suppose that most Jews no longer believed that sacrifice was essential to the fulfillment of Jewish religion. On the contrary, their feelings more accurately correlate with the words of the lamentation cited at the beginning of this essay. Sacrificial worship was for them exceedingly meaningful, an intense experience, not merely a formal activity. We should not be misled by the tone of the persistent criticisms of cultic religion that are found in biblical literature; all forms of worship can be genuinely meaningful for most people.

In God-centered religions, the operative theory holds that a "present" God may be expected to be more responsive to human needs, more approachable than a deity perceived to be distant, in the far heavens. This very powerful perception dictates the main objective of worship: to create an environment conducive to establishing a relationship that allows humans, individually and collectively, to bring their needs to the attention of God, the source of power and blessings.[2] This objective has not changed appreciably since earliest times, although the dynamics of worship in Judaism have changed radically.

All that remained once the Temple was destroyed were words—prayers, blessings, and readings from Scripture and the other canonical sources. The difference between sacrifice and prayer may be compared with the difference between actual service to God and saying that one is serving Him; between offering an actual gift to God, whom one loves, and saying that one loves God. A sacrifice represents an actual gift, offered to God in a sacred environment in which He is thought to reside and in which consecrated priests minister to Him in purity. Whenever humans and God shared a sacred meal a bond was acknowledged to exist between them: a veritable covenant. A "personal" basis was established and reinforced, one that allowed humans to petition God, to seek His help. Ever pressed by real needs, human communities find considerable security in the belief that God is near and attentive (Ps. 145:18).

Could Jewish religion continue to be effective, to answer the needs of its worshipers without the experience attendant upon the sacrificial worship of God? Could words compensate for gifts, and were there deeds or acts of a different sort that could produce something akin to the experience of sacrificial worship?

It might be of interest to explore what other religious communities have done to meet the needs of their adherents. Christianity adopted the policy of sanctifying space, as Judaism had once done. Christian worship in the form of the traditional mass affords the devout an experience of sacrifice, of communion, and proclaims that God is present.[3] The Christian church, then, is a temple. Islam, however, followed the example of Judaism in opting for nonsacral worship, thereby making of the mosque an institution more similar to the Jewish synagogue. But Islam operates with sacred space as well, most notably in Mecca, the

focus of pilgrimage for all Muslims.[4] Judaism, deprived of its unique, sacred space, the Temple of Jerusalem, has operated without sacrificial worship and without sacred space since late antiquity. This situation has necessarily undercut the intensity of religious experience. Jewish pilgrims, when they arrived in Jerusalem, saw only the scene of ancient ruins and retaining walls. They were afforded only sad memory and could experience only fierce hope.

Nevertheless, human needs do not change appreciably, even over long periods of time, as regards religious experience: The need for perceptible demonstrations of God's nearness and Presence has not diminished among the devout, even to this day. In theory, despite the destruction of the Temple, Jewish religion never renounced sacrificial worship permanently—at least not until modern times, when certain Jewish religious movements altered the traditional liturgy to avoid references to the restoration of sacrifice. Through the centuries since late antiquity, Jewish liturgy has expressed the hope for the reinstitution of sacrificial worship as part of the larger hope for the restoration of the Jewish people to the Land of Israel. At the present time, when the Land of Israel has been rebuilt, renewed proximity to the locus of ancient worship has, indeed, awakened a deep sense of the sanctity of space and released feelings that were previously unexpressed. It is too soon to project the course of future developments in Judaism relevant to sacred space, but we should expect that the factor of space will play a greater role than it had during the long centuries of dispersion.

The Centralized Cult

The course of Jewish religion—and the legacy of Leviticus—in later periods was of course influenced by decisions made in the preexilic period of biblical history. We are thinking in particular of severe limitation of sacred space to a unique site. When that place—the Temple in Jerusalem—was no longer functional, sacrifice likewise became impossible. There had, after all, been other possibilities. In earlier periods Israelite religion had functioned with ubiquitous sacrificial worship in the Land of Israel; temples and cult sites had been manifold. But prior to the Babylonian exile of 586 B.C.E., young King Josiah of Judah, instructed by devout priests, sought to repurify the cult, which had been compromised by a predecessor, Manasseh. Josiah centralized the cult in Jerusalem, requiring that henceforth all sacrificial worship of the God of Israel take place exclusively in the Temple. We now know that Josiah's edicts represented an advanced phase of a long, but delayed, movement toward cult centralization that had first emerged in the northern kingdom of Israel before its downfall in the late eighth century B.C.E..

We are not entirely clear as to the underlying motivations of this movement. Undoubtedly, centralization was held out as a means of greater control, the better to purify the Israelite cult of pagan elements and other improper forms of worship. Experience had shown how vulnerable the cult was to pagan influence. The eighth-century prophets condemned the religious situation in the northern Israelite kingdom, with its temples and altars. They saw in them mere tools of royal policy, instruments of state religion, and envisioned in their stead a new temple at a site to be designated by God, where loyalty to God would be more important than loyalty to kings.[5]

Though hardly obeyed promptly or consistently throughout the land, Josiah's "reforms," as they have come to be known, became definitive in the long term, the real test

coming in the exilic period. With the destruction of the First Temple of Jerusalem in 586 B.C.E. by the invading Babylonians, large numbers of the populace were exiled, and a Jewish Diaspora emerged in Babylonia and other parts of the Near East. For a time, both those Judeans who remained in the land and the Jews in the Diaspora were left without a central temple in Jerusalem. When the restoration became a real possibility, pursuant to the edict of Cyrus the Great, issued in 538 B.C.E., the only acceptable program was the rebuilding of the Temple on its former site in Jerusalem, although the hiatus of the exilic period had given Jewish leadership pause to consider a new and crucial set of alternatives: Should the God of Israel be worshiped through sacrifice in the Diaspora? Should altars and temples be built for this purpose in Babylonia, for example? There were certainly plenty of priests available in Babylonia to officiate at sacrificial worship. In a sense, this option had been foreclosed earlier by Josiah's edict. If sacred space within the Land of Israel, itself, had been officially restricted to a single site, how much more unacceptable would sacrificial worship be in the impure lands of the gentiles, who worshiped idols.

Nevertheless, we find allusions in the exilic biblical literature to an ongoing debate on the question of sacrificial worship in Babylonia. The Book of Ezekiel may well refer to this subject, although admittedly in cryptic fashion. In chapter 20 we read that elders of Israel approached the prophet Ezekiel with a certain inquiry and that he emphatically refused to sanction their proposal. The language is elusive, and we can infer the gist of the inquiry only from the prophet's response. He tells the elders that only when God restores His people to His holy mountain, in the Land of Israel, will it be possible for Jews to worship Him once again.[6] Until then, God will demonstrate His Presence among His people by being "something of a sanctuary" (*mikdash me'at*) in the lands of the exile (Ezek. 11:16–20). Ezekiel, who envisioned a rebuilt Temple in Jerusalem, would certainly have endorsed the edicts of Josiah. In the Commentary we maintain that the laws of Leviticus 17 regarding proper worship also reflect the principle of centralized sacrificial worship.

There were some exceptions to this principle. The only "Jewish" temple to be built elsewhere in the Land of Israel subsequent to the restoration was the Samaritan temple (now excavated) atop Mount Gerizim. The Samaritans, denied permission to participate in the establishment of the Jerusalem Temple, built one of their own. For the rest, it was to the Temple in Jerusalem that Jewish worshipers repaired to offer sacrifice. There were, in addition, a few Jewish temples in the Diaspora, especially in the Egyptian Diaspora, which began earlier than the Babylonian. The Jewish temple at Elephantine, in Upper Egypt, operated throughout most of the fifth century B.C.E. But such institutions did not speak for the main body of Jewry and seldom endured.[7]

With the rebuilt central Temple in Jerusalem sacrificial worship resumed under the aegis of a consecrated priesthood. During the period of the Second Temple, which lasted approximately six hundred years, the Levitical system was thus very much in evidence. But during that period the demography of the Jewish people had changed, the large majority living outside the Land of Israel. Thus, with sacrifice restricted to the only proper location and the population of Jews so dispersed, the bond between people and Temple became more attenuated, and those out of touch with the Temple required alternative modes of worship. There emerged the institution that came to be known as the synagogue (*beit ha-kenesset*, "house of assembly"). But even so the mentality of Jews during the period of the Second Temple should not be misunderstood. For the most part, they did not regard sacrificial worship as passé. Within its limited sphere, it was vital to the Jewish people. Even though they could not participate directly, Jews everywhere were concerned that the full

regimen of sacrifices continue without interruption or interference in the Temple of Jerusalem. It was precisely during this period, through sequential imperial dominations and brief opportunities at autonomous rule, that the Temple of Jerusalem and its priesthood enjoyed considerable power and prominence. The priesthood of Jerusalem represented Judea to imperial authorities at various times and also exercised governance within the Land of Israel. In religious matters, it often spoke for world Jewry.

This was a period when the *torot* of Leviticus were fully operative in Jerusalem. From the Books of Chronicles, a composition of the Persian period (538–ca.330 B.C.E.), we learn of the elaborate organization of the priesthood into assigned tours of duty (*mishmarot*). Second Temple literature and the writings of Josephus, for example, inform us of the role of the priesthood in Greco-Roman times. The Mishnah preserves evidence of Temple operations during its last phases. The overall impression is one of great activity in Jerusalem: of pilgrimages and delegations (*maʿamadot*) coming from all over the Diaspora, of financial support for the Temple establishment, and of written correspondence on matters of religious significance.[8]

It is interesting to note that during the Antiochan persecutions of the second century B.C.E., which provide the historical background of the Hanukkah episode, there was a very brief period during which the public cult of the Temple of Jerusalem was suspended. We are fortunate in having considerable documentation of that episode, which allows us to observe how great was the anxiety within the Jewish communities at the time.[9] We must conclude that there is no cause to discount the significance of the sacrificial cult, even though its performance was centralized and restricted, and even though most Jews could not actually participate in it directly.

Post-Temple Judaism

What became of the substance of Leviticus in post-Temple Judaism? How was the eventual loss of sanctity compensated? Unprecedented until the destruction of the Second Temple was the need to rely *exclusively* on nonsacral worship. Public prayer had coexisted with the cult—in the Temple precincts proper. Synagogues functioned in the Land of Israel and in the Diaspora. But these activities and these institutions did not have to be fully self-sufficient. There had always been the Temple.

A key to the answer lies in an analysis of the priestly components of the Torah. The two pillars of Leviticus are sanctity and purity. Between them, these two dimensions of law and ritual account not only for the content of Leviticus but also for the structure and organization of the book, as has already been shown. Jewish leadership in the post-Temple period saw an opportunity to compensate for the vacuum left by the cessation of sacrificial worship by placing a greater emphasis on purity. This process actually began long before the Roman destruction, as we now know from sectarian literature, such as the texts from Qumran.

Purity and sanctity had enjoyed a subtle relationship in ancient Israel. Viewed from the perspective of the cult, purity was a precondition: What was sacred had to be pure in the first instance; its purity had to be preserved and any defilement redressed. In the biblical period, purity legislation was stimulated primarily by the need for a pure sanctuary and a pure priesthood.

In itself, however, the *concept* of purity, the essential notion that certain places, objects,

and species of animals, for instance, were pure, whereas others were impure, had most probably emerged independently of the cult, to begin with. The priesthood, in effect, appropriated preexisting concepts of purity and applied them to the requirements of the cult. A good example is provided by the dietary legislation of Leviticus 11. Accepted criteria of pure and impure living creatures were adopted as a basis for determining which animals and fowl were suitable as sacrifices. These criteria also applied, however, to the diet of all Israelites.

So long as Israelite, then Jewish, religion was oriented to sacred space, toward a Temple, purity remained primarily a function of the cult. It affected priests and all persons, in varying degrees, in their relations with the Temple as a sacred environment. It was relevant to determine whether a person was pure because it was necessary to know whether such a person might or might not approach the Temple. In an extended sense, it meant that impurity threatened the status of the Temple which existed in the community.

Later Judaism progressively restored the distinction between purity and sanctity. What was lost by way of sanctity could not be replaced in kind when the Temple no longer stood. The efforts undertaken to generate alternative modes of worship and celebration could not, for all of their intensity, produce a religious experience of the same order as that afforded by sacrificial worship. But those aspects of purity that had always pertained to noncultic areas of life could continue to function in post-Temple Judaism, even if sacrifice itself was no longer possible.[10]

In post-Temple Judaism, purity remained operative in three principal areas: priesthood, family, and diet, all of which derive in great measure from the specific provisions of Leviticus.

The Purity of the Priest (Kohen) After the Second Temple of Jerusalem was destroyed, there remained little realistic need for priests. Furthermore, it became increasingly difficult to substantiate priestly lineage, which was hereditary, through the paternal line. After a time, priestly lineage became presumptive; it was merely a "claim" (*ḥazzakah*) to priestly status. Serious attempts were made to keep family records, and for a time, priestly status served as a social register. But with recurring dislocations and the distancing of Jewish communities from the Land of Israel, it eventually became impossible to prove such lineage conclusively.

Despite the relative little that remained of priestly function, so central to the Levitical system, there persisted an attitude on the part of the *kohanim* themselves, as well as on the part of the community, that saw value in having priests continue to obey the biblical restrictions imposed on them and occupy a respected position in synagogue and community. A recent study of the priests of Sepphoris, a town in Lower Galilee, sheds light on the status and religious role of priests during the centuries following the destruction.[11]

Two kinds of priestly restrictions have persisted in the absence of the Temple, one in the area of marital regulations and the other regarding contact with the dead.

According to the provisions of Leviticus 21, priests, as consecrated persons, are forbidden to marry certain women: a divorcée (*gerushah*), a harlot (*zonah*), and a woman classified as "a defiled woman" (*ḥalalah*), namely, one born of a union that had been forbidden to priests initially.

Sexual misconduct was regarded as a form of impurity and was the sole basis for divorce. According to the laws of Deuteronomy 24:1–4, a divorcée was stigmatized, it being assumed that she had been unfaithful to her husband. Being impure, she could not be

married to a priest. To be sure, later rabbinic law liberalized the grounds for divorce, but originally the restrictions on priestly marriage were a response to the strict letter of Mosaic law, as stated in Deuteronomy.

Rabbinic legislation retained the restrictive categories imposed in Leviticus 21, at times redefining them. Two classes of women forbidden to the priest were added: (1) a woman who had not been born a Jew but who had converted to Judaism (*giyyoret* in Late Hebrew), and (2) a woman rejected from levirate marriage (*ḥalutsah* in Late Hebrew). The latter prohibition represents an extension of the principle operative in banning divorcées: A woman rejected from levirate marriage (*yibbum*) was also viewed as stigmatized.

The ban on priestly marriage to a converted woman was derived hermeneutically from the prohibition of priestly marriage to a harlot, reflecting an admittedly disparaging view of the sexual behavior of gentile women in the rabbinic period. It was thought that one born in a state of impurity should not marry a *kohen*, even though the woman in question had subsequently purified herself through conversion to Judaism. Religious conversion—hardly envisioned in Leviticus—represents a later development in Jewish religion.

Now, a priest who transgressed the law and actually married a woman forbidden to him solely because of his priestly status defiled himself as a *kohen*. This defilement extended to all children born of the forbidden union. Such priests and their sons could not officiate, and they and their dependents would not receive priestly emoluments. But the marriage itself was legal and binding, and the children born of such marriages were of acceptable status in other respects. Until modern times, those who are of priestly lineage by their own reckoning have usually observed the ancient restrictions on marriage and, in traditional families, continue to do so.

The second area of priestly purity, namely, avoidance of contact with the dead, also derives from Leviticus 21, although the impurity itself and its regulation are addressed in Numbers 19.

In fact, contact with the dead defiles everyone, but nonpriests are permitted to defile themselves in this way because of the importance attached to proper burial of the dead. Priests, however, may render themselves impure in this extreme way only in order to attend to the burial of close relatives—a mother, father, son or daughter, and brother. Rabbinic law added one's wife to the exemption. The duty toward one's wife, implicit in biblical narratives, was never given a legal formulation in the Bible.[12]

Looking back over the centuries, it is remarkable to what extent men of priestly families have continued to adhere to these purity restrictions, notwithstanding the presumptive nature of their priestly status. Since the destruction of the Second Temple, no effective method has been available for priests (or for any Jews, in fact) to be purified after contact with the dead. (Proximity to non-Jewish dead does not, according to rabbinic law, render a Jew impure.) Talmudic literature gives ample evidence of the anxiety experienced over the impurity of the dead, as it became more difficult to identify Jewish graves in the Land of Israel during Roman times.[13]

Biblical religion regarded the dead as impure in the extreme and forbade priests from participating in funerary rites. In the Commentary it is maintained that this prohibition was aimed at preventing a cult of the dead from becoming part of Israelite worship. To the extent that a higher form of religious expression is served by avoiding a cult of the dead, the devotion of *kohanim* to the ancient purity restrictions has contributed significantly to this goal.

Certain priestly functions that survived in post-Temple Judaism, such as the redemp-

tion of first-born sons and the pronouncement of the priestly benediction, will be discussed in the section "Worship and Celebration."

The Purity of the Jewish Family Leviticus has a great deal to say about the definition of the family and about sexual behavior. As the primary statement of priestly law in the Torah, the book would logically tend to focus on such matters as incest and other forbidden sexual unions. The legalities of marriage and divorce and such problems as the misrepresentation of virginity in marriage are addressed elsewhere,[14] but it is in Leviticus that the inner workings of family life are discussed.

The law governing the immediate family, as it is projected in Leviticus 18 and 20, continued to operate in later periods of Jewish history. There were recurrent disagreements on the permissibility of marriage with first cousins and half sisters, for instance, but such matters hardly affected the basic incest system of the Torah. One notes that lesbian intercourse, not explicitly forbidden in Leviticus, was made so in rabbinic law, so that all forms of homosexuality were prohibited.[15]

New issues, unanticipated in Leviticus, began to affect the integrity of the Jewish family in later periods of Jewish history. Religious conversion to Judaism brought a new element to the family, and changing demographic and social conditions led to intermarriage. Eventually, the adoption of the matrilineal principle established the socioreligious identity of a child born out of an intermarriage as that of its mother, not its father.[16] Significantly, the illegitimacy of children, a subject rarely elaborated in the laws of the Torah, continued to be defined in limited fashion, rather than broadly. Only the offspring of incest or adultery was a *mamzer*, "bastard" (Deut. 23:3)—not one merely born out of wedlock, as was the case in some other legal systems. Only *mamzerim* were forbidden in marriage to Jews.[17]

But as a general rule, the provisions of Leviticus show more concern for sexuality per se than for legalities associated with it. There is great interest in the reproductive cycle of the female. The physiological processes involved in reproduction were defined as impure, and women undergoing such were distanced from the cult and Sanctuary. This function of impurity as a category of priestly law is explained in the Commentary. Though such impurity was relevant to the community because it could affect the Sanctuary, it was also relevant on the most intimate level to sexual relations within the family. That dimension of family purity survived and functioned vitally in post-Temple Judaism.

Menstruation, in particular, as well as the processes relevant to childbirth, were conditions that imposed restrictions on sexual intercourse between husband and wife and also required purification. In this area of behavior, purification had always affected personal life in other than cultic ways. These concerns are addressed in Leviticus 12 and 15. General prohibitions against having intercourse with a menstruating woman appear as well in Leviticus 18:19 and 20:18, in the context of family law.

Leviticus 15:19–23 (and cf. 12:1–8) deals with menstrual impurity. Intercourse is forbidden for seven days from the outset of the period. (Similar restrictions, but for longer periods, apply to a mother after childbirth). The law requires a woman to bathe at the conclusion of the seven days or following abnormal genital discharges that occur subsequently. Two factors are indispensable to the resumption of sexual intercourse: the passage of a fixed number of days and proper purification by bathing. The Torah does not, however, specify how bathing is to be carried out. Certain standards may be learned from a comparison with the purification of vessels, as delineated in Leviticus 11.

Rabbinic law defined bathing, an act conveyed by the Hebrew verb *raḥats*, as total

immersion of the body. Rabbinic law also specified the necessary quantity of water and determined its purity. Natural bodies of running water were optimal but hardly accessible in most situations. It became necessary to utilize man-made structures and to set standards and dimensions for them. In postbiblical sources, the "bath" used by women (and by others) is called *mikvah*, "a gathering, container of water."

The masculine form, *mikveh*, occurs in biblical Hebrew and designates natural bodies of water (Gen. 1:10; Exod. 7:9). In Leviticus 11:26, *mikveh mayim*, "a spring," is mentioned in connection with the purification of certain types of vessels. But it is in Isaiah 22:11 that the feminine form of the word, *mikvah*, appears, as synonymous with *berekhah,* "pool."

Mishnah Mikva'ot sets down the dimensions and specifications for a proper *mikvah*. The water (at least most of it beyond a certain minimum quantity) must be fresh; it may not be "drawn water" (*mayim she'uvim*), which is not sufficiently pure. The *mikvah* had to be large enough to allow for total immersion. Proper bathing meant that no substance could intervene between one's skin and the water. Such intervention was termed *ḥatsitsah*. Loose clothing could be worn, however.

Archaeological excavations have revealed actual examples of ancient *mikva'ot* at such sites as Masada.[18] All through the centuries, Jewish communities maintained *mikva'ot*, and until recent times adherence to the rites of purification seems to have been widespread. Practice today is mostly limited to traditional families.

Mishnah Niddah deals with menstruation in great detail. The period of seven days is absolute regardless of how long the actual flow lasted. At the close of the seven days, after dark, a woman must bathe properly. Abnormal discharges (*zivah* in rabbinic Hebrew; *zov* in Leviticus) also rendered a woman impure. Rabbinic law provides for various contingencies, depending on how long the discharges lasted, and special provisions were made for pregnancy and childbirth.

A woman who has not bathed properly in order to purify herself subsequent to her last period remains sexually forbidden to her husband. Other restrictions were imposed in order to prevent the kind of physical intimacy that might lead to intercourse, but nothing was done to interrupt normal conditions of family life during menstruation. A woman is expected to examine herself and monitor her menstrual period and to be honest and forthcoming with her husband. The purity associated with menstruation has no direct bearing on the legitimacy of children.

In antiquity it was assumed, and with good reason, that Jewish women would not engage in sex before marriage, which, in any event, usually occurred at a relatively young age. A young woman would therefore immerse herself for the first time before her marriage and continue to do so from then on.

The communal *mikvah* may also be utilized for the purification of vessels. Men may also use *mikva'ot*. In this connection it is worthwhile to contrast the impurity of males with that of females in post-Temple Judaism. The impurity of the male suffering from genital discharges was quite severe, according to the requirements of Leviticus 15. Yet such impurity soon lost its relevance, precisely because it had been cult related. But menstruation, because it had other applications deriving from its relation to human reproduction, became a major focus of purity legislation in later Judaism.

This is the most logical place to discuss circumcision, although it differs somewhat in its phenomenology. The only statement regarding this rite in Leviticus appears in 12:3, in the context of childbirth. The principal Torah source for the rite of circumcision is Genesis 17, where it is related to the life of the patriarch Abraham.

Circumcision must take place on the eighth day after birth. This requirement overrides

all other religious considerations. If the eighth day falls on Sabbath or on the Day of Atonement, for that matter, circumcision is performed as scheduled. Medical or potentially life-threatening conditions provide the only basis for postponement. Hemophilia, for example, is discussed in rabbinic law; and there are situations in which circumcision may actually be forbidden for medical reasons.

Rabbinic sources discuss fairly obvious considerations left unspecified in the Torah. The operation must be performed in specific ways, and there are personal and professional requirements as to who may perform this rite. The religious duty rests with the child's father. It is he who is commanded to circumcise his son, but as a practical matter, a professionally trained adult male Jew performs the operation on behalf of the father. Such a person is called *mohel*, "circumciser," and the rite itself is known as *milah*, "circumcising," or *berit milah*, "the covenant of circumcision." The circumcision is the physical mark, or "sign" (*'ot*), of the covenant between God and Israel, first enacted between Abraham and his family and God.[19]

Circumcising one's son is a religious duty commanded in the Torah, and it is therefore accompanied by blessings (*berakhot*) that express compliance with God's command. The *mohel* states that his act complies with the commandment "concerning circumcision" (*'al ha-milah*), whereas the child's father states that God commanded us "to initiate him in the covenant of Abraham, our patriarch" (*le-hakhnisso bi-verito shel 'avraham 'avinu*). The traditional liturgy refers, of course, to the covenant sealed in the flesh of all male Jews. In turn, the theme of covenant evokes the promise of redemption for the Jewish people. Ultimately, this is what brought the prophet Elijah into the act. In the later tradition, based upon 1 Kings 19:10,14, Elijah became an angel, the "angel of the covenant" (*mal'akh ha-berit*), the herald of the redemption to come (Mal. 3:23), when all who are circumcised will be saved from damnation.

As a rite of passage, one of a series of such rites that punctuate the life cycle, *milah* is linked thematically to other important moments. For this reason the liturgy of the *berit milah* expresses the hope that the child now being initiated into the covenant will, in due course, enter into the study of Torah (*torah*), into the marriage canopy (*ḥuppah*), and into a life of good acts (*ma'asim tovim*). Historically, circumcision has been the primary mark of Jewish identity. Those like the Roman emperor Hadrian, who sought to obliterate that identity, forbade circumcision. On the other hand, Hellenizing Jews of an earlier period, who had sought to conceal their Jewish identity completely, tried to alter the physical mark of their circumcision.

Generally, Jews have been extremely loyal to the duty of *milah*. It should be borne in mind that more than a medical operation is required. The operation must be performed in such a way that it reflects the "conscious intent" (*kavvanah*) of the religious rite.

Dietary Purity Leviticus 11 is the most elaborate text on the subject of the dietary laws, which, with some differences, are also presented in Deuteronomy 14. Both codes of law are addressed to the entire people of Israel, and not only to the priests, a fact that will prove to be significant in the ensuing discussion.

Historically, *kashrut*, "fitness," the name given to the overall dietary regimen, has proved to be an effective system of purity in post-Temple Judaism. It has lent to the Jewish home an atmosphere of purification. More than one midrash notes that the Hebrew word *shulḥan*, "table," may also designate an altar. When the prophet Ezekiel beheld the altar of

his visionary Temple he proclaimed: *zeh ha-shulḥan 'asher lifnei* YHVH, "This is the table that stands before the LORD" (Ezek. 41:22).[20]

Perhaps the clearest way of tracing what became of the dietary laws of Leviticus in later Judaism would be to list the principal features of biblical law and then review what became of each of them.

1. The Torah generically prohibits eating the meat or substance of certain living creatures and classifies them as impure. In some cases observable, physical criteria are stipulated, whereas in other instances, a list of forbidden creatures is provided (Lev. 11; Deut. 14).

2. It is forbidden to ingest the blood of any animal (including "beasts," such as deer) and of fowl. (Fish and insects are not included in this ban on blood.) It follows, therefore, that methods of slaughtering animals and fowl should allow for as much blood as possible to leave the body of the animal or bird. To remove residual blood, salted meat was left out to drain. The use of salt is mentioned in the context of sacrifice (Lev. 2:13). The Torah says nothing about the tools to be used for slaughter or about how slaughter is to be performed.

Akin to the prohibition against ingesting blood is that forbidding consumption of animal fat (*ḥelev*; Lev. 7:23–25). A specific statement in Genesis 32:31–32 prohibits eating the sciatic nerve (*gid ha-nasheh*), which could be plucked out by those expert in this task.

3. The Torah forbids eating the meat of the carcass (*nevelah*) of dead animals and fowl. It likewise prohibits eating meat from animals and fowl torn by beasts (*terefah*; Lev. 7:34; 17:15; 22:8). It is also forbidden to eat flesh from any creature while it is still alive (Gen. 9:4).

4. Leviticus 11 legislates detailed purity requirements for those vessels and utensils used to store, prepare, and serve food—the purpose being to preserve food from contamination. Impurity was thought to be conducted from one substance to another by actual contact, as well as in other ways.

5. In three separate statements (none of which appears in Leviticus) the Torah forbids boiling a goat in its mother's milk (Exod. 23:19; 34:26; Deut. 14:2). These prohibitions were similar in spirit to the ban on sacrificing a mother animal and her offspring on the same day, or the offspring immediately after birth (Lev. 22:26–28). In the later religious traditions, these three statements became the basis for separating meat and dairy products from each other. Of a similar character is the prohibition of eating leaven during the Passover festival (Exod. 12, 13, etc.); in both cases, the prohibition is relational, not intrinsic.

6. Torah legislation, much of it in Leviticus, prohibits Israelites from partaking in or benefiting from various foodstuffs until these are desacralized. The operative principle is that the crop, or yield, is forbidden to humans until God receives His share or until God's prior claim is satisfied, at which time the rest of the lot becomes available for use.

A good example of this is grain set aside for the tithe (*ma'aser*) or for priestly levies (*terumah*). Until these dues were withheld, the crop could not be used or prepared as food. The same prohibition of use would affect the fruit of young trees (*'orlah*) until after the fourth year, when it was to be devoted. First fruits (*bikkurim*) were to be devoted, and firstlings (*bekhorot*) of man and beast belonged to God. Unless fit for sacrifice, they were to be redeemed—and could not be used until then. All that grows during the Sabbatical year, "the fruit of the seventh year" (*perot shevi'it* in late Hebrew), may not be marketed.

The upshot of all of these laws is that certain otherwise permissible foodstuffs were forbidden for consumption ephemerally.[21]

What became of all these kinds of dietary restrictions in post-Temple Judaism?

1. The generic prohibitions have remained in force until the present day. At times, the pig has been regarded as the height of impurity. There is no basis for this distinction in religious law, but there are cultural and historical reasons for it. It has been necessary at times to decide the status of certain fowl unknown in the biblical period and to resolve ambiguities concerning certain species of fish. But by and large, the ancient system has persisted with remarkable precision.

2. The prohibition against ingesting blood interacted with the regulations governing *nevelah* and *terefah* to yield a method of slaughter and a system of inspection aimed at satisfying the cumulative requirements of biblical law.

In Mishnah Ḥullin we find the basic regulations governing *sheḥitah*, "slaughter." This term is a form of the same verb often used in the Torah, namely, *shaḥat*, "to slaughter." Rabbinic law defined this verb in practical terms by stipulating which tools may be employed in the process of *sheḥitah*.[22]

The verb *shaḥat* is defined as a cutting, or slicing, action, whereby a blade is drawn over a certain area of the neck. Stabbing, or piercing, is unacceptable. Tools made of various materials may be used, so long as their form makes them suitable for accomplishing an uninterrupted cutting action. Such tools must be sharp and devoid of nicks. The objective is to cut open the esophagus (*veshet*) and the windpipe (*kaneh*) so that the blood gushes forth rapidly. Rabbinic law also stipulates who may perform *sheḥitah*, and relatively few restrictions are imposed. The slaughterer is not a cleric or consecrated person by any means, only a skilled person. The functional meanings of the terms *nevelah* and *terefah* underwent significant adaptation in the later tradition. *Nevelah*, for example, was defined as meat from any animal (beast) or fowl that had not met its death through proper *sheḥitah*.

There is a rather subtle aspect to this definition because the Torah explicitly provides for hunting (e.g., Lev. 17:13–14; Deut. 12:15), and Leviticus 1:15 provides for snapping the nape of fowl offered as sacrifices. The blood of hunted animals and fowl need only be drained and buried, and the list of permitted animals in Deuteronomy 14:3–5 includes several types of deer, which were normally hunted. The rabbis were, of course, fully aware of the biblical sanction for alternative methods, but over time they standardized practice. It was a positive commandment (*mitsvat ʿaseh*) to slaughter all meat, to perform *sheḥitah*.

3. No meat may be eaten as food until the animal or bird from which it was taken has actually expired, a requirement based on Genesis 9:4. In rabbinic terminology, such forbidden meat is called *ʾever min ha-ḥai*, "a limb from a living creature."

Of particular significance is the rabbinic definition of *terefah*. Using subtle hermeneutics, the rabbis defined *terefah* as the condition of a living creature (including a human being) that was expected to die or that was on the verge of death. This would include a severely diseased animal, for example. A kind of autopsy was performed immediately after *sheḥitah* in order to ascertain whether the animal or bird had been healthy at the time of slaughter. This entailed examination of the internal organs, with the lungs most often mentioned. This inspection is known as *bedikah*. If it was determined that the animal or bird had been about to die—that is, it might have died on its own before *sheḥitah*—that animal or fowl was declared *terefah* and could not be used as food.

The prohibition against ingesting blood was addressed, in the first instance, by proper slaughter. Meat was then to be salted and the blood allowed to drain for a time so as to remove residual blood. Preparation over an open fire would also accomplish this objective.

4–5. We combine two features of biblical legislation that came to be associated with one another in later rabbinic law: the purity of vessels and the separation of meat and milk

products from one another. This extremely complex aspect of law underwent considerable development in postbiblical times. Rabbinic law in this area, concentrated in Mishnah Kelim, defines the biblical term *keli*, "vessel," in functional terms; and Mishnah Makhshirin deals with factors that "condition" (*makhshir*) substances so that they are susceptible to impurity. Thus, water conditions grain and makes it susceptible to impurity, whereas dry grain does not become contaminated.

Vessels manufactured of certain materials could be purified subsequent to defilement; others could not and had to be destroyed. Milk and meat were regarded as impure with respect to each other in their admixture, so that vessels used for one could not normally be used for the other. In a similar way, leaven (*ḥamets*) was functionally impure during the Passover festival, so that special cooking and eating vessels had to be used at that time. Heat is another factor that affects purity, since it is thought that porous materials absorb food when either the food or the vessel, or both, are heated. Biblical prohibitions are often stated in terms of boiling or cooking. After eating meat products, there was to be a waiting period before partaking of dairy products, and the two were not to be eaten together. Forbidden *ḥelev*, "fat," was normally removed after slaughter and rarely reached the consumer. Where experts were available to pluck out the sciatic nerve, the sirloin portion could be used. Otherwise, it was disposed of entirely.

The totality of later legislation yielded a highly systematic regimen of food preparation and of dining procedures: Only permitted foods could be eaten to start with, and the purity of these foods had to be preserved in specific ways.

Quite clearly, the regulations governing vesssels and utensils were aimed at achieving an effect similar to that of pure, sacrificial offerings. We read in talmudic literature of contemporary Jews who endeavored to attain a cultic standard of purity in their domestic diet. Down to modern times, *kashrut* has been practiced in Jewish communities all over the world, with some differences in custom.[23]

6. For some time after the destruction of the Second Temple efforts were made to support priestly families and to refrain from benefiting from whatever the Torah had originally assigned to the priesthood and to the Temple. Eventually, such taxes as tithes, priestly levies, and firstlings of the herds and flocks were discontinued, as such, and payments were collected by communal agencies for philanthropic purposes and other necessary functions. To a considerable extent, the practice of *tzedakah*, "philanthropy," replaced cultic donations. This redirection of communal energy and religious commitment is actually a fascinating process, which has been studied in considerable depth in recent years, but it goes far beyond the subject of dietary restrictions.[24]

Opinions differ even today—with the Land of Israel once again settled and yielding seasonal harvests—as to whether such regulations as tithing and setting aside the produce of the Sabbatical year are in force, given the fact that no Temple is currently operative. In the market places of Israel one can observe signs informing the consumer that tithes and priestly levies have been duly set aside or that the produce being marketed was not grown in the land during the Sabbatical year, known as the year of *shemitah*. It is still customary to cast a fistful of dough into the oven when baking, a practice known as *hafrashat ḥallah*, "the setting aside of hallah," which commemorates the *'azkarah*, "taken portion of the grain offering" (Lev. 2:2), and also most probably the *todah*, which is the thanksgiving offering ordained in Leviticus 7:12–13.

There are a few additional dietary regulations not mentioned in the above survey. It is forbidden for Jews to drink wine used in pagan libations because to do so would constitute

participation in idolatrous rites, at least indirectly so. This prohibition is derived from Deuteronomy 32:38, where those who drink pagan libations are condemned alongside those who partake of idolatrous sacrifices. The rabbinic system tended to maximize this prohibition, with the result that all wine produced by gentiles, or, in the opinion of some, even handled by them, was suspect and regarded as *yein nesekh*, "wine of libations." From the New Testament and other early sources, we learn that a debate ensued in Christendom on the subject of partaking of pagan sacrifices, whereas in Judaism this question was emphatically settled by a continuing commitment to the dietary regimen prescribed in the Torah.

The subject of wine produced by gentiles raises a problem of persistent concern, namely, policy regarding foodstuffs processed by gentiles or prepared under unsupervised conditions. This situation concerns such foods as cheeses, for example. All such considerations are still being addressed by religious authorities. *Kashrut* emerges as a dynamic system in religious life, not a static one.

In summary, post-Temple Judaism was enriched by efforts to redirect purity from Temple and cult to home and community. The area of *kashrut* owes a lot to Leviticus, specifically, because it is here that the factor of purity predominates, a purity that extends as well to vessels and utensils. The social and spiritual ramifications of *kashrut* continue to be important, strengthening the identity of Jewish families and communities, an objective basic to the biblical system itself.[25]

Worship and Celebration

A good deal has already been said about the loss of sanctity sustained by the Jewish people with the destruction of the Second Temple of Jerusalem and the demise of the sacrificial cult. A system of nonsacral worship was progressively introduced, one designed to enable Jews everywhere to worship God meaningfully. This process had already commenced during the period of the Second Temple—prayers and psalms were associated with Temple worship, and the Books of Chronicles and Ezra and Nehemiah tell of Levites who were singers (*meshorerim*).[26] But subsequently the process took on new urgency when the main event, sacrificial worship, was no longer possible and there was no longer a role for the consecrated priesthood. What changed pursuant to the destruction of the Second Temple was that henceforth there would be *sole* reliance on words: blessings, prayers, and readings from Scripture and from other canonical sources, such as the rabbinic texts. In this way an attempt was made to compensate for the experience that had been provided by sacrificial worship in earlier times.

Liturgy This approach to worship is epitomized in many midrashic interpretations, including the following: A clause in the second paragraph of the Shema, originating in Deuteronomy 11:13b, was interpreted to mean that prayer was a proper form of worship in its own right. The Israelites, addressed in the second person, are commanded to obey God's *mitsvot*: *ule-ʿovdo be-khol levavkhem*, "and to serve [= worship] Him with all your heart." The sages comment that *ʿavodah ba-lev*, "worship in the heart," is *tefillah*, "prayer."[27] The institution within which public prayer worship developed was the synagogue, or *beit ha-kenesset*, "house of assembly." Virtually everything about the synagogue is antithetical to what the Temple represented. The space of a synagogue structure was not consecrated. In fact, prayer, in contrast to sacrifice, could take place anywhere, at a moment's notice, and

no structure at all is necessary for its performance. No consecrated clergy is needed to officiate at public prayer worship. If *kohanim* are present, they bless the congregation in the words of the priestly benediction. It is customary to show *kohanim* respect by calling them first to the reading of the Torah. But if no priests are present, or if the priests excuse themselves, prayer proceeds all the same.

For a time, attempts were made to preserve a degree of purity in the synagogue. Males, who were impure due to seminal emissions and abnormal discharges from the genitals (the subject of Lev. 15), were initially required to undergo purification prior to entry. In earlier times, the impurity of discharges had been classified as quite severe, but it quickly lost its relevance to the synagogue, as we read in talmudic sources. It did not take long to divorce the synagogue from all rites of purification. Contrary to popular opinion, which is often uninformed, menstrual impurity, a major category of domestic religious law, hardly figured in synagogue worship. Men and women occupied separate parts of the synagogue to be sure, but there is no indication that this practice was based on menstrual impurity. The synagogue was most assuredly not a Temple, and it had no claim to the kind of sanctity that is legislated in Leviticus or addressed in priestly law generally.[28]

What, then, would remain of the legacy of Leviticus in the synagogue and in the religious life of individual Jews and their families and their communities?

In the first instance, public prayer was scheduled and structured in ways that paralleled the schedule of public sacrifices in the Temple.[29] Once we reconstruct a composite of public worship as it operated in the Second Temple, it should become evident just how this parallelism was generated in post-Temple Judaism. As it happens, Leviticus has relatively little to say about daily sacrifice, except for the daily incense offering of the High Priest (6:12–16) and the lamp kindled by the High Priest every day (24:2–4). It is Numbers 28–29 that provide the detailed information about daily, public sacrifice. When we add to this information that is provided in certain tractates of the Mishnah, such as Tamid, we can describe what occurred in the Temple in the last period of its existence. There is also considerable information available from other sources.

Every morning after dawn, a regimen of sacrificial offerings was presented at the altar. This time frame was known as *shaḥarit*, "in the morning." In the afternoon, a series of sacrifices known as *minḥah* was offered. This total structure of worship was called *tamid*, "regular, daily worship." All day long the altar was laden with other offerings: votives, expiatory sacrifices, and so on. This daily regimen continued on an uninterrupted basis. On Sabbaths and other sacred occasions of a seasonal nature, an additional regimen of offerings known as *musaf*, "additional offerings," was presented at the altar. These occasions are enumerated in Leviticus 23, which is a liturgical calendar; and what is missing there appears in Numbers 28–29. The occasions scheduled for additional sacrifices are Sabbaths, New Moons, the three annual festivals (the seven days of Passover, Shavuot, the seven days of Sukkot, and Shemini Atzeret [the assembly of the eighth day], immediately following Sukkot), the New Moon of the seventh month, Tishrei (which was later referred to as Rosh Hashanah), and Yom Kippur, on the tenth day of the month. The sacrifices ordained in Leviticus 23:10–14 for the day on which the first sheaf of new grain (the *ʿomer*) was to be presented were regarded in the later tradition as private worship, although certain Jewish sects seem to have considered this day as a public celebration.[30]

In all cases the main event occurred in the morning. There were no public sacrifices after nightfall. In the Second Temple period the paschal sacrifice, which occurred once a year, was performed in the afternoon, before evening. Now, if we transfer this schedule to

synagogue worship, we emerge with daily prayers: morning (*shaḥarit)* and afternoon or early evening (*minḥah*), before nightfall. We find additional prayers designated for the same sacred occasions as just listed. Evening prayers (*ʿarvit*) were introduced on an optional basis, and even though they have come to be perceived as a requirement of religious life, they never attained the same official status as the morning and afternoon prayers precisely because there was no nocturnal sacrifice in the Second Temple.

On the first level, therefore, the Synagogue worshiper would sense that he was following a specific schedule modeled after the cult of the Temple. This awareness was reinforced by the actual content of the prayer services themselves.[31]

The components of prayer were several. The rubric, or framework, of prayer was normally provided by *berakhot*, "blessings." Formally, a *berakhah* is a statement addressed to God or one that speaks of God; it usually contains the formula *barukh ʾattah* YHVH, "You are blessed, O Lord." This formula has more than one nuance, however: It may convey the wish that God "be blessed," or it may represent a normative statement that God ought to be blessed, that blessings are due Him.

There is no end to the variety of subjects addressed in the *berakhot*. In some cases, they are formulated so as to convey compliance with God's commandments (*mitsvot*): *ʾasher kiddeshanu be-mitsvotav ve-tsivvanu* . . . , "who has sanctified us by His commandments, and has commanded us . . . ." This formulation is significant because it expresses the notion that fulfillment of God's's *mitsvot* generates sanctity, that God has provided us with effective ways of attaining holiness. Even if so many sacred acts commanded in the Torah had become impossible to fulfill, others may be performed. By so doing, it may be possible to attain a degree of sanctity. The *berakhot* function as a means of increasing awareness and thereby enhancing the meaningfulness of religious activity. They also tell of God's acts—as Creator of the world and of mankind, as the redeemer of Israel, as guarantor of the necessities of life, and as a protector.

The major collection of *berakhot* included in the regular prayer liturgy is known as Amidah, the prayer that is said "standing." The daily Amidah contains nineteen *berakhot*. On Sabbaths and sacred occasions, another Amidah is recited as well as an additional (Musaf) one.

In addition to *berakhot*, Jewish liturgy incorporates readings from Scripture and from rabbinic sources, such as the Mishnah. These canonical selections serve an important function: They associate prayer with sacrifice, as it was performed in the Temple. Thus, the *shaḥarit* prayers include readings from the Torah and the Mishnah that describe the daily sacrifices once offered in the Temple. Normally, citations from Numbers 28–29 are preferred over Leviticus because of their greater detail. The Amidah actually includes a blessing that petitions God to restore the cult of sacrifice and, as a corollary, to accept the prayers of His people, Israel. The additional blessings for special occasions even more noticeably feature citations from the Torah relevant to the particular sacrifices ordained for those occasions, as if to say: What we are saying here is in place of what was enacted in the Temple on Sabbaths, festivals, and other occasions.

But readings from canonical sources served yet another purpose in post-Temple Judaism: the study of God's words. Here was a *mitsvah* that could be fulfilled always, without recourse to the Temple or sacrifice. By reciting relevant passages from Scripture, especially, one would ipso facto fulfill the duty of studying the Torah, all in the course of worship. The entire Torah was read sequentially as part of public worship in the synagogue, on Sabbaths

and other occasions, including Mondays and Thursdays, the customary market days. Such practices indicated the growing emphasis on education in later Judaism.

Perhaps the best-known collection of Torah passages included in Jewish liturgy is *keri'at shema'*, "the readings of the Shema," a collection of three Torah paragraphs (Deut. 6:4–9; 11:13–21; Num. 15:37–41). In the first paragraph, we find a proclamation of God's uniqueness and unity. We read of the duty to worship God sincerely and to obey His commandments by teaching them to one's children and speaking of them continually. The second paragraph is an admonition, promising a reward for the love of God and obedience for his *mitsvot* and punishment for disobedience. The final paragraph enjoins Israelites to affix fringes to their garments as visible reminders of God's commandments, the fulfillment of which will enable Israel to become a holy people.

Once again, we note that those Torah passages selected for inclusion in the liturgy of prayer emphasize the connection between *mitsvot* and holiness. We can say with assurance that the fulfillment of the *mitsvot* represented a system of *acts*, not merely of words, that in post-Temple Judaism helped to compensate for the loss of sacrificial worship.

The three paragraphs of the Shema have yielded three symbolic objects functional in Jewish religion to the present time: the *mezzuzah,* placed on the doorpost of one's home; the *tefillin* (phylacteries), worn by adult Jewish males, primarily during weekday prayer; and the *tsitsit* (fringes), worn during the daylight hours, and at some prayer services as a *tallit* (prayer shawl).

None of the above derives specifically from Leviticus, which, in fact, refers to only two kinds of prayers—to the confessional and to the priestly benediction, the text of which actually appears in Numbers 6:22–26. And yet, the spirit, if not the letter, of Leviticus is preserved in Jewish liturgy. Certain themes emanating primarily from Leviticus have found expression in later blessings and prayers.

Expiation of sins was one of the basic objectives of sacrificial worship. In terms of human needs, little could compare with the urge to secure God's forgiveness. Individuals and communities needed to be assured that they were acceptable in God's sight as well as in the sight of man. The loss of the altar of expiation (*mizbaḥ kapparah*) was a major deprivation. The principal expiatory sacrifices (most notably the *ḥatta't*, "sin offering") and their disposition are prescribed in Leviticus 6–7. The rites of Yom Kippur, the annual climax of public expiatory activity, are set forth in chapter 16, which is actually read in the synagogue on Yom Kippur along with sections of the Mishnah taken from the tractate Yoma. These and other readings are collected in a part of the Yom Kippur service appropriately named the Avodah, "sacrificial worship." In the later tradition, the New Moon was also associated with expiation.

A petition for forgiveness is included in the daily Amidah. The prayers of the *'arvit* service, recited after nightfall, seem to emphasize the theme of sin and forgiveness, and there are reasons for this. In the ancient Near East, nocturnal rituals often expressed the theme of penitence, perhaps a reflex of the fears that are strongest at night.

The Epilogue to the Holiness Code (Lev. 26:3–46), known in the later tradition as the *tokheḥah*, "admonition," is read quietly in the synagogue when the relevant portion of the Torah comes due. Like its counterpart in Deuteronomy 28–30, it focuses on the themes of sin, guilt, confession, and repentance, in historic perspective.

Holiness, still another theme prominent in Leviticus, virtually pervades Jewish liturgy. The Holiness Code, which encompasses Leviticus 17–27 and comprises the second division

of the book, is so called because it emphasizes the duty of the Israelite people to pursue holiness. One of the opening blessings of the Amidah is known as ***kedushat ha-shem***, "the sanctity of God's name" (or, perhaps, "the *sanctification* of God's name"). It includes a choral recitation on the theme of sanctity. Other ***berakhot*** also speak of God's holiness. Leviticus is undoubtedly the major Torah source on the theme of holiness, although this subject is also addressed elsewhere.

Although, as we see, the legacy of Leviticus lives on in the liturgy of Jewish worship, it is in the realm of celebration that Levitical themes are most prominent in post-Temple Judaism. There were always two discrete dimensions to the celebration of sacred occasions: the public dimension, realized in the Temple, and the domestic and communal dimension, centered around the home and the family.

It is the latter dimension that became especially relevant after the destruction of the Temple. In priestly statements within the Torah itself, this domestic-communal dimension is occasionally emphasized. We encounter the formula: ***be-khol moshevoteikhem***, literally "in all your areas of settlement." The requirement of eating ***matsot*** on the Passover festival contains this provision, indicating that it was not a practice limited to public celebration (Exod. 12:20). In fact, the paschal sacrifice provides a unique example of a domestic sacrificial rite, originally intended to take place in proximity to one's home and to be performed by the family or clan as a unit. At a later period, when all sacrifice was centralized at the Temple in Jerusalem, the venue of the paschal sacrifice shifted, but even subsequent to that time it was performed by families who assembled at the Temple mount.[32]

The prohibition against kindling fire on the Sabbath (Exod. 35:3) similarly contains a reference to all of the Israelite habitations. What is most significant for the present discussion is the fact that in Leviticus 23, we find the formula ***be-khol moshevoteikhem*** repeated most often: in verse 3, with reference to the Sabbath; in verse 14, regarding the presentation of the first sheaf (*ʿomer*); in verse 21, for Shavuot, the festival of first fruits; and in verse 31, with respect to the prohibition against performing assigned tasks (*melaʾkhah*) on Yom Kippur.

When the demographic pattern of Jewry began to change after the first destruction and continued to become more diffuse throughout the period of the Second Temple, the importance of religious activity undertaken in the home and community understandably grew. When the Second Temple was destroyed, this dimension of religious celebration assumed even greater importance.

The Sabbath In its influence on the calendars of other cultures, the Sabbath is perhaps the most remarkable contribution of Judaism to world civilization in late antiquity. In post-Temple Judaism, the Sabbath was of paramount significance. One begins to read statements on its importance in biblical literature of the exilic and near-exilic periods, in the writings of Jeremiah, Ezekiel, and Deutero-Isaiah.[33] The marked emphasis on ritual which one observes in later, postexilic prophecy is a reflection of the changing conditions of communal life. Postexilic biblical literature expresses considerable interest in the Sabbath. In the late fifth century B.C.E., Nehemiah takes special measures to assure observance of the Sabbath in rebuilt Jerusalem.[34] And later on, in the Qumran sect, observance of the Sabbath was strictly enforced.[35] In other words, the domestic and communal dimensions of Sabbath observance were already steadily developing before the public cult of Jerusalem terminated.

It is precisely in the Holiness Code of Leviticus that the significance of the Sabbath is most prominent. The Sabbath day generated the week, as we know it. In the Holiness Code

we observe how the Sabbath, and the week ending on the Sabbath day, became the basis of computing the time between the Passover festival and Shavuot, as well as the Sabbatical year and the Jubilee year, every half century. Nowhere is the thematic function of the Sabbath more evident than in Leviticus, except perhaps for the association of the Sabbath with Creation and with the liberation from Egyptian bondage, stated elsewhere.

It was recognized that the laws governing activity on the Sabbath were like "mountains hanging on a hair": an abundance of legal hermeneutics (midrash) and a paucity of explicit laws and commandments in the Torah itself. The principal function of later tradition was to define what is meant by *mela'khah* in the biblical injunctions. The Torah only singles out a few types of prohibited labor—gathering wood and the use of fire. Prophecy adds transporting goods outside one's house (Jer. 17) and, in rather vague language, prohibits attention to one's daily affairs (Isa. 58:13).

As is well known and clearly stated in Mishnah Shabbat 7, thirty-nine (forty minus one) specific actions are forbidden on the Sabbath: These were defined as *mela'khah*. The rabbinic sages, and perhaps others who had preceded them, categorized the specific actions required for the performance of the sanctuary cult and then determined that these same labors would be forbidden everywhere outside the Sanctuary. Thus, if it was necessary to cut in the act of slaughtering a sacrificial animal, then cutting was prohibited anywhere outside the Temple. The same would apply to other actions such as cooking, baking, sewing, weaving, writing, and hammering. A statement on the observance of the Sabbath immediately follows, in Exodus 31:12–17, the precise prescriptions on the construction of the Tabernacle in Exodus 25:1–31:11. This sequence was regarded as meaningful, as implying a topical connection between the Tabernacle project and Sabbath observance.

It is in Leviticus, however, that we find the most detailed descriptions of the precise actions involved in preparing sacrifices, primarily in chapters 1–7. In a real sense, therefore, the list of prohibited actions derives, in some measure, from the *torot* of Leviticus.

In summary, the prohibitive aspect of Sabbath observance, as it was systematized in rabbinic Judaism, ultimately owes much to the detail of sacrificial performance found in Leviticus. On the positive side, the key themes of the Sabbath are common to Torah literature: the commandment to remember and keep the Sabbath and to sanctify it, a notion conveyed by the verb *kiddesh*. These themes receive elaboration in later Judaism, and specific *berakhot* are formulated to dramatize compliance with, or fulfillment of, the biblical injunctions. Best known is the blessing called Kiddush, "sanctification," which is recited before the Sabbath evening meal. It is not necessary to go into detail about the various domestic observances traditional for the Sabbath. Pleasure (*'oneg*) is mentioned in some biblical statements on the Sabbath. This was interpreted in various ways, including sexual intercourse, which was encouraged on the Sabbath between husband and wife.

The Sabbath of post-Temple Judaism, in its domestic-communal dimension, covered a minimum twenty-four hour period, lasting from evening to evening. Shops were closed, Jews flocked to the synagogue for public worship, and, in the context of home and family, there was celebration around the dining table. Candles were lit before the onset of the Sabbath, and appropriate blessings were recited. Food was prepared in advance, of course, since no cooking was permissible on the Sabbath. Study of the Torah was encouraged on the Sabbath—a day off that afforded time for such important activity. In all, rabbinic legislation was highly effective in preserving those aspects of the Sabbath that allowed of fulfillment after the Temple was destroyed.[36]

Other Sacred Occasions Leviticus has relatively less to say about the Passover festival than does Exodus, for example. It also says little about Shavuot, although the period between the two festivals is most explicitly addressed in Leviticus 23. We shall return to these festivals presently.

As regards Sukkot, it is Leviticus that, more than any other Torah source, provides the basis for the observance of this festival in later Judaism. Leviticus 23 is the only source in the Torah that specifically ordains that Israelites dwell in booths (*sukkot*) during the seven days of the festival and that explains this requirement in historical and commemorative terms. In this same chapter, the use of fruit and greenery was specified for the Sukkot celebration. The fruit was later determined to be a citron (*'etrog*), and the greenery consisted of palm branches and willows, as explicitly mandated in the biblical text, and myrtle, as defined by tradition. It is in Leviticus that Shemini Atzeret (the assembly of the eighth day) is first ordained.

When the public, cultic dimension of Sukkot could no longer be celebrated and when the pilgrimage (*ḥag*)—which had been the major pilgrimage of the year—was no longer a reality, it was still possible to construct booths and celebrate the festival symbolically. It was still possible to rejoice on Sukkot, a theme expressed particularly in Leviticus 23. In later periods of Jewish history, when the cycle of Torah portions read in the synagogue reached its conclusion in the autumn of the year, as was customary in many Jewish communities, the "rejoicing" of Sukkot was directed toward the Torah. The assembly of the eighth day celebrated the Torah itself, and was known as Simhat Torah.

But let us return to Passover and Shavuot, in the spring of the year. The Passover festival, the essential character of which is revealed in Exodus and Deuteronomy rather than in Leviticus, included from its inception dimensions that could be realized apart from its cultic celebration. *Matsot* were to be eaten and leaven avoided. As has been noted, the paschal sacrifice itself was originally conceived as a domestic rite, and it never fully lost that character. The Passover Seder is a remarkable liturgical creation, which dramatizes through symbol and recitation the meaning of the occasion.[37]

The prohibitionary aspect of the Passover observance could function in post-Temple Judaism, of course. We see that the prohibitions of the Torah regarding leaven underwent a process similar to other aspects of the dietary laws. The Jewish home was searched for *ḥamets*, "leaven," which was to be removed before the outset of the festival, in compliance with biblical law. Other measures were taken to assure that the home and property of Jews were free of leaven for the duration of the festival.

The commemorative character of Passover could most certainly be expressed quite apart from reliance on sacrificial worship. Excursus 8 explains that whereas Shavuot and Sukkot were truly seasonal festivals, linked to the agricultural economy of biblical Israel, Passover, from its inception, was a commemoration of the Exodus from Egypt, an occasion expressive of historical memory. Perhaps for this reason, so much of its ancient character could remain functional in post-Temple Judaism.

This historical association brings us directly to Shavuot, originally a festival of first fruits (*bikkurim*), but in later Judaism, conceived as the occasion of the giving of the Torah at Mount Sinai. Like Passover, it had a historical dimension: its association with events subsequent to the Exodus. The Ten Commandments are read in the synagogue on Shavuot. We know that there was a rabbinic chronology of the early history of Israel, which may be reconstructed from midrash and commentary, in which specific dates were assigned to important events, such as the giving of the Torah and the birth and death of leading

figures. At some time, it became the practice to read certain of the biblical *megillot* on the three festivals: Song of Songs on Passover because it speaks of springtime, after the rains have passed; Ruth on Shavuot because its story takes place at the time of the wheat harvest; and Ecclesiastes on Sukkot because autumn turns one's thoughts to the cessation of life. The period of counting (*sefirah*) between Passover and Shavuot, a time highlighted in Leviticus 23, received attention in post-Temple Judaism and came to be associated with later historical events.

Beginning in the period of the Babylonian exile, we perceive a heightened sense of penitence and increased expression of individual as well as collective guilt. The early-postexilic prophet Zechariah (7:5) speaks of two annual fast days, one in the fifth month, Ab, commemorating the destruction of the Temple, and the other in the seventh month, namely, Yom Kippur. Isaiah (58:3–4) also speaks of the solemn character of Yom Kippur. We read in Ezra and Nehemiah of fasting and public confession. Although such practices in themselves are very ancient, interest in them seems to have peaked in the exilic period, in the wake of national tragedy. What happened after the first destruction recurred after the Second Temple was destroyed; only this time, the tragic effects were permanent.

Undoubtedly, the ascendance of Rosh Hashanah and Yom Kippur and of the ten-day period between them that characterizes later Judaism is attributable, in large part, to the continuing need for expiation and forgiveness, in the absence of the Temple and its "altar of expiation."

The New Moon of the seventh month became *the* New Year (Rosh Hashanah). The calendar had shifted to an autumnal inception of the year, and Yom Kippur became the major occasion for communal penitence. Leviticus 16 already gives evidence of a development in this direction in that the last part of the chapter (vv. 29–34) redirects emphasis from the Sanctuary to the people and speaks of self-denial and fasting. This need was sufficiently strong to make Yom Kippur the most solemn day of the year. The celebration of the New Moon survived in post-Temple Judaism, along with accompanying rites relevant to the birth and phases of the moon, but this complex does not derive specifically from Leviticus.

In summary, Jewish religion has effectively preserved—in the absence of a Temple and without the realistic possibility of pilgrimages—as much as could be preserved of the annual festivals and of the weekly Sabbath. Much of the ancient character of the festivals is revealed in Leviticus. That is, even without the cult, Jews everywhere could rest from work on all festivals and sacred occasions.

The Daily Experience of Religion We have already discussed the daily regimen of worship in the synagogue. We now proceed to characterize the daily practice of religion, with reference to the background of Leviticus, in the life of the individual and his family and of the community outside the synagogue.[38]

Circumcision, a family rite, has already been discussed in the context of purification, where some mention was made of the life cycle of the individual Jew. There has also been reference to the distancing of funerary rites from the Temple because of considerations of purity and the prohibition against the participation of the priests (*kohanim*) in the burial of the dead.

Another family obligation that has survived to the present time is the redemption of the first-born son (*bekhor*), known traditionally as *pidyon ha-ben*, "the redemption of the son." The Torah commands Israelites to hand over to God the first-born of man and beast (Exod.

13:2ff.; 22:28; 34:20; Deut. 15:19ff.). It is from Leviticus 27:2ff., however, that we learn how one was to redeem his first-born son, for that was the intent of the law. Leviticus establishes a system of evaluations, or equivalents (Late Hebrew *ʿarakhin*). An Israelite would redeem his first-born son through the good offices of the priest at the rate established for the age group of thirty days to five years. This amounted to five shekels by the sanctuary weight. (A child was considered viable at the age of thirty days.)

Traditionally, a *kohen* is invited to the home, and the redemption is dramatized. The five shekels (or other current units of money) are often returned to the father or donated as *tzedakah*, since, technically, the *kohen* may not keep them because his status is only presumptive. Blessings are recited; these state that the duty to redeem one's first-born son is a *mitsvah* of the Torah. This ritual, which is extraordinary in its occurrence (that is, it occurs only after the birth of the first issue of the womb if that issue is a male child) relates to an enduring theme in post-Temple Judaism: desacralization, which has already been mentioned in the discussion of dietary purity.

Desacralization requires that before humans may derive benefit from any of God's creation, God's prior claim to His creation must be satisfied. This principle is epitomized in the statement: "The earth is the LORD's and all that it holds" (Ps. 24:1). The theme of desacralization underlies a complex of *berakhot* known as *birkhot ha-nehenin*, "the blessings of the beneficiaries." (In Late Hebrew, the participle *nehenin* means "deriving benefit.") A variegated list of *berakhot* covers most of the daily experience of a human being but relates especially to eating food for sustenance. Before partaking of food, a Jew is required to express thanksgiving to God for allowing His creatures to derive benefit from His creation. The Grace after Meals (*birkat ha-mazon*) is a collection of *berakhot* recited upon the completion of a meal, in compliance with the commandment of Deuteronomy 8:10: "When you have eaten your fill, give thanks to the LORD your God for the good land which He has given you."

Conclusion

It is hardly possible in this limited space to do justice to all of the themes expressed in Leviticus or to trace their later applications in post-Temple Judaism. The intent was merely to show how a system of worship and purification that was essential to religious life in antiquity was restructured and redefined so as to enable Jews everywhere to worship the God of Israel meaningfully and to realize a degree of sanctity in their lives.

Along with purity and sanctity, Leviticus also held forth the vision of redemption and freedom. Speaking in the context of economic freedom, Leviticus 25 proclaims the Jubilee year as a time when *deror*, "release," will be granted to all those Israelites who are bound by debt and indenture and when *geʾullah*, "redemption," will be realized for land that had been lost to its owners.

These themes, which are given legal expression in Leviticus, are conceived as national redemption in the words of an exilic prophet, who foresaw God restoring the captives of Israel to the Land of Israel. Leviticus 25:10, conventionally translated, "Proclaim liberty throughout the land and to all the inhabitants thereof," is inscribed on the Liberty Bell, enshrined in Philadelphia, Pennsylvania. Leviticus 25:24b, *geʾullah tittenu la-ʾarets*, "You must provide for the redemption of the land," became the byword of the Jewish National

Fund, whose goal is the reclamation of the soil of the Land of Israel. "Love your neighbor as yourself" (Lev. 19:18) is the embodiment of God's will for humankind, and according to Rabbi Akiba, "a cardinal principle in the Torah."

Notes to Leviticus in the Ongoing Jewish Tradition

1. A passage from the prayer introduced into the Amidah of the Musaf service, when the New Moon falls on the Sabbath. See S. Baer, *Seder 'Avodat Yisrael* (Berlin: 1936–1937), 238. A similar prayer appears in the Musaf for festivals (ibid., p. 352).

2. See B. A. Levine, "On the Presence of God in Biblical Religion," in *Religions in Antiquity*, ed. J. Neusner (Leiden: Brill, 1968), 71–87.

3. See Monika K. Hellwig, *Encyclopedia of Religion* (1987), s.v. "Eucharist," for Christian concepts of communion.

4. See Richard Martin, in *Encyclopedia of Religion* (1987), s.v. "Muslim Pilgrimage."

5. See B. A. Levine, "Critical Junctures in Biblical Religion," *AJS Review* XX (1987), 143–157.

6. Especially Ezek. 20:1ff.,29,40ff. The text speaks of idolatry, but a close reading suggests that the issue is improper worship. V. 29 alludes to a *bamah*, "cult installation, high place," where some Jews may have been offering sacrifices in Babylonia. The late Professor Shalom Spiegel first pointed to the relevance of Ezek. 20 for the edicts of Josiah.

7. On the Jewish temple at Elephantine, see B. Porten, *Archives from Elephantine* (Berkeley: University of California Press, 1968).

8. See B. A. Levine, IDBSup, s.v. "Priests"; and idem, "*The Encyclopedia of Religion* (1987), s.v. "Levites." See also EncJud, s.v. "Priests and Priesthood," especially discussion by M. Haran and M. Stern.

9. See J. A. Goldstein, *Anchor Bible*, vol. 41, *I Maccabees* (Garden City: Doubleday, 1976), 205–207 for the comments on 1:20–64, and 221 for notes to lines 44–45 on the harsh edicts of Antiochus IV Epiphanes and the reaction to them.

10. See J. Neusner, *The Idea of Purity in Ancient Judaism* (Leiden: Brill, 1973). Neusner has produced a monumental edition of the order Tohorot of the Mishnah, *A History of the Mishnaic Law of Purities*, 22 vols. (Leiden: Brill, 1974–1977). Included is a new translation of the mishnaic text and extensive discussion of the talmudic system of purity. Throughout our discussion when reference is made to various tractates of Tohorot, such as Mish. Mik., Mish. Kelim, etc., the reader may consult relevant volumes of Neusner's edition. Vol. 22, *The Mishnaic System of Uncleanness: Its Context and History*, provides valuable insights into the functioning of purity in post-Temple Judaism.

11. The principal mishnaic sources are Mish. Ket. 1:10 and Mish. Kid. 4:5. The relevant formula is *massi'in la-kehunah*, "they may marry off [their daughters] to the priesthood." This refers to Jewish families considered properly observant of the laws of marriage and divorce. Also see EncJud, s.v. "Priests and Priesthood," 1087–1090. An interesting glimpse into the activities of priests in post-Temple period Palestine is provided by S. S. Miller, *Studies in the History and Traditions of Sepphoris* (Leiden: Brill, 1984), 103–127.

12. See the Comment to Lev. 21:4.

13. See Mish. Naz. 9 for laws pertaining to the treatment of grave sites in ancient Palestine and measures taken to avoid contact with burial plots.

14. See Deut. 21:15, 17; 22:13–23:7; 24:1–6; 25:5–10.

15. See the Comment to Lev. 18:22.

16. See the symposium, "The Issue of Patrilineal Descent," *Judaism* 34 (1985), especially articles by Shaye J. D. Cohen, "The Matrilineal Principle in Historic Perspective," and by Lawrence H. Schiffman, "Jewish Identity and Jewish Descent."

17. The basic statement of law is found in Mish. Ket. 3:12.

18. See Y. Yadin, *Masada: Herod's Fortress and the Zealots' Last Stand* (New York: Random House, 1966), 164–167.

19. See L. V. Snowman, EncJud, s.v. "Circumcision."

20. See Ber. 55a: "The verse opens with reference to an altar, and concludes by referring to a table! R. Johanan and R. Eleazar have both said: 'So long as the Temple was in existence, the altar would atone for Israel. But now, it is a person's table that atones for him.'" The same verse from Ezekiel is cited in Mish. Avot 3:3 to emphasize the importance of discussing Torah around the table.

21. The tithe is mentioned as a known obligation in only one section of Leviticus (27:30–32). The duty to desacralize the fruit of trees is prescribed in Lev. 19:23–25. The priestly levy (***terumah***) is referred to several times, in different connections (Lev. 7:14; 10:15; 22:12). First fruits are to be desacralized according to the provisions of Lev. 2:14; 23:16ff., and firstlings of man and beast, according to Lev. 27:26. The fruits of the seventh year are bound by the regulations of Lev. 25.

22. See relevant mishnaic sources in Mish. Bik. 2:11 and Mish. Ḥul. 9:7–8.

23. See H. Rabinowitz, EncJud, s.v. "Dietary Laws," for a summary of the Jewish dietary system.

24. See Richard Sarason, *A History of the Mishnaic Law of Agriculture* (Leiden: E. J. Brill, 1979), for a discussion of the shift from cultic gifts to philanthropy.

25. See S. Dresner, *The Jewish Dietary Laws: Their Meaning for Our Time*, with a guide to observance by S. Siegel (New York: Burning Bush Press, 1959).

26. On the Temple singers, the members of Levitical clans, see Ezra 2:64; Neh. 7:67; 1 Chron. 6:18; 9:33; 2 Chron. 20:21.

27. See Sif. Deut. par. 41, on Deut. 11:13b.

28. See L. I. Rabinowitz, EncJud, s.v. "Synagogue."

29. See Ber. 26b; the talmudic formula is ***keneged ha-temidim***, "corresponding to the daily sacrifices." The lengthy beraita expands on the parallelism in the scheduling of the prayers as counterparts to the sacrifices.

30. This is indicated by the importance attached to this occasion in the Qumran Temple Scroll, for instance. See Comment to 23:11.

31. A fine treatment of early Jewish prayer is by J. Heinemann, *Prayer in the Talmud: Forms and Patterns* (Berlin and New York: W. de Gruyter, 1977). An earlier study, which has become a classic, is I. Elbogen, *Der jüdische Gottesdienst* (Berlin and Jerusalem: Devir, 1924). See also Lawrence Hoffman, *The Canonization of the Synagogue Service* (Notre Dame, Ind.: University of Notre Dame Press, 1979).

32. See the Excursus for a discussion of the early development of the paschal sacrifice.

33. See Jer. 17:22ff.; Ezek. 20, 46; Isa. 56:2–6; 58:13; 66:23.

34. See Neh. 9:14; 10:32; 13:15–22.

35. On the elaborate code of Sabbath observance at Qumran, see L. H. Schiffman, *The Halakhah at Qumran* (Leiden: E. J. Brill, 1975), 177–133.

36. See EncJud, s.v. "Sabbath."

37. See the recent study by B. Bokser, *The Origins of the Seder* (Berkeley: University of California Press, 1984). Bokser's treatment of the development of the Seder rite and its relation to the paschal sacrifice is relevant to the approach taken in this essay, generally.

38. The reader may wish to peruse a Siddur, a book of Jewish prayers, for the actual content of the prayers and blessings. A useful prayer book is P. Birnbaum, *Prayerbook for Sabbath and Festivals* (New York: Hebrew Publishing Co., 1950 [Sephardic version, 1965]). The various religious movements within American Jewry have published their respective versions of the prayer book.

EXCURSUSES

EXCURSUS 1

That Person Shall Be Cut Off (chap. 7)

We encounter, for the first time in Leviticus, explicit references to the penalty of being "cut off" in chapter 7 (vv. 20–21, 25–27). This penalty is usually formulated as follows: *ve-nikhretah ha-nefesh ha-hi' me-'ameihah,* "That person shall be cut off from his kin," or similar wording. As a penalty specified for a variety of religious offenses, it is distinctive to the priestly texts. In rabbinic literature the penalty is called *karet,* "cutting off."[1]

To understand its priestly function, the nonlegal background of the penalty of *karet* must first be investigated. On the most elemental level, "cutting" a person off is a metaphor borrowed from the felling of trees and other forms of vegetation. Such actions are often conveyed by the verb *k-r-t*.[2] A metaphor of this type is preserved in the words attributed to Jeremiah's enemies, who plotted against his life: "Let us destroy the tree with its sap,/ Let us cut him off (*nikhretennu*) from the land of the living./ That his name be remembered no more!"[3] In a similar way, Isaiah of the exile used the metaphor of the tree in reassuring those foreigners and eunuchs who had attached themselves to the people of Israel that they would be redeemed along with the Judean exiles: "Let not the foreigner say, . . . 'The Lord will keep me apart from His people';/ And let not the eunuch say,/ 'I am a withered tree.'/ For thus said the Lord: '. . ./ I will give them, in My house and within My walls,/ A monument and a name/ Better than sons and daughters./ I will give them an everlasting name/ Which [literally] shall not be cut off (*'asher lo' yikkaret).*' "[4]

Job provides an interesting variation on this theme. He contrasts the fate of a tree with that of a person: "There is hope for a tree;/ If it is cut down (*'im yikkaret*) it will renew itself;/ Its shoots will not cease./ If its roots are old in the earth,/ And its stump dies in the ground,/ At the scent of water it will bud/ And produce branches like a sapling./ But mortals languish and die;/ Man expires; where is he?"[5] Job's depressing contrast hardly invalidates the graphic sight of a tree cut down and left as a decaying stump. The point is that, once felled, most trees do not grow again, certainly not to their earlier stature.

In priestly literature, the penalty of *karet* was understood to include a series of related punishments at the hand of God, ranging from the immediate death of an offender, as in 20:17, to his premature death at a later time, and even to the death of his descendants. In Mishnah Sanhedrin 9:6 and Mishnah Keritot 1:2, this penalty is characterized as *mitah bi-ydei shamayim,* "death at the hands of heaven." Since in 20:21 *karet* is mentioned in the same context as childlessness (*'ariri*), there is the implication that it took that course as well.

Some have pointed to the curse pronounced over the house of Eli, the priest of Shiloh, whose sons offended God. In 1 Samuel 2:33 God decrees that although Eli's descendants will not be "cut off" from the priestly office altogether, none of them will reach old age. The statement is best rendered, "all the increase in your house shall die while still in their prime."

This introduces another possible aspect of the penalty of *karet:* being "cut off" from a particular office or status. Thus, in 1 Kings 2:45, David is assured that literally "no person of your line shall be 'cut off' from the throne of Israel."[6] It has also been suggested that at times *karet* took the form of banishment or ostracism. In the ancient Near East, especially in sparsely inhabited areas, banishment would often have resulted in death, or at least in the extinction of a family or clan as a social unit. Hagar and her son Ishmael almost died after their banishment, as we read in Genesis 21:16f., and they were only spared by God's intervention. The wilderness is known in Leviticus 16:22 as the land "cut off" (*'erets gezerah*) from the living, which expresses the same theme in other words.

An interesting case of the effects of ostracism may be seen in the aftermath of the internecine war between the league of Israelite tribes and the tribe of Benjamin, as told in Judges 20. After avenging a Benjamite atrocity, the other tribes swore not to allow their sons to marry Benjamite women. Later, they experienced remorse, fearing that if this ban continued for very long, a whole tribe would be "missing," "cut off" (*nigda'*), or "wiped out."[7]

Against the background of metaphor and social reality, we may now focus on the more distinctly priestly applications of the penalty of *karet.* The priestly conception of God was pervaded by an awareness that He punishes offenders severely for violations of religious law. Priestly writers appropriated widespread notions of death at the hand of God and saw this process at work in specific situations. Uzzah was struck down for merely touching the ark, according to 2 Samuel 6:5–8. Two of Aaron's sons, Nadab and Abihu, were blasted by God's fire because they offered "hateful" incense, recounted in the episode of Leviticus 10:1f. Korah and his band were suddenly destroyed for attempting to usurp the priesthood from Aaron's clan, as we read in Numbers 16–17.

In priestly law, the certainty of God's punitive wrath was institutionalized in the penalty of *karet.* It was stipulated for the following offenses: (1) violation of the Sabbath and improper observance of festivals and holy days;[8] (2) violations of certain laws of purity;[9] (3) certain prohibited sexual unions, also regarded as a form of impurity;[10] (4) cultic offenses, such as eating blood and fat and mishandling sacrificial substances;[11] (5) failure to circumcise one's male children at the age of eight days, as ordained in Genesis 17:14 and Leviticus 12:3.

In the Sabbath law of Exodus 31:14–15, we observe a curious interaction of human and divine punishment that helps to clarify the penalty known as *karet.* We are told twice that one who desecrates the Sabbath "shall be put to death" by human agency, which is what the Hebrew formula *mot yummat* means. In Numbers 15:32–33 we actually read about one Israelite who was apprehended gathering wood on the Sabbath and was put to death by the congregation, on explicit instructions from God to Moses. How is it, then, that Exodus 31:14–15 stipulates *karet* as the punishment for violating the Sabbath? The accepted explanation is that if the community failed to punish the offender or failed to uncover the offense, God would mete out punishment in His own way and in His own good time.

The policy that a person, family, or tribe would be "cut off" and banished from the larger community because of an offense on the human level translated itself into the perception that God would similarly "cut off" those who had offended Him, if human agencies had allowed such offenses to go unpunished.

EXCURSUS 2

The Meaning of the Dietary Laws (chap. 11)

By classifying certain living creatures as *tame'*, "impure," the laws of Leviticus 11 and of Deuteronomy 14 place them in a broad "avoidance category," thereby helping to ensure that they would not be used as food. These laws became part of an elaborate system of purity and impurity affecting the sanctuary and the priesthood as well as the lives of individual Israelites, their families, and the community as a whole. Avoidance of the impure is a prerequisite for the attainment of holiness. Conversely, impurity is incompatible with holiness: It detracts from the special relationship between God and the people of Israel and threatens Israel's claim to the land. This is stated most clearly in 20:22–26:

> 22You shall faithfully observe all My laws and all My regulations, lest the land to which I bring you to settle in spew you out. . . .
>
> 24bI the LORD am your God who has set you apart from other peoples. 25So you shall set apart the clean beast from the unclean, the unclean bird from the clean. 25bYou shall not draw abomination upon yourselves through beast or bird or anything with which the ground is alive, which I have set apart for you to treat as unclean. . . .
>
> 26You shall be holy to Me, for I the LORD am holy, and I have set you apart from other peoples to be Mine.

These statements express several interrelated themes, all basic to the meaning of the dietary laws. On the basis of these and other similar statements, including verses 44–46 of this chapter and Deuteronomy 14:21, the rabbis classified the impurity associated with forbidden foods as *tum'at kodesh,* "impurity pertaining to holiness."[1] In the rabbinic law, the same category included the major sexual offenses set down in Leviticus 18 and 20. Maimonides likewise included both of these categories—forbidden foods and forbidden sexual unions—in Sefer Kedushah (The Book of Holiness), one of the fourteen sections of his Mishneh Torah.[2]

From the biblical point of view, there is a third category of transgressions that is also linked conceptually and legally to the dietary restrictions and the sexual prohibitions, namely, pagan worship. The nexus of all three categories is epitomized in the concept of *to'evah,* "abomination," closely identified with impurity. In the introduction to the dietary laws of Deuteronomy (14:3) we read: "You shall not eat anything abhorrent (*to'evah*)." The chapter continues with a list of forbidden living creatures, classifying them as *tame'*, "impure." Leviticus 18:24–30, in the concluding verses of the sexual code, warns that forbidden sexual unions are *to'evah* and at the same time *tame'*, "impure." Pagan worship is *to'evah,* a theme dramatized in Deuteronomy 7 and elsewhere in the Torah. It constitutes a major source of defilement.[3]

A triad of religious sins emerges—dietary, cultic, and sexual—all associated with impurity and all linked to the destiny of the Israelites as a people distinguished from other nations. The prophet Ezekiel (33:25–26), in one of his severe condemnations of the people who are in exile, alludes to the same three categories, adding the charge of murder and violence: "Thus said the Lord GOD: You eat [meat] with the blood, you raise your eyes to your fetishes, and you *shed* blood—yet you expect to possess the land! You have relied on your sword, you have committed abominations (*to'evah*), you have all defiled other men's

wives—yet you expect to possess the land!" In a positive sense, then, the laws of the Torah make the observance of a dietary regimen essential to the achievement of the collective humaneness of the people of Israel. They offer a means by which individual Israelites and their families—the nonpriests—may contribute to the attainment of holiness.

Underlying all the dietary regulations is a broad social objective: maintaining a distance between the Israelites and their neighbors, so that the former do not go astray after pagan religions. The introductory Comment to chapter 18 notes that biblical perceptions of the sexual habits of the Egyptians and Canaanites may have been imprecise in certain respects; the same is true of biblical characterizations of pagan religions. This reality does not, however, alter the *stated* intent of any of these laws. They condemn what they perceive to be the abominable ways of others, especially the Canaanite peoples of the land. This attitude is basic to the interpretation of the dietary laws.

A variation on this theme is the notion that the "lands" of exile are impure, that is, that the peoples of these lands follow an impure way of life. As a consequence, in the land of their exile Israelites will eat impure foods, just as they will be compelled to worship false gods. Prophetic utterances regard this as a form of divine retribution: Those who transgress against the laws of purity in their own land, where they may choose between obedience to God's laws or perverseness, must eventually, inevitably, commit the same sins in the lands of their enemies. This recalls the theme that Israel will retain its hold on the promised land only so long as the land remains pure. As far as the legislation of the Torah is concerned, this definitely includes observance of the dietary laws.[4]

Thus far, we have considered the expressed intent of the dietary laws. The question now arises as to what lies behind those laws. How were the particular prohibitions set forth in Leviticus 11 and Deuteronomy 14 arrived at? Is there a common denominator, or organizing principle, that can account for the designation of certain living creatures as pure and others as impure? There is an extensive literature on this question, extending from antiquity to the present.[5] In modern times this subject has been of particular interest to anthropologists and historians of religion, who have noted that the Torah's detailed classifications of the dietary laws are virtually unreflected in the rest of biblical literature. This absence is in itself a major problem of biblical interpretation. Only in two late passages of Deutero- (or Trito-) Isaiah do we find statements condemning the sacrifice of dogs, mice, and swine.[6] Ezekiel (4:14) once protested his innocence by insisting that he had never partaken of meat torn by beasts (*terefah*), carcasses (*nevelah*), or spoiled sacrificial flesh (*piggul*).[7] In Judges 13:4–7 Manoah's wife is admonished against eating anything impure (*tame'*) or drinking intoxicants prior to the birth of her son, Samson. The reference there is to the ritual status of foods generally, not to any particular kind of forbidden food. In the literature of a later era, we read that, while in Babylon, Daniel and his three friends refused to defile themselves by eating the usual food allotted to courtiers;[8] and 1 Maccabees 1:12–63 relates that, during the persecutions of Antiochus IV Epiphanes, the pious suffered death rather than eat the flesh of swine. These few references to dietary restrictions are both late and limited in scope; they do not provide us with historical evidence that the dietary laws of the Torah were practiced in earlier periods.

In the text of the Torah, a generic distinction between pure and impure animals first occurs in Genesis, in one of the versions of the Flood story. There are three versions of the story, and critical scholarship considers the Jahwistic (J) version of Genesis 7:2–3 to be the oldest. It is there that we read about seven pairs of pure animals and birds being taken into the ark by Noah, but only two pairs of impure animals. There, too, Noah offers only pure

species as sacrifice to God after the Flood. In the priestly version of the Flood story, as preserved in Genesis 6:19–25, no such distinctions are drawn; it simply states that two pairs of every species are taken into the ark.

There are probable reasons why the priestly version, which we would logically expect to be concerned with purity, fails to distinguish between pure and impure species in this context. It seems to be the priestly view that the regulations governing purity were particular to the Israelite people and were first ordained at Sinai. For purposes of our discussion, it is important to note that an early biblical tradition, not specifically linked to the priesthood, knows of a distinction between pure and impure species, although it does not specify which animals and birds are pure and which are impure. The laws of Deuteronomy and Leviticus serve to elaborate the specifics of the earlier, accepted distinction.

It is the priestly tradition, nonetheless, that affords us an insight into the meaning of the dietary system in the context of the Flood stories of Genesis. This clue is to be found in the dispensation stated in Genesis 9:2–3, allowing humans to use living creatures as food: "The fear and the dread of you shall be upon all the beasts of the earth and upon all the birds of the sky—everything with which the earth is astir—and upon all the fish of the sea. . . . Every creature that lives shall be yours to eat; as with the green grasses, I give you all these." This etiological statement explains how humans came to hunt and kill living creatures for food. In the aftermath of the Deluge the primeval relationship between humankind and the natural world was altered, placing human beings on a higher order. This status is already presaged in the priestly version of Creation, Genesis 1:28–29, according to which humankind is given dominion over all living creatures as well as over the earth itself. Indeed this priestly statement goes even farther: It grants humans a dispensation to subdue other living creatures. According to this tradition, the human response to the divine dispensation—the functional application of "the fear and the dread"—is the domestication of animals, fowl, and fish. In other words, God would make other living creatures submissive to man.

Analysis of the lists of permitted living creatures reveals certain common features. James Frazer observed that even those undomesticated land animals that may be used as food, such as deer, exhibit the same physical features as permitted domesticated cattle and sheep; they have split hoofs and chew their cud.[9] It is likely, therefore, that these two criteria were not the initial basis for the distinction between pure and impure animals but were, rather, a pair of observable physical features common to animals in an already established category. The initial basis for the various classifications of living creatures as pure and impure should be sought elsewhere.

Like many other ancient peoples, the Israelites personified the animal world, projecting onto it their own preferences and dislikes. The traditions of Genesis relate that "all flesh" had corrupted its ways.[10] Even in the postdiluvian dispensation, beasts are still held accountable for the murder of humans. God's covenantal promise never again to bring total destruction upon the world is phrased in terms of the sins of every living creature, not only those of humankind.[11] Certain laws of the Torah also address this issue. According to Exodus 21:29–32, the goring ox is to be judged and executed in the manner of a human murderer. Certain laws of war require that livestock captured from Israel's sworn enemies must be destroyed and may not be used as food or even offered as sacrifices. This is, to some extent, because such were closely associated in the minds of the people with the enemies themselves.[12] And in the story of Jonah not only does the citizenry of Nineveh fast and repent of their wickedness, but herds and flocks as well.

Each of these instances indicates a mentality that regarded domesticated livestock as members of the community; even wild beasts were held accountable for their actions. It follows that habits and behavior of animals, birds, and even fish had religious significance. In particular, the food that animals and birds themselves ate and how they obtained it were factors in determining their classification as pure or impure. This is readily evident in the list of prohibited birds: Almost all of them are birds of prey, by day or by night, who feed on carrion and tear the flesh of other living creatures in their pursuit of food. As such they were considered unfit as food for a people forbidden to eat blood and commanded to avoid flesh that had been torn by preying creatures. By contrast, those birds considered pure (identified by process of elimination), such as hens, doves and pigeons, quail, and certain types of geese, feed on grain and spend more time on the ground in proximity to human beings, to whom they are more submissive. In the early version of the Flood the raven, an impure bird, provides a contrast to the dove, a pure bird. Once released, the raven never returned to the ark, but the dove thrice returned![13] Elsewhere in the Torah, God brings the quail, a pure bird, to the Israelite settlements in Sinai to provide food for his people.[14]

Certain living creatures are not mentioned at all in the dietary laws of the Torah simply because they were not part of the diet. Dogs, horses, mules, and donkeys were not used as food, whereas certain reptiles, rodents, and insects were. Mary Douglas is correct in stressing the prominence of borderline cases in the formulation of the dietary laws.[15] Certain impure animals could be confused with pure species. Each of the four land animals singled out as being forbidden—the camel, the daman, the hare, and the pig—exhibits one, but not both, of the requisite criteria for purity. Pigs, for example, were raised extensively in the biblical environment, as we now know from archaeological evidence.[16]

Two features predominate in determining an animal's purity or impurity: digestion and locomotion. Ruminants met the criterion of proper digestion. As regards locomotion, paws were considered bestial, whereas the two "toes" common to animals with fully cleft hoofs were not repulsive.

In modern discussions of the dietary laws certain theories have predominated. One is the notion that the dietary laws are based on cultic norms: that what was suitable in the first instance for sacrifices was pure. It would seem, however, that the reverse is true: that sacrificial animals were selected from larger groups of animals and birds already considered to be pure. The generic distinction between pure and impure living creatures may well have antedated the specific laws of sacrifice.

Another notion is that the dietary laws constitute a taboo system. Thus William Robertson Smith, the nineteenth-century student of comparative religion, claimed that impure animals were really sacred creatures to be revered and sacrificed only under unusual and extreme conditions. Israelites were forbidden to use them as food precisely because they were reserved for special cultic utilization.[17] The evidence for this theory is exceedingly questionable, however. Smith calls attention to Ezekiel 8:10–11, where the prophet describes what he saw in a room of the Jerusalem Temple: "I entered and looked, and there all detestable forms of creeping things and beasts and all the fetishes of the House of Israel were depicted over the entire wall. Before them stood seventy men, elders of the House of Israel. . . . Everyone had a censer in his hand, and a thick cloud of incense smoke ascended."

What Ezekiel saw, in fact, was the defilement of the sacrificial cult. Like the fetishes, the depictions of beasts and creeping creatures were features of pagan cults imitated by the heterodox Israelites. If the dietary laws had indeed constituted a taboo, one would have expected the sacrifice of the prohibited living creatures—forbidden as food—to figure in

the priestly system. As an example of a genuine taboo, one may cite the prohibition against eating blood. Blood served several functions in sacrifice and purification, and was strictly reserved for these sacred purposes.[18]

The case of the kid goat (*saʿir*) is also instructive, but in a different way. We know that there was once a cult of goat worship in ancient Israel and in nearby areas, since this reality is referred to in 17:7: "that they may offer their sacrifices no more to the goat-demons (*seʿirim*) after whom they stray." Quite clearly, the ritual of the scapegoat relates to this cult, as does the fact that kid goats are frequently designated as sin offerings.[19] And yet, there is no prohibition against consuming the flesh of goats! What we observe is not a taboo system, in which the "sacred" goat is normally prohibited and reserved for special offerings, but rather a sympathetic magical system, in which the good goat combats the demonic evil goat associated with sinfulness.

On this question of a taboo system, therefore, the dietary laws give no evidence of a pattern wherein prohibited animals were ever revered or offered as sacrifice. Nor is there evidence of the opposite phenomenon, that any animal or bird suitable for sacrifice was ever prohibited as food. In the case of the kid goat, an animal formerly revered was retained as particularly suitable for sin offerings and riddance rituals, such as the dispatch of the scapegoat, but it was considered a pure animal in the diet.

Still another notion characteristic of modern discussions of the dietary laws is the disproportionate amount of attention given to the pig as a prohibited animal. There is no biblical evidence that there was a demonic mythology about the pig, in particular, although we must allow for the possibility that such a theme might have been suppressed. Comparativists point to Egyptian myths in which the pig figures prominently. In the story of Horus and Seth, the antagonist is a pig who wounds Horus. According to Herodotus, the pig was sacrificed in Egypt on the full moon because the moon was identified with Horus.[20]

In Canaan, the pig was simply part of the domestic economy during biblical times. Along with other animals, it was used by the Canaanites for sacrifice. Israelites had to be admonished not to eat it and to regard it as impure. Mesopotamian records often list pigs as sacrificial animals to be delivered to the temples.[21] In Ugaritic literature, *ḥnzr* (Heb. *ḥazzir*), "pig," is the eponym of a clan, in the same way that animals often served as personal names, and still do.[22]

The special attention given by scholars to the pig may be a result of the relatively abundant evidence about it available from comparative sources. It is also likely that since the pig later became a test of loyalty to Judaism, as it was during the Antiochan persecutions of the second century B.C.E., it was anachronistically assumed that in earlier biblical times it also had unique significance as the impure animal par excellence.[23] There is, however, nothing in the dietary codes or in biblical literature to indicate that that was so. Rather, the pig was singled out for mention because it was a borderline case, the only domesticated land animal in the biblical diet that has a fully cleft hoof, yet does not chew its cud.

The dietary laws of the Torah institutionalize the basic distinction between pure and impure living creatures. A practical system of food selection emerges, in which several factors interact. (1) There is a clear preference for domesticated land animals and birds, and this perception may even carry over to fish. (2) Within this larger framework, concern is shown for the diet and digestive processes of living creatures, as if to ensure that nothing forbidden to the Israelites as food had been eaten by the living creatures themselves. If it was, there was concern that such food had been digested as thoroughly as possible or, at the

very least, could be separated from the creature after slaughter. The permitted animals are herbivorous ruminants, whereas virtually all forbidden birds are carnivorous creatures of prey. The torn flesh of a land animal (*terefah*), the evidence of violent preying, is strictly forbidden, just as humans may not eat flesh that they have torn from a living creature. (3) Empirical evidence shows a correlation between methods of locomotion and patterns of feeding and digestion: In most cases, herbivorous ruminants have a cleft hoof. On this basis, creatures with truly cleft hoofs, two "toes," were considered domesticated, thus permitted; living creatures with paws were undoubtedly regarded as bestial and, hence, forbidden. (4) As regards fish, the biblical inventory is extremely limited. Preference for undulatory locomotion with fins probably correlated with observable feeding behavior. Crustaceans, for example, were perceived as scavengers.

Measured against current scientific knowledge, these classifications may appear imprecise and rudimentary, but they undoubtedly reflect the honest observations of ancient man. An equation emerges: Pure creatures are (with respect to the totality of possible diet) to impure creatures as the Israelites are to the other nations. A pure people eats pure creatures in a pure state. A carcass is forbidden because the dead are impure, as we read in Deuteronomy 14:21: "You shall not eat anything that has died a natural death; give it to the stranger in your community to eat, or you may sell it to a foreigner. For you are people consecrated to the LORD your God."

A socioreligious intent clearly underlies the dietary classification system. Ideally, humankind should be sustained by the produce of the earth. When, instead, other living creatures are used as food, as is permitted, such use should be restricted to living creatures that sustain themselves with what grows on the earth and that do not prey on other living creatures or attack man. In eating the substance of other living creatures, care must be taken not to eat their "life," which is to say "their blood." To do so would be a form of murder. The equation of human "life" with the "life" of other living creatures is unmistakable in the postdiluvian dispensation of Genesis, as well as in Ezekiel's condemnation of the Judean exiles. Eating blood is like shedding blood.

The Israelites must adhere to this ideal way of life although other nations do not. Required along with avoidance of improper sexual unions, which would corrupt the family of Israel, and avoidance of pagan worship, which would alienate Israel from God, is the avoidance of unfit food. By such avoidance, Israelites are kept from bestiality; their humaneness is enhanced. Such a pure people deserves to live in its own land, unmolested.

Finally, there have always been those who have sought a hygienic, or health-related, explanation for the dietary selectivity evident in the laws of the Torah. The survival instinct usually affects the acquired feeding habits of human groups. Aversion to certain food sources may, at times, reflect the observation that certain foods were demonstrably unhealthy, especially under particular conditions of preservation and preparation. There is no evidence, however, of a broad nutritional or health-related basis for the specific dietary classifications of the Torah. It is more reasonable to assume a socioreligious basis for them, as has been set forth in this discussion.

EXCURSUS 3

The New Mother (chap. 12)

The provisions of chapter 12 have long been a subject of intense discussion by modern scholars. It is difficult to explain why a new mother, after the awaited event of childbirth, should be considered impure, especially for such extended periods of time. There is also sex differentiation, whereby the birth of a male child obligates the mother to a less extended period of impurity than does the birth of a female.

Recent insights into the meaning of ritual make it possible to place the provisions of chapter 12 in proper perspective. The rituals prescribed in the Torah regularly utilize the category of impurity for dealing with conditions that are life threatening. In ancient usage, "pure" and "impure" correspond to what in modern health care would be referred to as immune and susceptible, respectively. Although the new mother was a source of joy to the community, and her new child a blessing, she generated anxiety—as did all aspects of fertility and reproduction in ancient society. The childbearing mother was particularly vulnerable, and her child was in danger too, since infant mortality was widespread in premodern societies. By declaring the new mother impure, susceptible, the community sought to protect and shelter her.

In ancient times, concern for the welfare of the mother and child was most often expressed as the fear of destructive, demonic, or antilife forces. This fear is evident in other ancient Near Eastern texts contemporaneous with the biblical period; they are replete with incantations and spells against demons and witches who were thought to kill newborn children and afflict their mothers.[1] It is reasonable to assume that similar anxieties were current among the ancient Israelites as well. And although biblical religion certainly did not permit magical spells and the like as the proper means for overcoming these perceived threats to life, it did provide ritual means, as well as practical methods, to accomplish for the Israelite mother and her community what magic was supposed to accomplish for a pagan mother.

Thus, chapter 12 presents a seemingly paradoxical situation: new life but also a new threat to life. Going beyond the protection of mother and child, the legislation also aimed at safeguarding the purity of the sanctuary and the surrounding community from defilement. To this end, the new mother was barred from the sanctuary and from contact with sacred things, out of the apprehension that the antilife forces, which prey upon the newborn and the mother in her state of vulnerability, would be carried with her into the sanctuary. That, in turn, would cause divine displeasure in the same way that it was aroused by any other carrier of "impurity."

In this connection, it is interesting to note the comment of the Sifra on 12:2: "'When a woman at childbirth bears a male.' What are you to conclude from this verse? Since it is stated (Lev. 15:31): 'You shall put the Israelites on guard against [literally] their impurity, lest they die through [literally] their impurity by defiling My Tabernacle which is among them'—I understand that the Tabernacle might be defiled not only from the inside, but also by contact with its outer side. You are to learn therefore: 'She shall not enter the sanctuary.' Only through actual entry into the sanctuary does one defile it." Although this statement seeks to limit the effects of the law, it expresses an awareness on the part of the

rabbis that defilement involved a risk of death through divine wrath. The God of Israel, provoked by the proximity of impurity, punishes the community as a result.

This interpretation may provide a clue to the systematic distinction drawn between male and female children. Ramban tried to rationalize this distinction by referring to notions, current in his day, about bodily emissions. He insisted that the birth of a female caused a mother to sustain discharges for a longer period of time. It is more likely that the doubling of the initial period of impurity and the waiting period for a female had a different basis.

It may have reflected apprehension and anticipation regarding the infant daughter's potential fertility, the expectation that she herself would someday become a new mother.

The regulations governing a new mother may also represent a strong response to the emphasis on fertility in ancient Near Eastern polytheism. By contrast, there could be no place in the Israelite sanctuary for the celebration of birth because such would promote a mythological attitude toward God Himself. We know from the literature of other ancient Near Eastern societies that, within the pagan temples, birth dramas were enacted and myths of birth were recited. Both dramatized the birth of gods and goddesses and their sexual union in celebrations that expressed the human drive for fertility.[2] The biblical restrictions, which excluded the new mother from religious life until she and her child had survived childbirth, created a distance between the event of birth and the worship of God, for God rules over nature and grants the blessing of new life, but He is not, of course, subject to the natural processes of procreation.

EXCURSUS 4
The Scapegoat Ritual (chap. 16)

James Frazer devoted an entire volume of his monumental study of religion and folklore, *The Golden Bough,* to the subject of the scapegoat.[1] He was able to document similar practices in diverse societies all over the world, in many periods of human history. The transfer of sins or other forms of impurity to an animal (or to a person or object) by means of procedures calculated to destroy it or prevent its return clearly reflects the magical objectives of demonology and exorcism. This observation raises a crucial question for our understanding of biblical religion. Is there a place for magic in a monotheistic religion that is based on the proposition that one God rules the universe by His supreme will? In other words, are not magic and monotheism, as understood in biblical theology, mutually exclusive?

Some insight into this question can be gained from a more detailed differentiation of the various kinds of magic. The Torah and the rest of the Bible voice vigorous opposition to almost all forms of divination, to the use of omens and incantations, and to necromancy and sorcery.[2] At the same time, there is no explicit objection to certain forms of therapeutic magic, such as might be employed in the healing process or in protecting against infection and illness. This omission allows us to propose that therapeutic magic may well have been permitted. Nevertheless, afflictions had to be treated by a proper Israelite priest and in the prescribed manner. In fact, the rites of the scapegoat have frequently been compared with those prescribed for the treatment of certain ailments and infections. Thus, an individual afflicted with the symptoms of *tsaraʿat,* a skin disease, was to be purified by means of a

complex ritual involving two birds, one to be slaughtered and the other to be sent forth into the open sky after being dipped in the blood of the first.[3]

The release of the bird, like the dispatch of the scapegoat, expresses the phenomenology of riddance, the elimination of what is to be avoided. Such ritual procedures were accompanied by other measures of a practical nature—quarantine, diagnosis and observation, shaving of body hair, and so forth. All of these measures clearly indicate that a real danger was perceived. Therefore these rites were not merely symbolic but were related to the existence of injurious forces or demons.

Would it be entirely accurate, however, to equate such procedures—in the domain of private ritual and involving illness and infection—with the ritual of the scapegoat, which was part of the public cult and which represented a unique instance of such presumably magical rites in the sanctuary cult?

In the case of the former category, the laws of Leviticus subsume all diseases and infections under the broad category of *tum'ah,* "impurity." The actual *metsora',* one whose skin disease was diagnosed as permanent and who was consequently banished, was declared *tame',* "impure."[4] Hence it would be correct to conclude that at least some forms of impurity were perceived as being dangerous, since both illness and sinfulness were forms of impurity. And in effect most of the "sins" of the priesthood and of the people, those very sins that were to be expiated on Yom Kippur, consisted of violations of the laws of purity. There was, therefore, a common denominator that linked disease and illness to sinfulness. This link is expressed in the concept of *tum'ah,* which bridges the gap between actual illness and ritual impurity. In this sense, one may argue for the magical character of the ritual of the scapegoat and for the claim that sinfulness, when left unexpiated, constituted a real danger. The priestly ideology was thus based on an awareness that, even in a world ruled by God, evil forces were at work—forces that had to be destroyed if God's earthly home, His sanctuary, was not to be defiled.

Another dimension of the ritual of the scapegoat further suggests its magical character: the destination of the scapegoat. In comparing the details of this chapter with the dispatch of a bird in chapter 14, we observe a significant difference. The bird is released into the open sky, carrying with it the impurity of disease, but no specific destination is mentioned. Its dispatch dramatized the fervent wish that illness and infection would never return. By contrast, the scapegoat was driven into the wilderness—to Azazel. As noted in the Comment to verse 8, Azazel is most likely the name of a wilderness demon, a goat-demon, similar to the *se'irim,* "goat-demons," mentioned in 17:7 and once worshiped by Israelites.[5]

The identification of Azazel as the demonic ruler of the wilderness enjoyed some currency in late antiquity. In the apocryphal Book of 1 Enoch 6–13, *'Aza'el* (also written *'Azaz'el*) was one of the deposed angels who had cohabited with human women (as recounted in Genesis 6:1–4), the archangel who was given jurisdiction over sorcery, acts of war, and harlotry—all exemplifications of evil. Cast into the wilderness by the archangel Raphael, Azazel was confined under jagged rocks to live there in darkness until Judgment Day. In this manner, he came to rule the wilderness. Although this myth is a transparent attempt to identify Azazel by utilizing an angelology foreign to the original, priestly conception, it nevertheless points to the image of the wilderness as a place of sinfulness and evil, itself a very ancient belief.[6]

All of the foregoing is relevant to the evident association of he-goats with the theme of sinfulness. Many sin offerings, including the one supplied by the people on Yom Kippur, consisted of he-goats.[7] This association would seem to be predicated on the notion of the

wilderness as the domain of impurity and sinfulness and of the goat as personification of the wilderness (just as the bird is the personification of the sky). The connection between the scapegoat and the cult of *seʿirim* referred to in 17:7 was, in fact, perceived by Ibn Ezra, who, in a cryptic comment on 16:8, stated: "If you are able to understand the mystery of the word 'Azazel' you will comprehend both its mystery and the mystery of its name, for it has analogues in Scripture. And I will disclose to you a bit of the mystery: When you understand thirty-three, you will know it." Now, 17:7, which refers to the ancient cult of the *seʿirim,* is the thirty-third verse after 16:8, where the name Azazel is first mentioned in our chapter.

Ramban provides a lengthy comment on 16:8, in which he elaborates on the legendary identity of Azazel: "There were worshipers of other deities, that is, of the angels, who offered sacrifices to them. . . . But the Torah utterly forbade the acknowledgment of their divinity, or any worship of them. . . . Rather, the Holy One, blessed be He, commanded that on Yom Kippur we dispatch a he-goat into the wilderness to the prince who rules over the areas of destruction. . . . And the intention with respect to the he-goat that is dispatched is not that it be a sacrifice from us to him (i.e., Azazel), God forbid, but rather that our intention be to do the will of our Creator who so commanded us." Ramban was aware of the traditions that portrayed Azazel as an angel or prince (*sar*) who ruled the wilderness. More significant is that he sensed the difficulty posed by the Azazel ritual of Yom Kippur, for he openly acknowledged its affinities to polytheism. His resolution of the problem, though stated somewhat cryptically as "to do the will of our Creator who so commanded us," reveals an understanding of the transformation that had occurred in biblical religion. The dynamics of the ritual, although changed, still retained a real function; and the imagery and associations with the premonotheistic experience of the people were still expressed. To be specific: Chapter 16 mirrors in official Israelite religion the ancient rites forbidden in the law of 17:7! Chapter 16 transforms the sacrificial worship of demons into a set of rites that coerce and subjugate the sinful and evil forces identified with the demon. The High Priest, acting in accordance with the command of the God of Israel, forced the iniquities of the people back on Azazel. When the he-goat returned to the wilderness, a return that the demonic prince of the wilderness was powerless to prevent, a boomerang effect was produced: Evil returned to its point of departure, to the wilderness!

This entire complex of rituals seems to be predicated on magical perceptions. The High Priest subdues Azazel by sending against him another goat—an application of the principle of sympathetic magic, by which similar powers are pitted against each other. The underlying theory is that danger must be countered in kind. The best biblical example of this phenomenology is the utilization of a copper serpent as an antidote to snake bites. In Numbers 21:6–9, we read that the Lord had dispatched snakes to bite the Israelites as a punishment for their lack of faith in Him. To alleviate the suffering of the people, Moses was instructed to mount a copper serpent atop a standard. All who gazed at the copper serpent would be healed of their snake bites, as if, in effect, the good serpent had defeated the evil serpent. At a later period Hezekiah, king of Judah in the late seventh century B.C.E., broke the copper serpent into pieces because it had become a focus of sacrifice, as recounted in 2 Kings 18:4. In chapter 16, similarly, the good goat defeats the evil goat.

The above interpretation of the ritual of the scapegoat is unacceptable to many modern students of the Bible, as it was to certain traditional schools. It is regarded as straining the limits and consistency of the monotheistic idea central to biblical religion and, most assuredly, fundamental to the priestly writings of the Torah. To some, the rites of riddance,

ordained in connection with the scapegoat, were merely symbolic in significance. They were carry-overs from premonotheistic practice that, even prior to their incorporation into the Torah, had already lost their original magical character. According to this view, such rites were retained for their dramatic effect, not because it was actually believed that demonic forces had to be eliminated or subjugated before purification could be achieved.[8]

Whatever its origin or ancient significance, the ritual of the scapegoat continued to function for centuries as an essential component of the Temple cult in Jerusalem. Talmudic sources provide detailed accounts of its enactment on Yom Kippur. To this day, both the biblical and the more elaborate talmudic descriptions remain part of the traditional liturgy of Yom Kippur.[9]

EXCURSUS 5

Family Structures in Biblical Israel (chap. 18)

In order to establish the family structures prevalent among the Israelites it is necessary to compare the provisions of chapters 18 and 20 with other information available to us from the Bible. Some of the regulations governing marriage, as set forth in chapter 18, contradict what we know about the marriages of the patriarchs, the clan of Moses, and the Judean royal family in the generation of David.[1]

The major differences are the following: All Torah legislation forbids marriage with half sisters. This is explicitly stated in Leviticus 18:9 and 20:17 and in Deuteronomy 27:22. Yet, according to Genesis 20:12, Abram claimed that Sarai, his wife, was his half sister—his father's daughter from another wife. In 2 Samuel 13:13 we read of Tamar's appeal to her half brother, Amnon, not to rape her. She insists that David, their father, would not deny her to him as a wife, perhaps indicating that a father might have permitted such a marriage at certain periods of biblical history. In effect, the above biblical sources know of no prohibition against marriage with half sisters of the same father.

Both Leviticus 18:12–14 and 20:19–20 forbid marriage with any of a man's three possible aunts. Yet Exodus 6:20 records, as part of a priestly genealogy, that Amram married his aunt Jochebed, who bore him Moses and Aaron.

Finally, Leviticus 18:18 forbids marriage to the sister of one's wife while that wife is alive. Yet Genesis 29:21–30 relates that Jacob married Leah and Rachel, who were sisters.[2]

It is likely, therefore, that the rules governing incest underwent considerable development. In the earlier periods of Israelite history it was permissible to marry a half sister with whom one shared a common father. (There is no explicit evidence to allow for marriage with a half sister from the same mother.) Similarly, one must conclude that the prohibition against marriage with a woman and her sisters is a later development, as is the injunction against marrying aunts (at least of the kind Jochebed was to Amram). Absent from the Torah legislation is any prohibition against marrying cousins; indeed, marriage between patrilineal cousins or between a man and the daughter of his patrilineal cousin was a preferred arrangement. Rebekah was the granddaughter of Isaac's uncle, Nahor, according to Genesis 22:22–23 and 24:24. Jacob's relationship to Laban, his father-in-law (and, of course, to his wives) was even more complex: Laban was Jacob's patrilineal relative, descended from Nahor, but he was also a matrilineal relative—the brother of Jacob's mother, Rebekah. Marriages with cousins and their children within the patrilineal clan

produced other such cross-generational situations as well. Genesis 28:9 recounts that Esau, in an effort to please his father, Isaac, married his uncle Ishmael's daughter, Mahalath, in other words, his patrilineal first cousin. According to 2 Chronicles 11:20, King Rehoboam of Judah married Maacah, the daughter of his paternal uncle Absalom, again, a first cousin.

Marriages within the extended clan, called the *mishpaḥah,* were encouraged, and there was a tendency toward endogamy, that is, marrying within one's own group. Such marriages helped to insure the retention of the ancestral estate within the clan. This explains the dispensation to marry the widow of one's brother, stated in Deuteronomy 25:5–10, in cases where the deceased brother had left no male heir. The heir produced by levirate marriage would carry on the estate. The story of Ruth illustrates the desirability of finding a man of the same clan. Such a one, in marrying the widow of his deceased relative, would then redeem the estate of a deceased relative and keep it within the clan. The episode of Zelophehad's daughters, in Numbers 36, also indicates the importance of keeping an inheritance within the same clan. Because there were no sons, these daughters were granted the right to inherit their father's estate but were required to marry men of their father's clan. Since the estate would come into the possession of their husbands upon marriage, it was imperative that they not marry outside the clan.[3]

Although all of these complex cases differ from each other in important respects, they have in common the perception that desirable marriages are those that keep the patrilineage intact down through the generations. Seen in the context of a society that was organized according to patrilineal clans that owned the land, the incest laws of the Torah can be understood as an attempt to prevent too much inbreeding within families that were otherwise bound together as socioeconomic units. The laws of ancient Israel kept certain channels open, while shutting others.

The prohibition of incest reflects the almost universal, natural feelings of a person toward those with whom he has been reared and toward those with whom his closest relatives have had sexual relations. What is perhaps most significant is that by their negations, the Torah laws provide a definition of the nuclear family. The sum of this data is tabulated and displayed in two charts (p. 255). In these charts the male head of the family, the individual addressed in the laws and commandments, is designated "EGO." His relationships to other members of the family are indicated by dotted lines, leading from him to his relatives. Arrows indicate how the prohibitions based on "flesh" relationships and affinal relationships were generated.

FIGURE 1: PROHIBITIONS GENERATED BY "FLESH" RELATIVES

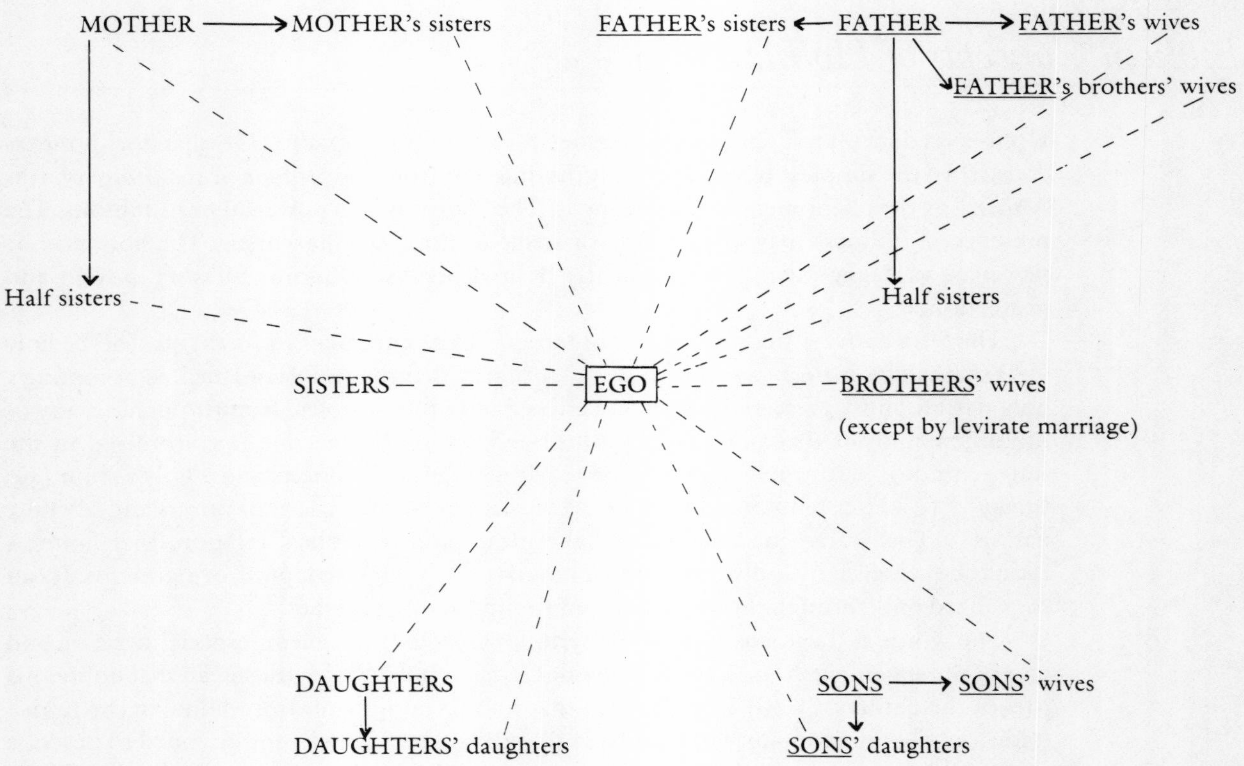

FIGURE 2: PROHIBITIONS OF MARRIAGE GENERATED BY THE AFFINAL RELATIONSHIP BETWEEN A MAN AND HIS WIFE

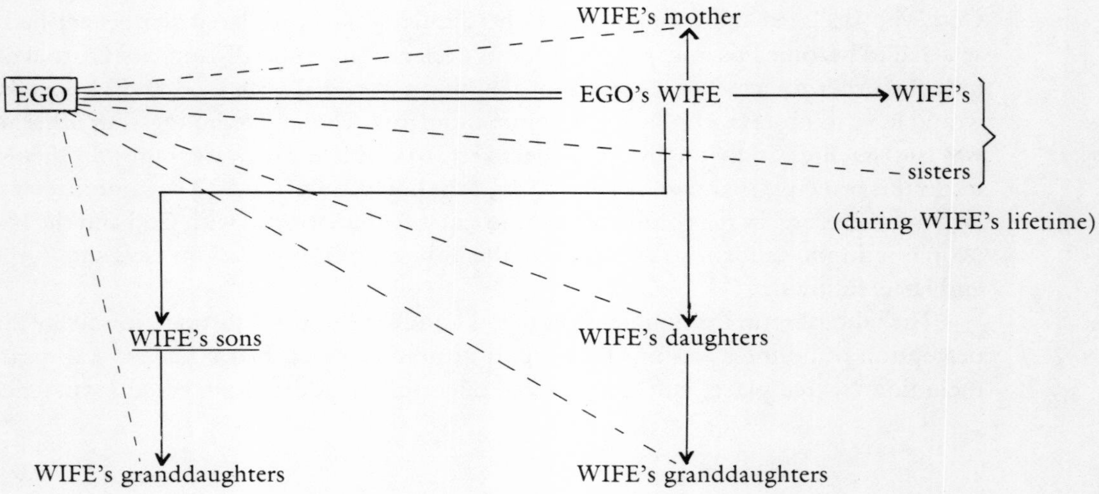

EXCURSUS 6

Biblical Concepts of Holiness (chap. 19)

Holiness is difficult to define or to describe; it is a mysterious quality. Of what does holiness consist? In the simplest terms, the "holy" is different from the profane or the ordinary. It is "other," as the phenomenologists define it. The "holy" is also powerful or numinous. The presence of holiness may inspire awe, or strike fear, evoke amazement. The holy may be perceived as dangerous, yet it is urgently desired because it affords blessing, power, and protection.

The Sifra conveys the concept of "otherness" in its comment to 19:2: You shall be holy—"You shall be *distinct (perushim tiheyu),*" meaning that the people of Israel, in becoming a holy nation, must preserve its distinctiveness from other peoples. It must pursue a way of life different from that practiced by other peoples. This objective is epitomized in the statement of Exodus 19:6: "you shall be to Me a kingdom of priests and a holy nation (*goy kadosh*)." (A better rendering might be: "You shall be My Kingdom of priests and My holy nation.") This statement also conveys the idea, basic to biblical religion, that holiness cannot be achieved by individuals alone, no matter how elevated, pure, or righteous. It can be realized only through the life of the community, acting together.

The words of Leviticus 19:2 pose a serious theological problem, especially the second part of the statement: "For I, the LORD your God, am holy." Does this mean that holiness is part of the nature of God? Does it mean that holiness originates from Him? In the Jewish tradition, the predominant view has been that this statement was not intended to describe God's essential nature, but, rather, His manifest, or "active," attributes. To say that God is "holy" is similar to saying that He is great, powerful, merciful, just, wise, and so forth. These attributes are associated with God on the basis of His observable actions: the ways in which He relates to man and to the universe. The statement that God is holy means, in effect, that He acts in holy ways: He is just and righteous. Although this interpretation derives from later Jewish tradition, it seems to approximate both the priestly and the prophetic biblical conceptions of holiness.[1]

In biblical literature there is a curious interaction between the human and the divine with respect to holiness. Thus, in Exodus 20:8, the Israelites are commanded to sanctify the Sabbath and to make it holy; and yet verse 11 of the same commandment states that it was God who declared the Sabbath day holy. Similarly, God declared that Israel had been selected to become His holy people; but this declaration was hardly sufficient to make Israel holy. In order to achieve a holiness of the kind associated with God and His acts, Israel would have to observe His laws and commandments. The way to holiness, in other words, was for Israelites, individually and collectively, to emulate God's attributes. In theological terms this principle is known as *imitatio dei,* "the imitation of God." The same interaction is evident, therefore, in the commandment to sanctify the Sabbath, with God and the Israelite people acting in tandem so as to realize the holiness of this occasion. God shows the way and Israel follows.

The biblical term for holiness is ***kodesh.*** Though the noun is abstract, it is likely that the perception of holiness was not thoroughly abstract. In fact, ***kodesh*** had several meanings, including "sacred place, sanctuary, sacred offering." In addition, in certain syntactic posi-

tions, Hebrew nouns function as adjectives. Hebrew *shem kodsho,* for example, does not mean "the name of His holiness" but, rather, "His holy name." This leads to the conclusion that in the biblical conception holiness is not so much an idea as it is a quality, identified both with what is real and perceptible on earth and with God. Indeed, the only context in which a somewhat abstract notion of "holiness" is expressed relates to God's holiness. God is said to swear by His holiness, just as He swears by His life, His faithfulness, and His power. When speaking of God, it is recognized that holiness is inextricable from His Being; it is a constant, divine attribute.

The overall content of chapter 19, with its diverse categories of laws and commandments, outlines what the Israelites must do in order to become a holy people. It includes many matters of religious concern, as we understand the term: proper worship, observance of the Sabbath, and also the avoidance of actions that are taboo, such as mixed planting and consumption of fruit from trees during the first three years after planting. What is less expected in ritual legislation is the emphasis on human relations: respect for parents, concern for the poor and the stranger, prompt payment of wages, justice in all dealings, and honest conduct of business. Even proper attitudes toward others are commanded.

In this latter respect, chapter 19 accords with prophetic attitudes indicating that the priesthood was highly receptive to the social message of the Israelite prophets. Holiness, an essentially cultic concept, could not be achieved through purity and proper worship alone; it had an important place in the realm of societal experience. Like the Ten Commandments and other major statements on the duties of man toward God, this chapter exemplifies the heightened ethical concern characteristic of ancient Israel.

Holiness, as a quality, knows no boundaries of religion or culture. Very often, the reactions it generates are perceived by all, regardless of what they believe. Similarly, places and objects as well as persons considered to be holy by one group may be perceived in the same way by those of other groups. There is something generic about holiness, because all humans share many of the same hopes and fears, and the need for health and well-being. A site regarded as holy by pagans might continue to be regarded as such by monotheists; indeed, some of the most important sacred sites in ancient Israel are known to have had a prior history of sanctity in Canaanite times, although the Bible ignores the pagan antecedents and explains their holiness solely in terms of Israelite history and belief.[2]

Despite many differences between Israelite monotheism and the other religions of the ancient Near East, the processes through which holiness was attributed to persons, places, objects, and special times did not differ fundamentally. Through ritual, prayer, and formal declaration sanctification took effect. In biblical Hebrew, these processes are usually expressed by forms of the verb *k-d-sh,* especially the Piel stem *kiddesh,* "to devote, sanctify, declare holy."

The gulf between the sacred and the profane was not meant to be permanent. The command to achieve holiness, to become holy, envisions a time when life would be consecrated in its fullness and when all nations would worship God in holiness. What began as a process of separating the sacred from the profane was to end as the unification of human experience, the harmonizing of man with his universe, and of man with God.

EXCURSUS 7

The Cult of Molech in Biblical Israel (chap. 20)

Few subjects have aroused as much controversy among biblical scholars and historians of ancient religions as the references in the Hebrew Bible to the cult of Molech (Moloch). This is attributable to a number of factors. First of all, there is abundant evidence for the practice of child sacrifice; and much of it has been known to modern scholars for quite some time, both from the writings of ancient historians and from archaeological excavations at such sites as Carthage. In recent years, renewed work at Carthage and other sites of the western, Punic commercial empire, such as Sardinia, have added significantly to the cumulative evidence available on child sacrifice in antiquity.

Then, too, the subject of child sacrifice, and of human sacrifice generally, is intrinsically provocative. References to the cult of Molech in the Hebrew Bible raise the specter of cruel religious practices among the Israelites, practices abhorrent to the biblical way of life. Some assume an apologetic posture in claiming that such practices were not actually extant at all. By way of contrast, others make overly harsh assessments as to the extent of child sacrifice. Neither point of view is accurate.[1]

The first reference to the cult of Molech in the Torah occurs in Leviticus 18:21, and it is soon followed by the statements in 20:1–5. The verbs used in these statements, *natan,* "to give, devote," and *heʿevir,* "to hand over," do not inform us precisely how Molech worship was carried out. Deuteronomy 18:10, however, forbids one to sacrifice children by literally "passing" them through fire (*maʿavir . . . ba-ʾesh*). This idiom is also used in the most explicit historical reference to the cult of Molech in the Bible, namely, 2 Kings 23:10. That passage recounts the actions of King Josiah of Judah, who, in his zeal for the purification of the Israelite cult, attempted to put an end to child sacrifice: "He also defiled Topheth, which is in the Valley of Ben-hinnom, so that no one might consign his son or daughter to the fire of Molech."

It is quite clear that Deuteronomy 18:10 refers to the same phenomenon, notwithstanding the absence of specific reference to Molech. In 2 Kings 16:3, we read that King Ahaz of Judah (living about a century earlier than Josiah) burned (*saraf*) his own son in fire, in imitation of the abominations of the gentiles. The same verb, *saraf,* is used in Deuteronomy 12:31 in reference to the abominations of other nations.

Mention of the pagan cult site called Topheth, located in the environs of Jerusalem, recalls Isaiah 30:33, which is part of an oracle predicting the utter defeat of Israel's enemies. The prophet pictures the destruction of the enemy in a firepit, in the same way that human sacrifices were consumed in the fire of Topheth: "The Topheth has long been ready for him;/ He, too, is destined for *Molech*—/ His firepit has been made both wide and deep. . . ."[2]

The two idioms *heʿevir ba-ʾesh* and *saraf ba-ʾesh* are virtually equivalent in meaning, as has been demonstrated by Morton Smith. They both mean "to burn in fire." This is proved by Numbers 31:22–23, the only passage in the Bible, in fact, where "passing through fire" does not refer to human sacrifice! There we read that spoils of war had to be purified before they could be used by the Israelites: "Gold and silver, copper, iron, tin, and lead—any article that can withstand fire—these you shall pass through fire and they shall be pure . . . and anything that cannot withstand fire you must pass through water." This statement

demonstrates that when something was "passed through" (*heʿevir be-*) it was submerged, or immersed, in either fire or water, as the case may be.[3] Now, it is true that metals could be removed from the fire after they had been purified, whereas the children "passed through" fire could not. Ezekiel 23:37–39 is particularly instructive regarding idiom and usage; as the following translation demonstrates: "And their sons which they bore Me they have given over to be consumed (*heʿeviru le-ʾokhlah*). . . . On the very day that they came to My temple, they slaughtered their children to their abominations."

It has been necessary to dwell at length on the specific language used in the various biblical statements on the cult of Molech in order to make an important point. The ambiguity of such verbs as *natan,* "to offer, devote," and *heʿevir,* "to hand over, pass through," cannot be construed to mean that child sacrifice was *not* the target of the Levitical prohibitions of chapters 18 and 20. Historically, the denunciations of human sacrifice by the prophets Jeremiah and Ezekiel may, in the spirit of tirade, have overstated the extent of the cult of Molech; but these prophets hardly invented the fact of royal sponsorship of this cult during the reign of Manasseh and Amon, kings of Judah, who ruled in the seventh century B.C.E., just prior to Josiah. On the other hand, we don't know how to evaluate the reference in 2 Kings 16:3 to such practices on the part of Ahaz, king of Judah, in the eighth century B.C.E., since there is no other evidence of the cult of Molech at that period, at least not in Judah. It is possible that it existed in the northern Israelite kingdom at that time.

In order to shed light on the history of the cult of Molech in biblical times we must, first of all, understand the phenomenon in religious terms. Did some Israelites believe that the God of Israel desired the sacrifice of children? Was the cult of Molech their way of worshiping the God of Israel? Or, were the injunctions against child sacrifice instead really part of the prohibition of pagan worship—of idolatry and the worship of other gods? Some, pointing to Deuteronomy 12:21, argue that Israelites and their kings had to be admonished against worshiping the God of Israel in such abhorrent ways. The same may be suggested by Micah 6:6–7: "With what shall I approach the LORD . . ./ Shall I approach him with burnt offerings . . ./ Shall I give my first-born for my transgression,/ The fruit of my body for my sins?" The story of the binding of Isaac, in Genesis 22, could be taken in the same way. God's demand for the sacrifice of Abraham's son, as a test of obedience and faith, is incomprehensible unless Abraham is presumed to have thought that God might desire such a sacrifice. When, however, God Himself provides a ram as a substitute, the point is unequivocal that Abraham's initial perception was wrong.

Certainly, child sacrifice was part of the ethos in ancient Canaan, to be used in extreme circumstances. For example, 2 Kings 3:27 relates that a Moabite king sacrificed his son and successor in the heat of battle and was subsequently granted victory. The story of Jephthah's daughter, recounted in Judges 11, is admittedly cryptic, but it, too, implies that Jephthah eventually sacrificed his daughter in fulfillment of a vow, again in the context of military victory. The curse pronounced in Joshua 6:26 against anyone who would rebuild Jericho—that it would be at the cost of his sons' lives—is reminiscent of similar execrations known from elsewhere in Near Eastern literature. This curse, fulfilled in 1 Kings 16:34, recalls one of the oldest forms of human sacrifice, the foundation burial. Usually, a child was buried in the foundation of a newly built or restored city to assure its future prosperity. And so, a case could be made that Israelites perceived child sacrifice as a valid way of worshiping the God of Israel and that prohibitions and denunciations of it were intended to correct that mistaken notion.

It is more likely, however, that the Torah laws, and biblical statements generally, are aimed at the worship of other gods rather than at religious syncretism, which is the blending of religious rites of diverse origins in a ritual composite. The God of Israel was the only deity to be worshiped, and no others were to be worshiped alongside Him! The situation under attack is described in 2 Kings 17:41. The foreigners who settled in Samaria after its fall at the hands of the Assyrians in 722 B.C.E. are characterized as follows: "Those nations worshiped the LORD, but they also served their idols. To this day their children and their children's children do as their ancestors did." This is the very thing said of the Sepharvites, one of the deported peoples, some verses earlier: "and the Sepharvites burned their children [as offerings] to Adrammelekh and Anammelekh, the gods of Sepharvaim." These Sepharvites most likely came from a locality in Syria, in the vicinity of Hamath. They were known to burn their children as offerings to gods whose names included *melekh*, "king," as a component, such as Adrammelekh, which is a misspelling of Addadmelekh, "Addad-is-King!"

It has been suggested, given the clear reference to the burning of children in Syria in the late eighth century B.C.E., that the cult of Molech described in biblical literature and condemned in the law codes of the Torah was linked historically to the Syro-Assyrian cults that flourished among the Arameans of Syria during a good part of the monarchic period in biblical Israel. Like Syrian art and architecture, Syrian religious practices, including the burning of children, may have been imitated by the kings of Israel and Judah. This historical reconstruction would support the conclusion that the name Molech is a conscious misvocalization of *melekh*, "king," intended to convey antipathy.[4]

Although this reconstruction accords with the times and places reflected in the biblical references to the cult of Molech, it does not exhaust the historical possibilities. It is, of course, more persuasive than the traditional attribution of this cult to ancient Phoenicia. But two other factors should be taken into account. It is likely that more than one cult in the ancient Near East included the burning and sacrificing of children. Then, too, gods with the same names may have been worshiped in different ways, in different places, and at different times. Recently attention has been drawn to Egyptian reliefs from the period of the New Kingdom that depict children being burned and hurled from the walls of besieged cities in Syria and Canaan. An attempt has been made to correlate these reliefs with Ugaritic literary descriptions of sacrifice that date from about the same period; this would suggest that the Ugaritic texts are actually describing the burning or killing of children. This correlation is highly questionable, however, and it is more likely that the Ugaritic texts in question are describing the sacrifice of animals and other usual foodstuffs.[5] So, we lack clear evidence of this cult at Ugarit.

In conclusion, then, definitive judgments concerning the extent of the cult of Molech in biblical Israel will have to await further evidence. For now, it can be reliably stated that this cult was sponsored by Manasseh and Amon, kings of Judah during the seventh century B.C.E., and that it involved the burning of children as sacrifices. How long these practices persisted and how widespread they were are not presently known.

EXCURSUS 8

The Development of the Biblical Festivals (chap. 23)

The Sabbath and the annual festivals have played a major role in the religious civilization of the Jewish people since antiquity. They were a factor in defining the social structure of Israelite society in biblical times and, in later centuries, in determining the organization of the dispersed Jewish communities that flourished around the world. The Sabbath and festivals have served to foster close family ties and provide meaningful religious experience. These occasions are the *sancta,* the religious celebrations that lend to any community its distinctive character and that reinforce its sense of unity and common purpose. They keep the memory of the past alive and enhance the awareness of a common destiny.

The first general observation to be made about religious festivals is that everything about them is significant—including the names by which they are called, the dates scheduled for their observance, and the manner of their celebration. All of these aspects underwent change in ancient Israel, and various biblical sources offer differing conceptions of the Sabbath and festivals, reflecting differences of time and place. The religious worshiper tends to accept traditional forms as they have come down from the past. The historian of religions, on the other hand, must insist on discovering, to the extent possible, how these forms have changed.

The Sabbath

So far as is currently known, the Sabbath is an original Israelite institution. The proposed identification of the biblical Sabbath with other ancient Near Eastern sacred days, such as the Mesopotamian *shapattu,* a day associated with the phases of the moon, is highly doubtful. To the contrary, the biblical Sabbath has nothing to do with the lunar cycle. It has been shown that the division of time into regular weeks that end in the Sabbath day represents a departure from the system of lunar "months" that predominated in the ancient Near East.[1] The Sabbath is to be seen as innovative, even within Israelite society itself.

The Sabbath is attested outside of Torah literature in fairly early biblical texts, although it seems to have gained in importance late in the seventh century B.C.E., during the period preceding the Babylonian exile. It is mentioned by the prophets Isaiah (1:13) and Amos (5:8) in the eighth century B.C.E. Hosea's reference to the Sabbath (2:13) is even more significant historically because the first three chapters of Hosea may date from the ninth century B.C.E.[2]

The commandment to observe the Sabbath by desisting from *mela'khah,* "assigned tasks," is found in the oldest collection of laws in the Torah, the Book of the Covenant, in Exodus 23:12. Both versions of the Decalogue, in Exodus 20:5f. and in Deuteronomy 5:12f., also command this observance, and it is emphasized repeatedly in priestly laws. As is true of all sacred days, observance of the Sabbath incorporated both cultic and more personal dimensions. In the sanctuary (or sanctuaries) priests celebrated the Sabbath with sacrifice and prayer, attended by the populace; and in the Israelite settlements and towns, the family observed the day by rejoicing and desisting from daily work.

The particular formulation of the Sabbath law in Leviticus 23 most closely resembles that of Exodus 31:12–17 and 35:1–3, as noted in the Commentary. All of these priestly

statements seem to be modeled, in turn, after the Exodus version of the Decalogue, the most emphatic affirmation of the aspect of sanctity. The Deuteronomic version of the Decalogue, while stating, of course, that the Sabbath is to be observed as a sacred occasion, stresses the ethical aspects of the Sabbath as a day of rest from labor. Consequently, rather than regarding the Sabbath as a reminder that the Creator had rested on the Sabbath of Creation, Deuteronomy links Sabbath rest to the Exodus: Sabbath rest is the expression of freedom and the negation of bondage.[3] The emphasis on sanctity, to be expected in priestly legislation, is epitomized in the term ***mikra' kodesh,*** "a sacred assembly," a term that probably originates in the Holiness Code (Lev. 17–26). It occurs no fewer than ten times in chapter 23, in various connections. Even the term ***shabbaton,*** also an innovation of priestly literature, echoes this theme. Sacred occasions are "Sabbath-like," and the characteristics of the Sabbath day serve as a paradigm for the festivals, as well.

The provisions of chapter 23 and of the Holiness Code, generally, with their strong emphasis on sanctity, seem to correlate with Jeremiah 17, Ezekiel 20 and 22, and the words of the exilic prophet—Deutero-Isaiah—on the subject of the Sabbath's holiness.[4] In Ezekiel 44:24 and 46:1–11 we read that the future prince of the restored Israelites will officiate at special rites in the Temple of Jerusalem on the Sabbath day. In the late fifth century B.C.E., Nehemiah, leader of the restored community, expresses concern over the proper observance of the Sabbath as a sacred day in Jerusalem and its environs.[5] No doubt the cruel experience of the exile made it more difficult, yet more vital than ever, to observe the Sabbath.

The primary regulation governing the Sabbath is the prohibition of ***mela'khah,*** "assigned tasks." Exodus 35:3 expressly forbids use of fire; and the gathering of wood for that purpose is presupposed as forbidden in the narrative of Numbers 15:32f. From Exodus 16:5f., a narrative about the manna, which served the Israelites as food in the Sinai wilderness, we may infer that the gathering of food as well as cooking and baking were forbidden on the Sabbath day. Jeremiah (17:21) objected to transporting goods outside one's house, which may represent his understanding of the Decalogue's rule against using work animals on the Sabbath.[6] These regulations further correlate with the admonitions of the exilic prophet, in Isaiah 58:13, against pursuing one's affairs on the Sabbath day.

The elaborate laws governing forbidden tasks, characteristic of later Judaism, developed through the hermeneutic interpretation of biblical pronouncements. They also relate to the Temple cult, in that those tasks necessary for the performance of the cult—carried out even on the Sabbath—became a model for defining the very tasks generally forbidden to Israelites. For example, slaughter, prerequisite to the act of sacrifice, is forbidden on the Sabbath.[7]

Just as festivals are occasions for rejoicing, so is the Sabbath. Special sacrifices were offered in celebration.[8] Each Sabbath the bread of display (*leḥem ha-panim*) was set before God in the sanctuary, to be left until the following Sabbath.[9] From 2 Kings 16:18 we learn that during the period of the Judean monarchy, kings had a role in the celebration of the Sabbath in the Temple of Jerusalem. Ahaz, who reigned in the eighth century B.C.E., installed a passageway leading from his palace to the Temple, so that he could enter it conveniently on the Sabbath. From 2 Kings 11:5–7 we learn that priestly tours of duty lasted from one Sabbath to the next.[10]

Psalm 92, entitled "A psalm. A song; for the sabbath day," speaks of praising God with music and of proclaiming His sovereignty. The emphasis on God the Creator echoes the Exodus version of the Decalogue, whereas in the victory of righteousness over wickedness,

where God is the triumphant warrior, we hear an echo of the Exodus saga, the liberation from Egypt.[11]

The exilic author of Isaiah 66:23 foresees a time when all the peoples of the earth will worship the God of Israel in the Temple of Jerusalem, on Sabbaths and New Moons.

The Annual Festivals

A reconstruction of the development of the biblical festivals has by and large eluded modern scholarship primarily because the priestly laws of the Torah, which provide most of the detailed information on festival observance, cannot be dated precisely. Put differently, we are not certain of the chronological relationship of the Torah and its laws to the historical books of the Bible and the writings of the prophets.

In particular, there has been uncertainty about the origin and date of Deuteronomy in relation to the priestly laws of Exodus, Leviticus, and Numbers. Deuteronomy is pivotal because its provisions call for a basic change in religious celebration. The three annual festivals are called *ḥag,* "pilgrimage," in the earliest laws of the Torah, preserved in Exodus 23:15f. This meant that an Israelite wishing to celebrate the festival fully was obliged to undertake a pilgrimage to a cult center or to a temple. According to the early law of Exodus 20:24, God may be worshiped at any properly constructed altar at which worship is conducted in the correct manner. There were cult centers throughout the Land of Israel suitable for such festival celebrations.

Deuteronomy 12 and 16 invalidate this pattern. All sacrifices, including, of course, those for festival celebrations, were to be carried out at one, unique, central Temple, to be designated by God. In practical terms, this meant that the duty of pilgrimage could no longer be fulfilled at local and regional cult centers, but exclusively at the central Temple. As we shall see, this restriction altered the character of the annual festivals in basic ways, affecting their scheduling, duration, and manner of observance.

In a recent study, H. L. Ginsberg has shed new light on the origins and promulgation of the Deuteronomic doctrine of a centralized cult and its effects on Israelite religion and later Judaism. He traces the derivation of the core of Deuteronomy, where the new legislation is found, and addresses the question of whether or not the priestly laws of the Torah reflect Deuteronomic teachings.[12]

In Ginsberg's view, the core of Deuteronomy comes from the northern kingdom of Israel and was first formulated in the mid to late eighth century B.C.E. The original intent of Deuteronomy was to advocate the establishment of a new, central Temple in northern Israel, where all proper worship of the God of Israel would be centralized. This doctrine was a response to the heterodoxy rampant at the time and is presaged by Hosea, who finally conceded that not only were the smaller, local shrines of northern Israel abominable, but even Bethel, as well.

After the downfall of northern Israel, annexed by the Assyrians in 722 B.C.E., the core of the Book of Deuteronomy found its way to Jerusalem. It was the Deuteronomic doctrine that impelled Hezekiah, king of Judea, to attempt the centralization of the cult. That attempt failed for a number of reasons, since Hezekiah's reign was followed by the long reign of the heterodox king, Manasseh. The doctrine of cult centralization survived underground, kept alive in certain circles. When Josiah, a young monarch instructed by devout priests, ascended the Judean throne, he revived the idea of purging the cult of its heter-

odoxy by limiting sacrificial worship to the Temple of Jerusalem. He may have learned this doctrine from a version of Deuteronomy found in the Temple. Thus, Hezekiah and Josiah effectively translated the Deuteronomic idea of a central temple, perhaps intended originally to be located on Mount Gerizim in Shechem, into the doctrine that the Temple of Jerusalem was that central Temple, the exclusive site of proper worship.

Ginsberg compares and contrasts the earliest pre-Deuteronomic laws on the celebration of the festivals with the priestly laws of Leviticus and Numbers. In the earliest laws preserved in Exodus 21–23, we find the following information: three festivals are called *ḥag,* "pilgrimage": (1) *matsot,* the festival of unleavened bread, (2) *katsir,* "reaping," a spring harvest festival, and (3) *'asif,* "ingathering," an autumn festival.

The pilgrimage festival of *matsot,* "unleavened bread," precedes the ripening of the grain in the spring of the year. By its very nature it is an historical commemoration, not an agricultural festival at all, as is stated in Exodus 23:15: "You shall observe the Feast of Unleavened Bread—eating unleavened bread for seven days as I have commanded you—at the advent of the new moon of the season of soft-seeded grain ears. For it was then that you went forth from Egypt; and none shall appear before Me empty-handed." To explain the translation, it should be realized that the Hebrew word *ḥodesh,* which is the normal term for "month," is taken here to mean the "new moon." In this verse, the clause "as I have commanded you" refers to Exodus 13:4–9, which contains the same essential provisions, except that it specifies the exact time of the pilgrimage itself. The pilgrimage is to take place on the seventh day after the New Moon, as a finale to the festival celebration.[13]

According to Exodus 12:21–28, the paschal sacrifice that initiates the festival is to be offered by Israelite families near their homes. They are to slaughter sheep or goats and smear some of the blood on the lintels and doorposts of their homes. This rite is to be performed sometime in the evening, and no person is to leave his house subsequent to it, until morning.

Exodus 23:18 states the primary relationship between the *matsot* festival and the paschal sacrifice: "You shall not offer the blood of My sacrifice with anything leavened." This means, in effect, that the festival opens with the paschal sacrifice, at which time the prohibition against eating leaven also begins.

Exodus 12:1–20, a priestly passage that may contain ancient material, ordains that the paschal sacrifice be roasted whole over an open fire, with no bones broken and no sectioning of the animal. This differed from the practice in altar sacrifices. In fact, no altar was used at all. Bitter herbs were to be eaten together with *matsot.* The sacrifice was to be offered in the early evening (*bein ha-ʿarbayim*).

The two agricultural pilgrimage festivals were *katsir,* "reaping," and *'asif,* "ingathering." The year was perceived as being divided into two primary seasons, *dagan,* "grain," and *tirosh,* "wine" (sometimes *yitshar,* "oil").[14] Thus, we read in Exodus 23:16f., in the continuation of the early festival law: "And the Pilgrimage Feast of the Harvest, of the first fruits of your work, of what you sow in the field; and the Pilgrimage Feast of the Ingathering, at the outset of the year, when you gather in the results of your work from the field." No date is given for the spring grain harvest festival, although it was clearly intended to celebrate the reaping of barley, the first grain of the spring. The autumn festival was scheduled for "the outset of the year." Its time can be fixed on the basis of the ancient Gezer calendar, in which the agricultural year began in autumn. That calendar mentions a two-month-long season called *'asif,* "ingathering," the same as the name of the festival. We can fix the season of autumn ingathering as Tishrei-Heshvan, our September-October. Work-

ing ahead in time from autumn to spring, we can fix "the month of reaping (*yrḥ qtsr* in the Gezer calendar) as Iyyar, our month of May. Most likely, each farmer would present his first fruits on a date of his own choosing. The pilgrimage festival called *'asif* occurred, therefore, at the outset of this two-month period. One might have expected it to fall on the New Moon of Tishrei, but we are informed that the actual pilgrimage was to occur at the full moon, at the middle of the month.[15]

To summarize what we know of the three pilgrimage festivals, based on laws that clearly antedate Deuteronomy, we can state the following: (1) The *matsot* festival began on the New Moon of the month just preceding the hardening of the barley (Nisan-April). It lasted seven days, and on the seventh day the pilgrimage took place. A sacrifice was to be offered outside one's home on the eve of the first day of the festival. *Matsot* were to be eaten and leaven avoided for all seven days. (2) The barley harvest festival (*katsir*) occurred when reaping started, at the beginning of the month of reaping, namely, sometime near the beginning of Iyyar-May. The pilgrimage lasted one day. (3) The festival of ingathering (*'asif*) occurred on the full moon of the former two-month season of the month of ingathering (Tishrei-September). The pilgrimage lasted one day.

Ginsberg in his analysis then addresses the question of how Deuteronomy's doctrine of cult centralization altered this system. A careful reading of Deuteronomy 16 reveals that, first of all, the spring barley harvest festival was deferred seven weeks and its name was changed from *ḥag ha-katsir,* "the Pilgrimage Festival of Reaping," to *ḥag shavu'ot,* "a Pilgrimage Festival of Weeks." This occasion could no longer appropriately be called *katsir* because it was not to be celebrated at the beginning of the grain harvest.

The reason for the postponement was practical. When pilgrimage had been only a short trip to a nearby cult center a farmer could manage the brief absence from his fields at the beginning of the grain harvest. Once a longer journey to a central Temple was involved, leaving the fields became virtually impossible; the spring harvest festival was necessarily postponed. One counted seven weeks from "when the sickle is first put to the standing grain" (Deut. 16:9) and then celebrated the pilgrimage festival—at a time when absence from the fields was possible.

Deuteronomy deals in much the same way with the Festival of Ingathering. In Deuteronomy 16:13–17 we read of a seven-day pilgrimage festival. It is not called *'asif,* "ingathering," but rather *ḥag ha-sukkot,* "the Pilgrimage Festival of Booths." No longer celebrated when produce was first brought in from the field, it was delayed until after the produce had been processed on the threshing floor and the vat. Once the spring harvest festival had been postponed for practical reasons, it became necessary to postpone the autumn pilgrimage as well, so that they would not occur in too close a succession. We do not have the precise date during the year of the Deuteronomic Sukkot festival, but its new name is readily understandable. Once the festival was extended to seven days to be celebrated in the religious capital, it became necessary to provide temporary housing for pilgrims in and around the city. Huts were erected for this purpose. Nehemiah 8:13–18 provides a description of such a Sukkot celebration in postexilic times.

The most thorny problem created by Deuteronomy's restriction of sacrificial worship to one central Temple concerned the paschal offering and the *matsot* festival. The paschal sacrifice could no longer be offered near one's home. Not only rescheduling, but restructuring the entire celebration was called for. Israelites would have to arrive at the religious capital before the eve of the *matsot* festival and then remain there, in most cases, until the seventh day of the festival, when the pilgrimage was celebrated. They might not have time

to get home and back in a period of six or seven days. It was therefore ordained in Deuteronomy 16:1–8 that the paschal sacrifice be offered later in the evening: ***ba-ʿerev ke-voʾ ha-shemesh,*** "in the evening when the sun sets." In this way, the paschal sacrifice could also serve as the sacrifice of the first day of the *matsot* festival. This explains why, according to Deuteronomy 16:8, *matsot* must be eaten for six days, not for seven, as in earlier laws. The paschal sacrifice counted as part of the pilgrimage, which now occurred on the first, not the seventh, day of the festival, thus leaving only six remaining days. The morning after the paschal sacrifice an Israelite returned "to his tent." He was required to eat *matsot* until after the seventh day of the festival and to observe the seventh day as an *ʿatseret,* "concluding assembly," a day on which labor was forbidden. This *ʿatseret* was a remembrance of the *ḥag* that had formerly occurred on that day.

In effect, Deuteronomy transformed the paschal sacrifice into the pilgrimage sacrifice, and in so doing, prescribed the same mode of sacrifice as obtained for a normal *zevaḥ,* "sacred feast": It was to be boiled in pots and might consist of large or small cattle.[16] The paschal sacrifice did double duty in commemorating the Exodus, as before, but also in representing the offering required on the pilgrimage day. Deuteronomy 16:1 even declared the moment of the Exodus to have been at night, so that technically it could be commemorated on the first day of the festival, not on the eve of the festival. The unusual fact that the initial sacrifice had been set for the eve of the festival was utilized in its restructuring. This remarkable accommodation is subtly expressed in Exodus 34:25, a paraphrase of Exodus 23:18 with Deuteronomic overtones:

Exodus 23:18	***Exodus 34:25***
You shall not offer (*tizbaḥ*) the blood of My sacred feast (*zivḥi*) together with anything leavened; nor shall the fat of My pilgrimage offering (*ḥaggi*) be left until morning.	You shall not slaughter (*tishḥat*) the blood of My sacred feast (*zivḥi*) together with anything leavened; nor shall the sacred feast of the *pesaḥ* pilgrimage festival (*zevaḥ ḥag ha-pesaḥ*) be left until morning.

Whereas Exodus 23:18 speaks of two separate sacrifices—the paschal sacrifice and the pilgrimage sacrifice, which were to occur on two successive days—Exodus 34:25 produces a synonymous parallelism, whereby both parts of the verse refer to one and the same sacrifice!

This reconstruction helps explain the terms of Josiah's edict of 622 B.C.E., recorded in 2 Kings 23:21–23. The king commanded that the paschal sacrifice be offered in the Temple of Jerusalem, thus discontinuing the customary domestic sacrifice. This had never occurred before and was clearly in accord with the provisions of Deuteronomy 16:1–8. In Josiah's edict there is no mention of the pilgrimage because that was not problematic. The pilgrimage of the *matsot* festival had always brought Israelites to the Temple of Jerusalem and to other cult centers, but the paschal sacrifice had not.

Against the background of the Deuteronomic laws, which sought to accommodate earlier practice to the centralization of the cult, we can proceed to place the priestly laws governing the festivals in historical perspective. The primary priestly source is this chapter. The Holiness Code, which includes Leviticus 23, accepts Deuteronomy's seven-week postponement of the spring pilgrimage festival. Thus 23:15f. restates the duty to count seven

weeks, here calculated from the offering of the first sheaf of grain. Consonant with the emphasis of the Holiness Code on the importance of the Sabbath, seven Sabbatical weeks (weeks ending on the Sabbath) are to be counted, in Hebrew *shabbatot*, not *shavu'ot*. This postponement is understandable only as a response to Deuteronomy's deferral of the spring harvest festival.

Actually, chapter 23 has only two pilgrimage festivals, instead of three: *matsot* and *sukkot*. The *ḥag* called *shavu'ot* in Deuteronomy 16:10 was henceforth to be celebrated in the sanctuary and in the Israelite settlements ("from your settlements—*mi-moshevoteikhem*"). Loaves of leavened bread, made of semolina wheat flour (*solet*), were delivered to the sanctuary and there offered to God. In 23:15f., the spring harvest festival is not designated *ḥag*—there was no pilgrimage!

The *matsot* festival of Leviticus 23 accords with Deuteronomy in some respects and differs in others. The paschal sacrifice is to be offered in the sanctuary, as Deuteronomy insists. It is clear, therefore, that in this regard Leviticus 23 is dependent on Deuteronomy 16. Nevertheless, Leviticus 23 reverts to the practice of offering the paschal sacrifice in the late afternoon, rather than after sunset. Furthermore, the date of the festival had been changed to the fifteenth day of the month, to the time of the full moon, placing the paschal sacrifice late in the afternoon of the fourteenth day. The pilgrimage lasted for seven days, and the first and seventh days were sacred assemblies, on which labor was prohibited.

It is not entirely clear why the Holiness Code reverts to this older pattern. Perhaps there was a realistic sense that pilgrims would not flock to Jerusalem for the *matsot* festival, in any event. From Numbers 9:4–15 we learn that impure persons, or those very distant from the sanctuary, could offer the paschal sacrifice in the second month, instead of the first month. This dispensation betrays Deuteronomic influence, because it is only comprehensible once sacrifice was restricted to one, central Temple.

The Deuteronomic Sukkot festival is adopted in Leviticus 23, but its postponement had become unnecessary. Its earlier date, on the full moon of the seventh month, was therefore restored, and once again, in Leviticus 23:39 we read of ingathering of produce from the field, not of its processing. The Deuteronomic requirement of a seven-day pilgrimage is, however, retained and understood historically as a commemoration of the Sinai wanderings.

How shall we explain the unusual *'atseret,* "concluding assembly," of the eighth day, ordained in Leviticus 23:36? Deuteronomy 16 gives no date for Sukkot, but it is probable that in the Deuteronomic schedule Sukkot occurred during the last seven days of the year, as it was then reckoned, in the Hebrew of Exodus 34:22: *tekufat ha-shanah,* literally "the turn of the year." This means that the day following the festival was the New Year, or the New Moon of the first month, according to the calendar then in use. When the Holiness Code restored the festival to its earlier date, so that it no longer occurred at the end of the year, it merely took the Deuteronomic New Year along and called it *'atseret.* It was a vestige of the old New Moon of what had been the first month of the year.

All of these changes in schedule are enumerated by a new scribal system, in which months are listed ordinally, "the first month," "the seventh month," and so forth. This system came into vogue in the near-exilic period, beginning in the late seventh century B.C.E. It is used in Jeremiah, in 2 Kings 25:1,25, and in contemporary epigraphy. It occurs from level six in the Arad ostraca, dated to the years just prior to the Babylonian destruction of the early sixth century B.C.E.[17]

In addition to festivals known from nonpriestly sources, Leviticus 23 ordains two

additional occasions in the seventh month. The first day of the seventh month is a time for blasting the shofar and is designated "a sacred assembly" when labor is prohibited. The Holiness Code probably took its cue from Psalms 81:4: "Blow the horn on the new moon." This was the New Moon preceding the principal pilgrimage festival of the seventh month, *ḥag ha-sukkot.* The Day of Atonement, which falls on the tenth day of the seventh month, is prescribed as a day of complete rest. The date of Yom Kippur is first indicated in Leviticus 16:29–34, an addendum to chapter 16, which is the primary source of information on the purification rites of Yom Kippur. In fact, Leviticus 23 may well be the source of Leviticus 16:29–34. The timing of the annual purification of the sanctuary is suggestive. Before the major, annual pilgrimage on the Sukkot festival it was appropriate to purify the sanctuary. Many worshipers would already have arrived a few days in advance of the festival.

The further development of the festivals may be traced through the laws of Numbers 28–30, but that would carry us beyond Leviticus.

EXCURSUS 9

Retaliation and Compensation in Biblical Criminal Law (chap. 24)

Chapter 24 (vv. 17–22) figures prominently in the talmudic discussion of the law of retaliation, or *lex talionis*, as it is known in Roman jurisprudence. The sages insisted that the original intent of the Torah was to allow compensation for bodily injuries, even when intentionally inflicted, and not to inflict the same injury on the offender. The only exception was murder, since Numbers 35:31 expressly prohibits compensation and demands the life of the murderer. The broad scope of the talmudic discussion in Bava Kamma 83bf. reflects an intense polemical effort on the part of the rabbis to demonstrate the milder intent of biblical law. Because this law is so often the subject of conflicting assessments of the humaneness of biblical law, or its harshness, it might be well to review the talmudic discussion in detail.

On the hermeneutic level, verses 17–22 of our chapter suggested to the rabbis an analogy between damage to property involved in the killing of another's animal and injury to persons. Verse 18 speaks of compensating for an animal one has killed, referring to such payment as *nefesh taḥat nefesh,* "life for life." In the biblical context, this undoubtedly meant that the guilty party was expected to provide either an animal in place of the one he killed or its equivalent value. The talmudic sages make the comparison with the same formula, *x taḥat x,* that is stipulated for bodily injuries in humans, as in "an eye for an eye," and so forth. They reason that if *x taḥat x* meant compensation in the case of animals it would mean the same in the case of injuries inflicted on humans. Their case seemed to be reinforced by the fact that in verse 21 the law repeated the principle of compensation or the replacement of destroyed animals.

However, this hermeneutic interpretation is problematic in that it compares humans with animals. The interpretation is finally sustained on the basis of an analogy drawn between chapter 24 and Deuteronomy 22:29. There it is stated that if one rapes a virgin he must pay her father an amount of silver in compensation *taḥat 'asher 'innah,* literally "in lieu of having forced her." Just as *taḥat* in that instance indicates compensation, so in our law, *taḥat* would indicate compensation. Both laws deal with humans, after all.

Modern scholars have for the most part reacted against these arguments, which they regard as an apologetic line of interpretation: they insist that the original laws of the Torah

are to be understood literally. Some comparativists, on the other hand, endorse traditional interpretation on the grounds that in other, even older Near Eastern legal systems, the principle of compensation in the case of humans was recognized. It would not be unprecedented if the Torah laws incorporated the principle of compensation, as well.[1]

The matter to be ascertained is whether the biblical criminal system is best understood as having literal intent where bodily mutilation is the stated penalty. Both capital and corporal punishment were operative in the biblical system. Deuteronomy 25:12 ordains that the hand of a woman be severed in the event she seized the genitals of a man who was fighting with her husband. Surely, this punishment must be understood literally as a form of retribution. Numbers 16:14 provides a taunting reference to plucking out one's eyes as a punishment. This probably also reflects reality and implies that doing so was a well-known form of punishment, although we find few actual references to it.

In a curious way, the talmudic discussion of *lex talionis* betrays a realization that—in a legal system that elsewhere provides for corporal and capital punishment—only by hermeneutic argument can it be demonstrated that the original intent was to impose compensation, not to inflict mutilation on the offender. Let us review that discussion: There is, first of all, an appeal to equity. The Torah states *mishpat 'eḥad yihyeh lakhem,* "one standard shall apply to you." This the sages interpret to mean *mishpat ha-shaveh le-khulkhem,* "justice that is equitable to all of you"; and they point to cases where imposition of bodily injury as a punishment would not be equitable. In the case of a criminal already blind in one eye, plucking out his remaining eye would disable him more than his own act disabled the victim, who had two good eyes at the outset. This argument, however, is refuted in the talmud in several ways. Most interesting, perhaps, is the observation that since similar inequities did not invalidate capital punishment as an institution they should not invalidate the principle of mutilation.

There is also an objection registered against the criterion of feasibility. Merely because the literal penalty cannot always be imposed does not invalidate the principle; for example, in the case of a man already blind who blinded another in one eye, retaliatory punishment cannot be imposed on the offender. The rabbis observe, in this regard, that although a murderer may die naturally before the capital sentence is carried out, one would not suggest doing away with capital punishment altogether. Clearly, when the sentence can be carried out, it is; and when this is not possible, obviously, it is not. Intent, likewise, is not a consistently valid criterion. Legal penalties are not totally discarded because in certain circumstances their implementation may overstep the intent of the law. Flogging is retained as a means of punishment even though the criminal being so punished may die under the lash. In such cases, the court is not liable for his death.

Compensation is a very ancient alternative to mutilation in Near Eastern law. The Code of Hammurabi ordains bodily mutilation in some cases and legislates compensation in still others. The Code of Eshnunna frequently allows for compensation in cases of bodily injury. The same is true in the Hittite laws. According to the Middle Assyrian laws, one who strikes the daughter of one who shares his rank and thereby causes a miscarriage may compensate, but if the injured woman is another man's wife, even of his own rank, he must pay with his life.[2] In these other codes there are several variables that determine the type of penalty imposed. Often the criterion is social status. Injuries inflicted on slaves seldom require retaliatory punishment. A form of stratification also figures in biblical law. Exodus 21:26–27 stipulates that one who struck out the eye of his slave must give him his freedom, which is a form of compensation.

The point is that in a system that recognizes both retaliation and compensation and

employs both modes of punishment selectively, which kind of penalty applies is a matter to be determined case by case. Thus, if an injury to a slave may be punished by compensation, we may deduce that a similar injury to a free Israelite could not be compensated or else the text would clearly state as much. It is reasonable to conclude that the law of the Torah was severe in the area of bodily injuries inflicted intentionally by one Israelite upon another. Later Jewish authorities thought that mutilation was unconscionable as a punishment. This testifies to their own sensibilities; they resorted to hermeneutic interpretation in a humane cause. This does not, however, alter the realities of biblical law in its original context, the realities of which the talmudic sages may well have been aware.

EXCURSUS 10

The Inalienable Right to the Land of Israel (chap. 25)

Leviticus 25 is the only collection of laws preserved in the Torah that defines the legal status of land held by clans and individuals in ancient Israel. The procedures it establishes for the sale and transfer of land guarantee the rights of owners. The chapter also deals with the use of land as security for debts and with the system of indenture whereby debtors repay their indebtedness with their own labor and with that of members of their families.

Underlying this legislation is a theory of land tenure that may be formulated quite simply: The God of Israel, to whom all land ultimately belongs, has granted the Land of Israel to His people, Israel, as an everlasting *'aḥuzzah,* "holding." In so doing, he has imposed on them certain conditions of tenure. Foremost among these is denial of the right to alienate land through its permanent conveyance to a purchaser—a right that is usually considered an intrinsic element of ownership.

Leviticus 25 represents a valuable source of knowledge, encompassing both theory and practice, relating to a central concern: the right of the people of Israel to its land. It is surprising how little the Hebrew Bible has to say on the subject of land ownership. Neither the Book of the Covenant (Exod. 21–23) nor the laws of Deuteronomy deal with this subject in detail. Deuteronomy 19:14–15 prohibits encroaching on another's property by altering established boundary limits. This law resembles many similar provisions in ancient treaties that forbid removal of boundary stones.[1] Numbers 27, whose provisions are presupposed in Numbers 36, sets down rules of inheritance governing family property. In addition, prophets condemn the tendency of the rich and powerful to foreclose on the land of the poor: "Ah,/ Those who add house to house,/ And join field to field."[2] And the story of Naboth of Jezreel, preserved in 1 Kings 21, confirms that even a king of northern Israel, ruling in the ninth century B.C.E., could not legally compel one of his subjects to sell any part of his family estate.

The diverse contents of chapter 25 should be studied against the background of several biblical institutions that bear on the role of arable land in an agricultural economy. First among these is the law of the seventh year, called the sabbatical year in chapter 25. There are three basic statements in the Torah relating to the seventh year: Exodus 23:10–11; Deuteronomy 15:1–6; and in this chapter, verses 1–24. The Exodus passage, which is the earliest, speaks of agrarian pursuits. All Israelites are to let their fields lie fallow every seventh year. During that year sowing the fields and tending the vineyards and groves are expressly forbidden; and the needy among the people must have free access to all that grows on its

own. The key verb in the passage is *shamat,* "to let go, release." The provisions of Deuteronomy 15:1–6 say nothing about agriculture or land per se. In the view of some modern scholars, these verses do not provide for an agricultural release of the land at all, but are concerned only with indebtedness, ordaining a moratorium on debts every seventh year. From the verb *shamat,* "to release," applied in Exodus 23 to fallow land, Deuteronomy derives the noun *shemitah,* "release"—that is, from indebtedness.

Talmudic law regarding Exodus 23:10–11 and Deuteronomy 15:1–6 views them as complementary, calling the requirement of Exodus, *shemitat karka'ot,* "release of lands," and of Deuteronomy, *shemitat kesafim,* "release of monetary claims."[3] The talmudic sages were correct in making this association. It is decidedly more reasonable to see Deuteronomy 15 as continuing the legislation of Exodus 23 by extending it to the matter of indebtedness. We therefore translate Deuteronomy 15:1ff. as follows: "Every seventh year you shall execute a release. The following shall [also] be the subject of the release: Every owner shall release the pledge that he claims from his neighbor." In agrarian economies, virtually all indebtedness was linked to the soil. It often became necessary to borrow seasonally in order to secure seeds for sowing, implements, work animals, and the means to pay workers. The vicissitudes and uncertainties of agriculture—poor crop yields, drought, blight, and crippling taxation—were the factors that most often drove farmers into long-term debt and, subsequently, to indenture, when all other means failed to alleviate indebtedness.

The alignment of the legal statements of the Torah on the subject of indebtedness and indenture, on the one hand, and the release of the land, on the other, raises a basic question. Is the law of Deuteronomy 15:1–6, which imposes a moratorium on debts every seventh year, linked to the statute that limits the duration of indenture in verses 12–18 of the same chapter? That is, was indenture to last only until the next scheduled year of release from indebtedness, or was it to last a full six years—unrelated to the release of the land? This question has been studied by Nahum M. Sarna on the basis of the evidence in Jeremiah 34. Sarna explains that the prophet understands the law of the Torah to mean that the release of indentured servants is to occur every seventh year, regardless of when indenture had begun.[4] As recounted in Jeremiah, with the Chaldeans at the gates of Jerusalem, King Zedekiah ordered the immediate release of all indentured servants, much in the manner of a Babylonian king issuing an edict of *mesharum,* "equity."[5] His motive was probably to provide fighting men to defend Jerusalem; and the edict of release was, in reality, a form of conscription. When the crisis eased, many of the indentured servants were summarily repossessed by their creditors. Jeremiah (34:14), denouncing this procedure, states that the Torah commands that literally "every seventh year" (*mi-kets sheva' shanim*) indentured servants are to be permanently released.

This prophetic statement represents a meaningful interpretation. Although in Deuteronomy 15:1 the formula "every seventh year" pertains to monetary claims, not indentured servants, Jeremiah 34:14 applies it to indentured servants, which is the subject of Deuteronomy 15:12–18. For the prophet, the fact that the two Deuteronomic laws are separated in the text does not mean that they are legally unrelated. He explains indenture as being limited to the interval between the scheduled years of release. In fact, the same is probably true of the laws of Exodus 21, 23. The law of indenture is found in Exodus 21:1f., whereas the agricultural release is ordained in Exodus 23:10–11. Nevertheless, it is reasonable to assume that from earliest times the limit on indenture was a function, or feature, of the seventh year, not an absolute statute of limitations.

Once a law requiring cessation from agricultural pursuits every seventh year was in force, certain economic problems ensued. Landowners, having no need for indentured servants during the seventh year because they were not at work, would not provide them with room and board. Such needy persons would have to sustain themselves on gleanings, indeed, exactly the situation reflected in the words of Exodus 23:11. The needy among the people must be allowed free access to what grows on its own in the seventh year. In similar circumstances, Deuteronomy 15:7f. uses the term *'evyon,* "needy person," the same characterization that occurs in Exodus 23. It would have been the height of cruelty were creditors to reimpose indenture on such needy persons after the seventh year. Those unable to repay debts in times of normal agricultural activity could hardly have done so after a year of unemployment. The result would have been serfdom, a condition of permanent disenfranchisement from the land. Deuteronomy 15 actually reinforces the linkage of indebtedness and indenture to the seven-year agricultural cycle. In commanding the liberation of all Israelites every seventh year, it even abolishes the ancient distinction (retained in Exod. 21) between male and female servants.

The practice of allowing arable land to lie fallow periodically was a necessary aspect of ancient agriculture, especially where extensive irrigation was utilized. It served to reduce the quantity of alkalines, sodium and calcium, deposited in the soil by irrigation waters. In modern times, with the use of fertilizers, the soil is replenished through crop rotation. So, although the scheduled release of land every seventh year may smack of artificiality, expressing the cyclic thinking of the ancient Israelites, the agricultural advantages were real.

In this regard, we know that one of the major causes for the decline of the once prosperous Neo-Sumerian economy of Mesopotamia early in the second millennium B.C.E. was the high alkaline content of the soil in areas of the Diyala River region, where irrigation was extensively utilized. Crop yields fell drastically, and the economy failed.[6] There is also evidence that Near Eastern farmers in more recent periods have left different plots of land fallow each season, so that over the course of a period of years all of their fields underwent replenishment.

Notwithstanding its long-term benefits, periodic cessation of agricultural cultivation created severe economic problems, not unlike those resulting from drought or crop failure. A glimpse of this reality comes from Genesis 47, where we read that Joseph, viceroy of Egypt, planned for the anticipated lean years by storing huge quantities of grain in royal granaries. During the crisis, when the Egyptians had no more silver to buy grain, they were compelled to hand over their livestock as payment. When that source was exhausted, the people cried out: "nothing is left at my lord's disposal save our persons and our farmland" (Gen. 47:18). In this way—by forfeiting their land and indenturing themselves—the Egyptian people were disenfranchised.[7]

In Leviticus 25 we observe, curiously enough, a similar process. Release from indebtedness and indenture every seventh year is nowhere mentioned, the only exception being 25:47f., which exhorts Israelites of the same clan to redeem relatives who have become indentured to gentiles. Otherwise, an Israelite indentured to another, who is bereft of means or of concerned relatives, must await the Jubilee year. And this in a system that retains the requirement to let arable land lie fallow every seventh year! We find exhortations to treat indentured fellow Israelites kindly, to come to the aid of distressed clan relatives, to redeem mortgaged or sold land, and to lend funds to fellow Israelites without interest. But there is no legal obligation to release debts or indenture every seventh year.

In sharp contrast to its neglect of the distressed individual, chapter 25, building on the

ancient law guaranteeing ownership of ancestral land, nullifies and voids the actual alienation of agricultural land. Legally speaking, all lands sold or mortgaged are merely leased to others for a period never to exceed fifty years, until the next Jubilee year. At that time, such lands as had not been redeemed would revert to their former owners. Indenture would also cease, and all Israelites would "return" to their homes.

How this system operated may be learned from Nehemiah 5, which pertains to the late fifth century B.C.E., or even later, when Jerusalem and Judea were under Persian domination. Nehemiah, a Jew and the Persian governor of Judea, heeds the outcry of the people, who complain that they are unable to feed their large families. Their fields and vineyards, which they had mortgaged to their debts, are being lost to their creditors. They cannot pay the royal tax, the *middah* (Akk. *mandattu*), and have no grain in time of famine. Their sons and daughters have been indentured, with little or no hope of release. They bewail the deplorable irony that, after redeeming fellow Judeans indentured to gentiles (a duty stated in Lev. 25:47f.), they now find their own sons and daughters remaining in servitude to other Judeans.[8]

Nehemiah immediately cancels all indenture and all monetary claims; land holdings are restored to their original owners. In effect, he proclaims a "release," although the term *deror,* used in Leviticus 25, does not appear. In essence, Nehemiah attempts to remedy a situation that had developed at least over the twelve-year period of his administration as governor and that may well have existed even prior to that time. His apologia for his own policies is also revealing. In contrast to earlier Persian governors he had never demanded "the *Peḥa*'s bread" (the governor's food allowance), which is a way of saying that he had not imposed additional taxes on the people. He had also subsidized construction out of his own resources and had provided for the needs of the bureaucracy. All of this he had done out of "fear of the Lord" and because the people were already so pressed. Reference to the "fear of the Lord" recalls the exhortation repeatedly emphasized in Leviticus 25 and in the Holiness Code, generally, that all laws are to be obeyed out of "fear of the Lord." Whereas the language of Nehemiah 5 shows some Deuteronomic features, for the most part it is based on the specific legislation of Leviticus 25.

The first verse of chapter 25, as well as its closing statements in verse 46 (cf. 27:34), recalls that the laws contained therein were communicated by God to Moses on Mount Sinai, before the Israelites entered their land. Modern scholarship regards such statements as traditional, not historical, and continues to search for the historical setting reflected in the laws themselves. At the present time, two views predominate as to the historical order of the biblical collections of laws dealing with the seventh year. One view arranges the codes of law as follows, in accordance with the canonical order of the books of the Torah: (1) Exodus 21, 23, (2) Leviticus 25 (and 27), and (3) Deuteronomy 15. Another view arranges the relevant law codes differently: (1) Exodus 21, 23, (2) Deuteronomy 15, and (3) Leviticus 25 (and 27). Following this sequence, would not the legislation of Leviticus be retrograde, undoing the benefits extended by Deuteronomy? According to the interpretation presented in the Commentary, Deuteronomy not only endorses the agricultural year of release, but adds to the economic relief afforded to the needy. Leviticus 25 effectively withdraws the benefits of release every seventh year. Some argue that it must, therefore, precede Deuteronomy.

Nevertheless, based on a variety of interacting factors, it seems preferable to regard Leviticus 25 as coming at the end of the sequence, namely, subsequent to Deuteronomy 15. Rather than regarding the provisions of Leviticus 25 as retrograde and arguing for the relative antiquity of the chapter, as some scholars do, we should perhaps see in it an attempt

to deal with a radically new situation. The legislation enacted in response to this new situation sought, as its paramount objective, to prevent the loss of land by Israelites and their families. The close parallels with Nehemiah 5, discussed above, suggest a common, historical setting for both sources: the situation of the Judean community under Persian domination. Leviticus 25:45f. recalls the complaints of the citizenry in Nehemiah 5 and betrays the probability that both reflect the life of the postexilic community. Leviticus 25 speaks of Israelites indentured to non-Israelites, suggesting a mixed population. The prohibition against the permanent alienation of family land may also have been motivated by the fear of the loss of land to gentiles and foreigners to whom Israelites were indebted. As bad as conditions may have been under the Judean monarchy, there was little danger that foreigners or gentiles would gain possession of family lands or that Israelites would be indentured to non-Israelites. The only economic factor missing in Leviticus 25, but which figures in Nehemiah 5, is that of taxation. But, then, Torah legislation never refers to governmental taxation. Its laws are presented as a program revealed to the Israelites before they entered Canaan; and it never goes beyond envisioning the likelihood of a monarchy.

Historically, the returning Judean exiles were repatriates allowed to resettle in their ancestral land and to rebuild their Temple in Jerusalem. These terms were granted by the edict of Cyrus the Great, issued in 538 B.C.E., after the Persians had assumed hegemony over the territories of the Neo-Babylonian empire. But that edict did not guarantee that Judeans would recover their former lands or take possession of other lands within their new areas of settlement, although that occurred in some cases. Benjamin Mazar has shown, for example, that some prominent Judean families returned to the areas of their preexilic habitation. It is even likely that some Judeans remained in the land and retained uninterrupted possession of their estates throughout the political changes that came in the wake of the Babylonian and Persian conquests.[9] Nevertheless, it was undoubtedly necessary in many cases to repurchase land from non-Judeans, and there was probably conflict over rights of ownership. In Ezra, we read of disputes related to the Temple and the city of Jerusalem and of the intervention of Persian imperial agencies. We are warranted in supposing that similar disputes arose over the ownership of family estates.[10]

The priestly leaders of the repatriated Judean community formulated a theory to legitimize their situation: God had granted the Land of Israel to his people as an everlasting *'aḥuzzah,* "holding." His people were His tenants and were granted the right to work the land and enjoy its fruits. They were, however, denied the right usually considered a *sine qua non* of ownership, the right to alienate what one owns. Following this line of reasoning, the edict of Cyrus was translated into a divine land grant. In the prophecies of Deutero-Isaiah it is stated explicitly that the God of Israel commissioned Cyrus to restore His people.[11] It was hoped that the returning exiles, some of whom were impoverished when they arrived, would be helped by their coreligionists in Babylonia and that they would band together, clan by clan, to help each other. Relatives were to redeem threatened lands. The goal was to regain control over the land. The institution of *ge'ullah,* "redemption," first encountered in Jeremiah 32, and the theme of *ge'ullah*, accentuated by Deutero-Isaiah during the exile, assumed new meaning for the Judean community.[12] Leaders like Nehemiah were needed to restrain the usual greed for land and wealth, so that these worthy goals could be achieved.

There is much more that could be said about the historical setting of Leviticus 25. Only further research will determine whether the reconstruction proposed here is historically accurate.[13]

EXCURSUS 11

A Priestly Statement on the Destiny of Israel (26:3–46)

The Epilogue to the Holiness Code is patterned after other biblical blessings and curses and after other similar ancient Near Eastern compositions. Its position is the key to its function in the text. It comes directly after a collection of laws and commandments. All three Torah collections of laws are followed by admonitions, and the same is true in the rest of ancient Near Eastern literature generally. The Code of Hammurabi concludes with an Execration, and curses follow the provisions of boundary stones and royal decrees. The Egyptian "execration texts" are so called because they contain curses. Execrations were pronounced over towns and provinces that failed to pay tribute to the Pharaohs or were disloyal in other ways. One cannot be punished without being first admonished.[1]

Well-being, peace, and prosperity, in short all the blessings individuals and nations seek to secure from divine powers, are contingent on obedience to laws, treaties, oaths, and royal edicts. Divine wrath is the misfortune of the disobedient. Our Epilogue presents particular priestly notions of the meaning of the covenantal relationship between God and Israel. The most awful punishment threatened for violation of the covenant is exile because it brings with it the danger of extinction in hostile lands.

In the Commentary, the Epilogue is treated as a unified composition. Literary analysis shows, however, that Leviticus 26:3–46 is actually a composite document, including a primary Epilogue and several significant additions. The primary section, which will be identified in the outline that follows, ends on a note of doom with the destruction of the land and the dispersal of the people into exile, like the conventional ending of an ancient Near Eastern execration. The additional sections, however, express perceptions that emerge from the actual experience of exile, most poignantly, the hope for God's forgiveness and the prospect of restoration. Historically, the primary Epilogue could have been written, at the very earliest, right before the exile, which came in stages during the ten or so years prior to 586 B.C.E., the date of the final destruction of Jerusalem by the Babylonians. It could have been written considerably later, however, because predictions of doom may actually convey the thinking of those who have already experienced it. In any event, the additions to the primary Epilogue postdate the deportations and may even reflect the thinking of biblical writers at the end of the exile.

As presented, the Epilogue is addressed to the Israelites, who are about to enter the promised land. It informs them of the conditions of their sovereignty over the land and of the circumstances that might bring about the loss of the land. Modern scholarship respects this traditional frame of reference; at the same time, it seeks to identify the historical frame of reference reflected in the Epilogue—by means of an analysis of language and diction and by comparisons with other biblical works pertaining to the themes of exile and divine punishment. This methodology allows us to come to some understanding of how biblical writers interpreted important historical events.

H. L. Ginsberg has proposed an outline of the Epilogue that is enlightening in terms of its literary-historical analysis. It is followed here, with only slight variation, and is supplemented in order to cover the entire Epilogue: (1) The primary Epilogue (vv. 3–33a, 37b–38); (2) the first "postcatastrophe" addition (vv. 39–40b, 44–45); (3) later additions: (a) the theme of desolation and the fears engendered by exile (vv. 33b–37a) and (b) more about desolation, Israel's submission to God, the atonement of both people and land personified, and the theme of the patriarchal covenant (vv. 40b–43).[2]

The structure of the primary Epilogue reveals a symmetry of contrasts, as between the promise of reward and the threat of punishment. The land will be fertile (vv. 4–5,10)—the land will be utterly unproductive (vv. 16,19–20,26). God will turn with favor toward His people (v. 9)—God will set His face against them (v. 17). Israel will repulse its enemies (v. 9)—Israel will be battered by its enemies (vv. 17,25). The land will be rid of wild beasts (v. 6)—wild beasts will devour people (v. 25). No sword will traverse the land (v. 6)—a sword will bring destruction (v. 25). Obedience brings secure settlement (v. 5)—disobedience brings exile (v. 33a). It is also possible that Hebrew *tekumah,* literally "the ability to stand up," in verse 37b at the end of the curses may be a subtle reflection of *komamiyyut,* "at full stature," in verse 15 at the conclusion of the blessing. Instead of remaining free as Israel was when it left Egypt, after the bars of its yoke had been broken, it will be bent over, captive in exile.

As noted in the Commentary, the punishments of the primary Epilogue escalate in magnitude; if one set fails to secure Israel's obedience, worse will follow. This escalation is emphasized by periodic refrains, which may be outlined as follows: Israel's failure to obey results in sevenfold punishment (v. 18); Israel's coldness to God, in addition to its failure to obey, results in sevenfold punishment (v. 21); Israel's failure to be chastised, in addition to Israel's coldness to God, results in God's coldness toward Israel and sevenfold punishment (vv. 23–24); Israel's failure to obey, in addition to Israel's coldness to God, results in God's coldness and sevenfold punishment (vv. 27–28).

The effect of the escalation—which virtually tabulates a process of action and response, of mutual hardening of attitudes between Israel and God—is both disheartening and, in a curious way, consoling. God, for His part, will not relent and will respond to disobedience with increasing severity, to the point of exiling His people as He has threatened. On the other hand, the conditional formulation of the curses leaves an opening for Israel—at any of several stages—to renounce its disobedience, at which time the punishments would cease. One is immediately reminded of the saga of the ten plagues in Egypt, recounted in the Book of Exodus. Unfortunately for the victims, in both instances, submission came too late!

The overall structure of the primary Epilogue is reminiscent of an oracle preserved in Amos 4:6–11, according to which God punished the Israelites repeatedly, but at no time did they return to Him.

> I, on My part, have given you
> Cleanness of teeth in all your towns . . .
> Yet you did not turn back to Me
>
> —declares the LORD.
>
> I therefore withheld the rain from you
> Three months before harvesttime . . .
> Yet you did not turn back to Me
>
> —declares the LORD.
>
> I scourged you with blight and mildew;
> Repeatedly your gardens and vineyards . . .
> Yet you did not turn back to Me
>
> —declares the LORD.

I sent against you pestilence
In the manner of Egypt . . .
Yet you did not turn back to Me
—declares the LORD.

I have wrought destruction upon you
As when God destroyed Sodom and Gomorrah . . .
Yet you have not turned back to Me
—declares the LORD.

The primary Epilogue is stated in stark terms, without the exhortations that we find in some other biblical admonitions, such as Deuteronomy 11:13–38. There we read that God urges the people to beware of the temptation to go astray and urges upon them the life-affirming choice of obedience, as against disobedience. Here we have only the presentation of cold, matter-of-fact alternatives: to obey or to disobey.

Our Epilogue resembles Deuteronomy 28:1–48 in terms of literary composition, although as regards diction and forms of expression the two texts have little in common. The same sort of mitigations observable in the additions to our primary Epilogue are also evident in Deuteronomy, as has been noted. Thus Deuteronomy 30:1–10, part of the conclusion of the Book of Deuteronomy, states that Israel will be restored to its land if it returns to the Lord sincerely. The same thought is expressed in Deuteronomy 4:25–31f., part of the introduction to the book. In both Deuteronomy and Leviticus, the classic curse, which ends in doom, is amended to allow for survival.

Deuteronomy 28:1–48 and our Epilogue resemble in their composition the epilogue to the Code of Hammurabi. King Hammurabi adjures his successors to uphold the laws he has promulgated, to honor his name, and so on. He poses the same alternatives as we find in the Epilogues of the Torah: "If that man (i.e., the king who shall be raised up in the land) has heeded my words, which I have inscribed on my monument, has not made light of my commandments . . . may Shamash enlarge that man's empire like mine, the just king, and may he lead his people in justice. If that man has not heeded my words, which I have inscribed on my monument . . . may the great god, Anum, father of the gods, deprive that man . . . of royal splendor, break his scepter, curse his destiny. . . ."[3] There are, of course, basic differences between our Epilogue and that of the Code of Hammurabi, but the similarities are nonetheless striking.

Having placed the Epilogue to the Holiness Code into a wider context of blessings and curses, we can now move on to other considerations. Diction, for example, pertains to the precise manner in which an author expresses ideas. It concerns phrases and idioms and the choice of words, and is often the key to historical setting. This is especially true of our Epilogue, in which diction both broadens our perspective and focuses our sights. To the extent that our Epilogue reveals conventional diction, we are able to understand its general literary origins. But in those instances where its diction is linked to specific biblical sources, and to no others, we can identify precise periods of Israelite history and particular schools of biblical writers.

The most obvious parallel to our Epilogue is found in Deuteronomy 28; and Deuteronomy 27 is relevant to our comparisons as well. Both Deuteronomic chapters use ***berakhah*** and the adjective ***barukh*** to express blessing and forms such as ***'arur,*** "accursed," to express the opposite. These terms are absent from our Epilogue, although, to be sure, it deals with these same realities and simply expresses themes differently, most notably by the verb ***shama',*** "to heed, obey," which also occurs in Deuteronomy 28. On the other hand,

our Epilogue emphasizes the idea of *berit,* "covenant," a term absent from Deuteronomy 28:1–48.

There are several clichés that are common to our Epilogue and to Deuteronomy 28. Both mention the same pair of diseases, *kadaḥat* and *shaḥefet* (Lev. 26:16; Deut. 28:22). Both refer to skies of iron and soil of bronze (Lev. 26:19; Deut. 28:33) and to eating the flesh of children (Lev. 26:29; Deut. 28:33). Both curses speak of being battered by enemies, using the verb *niggaf* (Lev. 26:17; Deut. 28:7,25). Both refer to exhausted eyes and languishing bodies (Lev. 26:16; Deut. 28:65). Both contain references to rains in their season (Lev. 26:3; Deut. 28:12). Finally, the term *mitsvah,* "commandment," is found in both compositions.

What is common to both Epilogues is conventional, not only within biblical literature, but throughout the ancient Near East. Thus, eating one's children is depicted in a number of other biblical sources having to do with war and destruction and is, in fact, also projected in the vassal treaty of Esarhaddon, the Assyrian king of the seventh century B.C.E. In that treaty drought is depicted as iron soil and bronze heavens, an inversion of the very cliché we find both in our Epilogue and Deuteronomy.

Recent discoveries have provided additional parallels that show how intimately biblical and other ancient Near Eastern curses are related in their diction. Perhaps the most recent of these discoveries is a bilingual statuary inscription, written in Aramaic and Akkadian, from Tell Fekherye in northeast Syria near Tell Halaf (biblical Gozan). It probably dates from the ninth century B.C.E. Like all such royal inscriptions, this text includes a section of curses. In line 22 of the Aramaic version we read: "May one hundred women bake bread in a single oven, but let them not fill it!" The Akkadian is a bit more poignant: "May one hundred baking women not even fill a single oven!" These statements recall Leviticus 26:26: "When I break your staff of bread, ten women shall bake your bread in a single oven."[4] In the vassal treaty of Esarhaddon, mentioned above, we find similar imagery: "May your fingertips not dip in the dough; may the dough be lacking from your kneading troughs." The Assyrian curse recalls Deuteronomy 28:5,17, where blessing means that the kneading troughs of those who obey God will contain abundant dough.

Depicting exile as the "scattering" of a people is also common in ancient Near Eastern diction. The Hebrew verb *zerah,* "to scatter, disperse," used in verse 33 of our Epilogue, is paralleled by a statement in the epilogue to the Code of Hammurabi, which speaks of *na-ás-pu-úḫ ni-ši-šu,* "the scattering of his people." The image of defeat as the inability to "stand up" before enemies, conveyed in our Epilogue by the noun *tekumah* in verse 37, is paralleled in the vassal treaty of Esarhaddon by the statement: "May you not stand (*la ta-za-za-a-ni*) before your enemies!"

The threat in verse 31 of our Epilogue that God will not accept the sweet savor of Israel's sacrifices is also a typical theme. In the aforementioned bilingual inscription from Tell Fekherye, we find a similar idea. The king who erected and dedicated the statue warns his people: "Whoever would remove my name from the vessels of the temple of Hadad, my lord, may my lord Hadad not accept his food and water offerings from his hand!" A thorough investigation would turn up many more similar parallels. It is clear, even from this sample, that our Epilogue represents a genre of ancient Near Eastern literature, quite apart from its special significance within the Bible.

It is now appropriate to explore the other side of the coin, the value of diction in enabling us to pinpoint how our Epilogue fits into the treatment of the themes of exile and restoration in biblical literature. Ginsberg has provided a reliable point of departure for a discussion of diction as the key to identifying historical setting. He observes that in the first

postcatastrophe addition to the primary Epilogue (in vv. 39–40a,44–45) we find a theme clearly expressed in Ezekiel 20.

In the year 591 B.C.E., after the first deportations by the Babylonians, the prophet Ezekiel reviews the history of Israel's covenantal relationship to God. He perceives a chain of disloyal acts on Israel's part. At several critical junctures of Israel's history, God was all but ready to nullify the covenant He had enacted at the Exodus, on the grounds that Israel had violated its terms by failing to obey His laws and commandments. Each time, He stopped short of doing this out of concern for His "Name." Since He had sworn to uphold the covenant "in the sight of the nations" (*le-ʿeinei ha-goyim*), to nullify it would lead to the desecration of His Name. This is expressed in Ezekiel 20:8–9,17,21–23 and is repeatedly emphasized in that chapter. Finally, God executed His threats: He exiled His people and allowed the land to be devastated. But all is not lost, Ezekiel tells us, for God will again restore at least part of His people.

Now, the Hebrew phrase *le-ʿeinei ha-goyim,* "in the sight of the nations," appears exclusively in our Epilogue (v. 45); in Ezekiel, who employs it in several oracles; and in Isaiah 52:10, in an oracle of restoration, where we find *le-ʿeinei kol ha-goyim,* "in the sight of all the nations." The prophet of the beautiful oracle of restoration of Isaiah 52:7–10, composed at the end of the exile, echoes Ezekiel 20. Ginsberg further calls attention to another item of Ezekiel's diction, his use of the rare verb *m-k-k,* "to melt, waste away." In verse 39, part of the first addition to the primary Epilogue, we read: "Those of you who survive shall be heartsick over their iniquity (*yimmakku ba-ʿavonam*)." Only our Epilogue and Ezekiel know of this idiom. In terms of literary-historical analysis, the dependence of the first additions to the Epilogue on Ezekiel means that we are well into the sixth century, the period of the exile. If this is so, the additions in Leviticus 26, in verses 33b–37a and 40b–43, must be regarded as being even later. Indeed, we are fortunate in having a clue to this effect.

In verses 34–35, and again in verse 43 of the later additions, we find a usage that is elsewhere attested only in Isaiah 40:2, an oracle written near or at the end of the Babylonian exile. The idiom is *ratsah ʿavon,* "to atone for, expiate a sin." "Comfort, oh comfort My people,/ Says your God./ Speak tenderly to Jerusalem,/ And declare to her/ That her term of service is over,/ That her iniquity is expiated (*ki nirtsah ʿavonah*)." In verse 43 of our Epilogue both the land and the people atone for their sins: the people, through submission to God after the prolonged sufferings of the exile; and the land, by compensating for its neglected sabbatical years. The sabbatical theme, so prominent in chapters 23 and 25 of the Holiness Code, is here expressed with cruel irony: Because the land was not allowed to lie fallow every seventh year while the Israelites lived in it, it will now lie desolate involuntarily, bereft of its inhabitants. This diction leads us to Isaiah of the exile. Of interest, too, is the echo of our Epilogue in 2 Chronicles 36:20–21: "Those who survived the sword he exiled to Babylon . . . in fulfillment of the word of the LORD spoken by Jeremiah, until the land paid back its sabbaths; as long as it lay desolate it kept sabbath, till seventy years were completed."

In another connection Ginsberg again uses diction to clarify the literary-historical analysis of the later additions to the Epilogue. Verse 42 speaks of a covenant with the patriarchs, most probably an exilic idea. Preexilic biblical sources know only of the conditional Sinaitic covenant, which depended on Israel's loyalty; the advent of exile was a sign, in religious terms, that God had abrogated it. The covenant with the patriarchs is first expressed in Exodus 6:2–9, part of priestly literature. There, the three patriarchs—

Abraham, Isaac, and Jacob—are mentioned in the usual order. Verse 42 of our Epilogue reverses the order, beginning with Jacob. This suggests an adaptation of the original version. The unconditional covenant with the patriarchs—in contrast to the severed Sinaitic covenant—was to last forever; for those living in exile, it held forth hope of a restoration to the land. It seems, therefore, that the two dominant themes of the later additions to the Epilogue, those subsequent even to the first postcatastrophe additions, express exilic ideas. We may speak of three stages in the composition of the Epilogue as we have it: the primary Epilogue, the first postcatastrophe addition, and the later additions. At the earliest, the completed Epilogue takes us to the end of the exile, possibly to the first period of return after the edict of Cyrus the Great, issued in 538 B.C.E. It is quite probable that the same criteria that endorse an exilic setting for the additions to the primary Epilogue suggest as well the influence of Ezekiel's diction since Ezekiel went into exile. There is evidence of themes received from the prophecies of Ezekiel and, also, from Jeremiah.

The author of the primary Epilogue probably appropriated the idiom *ga'al nefesh,* "to spurn," from Jeremiah 14:19f.: "Have You, then, rejected (*ha-ma'os ma'astah*) Judah?/ Have You spurned (*ga'alah nafshekha*) Zion?" For Jeremiah, the verb *ga'al,* "to spurn," marks the critical juncture at which God determined that there is no return, that matters have gone too far to avert destruction and exile. Jeremiah is making a last appeal, for, in the ensuing oracle of chapter 15, he announces God's refusal to reconsider, and the exile is finally decreed. In similar fashion, the author of the primary Epilogue also uses this verb to mark critical junctures. The process begins in verse 11, where Israel is assured that if God's laws and commandments are obeyed, God will *not* spurn (*ga'al*) Israel. In verses 14–15 the first punishments are introduced, precisely when Israel "spurns" His laws and statutes. The punishments escalate until, in verse 30, God "spurns" Israel, at which point no opportunity remains for averting the final disaster. The conclusion to the primary Epilogue, verses 31–33a, project destruction and exile.

The author of the first postcatastrophe addition adopted the same code word, the verb *ga'al.* In verses 44–45, he states that redemption is possible because God had not ever actually "spurned" Israel; for this would have led to their extinction in exile, which had not occurred. If God had spurned Israel, His reputation would have been damaged in the sight of the nations. Thus, after Israel shows remorse and confesses its sins, God will reaffirm the covenant enacted at Sinai. Again, the dynamics of the first addition revolve around the verb *ga'al,* "to spurn." Even the authors of the later additions, who hold a different concept of the covenant, knew and used the code word *ga'al.* The exile had endured and expiation was delayed because Israel had persisted in "spurning" God's laws and statutes.

The hypothesis that the author of the primary Epilogue and those authors who came after him drew on Ezekiel's themes is strengthened by still other similarities of diction. Note the following examples: (1) The verb *zerah,* "to scatter," is used to characterize exile in verse 33a of our Epilogue. Ultimately, this usage can be traced back to Jeremiah (31:10; 49:32; 51:2). Ezekiel then elaborates on the theme (Ezek. 5:10; 6:15,8; 12:14–15; 20:2,23; 22:15; 29:12; 30:26). (2) In verse 19, our author speaks of "your powerful glory" (*ge'on 'uzkhem*), his way of referring to the land, for he goes on to speak of drought and the failure of the soil to yield its produce. This locution is known elsewhere only in Ezekiel—in 7:24; 30:6,18; and 33:28, in various connections. (3) Only Ezekiel and our author know of the idiom *herik ḥerev 'aḥarei,* literally "to unsheath the sword after." Our author uses it in verse 33a, as does Ezekiel in 5:2 and 12:14. Only our author, in verse 6, and Ezekiel 14:17 know of the

combination *ḥerev ʿavar,* "the sword traverses." Only our author, in verse 25, and Ezekiel (5:11; 6:3; 11:8; 14:17; 29:8; 33:2) know the idiom *hevi' ḥerev ʿal,* "to brandish the sword over." (4) On the theme of sustenance, both our Epilogue (v. 26) and Ezekiel (4:16; 5:16; 14:13) use the idiom *matteh leḥem,* "staff of bread." Elsewhere it is found only in the late Psalms 105:16. In Isaiah 3:11 the idiom is *mishʿan leḥem,* "support of bread." (5) It has been noted in the Commentary that verses 3–13 of our Epilogue bear remarkable similarities to Ezekiel 34:25–28; the same is true of the similarities between Ezekiel 6 and verses 30–31 of our Epilogue.

Given the situation outlined here, we are warranted in attributing much of what the author of the primary Epilogue says to the influence of prophecy and, more precisely, to that of Ezekiel and, to a lesser extent, Jeremiah. We are not dealing with isolated parallels, but with major, pervasive themes that are expressed in precisely the same ways.

It is impossible to say exactly when each of the three strata of the Epilogue was composed. The differentiation of the final composition into three strata is, however, important for understanding how the ideas it expresses emerged in stages. The author of the primary Epilogue, stunned by the initial shock of the exile, thought all was lost. His curses end in doom; the people of Israel are pursued into the lands of their captors, unable to stand up before them. The author of the first addition to the primary Epilogue introduces two variables into the equation: God, for His part, will yet uphold the Sinaitic covenant for the sake of His Name because He swore to uphold it in the sight of the nations. Israel, for its part, will confess its sins and respond contritely to the sufferings of exile. Those who survive will then be restored. The authors of the still later additions sought to explain the delay in realizing this restoration. The prolongation of exile was explained in two ways. First, the expiation of the people and the land would of necessity take a long time, for the sins of the people, as they affected the land, had lasted for many generations. Redemption would require patience. Second, a new understanding of the covenant was needed to replace the conditional, Sinaitic covenant that had been annulled by God when He exiled His people.

The author of the first postcatastrophe addition to the Epilogue still believed that the original Sinaitic covenant would assure restoration, if only Israel confessed its sins. But the authors of the later additions no longer held to this view. The sins of Israel had been too grievous, their breach of the covenant too damaging. Only the unconditional covenant with the patriarchs could be invoked so late in the exile. Any hope for restoration derived from God's promise to the patriarchs to grant their descendants the land of Canaan, a promise that was not made contingent on any merit on Israel's part.

Our Epilogue contains the only biblical reference to God's remembrance of a personified land in verse 42. This unique reference expresses a great love for the Land of Israel and a yearning for it.

The Epilogue to the Holiness Code grapples with the question of the destiny of the people of Israel in the face of the cataclysmic destruction of Jerusalem and Judea. It reflects the influence of the prophets Jeremiah and Ezekiel on the thinking of the Israelite priesthood, in exile and during the early period of return. New hope was engendered through new understandings of covenant and new responses to disaster and exile.

NOTES TO THE EXCURSUSES

Excursus 1

1. In Mish. Ker. 1:1f. we find later laws dealing with the penalty of *karet.* See M. Tsevat, "Studies in the Book of Samuel," HUCA 32 (1961): 191f.

2. Cf. Deut. 20:19–20; Isa. 14:18; Jer. 22:7.

3. Jer. 11:19; and cf. Isa. 18:5; Pss. 34:17.

4. Isa. 56:3–5; and cf. Josh. 7:9; Pss. 109:13.

5. Job 14:7.

6. Cf. Jer. 33:17–18; 35:19.

7. Judg. 21:4–6; and cf. Num. 27:4; Deut. 25:6.

8. Exod. 12:15–19; 31:14; Lev. 23:29; Num. 9:13.

9. Cf. Lev. 7:20–21; 22:3; Num. 9:13,20.

10. Cf. provisions of 18:19; 20:17–18.

11. Exod. 30:33,38; Lev. 3:17; 7:25–27; 17:4,9; 19:8.

Excursus 2

1. See chap. 11, n. 1.

2. See the discussion in I. Twersky, *Introduction to the Code of Maimonides* (New Haven: Yale University Press, 1980), 238ff., especially 264f.

3. On the prohibitions called *to'evah,* see Deut. 12:31; 13:5; 18:11–12; 27:15; Isa. 1:13; 44:19.

4. This theme is developed in Deut. 28 and in Lev. 26:3f. See Excursus 11.

5. See chap. 11, n. 5.

6. Cf. Isa. 65:3–4,17.

7. See Comment to 7:18.

8. Cf. Dan. 1:5f.

9. See J. Frazer, *The Golden Bough,* vol. 2 (London, New York: The Macmillan Co., 1900), 154, 212f., 299f.

10. Cf. Gen. 6:12–13.

11. Cf. Gen. 7:4–5, 10-17.

12. Cf. 1 Sam. 15:9, in the context of the Amalekite wars.

13. See Gen. 8:6–12.

14. Cf. Exod. 16:13; Num. 11:31–32. Mish. Ḥul. 3:6 defines a pure bird as one that has an extra talon, characteristic of birds that eat grain and seeds; has a craw, or throat; and has a stomach that can be peeled off, so that undigested contents can be disposed of separately.

15. See M. Douglas, *Purity and Danger* (London: Routledge and Kegan Paul, 1966), 41ff.

16. See the article by G. J. Botterweck, TWAT, s.v. *ḥazir.*

17. See W. R. Smith, *Lectures on the Religion of the Semites* (New York: Ktav, 1969), 357ff.

18. See Comment to 17:11 on the cultic uses of blood.

19. See Excursus 4 for a discussion of the scapegoat theme.

20. See Herodotus, *Histories* 2.46–48 (Loeb Classical Library, pp. 333f.).

21. See F. Blome, *Die Opfermaterie in Babylonien und Israel* (Rome: Pontifical Institute, 1934), 120f.

22. See R. E. Whitaker, *A Concordance of the Ugaritic Literature,* s.v. *ḫnzr,* in Ugar. personal names or clan affiliations: *bn ḫnzr,* "member of the Ḫinzir clan," or the like.

23. See J. Goldstein, *I Maccabees* (AB), Introduction 157f., on the sacrificing and eating of swine in Seleucid times.

Excursus 3

1. As an example we may cite the Arslan-Tash inscriptions of the seventh century B.C.E., which contain incantations against demons. These Syrian inscriptions sought to ward off demons who were thought to strangle infants. Similarly, in Ugar. texts of the fourteenth to twelfth centuries, also from Syria, we read of "the two strangling goddesses" (Ugar. *iltm ḫnqtm,* in C. F. A. Schaeffer, *Ugaritica V* [Paris: Imprimerie nationale, 1968], 594). See J. Gibson, *Textbooks of Syrian Semitic Inscriptions* (Oxford: Clarendon Press, 1971), 82d, nos. 23–24. Also see the Egyptian incantation entitled "Magical Protection for a Child," in ANET, p. 328.

2. A Ugar. poem celebrates the birth of twin gods. See J. Gibson, *Canaanite Myths and Legends* (Edinburgh: T. and T. Clark, 1977), 28f., texts 123f.

Excursus 4

1. See J. Frazer, *The Golden Bough,* vol. 3 (London, New York: The Macmillan Co., 1900), 1–134.

2. The casting of lots is an approved form of divination, as is explained in the Comment to 8:8. The major prohibitions of magic in Torah literature are to be found in Exod. 22:7; Lev. 19:26–28; Deut. 18:9–11.

3. See 14:33f.

4. See 13:46.

5. Isa. 13:21 and 34:14, both late passages, speak of *se'irim* in the wilderness. It may be significant that in Dan. 8:21 the inimical Greek empire is called *ha-tsefir ha-sa'ir,* "the buck, the he-goat."

6. See J. T. Milik, ed., *The Books of Enoch: Aramaic Fragments of Qumrân Cave 4* (Oxford: Clarendon Press, 1976), 313, s.v. plate 31, line 6: *'z'[z]l.* Also note sources cited by Milik, such as two Heb. texts from Qumran (4Q 180.1, line 6, on p. 249; 4Q 181.1, line 22, on p. 314), both of which mention Azazel. Also note "The Midrash of Šemḥazai and *'Azā'ēl,*" on p. 322f.

7. See 16:5, and cf. Lev. 4:22f.; 5:6; 9:3; 23:19; Num. 7; 15:24; 28:15; 29:5; Ezek. 43:22,25; 45:23.

8. See the critique of the view of Yehezkel Kaufmann and references to his work, in B. A. Levine, *In the Presence of the Lord* (Leiden: E. J. Brill, 1974), 77f.

9. See the study by H. Tawil, "*'Azazel* the Prince of the Steppe: A Comparative Study," ZAW 92 (1980): 43–59; and S. Ahituv, EB (Hebrew), s.v. *'aza'zel.*

Excursus 5

1. A good summary of the biblical evidence may be found in the article by C. R. Taber, IDBSup, s.v. "Marriage."

2. Some scholars have cited 1 Chron. 2:24 as an indication that a man was permitted to marry his father's widows. The Masoretic text of that verse appears to be deficient, and the Septuagint reads "After the death of Hezron, Caleb married Ephrathah, the wife of Hezron, his father." See J. M. Myers, *I Chronicles* (AB) to 2:24.

3. See B. A. Levine, "In Praise of the Israelite *Mišpāḥa:* Legal Themes in the Book of Ruth," in *The Quest for the Kingdom of God: Studies in Honor of George Mendenhall,* ed. H. Huffmon et al. (Winona Lake, Ind.: Eisenbrauns, 1983), 95–106.

Excursus 6

1. See A. Altmann, EncJud, s.v. "Attributes of God." See also further bibliography in Introduction to Leviticus, note 1.

2. An example is Bethel, which has been extensively excavated in recent decades. And yet one would not know of this background from Gen. 28:10–22.

Excursus 7

1. See R. de Vaux, *Studies in Old Testament Sacrifice* (Cardiff: University of Wales Press, 1964), 52–90. De Vaux argues for the existence of child sacrifice in biblical Israel. M. Weinfeld, "On Burning Babies," UF 4 (1972): 133–154, argues that actual child sacrifice was not involved in the Molech cult in biblical Israel.

2. The Masoretic text reads *melekh,* "king," but the new JPS translation correctly notes that the reference is actually to Molech.

3. M. Smith, "A Note on Burning Babies," JAOS 95 (1975): 477–479.

4. See M. Cogan, *Imperialism and Religion* (Missoula, Mont.: Scholars Press, 1974), 77–83.

5. See A. Spalinger, "A Canaanite Ritual Found in Egyptian Reliefs," Journal of the Society *for the Study of Egyptian Antiquities* 8 (1978): 47–60, and plates.

Excursus 8

1. See W. W. Hallo, "New Moons and Sabbaths: A Case Study in the Contrastive Approach," HUCA 48 (1977): 1–18.

2. See H. L. Ginsberg, "Studies in Hosea 1–3," in *Yehezkel Kaufmann Jubilee Volume,* ed. M. Haran (Jerusalem: Magnes Press, 1960), 50–69.

3. Cf. the two versions of the Decalogue, Exod. 20:5f. and Deut. 5:12f.; and also Exod. 34:21.

4. Cf. Isa. 56:4; 58:2,6,13; 66:23.

5. See Neh. 9:14; 10:32–34; 13.

6. Cf. Neh. 10:32; 13:15–16,21.

7. See Mish. Shab. 7:2.

8. Cf. Num. 28:9–10; Ezek. 44–46; Hos. 2:3.

9. Lev. 24:8; 1 Chron. 9:32.

10. A later record of this system is mentioned in 2 Chron. 23:4–8.

11. See N. Sarna, "The Psalm for the Sabbath Day," JBL 81 (1962): 155–168.

12. H. L. Ginsberg, *The Israelian Heritage of Judaism* (New York: Jewish Theological Seminary of America, 1982), especially 55–83.

13. Ginsberg adopts an earlier suggestion by A. Ehrlich that here, as in other relatively early passages, such as Isa. 1:13; 1 Sam. 20:5,18; 2 Kings 4:13, *ḥodesh* means "new moon" specifically, and not simply "month." Ginsberg also refers to the pre-Islamic Arab festival of the month of Rajab in the spring. The festival begins on the new moon and lasts for eight days. Bedouin eat herb-flavored yogurt and also crispy bread. The practice of not breaking the bones of roasted small cattle is also typical of the Bedouin.

14. Cf. Exod. 23:14; Pss. 4:8.

15. This is suggested in Pss. 81:4: "Blast the horn on the new moon, on the full moon for the day of our feast day." For the text of the Gezer calendar, see J. Gibson, *Textbooks of Syrian Semitic Inscriptions,* vol. 1 (Oxford: Clarendon Press, 1971), 2f.

16. See Deut. 16:7, and see the introductory Comment to chap. 3 on the usual preparation of the *zevaḥ.*

17. See Y. Aharoni et al., *Arad Inscriptions* (Jerusalem: Israel Exploration Society, 1981), no. 20, lines 3f., *la-ʿasiri be-l la-ḥodesh ʿad ha-shishah la-ḥodesh,* "of the tenth (month), on the first of the month, until the sixth of the month."

Excursus 9

1. See J. J. Finkelstein, "Ammiṣaduqa's Edict and the Babylonian 'Law Codes,'" JCS 15 (1961): 91–104.

2. Cf. the provisions of the Code of Hammurabi, pars. 196f. (ANET, p. 175); of the laws of Eshnunna, pars. 42–48 (ANET, p. 163); and of the Middle Assyrian laws, par. 21, contrasted with pars. 50–52 (ANET, pp. 181,184–185).

Excursus 10

1. See sources cited in chap. 25, n. 11, and Excursus 11.

2. Cf. Isa. 5:8; Mic. 2:1–2.

3. See Git. 36a and MK 2b. "Scripture is speaking of two *shemitot:* both the abandonment of land and the abandonment of funds."

4. See the study by Nahum M. Sarna, "Zedekiah's Emancipation of Slaves and the Sabbatical Year," *Orient and Occident: Essays Presented to Cyrus H. Gordon,* ed. H. A. Hoffner (Kevelaer: Butzon and Bercker, 1973), 143–149.

5. See sources cited in chap. 25, n. 10.

6. See T. Jacobsen, *Salinity and Irrigation Agriculture in Antiquity* (Malibu: Undena Publications, 1982).

7. This comparison was pointed out to me by H. L. Ginsberg, in a verbal communication.

8. Also cf. Neh. 9:36–37.

9. See B. Mazar, "The Tobiads," IEJ 7 (1957): 137–145, 229–238.

10. See Ezra 4–6.

11. See Isa. 45:1f.

12. See Isa. 43–44; 47–49.

13. See B. A. Levine, "Late Language in the Priestly Source: Some Literary and Historical Observations," in *Proceedings of the Eighth World Congress of Jewish Studies* (Jerusalem: World Union of Jewish Studies, 1983), 69–82.

Excursus 11

1. See G. R. Driver and J. C. Miles, eds., *The Babylonian Laws,* vol. 2 (Oxford: Clarendon Press, 1955), 95–107, for the epilogue to the Code of Hammurabi. The boundary stones (Akk. *kudurru*) were inscribed, and in these inscriptions curses were called down on all who would alter established boundaries. See L. W. King, ed., *Babylonian Boundary-Stones and Memorial-Tablets in the British Museum* (London: British Museum, 1912). Cf. Deut. 27:17 for a similar prohibition against moving boundary stones. For a translation of the Aram. treaty from Sfire, which contains many curses pronounced over would-be violators, see ANET, pp. 659f. For Akk. treaties, see ANET, pp. 531f. For Hittite treaties, see ANET, pp. 199f. Some Egyptian execration texts are translated in ANET, pp. 326f. Phoen. and early Aram. building inscriptions also contain curses. Some are translated in ANET, pp. 653–655.

2. See H. L. Ginsberg, *The Israelian Heritage of Judaism* (New York: Jewish Theological Seminary of America, 1982), 79f., 100f., 107, and n. 136. In one particular, I differ from Ginsberg's analysis. In v. 40, the words *be-maʿalam 'asher maʿalu bi,* "when they broke faith with Me," could just as well be part of the first addition to the Epilogue. They paraphrase Ezek. 39:26 and have the same sense here as they do there. See also B. A. Levine, "The Epilogue to the Holiness Code: A Priestly Statement on the Destiny of Israel," in *Judaic Perspectives on Ancient Israel*, ed. J. Neusner *et al.* (Philadelphia: Fortress Press, 1987), 9–34.

3. See the literature cited in n. 1 for the text of the epilogue to the Code of Hammurabi.

4. See J. C. Greenfield and A. Shaffer, "Notes on the Curse Formulae of the Tell Fekherye Inscription," RB 92 (1985): 47–59, and literature cited.